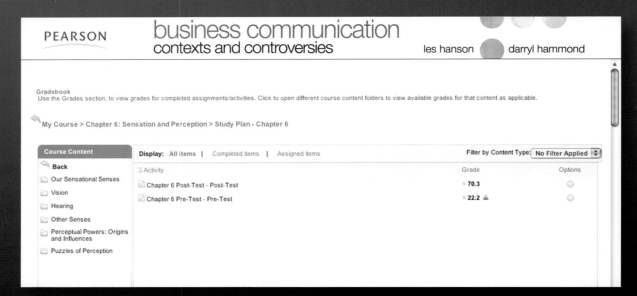

Pearson eText

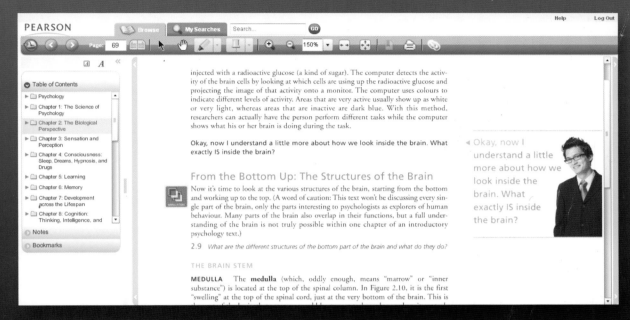

Pearson eText gives students access to the text whenever and wherever they have access to the internet. eText pages look exactly like the printed text, offering powerful new functionality for students and instructors.

Users can create notes, highlight text in different colours, create bookmarks, zoom, click hyperlinked words and phrases to view definitions, and choose single-page or two-page view.

Pearson eText allows for quick navigation using a table of contents and provides full-text search. The eText may also offer links to associated media files, enabling users to access videos, animations, or other activities as they read the text.

Save Time. Improve Results. www.mycanadianbuscommlab.ca

Get the Writing Help You Need

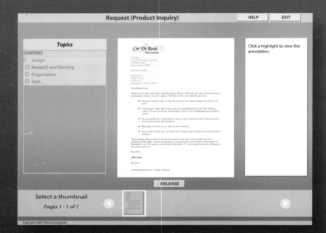

Model Document Practice

In MyCanadianBusCommLab you can see real business-world samples of documents that you will need to write when you begin your career. These "Model Documents" and "Model Document Makeovers" allow you to apply what you have learned.

Help with the Writing Process

MyCanadianBusCommLab provides help with every step of the writing process and will help you prepare to communicate effectively in the business world. Activities include a tutorial on writing formal reports. A "Composing" space provides resources at your fingertips as you research, draft, and revise. You get the help you need when you need it, without ever leaving your writing environment. Improve your writing skills, improve your grade, improve your chances of succeeding in your career.

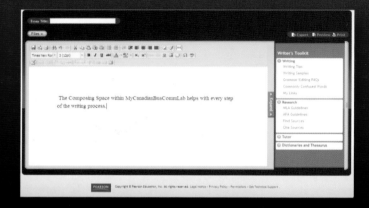

Save Time. Improve Results. www.mycanadianbuscommlab.ca

business communication
contexts and controversies

les hanson
red river college

darryl hammond
red river college
university of manitoba
university of winnipeg

business communication
contexts and controversies

Pearson Canada
Toronto

Library and Archives Canada Cataloguing in Publication

Hanson, Les, 1956–
    Business communication: contexts and controversies / Les Hanson, Darryl Hammond. — 1st ed.

Includes bibliographical references and index.
ISBN 978-0-13-814498-2

    1. Business communication—Textbooks.
I. Hammond, Darryl, 1964– II. Title.

HF5718.H35 2010   651.7   C2009-904828-0

ISBN 978-0-13-814498-2

Vice-President, Editorial Director: Gary Bennett
Editor-in-Chief: Ky Pruesse
Acquisitions Editor: David S. Le Gallais
Signing Representative: Duncan MacKinnon
Marketing Manager: Loula March
Senior Developmental Editor: Patti Altridge
Managing Editor: Söğüt Y. Güleç
Substantive Editor: Cheryl Cohen
Copy Editor: Dawn Hunter
Proofreaders: Audrey Dorsch, Sharon Kirsch
Production Coordinator: Avinash Chandra
Composition: MPS Limited, A Macmillan Company
Photo Research: Mary Rose MacLachlan
Art Director: Julia Hall
Cover and Interior Design: Anthony Leung
Cover Image: Veer Inc.

2 3 4 5   14 13 12 11 10

Printed and bound in USA.

Thanks to our families
for their patience and support.

Brief Contents

Contents

7 Oral Presentations: The Counterintuitive Speaker   137

8 Writing Routine Letters, Memos, and Emails   170

9 Writing Persuasive Messages   211

10 Dealing with Negative Information *232*

PART 3   Longer Documents

11 Writing Instructions, Explanations, and Definitions *257*

16 Networking, Developing Effective References, and Succeeding in Employment Interviews   393

17 Interpersonal Communication: Surviving Life on the Cube Farm   423

Appendix: Grammar, Punctuation, and Plain English   449

ISSUES *in* Communication

Preface

We had reservations about writing a new textbook when we were first approached with the idea because there are many good business communication textbooks on the market. Before we agreed to the project, we had to assure ourselves that there was a genuine need for a new book.

Having taught the subject for many years, we have read dozens of business communication textbooks. We looked again at many of these and made lists of the problems that we (and our students) had found with them. Some included profiles of business leaders or companies that we had found boring. Others included exercises that required little thought or imagination or ones that required students to "make up additional details when necessary." Some books ignored emerging areas of communication such as the use of smart phones. In others, email seemed to be tacked on as if it were a recent innovation. We noted that students were distracted by grammar exercises that dealt with multiple kinds of problems. Some books placed too much emphasis on having students memorize obscure details rather than helping them to write clearly.

We were convinced.

Business Communication: Contexts and Controversies overcomes these problems by

- allowing students to relate information in the book to real-world situations
- including interesting assignments
- providing provocative discussion questions
- promoting active learning
- illustrating some explanations with humorous examples
- using simple explanations

FEATURES

Business Communication: Contexts and Controversies includes a number of features that are not found in other textbooks or that offer improvements over those found in existing books.

Up-to-date Coverage of Communication Technology. Social networking, texting, cell phone etiquette, viral marketing, and multi-tasking are just some of the topics that have been included because of the influence that technology has had on communication.

Issues in Communication. Each chapter includes an "issue in communication" that illustrates a real-life situation relating to the topic of the chapter. The chapter on business plans describes a unique business idea that won a Nobel Prize, for example, while the chapter on writing routine messages describes attempts to promote a paperless office. Each Issue in Communication box includes questions that are intended to promote discussion.

Business Plans. *Business Communication: Contexts and Controversies* includes a chapter that provides an introduction to the writing of business plans—a task that will be faced by many business students before (and after) they graduate.

Instruction Manuals. While guides for writing instructions are frequently found in technical communication books, an increased reliance on computers and other hi-tech devices means that more and more people in business are being called upon to explain things to other people. Most of Chapter 11 (Writing Instructions, Explanations, and Definitions) deals with different aspects of instruction manuals.

Behavioural Interviews. While behaviour-based interviewing has been a key tool of human resources departments for years, most communication textbooks have ignored the topic or given it only limited coverage. *Business Communication: Contexts and Controversies* provides detailed advice to people on preparing for this type of employment interview.

Take It Further. While many textbooks contain sidebars summarizing the key points found on each page,

Business Communication: Contexts and Controversies sidebars contain interesting tidbits of information that are not included in the body of the text. Each sidebar ends with a provocative question intended to promote discussion of the material found in the chapter.

Thinking and Writing Exercises. The writing assignments included in the chapters dealing with letters and emails are much more detailed than those found in other textbooks. Just as real-life writing requires people to make decisions about what information to include, many of these exercises require students to sort extra information to find the details that need to be included in their final submissions.

Writing Skills Checkup. Unlike the writing improvement exercises found in most textbooks, those in *Business Communication: Contexts and Controversies* deal with a single topic in each chapter, along with a brief explanation of the guiding principles behind it. This allows students (and instructors) to concentrate on a single language-use problem at a time without getting distracted by other types of errors.

ORGANIZATION

Part 1 Foundations

Foundations is made up of five chapters that provide students with the principles on which all business communications are based:

Chapter 1, "Business Communication in the Twenty-First Century," the book's introductory chapter, looks at some of the ways that business communication has changed in recent years. It uses these to explain the book's premise that communication involves the interaction of ideas, words, and media.

Chapter 2, "Ideas: Planning the Writing Process" emphasizes the need to plan all types of business communication based on the purpose of the document and the audience for whom it is intended. It provides instruction on brainstorming and sample outlines.

Chapter 3, "Words: Looking at Your Language" explores the impact of the words we use in business. It explains the need for simplicity in language and discusses how euphemisms can sometimes be used (or abused). The chapter contains detailed guidelines on the use of non-discriminatory terminology along with examples from current Canadian usage.

Chapter 4, "Media: Choosing Your Channel," compares the features of various oral and written communication channels to help students choose the most appropriate medium for their messages. In addition to the traditional tools for business communication, it includes sections dealing with some of the newer forms of communication to emerge, such as blogs, social networking, and viral marketing.

Chapter 5, "Intercultural Communication," explores the impact that culture has on business communication. In a world that has been made smaller by cheaper and faster forms of communication, the chapter shows how the cultural background of an audience can affect how messages are received.

Part 2 Routine Communications

Routine Communications consists of five chapters that concentrate on the forms of communication that take place every day in most places of business.

Chapter 6, "Meetings," explains how to plan meetings to make the most effective use of time. It explains the various duties that people can expect to perform during a meeting and shows people how they can contribute to the success of a meeting.

Chapter 7, "Oral Presentations: The Counterintuitive Speaker," provides readers with ways to give speeches and presentations that capture the attention of the audience and present them with memorable information. It also explains how to prepare visual aids that enhance a presentation instead of boring the audience.

Chapter 8, "Writing Routine Letters, Memos, and Emails," looks at the mainstay of most office communications—email—and explains how to write messages that begin with a central idea and include all necessary details. It shows how the same principles should also be applied to letters and memos. Examples of good and bad communication are provided throughout the chapter.

Chapter 9, "Writing Persuasive Messages," identifies different types of situations where persuasion is necessary and then provides a range of strategies for convincing an audience. It discusses the merits of emotional and logical appeals and provides examples of how they can be applied to business communication.

Chapter 10, "Dealing with Negative Information," provides strategies for dealing with some aspects of communication that many people find uncomfortable: making complaints, answering complaints, and making apologies. It explains how bad news can be used effectively and shows techniques for retaining the goodwill of clients under difficult circumstances.

Part 3 Longer Documents

Longer Documents includes four chapters that deal with writing detailed documents.

Chapter 11, "Writing Instructions, Explanations, and Definitions," demonstrates the need for people to write explanations that are based on the needs of their readers. It explains how to deal with technical language and to write instructions that people will actually understand.

Chapter 12, "Preparing to Write Proposals, Reports, and Electronic Presentations," examines the initial processes needed to write effective reports and proposals. It covers different types of research and search techniques, proper referencing, and the best methods for presenting results visually.

Chapter 13, "Writing Proposals and Reports," describes strategies for presenting solicited and unsolicited proposals and examines informational and analytical reports. It shows how to assemble various parts of a report including graphs, tables, and other visual aids, and includes examples of completed reports and proposals.

Chapter 14, "Writing Business Plans," deals with one of the most important (and detailed) documents that any entrepreneur will ever create. It describes the various sections that go into a typical business plan and explains how to present the information that most investors will require before approving the plan.

Part 4 Employment

Employment consists of three chapters intended to help students apply for jobs and keep them.

Chapter 15, "Writing Resumés," provides guidelines for preparing several types of resumés, including online applications, as well as for writing persuasive application letters. It includes examples of all of these documents.

Chapter 16, "Networking, Developing Effective References, and Succeeding in Employment Interviews," discusses developing a career network to help

with successful job searches. It not only contains advice on obtaining interviews and answering common interview questions but also deals extensively with performing well during behavioural interviews.

Chapter 17, "Interpersonal Communication: Surviving Life on the Cube Farm," is based on the principle that students must have the interpersonal communication skills that will allow them to keep that important first position. It includes sections on office etiquette, emotional intelligence, and dealing with frontline workers.

Appendix

"Grammar, Punctuation, and Plain English" teaches and reviews the basic concepts of grammar while employing humour and interesting visuals.

mycanadianbuscommlab

MyCanadianBusCommLab is a website that offers videos, sample documents, and interactive exercises to improve communication skills. Throughout the textbook, icons highlight material where related activities or samples are available on MyCanadianBusCommLab.

> **Explore** Explore dozens of **Writing Samples,** from letters to emails to reports, that model effective communication.

> **Practise** Interactive **Document Makeovers** provide practice in correcting ineffective communication; feedback guides students to understand the problems and find solutions.

STUDENT SUPPLEMENTS

MyCanadianBusCommLab This state-of-the-art, interactive, and instructive solution for business communication is designed to be used as a supplement to a traditional lecture course or to completely administer an online course. See the opening pages of this text for details. Visit www.mycanadianbuscommlab.ca.

MyCanadianBusCommLab includes a Pearson eText, which gives students access to the text whenever and wherever they have access to the internet. eText pages look exactly like the printed text, offering powerful new functionality for students and instructors. Users can create notes, highlight text in different colours, create bookmarks, zoom, click hyperlinked words and phrases to view definitions, and view in single-page or two-page view. Pearson eText allows for quick navigation to key parts of the eText using a table of contents and provides full-text search. The eText may also offer links to associated media files, enabling users to access videos, animations, or other activities as they read.

A student access card for MyCanadianBus-CommLab is packaged with every new copy of the text. Access codes can also be purchased through campus bookstores or through the website.

CourseSmart for Students. CourseSmart goes beyond traditional expectations—providing instant, online access to the textbooks and course materials you need at an average savings of 50%. With instant access from any computer and the ability to search your text, you'll find the content you need quickly, no matter where you are. And with online tools like highlighting and note-taking, you can save time and study efficiently. See all the benefits at **www.coursesmart.com/students.**

INSTRUCTOR SUPPLEMENTS

- **MyTest** from Pearson Canada is a powerful assessment generation program that helps instructors easily create and print quizzes, tests, and exams, as well as homework or practice handouts. Questions and tests can all be authored online, allowing instructors ultimate flexibility and the ability to efficiently manage assessments at anytime, from anywhere. To access MyTest please go to **www.pearsonmytest.com.**

- **Instructor's Manual** provides chapter outlines, suggested solutions to the exercises, and formatted letters for the cases in the letter-writing chapters.

- **PowerPoint Presentations** cover the key concepts in each chapter.

These instructor supplements are available for download from a password-protected section of Pearson Canada's online catalogue (**vig.pearsoned.ca**).

Navigate to your book's catalogue page to view a list of those supplements that are available. See your local sales representative for details and access.

CourseSmart for Instructors. CourseSmart goes beyond traditional expectations—providing instant, online access to the textbooks and course materials you need at a lower cost for students. And even as students save money, you can save time and hassle with a digital eTextbook that allows you to search for the most relevant content at the very moment you need it. Whether it's evaluating textbooks or creating lecture notes to help students with difficult concepts, CourseSmart can make life a little easier. See how when you visit **www.coursesmart.com/instructors.**

Technology Specialists. Pearson's Technology Specialists work with faculty and campus course designers to ensure that Pearson technology products, assessment tools, and online course materials are tailored to meet your specific needs. This highly qualified team is dedicated to helping schools take full advantage of a wide range of educational resources, by assisting in the integration of a variety of instructional materials and media formats. Your local Pearson Canada sales representative can provide you with more details on this service program.

Please speak to your Pearson Canada sales representative for more information about these and other ancillary materials.

ACKNOWLEDGMENTS

We have many people to thank for making this book a reality. First and foremost, this project would not have been possible without the support of our families who waited patiently for the keyboard to become quiet, sometimes late into the night, and did not complain as home repairs went undone and social events were missed.

Next, a thanks to our current colleagues and past students, always a source of inspiration and example. Finally, a heartfelt thank-you to our Pearson team: David Le Gallais (Acquisitions Editor), Patti

Altridge (Senior Developmental Editor), Söğüt Güleç (Managing Editor), Cheryl Cohen (Substantive Editor), and Dawn Hunter (Copy Editor). Thank you all.

We also want to thank the following conscientious and knowledgeable reviewers, listed below in alphabetical order, whose suggestions have helped shape this first edition of *Business Communication: Contexts and Controversies:*

Denise Blay, Fanshawe College
Kathy Cocchio, Northern Alberta Institute of Technology
Lyle Cruickshank, Concordia University
Lyndsay Dustan, Southern Alberta Institute of Technology
Daniel Guo, Conestoga College
Dana Hansen, Humber College
Sharon Josephson, Okanagan College

Chris Legebow, St. Clair College
Diana Lohnes-Mitchell, Nova Scotia Community College
Peter MacDonald, Seneca College of Applied Arts and Technology
Marlene MacInnes, Cape Breton University
Peter C. Miller, Seneca College of Applied Arts and Technology
Sonia Perna, Southern Alberta Institute of Technology
Patricia A. Post, University of New Brunswick
Marion Ross, Georgian College
Rhonda Sandberg, George Brown College
David Thomson , University College of the Fraser Valley
Katherine Woodward, Grant MacEwan University

Les Hanson
Darryl Hammond

About the Authors

Les Hanson has over 30 years' experience teaching in locations ranging from the highlands of Papua New Guinea to fly-in communities in Northern Manitoba. He has a Bachelor of Education degree from the University of Manitoba and a Master of Arts degree in community college education from Central Michigan University. For the last 20 years, he has taught business communication at Red River College in Winnipeg. He recently assumed the position of coordinator in the Business Administration and International Business programs. His current academic interest is in the use of laptop computers in education.

His personal interests include cross-country skiing, bicycling, and in-line skating, as well as auto mechanics and home renovation. He continues to live in Winnipeg with his wife and two children.

Darryl Hammond is a communications and marketing specialist with over 20 years of business managing and post-secondary teaching experience. Having worked in the public, private, and not-for-profit sectors, he has gained a unique perspective of effective business communications from many angles. After building a successful career in senior management with the provincial government, specializing in social marketing, Darryl opened Hammond Communications; a marketing and communications firm with provincial and national accounts. In addition, Darryl began teaching part time at the University of Manitoba and later at the University of Winnipeg. More recently he has turned a part-time teaching passion into a full-time focus. Darryl now teaches business communications and management at Red River College. He also continues teaching at Manitoba's two universities in the areas of social marketing, business administration, and economics. He is a contributing author in a number of Pearson publications in the areas of business administration and communications. Darryl's hobbies include water-skiing, snowboarding, reading, and music, which he enjoys with his wife and their four children.

About the Contributors

James Swingle worked in the financial industry in New York City for over 15 years, most recently as vice president in charge of project management for Reuters Consulting. In 2006, he moved to British Columbia, where he lives with his wife and 14-month-old son. Mr. Swingle works as a trainer and consultant for industry. He has been an adjunct professor at Pace University in New York City and at the University of British Columbia—Okanagan. He currently teaches in the MBA and undergraduate business programs at Thompson Rivers University.

James Swingle authored Chapter 4, "Media: Choosing Your Channel"; Chapter 5, "Intercultural Communication"; and Chapter 9, "Writing Persuasive Messages."

Joan Flaherty is a faculty member in the School of Hospitality and Tourism Management at University of Guelph, where she teaches communications to both undergraduate and graduate students. With over 20 years' teaching experience, she has been a frequent speaker at educational conferences, including The Teaching Professor Conference in the United States and The Society for Teaching and Learning in Higher Education Conference in Canada. A profile of her research interests and publications can be found at **www.htm.uoguelph.ca/joan-flaherty.shtml**.

Joan Flaherty authored Chapter 7, "Oral Presentations: The Counterintuitive Speaker."

Kathryn Davis works in Red River College's Mechanical Engineering Technology (MET) program and has a background in technical writing, technical editing, course development, and teaching. She teaches technical communication and facilitates MET's co-operative education program as well as freelancing and teaching courses for continuing education, distance education, and industry. Kathy has a broad range of experience in producing technical documentation for gas turbine engines, telecommunications, hardware, software, military equipment, HVAC, electronic and industrial instrumentation, CSA applications, ISO 9000, and marketing and sales. Kathy is a senior member of the local chapter of the Society for Technical Communication (STC).

Kathryn Davis authored the Appendix, "Grammar, Punctuation, and Plain English."

business communication
contexts and controversies

Business Communication in the Twenty-First Century

CHAPTER

1

LEARNING OUTCOMES

After completing this chapter, you should be able to do the following:

1.1 Discuss the benefits of communicating effectively in the workplace

1.2 Describe the interaction of three major elements of communication: (1) ideas,

(2) words, and (3) media

1.3 List some challenges and opportunities that modern business communication provides

1.4 Discuss how the increased need to multi-task and use new technology could affect those involved in business in the twenty-first century

CHANGING COMMUNICATION TECHNOLOGY

You won't find identity theft, electronic mail, and spam mentioned in older textbooks. Although these topics have been in the news often in the past few years, they simply did not exist in the 1980s or earlier. Communication is changing, and advances in communication technology have led to the biggest changes in business communication.

Fortunately, not all aspects of business communication have changed dramatically over the past 20 years. The following two major elements, for example, have changed little:

1. *Letters.* Those written today follow the same format as those written 20 or even 50 years ago.

2. *Business language.* It is largely the same. A changing world has brought new terms, such as *Google* and *blind copy*, and increased sensitivity has removed sexist terms, such as *girl Friday* to describe office assistants, but these changes are relatively small.

The timeline in **Table 1-1** shows some of the most important changes in office communication technology over the past 150 years. Notice how many of these technological innovations have occurred within your lifetime.

Communication is an essential part of all office work.

TABLE 1-1	Timeline of the Introduction of Communication Technologies		
1867	Modern typewriter	1976	Commercial laser printer
1876	Telephone	1979	Cellphone network
1898	Telephone answering machine	1980	Sticky notes
1938	Ballpoint pen	1981	IBM personal computer
1946	Commercial computer (ENIAC)	1984	Inkjet printer
1958	Office photocopier	1994	World Wide Web
1966	Fax machine	1999	BlackBerry personal digital assistant
1967	Pocket calculator	2000	Camera telephone
1975	Apple personal computer	2007	iPhone

Source: Adapted from Bellis, Mary. "The History of Communications." About.Com: Inventors. Web. 25 May 2009.

The dates in the table are approximate; in most cases the technology did not come into common usage until well after its invention. Laser printers and cellphones, for example, were introduced to the market in the late '70s but did not come into widespread use until the 1990s.[1]

This book deals with various aspects of business communication that you will encounter in your career: writing letters and emails, delivering presentations, and preparing reports. Each chapter also contains an issue in communication that relates the communication concepts to the world at large.

ISSUES *in* Communication

BlackBerry or Crackberry?

A BlackBerry is a wireless computer a little bigger than a cellphone that a person can use to connect to the internet, send and receive email and text messages, store documents, and make phone calls.

BlackBerrys, manufactured by Canadian company Research in Motion (RIM), are at the forefront of the technological revolution, although Apple's iPhone is beginning to receive support from some corporate clients now that security features of the device have been improved.[2]

People in business and in government have been adopting the technology for a variety of purposes. One recent survey reported that two-thirds of large organizations make some use of handheld communication devices. Usually these devices are supplied only to those people who need them most: upper management, sales representatives, information technology staff, and teleworkers.[3]

BlackBerrys have become an extension of the office, allowing people to answer emails and update their schedules from almost anywhere: in airports and hotel rooms, during meetings and conferences, or while at home or driving a car.

Communication technology can be addictive and dangerous.

Some people are concerned that this degree of flexibility poses problems. They worry that BlackBerrys have become leashes that tie people to their jobs and that the devices can become so addictive that they interfere with employees' personal lives. Because they are so portable and easy to use, BlackBerrys are blurring the distinction between work and personal time.[4]

Bringing home work in a briefcase requires a deliberate decision to sit down, take out the documents, and begin working, but technology, such as the BlackBerry, makes it easy to do anywhere. The device you use to check your email quickly in the evening may draw you back into your work. That is why more and more people who use BlackBerrys for work call them "crackberries," just as some Facebook users talk about "crackbook."

BlackBerrys are examples of personal digital assistants (PDAs). A survey conducted by AOL in June 2007 revealed that 43 percent of the American users polled left their PDAs close to their beds to listen for incoming messages at night, 37 percent checked their messages while driving, and 12 percent admitted to checking messages in church.[5]

An article in the British journal *Personnel Today* cited research showing that 90 percent of 18- to 25-year-olds took their cellphones with them everywhere, while 40 percent "couldn't cope" without them. The same article described survey results indicating that two-thirds of British bosses would take a BlackBerry on holiday to access work-related emails and to stay in touch with their colleagues. According to 12 percent of these bosses, checking emails while on vacation gave them a "welcome break from the family." The article noted that the symptoms of communication technology addiction are similar to those experienced by gambling addicts and could damage the mental health of workers.[6]

NEW TECHNOLOGY, NEW RULES?

Immediacy is highly valued in the workplace. People want immediate answers. Waiting a day for a response to a question can be unacceptable to the BlackBerry addict. This kind of technology may be creating a culture of instant gratification in which people and information are expected to be instantly available.

Personal digital assistants are becoming more common in meetings and conferences. Meetings can be held on two levels: the main level, with people openly discussing agenda items, and the underlying level, with people using BlackBerrys, iPhones, or other PDAs under the table to communicate privately. Text messages can be even more intrusive than cellphone calls—people who would not consider taking a call during a meeting or phoning a co-worker at home may be tempted to send a text message because it is not as disruptive.[7]

The arrival of the internet in the workplace in the 1990s led to rules about the use of personal email and access to personal websites. Now, the spread of personal digital assistants may force employers to introduce or update rules governing what is an acceptable use of technology in the workplace.

DISCUSSION

1. In many forms of communication, a delay occurs between the time an idea forms and when it is transmitted over a channel; along the way, it is put into words. With a letter that time lag can be a few days. Even with email, we don't normally expect instant responses. PDAs have reduced that time lag to minutes. How might this affect the communication process? What are the positive implications? What are the negative possibilities?

2. Under what circumstances should BlackBerrys be allowed in meetings? Should they be banned outright, the way cellphones are now? If they should be allowed, what etiquette, or rules of conduct, should users follow? What are the possible positive uses during a meeting?

3. If you were given the option of having a BlackBerry—which your employer would provide—would you accept it? Why, or why not?

4. Some jurisdictions ban drivers from using cellphones; discuss whether the bans should be extended to other devices, such as PDAs. Are such laws reasonable? Are they enforceable? Do you use your cellphone while you are driving?

TAKE IT FURTHER

U.S. Presidential BlackBerry

In 2009, Barack Obama became the first U.S. president to use a BlackBerry while in office. His PDA contains special security features and is used only to communicate with a select group of family and colleagues.[8]

Aside from issues of security, why are so many political leaders—compared with business leaders—reluctant to use such communication tools?

WHY STUDY COMMUNICATION?

�֍ Explore

Look through the Careers section of any newspaper and you will see many ads similar to that shown in **Figure 1-1**.

Most professional jobs require strong communication skills, but communication can take many forms. Some jobs require us to address large groups of people. Others require that we write reports or emails. Sometimes communication involves selling products or dealing one on one with clients. In other situations it requires the ability to type quickly, or to speak a second or third language. Communicating with other people is an essential skill in all professions, and in business, miscommunication can cost millions of dollars.

At one time professionals could depend on secretaries to check their grammar or revise their first drafts. The business world now seldom hires employees to take dictation and type letters. Technology, such as word processors and photocopiers, has made the personal secretary largely a relic of the '50s and '60s. Secretaries have now become administrative assistants whose duties usually entail far more than polishing someone else's writing.

Most office workers have access to computers and are expected to write their own letters, reports, and emails. Most word-processing programs do come equipped with spelling and grammar checkers, but even such tools as these are useful only if the operator is able to understand the advice being offered and put it in place.

Communication drives the world of business: Suggestions are made, ideas are pitched, products are sold, and deals are negotiated. Effective communication, in dozens of forms, makes these things happen.

Practise | FIGURE 1-1 | **The Importance of Communication Skills**

BUSINESS ANALYST
WOMEN'S ENTERPRISE CENTRE
OF MANITOBA

THE ORGANIZATION

the company described

The Women's Enterprise Centre of Manitoba assists entrepreneurial women as they start, operate, expand and transition their businesses. The Centre provides a range of value-added business services including seminars, business counsel and loans up to $100 000.

THE OPPORTUNITY

the position described

We are looking for a business generalist who has experience assessing business plans, counselling for business development and delivering seminars on business topics relevant to entrepreneurship.

THE PERSON

We are seeking an individual experienced in business start-up and expansion who will work collaboratively with our team delivering client-centred business services and heightening the community's awareness about the Centre and its services for women entrepreneurs.

Success equals exceptional communication skills.

The successful candidate will have excellent analytical financial and problem-solving skills, exceptional verbal and written abilities, and strong presentation skills. Relevant post-secondary education and/or related business experience is necessary. Business ownership, experience with commercial lending, and a second language will be considered assets.

Please submit your resume in confidence to
Women's Enterprise Centre of Manitoba
by Monday, April 14, 2008

Technical skills plus communication skills lead to an interview.

Only those candidates selected for an interview will be contacted.

WOMEN'S ENTERPRISE CENTRE
CENTRE D'ENTREPRISE DES FEMMES

Source: Reprinted with permission from the Women's Enterprise Centre of Manitoba

The people who deal with your writing—clients, co-workers, supervisors—will not necessarily tell you that they are judging you. They may not even realize it themselves, but they will form an impression of you based on the way you communicate. That impression is one feature that can easily separate those who rise through the ranks of an organization from those who spend their careers in dead-end jobs.

Hard Skills and Soft Skills

Most people enrol in higher education to strengthen their hard skills—the skills that are directly related to the job. Hard skills, such as accounting, computer use, and working with statistics, are important, but proficiency in these areas will provide you with the bare minimum needed to land a job. If you want to keep that job and, more importantly, be promoted to higher positions, you will need to develop your soft skills. Soft skills are not as easy to define but usually include interpersonal skills, perseverance, and communication ability. Soft skills help people function effectively in complex business environments. In a recent survey of 1400 financial executives, 75 percent of those polled said that verbal, written, and interpersonal skills are more valuable now than they were five years ago.[9]

Hard skills may get you a job, but soft skills will help you keep that job.

Some soft skills are difficult to acquire in a school environment. A post-secondary school is unlikely to be able to teach students to be honest, hard-working, or ambitious, for example. Such characteristics as these are often acquired more through upbringing than through education. Business communication, though, is a skill (or collection of skills) that students can learn and develop. Some aspects of communication involve learning principles of grammar and language use, and then applying them to writing. Other aspects involve developing sensitivity toward the needs of the reader. Good communication will also require you to learn some basic writing formulas and then apply them—similar to the equations that enable you to balance algebraic expressions.

The Conference Board of Canada, a non-profit applied research organization, assembled a list of the key skills necessary to progress in the working world, and you can study them in **Table 1-2**.[10]

How Business Communication Differs from High School English

After studying English in high school, students entering college or university are often disappointed to find that they will be forced to take yet another similar course. Many high school English courses emphasize sentence structure, grammar, and organization, and they do it well. Business communication courses often deal with the same topics, though usually in more detail. English courses involve a good deal of reading, along with library research; so does business communication.

The main difference is one of focus. English courses tend to have a literary focus—students study plays, poetry, and great novels. One purpose of such courses as these is to expose students to some of the world's great writers and to ideas and settings they might not have encountered yet.

The goal of business communication courses is far narrower, and they focus more on simplicity and clarity than on art. Business communication is practical. The objective is to get the job done simply, clearly, and effectively.

TABLE 1-2   **The Conference Board of Canada's Employability Skills 2000+**

The skills you need to enter, stay in, and progress in the world of work—whether you work on your own or as a part of a team.
These skills can also be applied and used beyond the workplace in a range of daily activities.

Fundamental Skills	Personal Management Skills	Teamwork Skills
The skills needed as a base for further development	The personal skills, attitudes and behaviours that drive one's potential for growth	The skills and attributes needed to contribute productively
You will be better prepared to progress in the world of work when you can:	*You will be able to offer yourself greater possibilities for achievement when you can:*	*You will be better prepared to add value to the outcomes of a task, project or team when you can:*
Communicate – read and understand information presented in a variety of forms (e.g., words, graphs, charts, diagrams) – write and speak so others pay attention and understand – listen and ask questions to understand and appreciate the points of view of others – share information using a range of information and communications technologies (e.g., voice, e-mail, computers) – use relevant scientific, technological and mathematical knowledge and skills to explain or clarify ideas	**Demonstrate Positive Attitudes & Behaviours** – feel good about yourself and be confident – deal with people, problems and situations with honesty, integrity and personal ethics – recognize your own and other people's good efforts – take care of your personal health – show interest, initiative and effort	**Work with Others** – understand and work within the dynamics of a group – ensure that a team's purpose and objectives are clear – be flexible: respect, be open to and supportive of the thoughts, opinions and contributions of others in a group – recognize and respect people's diversity, individual differences and perspectives – accept and provide feedback in a constructive and considerate manner – contribute to a team by sharing information and expertise – lead or support when appropriate, motivating a group for high performance – understand the role of conflict in a group to reach solutions – manage and resolve conflict when appropriate
Manage Information – locate, gather and organize information using appropriate technology and information systems – access, analyze and apply knowledge and skills from various disciplines (e.g., the arts, languages, science, technology, mathematics, social sciences, and the humanities)	**Be Responsible** – set goals and priorities balancing work and personal life – plan and manage time, money and other resources to achieve goals – assess, weigh and manage risk – be accountable for your actions and the actions of your group – be socially responsible and contribute to your community	**Participate in Projects & Tasks** – plan, design or carry out a project or task from start to finish with well-defined objectives and outcomes – develop a plan, seek feedback, test, revise and implement – work to agreed quality standards and specifications – select and use appropriate tools and technology for a task or project – adapt to changing requirements and information – continuously monitor the success of a project or task and identify ways to improve
Use Numbers – decide what needs to be measured or calculated – observe and record data using appropriate methods, tools and technology – make estimates and verify calculations	**Be Adaptable** – work independently or as a part of a team – carry out multiple tasks or projects – be innovative and resourceful: identify and suggest alternative ways to achieve goals and get the job done – be open and respond constructively to change – learn from your mistakes and accept feedback – cope with uncertainty	
Think & Solve Problems – assess situations and identify problems – seek different points of view and evaluate them based on facts – recognize the human, interpersonal, technical, scientific and mathematical dimensions of a problem – identify the root cause of a problem – be creative and innovative in exploring possible solutions – readily use science, technology and mathematics as ways to think, gain and share knowledge, solve problems and make decisions – evaluate solutions to make recommendations or decisions – implement solutions – check to see if a solution works, and act on opportunities for improvement	**Learn Continuously** – be willing to continuously learn and grow – assess personal strengths and areas for development – set your own learning goals – identify and access learning sources and opportunities – plan for and achieve your learning goals	
	Work Safely – be aware of personal and group health and safety practices and procedures, and act in accordance with these	The Conference Board of Canada **Insights You Can Count On** 255 Smyth Road, Ottawa ON K1H 8M7 Canada Tel. (613) 526-3280 Fax (613) 526-4857 Internet: www.conferenceboard.ca/nbec

Source: From Employability Skills 2000+ Brochure 2000 E/F. *Conference Board of Canada. May 2000. Web. 29 Oct. 2007.*

If you have begun reading this book with the idea that business communication involves throwing around phrases like "as per your request" and "the aforementioned wishes to advise you that," it is time to abandon that notion. Good business communication does not use pompous, empty phrases. The fact that you may have seen such phrases simply justifies the need for courses that teach business students to write effectively.

Good business writing is easy to understand, well organized, and brief. Reading at work is usually a chore—few of us would willingly choose annual reports as vacation reading—so people will be appreciative if you express your ideas concisely. When people judge you on your writing, they will admire you more for communicating all the necessary information with no extra frills or bureaucratic language than they will for trying to overpower them with wordy documents and meaningless nonsense.

Our aim in this book is to show you techniques for writing that will allow you to communicate as efficiently as possible. That way, you will be able to concentrate on getting the job done and not have to worry about how your communication skills are being judged.

ELEMENTS OF COMMUNICATION

Your first task as a communicator is to make the decision to communicate. Sometimes this decision is so obvious as to go unnoticed. For example, when the phone rings, the first impulse most people have is to answer it. Others make a conscious decision not to answer the phone—they let it ring in the hope that the person at the other end will go away; they screen their calls by looking at the phone numbers; or they let the call go to voicemail. Even those actions are aspects of communication.

In some situations, the decision of whether or not to communicate comes only after much consideration. When a prospective employer takes you to lunch, for example, you may think carefully before you tell her that you are scheduled to meet with a representative from a rival company the following week.

When you do choose to actively communicate something to someone, you need to make decisions about three separate but related areas: what to say, how to say it, and how to send it, or, more simply, (1) ideas, (2) words, and (3) media. (See **Figure 1-2**.)

We are numbering these three areas to help you remember them. In real life, they do not necessarily occur in a fixed order. When you pick up a ringing telephone, the decision about media has already been made. However, the decisions you then make about ideas and words are almost simultaneous—until you reach an awkward moment and struggle to find the correct word to express a complicated or emotionally delicate idea. Such moments are usually accompanied by an awkward pause in the conversation. At other times people babble non-stop and then sometimes say things that they had not intended to say—moments that are usually followed by periods of forehead thumping and self-recrimination.

✳─[Explore **FIGURE 1-2**   **Elements of Communication**

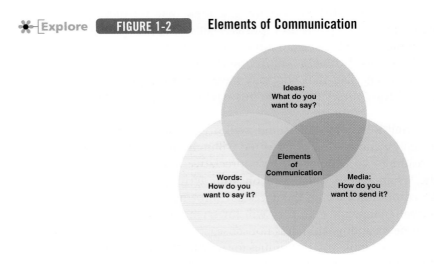

Writing in any media (email, letter, or report) usually begins with ideas that are jotted down at random and then organized into an outline. This skeleton is fleshed out with the exact words needed to express the ideas, but even then the sequence is not carved in stone. People frequently return to their outlines and revise them midway through the writing process. Or they may change their choice of medium—such as when they phone someone, receive no answer, and decide to write an email instead. The order is not fixed. People often switch back and forth between decisions about words, ideas, and media.

Usually media choice is made early in the communication process. Decisions about words and ideas, however, frequently cause problems for people. One challenge of good communication is managing these three elements.

1. Ideas

Communication, by its very definition, requires the exchange of ideas. Making the decision on which ideas to use and when to use them may involve difficult choices.

Many people start with a brainstorming approach, jotting down as many ideas as they can think of and then pruning the list. When putting together a resumé, for example, people usually begin by making lists of everything they have done in their work and education. They then decide whether to mention short-term jobs or courses that they started but did not complete.

When planning how to sell a product, marketers look at their customers' characteristics and decide the best way to create a need for the product. They may do this by listing the features of the product and then deciding which to mention and which to leave out.

Alternatively, they may take an entirely different approach and try to associate their product with something else: sex, fun, youthfulness, or prestige, for example. Think about beer commercials. Some will talk about the premium hops and the high-quality barley that they use. Others try to associate their product with good times: skiing, parties, or exotic vacations. The main selling point of one popular brand of beer focuses on the fact that it is cold—an idea that should not come as a revelation in a country where most people have access to refrigerators.

Ideas are not always presented in a logical manner, and sometimes they don't have to be.

Many messages contain emotional elements, such as humour, happiness, sadness, or anger. Exactly how much emotion to include is one of the decisions you need to make when you send a message. Once again, it's an important decision. Pity the job applicant who includes a letter describing the madcap and zany practical jokes she played on co-workers at her last position.

You live in an age of information. Computers and the internet put a wealth of information at your fingertips. A major part of the communication process is filtering that information and deciding what needs to be delivered. When you decide to communicate—whether by answering the phone or by picking up a pen—questions arise about what ideas to send.

Ideas in Action   Imagine that you are the manager of a business that is suffering financial difficulties, and the district manager has told you to reduce your operating expenses. You examine the various ways you could do this:

- by increasing efficiency
- by reducing services
- by finding other cost-saving measures

You study all the available options, crunch some numbers on a spreadsheet, and perhaps consult with other people. Eventually, you arrive at a solution.

Assume that your decision is to reduce the number of staff. Once again, you have to make decisions, this time about which employees to lay off. You have to examine various factors, including

- employees' seniority
- their value to the organization
- the cost of their salaries

Making decisions of this nature is difficult. Eventually, however, you decide which staff members to let go.

Once that idea is formed, you have further issues to work out:

- severance pay
- layoff dates
- redistribution of the laid-off workers' duties

The next task is to inform the unfortunate workers. You still have decide on the wording of the message and the medium you will use to inform them.

2. Words

Choosing the words for a business communication is a fairly straightforward task if the only goal is to convey the information. A far greater challenge is choosing words that convey the intent of a difficult message—such as a layoff notice—honestly while still showing compassion.

Emotional topics present numerous choices of less offensive words that may be used to deal with the situation. Such words are called *euphemisms*. Delicate subjects frequently spawn words with subtle differences in meaning to allow people to convey the exact meaning that they require under the circumstances. People have dozens of ways of expressing the concept of death, for example:

- *Passed away* might be a suitable term to use at a person's funeral.
- *Slaughtered* might be an appropriate term to refer to animals in a meat-packing plant.
- *Expired* could be used to refer to a patient in a hospital setting.

A mistake in word choice could be devastating. Hearing your doctor refer to a dead patient as a *casualty* would not likely inspire confidence.

Words, no matter how carefully they are crafted, can never alleviate the devastating impact of serious life events, but they can help you convey your sympathies.

Words in Action   Writing a layoff notice requires the writer to relay the information in such a way that neither the employer nor the laid-off worker looks unnecessarily bad. Word choice is critical.

The concept of a layoff can be expressed in numerous ways. Most people would consider such words as *fired, terminated,* or *getting the axe* to be unduly harsh for the announcement of a layoff. Although the recipients of layoff notices might use such terms in an informal sense to describe what happened to them, they would not appreciate seeing such words in official documents.

Terms commonly used to describe layoffs include the following:

- restructuring
- downsizing
- workforce reduction
- staff adjustments

Many (but not all) people would consider these to be acceptable terms that are intended to preserve the dignity of everyone involved.

Other terms, such as *rightsizing, corporate realignment,* or *human resource rebalancing,* are often viewed as attempts to give too positive a look to what is a negative event, and most of the people affected would likely greet such terms with scorn.

It is never possible to choose words that satisfy everyone. Even though many people would accept such a word as *downsizing* as an effective compromise between the harshness of *fired* and the vagueness of *human resource reengineering,* some people would consider it a deliberate attempt to avoid taking responsibility for an unpleasant decision. A certain number of people will always prefer the bluntness of such terms as *fired* or *laid off.*

When choosing words for this situation, the most important communication factors are giving people as much notice as possible that layoffs are pending and delivering the news in as sensitive a way as possible.

TAKE IT FURTHER

Media

The word *media* is the plural form of the word *medium.* A newspaper is one medium for receiving news. Radio, television, and the internet are other common news media sources.

If we start the list with Twitter, what media can you imagine using in modern business communication (1) within the workplace and (2) from the workplace to the outside world?

3. Media

Many communication tasks involve making choices about how the message is to be delivered. If you need to inform your staff of a layoff, you have various options:

- call everyone together and give them the bad news in a meeting
- send a letter to the people involved
- send an email to all staff
- call each affected employee to your office and tell them one by one
- visit their offices individually and inform them
- tell them over the telephone

The choice of media depends on dozens of pieces of information about the situation that have not been provided here. You do not know how many staff are employed by this fictional organization or how many are to be laid off. You do not know anything about the work environment—whether the workplace is an office with private areas that would allow people to talk, or whether it is a noisy factory assembly line. You know nothing about the workers themselves: their relationship with the company, their levels of expertise, or their years of experience.

These and dozens of other factors influence the choice of media in such situations as these. The methods used to inform summer students of a layoff at a beach-front resort in late August would be quite different from those used to announce a mine closure in a one-industry town. Making a poor decision could result in hurt feelings, angry people, and a poor public image of the organization that you represent.

Media Choice in Action   Consider what your own reaction would be if you came into your office on a Monday morning to find that your network password no longer worked and that an envelope containing a layoff notice and instructions to have your desk cleaned out by noon had been taped to your computer terminal.

Although it may be tempting for managers to use such indirect communication methods to avoid unpleasant confrontations, the backlash that often results from such callous treatment of employees can produce worse results.

When Radio Shack laid off 400 workers by using an email notice in 2006, people all over North America criticized the approach. The company received far more negative publicity than it would have received had the people responsible for the decision used a more conventional approach.[11]

Medium Is the Message   Marshall McLuhan, the famous Canadian communications theorist, coined the phrase "the medium is the message" to describe the social impact that our media choices have on the communication process.[12] Even before people begin to put their messages into words, the channel they chose to send that message has already communicated a great deal. Consider the impact of a politician who makes an appearance on a controversial television talk show. What the politician says on that show may be

This advertisement from Telus illustrates the importance that media choices have on the way that a message is received.

remembered less than the fact that he or she appeared on the show. Likewise, an invitation to a banquet that arrives in an embossed envelope will likely attract more attention than the same message transmitted by fax machine.

McLuhan compared the effects of media choice to the impact of the historical opening of railways across a frontier. The actual freight that was carried on the trains had less of an impact than the existence of the railway itself. In the long run, it did not matter whether the trains carried bricks or cattle or mail. Their very existence affected the way cities were constructed and changed many aspects of human interaction.

The hero in William Saroyan's novel *The Human Comedy* is a boy who delivers telegrams during the World War II. So omnipresent was the use of the telegraph to inform families of tragic news that the message was communicated even before the messenger entered the person's home.[13]

Your choice of medium, or media, will have a major impact on the way your message is received. You have probably heard stories of various romantic ways that people chose to propose marriage: with messages strategically placed on giant billboards or on video screens at football games, with a diamond ring that dramatically appears at the end of a romantic dinner, or even with the traditional face-to-face approach. Compare these strategies to that of the person who sends a text with an offer of marriage. Even though the words and intent may be the same, the way the message is received will be greatly affected by the choice of medium.

McLuhan did not intend to completely downplay the importance of content in a message. The following quotation comes from an interview published in 1969:

> By stressing that the medium is the message rather than the content, I'm not suggesting that content plays no role—merely that it plays a distinctly subordinate role. . . . By placing all the stress on content and practically none on the medium, we lose all chance of perceiving and influencing the impact of new technologies on man, and thus we are always dumfounded by—and unprepared for—the revolutionary environmental transformations induced by new media.[14]

Some would argue that even this position places too much emphasis on form over substance. Ultimately, you will have to arrive at your own opinion on the matter. As you are thinking about such issues, remember that this interview took place in 1969—before the internet, cellphones, banking machines, MP3s, and YouTube. Imagine what changes McLuhan might have made to this statement had he lived at a time when these technologies existed.

Choosing the Right Medium   Numerous factors influence a person's media choice, including the following:

- cost
- speed
- audience size
- opportunities for feedback
- need for permanence
- level of personal contact required

These factors vary according to the situations in which they are used. Decisions relating to media choices are usually based on a number of factors.

Examining a media choice by using one factor alone, cost, can produce problems. If, for example, it was necessary to discuss a matter with a client in Australia, two obvious choices would be email or telephone. Although email may cost less to send, a telephone call may be cheaper than an email message if you consider other factors that can affect the situation. The telephone makes it simple to ask and answer questions immediately, making it easier to resolve problems quickly. It also has superior capabilities for communicating emotion. Either one of these characteristics may, in some situations, be far more important that the mere cost of the call.

However, an international call may require that you consider other hidden costs. When it is 3 p.m. in Toronto, it is 6 a.m. in Sydney. Finding a mutually convenient time for a call could mean having one person stay late at work or another person arriving early, either of which could involve overtime expenses or missed calls.

TAKE IT FURTHER

The Cost of Long Distance

The cost of long distance calling is one of the few things whose cost has declined considerably over the years. In 1921, a three-minute call between Montreal and Vancouver cost $14.50; in 1950 the same call was $4.70; by 1975 it was $3.15.[15] Today, that call might be $1.75.[16]

How have such reductions in communication costs changed the way people do business in North America?

Spam

The *Oxford English Dictionary* says that spam (lower case) has been used since 1991 to mean flooding computers with unwanted information by email.[17] The Hormel Corporation, maker of SPAM (upper case) luncheon meat, attributes the lower-case usage to the British television show *Monty Python's Flying Circus*, in which a Viking chorus drowns out other speakers by repeating the word.

Can you name other consumer products that have been subverted by popular culture?

 Explore

Accents may also pose issues. Although a rural Newfoundlander may have no difficulty understanding written communication from a northern Queenslander, the very different speech patterns of the two people may present communication difficulties when they talk on the telephone.

One final cost to consider relates to the volume of information that you can transmit over the two channels. An email message can contain far more information than a phone call. It is not necessary to keep a pad and a pen handy when reading email; you can always read the message again if you miss something. With a phone call, if you are likely to need any information later, you have to remember it, write it down, or record the call.

Oral communication channels may be useful for their interactive nature, but they do not work well when you need to transmit large amounts of information.

Email: Benefits and Pitfalls Email has become the channel of choice for much of the business communication taking place in the world today. It is fast, relatively cheap, and allows the transmission of both quick one-line messages and detailed multi-page documents. Yet email is far from the perfect medium. Its low cost and ease of use present disadvantages. *Spam* messages for get-rich-quick schemes or products of questionable quality can now be sent out so cheaply to such wide audiences that even though most people delete them immediately (if their service providers have failed to block the messages), enough people do respond to make it worthwhile for the sellers of this junk to continue. Meanwhile such messages waste millions of hours and try the patience of workers all over the globe.

Even legitimate email messages can be troublesome if not managed properly. Reading every email message as it arrives can distract people from other duties. People can waste time passing along jokes and gossip or insisting on sending copies of messages to people who have no need for the information. Some people have found that they spend more than an hour a day managing the email messages that come to them—time that they would otherwise have used for different purposes. Some organizations, such as Nestle Rowntree and Intel, have declared "email-free Fridays" to reduce information overload and promote more vocal interaction by using the telephone or face-to-face communication.[18]

No medium is perfect for all purposes. That is why we have so many different channels available. Some, like hieroglyphics or the telegraph, have vanished completely as technology finds better alternatives, but numerous other alternatives have replaced them.

COMMUNICATING IN THE TWENTY-FIRST CENTURY

A 2006 article in the American academic journal *Chronicles of Higher Education* was titled "Email Is for Old People"—and it reflected the feelings of many of the students interviewed. (The article discussed students' use of communication technologies.) They were all familiar with numerous forms of electronic communications but tended not to use email, sometimes missing important announcements from their instructors. The students preferred instant messaging, text messaging, and social websites for their own communications. Email, a technology that exploded onto the world less than 20 years ago, has now become a tool for old people.[19]

This does not mean that you should ignore the technology of email. Email and the telephone are the primary communication tools in business as we write this book and will likely remain that way for many years to come.

The medium used for communication has a significant influence on the level of formality required in any situation. Text messages are very informal and tend to disregard most of the traditional "rules" of grammar and spelling. Although the language used in emails is more formal than that of text messages, emails do tend to be less structured than letters or reports. It is often easier to ignore a minor error in a quick email than the same kind of error in a letter. A resumé that contains even a single spelling or grammatical error could cost an applicant a job opportunity.

You need to adjust your writing style to fit the medium you choose and the expectations of the intended audience. It would probably be unwise, for example, to inquire about a low mark on a writing assignment by sending your writing instructor an email message written entirely in lower-case letters.

In the same way that beach clothing is inappropriate for the office, the standards that people expect for most business communication are different from the level found in most text messages.

Text Messaging

> Txt msg ws an acidnt. no 1 expcted it. Whn the 1st txt msg ws sent, in 1993 by Nokia eng stdnt Riku Pihkonen, the telcom cpnies thought it ws nt important. SMS—Short Message Service—ws nt considrd a majr pt of GSM. Like mny teks, the *pwr* of txt—indeed, the *pwr* of the fon—wz discvrd by users. In the case of txt mssng, the usrs were the yng or poor in the W and E.[20]

Such writing as that in the quotation above does not normally appear in books. It is based on the text-messaging shorthand used on cellphones and wireless handheld devices. The shorthand makes it easier to type messages using only the thumbs. But is it correct writing? The answer depends on the situation.

When appearing on a portable screen, it would often be considered correct; the writing has intentionally been shortened to improve efficiency. In a textbook, such as this, it is correct only as an example of text messaging. Consider what would happen if the entire book were printed in this language. There would be complaints from people who insist on conventional spelling to honour tradition and to preserve consistency in language. But there are other reasons why this language would not be readily accepted.

The passage you read was only a half a dozen lines or so, but even if you are a skilled reader of text messages, it probably took you longer to read that with any understanding than it would take you to read the same message written in conventional English. Compare:

> Text messaging was an accident. No one expected it. When the first text message was sent, in 1993, by Nokia engineering student Riku Pinkonen, the telecommunications companies thought it was not important. SMS—Short Message Service—was not considered a major part of GSM [Global System for Mobile communications]. Like many technologies, the *power* of text—indeed the *power* of the phone—was discovered by users. In the case of text messaging, the users were the young or poor in the West and East.[21]

This version, although a few lines longer than the first version, probably took you half the time to read. Text messaging evolved not because it is easy to read, but because it is easy to write and easy to send. Articles, such as *a* and *the*, are usually omitted. Words are often written without vowels. Thus *speak* becomes *spk*. **Table 1-3** shows a few common SMS abbreviations.

Texting has also gone far beyond the realm of quick messages of just a few words. In the first six months of 2007, half of Japan's top-ten best-selling works of fiction were composed on cellphones—a phenomenon known as *keitai shousetsu*. Most of these cellphone novels are written by first-time writers for an audience of young female readers, who read them on the screens of their cellphones. Some of these works have since been published in hardcover as well, including one best-seller that sold more than a million copies and went on to become a movie.[22]

A 2007 British study showed that face-to-face communication was the first choice among people aged 14 to 24 for staying in contact with their friends. Texting on a cellphone was second, followed by instant messaging, speaking on a telephone, email, and social networking.[23]

TABLE 1-3	**Common Abbreviations in the Short Messaging System (SMS)**
Standard English	**SMS**
are	R
as soon as possible	**asap**
ate—either as a word or part of another word (late, hate)	8 (l8, h8)
be (before, because)	b (b4, bc)
for	**4**
see	C
thanks or thank you	Thnx or ty
to, too, two	2
why	**Y**
you	**U**

Living with PDAs

You may one day have a job that requires you to use a personal digital assistant. Employers often issue BlackBerrys to their sales representatives, information technology personnel, and managers. The tools are not rewards for good work—PDAs allow people to be contacted more easily and can improve their productivity. If your supervisor gives you a PDA—or perhaps something that has replaced it by then—you will have to learn to use it effectively. Part of the learning will relate to mastering the technology. The hard part, though, will be in preventing the technology from dominating your life.

The first, and probably the most important, feature that you will need to learn to use is the *off* button. You have a life outside of work.

Others have already learned that lesson. If you have trouble reaching someone, it could simply be because the other person is following a different schedule. Many people do not take their work home with them. Others refuse to answer their phones while they are driving. Even hands-free cellphones can be a distraction, and answering text messages while driving is extremely dangerous.

Once you have decided not to let technology dominate your life, you will have to figure out how to allow it to make you more productive at work.

The first point to remember is that text messaging is not instant. You should not expect an immediate reply to every message that you send, for several common reasons:

- Although you may have your PDA turned on, others may not.
- A problem could arise from people trying to deal with incompatible operating systems.
- A problem could arise with people who have trouble understanding the technology.

If you cannot get through and your text message is ignored, there is probably a good reason. Double-check the recipient's number before sending a message—especially if the message contains any sensitive information. Your boss might not enjoy reading the same witty observation about a co-worker that you sent to your friend.

Text messages may not be the best choice for all communication. Consider these factors, for example:

- The speed and informality of text messaging make it a good choice for transmitting short messages, but email or phone calls are better for messages longer than a sentence.
- Texting cannot replace the personal touch of face-to-face meetings or even phone calls.
- It should never be used to send formal invitations or to avoid speaking with someone.
- Under no circumstances should bad news be delivered by text message.

TABLE 1-4	Text-Messaging Etiquette
Generally accepted rules of conduct, such as the following, govern the use of text messaging as a form of business communication:	
Taboo	Composing a text message during a face-to-face conversation with someone is as rude as taking a phone call in a movie theatre.
Risky	If you use your PDA during meetings, you risk annoying the other people attending the meeting.
Content	Any text messages you do send during a meeting should contain only information that you would not be ashamed to read aloud to everyone.
Wording	Choose your words carefully so that recipients do not misinterpret an innocent comment. (Conveying a message with the appropriate tone can be difficult in the abbreviated format of text messages.)
Shrthnd	Think carefully about your text-messaging shorthand. It may not be realistic to expect your reader to understand all the text-messaging slang that you use in a non-work situation.

Text messaging is useful in four main areas:

1. for a quick exchange of brief information
2. for arranging appointments
3. for confirming meeting places
4. for sending quick messages

Text messaging comes with its own rules of etiquette. See **Table 1-4**.

These days, texting is mainstream. Its speed and efficiency are indisputable, and it has numerous uses both for workplace communications and for personal use. Yet no medium is perfect. For messages with any detail or emotional content, a different media choice would be more appropriate. Even when it is used to deliver brief spurts of information, texting can come under attack because of its intrusive nature.

An incoming message can interrupt a person's train of thought. Composing outgoing messages can lead to multi-tasking.

Multi-tasking: The New Normal

The *Oxford English Dictionary* says the term *multi-tasking* first appeared in 1966 and was used to describe the simultaneous processing of two or more jobs by a computer. By 1999, the dictionary says, the term's meaning had expanded to include human activities, particularly among teenagers.[24] Today, multi-tasking is widespread.

Almost everywhere you will see people engaged in examples of multi-tasking:

- talking on the phone while driving
- watching television while using a computer

Texting can distract you from other things.

▪ listening to a lecture and taking notes, while checking text messages on a cellphone and downloading music on a laptop

The meteoric rise in multi-tasking is due largely to the vast improvements in computer technology over the last couple of decades. As noted, the term *multi-tasking* was originally applied only to computers. As the technology became more sophisticated and people acquired the ability to run several programs simultaneously, they also became more used to juggling multiple tasks. This phenomenon is not new, of course. Parents have always had to keep their eyes on their small children while preparing meals and doing housework.

Portable electronic technologies have greatly increased the amount of multi-tasking that people are able to attempt. The important word, though, is *attempt*. Whether people are attempting to juggle two jobs, a family, and an active social life, or a cellphone, a PDA, a laptop, and a staff of ten, they must examine their time-use strategies to determine whether multi-tasking is helping them to use their time effectively or causing so much inefficiency that they end up making mistakes or having to redo whole tasks.

In many situations, multi-tasking increases mistakes and wastes time.

A *New York Times* article cited several research reports showing that multi-tasking increased the chances of making mistakes and reduced workers' performance on the job. The article described one study at Vanderbilt University in Nashville, Tennessee, in which subjects were given two tasks involving sound and pictures. The first task was to press a specific key on a computer keyboard after hearing one of eight different sounds. The other task was to say the correct vowel after seeing one of eight pictures.[25]

No delay was seen when the subjects performed the tasks one at a time. The response to the second task was delayed by almost a second when the participants were given the two tasks at about the same time.

Although a one-second delay is insignificant in many circumstances, in other situations, such as driving a car, it can mean a great deal.

By mid-2009, five Canadian provinces had banned the use of handheld cellphones in cars: Newfoundland and Labrador in 2002; Nova Scotia and Quebec in 2008; and Manitoba and Ontario in 2009. Some critics argue that even these bans may not go far enough because they continue to allow people to use hands-free phones while driving. A Transport Canada study found that even hands-free headsets posed enough of a distraction to result in significant changes in driving behaviour.[26]

Some people argue that people born in the '80s and '90s, "the Millennials," have a greater capacity for multi-tasking because video games, computers, and cellphones have been a part of their lives almost since the day they were born.

The *New York Times* recently reported on an experiment at Oxford University in Britain in which a group of 18- to 21-year-olds was compared with a group of 35- to 39-year-olds on a task that involved processing a simple code. The younger people did better when uninterrupted, but performance was equal when both groups were interrupted with phone calls, indicating that the older people were better at coping with distractions.[27]

Although some may think that habitual computer use makes people immune from the problems of multi-tasking, the *New York Times* article also cites a study at Microsoft that found that workers took an average of 15 minutes to return to their writing or coding after responding to phone calls or instant messages. The brain requires a warm-up period to move from task to task. It takes a few minutes for people to remember where they left off when they move from one partially completed task to another. The more times in a day that people move from one job to another, the more time they end up wasting.

Multi-tasking is not necessarily a bad idea in all situations. It may be possible to combine some tasks and improve efficiency, but the tasks have to be those that involve little concentration. A person might sort through files while waiting for the photocopier to complete a job, sort through email on a PDA while waiting for an airplane, or shut down a computer while taking a phone call. But people who attempt to type emails while attending meetings, or who talk on their cellphones or send text messages while driving will—at best— miss important information and reduce their efficiency. At worst, they will become a hazard to themselves and others. A British study by the Transport Research Laboratory found that texting while driving is more dangerous than drinking and driving.[28]

Tips for More Efficient Time Management Rather than jumping from job to job, or trying to do three things at once, a truly efficient person will try to reduce the amount of time wasted in unproductive activities. The following tips may help:

1. *Set aside blocks of time in which to accomplish specific goals:* 15 minutes to read email messages, half an hour to look up information on a client, an hour to meet with a client.

2. Keep a date book to record the times for appointments, due dates for projects, and other time-sensitive information. Do not leave things to the last minute so that you are forced to multi-task.

3. Reduce time wasted while travelling. Combine trips when possible so that you can accomplish two or more things on the same trip. Use the telephone or email instead of driving.

4. *Learn to say no.* It is impossible to be all things to all people. There are times when you need to refuse or delay a request in order to accomplish something else.

Chapter Summary

Communicating with others is an important part of most jobs. It can take many forms: writing emails and reports, speaking face to face or over the phone, or delivering oral presentations. People with strong communication skills generally receive higher-paying jobs and faster promotions than poor communicators.

The ideas you choose to communicate, the words you select to convey those ideas, and the media you choose for sending those messages all have a major effect on the impact of the message. The sequence of these decisions may change with the individual circumstances.

You live in an age of information and have access to a wide range of communication tools that were undreamed of a generation ago. Although such tools as personal digital assistants and emails can make communication more efficient, they also make demands on people's time and can become electronic leashes. People need to develop strategies for using them so that they do not dominate their lives.

PEARSON mycanadianbuscommlab Visit **www.mycanadianbuscommlab.ca** for everything you need to help you succeed in the job you've always wanted! Tools and resources include the following:

- Composing and The Writer's Toolkit
- Document Makeovers
- Video Case Studies
- Grammar exercises and much more!

Thinking and Writing Exercises

1. **The Advantages of Texting**
   Make a list of the advantages of sending a text message over talking to someone over the telephone. Make a second list of the advantages of talking over sending a text message. Compare your lists with someone else's.

2. **The Impact of Audience**
   You have made arrangements to meet a friend but are 20 minutes late because your bus is behind schedule.

   a. Translate the following paragraph into a text message:

   "My bus is stuck in traffic and will be about 20 minutes late. I'll meet you for coffee at the Tim Hortons restaurant at the corner of Princess Street and William Avenue."

   Compare your answer with those of several other students in the class. What differences do you notice in the way that people have abbreviated various parts of the message? What, if any, potential difficulties could this present?

   b. Write the message a second time, this time assuming that the reader is a business client. Compare the two messages for style, grammar, and tone.

3. **Social Activism Using the Web**
   Go to a social networking website, such as Facebook, MySpace, or YouTube. Use the search function to find examples of how people in your city, province, or territory have posted material for a political purpose or to advance a social cause. Write a short summary of the material that was posted, and explain how the media used had an influence on the message that was sent.

4. **Multi-tasking**

   Which of these multi-tasking activities would allow a person to work more efficiently because they do not involve significant competition from two activities requiring focused attention?

   a. downloading a ring tone while riding the bus

   b. organizing notes while watching television

   c. heating a baby's bottle, listening to the radio, and painting a wall

   d. listening to your partner's problems as you check messages on a PDA

   e. participating in a conference call while viewing the notes for it on a computer file

   f. answering messages on a PDA while driving to your next appointment

   g. making a phone call on a handheld cellphone while driving to your next appointment

   h. making a phone call on a hands-free cellphone while driving to your next appointment

   i. driving to the bank, mailing a letter, and stopping at the grocery store on the way home from work

   j. mediating a dispute between two co-workers, planning a meeting, and answering an urgent telephone call

   k. listening to a lecture, checking instant messages, and completing an assignment that is due at the end of a class

5. **Colour-Coded Layoffs**

   Consider the following situation: All employees within an organization are told to attend a company-wide meeting. Each person is handed a coloured envelope as he or she enters the room and is then directed to a section of the room that matches that colour. Layoffs are announced at the meeting. Those with one colour are directed to return to their offices; those with the other colour are escorted from the room by security personnel and told that their personal belongings will be packaged for them and returned. They are then escorted to the parking lot.[29]

   a. Under what circumstances would such a technique be justified?

   b. If circumstances changed a few months after the layoff and it was possible to rehire some of the laid-off workers, what effect would this method of workforce reduction have?

   c. Suppose you were one of the "survivors." What would your reaction be? How would this affect your loyalty to the company?

6. **Updating Employability Skills 2000+**

   With the possible exception of the skills related to communicating and using numbers, most of the items mentioned on the Conference Board of Canada's Employability Skills list relate to soft skills, such as working with others or demonstrating a positive attitude.

   a. Why does the Conference Board's list not include more hard skills, such as accounting or welding?

   b. The original list was created about ten years ago. Suppose that you were given the task of revising it. Are there any items on the list that no longer apply to all jobs? Are there any items that should be added?

7. **The Meaning in the Medium**

   a. At some point in your life, if it has not happened already, you will need to apply for a job and go to an employment interview. After the interview, you may receive either a written response in the form of a letter or email message, or an oral response in the form of a telephone call. What is the likely meaning of the medium in each case? Why?

   b. How has the creation of YouTube, Facebook, MySpace, and other interactive websites changed the way the world communicates? How might the existence of these media be more important than the actual messages posted on such sites?

8. **Layoffs by Email**

   Discuss the Radio Shack layoff mentioned earlier. Company officials defended the practice by saying that employees had received earlier notice that layoffs were pending and had been told that these notices would come through an email message.

   a. Does this make the practice acceptable?

   b. What are the advantages from a manager's perspective of using text messaging, voicemail, video recordings, or email to deliver bad news, such as layoff notices? What are the disadvantages?

   c. When is it acceptable to use text messaging to inform an employee of good news, such as a promotion or salary increase?

Writing Skills Checkup: Sentence Errors

Each sentence below could be a run-on sentence, a sentence fragment, or correct. Identify and correct the errors. If you think a sentence is correct, put a check mark beside it.

> Example: If you write a text message at a staff meeting. You should do it only if you would not be ashamed to read it aloud to everyone.

> Correction: Fragment in original version. If you write a text message at a staff meeting, you should do it only if you would not be ashamed to read it aloud to everyone.

1. Texting is informal text messages should not be used to send formal invitations or to avoid speaking with co-workers.
2. Courtesy is always important, composing a text message while you're in a face-to-face conversation with someone is as rude as taking a phone call in a movie theatre.
3. Do not get annoyed. If you don't get an immediate reply. Before you text someone to complain at the lack of a response. Be sure that they know how to use the system. And that their PDA will accept messages from yours.
4. Tone is difficult to gauge in text messages or in email. Recipients sometimes misinterpreting an innocent comment.
5. Illegal in some places to talk on the phone while driving. Even hands-free telephones pose a distraction that could be dangerous never send text messages while you're driving.
6. Expecting your boss to understand all the text-messaging slang that you use.
7. Awareness of other people's schedules. Don't assume that because you are awake, that the person you're texting is as well, many people prefer not to take their work home with them.
8. If it's urgent, make a phone call, if you can't get through and your text message is ignored, there's probably a good reason.
9. Your text-messaging device has an *off* button. Important that you learn to use it.
10. Text messages not the best choice for all communication, texting cannot always replace face-to-face meetings. Even phone calls.
11. Deliver bad news by text message. Not.
12. Text messages only for short requests or immediate responses. Anything more than 150 characters should be an email or a phone call.
13. Check the recipient's number before sending the message, your boss might not enjoy the same witty observation that you sent to your friend.
14. If you use your PDA during meetings you may feel more efficient you may also lose the respect of other people attending the meeting.

Ideas: Planning the Writing Process

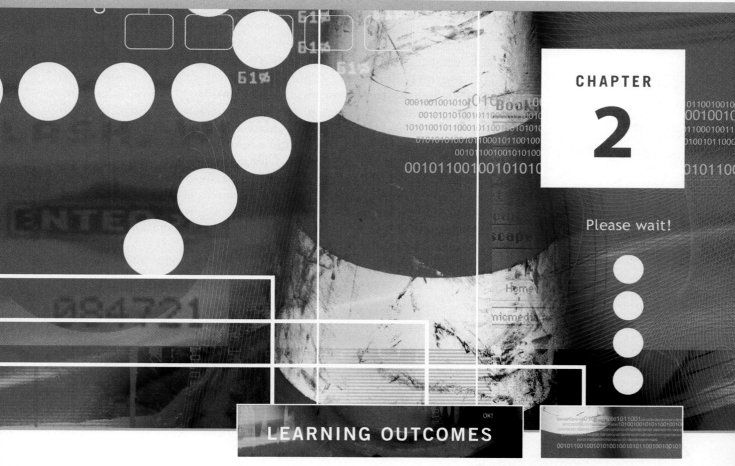

LEARNING OUTCOMES

After completing this chapter, you should be able to do the following:

2.1 Identify a key purpose for every document you create

2.2 Generate ideas through brainstorming

2.3 Construct outlines to organize content

2.4 Select information based on the purpose of your document and the needs of the audience

THE COST OF POOR PLANNING

When Mirabel Airport opened in 1975, it had largest area of any airport in the world. Located an hour's drive outside Montreal, it was supposed to become the transportation hub of northeastern North America, intended to process 17 million passengers a year. Many rural Quebecers were angered by the plan because farmland from 3000 local families was expropriated to make room for expansion.[1]

Instead, less than 10 percent of the expropriated land was ever used, and Mirabel carried only 3 million passengers in its peak year. A high-speed highway linking the airport to Montreal was never completed and another highway to Ottawa was never begun. High-tech vehicles used to shuttle passengers between planes and arrival decks broke down frequently. Passengers needing to transfer between domestic and international flights were forced to undergo a long and costly commute between Mirabel and the more centrally located Montreal-Trudeau airport. Although Montreal-Trudeau was supposed to close after Mirabel had opened, public opposition caused it to remain as Montreal's main airport. These problems occurred at a time when Toronto was overtaking Montreal in importance, and so airlines simply shifted their operations to Toronto's Pearson International Airport.

In 2004, Mirabel stopped all regular passenger flights and now handles cargo traffic alone.[2]

Poor planning contributed to Mirabel Airport's failure to attract business.

Operating at a fraction of its capacity, Mirabel today is being used as a location for movie production; it has been considered as a site for an amusement park, and land expropriated for its construction is gradually being returned to its original owners.[3] Billions of dollars invested in its construction have been written off as a loss.

Proper planning is a vital part of all business activities, including writing. When you are writing, good planning will save you time and money, and improve the quality of your work. Good planning involves establishing a purpose for writing, identifying the needs of your audience, gathering the information needed to meet those needs, and organizing your words in an effective way.

The Issues in Communication box deals with a twenty-first-century problem: the environmental problem that plastic bags pose and the ways that it is being dealt with in different places. As you read, notice the planning that went into the solutions.

ISSUES
in Communication
Banning the Bags

Plastic bags that clogged drains were blamed for flooding in Bangladesh.

In 2007, the isolated mining town of Leaf Rapids, Manitoba, became the first community in Canada to ban disposable plastic bags. The town implemented the change gradually—first imposing a levy on throwaway bags and then offering reusable bags at a discount when it imposed a complete ban—but its isolated location made it easier to put the bylaw into effect. Customers who do not like the bylaw have to travel for several hours to reach the next available store.

Dhaka, the capital city of Bangladesh, banned plastic bags after they clogged drainage ditches and caused flooding.[4] Bans have also been enacted in Ireland, China,[5] and San Francisco.

When bans on plastic bags are legislated, all businesses must operate under the same set of regulations. When businesses want to impose their own plans to reduce bag consumption in places that have not enacted such legislation, they face numerous challenges. They can seldom adopt Leaf Rapids' take-it-or-leave-it approach because consumers will take their business elsewhere.

It is not simply customers that retailers must consider. They have to answer to their own employees, to boards of directors, to stockholders, and to the general public and anyone else with an interest in the company. Informing people of such changes requires skilful management of information.

THE STAKES

Billions of plastic bags are manufactured each year, but their disposal has been responsible for the death of wildlife and the squandering of natural resources, as well as the cause of litter and waste disposal problems.

Conversely, a widespread moratorium on their use could undermine an entire industry. Some argue that a bag ban is unnecessary and have lobbied for voluntary bag reduction schemes and recycling programs. The Alberta Plastics Recycling Association cites figures that show Ireland's tax on plastic bags has simply resulted in people buying more heavy-gauge plastic bags for use in garbage disposal.[6]

The Canadian Plastics Industry Association provides information on alternatives to bag bans by offering advice on ways to reuse and recycle bags to reduce some of the environmental damage that the use of the bags is causing.[7]

COMMUNICATING THE MESSAGE TO DIFFERENT GROUPS

In places where bans have not been enacted (or perhaps to avoid the prospect), more and more Canadian businesses are reducing consumers' use of plastic bags by charging them for each bag that they use.

Even though the core message is essentially the same, communicating to customers, investors, employees and others requires businesses to adapt their message to the needs of the various groups.

The David Suzuki Foundation assembled a list of guidelines for communicating environmental messages. These guidelines can be used for many other messages as well:

- Customers and clients need information about what they can do to deal with the problem—preferably in the form of displays and other point-of-sale information.
- Employees need to know how they can take part in a successful program and they require opportunities to provide feedback.
- Investors want information about how the business is managing the change, how those changes compare with those made by other businesses, and how the business is benefiting from new opportunities.
- Media require independent proof of the claims, along with information about the reaction of customers and employees.[8]

Loblaws issued a news release that included the results of an independent survey on the public's attitude toward plastic bags, information about changes to the checkout process, and an announcement that partial proceeds from the plastic bag levy would be given to the World Wildlife Federation. Customers were reminded of the change with information cards, internal and external signs saying "Bring it," and teams of "Green Greeters" in the

stores to help during the transition.[9]

In its corporate social responsibility report directed at customers, colleagues, investors, and government, Loblaws provided data on the reduced consumption of plastic bags in its stores, along with information about its other waste-reduction plans.[10]

ENSURING LONG-TERM COMMITMENT

People who say in surveys that they support such environmental changes do not always follow through when faced with reality. A few years ago, British supermarkets found themselves overstocked with green products because consumers had said that they wanted to purchase environmentally friendly products, but they were then unwilling to pay extra for them.[11]

Loblaws, as well as its competitor Sobeys, anticipated that some customers would see the move to charge for bags as a cash grab and planned strategies to avoid such allegations. Both companies announced that they were donating some of the money from the sale of bags to environmental causes.[12] In addition, Sobeys offered a lifetime guarantee on its reusable bags. When one of its bags does wear out, it will be replaced free, thus saving consumers the cost of replacing bags while at the same time promoting customer loyalty.[13]

Achieving widespread social change relies on a multi-faceted approach that involves legislation, communication, and other types of social action. Similar widespread changes have occurred in the last few decades to deal with other problems: Public attitudes toward seatbelt use, smoking, and drunk driving have changed significantly in that time.

When communicating an environmental message (or any other information), it is important to analyze the information and the audience when deciding what aspects of that message to emphasize. Strategies that work well in some situations may be much less effective in others.

DISCUSSION

1. Do you believe that persuasion is sufficient to get people to act in more environmentally responsible ways, or is a stronger approach involving governmental regulation and taxation required?

2. Identify the most significant improvement to the environment that you can think of, and then identify the factors that have caused this change to occur.

3. What role do businesses play in promoting an environmental message? How can business be influenced to promote other types of less wasteful packaging?

4. How do you respond to the argument that the banning of disposable plastic shopping bags will simply result in people purchasing more plastic garbage bags?

TAKE IT FURTHER

The First Appearance of Plastic Bags

The first facility to make plastic grocery bags was started in 1973. Paper grocery bags were being phased out by 1976.[14]

What other businesses were affected by the switch from paper to plastic? ■

THE IMPORTANCE OF PLANNING

Leaf Rapids, Sobeys, and Loblaws began planning to phase out disposable bags well before they announced the changes publicly. Businesses and governments plan all major changes so that the tasks proceed smoothly. The same thing is true of writing. Many people resist the idea of devoting time to the preliminary work required to plan their writing. Some see this as a waste of time that prevents them from getting to the work at hand. They prefer to jump ahead to the actual writing rather than waste effort thinking about their readers, conducting research, and jotting down key points.

An experienced writer will often write a routine document in one draft without doing any apparent planning. When the topic is familiar, it's possible to store the important ideas in your head. Even so, a good writer will begin by jotting down the key points. Sometimes in their haste to send out a routine email, people forget to put in crucial information, such as the location of a meeting, thus annoying recipients who must then write back for the missing details. Longer documents, or ones that are not produced on a regular basis, require even more careful planning to ensure that all necessary information is included.

Some writers resist planning after having tried (and failed) to follow a structured approach in the past. Certain topics are far more difficult to write about than others. Compare the relative difficulty of planning a report describing the events of a sales trip to clients with the planning of a report presenting ways to deal with an economic crisis. See **Table 2-1.**

Although you will likely face such difficult challenges as the economic crisis report many times in your career, many of the business documents that you will prepare will require you to write about topics that are fairly straightforward.

✷ ⸢Explore   `TABLE 2-1`   **Simple versus Complex Report**

Simple Sales Trip Report	Complex Economic Crisis Report
– Contains concrete information based on notes gathered during the week	– Requires more open-ended thinking and much more planning
– Subdivided into separate sections for each location, with subsections containing specific information about each customer's order	– Requires the challenging task of gathering the necessary information about the crisis, its causes, and its effects; part of this challenge is deciding what available information is relevant to your report
– Ends with a quick summary of any changes that will take place	– Involves working out the best course of action, through discussion with others; the ultimate challenge is to arrive at a creative solution to a difficult problem
	– Ends with recommendations for dealing with the problem—which may not be agreed on by all people concerned

✷ ⸢Explore # Planning Routine Documents

Most of the writing that you do at work will probably take the form of routine documents: emails to co-workers, letters to clients, or progress reports to supervisors. *Routine* in this sense means that the documents will not usually require you to demonstrate any great insight. Your main goal in writing routine documents will usually be to communicate all the necessary information in a way that is easy to understand.

Deciding what information is necessary, and how to make it easy to understand, poses additional challenges that vary from situation to situation. Often the audience will affect your decisions. A strategy that is effective for communicating to one type of reader may not work at all for a different set of readers.

THREE-POINT PLANNING

Whenever you write in the workplace, you have three main goals in the initial stages (see **Figure 2-1** on page 36):

1. Determine your purpose.
2. Identify the needs of your audience.
3. Obtain and organize your information.

We discuss the principles involved in each of these points in the sections that follow. You can apply them to all the writing that you do in the workplace.

1. Establish Your Purpose for Writing

One of your first tasks when planning any business message is to identify your purpose. Sometimes you will be supplying other people with information;

sometimes you will be trying to sell something; and sometimes you will be looking for answers to your questions.

The purpose of your message is whatever you want the receiver to think or do as a result of your message. You may want to ask the reader to take some action. At other times your purpose will simply be to provide specific information—the only action required of the receiver will be to take note of the information. Sometimes your purpose will be to change your readers' opinion or to convince them to do something. Whatever your purpose, write it down as you are planning your message and refer to it frequently as you add the details to your outline.

The purpose you choose will affect everything else in the message. If, for example, your purpose is to let your supervisor know which dates you have chosen for your vacation, it is enough to simply include the relevant dates. If, however, the purpose is to convince the supervisor to approve your request for a vacation during a busy time of year when the office is already short-staffed, it might be necessary to provide reasons that you should be given special consideration.

Purpose in Action When you are deciding your purpose, it is often a good idea to ask the following questions:

- *Is the message necessary? Will the information change anything?* Although it may be necessary to let your supervisor and co-workers know about the dates for your vacation, a message complaining about the company's policy for scheduling vacations might be perceived as a waste of time if it is sent to people with no authority to change policies.

- *Are you the right person to deliver the message?* The identity of the person sending a message can have a major impact on the way it is received. A request to change a company's policy on vacation bookings will have a different effect depending on whether it comes from one individual, a union representative, or a person in upper management. One aspect of communication strategy is finding the correct person to deliver the message.

- *Does your message make sense? Is it logical?* People tend to resist making changes until they have a good reason to do so. The bigger the change, the more persuasion they will require. A routine vacation request may be approved automatically. Asking for an exception to standard procedures may require an explanation, which may or may not lead to the request being granted. Revamping the entire policy for allocating vacation days will require a very convincing argument backed up with evidence.

- *Is your timing appropriate?* Timing affects the way a message will be received. A request for a special vacation time has a better chance of success if it is delivered well in advance of the vacation period than if it is presented a week before the date.

Timing is often given careful consideration before a message is sent out. In many organizations, controversial news is delivered late on a Friday afternoon to allow people to assess the impact of the message over the weekend before responding.

TAKE IT FURTHER

The Impact of the Messenger

The year after golfer Tiger Woods turned pro, interest in the game increased dramatically, TV ratings soared, and more than $650 million of new money was poured into golf.[15] Celebrities have also been known to endorse political candidates and a variety of causes where they have no expertise.

Should such endorsements be regulated? If so, how?

✓• Practise ## 2. Analyze the Audience

The other key factor in the initial planning of messages is the audience. Different people have different requirements. Information that is vital to some people may be unnecessary to others. For example, in the aftermath of a fire, a business owner has to communicate the information to a variety of people. Insurance adjustors require the details of the damages, along with reports from the police and fire departments. Clients are more interested in the status of their own property and predictions on when business will resume. Investors need assurances that the damage was covered by insurance.

The audience has a major impact on the planning of any message. The following questions will help you to analyze your audience and provide them with the appropriate information.

Who Are the Primary and Secondary Audiences?   The larger your audience, the more decisions you will have to make about the information to include in a document. Information that is important to one person may be unneeded by another. In general, you can classify your readers into primary and secondary audiences. Primary audiences are the key decision makers, usually supervisors or clients.

Secondary audiences are other people who receive a message but are not deeply involved, such as lower-level workers needing to know how changes will affect them. The secondary audience may include the people who influence a decision or are to be affected by it but who do not hold the final authority. Secondary audiences may also be such people as higher-level managers who are removed from the actual details of an issue but are ultimately responsible for any decisions made.

When planning a document, it is necessary to deal with the secondary audiences as well. Although the report may convince upper management that a plan will reduce costs and improve efficiency, if that same plan creates headaches for the people responsible for implementing it, you can be sure that they will voice their objections.

In general, the more you know about your audience, the better able you will be to meet their needs. The key decision makers are concerned about practicality, costs, and efficiency. Those who influence a decision but have no formal say in it are concerned mainly about how the decision will affect them. You need to find out as much as you can about your audience to meet their needs.

What Is Their Background Knowledge?   The background knowledge of your audience will influence the way your message is received. In some cases your audience will have more expertise on the topic than you do. In other cases your readers may know very little about the topic. Even if you are writing to people with more authority than you have, remember that they may not have your level of expertise.

You will sometimes work on projects that require a specialized set of skills. You may be hired because of your accounting skills, but your supervisor may be an expert in marketing. Your supervisor, who will be responsible for many such projects, will expect you to be able to explain your work simply and briefly without getting bogged down in the technical details.

When you are writing for people with limited knowledge of the topic, use the simplest terminology possible and explain any technical terms or jargon that you must use. It is also necessary to clearly explain which parts of the information are facts that can be verified and which parts are opinions.

When you are writing to people who are knowledgeable in your topic area, do not provide basic explanations of things they already know. People find that condescending. Instead, give thorough explanations of the information they require, making sure that you have indicated how you obtained the information so that they can review your sources if necessary.

What Do They Know and What Do They Need to Know?   People rarely are totally ignorant about a topic. Most people have some knowledge about many topics. One of your objectives when planning a document is to find out what your audience knows and what they need to know. Then you can decide whether to give them a brief recap of background information (some of which they may know) to act as a bridge to any new information that you include.

The decisions about what new information to include are essential. Sometimes you will identify factors that your readers have not even considered. A business owner, for example, who requests an estimate for renovations to an old building will likely receive along with it some information about other changes required to bring the building up to the local building code: improvements to wiring and fire safety, changes needed to accommodate people with disabilities, details of asbestos removal, and other improvements needed to make the building conform to current environmental standards.

Supplying your audience with the information they have requested is a good starting point, but trust your own judgment, too.

3. Obtain and Organize Your Information

One challenge, whenever you write, is deciding what information your audience needs and then finding the best combination of primary and secondary research that provides the information.

- You may look through records or take notes on what you have seen. You may find, just as Loblaws did, that you require more information than your own observations can provide. Loblaws conducted surveys to find out the public's attitude toward plastic bags. Observation and surveys are two techniques in *primary research*, which involves assembling information that was not previously known.

- *Secondary research* is an often-used source of evidence. You can select information that has already been published elsewhere and use it to support your own arguments. This book, for example, includes a list of endnotes: sources that were assembled during the planning stages.

✴ Explore **FIGURE 2-1** **Planning a Business Message**

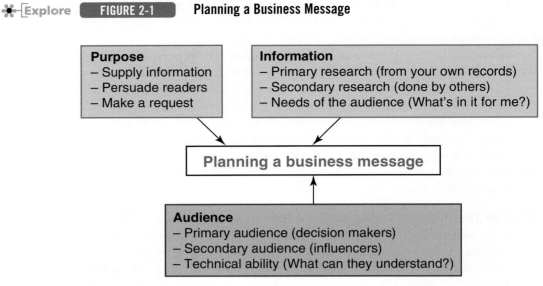

Purpose
— Supply information
— Persuade readers
— Make a request

Information
— Primary research (from your own records)
— Secondary research (done by others)
— Needs of the audience (What's in it for me?)

Planning a business message

Audience
— Primary audience (decision makers)
— Secondary audience (influencers)
— Technical ability (What can they understand?)

When you are planning any business message, think about its purpose, its audience, and the necessary information.

What's in It for Me?   When people receive new information, they frequently ask the question "What's in it for me?" They have a basic human characteristic to need to know how changes will affect them. Understanding this principle will allow you to structure information to show how it will affect the readers.

When the management of an organization decides to expand operations into a different location or to branch out in a new direction, they need to explain the consequences to all the people affected. Some employees will be anxious about whether their existing positions will change. Others will want to know about transfers to a new location and whether any such moves will be mandatory. Questions about wages and job security should be expected.

Customers and suppliers need to know how their operations will be affected, and stockholders need to know how the move will affect their investments.

The main focus of all their questions is "What's in it for me?"

Working with Others

The process of communication frequently involves collaborating with others. Large documents may require input from a variety of people. Presentations may be delivered by a team. Different people or departments may be expected to contribute sections of a project according to their areas of expertise. The modern world simply moves too fast to accommodate an individual labouring alone for years.

Collaboration is a common practice in many workplace writing assignments. Writing with a group allows different people to contribute specialized knowledge. It also allows the group to benefit from the collective wisdom of its members.

Whether you are working alone on a small project or working with a group on a larger assignment, all writing goes through the phases of planning, composing, and revising, in roughly that order. Whereas much of the composing is done by individuals working alone, the planning and revising are frequently done in teams.

Basic Tips   Teamwork of this sort may be more productive with the application of a few basic principles:

1. *Choose a leader.* At times, a person in authority will appoint the group leader or editor; at other times the group itself will make the choice. The leader should give direction to the group and sometimes mediate disputes, always focusing on the finished product rather than the individual pieces.

2. *Allocate duties.* Each person in the group should know exactly what he or she is expected to do. Sometimes the group will decide these duties, and sometimes the leader will. At times the task itself will dictate who does what (e.g., the sales team might report on marketing efforts, while engineers deal with production issues). When working on any team writing assignment, a well-constructed outline will ensure that key sections are neither accidentally left out nor repeated by two different writers. See the section "Organizing with Outlines."

3. *Establish deadlines.* Whether you are working alone or with others, setting realistic deadlines—and keeping to them—will ensure that the job proceeds smoothly. It may be necessary to set deadlines for various stages of a large project. The group will probably need to meet periodically to exchange information and share ideas, with each group member then going away to accomplish a task.

4. *Anticipate problems.* Inevitably, any group of people working together will encounter problems. Someone may have trouble meeting deadlines; another person may not be contributing enough; two people may disagree on the content of a section. A way of settling disputes needs to be established. The group leader may be assigned to mediate, or the other group members may be asked to decide. Problems should not be ignored in the hope that they will disappear. Minor differences of opinion will grow into major disputes if they are not dealt with, and anger and resentment can overshadow the group's solidarity.

Generating Ideas   Although much of your writing will involve creating routine documents, you will at times be expected to present a new or innovative solution to a problem. Then your first and possibly most difficult challenge will be to identify a solution. Ideas do not simply appear out of nowhere, even if it seems that way when someone receives a flash of inspiration. Such moments of brilliance usually come after long hours or even years of hard work, failed attempts, and careful preparation. Inventor Thomas Edison once said that "genius is one percent inspiration, ninety-nine percent perspiration."[17] Good ideas do not come easily. Hard work, intensive preparation, and persistence are necessary to produce creative ideas.

Ideas do not always come to individuals working alone. Sometimes the best ideas result from the collective effort of a group of creative minds.

MEETING IN PROGRESS

Teamwork may be more productive when a few basic principles are followed.

Brainstorming Brainstorming is a group technique for generating ideas. It was developed in the 1930s by advertising executive Alex Osborn to help groups generate creative solutions to problems.[18]

Problem does not necessarily mean something that is wrong, although it could. In this context, *problem* also means "challenge" or "opportunity." The important thing is that everyone starts with a specific question that defines the issue to be dealt with. Large challenges can be subdivided into smaller ones when necessary.

A problem that many employers face at some point, for example, is the amount of time employees spend getting to and from the workplace each day. Associated problems include the following:

- the environmental costs of commuting
- employees' commuting expenses
- actual travel times
- absenteeism during bad weather

TABLE 2-2	Alex Osborn's Brainstorming Guidelines
1. More Is Better	Try to generate as many ideas as possible. Many of these ideas will go unused in the end, but a large number of possibilities will give people more material to work with.
2. Delay Judgment	All ideas are good. Criticism or rejection of ideas is not allowed. People should contribute as much as possible—even if the ideas are half-baked or wacky.
3. Encourage Wild Ideas	Unusual ideas can lead to new ways of thinking. Participants should look at things from different perspectives or to find alternative ways of examining the issue.
4. Build on Each Other's Ideas	Often two or more partial ideas can be combined into one. People should be encouraged to take elements from other ideas and adapt them to the problem's solution.

Source: *Adapted from Osborn, Alex.* Applied Imagination: Principles and Procedures of Creative Problem Solving. *New York: Scribner's, 1963. Print.*

Solutions vary and can include subsidized transit passes, decentralized workplaces, and flexible work hours.

A group that is looking for solutions to such problems needs to identify specific restraints—budgetary restrictions, for example—that would prevent some solutions from being implemented. After that comes the difficult part—generating ideas through the actual brainstorming. During brainstorming sessions, everyone is equal. Seniority should not count because deferring to people in authority may inhibit the process of generating ideas.

Osborn set four guidelines for effective brainstorming. See **Table 2-2.**

Cluster Diagrams Tools that can aid the brainstorming process include cluster diagrams, or mind maps, that help people to group ideas and see relationships between the groups. Computer software can be used to create cluster diagrams, but blank sheets of paper work well too. Some people prefer to write their ideas on sticky notes so that they can group them in different ways.

The process involves many of the same rules as brainstorming. Participants build on each other's ideas, delaying judgment until the idea-generating process has ended. The difference is that cluster diagrams have a greater visual element. People start with the key problem in the middle of a blank sheet of paper, drawing lines to add new ideas or to connect related ideas. People are encouraged to free associate ideas and to use a variety of colours and shapes to help in the grouping process.

The mind-mapping process results in a more visual approach to idea generation that helps some people with the creative process. The cluster diagram in **Figure 2-2** shows the result of a planning session on ways to reduce office overcrowding.

When the group completes the process of generating ideas, group members can start examining the ideas more critically. Ideas that are obviously

TAKE IT FURTHER

Online Innovation Jam

In 2006, IBM held what may have been the world's largest brainstorming session, involving 100 000 people. It set up a website that went live at a predetermined time and invited ideas on a variety of general topics. IBM did not claim the rights to any of the suggestions, but it did promise to fund development of the strongest ideas.[19]

Can you think of other ways that online collaboration can be used to generate ideas?

FIGURE 2-2 Cluster Diagram

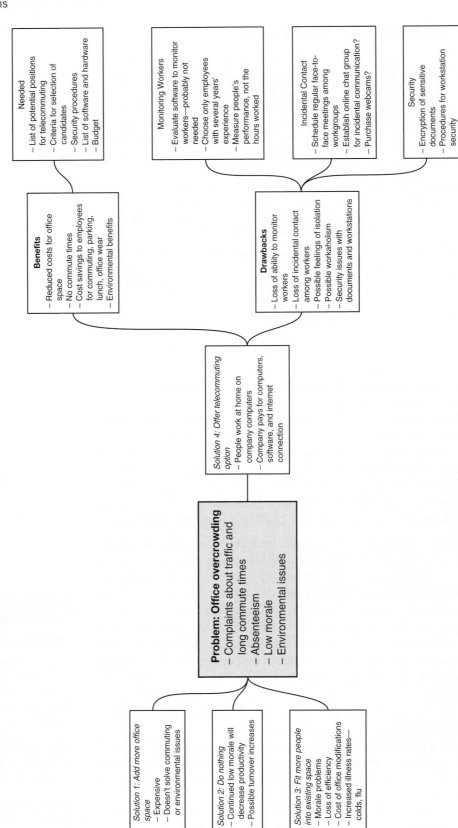

Problem: Office overcrowding
- Complaints about traffic and long commute times
- Absenteeism
- Low morale
- Environmental issues

Solution 1: Add more office space
- Expensive
- Doesn't solve commuting or environmental issues

Solution 2: Do nothing
- Continued low morale will decrease productivity
- Possible turnover increases

Solution 3: Fit more people into existing space
- Morale problems
- Loss of efficiency
- Cost of office modifications
- Increased illness rates—colds, flu

Solution 4: Offer telecommuting option
- People work at home on company computers
- Company pays for computers, software, and internet connection

Benefits
- Reduced costs for office space
- No commute times
- Cost savings to employees for commuting, parking, lunch, office wear
- Environmental benefits

Needed
- List of potential positions for telecommuting
- Criteria for selection of candidates
- Security procedures
- List of software and hardware
- Budget

Drawbacks
- Loss of ability to monitor workers
- Loss of incidental contact among workers
- Possible feelings of isolation
- Possible workaholism
- Security issues with documents and workstations

Monitoring Workers
- Evaluate software to monitor workers—probably not needed
- Choose only employees with several years' experience
- Measure people's performance, not the hours worked

Incidental Contact
- Schedule regular face-to-face meetings among workgroups
- Establish online chat group for incidental communication?
- Purchase webcams?

Security
- Encryption of sensitive documents
- Procedures for workstation security

Software is available to produce cluster diagrams, but many people use flip charts or sticky notes instead.

unworkable are removed, as are duplicate ideas. The remaining ideas are then organized, and the process of outlining starts.

Organizing with Outlines

One reason many people resist writing outlines is that they think the process involves a lot of work. There is some truth to this: Creating an outline is a great deal of work. Preparing an outline requires the writer to do all the initial research, the planning, and the creative work. The advantage of an outline is that once this preliminary work is complete, the rest of the writing task can move very quickly.

Most people would agree that outlines are a key requirement for long documents, such as reports and proposals—especially when the work needs to be divided among different people. However, when you are planning shorter types of communication, such as letters, emails, or even phone calls, outlines can save you time and improve the quality of your work.

Do not make the mistake of writing without knowing what to say in the hope that everything will work itself out on paper. That will not happen. Even a quick note telling someone that you will be late will require a certain amount of planning.

1. Outlines for Short Documents   Your word-processing program contains an outlining function that may be useful for complicated outlines, but shorter types

"O.K., we've set up the manufacturing facilities, organized the distribution network, hired the marketing expertise, and allocated the advertising budget. Any ideas for a product?"

Brainstorming does not always follow a sequential pattern.

of communication may require only a handwritten list on a notepad. Before making a phone call to a business associate, many people will jot down a list of the key points to be covered so they don't forget anything. Such informal outlines take little time to write and use either a simple numbering system or none at all, but they help to ensure that all the necessary information is shared.

Similarly, before writing a message about a routine matter, it may save time and improve efficiency to put the key points in a brief outline. The following outline may be useful for a number of situations.

Main idea   Most messages begin with the information that is most important. It contains the key idea that you want to communicate to your colleague or customer and may also contain a summary of the entire message.

Details (supporting details: dates, times, prices)   The details section may be the longest part of the message. When you are writing your outline, list all the data that should be included: dates and times for meetings, specific questions you want answered, or further information about the matter being discussed.

Outcome (What comes next?)   The outcomes section will often be the shortest part of the outline. The email or letter that develops from this outline will usually end by indicating what will happen next. If you are sending something to the reader, you would say so and indicate the date. The outline itself may simply include the words "Send package June 1" to remind the writer to specify the date.

Such outlines take only a few minutes to prepare. Appearance, spelling, and grammar are unimportant at this stage of the writing process. You can improve all these later in the writing process. The key purpose for an outline is to ensure that all the necessary information is included and well organized.

2. Outlines for Longer Documents   Outlines are indispensable when working with a group.

As documents become longer and more complicated the need for outlines, and their complexity, increase. A short report justifying the use of a new strategy to combat a city's litter problem requires a more structured approach than a request for new recycling bins in an office. The report will very likely require a formal outline.

Formal outlines usually include several sections, each of which is divided into subsections. Each section is described with a few key words or short phrases, which often are turned into headings later. Writers use various numbering schemes to help with the organization of the ideas. Since reports and long documents are frequently group efforts, creating a formal outline will not only improve the document's organization but also save time, effort, and money by helping the writers overlapping each other's work or, even worse, omitting important information.

A variation of the formal outline is the sentence-level outline, which, as the name suggests, uses whole sentences instead of words and phrases to outline the document. Creating this type of outline may take more time, but it will reduce the time needed during later phases of the writing process and may make it easier to collaborate with others.

Advantages of Outlines   Outlines aid writing in four ways:

1. They help generate ideas, allowing you to see how the separate ideas fit into the overall picture.

2. They facilitate group work. Different sections of a large project can be distributed to different people with minimal overlap.

3. They improve organization, making it easier to group similar ideas together and to rearrange blocks of ideas.

4. They ensure that nothing is left out. They act as a sort of shopping list— important sections can be checked off as they are completed.

Organization in Action: Getting Your Information in Order

When you have established the purpose of a document, determined the audience, and gathered the preliminary information, you need to choose the best way to organize the information.

Different documents require different strategies. A single document may use several of the following strategies in different places:

- *Chronological order:* Use this when you need to present information in a specific sequence. Instruction manuals or incident reports generally follow a timeline.

- *Spatial approach:* A good choice for documents organized around geographical factors or physical features. An analysis of several branch plants would focus on each location in turn.

- *Comparisons:* This usually reveals the most important overall factors. An analysis of equipment being considered for purchase might examine such factors as price, reliability, warranty coverage, and maintenance costs.

- *Problem-solution pattern:* This is used when presenting the reader with options on how to change an existing situation. You can identify the problems with the current situation and then suggest improvements.

Writers often use more than one strategy in different sections of a document. In a report evaluating different sites for a company's future expansion, for example, you could organize the information by using both the key decision-making factors and the locations. The same information could be organized in two different ways, both of which could be used effectively—see **Table 2-3** and **Table 2-4.**

Organizing around locations is preferred if the readers are expected to process all the details of each location at one time. This structure might be useful in a short report or for the summary section of a long report.

For a longer report or one that requires a more detailed comparison, the key factors in **Tables 2-3** and **2-4** would likely form the primary division.

TABLE 2-3   **A Comparison Report Organized by Location**

1. Moose Jaw	2. Medicine Hat	3. Yellowknife
A. Labour costs	A. Labour costs	A. Labour costs
B. Building costs	B. Building costs	B. Building costs
C. Taxes	C. Taxes	C. Taxes
D. Transportation costs	D. Transportation costs	D. Transportation costs

TABLE 2-4   **A Comparison Report Organized by Key Factors**

1. Labour Costs	2. Building Costs	3. Taxes	4. Transportation Costs
A. Moose Jaw	A. Moose Jaw	A. Moose Jaw	A. Moose Jaw
B. Medicine Hat	B. Medicine Hat	B. Medicine Hat	B. Medicine Hat
C. Yellowknife	C. Yellowknife	C. Yellowknife	C. Yellowknife

This would allow readers to form a detailed picture of the impact of each factor at all locations before moving on to a detailed discussion of the next factor.

Documents may have more than one level of heading. The report in the tables above has two levels. Longer documents may have three or more levels. The following guidelines will help you find a logical basis for subdividing your outlines into smaller sections:

Principles for Organizing Information   Common principles for organizing information include the following:

- Sections can be subdivided into two to five subsections.
- No subsection should consist of a single point.
- All subordinate points should relate to the main point of the section.
- The basis for division should not allow overlap between sections and should ensure that nothing is left out.

Do not be afraid to change your outline at any time during the writing process. Delete sections that do not belong. Add more information when necessary. Change the sequence. Always remember that outlines are simply tools to help you organize ideas. A good outline will allow you to make major changes to a plan with a minimal amount of work. It is far easier to change a few lines on an outline than to discard pages of carefully written text and begin again.

THE WRITING PROCESS IN ACTION

When you are ready to transform the ideas in your outline into sentences and paragraphs, you will find that the time and effort that went into the planning process were well worth it. The actual writing will progress quickly if you follow a few simple guidelines.

1. Set Objectives for Yourself

It is necessary to set long-term goals, such as completion dates for a project, but shorter-term objectives will also help you get the job completed. Along with these small tasks can come small rewards. Tell yourself that when you complete the section that you are working on, you will take a ten-minute break. Organize your schedule so that you can get the task completed within a reasonable amount of time.

2. Expect to Make Mistakes

Nothing you write will be perfect the first time. Do not interrupt the flow of thought by running for a dictionary to determine the correct meaning of a word or agonizing over a sentence that does not sound quite right. Concentrate on meeting your objective. You will revise your work later, so it is not necessary to get everything perfect on the first draft.

3. Feel Free to Shift between Sections

It is usually not necessary to begin your writing with what you expect to be the first word of your final document and to end with the last word. You may find it more productive to start with the section that is easiest to write. If you get writer's block while writing one section, you can always set it aside and work on a different section.

Consider writing your introduction last. Since one of the functions of an introduction is to present readers with a preview of the document, it will be much easier to do that once you have written the rest of the document. An exception might occur when you still need to work out for yourself what the document is going to say. In that case, writing the introduction first might make everything that follows much easier to write.

4. Set Your Work Aside When It Is Complete

Immediately after you finish a piece of writing, you may feel a sense of accomplishment. This satisfaction is only natural and is certainly desirable. However, it may cloud your objectivity and prevent you from making good critical judgments about your work. Plan your time so that once you have completed a section, you can set it aside for a day or two and look at it again after the sense of satisfaction has worn off and your objectivity has returned. You will find errors that you may not have noticed before and sections that could have been expressed more clearly. To do this, of course, you cannot leave your writing until the last minute.

5. Edit Your Work

After the work has had a chance to sit, pick it up again and begin revising your writing. With a letter or an email, the revision process may take only a few minutes and be completed soon after the initial writing is complete.

With a report or a longer document, especially one that has been written in collaboration with others, that process may take much longer. We suggest the following steps:

- Begin by reading the document and comparing it with your original outline. Make sure that you have included all the information you intended to put in.
- Decide whether you have accidentally repeated yourself or included information that is not needed.
- Decide whether you need to alter the sequence of your information.
- Check the accuracy of your data and your facts, and that your calculations are correct.
- Ask yourself whether you have expressed the ideas in a way that suits your purpose and audience.

Editing is more effective if you give your writing to someone else to read. You might know exactly what you intended to say, and the way you expressed it might seem perfectly clear to you, but if another reader does not agree, then you may need to revise your work. Sometimes you may need to rewrite or delete whole sections.

You will likely need to revise longer and more detailed pieces of writing several times before they are ready to present to the intended audience.

6. Proofread Your Work

The Problem with Spell "Chequers"

Every word in the following sentence is spelled incorrectly. Type it into a word processor and see how many errors the spell checker detects: Ewe cant trussed ah programme two fined awl you're righting miss takes fore yew.

Mark Twain said that he respected people who knew more than one way to spell a word.[20] Why do people in business place an emphasis on correct spelling?

Before any document can be considered finished, it must be proofread. Ideally the proofreading will be done several times by more than one person. Proofreaders concentrate on technical errors: spelling mistakes, typographical errors, grammatical problems, or words that have been used incorrectly. Of course, if they also find factual mistakes or other more serious problems, those must also be corrected.

The spelling and grammar checking tools that come with many word-processing programs are useful writing aids, but they are no better than the person operating the computer. The limited artificial intelligence of such devices cannot offer useful advice on how to correct some of the errors they identify (or even to identify many problems), nor will they catch all the errors that people commonly make. Problems, such as confusing *it's* (for *it is*) and *its* (as in *its coat*) or writing *of* instead of *off* may go unnoticed by the computer.

Take advantage of these tools, but remember that you are ultimately responsible for your own writing.

WRITING TEMPLATES

Business and government organizations frequently provide writing templates to assist people who are assembling large writing projects. Such templates help writers generate ideas and ensure the consistency of submissions for the readers.

Here is an example of one such template that has been adapted from the Business Development Bank of Canada (BDC; **www.bdc.ca/en/home.htm**). Each year BDC holds a contest for entrepreneurs aged 19 to 35. Entrants are judged on the originality of the business concept, the company's success, its potential for growth, and the company's social involvement.

To assess these qualities, BDC asks nominees to submit a description of the business organized into the four sections:

BDC Young Entrepreneur Awards   ✳–[Explore

Section 1: General Information

- company name, address, website, email, province or territory of registration or incorporation, date of establishment
- industry sector
- description of the type of products or services the company offers
- financial data for the past 12 months

Section 2: Company's Strategic Position

- accomplishments and challenges the entrepreneur faces
- company's competitive edge and general strategy
- factors that set the company apart from the competition

Section 3: Vision

- plans for the company's future
- strategies for achieving entrepreneur's goals

Section 4: Community Involvement

- membership in a business association
- charitable work[21]

Such lists clarify the BDC's expectations for the people entering the competition and make the planning of their writing straightforward. The onus is still on the writers to assemble the necessary information and to present it in a persuasive manner, but a template makes planning for that task much easier.

If the entrepreneurs entering this competition were part of a group, this template would simplify the allocation of the writing tasks. Different people could put together the background information on the company and its community involvement. Sections on the company's vision and plans for the future would require a more creative approach and would likely be prepared either by the group leader or by a committee of the business's key personnel.

Before submitting the application, those involved examine their information alongside the submission form to make sure that all the required information is provided.

Templates are often provided by organizations that request submissions, but many word-processing programs have similar templates that provide writers with headings or questions to answer. Such tools do improve the writing process as long as the writer realizes that generic templates seldom fit the writing task exactly. They usually require modification to ensure the final document meets the needs of both reader and writer.

Commercially Produced Templates

Numerous organizations produce writing templates that were designed with adaptation in mind. This is an excerpt from Microsoft's "Business Plan for Startup Business."

> **IV Products and Services**
>
> - Describe in depth your products or services (technical specifications, drawings, photos, sales brochures, and other bulky items belong in Appendices).
>
> - What factors will give you competitive advantages or disadvantages? Examples include level of quality or unique or proprietary features.
>
> - What are the pricing, fee, or leasing structures of your products or services?[22]

This is only a tiny fragment of a template that covers almost thirty pages. Other parts of the template call for information about the prospective business's goals and objectives, marketing strategy, and financial plan.

The Limitations of Templates

Templates, such as those discussed above, help people organize their writing and provide them with useful prompts that may help them to identify key factors. To use such a tool successfully, though, it is important to remember that a template is only a starting point. Templates are prepared with the needs of numerous people in mind. It is impossible for one to fit the exact needs of every user. When you are using templates, adapt them to your specific needs. Some sections will have to be modified, others added, and some left out completely.

All templates must be used with caution. Although a generic document may help you plan and organize your own writing, a one-size-fits-all approach cannot produce original ideas or replace the contributions of creative minds.

Chapter Summary

Writing outlines will save you time, reduce your workload, and make it easier for you to coordinate your work with that of your co-workers. Even if you have resisted making outlines in the past, try again. Business writing often deals with information that is more concrete than that needed for essays.

Even routine writing assignments, such as writing letters or planning phone calls, can be improved if you make a quick outline written on a notepad. Brainstorming techniques will help groups or individuals generate ideas.

Regardless of how the ideas are assembled, all writing requires you to begin with a purpose and pay attention to the needs of the audience. Before the document is delivered to the reader, it must be checked carefully, both for the ideas it contains and for the style in which it is written.

Thinking and Writing Exercises

1. **Vacation Policy**

   Think back to the vacation example mentioned earlier. Suppose you work for an organization that needs to maintain a consistent level of staffing year round. The number of weeks of vacation awarded to workers increases with seniority. New workers receive three weeks' annual vacation. Every three years another week is added to the total, so that after 21 years, an employee has ten weeks of vacation time each year. Vacation days are booked according to seniority. People with the highest levels of authority are given first choice for booking their vacation days. The newest employees are given the last choice. Thus a veteran worker could theoretically take all of July and August off and then have another two weeks over the winter holidays.

   Younger workers who have to settle for less popular dates have pushed for reforms. Some have started looking for jobs at companies with different policies for allocating vacation days. Others have been calling in sick on Fridays and Mondays during the summer.

   Create a cluster diagram analyzing the possible impacts of the solutions listed below. Include the benefits and drawbacks of each outcome. Then come up with an additional solution that is not listed below and identify its benefits and drawbacks. See **Figure 2-3**.

   - leaving the existing structure in place
   - reversing the existing selection process so that those with the least amount of vacation each year would receive first choice of dates
   - holding an annual lottery where the names of people in each department would be drawn from a hat and the winners would be awarded first choice of vacation dates
   - placing limits on the maximum amount of vacation time that can be taken during peak periods

2. **Selling a Transit Expansion**

   Suppose that you work for an urban transit commission and have been given the task of promoting the expansion of your city's mass transit service—a move that will likely cost taxpayers money. For each audience listed below, answer the following questions. Then identify the best approach for convincing these different audiences to support a tax increase to pay for improvements to mass transit.

   - students ranging in age from 16 to 30
   - young families with small children
   - middle-class office workers
   - retired people
   - upper-income business owners and executives

   a. Would they likely be regular users of mass transit?

   b. Would they be inclined to favour tax increases to improve a city's mass transit system?

   c. Which factors would likely be the most significant in convincing each audience to support tax increases for mass transit: environmental concerns; convenience; cost savings from not having to drive?

   d. The cost of the tax increase would likely be the most important factor that would cause people to oppose tax increases for mass transit. How could this obstacle be overcome?

3. **Reducing Transportation Costs**

   Rising fuel prices make life difficult for businesses and private individuals alike. Work in a small group to create a cluster diagram with the heading "Reducing transportation costs" at the centre. Then identify an audience that has been affected by the cost of fuel. One possible audience would be students at your college or university; another would be a small restaurant in your area that delivers pizzas or flowers; a third would be a large business, such as a trucking company or a paper mill. You will probably be able to come up with other businesses that have suffered because of rising transportation costs.

   Once you have identified the audience, list as many different approaches as possible that the selected audience could use to reduce transportation

FIGURE 2-3   Incomplete Cluster Diagram

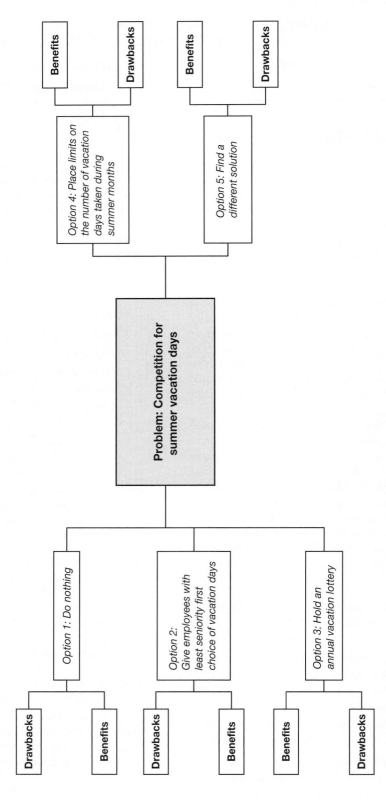

This cluster diagram shows possible outcomes of a change in vacation scheduling.

costs. Don't reject outlandish ideas. Your job is to produce quantity, not quality. Compare your results with those of other groups. When you have finished, review your ideas and identify several possible approaches for your target audience to reduce its transportation costs.

4. **Paper or Plastic?**
Work with a small group to put together an outline for a short report informing consumers about the advantages and disadvantages of paper, plastic, and reusable shopping bags. Start by brainstorming some of the factors that might be important to consumers. Then use the internet to conduct research, and list information about the advantages and disadvantages of each type of bag. Try to find information from a variety of sources, including environmental groups and the plastics industry.

As you uncover information, you will likely find factors that you had not considered during your initial brainstorming. If so, modify your outline to accommodate this new information.

5. **Keep It Clean**
Now that consumers are buying more and more reusable shopping bags, some people have expressed concerns about sanitary issues. Juices from meat or residues from cleaners could contaminate fresh fruit or vegetables.

Do some research on the problem and then write an outline that explains the various ways that consumers can prevent cross-contamination of their food in reusable shopping bags.

Writing Skills Checkup: Point of View Shift

Writing should have a consistent point of view. Readers find it confusing when the writer's perspective changes from *we*, to *you*, to *I*.

Incorrect: Even though we cannot refill aluminum cans in the same way that I can reuse glass bottles, in many provinces you can receive deposit refunds for recycling the cans.

Correct: Even though people cannot refill aluminum cans in the same way that they can reuse glass bottles, in many provinces they can receive deposit refunds for recycling the cans.

Correct the following:

1. Everyone should make an effort to reduce your use of paper, energy, and water in his workplace.
2. If anyone is interested in measuring their amount of greenhouse gases produced in our day-to-day lives, they should go to a carbon footprint calculator on the internet, which can be used to estimate our impact on the global environment.
3. Many people do not realize just how interconnected all species on this planet really are. If you think about the number of species of animals that have become endangered in our lifetime, they amount to a huge

environmental issue, as well as endangering the future of your children.
4. Whether we like to admit it or not, you can tell that the rapid population increase of people on this planet is the root cause of all the other environmental problems that they are facing.
5. Urban sprawl is a situation that exists when we abandon high-density areas in their inner cities, expand into new subdivisions, and take over land on the peripheries of our cities.
6. People are responsible for introducing many invasive species into areas in which they do not occur naturally. When we opened the St. Lawrence Seaway, they allowed parasites, such as sea lampreys, into the Great Lakes, which caused devastating losses to our inland fisheries.
7. We must be concerned about how our economic activities affect the world when I see places like the Aral Sea in central Asia, which has shrunk to less than 10 percent of its original volume after they diverted the rivers feeding it to irrigate your cotton crops.
8. The cars that you drive today produce much less pollution than the ones they drove in the '50s, they emit far less lead into the atmosphere, and we get better fuel efficiency.

Words: Looking at Your Language

LEARNING OUTCOMES

After completing this chapter, you should be able to do the following:

3.1 Communicate your ideas with simple, accurate words that are free of bureaucratic jargon

3.2 Choose words that express ideas

positively, without deceiving the audience

3.3 Choose words that have the appropriate tone for your message and your intended audience

3.4 Express yourself by using inclusive, non-discriminatory language

THE IMPORTANCE OF THE RIGHT WORDS

Steven Pinker began his book *The Stuff of Thought* with a description of the terrible events of September 11, 2001, when airplanes were deliberately flown into the two towers of New York's World Trade Center. He then posed the question of whether this constituted one act of terrorism or two.

Many people would respond to such a question by saying that the distinction was unimportant; the scope of the disaster made such philosophical issues meaningless. Yet, Pinker pointed out, the actual answer to that question is worth billions of dollars. As the insurance policies allowed for a maximum award of $3.5 billion for each "destructive event," the courts have been called on to decide whether the attack was one event or two. One side argues that the disaster was the result of two separate impacts, while the other argues that it came from a single plot.[1]

Although it is rare for such a large amount of money to be riding on the interpretation of a few words, it does point out the importance of the words that we choose. Words are the building blocks of language. Choosing the correct ones for a given situation can help you get a promotion, win a contract, or form a partnership.

This chapter deals with the words used in business and the factors that drive our changing language.

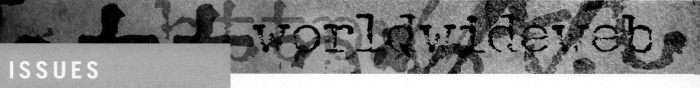

ISSUES
in Communication

New Words at Work: From Blogs to Bandwidth

The word *skyscraper* has at various times meant a large triangular sail, a tall horse, a high hat, and a person who rides a tall bicycle.[2] The fact that people no longer talk about skyscrapers passing them on the road is just one example of the dramatic changes in vocabulary that can takes place as new words and meanings come and go through the years.

The words people use change. Technological advances, for example, are a good source of new words. Before the internet, people had no need for such a word as *blog*. *Twitter* used to be something that birds did. Technological changes force language to adapt so that people can speak and write about the innovations as they take place.

New words or unusual uses of existing words are usually considered slang when they are first introduced. After they have entered mainstream usage, dictionaries begin to recognize them as standard English. Linguistics expert Mark Abley has pointed out that *teenager, takeover, throwaway,* and *acronym* are all products of the twentieth century.[3] These words

have gone past the slang stage and are now considered an appropriate part of standard English.

Popular culture creates new words (e.g., *bling*), as do many other areas of life—today, with the environment, it is the *carbon footprint*.

Words from other languages frequently enter our vocabulary when there is no English equivalent. *Parka* comes from the Aleut language[4] and *tuque* from Canadian French.[5] In much the same way, technical jargon sometimes passes from one field to another. The term *bandwidth* was once used only to describe radio frequencies but later was also used to refer to the transmission capacity of a computer network. The word is now sometimes used in business to mean "capacity" alone, without any of the

During the 1890s, the caption to a photograph like this would have said we were looking at a skyscraper.

technical implications, as in the sentence "We don't have the bandwidth to create that presentation."[6]

New words have a better chance of survival if they express an idea that cannot be expressed as well with existing words. *Blogging* describes a completely new concept. *Stocking cap* simply does not carry the same sense of Canadian identify as *tuque*. *Bandwidth* may not last long, though, because such words as capacity, capability, and facilities already meet some of the need for such a term.

People often feel a deep sense of discomfort over the changing meanings of words. During the 1960s, using the word *contact* as a verb instead of as a noun (e.g., in such a sentence as "I will contact you next week") was criticized as an "abomination" and a "barbarism,"[7] yet such usage is generally accepted today.

Language use can be just as much of an emotionally charged issue in business as in the rest of our lives.

Because the nature of business is essentially about buying and selling, businesspeople have long realized the importance of choosing words that present a positive image. Walk into any department store these days and ask for the complaint department and you are likely to be directed to customer service or consumer relations.

Words intended to reduce the emotional impact of sensitive topics are known as euphemisms. Such words are frequently used in everyday life. *Washroom, passed away,* and *sleeping with* are words that are commonly used to smooth over delicate topics.

Writers must always consider the purpose behind any euphemism they use. Is the purpose to reduce tension by showing sensitivity to the readers or is it to deceive? The answer is not always easy. For example, *food irradiation* is a process that extends the shelf life of food by exposing it to high-energy gamma radiation. The process does not make the food radioactive, but the process is controversial. Because such words as radiation can frighten people, the process of food irradiation is increasingly becoming known as *cold pasteurization,*[8] a far more comforting term but one that some find deceptive. Is cold pasteurization an example of deceptive language that is being used to increase corporate profits, or is it language intended to increase consumer acceptance of a safer food-preservation process? Both answers contain elements of truth.

Blog

The *Oxford English Dictionary* (OED) says that *blog* entered the language in 1999 as a shortened form of web log and is defined as "a frequently updated web site consisting of personal observations, excerpts from other sources, etc., typically run by a single person, and usually with hyperlinks to other sites; an online journal or diary."[9] Companies as diverse as PetroCanada, Microsoft, General Motors, and RBC, all host blogs.

What is a blog's value to a business? ∎

DOUBLESPEAK

William Lutz defined doublespeak as language that "pretends to communicate but really doesn't."[10] He listed four categories of doublespeak:

1. polite euphemisms: "restroom"
2. pretentious use of technical jargon: "organoleptic analysis" (sniff test)
3. bureaucratese intended to overwhelm an audience: "revenue enhancement" (tax increase)
4. inflated language to make the ordinary seen impressive: "preowned vehicles"

Lutz said that the language of doublespeak can sometimes be harmless or even amusing (such as when mechanics are referred to as "automobile internists"), but he argued that referring to a fire in a nuclear plant as an "energetic disassembly" corrupts language and makes people more cynical.[11]

When business or governments use doublespeak, they risk creating an atmosphere of mistrust. In 2007, for example, when representatives of the Asia-Pacific Economic Cooperation (APEC) member countries released a report on what they were doing to combat climate change, the president of a corporate communications agency criticized them for using the term "aspirational targets"—words that he said were "designed to suggest that you're doing something when you're really doing nothing."[12]

BRAND NAMES

Company and product names are designed to create a favourable image that the manufacturers hope will carry over to their products. For example, the names for Eveready, Duracell, and Energizer batteries were obviously created to make consumers think about reliability, durability, and power. Sometimes naming companies are brought in to help develop the right name—this was the case when Mutual Life of Canada changed its name to Clarica.[13]

When Coca-Cola translated its name into Chinese, the company tried to find a name that sounded similar to the original and presented a positive image of the drink. The result was *Ke-kou-kele*, which means "tastes good and makes you happy."[14]

PROCESS OF CHANGE

At times, organized groups have tried hard to change the words that people use. Sometimes they have succeeded, sometimes not. Feminists succeeded in getting the courtesy title *Ms.* into the language of business in 1952,[15] and now the term is used widely as the female equivalent of *Mr.*

Because of its possible derivation from the Algonquin words for "eaters of raw flesh," Aboriginal groups in Canada succeeded in having the term *Eskimo* replaced by the term *Inuit* ("people" in Inupik).[16] The use of *Eskimo* persists, however, in the United States and in other contexts: Eskimo roll in kayaking, the name of Edmonton's Canadian Football League team, and the American Eskimo dog breed.

Organized efforts to change the way people use language sometimes meet with resistance. The CBC began receiving complaints in 2000 when some of its news stories started using *fisher* to replace *fisherman*.[17] Common usage will eventually decide whether *fisher* or *fisherman* fades into distant memory, or whether both terms will coexist in the manner of Miss, Mrs., and Ms.

DISCUSSION

1. **The credit card that we now know as Visa was called Chargex until 1977. MasterCard changed its name from Master Charge in 1979. Discuss the possible reasons behind these companies' decisions to rename their products.**
2. **Under what circumstances is it appropriate to name sports teams after ethnic groups? Discuss the name choices of, for example, the Edmonton Eskimos, the Atlanta Braves, and the Boston Celtics. List other team names that have an ethnic connection. How do the teams' choices of symbols (such as the Celtics' Lucky the Leprechaun or the Braves' use of the tomahawk chop) affect your opinion?**
3. **Few businesses send cards wishing people "Merry Christmas" anymore, preferring instead to extend "Season's Greetings" or "the best of this Holiday Season." Why do you think this change came about?**

TAKE IT FURTHER

Lost in Translation

In 2003, General Motors renamed the Canadian version of the Buick LaCrosse after discovering that LaCrosse was a slang term in Quebec for masturbation. U.S. models were unaffected by the name change.[18]

Do you think that GM was correct to change the name of the LaCrosse?

STANDARD ENGLISH: USING DICTIONARIES AND STYLE GUIDES

The English language comes in dozens of forms, each with variations in vocabulary and grammar. To ensure continuity in written communications, most business documents are written in what is loosely defined as *standard English*, "the variety of English that is generally acknowledged as the model for the speech and writing of educated speakers."[19] At times, a business writer might not follow all these conventions strictly—such as when choosing to ignore the distinction between *who* (the subject of the sentence) and *whom* (the object) to sound less formal. However, using standard English in written documents reduces the possibility that someone will misinterpret your writing.

Dictionaries will help you to determine the precise meaning of words, while style guides will help you to deal with such issues as capitalization and grammar problems. Because the English language does not have any one standard body regulating what is correct, many different style guides exist, some produced by employers themselves to ensure that all employees' writing meets a certain standard.

Literal Meanings: Denotation

It is possible to examine the literal meaning of words from various perspectives. The obvious way of finding the meaning of an unfamiliar word is to look it up in a dictionary. There, you will find the denotation, or literal meaning, of the word, along with its pronunciation and origin, and perhaps a note on its usage.

Most dictionaries describe language use, but they don't prescribe it. They will sometimes provide suggestions as to appropriate usage—using such terms as *slang, informal,* or *abusive* to prevent people from accidentally using a word in an embarrassing way—but they don't make themselves the final authority on what is correct and what is incorrect.

When you are looking for the accepted way to pronounce such words as *lieutenant, buoy,* or *schedule,* you can consult the *Canadian Oxford Dictionary,* which lists the most common Canadian pronunciation first.

The *Oxford English Dictionary* traces the history of words and describes their use over time, but other than explaining the usage of a word, it does not try to determine its correctness. The *American Heritage Dictionary* takes a different approach and assembles panels of language usage experts who are asked whether they find a particular word or construction to be acceptable or not in formal standard English.

Many words have multiple meanings, and both reader and writer have to determine which of the words' meanings are intended. Furthermore, meanings sometimes change. The word *gay* once meant "bright or carefree," but the 2004 edition of the *Canadian Oxford Dictionary* labels such a meaning as "dated" and gives one word for its first definition: "homosexual." A 2008 draft revision of the *Oxford English Dictionary* also includes the slang meaning "foolish or stupid," which was introduced in 1978.[20]

Deciding Which Words Are Appropriate

As discussed earlier in this chapter, when word meanings change, the new meaning may first be considered slang. Later, if the new meaning becomes commonly used, dictionaries will begin to recognize this change. One example is the word *ridiculous*. When explaining its meaning, the OED uses such words as "absurd" and "outrageous,"[21] words that most of us would find appropriate. It also lists the slang meaning as "excellent." You have probably heard the word used in that complimentary way, but it has not yet entered mainstream usage to a point where most people would consider it standard English. As a result, you would be unwise to describe a colleague's presentation as *ridiculous*, regardless of your good intentions. The slang meaning of *ridiculous* may one day shift so that this usage becomes dominant. Until that happens, though, it is best to take a more conservative approach. Dictionaries will continue to keep track of the evolving usage of words, such as *gay* and *ridiculous*, providing advice on the appropriate way to use them.

Students and writers in many professions rely on style guides to determine correct usage within a specific context. Style guides often contain guidelines on word usage, capitalization, grammar, and other technical issues related to writing.

Suppose, for example, that you were concerned about the use of the word *anxious* in this sentence: "The employees are *anxious* to begin their vacations."

The *Canadian Oxford* says that the meaning "eager" is "disputed": "Many claim that *anxious* should not be used to mean *eager*, but this use is well established, and standard since the 18th c. [century]."

Almost half of the usage panel assembled by the *American Heritage Dictionary* accepted the use of *anxious* to mean "eager."[22] *Webster's Revised Unabridged Dictionary* say that its use to mean "eager" is fully standard but the dictionary does acknowledge that many people do consider it incorrect.[23]

The same question was asked in a survey of academics and high-level business executives. The results were similar. The people surveyed were less bothered by the *anxious/eager* distinction than they were by other common word difficulties, such as *its/it's*. However, older respondents and those from the academic world did tend to take a more conservative stand and considered *eager* to be preferable to *anxious* in the sentence.[24]

When you deal with issues relating to word use, consult a reputable guide first. If you receive conflicting advice, consider your audience. When writing for older people or an academic audience, choose the most conservative option. Even though some of the guides listed above did accept the use of *anxious* to describe an anticipated vacation, all of them would have considered *eager* to be correct in the same circumstance. Many other stylebooks are available that will also help you deal with some of the finer points of word usage, grammar, and punctuation.

Non-words   Be careful not to include non-words in your writing. Informal words, such as *ain't*, *copacetic*, and *ginormous*, may not be standard English, but they are words. Non-words have less legitimacy. Some of them are corruptions

TABLE 3-1	Non-words and the Options
Non-words	**Suggested Alternatives**
alot	a lot (for informal use only), many
commentate	comment
inflammable	flammable (for things that burn)
(technically not a non-word, but this word serves no real purpose and is rapidly disappearing)	non-flammable (for things that don't burn)
irregardless	regardless
seldomly	seldom
thusly	thus
unthaw	thaw

of legitimate words. Others use unnecessary prefixes or suffixes that don't contribute anything. Using any of the words in **Table 3-1** will convey a negative impression about you and your writing.

Connotation: Emotional Meanings

If sorting out the literal meaning of words is a skill, then figuring out their emotional meanings is an art. Words carry with them all sorts of emotional meanings that do not necessarily come through in their dictionary definitions. Words that may be listed as synonyms in a thesaurus can have a more positive connotation than other available word choices. The art is in deciding which word fits the connotation you want. For example, these words are all synonyms for *sell*: auction, bargain, deal, deliver, dump, hawk, hustle, market, merchandise, offer, peddle, push, retail, supply, trade, transfer, unload, vend, wholesale.

If you were trying to sell a product, you would likely have more success by telling potential customers that you were "offering it on the open market" than by saying that you were "hoping to unload it," even though the literal meaning of both expressions is the same.

✓●⌐Practise **USING THE APPROPRIATE STYLE AND TONE**

Your attitude toward your reader will be reflected in the tone of your writing. Be careful with the words that you choose. Unlike speech, which also uses body language and the sound of your voice to communicate tone, writing relies almost entirely on words. A joke could be misinterpreted, or subtle suggestions could be lost if your words are taken the wrong way.

You can express messages in various levels of formality, partly with the words you choose to express your ideas and partly with the way you express them. All styles have their uses, but as with any other communication tool, they must be used at the appropriate time with the appropriate audience.

Informal Style

A conversation between two co-workers complaining about the high cost of fuel might include a line like this:

> The oil companies keep jacking up the price of gas every time there's a problem somewhere, but I haven't seen them hurrying to lower the price when crude oil gets cheaper.

An informal style is often used in conversations. In presentations it is used to create an atmosphere in which the audience feels a sense of familiarity with the speaker. In writing, this style might be used in emails to peers or to friends.

It frequently uses contractions (*haven't, there's*), personal pronouns (*I, they*), and occasionally well-known slang (*jacking up the price*).

Academic Style

A more formal academic style might be used to express that idea in an academic paper or a formal report:

> The hasty increases in petroleum prices that have been precipitated in recent years by Middle Eastern conflicts or storms in the Gulf of Mexico have not been counterbalanced by a corresponding rapid reduction in consumer prices following the resolution of these crises.

Writers use an academic style to appear detached and objective, rather than emotional and subjective. They use very few personal pronouns (*I, we*) and instead sometimes say things like "One must come to the conclusion that. . . ." They often write sentences in the *passive voice* to try to increase the impression that they are being objective. A passive-voice sentence focuses on the result of an action ("a decision was reached"), whereas an active voice sentence focuses on the people responsible ("the committee members reached a decision").

Sentences written in an academic style may be quite long. Standard English is used throughout, along with any technical terms that may be needed. Contractions are never used and slang of any sort is unacceptable.

Business Style

The same idea might be written in a more businesslike style in a letter to an oil company or an article in a business magazine:

> Consumers have seen prices at the pump take a dramatic rise immediately after a hurricane in the Gulf of Mexico or a war in the Middle East. They've not seen similar price reductions when these problems have passed, however.

A business style falls somewhere between informal communication and academic writing in its level of formality. It does use personal pronouns (such as *you*), especially when referring to the reader. Sentences often use the *active voice*, with people—rather than things—as the subject. Contractions (such as *it's* for *it is* and *don't* for *do not*) are used at times. Standard English is used and correct grammar is important, but rules are occasionally broken. Business writers choose words mainly based on the way the words will affect the audience.

The Impact of Tone

The way we use words has an impact on the way that even simple messages are received. Consider the difference in connotation between these two sentences:

1. We cannot process your order because you failed to specify the model numbers you require.

2. Please specify the model numbers you require so that we can finish processing your order.

The sentences say essentially the same thing, but the first one uses such words as *cannot* and *failed*—words that will seldom make people happy—while the second avoids the negative wording and uses the word *please*. If your kindergarten teacher told you that *please* and *thank you* were magic words, that was not a lie. Politeness remains one of the more important tools for effective business communication.

Now compare the emails in **Figure 3-1** and **Figure 3-2** that each announces a plan to shorten workers' hours to avoid a layoff. The polite tone

| FIGURE 3-1 | **An Ineffective Email Announcement** |

The subject line has a negative tone.

The confrontational tone and legalistic language do little to persuade workers that the plan is a good idea.

The idea is presented negatively using complicated language.

From: management@nationalpaper.ca
To: staff@nationalpaper.ca
Cc:
Subject: Impending Layoffs
Sent: Thu 8/27/2009 10:28 AM

As you undoubtedly know, National Paper is facing severe economic hardships because of a reduced demand for our products. Thusly, National Paper will temporarily suspend operation of one of its paper machines until the company experiences a resurgence in demand for newsprint.

While National Paper has been striving to retain jobs, layoffs appear to be imminent. Until and unless an alternative plan is ratified by your collective bargaining committee, layoffs appear to be inevitable. Since your union has not demonstrated a propensity to conduct reasonable negotiations in the past, and since your overly generous union agreement does not allow us to force compliance with our completely reasonable proposal, all workers are henceforth given notice that if you will not accept voluntary cuts to your hours, the next step will be either to shut down the plant for several weeks or to impose mandatory workforce reductions upon a significant portion of the workforce. Your union agreement contains no legal impediments that will protect you from either of those measures.

Therefore, I implore you to accept the company's plan, which has been presented to your union negotiators, the gist of which has been set forth below:

Unless economic conditions improve to the point where all paper machines can be made operational again, workers will sacrifice one shift per week, seeing their 40-hour week slashed to 32 hours. Said hourly reductions will continue for a period that could last as long as six months or possibly even longer. Workers from the affected areas will be reallocated to other paper machines. If workers accept this reduction in hours, the company is sanguine that no further actual layoffs will be needed. Failure to ratify this proposal, however, will mean that upwards of 10% of our operating staff will be terminated for an indefinite period.

The choice is yours.

This email uses a tone that is unlikely to persuade readers.

| FIGURE 3-2 | **An Effective Email Announcement** | Explore |

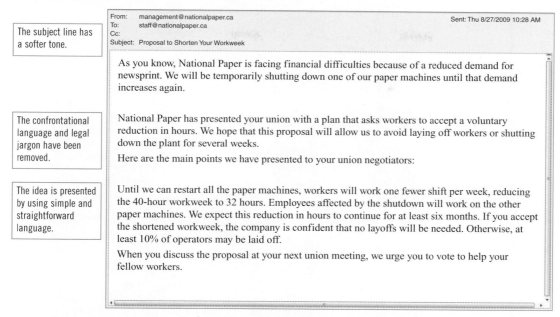

The subject line has a softer tone.

The confrontational language and legal jargon have been removed.

The idea is presented by using simple and straightforward language.

From: management@nationalpaper.ca
To: staff@nationalpaper.ca
Cc:
Subject: Proposal to Shorten Your Workweek

Sent: Thu 8/27/2009 10:28 AM

As you know, National Paper is facing financial difficulties because of a reduced demand for newsprint. We will be temporarily shutting down one of our paper machines until that demand increases again.

National Paper has presented your union with a plan that asks workers to accept a voluntary reduction in hours. We hope that this proposal will allow us to avoid laying off workers or shutting down the plant for several weeks.

Here are the main points we have presented to your union negotiators:

Until we can restart all the paper machines, workers will work one fewer shift per week, reducing the 40-hour workweek to 32 hours. Employees affected by the shutdown will work on the other paper machines. We expect this reduction in hours to continue for at least six months. If you accept the shortened workweek, the company is confident that no layoffs will be needed. Otherwise, at least 10% of operators may be laid off.

When you discuss the proposal at your next union meeting, we urge you to vote to help your fellow workers.

This email presents the same information by using simpler language and a tone that is less confrontational.

and more positive language of the second one help to make the proposal more acceptable.

Here are a few more rules that will improve the tone of your writing.

Focus on the Reader   People tend to be more concerned with their own needs than with yours. Even when they do not consciously realize it, people ask the question "What's in it for me?" any time they are dealing with others. You can use this basic fact of life in your business communications by answering this question without it being asked.

Place yourself in the shoes of your reader and look at things from the reader's perspective rather than your own. For example, this sentence centres on the writer's needs and has a rather harsh tone: "We will not process any orders if the forms have been filled out incompletely." You can remove some of that harshness by increasing the focus on the reader's needs: "Please ensure that all sections of the order form are completed so that your order will be filled promptly and accurately."

Be Positive   Another valuable lesson that you probably learned in kindergarten was to look on the positive side of things. "This cup is not half empty. It's half full." That principle can be applied to much of your writing. That does not mean that you should deny the existence of bad things.

You can, however, express your ideas by using positive language. Instead of telling a customer that an order "won't be ready until Wednesday," say that the order "will be ready on Wednesday." People have also been known, in some circumstances, to exaggerate and say, "Your order is scheduled for delivery on Thursday, but I'll see if I can pull a few strings and have it ready for Wednesday."

"IF HE SMILED MUCH MORE THE ENDS OF HIS MOUTH
MIGHT MEET BEHIND," SHE THOUGHT

"When I use a word," Humpty Dumpty said in rather a scornful tone, "it means just what I choose it to mean—neither more nor less."

"The question is," said Alice, "whether you CAN make words mean so many different things."

—*Lewis Carroll*, Through the Looking Glass

You can also use positive language to *upsell* (business jargon for making a larger sale) your product to your customers. Instead of saying that your cheapest model cannot be expected to last long, say that your deluxe model offers increased durability.

Advertisers have used such principles for years. Few consumers will be attracted to a label saying that a bottle of shampoo "contains 5% grease," but they will pay extra for one that claims to be "95% oil free."

Be careful about being deceptive though. When one brand of gasoline advertises that its product leaves engines cleaner than *inferior gasolines*, it implies that all other brands are inferior. The *other gasolines* referred to in the advertisements may not be available commercially in this country.

STREAMLINING YOUR WRITING

You can use various ways to make your writing easier to read. As discussed in the sections that follow, you can start by being aware of pitfalls, such as wordiness, archaic expressions, and needlessly complicated words. You can also use appropriate business jargon and acronyms to make your writing more concise.

Many people communicate in a complex code of business jargon that must be deciphered to be understood.

Avoid Wordiness

Big is not necessarily better. People do not want to read any more than they have to. Your job is to communicate your ideas clearly and briefly. Your writing will be less wordy if you eliminate wordy expressions and bureaucratic jargon, and look for simple ways to express your ideas.

Avoid Redundant Words and Wordy Expressions

Redundant means "unnecessary repetition." Repetition in writing is not always a bad thing—people sometimes repeat things for emphasis or place a key thought in several parts of a long document to ensure that it is not missed. However, when a person selling a car places an ad in a newspaper describing it as *blue in colour,* the words *in colour* are costing that person money. Although redundancy does not usually have a fixed cost attached to it, it does take up people's time, and it sometimes annoys them.

You can also streamline your writing by eliminating meaningless expressions, such as "needless to say," and reducing inflated expressions, like "on a monthly basis" to "monthly." See **Table 3-2** for a list of wordy expressions, along with suggestions for reducing them.

Avoid Outdated and Bureaucratic Expressions

We hinted in Chapter 1—and it is worth mentioning again—that many people assume that business documents need to be written by using outdated bureaucratic expressions, such as "as per your request" or "in lieu of," as

TABLE 3-2	Shortening Wordy Expressions		
Wordy Expression	**Revised Version**	**Wordy Expression**	**Revised Version**
an amount of $45	$45	in the near future	soon
at this point in time	at present, now	in the very near future	soon
close proximity	near	is authorized to	may
consensus of opinion	consensus	it is requested that	please
cooperated together on a joint project	cooperated on a project	large in size	large
due to the fact that	because	not later than July 7	by July 7
for a period of	for	on a weekly basis	weekly
has a requirement for	needs	past history	history
in a timely manner	promptly	plan ahead	plan
in order to	to	sum total	total
in the amount of	for	very intelligent assistant	intelligent assistant
in the event of	if	with reference to	about

Some people have trouble accepting the use of plain English in business writing.

though such words somehow make a document sound more professional or the writer seem more important. Many businesspeople and government officials do indeed write that way, but most people prefer the use of simple, straightforward words that actually communicate.

Many governments and business organizations have even put plain language policies into place to ensure that simpler language is used. Here is an example of writing that was revised by the City of Toronto's plain language consultant:

- *Before:* "The city, in its current fiscal position, is not in a position to attempt even a portion of the capital or operating implications contemplated by the Evergreen proposal."

- *After:* "At this time, the city cannot afford to implement any part of the Evergreen proposal."[25]

The revised version is 15 words instead of 28—almost half the length of the original and much easier to understand. If you do want to impress people with your writing, keep it simple. See **Table 3-3** for a list of common bureaucratic expressions and their suggested revisions.

TABLE 3-3	Revising Bureaucratic Expressions

Bureaucratic Expression	Simpler Alternative	Bureaucratic Expression	Simpler Alternative
addressee	you	implement	carry out
adjacent to	next to	in an effort to	to
advantageous	helpful	inasmuch as	since
adversely impact	cause problems	inception	start
afford an opportunity	allow	incumbent upon	must
apparent	clear	indicate	show
appreciable	many	in lieu of	instead of
approximate	about	in regard to	concerning
as per your request	as you requested	in relation to	about
ascertain	find out	interface with	work with
attain	meet	liaise	meet
capability	ability	necessitate	cause
caveat	warning	notwithstanding	in spite of
commence	begin	optimum	best
comply with	follow	parameters	limits
comprise	include	pertaining to	about
consequently	so	practicable	practical
constitutes	makes up	prioritize	rank
convene	meet	prior to	before
deem	think	pursuant to	relating to
depart	leave	required to	must
designate	appoint	reiterate	repeat
disclose	show	relative to	about
disseminate	distribute	remuneration	payment
effect modifications	make changes	reside	live
elect	choose	retain	keep
endeavour	try	solicit	ask for
equitable	fair	strategize	plan
evidenced by	shown by	subsequently	after
expedite	speed up	terminate	end
facilitate	help	the undersigned	I
finalize	complete	utilize	use
furnish	provide	Via	by
herein	here	viable	practical
heretofore	until now	vis-à-vis	in relation to
herewith	below, here	whereas	because
impacted	affected		

Use Caution with Business Jargon

Jargon is the specialized terminology that is used within any field. Doctors have medical jargon, instructors have teaching jargon, and athletes have sports jargon.

Likewise, people who specialize in ebusiness use jargon that includes such terms as *acceptable use policies* and *click-through rates*. Accountants talk about *accounts payable* and *audited financial statements,* while entrepreneurs write about *cost-benefit analyses* and *break-even points.* All these terms are useful ways to express specialized ideas.

Jargon becomes a problem, though, when it is used not as a form of easily recognizable shorthand but as a form of pompous writing in which many words say nothing. Such terms as *mission critical integrated solutions* or *leveraged synergistic opportunities* are more likely to confuse readers than help them understand more quickly.

Business jargon can save time when used among people who share a common code, but the specialized terms will confuse people who are outside that group. Before using any jargon, you need to think about whether the intended audience is likely to understand or not. If you have any doubt at all, explain the term or use a simpler alternative. Such a term as *third-party liability insurance* may require no explanation when used among people in an insurance office, but when that office is communicating with a client, the term should be explained.

Acronyms and Initialisms   Try saying *Registered Retirement Savings Plan* really quickly, and you will know why people often prefer shorter terms. Most people have trouble even with *RRSP,* so it is increasingly common for people to simply refer to such savings plans as *RSPs.*

Formal style guides often make a distinction between *acronyms* (where the combination of letters is pronounced as a word—NAFTA, AIDS) and *initialisms* (where the letters are pronounced individually—GIC, GNP). Either way, unless the shortened version is commonly used, it should be written out in full the first time it appears, with the acronym written in parentheses: North American Free Trade Agreement (NAFTA), acquired immune deficiency syndrome (AIDS), guaranteed investment certificate (GIC), and gross national product (GNP). After that, the acronym can be used alone, depending, of course, on the document's purpose and audience.

Acronyms are a form of jargon that can be a convenient form of business shorthand as long as everyone involved understands what they mean.

Commonly used initialisms and acronyms, such as *DVD, GST,* and *IKEA,* usually require no explanation.

Try not to subject your audience to a sea of specialized acronyms that they are unlikely to be able to remember from one paragraph to the next. The use of many unfamiliar acronyms will confuse and annoy most readers.

Use Simple Verbs

Verbs carry much of the meaning in your writing. Allow them to do their job. When people use such expressions as *make an application* rather than *apply,* they are substituting a less powerful word, *make,* for the forceful word *apply.*

Botox

The name for the drug Botox is a kind of word that is a relative of the acronym, called a *portmanteau.* It is derived from the words "botulinum toxin," a naturally occurring poison that in a diluted form is now used as a cosmetic treatment. Portmanteau words have been used by everyone from corporations (Microsoft) to celebrity watchers (Brangelina).

List several other examples of portmanteau words and explain the popularity of such terms.

TABLE 3-4	Alternatives for Hidden Verbs	
Hidden Verbs	**Uncovered Verbs**
Please give your approval to my request.	Please approve my request.
I am of the opinion that the formation of a partnership will be helpful to both of us.	I believe that forming a partnership will help us both.
If the minimum monthly fee of $50 is not paid, your card will be placed in suspension until the balance of the shortfall has been received.	If you cannot pay the $50 minimum monthly fee, you will not be able to use your card until you pay the remaining balance.

TABLE 3-5	Alternatives for Vague Words	
Vague	**Specific**
We will only host the event if we have enough volunteers.	We will host the event if *15* volunteers come forward.
I see several problems with the new legislation.	The new legislation has *three* problems.
We need to hire some good employees.	We need to hire some employees who are *honest*, *intelligent*, and *hard*-working.

Don't cover up verbs by turning them into nouns. **Table 3-4** gives a list of hidden verbs and their suggested alternatives.

Use Specific Words

Such words as *several*, *good*, or *enough* have their uses, but using more specific words will often make your writing easier to understand. See **Table 3-5.**

Use Content and Function Words Properly

All words can be classified as either *content* or *function* words, and knowing more about their uses can help you to improve the structure of your documents:

- *Content words* form the majority of words. They make up all the nouns, verbs, adverbs, and adjectives in a language. Any word that calls up an image in your mind is a content word. The words *puppy, chew, yappy,* and *bad* are all content words.

- *Function words* give structure to sentences. The list includes prepositions, conjunctions, and articles, such as *for, by, the, a, so*, and *but*. There are fewer than one hundred function words, but they are used frequently. Function words provide clues about the words that are coming, making it easier for people to read documents. Such words as *a* and *the* signal the arrival of nouns; *but* signals that something different is coming. Think of function words as the glue that binds language together.

| TABLE 3-6 | Balancing Content and Function Words |

Poor Wording	Improved Wording
No-fault auto insurance claim procedures	Procedures for making claims with your no-fault auto insurance
British Columbia's mountain pine beetle eradication efforts suffer from inadequate funding.	Efforts to eradicate the mountain pine beetle in British Columbia have suffered from inadequate funding.

A Common Error   Too often, people remove function words in a misguided effort to make things shorter, but they end up sounding like the announcer on a late-night infomercial. "Place whole fruits into patented Vinomatic combination food processor/fermentation unit, add yeast, and enjoy fresh homemade wine in minutes." Such writing does allow announcers to squeeze 60 minutes of dialogue into 30 minutes of television, and it may even be understandable when an enthusiastic narrator does the reading. However, a business document that contains long strings of content words, with few function words to bind them, is difficult to read.

Look for ways to restructure sentences or headings so that long groups of content words do not appear in one long string. See **Table 3-6,** where you will notice that the improved version is longer, in most cases, but far easier to read and understand.

SENSITIVITY 101: AVOIDING BIASED LANGUAGE

As society has become increasingly sensitive to the way that language use affects others, people have begun adopting a more culturally sensitive approach to language. Late-twentieth-century references to people with disabilities as *cripples* or to older people as *the elderly*, for example, are simply not acceptable today.

In general, this means that your writing should focus on people first and their other characteristics second—and only when those characteristics are relevant. Cultural sensitivity (which we touch on again in Chapter 5) includes four general categories:

1. references to gender
2. references to age
3. words that refer to race, religion, and culture
4. words that deal with disabilities

The process of language reform is not easy. People resist changes that they feel are being forced on them. The term *political correctness* is often used in a derogatory way to refer to language that has been modified to make it more culturally sensitive. One writer said that most people consider the use of the term *political correctness* as a "conservative assault on efforts to enforce speech codes."[26]

Political correctness carries with it all sorts of negative connotations, but the idea of using language that is culturally sensitive is simply common sense. In its most basic interpretation, *cultural sensitivity* means referring to people by using the words they prefer. Unfortunately, putting such guidelines into practice is sometimes difficult. People do not always know what they want to be called or have the words to express their thoughts in an inclusive manner.

Anthropologist Benjamin Whorf said that language and thought have a mutual influence on each other. Language is not only a tool for voicing ideas, it is also a way to shape thought.[27] The words people use affect the way they think, and the way they think influences the words they use. Thus, a person brought up in Canada will have no trouble identifying a dozen types of snow: *sleet, slush, powder, crust, drifts*, and so on, while a person from a tropical country, such as Papua New Guinea, may have difficulty differentiating between snow and ice. The New Guinean, however, will have numerous words for varieties of sweet potato (a staple food in that country) even though they all appear to be the same to most Canadians.

Words that are used to describe food or weather conditions do not usually have much effect on people. In contrast, consider the effect of such terms as *woman's work, gyp*, or *Dutch courage*. These terms reinforce stereotypes that promote inequality.

Remember that your primary goal is to communicate information and ideas, not to change the world. Find ways to express your ideas that are appropriate to the audience. If you are explaining computer use to people who are concerned with violent linguistic expressions, it is better to tell them to *press the Enter key* than to tell them to *hit Enter*. Even if your audience is not made up of pacifists, it's unlikely that anyone will realize you have deliberately chosen the safer alternative, so why not use it?

Gender

Women are equal to men, but centuries-old rules of usage that allow such words as *man* or *he* to refer to both genders make possible such absurd sentences as "Man, like other mammals, breastfeeds his young." Few people would object to a non-sexist revision of that sentence, and indeed, most people would find this far less cumbersome to read: "Humans and other mammals breastfeed their young."

Such terms as *master's degree* and *ombudsman,* however, do not yet have commonly used gender-neutral equivalents. Many people will continue using those terms until better alternatives are presented.

We should, however, try to specify gender only when it is a relevant issue. It is acceptable to refer to *the ladies' room* or to *men's shoes*, but neutral alternatives have now replaced such terms as *policewoman* and *male nurse*. See **Table 3-7.**

Pronouns   Pronouns, such as *his* and *hers*, can present problems because, traditionally, the male pronoun could be used to refer to both males and females. Such usage is no longer socially acceptable, but some of the options available, such as *s/he* or *her and his*, are awkward. **Table 3-8** presents options for using the pronouns in a non-sexist way in the following sentence: *Each student should read his handbook carefully.*

TABLE 3-7	**Neutralizing Sexist Terms**
Sexist Terms	**Gender-Neutral Alternatives**
man, mankind, man-made, man hours	person, individual, people, human beings, humanity, artificial, synthetic, staff hours
chairman, spokesman	chair, chairperson, coordinator, moderator, presiding officer, spokesperson, representative
policeman, fireman, postman, anchorman, cleaning woman, chambermaid, housewife, steward/stewardess	police officer, firefighter, mail or letter carrier, anchor, cleaner, homemaker, cabin crew, flight attendant
businessman, salesman, saleswoman, alderman	businessperson, executive, manager, business owner, salesperson, sales representative, sales associate, retailer, city councillor

TABLE 3-8	**Options for Using Non-sexist Pronouns**
1. Use a plural.	Students should read their handbooks carefully.
2. Address the reader directly.	You should read the handbook carefully.
3. Avoid the use of pronouns altogether.	Each student should read the handbook carefully.
4. Use the passive voice.	The handbook should be read carefully.
5. Use pronoun pairs.	Each student should read his or her handbook carefully.

Note that in the case of pronoun pairs, their use tends to produce awkward sentences; use these only when the other options fail. (If you do use them, reverse the order at times: "he or she" can be "she or he.") And although it is becoming increasingly common for people to fix the problem simply by changing *his* to *their* (Each student should read *their* handbook carefully), most guides have not yet accepted this as standard English.

Age

People are, at times, subjected to discrimination on the basis of their age. The people most affected tend to be those who are young and those who are old. When drivers refer to "the retirees who should have their licences revoked" or to the "reckless young kids who take too many chances" they are stereotyping a whole class of people based on the actions of a few. Indeed, some young people drive too fast and some older people should no longer be driving, but some people in both these groups are safe drivers. It is unfair to make judgments about people based on age alone. Consider these two sentences:

- Hector Gonzales, a senior citizen, continues to run his department efficiently, despite his advanced age.

- Hector Gonzales continues to run his department efficiently and has no plans to retire.

The second one is much better than the first. Better yet, unless Gonzales's age is relevant to the topic, all references to his age group should be left out entirely so that the sentence focuses only on his efficiency. The sentence would then read:

■ Hector Gonzales runs his department efficiently.

Race, Religion, and Ethnicity

A good rule of thumb is to ignore matters of race, religion, and ethnicity in the workplace. It is obviously better to say simply that "Ahmed occupies the corner office" rather than "Ahmed is the Muslim in the corner office." Nevertheless, religion and ethnicity do sometimes need to be discussed—when talking about religious holidays, for example.

Terminology When you have to deal with such topics as religion and ethnicity, use the appropriate terminology. Usually, this means using the terms that the people under discussion prefer. Remember, though, that preferences change over time and may even vary from person to person. When describing African Canadians, the term *coloured* was once used, followed by *negro*, followed by *black*, followed by *Afro-Canadian*, followed by *African Canadian*. The language has now almost come the full circle with *person of colour*.

Other terms that have connections to identifiable groups have also changed. Consider this list:

Unacceptable	Preferred
Gypsy	Roma
Laplander	Sami
Mohammedans	Muslim, Islamic
Oriental	Asian

TAKE IT FURTHER

Rule of Thumb

According to a commonly held myth, the term *rule of thumb* refers to a practice in British common law that permitted a husband to beat his wife with a stick no thicker than his thumb. The *Canadian Oxford Dictionary* explains it as a rule "based on experience or practice rather than theory,"[28] while the *Oxford English Dictionary* provides more than 20 examples of its use dating from 1692, none with a connection to spousal abuse.[29]

Look up the origins of the following terms and discuss the appropriateness of their use: kill two birds with one stone, beating a dead horse, devil's advocate. ■

The terminology used to identify First Nations peoples in Canada has also changed. *Indian* was one of the first terms used (and is still used today in informal and some legal contexts); it was largely the result of a mistake that the first Europeans to visit North America made. Aside from the fact that no one wants to be named mistakenly, *Indian* is also used to describe people from India (*East Indians*), so its use can result in confusion. In some parts of the world, the original peoples of North America are known as *Red Indians* to distinguish them from people from India. More precise terminology is used in Canada:

■ *First Nations* and *Native Canadians* are general terms to describe the original peoples of North America and their descendants.

■ *Metis* is used to describe people of mixed European and Native heritage.

- *Inuit* is used to describe people of the far North. (The singular is *Inuk*.)
- *Aboriginal people* is a broad term that includes First Nations, Metis, and Inuit.

Just as it is sometimes preferable to describe a European as a Swede or an Italian, it is often better to describe Native people by their specific ethnic grouping: Mi'kmaq, Cree, Haida, and so on.

Indian and Northern Affairs Canada capitalizes all of these terms in the same way that it would for other designations, such as *Arabic, Francophone,* or *Nordic*.[30]

Capitalization   Capitalization is a complicated issue. Generally, any term that applies to a specific language, religion, or ethnic group should be capitalized: *French, Hindu, Serbian.* More general terms do not receive capitals: *black, white, fundamentalist, northern.* Such words as *native* or *aboriginal* are capitalized when referring to people, but not when used in a more general sense: "*native* language" or "*aboriginal* forests."

However, there are grey areas in which even the experts do not always agree. Although most guides state that such words as *black* and *white* are not capitalized even when describing skin colour, the *Publication Manual of the American Psychological Association* recommends capitalizing colours when used as racial terms.[31] Some guides do not consider *anglophone* or *francophone* to be ethnic designations and do not capitalize them.

When you need detailed information, consult a style guide, but most importantly, use the rules consistently.

Going Too Far   Care is required so that language reformers are not seen as crusaders, imposing their beliefs on people unwilling to receive their message. In 1999, the mayor of Washington, D.C., accepted the resignation of an aide who had used the word *niggardly* (miserly) when describing a budget. While the aide was later rehired, the overzealous attack on a person for using a word that had only a coincidental connection to race left a bitter legacy and contributed toward the negative connotations of *political correctness*.[32] Similar problems arise from people's ignorant objections to inoffensive terms, such as *a chink in the wall*, or *calling a spade* a *spade.*

Disability

Since language communicates attitudes as well as ideas, it is important to remember that the language used to deal with people and disabilities should place people first and the disability second. Do not talk about *the disabled* or *the blind* as if the condition were more important than the people. Instead, refer to *people with disabilities* or *blind people.* Even then, the disability should be mentioned only when it is relevant.

People sometimes use such terms as *confined to a wheelchair* or *wheelchair bound*, when in fact wheelchairs increase the mobility of the people who

"My disability is that I cannot use my legs. My handicap is your negative perception of that disability, and thus of me."

—*Rick Hansen, wheelchair athlete and fundraiser, Rick Hansen: Man in Motion, 1987.*[33]

use them. Such problems can be solved easily by using less dramatic verbs—such as *has* and *uses*—when describing disabilities.

As with many other aspects of language, terminology evolves over time. At a time when many people believed that disabilities were a punishment from God, it was acceptable to refer to people as being struck blind. Although such terms as *imbecile* or *spastic* once had specific clinical meanings, they are

TABLE 3-9 Disability Sensitivity

Outdated Term	More Sensitive Term
afflicted with cancer	has cancer
crazy, insane, psycho	mental health problem
crippled	has a disability
dumb	has a speech impairment
epileptic	person with epilepsy
retarded	has a developmental disability or intellectual disability
normal (when used to describe people without disabilities)	non-disabled or able-bodied
Siamese twins	conjoined twins
spastic	person with cerebral palsy
suffering from AIDS	has AIDS

now considered offensive terms. Other terms, such as *mentally challenged* are rapidly moving in the same direction, because *challenged* has been used to ridicule others (e.g., with such terms as *follically challenged* or *vertically challenged* for bald or short people, respectively).

Handicapped and *disabled* are not synonyms. *Disability* refers to the condition itself; *handicap* refers to the way that condition affects the person's life or work. A person who is colour blind might have a minor disability, but it creates a handicap when it limits the person in some way—such as if the person is becoming an electrician or a fashion designer, or functioning in some other area that requires the ability to distinguish colours. The only people entitled to use handicapped parking spaces are those with disabilities that limit their mobility; a person who cannot hear would not have such a limitation. See **Table 3-9** for preferred terms.

Chapter Summary

Explore

The words that you choose not only affect people's understanding of the things you write but also create an emotional climate that influences their impression of you. The best word choices are generally the simplest. Try to avoid the use of complicated terms or wordy expressions.

Language is constantly changing. New words are added, meanings sometimes change, and old words fall out of use. Dictionaries and style guides can provide you with advice on word choices.

When dealing with words that describe people, find out which words your readers prefer so that you can avoid offending anyone. The traditional "rules" for some aspects of English are sexist, and so it is sometimes necessary to find ways to express ideas in an inclusive manner.

Thinking and Writing Exercises

1. Bias-Free Language

Revise the following sentences to make the language more inclusive. An example is shown:

> Poor: Each participant is required to supply his own computer.
>
> Improved: Please bring your own computer to the workshop.

a. We'd like to welcome Angus Ross, 48, to the accounting department.

b. Despite his mental retardation, Billy has become an essential part of Ms. Clermont's recycling team.

c. Man-made materials, such as plastic bags, take hundreds of years to break down in landfills.

d. Bob Longclaws is quite talkative for an Indian.

e. For someone who is only 22, Amina showed surprisingly good judgment and maturity.

f. Send an email to the webmaster if you find a problem with a hyperlink.

g. All members of the executive council and their wives will receive invitations to the banquet.

h. Each manager should inform his staff that the new contract will come into effect on January 1.

i. Even though he is a straight white man, Percy is a good dancer and has excellent fashion sense.

j. Confined to a wheelchair since a collision with a moose, Steven Fletcher has gone on to a distinguished career as a Member of Parliament.

2. Positive Language

Revise these sentences so that they have a more positive tone.

> Poor: Use the envelope that we have enclosed so that your order doesn't get lost in the mail.
>
> Improved: Please use the enclosed envelope to help us process your order quickly.

a. Please put your own groceries into bags so that our company can reduce its labour costs.

b. You are sadly mistaken if you think that you should receive special treatment ahead of our regular customers.

c. Of course the remote control wouldn't work. You neglected to insert batteries into it.

d. We will not be sending a service representative to your office unless you have a genuine problem with the photocopier.

e. It would be cheaper for us if you would send us your questions using email rather than by regular mail so that we don't have to pay postage to answer them.

f. You failed to attach the report to your email.

3. Word Connotation

For each neutral word listed below, find two words that have a more positive connotation and two words that are more negative. An example is given:

Neutral	Positive	Negative
expensive	luxurious	overpriced
	posh	exorbitant

a. fired

b. strike

c. inexpensive

d. capitalist

e. hard-working

f. difficult

g. forgot

h. intelligent

i. economic recession

j. price increase

4. **Up-to-Date Words**
Revise these sentences so that they use less bureaucratic language and more up-to-date words.

> Poor: Enclosed herewith are copies of our business plan and our loan agreement with the bank.

> Improved: We have enclosed copies of our business plan and our loan agreement with the bank.

a. The office staff members have accepted longer workdays in lieu of a pay cut.

b. As per your instructions, I have forgone further efforts to secure payment from our erstwhile client.

c. Unless an affirmative response is received forthwith, the undersigned will cease all further negotiations and seek out alternative vendors who offer more favourable rate alternatives.

d. If you no longer reside in the vicinity of our business establishment, you may order via our website.

e. Your remuneration will be forthcoming on the first Friday of next month and, subsequently, on the third Friday of each month.

f. In order to achieve optimum results, it is advisable to prioritize your functional goals.

g. Let me reiterate. For optimum performance pertaining to the status of negotiations, we need to touch base prior to liaising with the bargaining committee.

5. **Untangling Bureaucratese**
The following message is long, wordy, and filled with bureaucratic jargon that would be difficult for the average reader to understand. Translate it into standard English that would be appropriate for an office environment. Your final product should be shorter and clearer than the version you see below.

To: All Office Staff

From: Clark Gabble, Director of Office Services

Subject: Print and Graphic Centre Announcement

As part of Widgets-R-We's ongoing desire to "Drive Innovation through Technology," Widgets-R-We has partnered with CopyDoc Global Services (CDGS) for our Print and Graphic Services. The objective of this partnership, through qualitative change, will be to deliver a comprehensive service for document creation and to address the needs of users while managing the cost and environmental impact associated with producing documents.

By leveraging CopyDoc's best practices, together we will introduce new processes that will increase end-user satisfaction and accelerate productivity both in the office environment and in our Print and Graphic production site.

The CopyDoc Lean Six Sigma (LSS) approach will help our organization minimize the time and disruptions to achieve the "desired state" while maximizing employee satisfaction.

The project will see CopyDoc interact with Widgets-R-We to assess our current environment over the next few weeks, recommend where we could implement changes within a carefully orchestrated program of change management techniques, and culminate in the post-transition where we will ensure that the new processes achieve the desired outcome and become part of our best practices.

The CopyDoc team has proven experience, knowledge, and project management skills. Providing the Print & Graphic and CopyDoc teams with your utmost cooperation during this on-going project will definitely result in successes at all levels of our organization.

Thank you in advance for your anticipated cooperation. For any questions regarding the new CopyDoc partnership, please feel free to contact me at either cgabble@widgetsrwe.ca or 705-555-6543.

Writing Skills Checkup: Frequently Confused Words

Spell checkers are great tools, but they do not give any information on usage. All the words in the sentences that follow are spelled correctly, but only one of the words in parentheses in each group is used correctly. For each sentence, choose the correct word. Consult a dictionary when necessary.

The (complimentary, complementary) (stationery, stationary) that was supplied with (their, they're, there) room had the hotel's address printed at the top. _____ _____ _____

The complimentary stationery that was supplied with their room had the hotel's address printed at the top.

1. To solve the contract dispute, the two companies hired (a disinterested, an uninterested) retired judge to listen to (there, their, they're) arguments. _____ _____

2. (Perspective, Prospective) contractors are encouraged to examine the problem from various (perspectives, prospectives) before submitting proposals. _____

3. People should get others to check over (there, their, they're) work before submitting it to (there, their, they're) clients. Since the clients are paying the bills, (there, their, they're) the ones whose concerns are most important. _____ _____ _____

4. (Its, It's) a shame that confusion over these two small words causes so much confusion. When used as a possessive pronoun in sentences such as "Put the snake in (its, it's) cage" an apostrophe is not needed any more than one would be if the word *his* were used instead.

However, (its, it's) necessary to use an apostrophe to signify that either of the words is or has been condensed. _____ _____ _____

5. Business owners on the south side of the street felt that they were being (prosecuted, persecuted) when they were told that road repairs would take three months longer (than, then) the renovations faced by the owners on the north side. _____ _____

6. By parking in the spot reserved for drivers with disabilities, the chief of police (flouted, flaunted) the law that he had helped to create. _____

7. With most mortgages, more money is paid in interest than is applied toward the (principal, principle). _____

8. (Moral, Morale) within the (personal, personnel) department went into decline after a new (moral, morale) code was introduced that restricted employees' weekend activities. _____ _____ _____

9. It really doesn't matter (whether, weather) you agree with the new policy or not. All workers, (except, accept) those required to work weekends or nights, will now work four days a week instead of five but with the same (amount, number) of hours. _____ _____ _____

10. Purchasing new (stationery, stationary) and discarding several boxes of unused paper may not have been an environmentally sensitive move, but it resulted in far (fewer, less) complaints than when the old paper was used, because it had the company's address and phone number listed incorrectly. _____ _____

Media: Choosing Your Channel

LEARNING OUTCOMES

After completing this chapter, you should be able to do the following:

4.1 List several channels you should think carefully about for a particular communication

4.2 Choose a channel tailored to your audience and context

4.3 Determine whether a situation requires verbal or written communication

4.4 Decide when to use formal and when to use informal communication channels

4.5 Make informed choices about legal liability

CHOOSING THE RIGHT CHANNEL

Suppose you are sitting in an office and have to tell a manager that something has gone wrong. You probably have a pretty good idea about the *what* of your message, but it is not always simple, however, to decide on the *how*—that is, the best way to deliver that message. The method of communication often says as much as the content does—and sometimes even more. It is important that the channel you choose to communicate through conveys what you want it to.

Your choices might include verbal versus written communication and formal versus informal. The point to remember is that you can deliver your message through a number of channels or media, and they change the nature of the message itself. Some will enhance it, and others will undermine it.

This chapter looks at how the medium can change the way people receive the message and how using the right medium for the situation can help your message have the desired impact.

Some channels of communication will enhance your message, and others will undermine it.

ISSUES
in **Communication**
Viral Marketing

When a virus, such as the H1N1 virus, infects someone, it takes over the normal functions of that person's cells to create new copies of itself.[1] Viral marketing works on the same principle: Instead of trying to reach your target market directly with your marketing message, you give the message to a few well-chosen people, encourage them to pass it on, and hope that those new people in turn pass it on, and so on. Your marketing message spreads from one person who has been exposed to the next, in the same way that a virus spreads from infected individuals to the people they come into contact with.

A recent example of viral marketing was a video released on YouTube in which a bride-to-be "wigs out" over a bad haircut and hacks off her hair with a pair of scissors while her friends watch and try to help. The video looks as if it were shot by one of the women, perhaps by using her cellphone, and is unbranded—that is, the video contains no credits or references to the company that had it made or the ad company that produced it. Most viewers assumed the video was footage of a real bride-to-be having a bad emotional response to a haircut.[2]

It turned out the video was produced by the Toronto-based company Capital C Communications for Unilever Canada's Sunsilk shampoo. The company was launching a new ad campaign and wanted to highlight the word "wig-out" before the campaign started.[3]

In terms of inexpensive publicity, it worked out better than Capital C Communications or Sunsilk could have imagined. The video was produced for $3000. It was viewed by millions online and covered by network TV.[4]

Does viral marketing erode trust in the company or product? Is it ethical? Your judgment might change from case to case. This kind of marketing is certainly manipulative—the goal is to get people to pass on a message that will sell products or vitalize a brand. Viral marketing also makes use of deception. If a company creates a TV ad campaign, viewers know they are seeing a commercial made by that company and can judge its claims accordingly. If you read a blog entry about a great new investment opportunity, however, and you don't know that the writer of the blog was paid to make that recommendation, or perhaps even paid to post a recommendation that was written by the company's marketing department, you are apt to approach the claim with less skepticism than you would if you knew the source.

Whether or not you decide to use viral marketing in your career, it's important to know that it's used regularly. At the very least, you can protect yourself from being infected by a message you don't want to pass on.

DISCUSSION

1. **Doesn't all marketing manipulate the audience, whether it's by including images of happy users of the product, by paying famous people to be spokespersons, or by using some other method? Discuss how viral marketing differs from any other type of marketing campaigns.**

2. **What do you think of using a viral marketing campaign to sell (a) a video game and (b) an unproven dietary supplement?**

3. **Under what circumstances (if any) would you use viral marketing?**

4. **Do you think you've ever received a message created by a viral marketing campaign? When? What makes you think it was viral advertising?**

TAKE IT FURTHER

Guerrilla Marketing

Guerrilla marketing uses unconventional ways to create a large impact for little money. Rather than generating viewer interest, however, a Turner Broadcasting Network guerrilla marketing campaign generated fears of terrorism when they posted light boards around the city of Boston to publicize their new Adult Swim network TV show *Aqua Teen Hunger Force*. People did not know the devices were part of a guerrilla ad campaign and mistook them for bombs, tying up major roadways and wasting the time of emergency response teams. When the real purpose was found out, the two artists hired to do the campaign faced criminal charges, and Turner Broadcasting Network's handling of the situation was criticized by the police and by Boston's mayor.[5]

What responsibilities do companies have when planning to use a guerrilla marketing campaign?

VERBAL VERSUS WRITTEN CHANNELS

One of the first choices to make when communicating is whether to talk to someone about an issue or put it in writing. Some types of verbal and written channels of communication are listed in **Table 4-1.**

| TABLE 4-1 | Types of Verbal and Written Channels of Communication | |

Verbal Channels	Written Channels
Verbal channels include	Written channels include
— conversations — meetings — telephone calls — conference calls — podcasts	— emails — memos — letters — reports — press releases — webpages
They may involve some planning or they may be unplanned.	They usually involve careful planning.

As you continue to read this section, consider how you would apply what you are reading to a specific example: the scenario at the beginning of the chapter in which you have to let the boss know that something has gone wrong. Let's make this earlier example more specific:

You work for Innovate Tech Solutions (ITS), a large software company. ITS will bring in $200 000 a year in licensing fees if Thunder Bay Shipping, the sales lead that you have been pursuing, buys your software to help its business. Karen, your boss, thinks the sale is going to happen any day and is already counting the revenue toward her annual target. You just met with the CIO at Thunder Bay Shipping, and he told you they need a feature your software doesn't have. If your company doesn't add that feature, it's a deal breaker. You need to tell your boss.

In a situation like this, the words you choose are only part of the communication. You also have to decide *how* you are going to tell her.

We will come back to this example and discuss which choice might work best.

Verbal Communication

Verbal channels have both strengths and weaknesses, and they are summarized in **Table 4-2**, which comes after our discussion. We will start by looking at the positive side.

Strengths One of the strengths of talking to someone face to face is that you can see the reaction to your message and adjust both your words and delivery in response. If the person you are talking to does not understand a point you are making, you can go back and explain it again. If the person voices objections, you can address these as they arise. If the person reacts emotionally to the message, you can deal with the emotions right away. Even over the phone, when you cannot see how the person reacts, you can respond to the tone of his or her voice. The person can also ask questions if something is not clear. One of the most powerful aspects of verbal communication is that it allows you to modify your words and delivery as you are communicating, instead of having to imagine and account for all possible reactions.

A second benefit of verbal communication is the wide range of settings it supports. You can schedule a formal meeting to talk to someone, but you can also catch that person in the hallway, in line at the cafeteria, or wherever you usually run into each other. Further, you can often control where a meeting takes place. If you want to deliver a quick message without a lot of detail, catching your target person in the lunch line at the cafeteria might be a good strategy. Perhaps you know you are dealing with a complex issue, and you will need extra time to explain the situation. If you know the person you are meeting with is very busy all day, it might be better to stop by the person's office early in the morning, before the first appointment on his or her calendar. Verbal communication gives the person delivering the message options for the place and timing of the message.

Another aspect of verbal messages often is helpful, but sometimes it is a weakness (as we will discuss later): Verbal messages leave no written record.

This is a strength when you would rather not have a written record of the conversation. For example, if you are delivering a delicate message that could upset others in the company, you may want to ask yourself whether you want to risk sending an email that might be forwarded to the people it would most upset. Do you want to be the messenger who is remembered for delivering that bad news? In such a situation, dropping into one office for a quick talk is often the better approach. You can ensure the message is delivered but in a way that limits your words to the specific person or group of people you want to hear it.

Finally, verbal communication is, in most cases, the best way to express a concern the first time. Putting a problem in writing tends to make the problem bigger. At a certain point, that might be necessary, but if you believe that the person you need to deal with is not aware of the problem, it's usually best to simply chat. If you convey the problem in a polite, matter-of-fact, and

TAKE IT FURTHER

Grievances

Sometimes a problem is more than just a concern. You may have an official grievance against your firm or someone in it. Your human resources (HR) department should have policies in place to cover the situation. Check with your HR representative to find out the process you should follow in communicating your grievance.

Why is it important to have a defined process to follow when an employee cannot resolve an issue alone?

"Thank you for your enquiry. This is an automated response."

Choosing the right time and place to deliver your message in person is important.

non-threatening way, many times you may be able to resolve things right there. If the problem is not resolved, and you do have to make it into a bigger issue, the first question you hear will usually be whether you've talked to the other person. For this reason, if you have a concern, start by talking to the person or persons most directly involved.

Weaknesses One weakness of verbal communication is that it can be harder to structure and deliver your complete message in spoken language than it is in writing. In person, a listener can interrupt with questions or arguments, breaking the flow of your communication, possibly cutting you off altogether. This is a risk particularly in informal conversations, where there is no clear agenda. The other person may leave before you have made a crucial point or emphasized an important qualification. In that case, the listener takes control of the interaction, not allowing you to achieve your communication goals. The immediacy of a response might have been the very reason you chose verbal communication, but it isn't always a positive feature.

Being nervous can sometimes get in the way when it comes to verbal communication. Many people find this particularly true of public speaking, but even a one-on-one meeting can provoke anxiety. If confrontation is involved, both the meeting and the period leading up to it may be nerve-racking. Your nerves can also make you may say more than you had intended to, even if the listener does not interrupt you. You may ramble on, saying things that undermine your case or confuse the issue. If you are not careful, verbal communication can stray away from the topic and end up doing more harm than good.

Verbal communication usually leaves no record (except when a conversation is recorded—see Take It Further). This lack of a record can be a strength of verbal communication, as we have mentioned, but it can also be a weakness. If your boss tells you he's planning to give you a big promotion, that's great. But it's even better if he says so in writing. Even when they have the best of intentions, the two people involved may remember a conversation differently. These differences only increase with time. Going back to a conversation that took place months earlier often uncovers remarkably different views of what was agreed to.

Verbal Communication in Action Remembering what we have just said about verbal communication, let's look again at this chapter's scenario: You work for ITS, a software vendor, and your client, Thunder Bay Shipping, has just told you that unless your company can add a software feature, Thunder Bay Shipping won't be spending $200 000 a year to license the software package. You have to tell your boss, Karen.

What are the strengths of choosing a verbal channel to deliver the message to Karen?

You have good reasons for using face-to-face verbal communication in this situation. Verbal communication can convey a sense of urgency that email and voicemail often lack. The message itself is fairly simple, so there is little chance your message will be interrupted or cut off before you are finished. You can see how Karen responds and adjust your message to best

Sometimes you just have to get things in writing.

address her concerns as well as her emotional reaction. You don't have to worry about Karen forwarding your message in a way that could make you look bad. Finally, talking to Karen is more likely to create a sense of cama-raderie—the two of you trying to solve the problem together.

Are there any risks? Probably not. If you need to follow up with written communication, you can do that after talking to Karen. Further, if you do need to write something, you two can discuss which approach will help you both look as good as possible and provide the best chance of reaching your goal: getting the requested feature added to the software so that the sale to Thunder Bay Shipping will go through.

Given the facts in this situation, having a talk with Karen seems like a good idea.

Written Communication

As we look at both the positive and the negative sides of written communication, keep in mind what we discussed about verbal communication. At the end of this section we will review both forms of communication in the summary **Table 4-2**.

Strengths One of the most important strengths of written communication is that you can carefully structure it to make all the relevant points in the order best suited to the situation, leaving out anything that is irrelevant. Writing everything down means the reader has no chance to interrupt, and so you can ensure the communication stays focused on important issues.

Writing also gives you the chance to read and revise. It's extremely difficult to get something just right the first time. If the situation is complex, it's impossible to cover every angle immediately. Writing is ideal for working through a complex problem. Each draft allows you to capture more and more of the issue at hand, in an increasingly precise way. Each read-through allows you to identify places where a major point is missing, a supporting fact is needed, or the logic of the argument breaks down. The revision process helps you fine-tune not just the communication but also your thinking.

For this reason, it's a good idea to write an outline for important verbal communications before you open your mouth. Use the process of writing and revising your outline to make your verbal communications more effective. See Chapter 3 for information on how to write an outline.

Finally, written communication creates a record of the message. As we discussed when talking about verbal communication, that record can be a problem at times. But in most cases, it is one of the strengths of written communication. For example, imagine that you have been promised a refund for a product you cannot use and you arrive at the store involved to pick up your money. Would you rather have to say that a representative on the phone promised you the refund or be able to hand over a letter in which a representative stated you would get a refund? It's easier to get people to act on what they have promised if you have it in writing. And it's easier to make sure people don't expect you to do things you never intended if you have a written record of what you did and didn't promise.

Weaknesses Many of the limitations of written communication stem from the fact you are not usually present when it is read to address any issues or questions that might arise for the reader. If the reader has an emotional reaction to the message, you can't take the reaction into account and respond appropriately. You may have had that happen with an email, where you meant something humorously, and the reader didn't understand it was a joke and took offence. The reader may misunderstand your position, and you do not have the chance to immediately clarify what you mean. Or the reader may be lacking some background fact or explanation necessary to fully understand the message. This, in turn, can cause the reader to draw wrong conclusions. Since you aren't there to clarify immediately, the reader may pass on that misunderstanding or take an ineffective or even a counterproductive action based on that wrong understanding.

Another weakness of written communication is that although you can ensure the full message is delivered, you can't ensure the full message is read. The reader may possibly not get to all your key points or will bypass important warnings or considerations that require additional thought. In a conversation you will know immediately if anything was left out or if a key point was not heard.

Finally, written communication creates a written record, which can be a strength or a weakness. If you write an email, it may be forwarded to people you would rather not have read it. A report might be distributed to an unintended audience, which, in turn, may trigger personal or professional backlash. For example, you may send Karen an email that contains references to internal problems with delivery for Thunder Bay Shipping. If Karen mistakes your email for the answer the client is waiting for and forwards it to Thunder Bay Shipping, your client will know about problems you would rather solve than discuss with them.

Written Communication in Action Given the strengths and weaknesses of written communication, let's think about the example we looked at when examining verbal communication. You have to tell your boss, Karen, that your company, ITS, might not make the sale it expected to Thunder Bay Shipping because your company's software lacks a feature Thunder Bay Shipping needs. After discussing the strengths and weaknesses of verbal communication, we said that talking to Karen would probably be the best choice in this scenario. Could anything change that plan?

One possibility is that Karen could use a written report to raise the importance of the issue. You might start by talking to Karen, and then strategize with her to write a report asking for quick action to save the sale. Working with others to coordinate your choice of channel with their needs and goals is a key tool in creating powerful organizational communications.

To summarize, neither verbal nor written communication is better. Both have their strengths and weaknesses. What's important is to think about your goal, consider your audience, and then choose the form of communication that will reach them most effectively. Let's review the strengths and weaknesses of both forms of communication by using **Table 4-2**.

Legal Liability As we've discussed, one potential weakness of written communications is that they leave a record. Sometimes, the danger of that written record is simply that the wrong person will read it, creating a backlash against the writer. Other times, however, the problem goes further—the written record

TABLE 4-2	Summary of Strengths and Weaknesses of Verbal and Written Communication	
	Verbal Communication	**Written Communication**
Strengths	— Speaker can gauge and respond to listener's reactions — Method is usable in a wide range of settings — No written record is created — Good way to first raise an issue	— Writer can structure a message to deliver all important points in the most effective order — Writer can revise message before delivery — Revision process strengthens not just the message but the thinking behind the message — A written record is created
Weaknesses	— Message is harder to structure and deliver as intended (e.g., might be interrupted) — Speaker may ramble, saying things that are confusing or unhelpful — Nerves may be a concern — No written record is created	— Reader may misinterpret message — Reader may lack sufficient back-ground knowledge — Full message may not be read — Written record can have an unin-tended audience or create legal liability

creates a legal liability. Large companies, even the most ethical, law-abiding ones, can be sued by customers, former employees, or other parties.

Always remember that as a representative of your company, everything you send out in writing—even emails—is an official message from the company. This also applies to voicemail messages you leave. Think before you put something in writing, or leave a recorded message, that could later be, or *appear to be*, incriminating either to you or to your firm.

Also, be aware that once something is in writing, you can create more problems by trying to delete or destroy it. One highly publicized case occurred recently in the United States. The accounting and consulting firm Arthur Andersen destroyed documents relating to its client Enron, after being notified that a Securities Exchange Commission investigation of Enron had begun. This destruction of documents led to Arthur Andersen being indicted for obstruction of justice.[6]

The chances are small that a communication you write will later play a part in a legal investigation. We aren't suggesting that you spend your work-day being anxious about everything you write. But you should be aware that written documents have a long life, and sometimes they end up being used by parties you never thought would read them, to prove things you never intended to communicate.

FORMAL VERSUS INFORMAL CHANNELS

As well as choosing whether to communicate verbally or in writing, you must decide how formal your message should be. Unlike the choice between writ-ten and verbal methods, which is usually an either-or choice, you can choose

TABLE 4-3	Features of Formal and Informal Channels of Communication	
Formal Communication	**Informal Communication**
— Adheres to a standard format and structure — Follows an agreed-on agenda — Uses an elevated diction	— Does not adhere to strict standards for format and structure — Has little or no agreed-on agenda — Uses casual, sometimes even familiar, language and diction — Is available anywhere two people can have a conversation — Gives the appearance of less preparation time

to use a mixture of informal and formal channels, the general features of which are summarized in **Table 4-3**.

People often spend a good deal of time preparing to communicate in a formal way. The tendency is for written communication to be more formal and for verbal communication to be more informal, but that is not always the case. For example, someone who works for a large company may give a very formal verbal presentation to her board of directors but write a quick, informal email to a colleague.

Many informal communications are put together quickly or even delivered with no advance preparation. In other cases, much time and effort can be spent preparing a communication that ends up looking informal and quickly put together.

Let's look again at the ITS scenario, in which you need to tell your boss, Karen, that something has gone wrong.

You could choose an informal approach. You could call her on the phone, or walk down to her office and see if she has a moment. You could ask her to stop by your office, though since she's your boss, that doesn't seem like a good idea. You could wait to catch her in the hallway.

If you want to use a more formal approach, you could set up an appointment to meet with Karen. You could call a meeting to tell key people at ITS about the problem with the deal. You could choose to send an agenda before you meet, and plan to take minutes and circulate them after the meeting. When people are in the room, you could tell them the problem and open it up for discussion, or you could prepare a set of PowerPoint slides as a presentation, followed by a Q&A period.

Formal Communication

Formal communication has both strengths and weaknesses. They are summarized in **Table 4-4**, which comes after our discussion. We will start by looking at the strengths.

Strengths One strength of a formal method of communication is that it looks professional. It makes a positive impression on the audience when you take the time to create a polished formal report or to put together a well-designed and well-executed formal presentation. This professionalism adds to the authority

TAKE IT FURTHER

Q&A

Q&A is an abbreviation for "question and answer." It's common for business presentations to end with time set aside for the audience to ask the presenter questions.

Why do you think presenters do this?

"Sorry, black tie only!"

"I've never been a black tie man myself."

of the person delivering the information and makes the argument more persuasive. Psychologists use the term *halo effect* to describe the fact that a positive reaction generated by one thing rubs off on other things associated with it.[7] In this case, the impact created by the professionalism of the formal report or presentation rubs off on both the creator and the contents.

Another advantage of formal communications is that, in many cases, a structure is already available, developed specifically for the purpose at hand. Many firms have templates for many kinds of reports, meaning that you don't have to create a new format and section headers every time you want to write a progress report, document a new procedure, or perform a feasibility study. Companies often provide templates for letters and memos and for PowerPoint presentations intended for clients outside the company as well as those for audiences within the company. You can save time and create more effective communications if you start with these documents.

Another benefit of formal kinds of communication is that they often set up expectations, so that everyone knows the reason for the communication and what the desired outcome is. Some formal communications are defined by their purpose—an annual report, for example, provides information to stockholders and potential investors about a company's mission, sales, operations, and finances. Meetings can be called for many purposes, but sending an agenda to participants ahead of time is a formalized process that you can use to ensure everyone knows what the meeting will cover. (See Chapter 6 for more on meetings.) With both annual reports and agendas, people have a clear set of expectations about what they will get out of reading or attending.

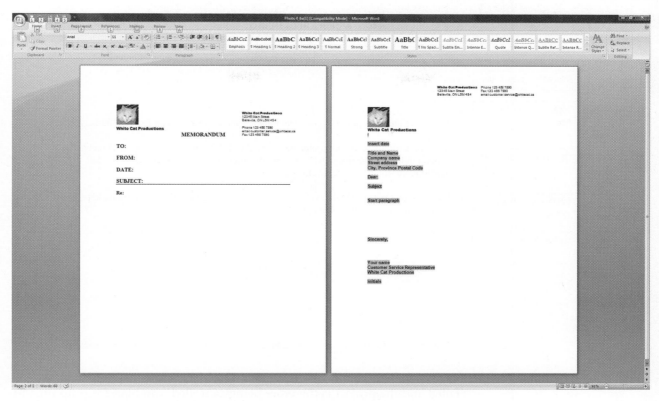

Companies use templates to give their documents a consistent, professional look.

Finally, formal communications focus specifically on the subject matter. Formal report structures leave little room for the personal comments that are often included in casual emails. A meeting with a set agenda and length, with someone attending to minutes and action items, can enforce a structured problem-solving approach in a way that's difficult to achieve in a spontaneous conversation in the company cafeteria.

Weaknesses One weakness of formal communication is that the structures can become bureaucratic. In other words, sometimes people go by the rules simply because the rules are there, rather than because the rules have value. For example, consider the following:

- Completing a full feasibility report before cancelling a project may be pointless if the only thing everyone needs to know is that the prototype failed.
- If you spend more time at your company meetings struggling with the rules for how meetings should be run than you do tackling the actual issues, you're not making the best use of everyone's time.

This increased bureaucracy creates overhead—that is, extra work—which, in turn, means tasks and processes take longer. If, instead of writing that full feasibility report, you send a quick email saying that the prototype

✳ Explore   **FIGURE 4-1**   **A Short but Effective Email**

informative subject line

positive tone to deliver news

clear and concise report

future action stated clearly

cordial closing

From: joh@swtech.ca   Sent: Thu 8/27/2009 10:28 AM
To: dsandeep@swtech.ca
Cc:
Subject: Data-Mining Prototype

Dear Divina,

Thanks for the go-ahead to test our data-mining idea. We learned a lot from the initiative.

Based on the response to our prototype, we've decided that this is not an application we can develop in-house. The research and testing we would need to create a system with full functionality would not be cost effective.

What we have learned will help us to select a third-party data-mining software package, if we decide to move ahead with that option.

Best,
Jeewong

failed and the project is therefore being cancelled, you have freed up time to work on something else. **Figure 4-1** shows an example of a short yet effective email about the prototype failure. If you move the focus from following every detail of the meeting rulebook to making sure you have a clear agenda and set of ground rules that centre on the problem that needs to be solved, you can ensure everyone's time is spent productively.

Finally, formalized communication can, at times, put style ahead of content. Sometimes PowerPoint slides look impressive but don't introduce any new information or provide insights. Creative gimmicks used in marketing materials may not tell you anything useful about the product or service. You have likely seen TV commercials that are memorable, but can you remember the product they were advertising? How effective are these?

Formal Communication in Action   Given these strengths and weaknesses of formal communication channels, let's look again at the ITS scenario. Why might you choose a formal approach to telling your boss, Karen, that the software sale to Thunder Bay Shipping is at risk?

Given the fact that you are delivering bad news, you may want to benefit from the halo effect that a well-executed formal presentation provides. Also, if you find yourself delivering an update on the situation to senior management, it makes sense to use a formal approach. This both encourages the halo effect and allows you to emphasize the facts and some constructive next steps. Aiming for specific results like this is helpful both in saving the sale and in keeping the conversation from coming around to how you lost the client. So, although a talk with your boss, Karen, is probably the best first step, if you are the one that must present the message to her bosses, choosing a more formal approach makes sense.

Informal Communication

The positive and negative sides of an informal approach are detailed below. At the end of this section we will review both forms of communication in the summary **Table 4-4**.

Strengths One strength of informal channels is that they are often faster. If it is urgent that someone receive a message right away, it is quicker to call or send an email than it is to write a formal report or prepare a formal presentation. In a fast-changing environment, the speed with which new information reaches the person who can act on it often becomes the most important factor. For instance, critical computer systems often send an automatic text message to support staff if a problem occurs.

Another benefit of informal communication is that it is extremely flexible—it can take place anywhere, at any time. Informal communication can involve simply calling someone on the phone, sending an email, or running into someone in the hallway. This flexibility makes informal communication useful in managing day-to-day problems as they arise, as well as in dealing with crisis situations, when formal processes might not be fast enough.

Finally, informal communication allows for emphasis on the relationship between the people speaking or corresponding. In a formal report, it would be inappropriate to include a question about how someone's newborn baby is doing. In an informal talk or an email between people who have worked together for a long time and gotten to know each other, however, it's often quite natural to ask about personal events, such as a recent vacation or the arrival of a baby. Business is not simply about data—it is also about the personal relationships between co-workers, between vendors and clients, and even between competitors. Informal communication can greatly strengthen those personal bonds that make business run more smoothly and make the workday more enjoyable.

Weaknesses A weakness of informal communication is that it can come across as sloppy. If you need to convey information to a group of people, you show professionalism, seriousness, and care if you send out a meeting agenda, use PowerPoint slides to present your findings, and follow up with meeting minutes. Not taking those formal steps increases the chance that the meeting will seem unprofessional, as if you didn't put enough thought into it, even if you present the same basic information. For this reason, it's a good idea to write a formal cover letter to accompany your resumé when applying for a job, even if you are submitting electronically. It makes you look professional. An informal email with an attached resumé does not have the same impact.

When using informal communication, people do not always feel compelled to follow the logical steps that a formal process requires. If you think a new company project is going to create more problems than it solves, then

✓•─│Practise   TABLE 4-4   **Summary of Strengths and Weaknesses
of Formal and Informal Communication**

	Formal Communication	Informal Communication
Strengths	− Has useful forms and structures already in place − Sets expectations − Emphasizes content	− Is quicker − Is flexible in terms of time and place − Emphasizes relationship
Weaknesses	− Can take time − Creates more overhead − Can emphasize style over substance	− Can seem sloppy − Can lack rigour − Can be too familiar

using a formal risk-assessment process and creating a report emphasizes that you have looked at all the relevant data and that you are presenting your conclusions based on that thorough analysis. Stopping by your boss's office to voice those same conclusions is much less convincing. Without the formal process behind the report, it's impossible to know whether all the important facts have been taken into account. The downside of the speed of informal communication is that it can turn out to be incomplete.

A final disadvantage of informal communication is that it can sound too familiar. If you have not met someone before, it is inappropriate, and will make a bad impression, to address that person as you would a friend or an acquaintance. This problem occurs particularly in email, where we sometimes default to an informal style. An email starting with an informal "Hey, John" is too familiar when addressing a senior manager you've never spoken with. The more you lack an existing relationship with someone, the more formal your communications should be.

To summarize, neither formal nor informal communication is better. Many degrees of formality exist between the extremes. What is important is to use the degree of formality or informality appropriate to the given situation. And remember, when in doubt, it's better to err on the side of formality. Let's review the strengths and weaknesses of both styles of communication by using **Table 4-4**.

ONE-TO-ONE, ONE-TO-MANY, AND MANY-TO-MANY CHANNELS

Another communication choice to consider is whether your channel is one to one, one to many, or many to many.

One-to-One Communication

One-to-one communication is useful when you want tight control over who knows about the information being communicated. Examples include

- exchanges between two people via email

■ face-to-face conversations

■ phone calls between two people

One-to-one communication is also good for building personal relationships. Additionally, it offers an excellent opportunity to hear and respond to the particular questions and concerns of one person. For instance, if it's important to know your boss's opinion on a matter, speaking one to one makes sure you are getting her feedback, without other participants sidetracking the conversation.

One-to-Many Communication

The greatest strength of one-to-many communication is that it allows you to communicate quickly to a large group of people. Examples include

■ a presentation to a group

■ an announcement during a conference call

■ a post on a blog

■ any communication in which one person delivers a verbal or written message to multiple readers or listeners

It might take all day, or even several days, to communicate a new development to staff members one to one, but you can communicate to the group as a whole through a single email or through a meeting for the whole group. Through email, web postings, and teleconferences, it is possible to deliver a message to a large, geographically diverse group of people. Further, one-to-many communication ensures the whole group hears the same message.

A message can change over the course of delivering it many times in one-to-one situations. A one-to-many approach conveys the same message to everyone. On the informational level, this method ensures that everyone starts with the same information. On the relationship level, it can build trust by making that information available to everyone.

Many-to-Many Communication

Many-to-many communication tends to be the most open-ended kind of communication. It takes place when a number of people both contribute and receive communications, such as in

■ a brainstorming session in the boardroom

■ an online discussion forum where everyone is allowed to post topics and replies

When many people are talking or writing, they can take the discussion in unintended directions. That's a weakness when you want to deliver specific actions to be followed as presented. It can be a strength, however, when you are trying to generate new ideas or when you are problem solving. Brainstorming during a meeting, or posting a problem on a forum and allowing everyone to reply, allows each participant to bring expertise to the subject. This interaction allows new options and possibilities to surface from the collective experience and skills of the group. The key is to have enough structure in place so that the discussion doesn't go off the subject altogether.

When deciding how best to communicate a message, each approach—one to one, one to many, and many to many—offers different strengths. To be an effective communicator, you need to consider which approach lends itself to the needs and objectives of your situation.

THE NEW CHANNELS

What do blogs, Facebook, YouTube, and the other new media mean for the office environment? In one sense, nothing is new. Before the internet came along, companies wanted their employees to be productive, just as they do today. But old cartoons show staff gathered around the water cooler, exchanging gossip. Companies wanted the resources they supplied to be used for company business, but pens and legal pads made their way back to employee homes to be used for grocery lists. In that sense, an employee taking company time to log on to Facebook, using a company computer and bandwidth to connect, is nothing more than the latest version of the old push-pull between an employer's desire to get the most productivity from employees and an employee's desire to take a break from her workload.

That said, new technology certainly has changed the scale of an employee's ability to check out for a while during the workday. If they sit in such a way that no one can see their computer screens, employees can spend hours reading blogs and playing games on Facebook, all the while appearing to an outside observer no different from those who are trying to finish their spreadsheets for the Friday deadline.

Of course, usually a computer log will be sitting on some server, capturing every webpage request each employee makes. If anyone takes the time to look, an employee might have to explain what possible business reason she had for spending all morning on MySpace, followed by an afternoon watching videos on YouTube.

Privacy and the New Media

Beyond what we do at work, new technology has made it possible for employers to get glimpses of what we do and think in our private lives. A hiring committee or manager can locate anything you've posted on the internet under your own name—from rants about former bosses on your blog to camera-phone pictures a friend posted of you sprawled drunk across the floor of a restroom in a bar. Even if you've posted something anonymously, if the facts are revealing enough, someone might figure out it's you.

Placing restrictions on who can view your account often leaves some things still visible. You might allow only friends to access your Facebook account, but is your profile picture—the one of you sunbathing in your backyard—still visible to all? Even if you're careful with your own posts and

Facebook circa 1953

pictures, there's that friend with the camera phone. Further, once something is on the internet, it can hang around forever: Deleted webpages are archived on Google.

Our point is not to scare you into spending the rest of your life outside work sitting at home. With so much information on the internet, chances are no one will take the time to research what's been posted by or about you on the internet, unless you're doing something in the public eye, such as running for elected office. And with this flood of information and pictures now readily available, standards are changing. Think about how many incriminating stories, pictures, and videos have been discovered about celebrities, without any significant negative impact on their careers.

It's up to you to decide on the proper balance between what you do in your private life and what you do for your professional life. You might decide you are going to share what you want with your friends online, and you do not want to work for any company that has a problem with that. You might decide that expressing your political beliefs is so important it is worth the risk of losing a job opportunity. You might decide that freedom of artistic expression, even if it might offend a potential employer, is central to who you are as a person. You can post funny pictures, strong opinions, or artistic expression, but you need to realize the posts might have consequences. Make sure what you post is important enough to you that you are willing to deal with those consequences.

TAKE IT FURTHER

Border Bashes

Canadian border guards were recently caught posting pictures on Facebook of officers drinking while wearing their uniforms. Drinking alcohol in uniform, whether on duty or off duty, violates the Canada Border Services Agency's code of conduct.[8] Other officers made jokes about how they would be receiving their guns soon.[9]

When do you think it is okay for an employer to hold an employee responsible for what he or she posts on a website like Facebook?

Chapter Summary

The medium you choose for your message can be the difference between effective and ineffective communication. Whether you want to tell someone he did a good job, suggest a new approach, or make people aware of a problem, don't just pick up the phone or fire off an email—stop to think about the medium that best fits the needs of the situation. Consider whether the situation calls for written or verbal communication. Think about the strengths and weaknesses of formal communication versus an informal mode of communication. Decide whether a one-to-one, one-to-many, or many-to-many channel best fits the situation. Identify whether any issues of legal liability are involved. And take a second to consider whether any of the newer communication technologies offer a creative approach. Your department has always had weekly team meetings on Friday mornings. Perhaps setting up an online forum for the team, and giving up the weekly meeting, will allow for greater participation, more constructive contributions, and less wasted time.

Choosing the best medium is both an important first step in the communication process and a chance to exercise some creativity. Don't be afraid to experiment a bit with the various media available, and learn first-hand what works best for you in different situations.

---

mycanadianbuscommlab Visit **www.mycanadianbuscommlab.ca** for everything you need to help you succeed in the job you've always wanted! Tools and resources include the following:

- Composing and The Writer's Toolkit
- Document Makeovers
- Video Case Studies
- Grammar exercises and much more!

Thinking and Writing Exercises

1. **Evaluating Communication Choices**
   For each situation below, decide whether the form of communication chosen is well suited to the needs of the situation. Explain why you think the form chosen works or doesn't work.

   a. Manon has been project managing a nine-month project to install a new software package in multiple offices at her firm. The project is due for completion in three weeks, but the final launch will occur at least a month after the scheduled due date. Manon calls a meeting for the earliest possible date, which turns out to be the following week, to announce the delay to the people with the biggest interest in the project.

   b. Guy is a precious metals trader. He arrives at 6:30 a.m. to find the overnight batch processor for the trading system has failed. He sends system support a text message with the problem and his phone number.

   c. Benny is a salesperson for a payroll services company. His firm is launching a new service to handle payments to foreign employees in their local currency. Benny thinks one of his client firms might be interested. He calls the manager that he's dealt with most often among that client's staff to tell him about the new service.

   d. Shari has an idea for a new feature that she thinks could greatly increase the market for her firm's product. She spends several weeks preparing a feasibility study for the new feature, as well as a market analysis, including the estimated ROI (return on investment). When she has those completed, she puts together a PowerPoint presentation and meeting agenda, and then sends out invitations to key managers in marketing, sales, and product development.

   e. Lawrence is a senior manager who knows numerous rumours are going around that the company will be laying off people soon. The company has no plans to lay anyone off. Lawrence wants to put an end to the rumours, so he sends an email to everyone telling them they must attend an emergency meeting the next morning at 9 a.m. sharp.

2. **Choosing the Best Communication Medium for the Situation**

   In each situation below, what medium (e.g., letter, email, informal conversation, formal presentation, a combination of media) would you use to communicate your message. Why? What benefits does your choice offer in the given situation? Does it carry any particular risks?

   a. You've been a junior project manager for two years. Most of the time, your current role involves assisting senior project managers with documentation and administrative tasks on their projects. You feel that you've done an excellent job and learned a lot, but you have reached a point where you are no longer learning new skills and growing professionally. You want your manager to give you the chance to manage your own project.

   b. You manage a bookstore. Your store offers a discount to employees and their immediate families, but recently the number of books sold with employee discounts has gone up greatly, leading you to suspect some employees are offering their discounts to a wider group of people than their immediate family. You need to remind your salespeople that the employee discount is only for employees and their immediate families.

   c. You are in charge of vendor relationships for a large manufacturing company. Your company has recently adopted ISO 9000 standards, and you are requiring your suppliers to adopt the standards too. Those not already complying will have 18 months to bring their companies into compliance. You need to make all your firm's suppliers aware of this new requirement.

   d. You decide to give a lunchtime talk at your firm on an area of person expertise. You think the subject might be of interest to many of your co-workers. You need to let them know both the subject of your talk and the logistical details of the event (e.g., noon, Room 308, bring your lunch, drinks will be provided).

   e. Your department team is spread over a wide geographic area, and you feel that everyone is working on projects in isolation. You think your team would benefit from hearing each other's input on opportunities and problems that arise. You need to provide a way to allow the whole team to be aware of each other's issues and to provide feedback, insights, and suggestions.

3. **In Your Experience**

   Come up with four examples from your life in which someone communicated to you by using a channel that was highly effective. For each example provide the following:

   a. a brief background describing the situation

   b. the channel the communicator used

   c. a reason why it was an effective choice for the situation

4. **Available Communication Channels**

   In small groups, brainstorm as many examples as possible of each of the following types of communication channels:

   a. formal written communication

   b. informal written communication

   c. formal verbal communication

   d. informal verbal communication

   e. written many-to-one communication

   f. verbal many-to-one communication

   g. written many-to-many communication

   h. verbal many-to-many communication

5. **Researching New Media**

   Choose one of the new media (e.g., blogs, Facebook, YouTube) that are now appearing in the office environment. By using online and library resources, compile lists of the strengths and weaknesses of the medium you chose. Which of the items on your lists do you think are the most important to remember when using the new medium?

6. **For Discussion**

   a. In what situations in your life have you found verbal communication more effective than written communication? How about situations in which written communication has been more effective? What criteria have you used when choosing whether to deliver a message verbally or in a written format?

   b. In what situations in your life have you found a formal style of communication more effective than an informal one? How about situations in which informal communication has proven more effective? What criteria have you used when choosing a formal or informal style for communicating?

c. Do you think viral marketing is ethical? Why or why not? If you're concerned in general about viral marketing, are there any circumstances under which you would use it? If you're not concerned in general about viral marketing, are there any circumstances under which you would never use it?

d. A firm announces that it reserves the right to do internet searches on all existing and potential employees. First, imagine that you work in the firm's human resources department and are responsible for writing a memo to employees explaining and justifying the policy. What arguments would you make to support the new policy? Second, imagine you are an employee who wants to protest the policy. What arguments would you make?

Writing Skills Checkup: Apostrophes and Possessives

For each sentence below choose the correct form of the possessive from the pair offered. (Some sentences have more than one pair.)

Example: Tom drove to his sister (Mary's, Marys') house.

In this sentence, the correct choice is Mary's.

1. The most useful feature of the website is (its, it's) _____ page of links to other relevant sites.
2. Samantha's (baby's, babies') _____ rattle was lost when the fire department checked all the (baby's, babies') _____ car seats for safety.
3. (Who's, whose) _____ laptop is that?
4. The CEO signed off on the (company's, companies') _____ marketing plan.
5. The members of the sales force retained (there, their) _____ competitive edge by delivering professional communications to (there, their) _____ clients.
6. The advantage is (hers, her's) _____.
7. The regional (offices', offices's) _____ proximity to major airports made travel to corporate headquarters convenient.
8. (Charles's, Charles') _____ antivirus software is out of date.
9. The firm sent out cards wishing (Season's Greetings, Seasons Greetings) _____ to customers.
10. Every (policy's/policies') _____ introduction should clearly state the purpose of the policy.

Intercultural Communication

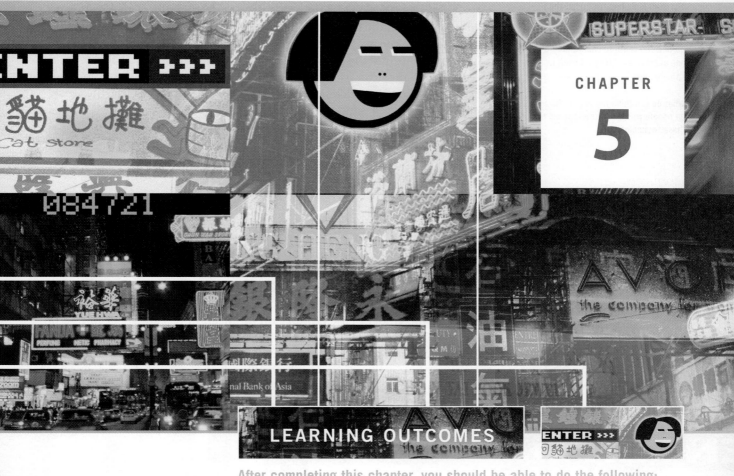

LEARNING OUTCOMES

After completing this chapter, you should be able to do the following:

5.1 Recognize communication between men and women as one form of cross-cultural communication

5.2 Describe the differences between high-context cultures and low-context cultures

5.3 Describe the differences between cultures that focus on individualism (the needs of the few) and those that focus on communitarianism (the needs of the many)

5.4 Understand the history of different cultures and the way different cultures explain themselves

5.5 Identify non-verbal behaviours that differ among different cultures

LIVING IN THE GLOBAL VILLAGE

TAKE IT FURTHER

The Global Village

Marshall McLuhan first used the phrase "global village" to describe the way technology now allows people around the world to communicate with one another as if they all lived in the same village.

What do you think the impact is on people who don't have access to these technologies?

Technology is quickly intertwining the lives of people around the world. As a result, it is increasingly important to be able to communicate respectfully and cooperatively across cultures. From anywhere in the world, a person with an internet connection can join online communities made up of people from every continent sharing a common interest—from politics to hip-hop to what happened on the latest episode of *The Office*. If you want to get together face to face with the people you meet online, you can catch an airplane to and from cities all around the globe. Right now, Travelocity.ca lists 31 flights from Singapore to Vancouver for next Wednesday. Even apart from technology, we are learning about the ideas and cultures of people from all over the world from many sources, including the following:

- foreign students we meet
- novels we read
- music we listen to
- films we watch

These days, because of increased communication and travel around the world, what happens in countries far away—elections, inventions, religious unrest, crops destroyed by insects—affects us. What we do in Canada also affects the people in other countries.

For businesspeople, only a lack of creativity and the ability to work with other people limits the opportunities for new ideas, new partners, and new markets in the global marketplace. Communication has always been one of the single biggest factors in a businessperson's success. As the world becomes more interconnected, communication skills become even more important. As more and more co-workers and clients come from around the globe, cultural sensitivity and competence in intercultural communication will be skills that every company will look for in its employees.

ENTER >>>

ISSUES *in* Communication
Men and Women as Different Cultures

In September 2008, the *Globe and Mail* ran an article titled "Tougher for women to work for women: Study finds more mental, physical problems than if they work for a man."[1] Certainly many people—women and men—believe the stereotype that it is harder for women to have a woman boss. But is that true? Is that even what the researchers said?

As it turns out, the researchers said that the study did *not* allow for conclusions as to why women who report to women have more mental and physical problems. One possibility, they said, is that women who have a female manager "might tend to cluster in the kinds of work or in certain sectors that involve stressful activities that our survey didn't identify."[2]

TV, books, magazines, and the internet report endlessly about the gender wars. Sometimes, as in the headline cited above, they place the blame more on women. At other times, men are to blame.

In her book *You Just Don't Understand*, Deborah Tannen suggests the reason that the relationship between the sexes causes problems is that male-female communication is cross-cultural. "Many frictions arise because boys and girls grow up in what are essentially different cultures, so talk between women and men is cross-cultural communication."[3] To capture this cross-cultural aspect of communication between men and women, Tannen uses the term *genderlects* to refer to these different dialects spoken by male culture and female culture.

Tannen says that male culture teaches a man to view himself "as an individual in a hierarchical social order in which he is either one-up or one-down."[4] In such a world, a man must always guard against attempts to knock him down on the social order. He must be ready to fight to keep his position in the hierarchy. Female culture, Tannen argues, teaches a woman to see herself "as an individual in a network of connections."[5] In this world, a woman wants to give and receive support. She wants to find community. Tannen acknowledges that men also want community and that women also want success. The point she is making is that the focus is different for men and women. This differing focus leads to misunderstandings and potential breakdowns in communication when men and women talk to each other.

One specific difference Tannen identifies is the difference between *report talk* and *rapport talk*. Men use report talk: They want to maintain independence and status by "exhibiting knowledge and skill, and by holding center stage through verbal performance such as storytelling, joking or imparting information."[6] Women, conversely, use conversation "primarily [as] a language of rapport: a way of establishing connections and negotiating relationships."[7] So men and women often work toward different goals in a conversation.

One of the strengths of Tannen's approach is that it does not place any blame or judgment on either style. Neither style is right nor better. Men and women simply have different communication styles, the same way people from Japan learn a different communication style than people from Canada do. We need to understand both styles if we want to communicate effectively across that cultural divide.

A look at recent book titles suggests the sexes are still looking for help understanding each other.

DISCUSSION

1. What are some examples of negative stereotypes of men and women you have seen in the media?
2. Do book titles such as *Men Are from Mars, Women Are from Venus* exaggerate the differences between men and women?
3. What is your personal experience with male and female communication styles? Are they very different, or do you think the differences have been exaggerated?
4. What benefits are there to identifying differences between male and female communication styles? How could that help you communicate more effectively?

Intercultural and Cross-Cultural

The ITP Nelson Canadian Dictionary of the English Language defines *intercultural* as "of, relating to, involving or representing different cultures,"[8] and *cross-cultural* as "comparing or dealing with two or more different cultures."[9] The terms are often used interchangeably. However, you might come across writers who make a distinction between the two words.

To what extent do you think different companies create their own cultures?

✓—Practise CULTURAL BALANCING ACTS

Most people would agree that being sensitive and skilful in communicating with people from other cultures is vital to career success. But what exactly does that mean? Clearly, to achieve those goals, you need to know how to be sensitive to someone from a different culture even if you don't know the specifics of his or her cultural expectations and meanings. It can be easy to offend without intending to. In Arab cultures, for example, it's considered offensive to point the bottoms of your feet at someone.[10] If you didn't know this, you might sit down and cross your legs, as is customary for many Canadians, and offend someone without meaning to.

As you learn more about any culture, you also need to balance cultural norms against individual variation. On the one hand, effective intercultural communication requires you to be aware of the differences in communication styles in different cultures and countries. On the other hand, effective communication begins with respect for the individual you are communicating with.

Intercultural communication requires a balance of two needs:

1. to learn about and respect cultural norms and styles other than your own
2. to learn about and respect an individual's own communication styles and preferences, regardless of the person's culture or country of origin

If you are afraid to generalize about a culture, you aren't going to identify any useful guidelines. But if you treat all members of a culture as though they must fit those generalizations, you will act as if the world is full of stereotypes instead of real people. As you read this chapter, it is important to make generalizations to learn, and just as important to remember that each person you meet is different. Take the person himself or herself into account.

Finally, it is important to remember no generic "other culture" exists. You cannot learn a one-size-fits-all "other culture communication style" to use when speaking with non-Canadians. No such communication style exists. What you can learn about are the communication styles of specific cultures and countries.

Fortunately, some general guidelines are available for approaching situations that require communication between cultures or countries. See **Table 5-1.**

The section that follows describes some cultural patterns that can help you to better understand how the communication styles of other cultures differ from your own.

TAKE IT FURTHER

Ethnography

One approach to studying a culture is ethnography, which means that the researcher cannot study the different aspects of a culture in isolation and must look at the culture as a whole. That often involves living in the culture being studied. An example of ethnography to better understand the business world is Michael Pacanowsky's writings on corporate culture at Gore-Tex. He states that organizations as well as societies are cultures.

How would you describe the culture of your college or university?

TABLE 5-1	**Intercultural Communication Tips**
Always remember to do the following:	

— Approach cultural differences descriptively. That is, identify the practice but don't judge it.
— Take the time to research and learn about the specific cultures you communicate with regularly.
— Talk to and correspond with the person, not a cultural stereotype.

High-Context and Low-Context Cultures

One difference in communication style is the distinction between high context and low context.[11] These refer to the degree to which the communication takes elements other than the words themselves into account for the understanding of what is meant:

- *Low-context communication* conveys meaning mainly through the words used.

- *High-context communication* involves a great deal of meaning that is never actually stated—it is understood from the situation in which the communication occurs.

We all make use of both low-context and high-context communication. Consider these examples:

- *Low-context communication:* A friend comes over and you ask her, "Do you want some pop?" In this case, you likely want to know whether she would like to drink some pop. The words say what they mean.

- *High-context communication:* A wife goes out to dinner with her husband. He has a history of drinking problems, but he hasn't had a drink in the past six months. She sees him standing at the bar, signalling the bartender. She goes over to him and asks, "Do you want some pop?" In this case, her meaning is not a simple inquiry whether he would like to drink some pop. Given the context, her words suggest another meaning, such as "Please, you don't want to go back to drinking alcohol. Drink some pop instead of something alcoholic."

Just as individual communications are positioned all the way along the line from low context to high context, different cultures have communication styles that are lower context or higher context:

- Asian cultures tend to be higher context.

- European and North American cultures tend to be lower context.

- Within such general categories are variations among individual countries and cultures: France is higher context than the United States, for instance.

These examples do not mean that every communication by someone from China will be high context, while every communication by someone from the United States will be low context. They simply mean that, in general, communication in high-context cultures relies more on things that aren't actually said, while communication in low-context cultures relies more on the words themselves.

People raised in mainstream Canadian culture tend toward the low-context side of full spectrum. That means that the biggest communication problems for most Canadians come when dealing with high-context cultures. Those who were raised in high-context cultures and come to Canada can reduce misunderstandings by being aware of the features of low-context cultures.

To lessen the chance of misinterpretation, be aware of the differences outlined in **Table 5-2.**

TAKE IT FURTHER

Edward T. Hall

Edward T. Hall's book *Beyond Culture* introduced the concept of high-context and low-context cultures. He was serving in the U.S. Army during World War II when he first noted the difficulties that failures of intercultural communication can create.[12]

Why do you think reading his book could be of help to a businessperson?

✳ Explore

TABLE 5-2	Features of High- and Low-Context Cultures
High-Context Cultures	**Low-Context Cultures**
− Much of what is communicated is non-verbal. − Relationship building is crucial to long-term success. − Decisions are reached more slowly. Indirect approaches to the decision-making process are often necessary. − There is a strong subtext regarding issues of status and face-saving—this subtext must be respected.	− People say what they mean. − Indirect approaches that work in a high-context culture go unnoticed. − The focus is on the issue at hand, not the status of the participants. − People make direct, even blunt, statements about a situation to address the issue. The statements are not intended to offend.

> *"The needs of the many outweigh the needs of the few or the one."*
>
> — Mr. Spock
>
> *Star Trek: The Wrath of Khan*

Particularly in the case of people from low-context cultures communicating with people from high-context cultures, the wide number of non-verbal factors and underlying relationships can be overwhelming for someone. In addition to the guidelines in **Table 5-2**, it is useful to look at the way members of a high-context culture respond to what is said to get clues about how best to respond.

The Needs of the Many and the Needs of the One

In 2005, three Japanese aid workers who had gone to Iraq to start a non-profit organization to help street children were taken hostage. When they were released and they returned to Japan, they were not greeted with relief but with strong disapproval. A sign held up at the airport said, "You got what you deserve."[13] A post on one of their websites read, "You are Japan's shame."[14] Japan's government billed them $6000 for their airfare home.[15] The three were forced to go into hiding.

Colin Powell, U.S. secretary of state at the time, said of them, "Well, everybody should understand the risk they are taking by going into dangerous areas. But if nobody was willing to take a risk, then we would never move forward. We would never move our world forward."[16]

Yasuo Fukuda, then Japan's chief cabinet secretary, said, "They may have gone on their own but they must consider how many people they caused trouble to because of their action."[17]

The differing reactions of the U.S. and Japanese officials highlight the difference between the views of communitarianism (the needs of the many) and individualism (the needs of the one).[18] Individualism sees individuals as primarily self-determined. They may belong to social networks, but they really exist outside of those networks. People create their own identities. Communitarianism sees individuals as produced by their networks and as ultimately understandable only as part of those networks. Social networks and relationships create people's identities.

TAKE IT FURTHER

Communitarianism, Collectivism, and Communism

Dutch writer Geert Hofstede uses the term *collectivism* to refer to societies that focus on the needs of the group. We've used the word *communitarianism* to avoid confusion, because collectivism is also used as a synonym for communism. In this context communitarianism and collectivism refer to a cultural pattern that places emphasis on the whole social group over individual members. Japan has a communitarian culture, but not a communist government.

Can you think of any general workplace in Canada that might have a communitarian approach? ◼

Given how close Canada is to the United States, a country that has strong traditions of "rugged individualism" and "the self-made person," Canadians may at times feel they are communitarian in contrast to U.S. individualism. In the context of world cultures, however, mainstream Canadian culture also places a high degree of importance on individualism. When a Canadian reads about the Japanese aid workers' story above, she is likely to have sympathy for the aid workers and feel that their reception on returning home was unfair. After all, the aid workers saw a problem—the plight of the Iraqi street children—and they took action, at great personal risk, to help those in trouble. From the point of view of individualism, they were heroes.

Nothing is wrong with that view, but individualism is not the only lens through which to view the events. From a communitarian perspective, the aid workers acted without thinking about the cost their actions might carry for their government and community. When they were taken hostage, it became Japan's problem, and Japan had to negotiate for the hostages' release. From the point of view of communitarianism, they were selfish.

If you were raised in mainstream Canadian culture, you can reduce misunderstandings by remembering the common features of communitarian cultures listed in **Table 5-3**. If you were raised in a communitarian culture before coming to Canada, you can reduce misunderstandings by being aware of the common features of individualist cultures listed in the same table.

Listening to Cultural Narratives

On October 15, 2007, Chief Kim Baird of the Tsawwassen First Nation spoke to the British Columbian legislature. The provincial legislature was about to begin debate on the ratification of the first urban treaty. Chief Baird's speech was positive and optimistic, proud of the First Nations' heritage and looking to its future (see sidebar quotation on the next page).

In High Noon, *Gary Cooper takes on the outlaws alone when the townspeople turn their backs on him. American culture emphasizes individual action.*

TABLE 5-3	Common Features of Communitarian and Individualist Cultures
Communitarian Cultures	**Individualist Cultures**
— The impact of a decision on your family, community, and nation is the determining factor. — Actions that hurt the group are to be avoided. — The decisions and actions of the individual reflect on that person's family and country. — The existing hierarchy is respected.	— Whether a decision helps you achieve your goals is the determining factor. — The impact of your actions on others is ultimately their issue to deal with. — Decisions and actions reflect on the person making the decision and not on anyone else. — No hierarchy is recognized—everyone is equal.

"For the Tsawwassen people, this is a time of great hope and optimism— a challenging, yet exciting time. It is a time for revival and renewal. It is a time when we will take back our rightful place as a community, equal to others, through our treaty.

I say 'take back our rightful place' because we have a long and proud history that predates the birth of this province. For thousands of years, we used and occupied a large territory that was abundant in fish, shellfish, wildlife and other resources."[19]

— Chief Kim Baird

Chief Kim Baird of the Tsawwassen First Nation

Intercultural communication is not only about talking to people from outside Canada. Canada was built on three cultural traditions:

- First Nations
- French
- English

Today Canada contains many cultures, and Canadian businesspeople broaden their opportunities when they understand and communicate effectively with them.

A culture's understanding of itself is influenced by its history, so one important step in better understanding another culture is to learn about its history. You can learn about a culture's history through regularly reading newspapers and news magazines, reading history books, reading fiction, and seeing movies. Of course, you'll want to double-check that the movie is at least largely accurate, not a romanticized version of the event in question. Movies often take a great deal of artistic licence with the truth. Also, be curious when you meet with people. Instead of talking about sports to get the conversation going, for example, maybe ask about a local restaurant or building of interest. That way you will combine learning about a person's culture with expanding your personal relationship with them.

It is not enough to just learn the history, though. *History* likely makes you think about what happened in the past. A culture's narrative, the way it understands itself, is very much alive and in the present. For example, the vote was not extended to all Aboriginal peoples living in Canada until 1960—that means people you do business with might have been denied the vote or have grown up hearing from their parents or grandparents how they were denied the vote. Again, this is not only history—it is also a living and current part of the self-narrative of Aboriginal experience in Canada.

If you want to understand and communicate effectively with people from another cultural background, one of the most important things is to listen—listen to their history and to their story, listen to the narrative they tell about themselves. With that in mind, let's end this section by listening to one more passage from Chief Kim Baird's speech (see sidebar).

Non-verbal Aspects of Communication

A number of non-verbal behaviours, or codes, differ among cultures. Becoming aware of differences among cultures in their attitudes toward these non-verbal aspects of communication is another way to reduce misunderstanding and ensure effective, respectful communication. Let's look at five such non-verbal behaviours.

"Today, I have two girls, aged 4 and 10 months. I am confident they will study, work and live in a new and different world, defined by hope and fuelled by optimism, while being proud of their heritage.

I have to add that I am also glad that in the future when my girls visit this building, they will not feel embarrassed by how their ancestors are portrayed on those murals. The future is very bright for my children, and all the children and future children of my community if this treaty is signed by all three parties. I hope their world will be so much better than the one their ancestors faced for too long. We are decolonizing through accommodation of our differences—not assimilation."[20]

— Chief Kim Baird

Emblems and Gestures Researchers in intercultural communication use the term *emblems* to describe gestures whose meaning is culturally determined. Gestures, or emblems, can have meanings within a culture (see **Figure 5-1**). For example, holding up your thumb is a signal of victory or success within North American culture, whereas holding up your middle finger is an insult. However, in Arabic cultures, the thumbs-up gesture is an insult, with a meaning similar to holding up a middle finger in North American culture.

Cultural gestures are particularly tricky because they are arbitrary. That is, there is no particular reason that a given gesture should mean what it does—there is no reason that holding out your hand and raising your thumb should mean "good job" or that it should be an insult. The meaning exists only within the context of a specific culture. Consequently, you have no way

FIGURE 5-1   Gestures of the World

	Gesture	What It Means in Canada	What It Means Elsewhere
	Thumbs up	Victory, success	In Arabic cultures, it is an insult, similar to holding up the middle finger in Canada.
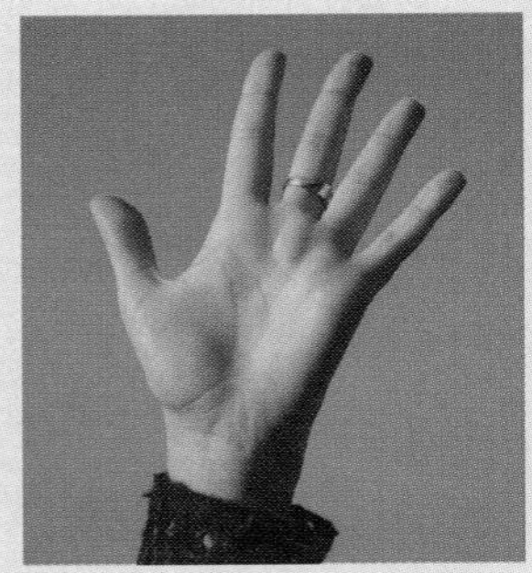	Waving with your palm out, fingers up	Hello, goodbye, or a way of getting someone's attention	In Europe, it signals "no."
	Calling someone over by beckoning with your forefinger	Could you come over here?	In Indonesia it means the same thing, but it is *used only to call an animal.*
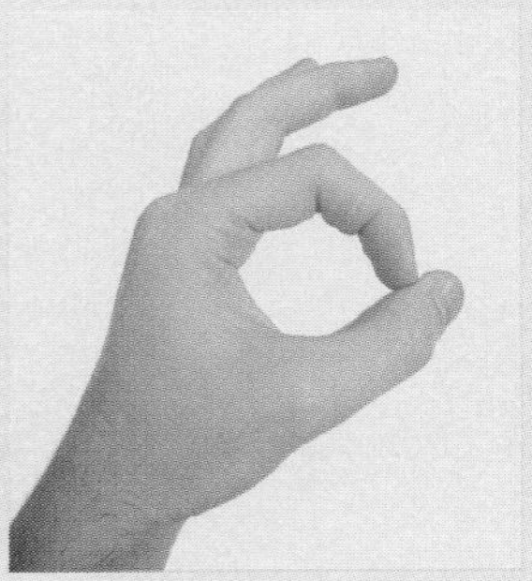	Circling thumb and forefinger in the OK sign	OK	In Brazil, it signifies a part of the female anatomy and is considered a very rude gesture.

Sources: Examples in this chart were compiled from "Africa & Middle East: United Arab Emirates, Country Profile." Berlitz Career Services. Berlitz International Inc. Web. 23 Aug. 2008; Axtell, Roger E. Gestures: The DO's and TABOOs of Body Language around the World. *Rev. ed. New York: John Wiley and Sons, 1998. Print.*

to know whether a gesture will be positive, negative, or neutral except by learning through study or direct exposure.

This is particularly difficult when it comes to gestures that are neutral within your own culture but have negative meanings within another. As mentioned earlier in the chapter, crossing your legs is a neutral gesture in Canada—it has not been assigned a cultural meaning. However, pointing the bottoms of your feet at someone is an insult in Arab culture. It is important to research and find out what potentially offensive emblems exist within cultures you communicate with.

Regulators Regulators are the pauses, gestures, and verbal behaviours that let participants manage the flow of the conversation and know when it is appropriate to speak. For example, one regulator is simply waiting for the correct amount of time after another speaker has finished before you begin speaking. In a culture that expects a shorter pause, speakers will start talking as soon as that short period has passed. People in other cultures, expecting a longer pause, will wait for that longer time to pass before assuming a speaker is finished and starting to talk themselves.

Tension can arise when people from a culture that expects very short pauses between speakers interact with people from a culture that expects longer pauses. The people expecting the longer pause may judge speakers who jump in after the shorter pause as rude and as interrupting. People who are used to the longer pause will have trouble entering the conversation. On the other side, people who expect a shorter pause may find speakers who allow for the longer pause slow and even make the assumption that such speakers are less intelligent.

Differences between how long a listener should pause before saying something can exist within the same country, between different geographic regions. For example, New Yorkers expect a much shorter pause between speakers and therefore can come across as pushy or rude to Americans from other regions. On the other hand, people from the Southern states allow a longer pause between speakers and therefore may be underestimated by people from New York.

The best way to approach regulators is by doing research in advance to make sure you have a good sense of what to expect when talking to people from a given culture. Also, if you find yourself frustrated that you aren't getting a chance to say what you want to say, or if you find yourself thinking the people you are talking to seem a bit slow, remember to step back and approach the situation from a descriptive point of view. Different cultures have different styles, but one style isn't better than another—they're just different. Once you have that objective perspective, you can plan how you might change your own behaviour to make the conversation more productive for everyone.

Personal Space People designate a certain amount of space surrounding themselves as their personal space. If someone enters this personal space uninvited, it can cause anxiety or make you feel threatened. This experience is universal. What differs between cultures is the size of the personal space zone. For example, North Americans consider a larger zone their personal space than Arabs do. From the standpoint of intercultural communication,

We should learn from members of the other culture what level of touch is regarded as appropriate.

the problem occurs when someone from a culture who expects less personal space stands at a short distance from someone who expects a larger zone of personal space.

As always, a good way to prepare is to research in advance what a given culture's sense of personal space is relative to your own. The other important step to take is to monitor your reactions. If you find yourself feeling crowded, ask whether that might be due to different expectations regarding personal space. If you are from a culture where the zone of personal space is smaller and you find yourself constantly moving closer to Canadians only to have them back away, see whether maintaining a distance that is slightly farther than you normally would helps.

Touch Cultures have very different expectations about touch—who can touch whom, where they can touch that person, and under what situations it is appropriate. In general, North Americans touch each other less than many other cultures. For instance, in Latin America, it is not uncommon for business associates of the opposite sex to kiss each other on the cheek in greeting. In North America, leaning in to kiss a business associate on the cheek would most likely result in a lecture from your human resources department, if not worse.

As with other non-verbal behaviours, you should do research into cultural expectations and norms. You should also learn from members of the other culture what level of touch is regarded as appropriate. However, given the risk of offence if you touch someone inappropriately, it is best to err on the side of not touching someone, unless you are sure. The best way is to mirror the behaviour of people you meet. That is, let them take the lead in determining what is normal within their culture, and respond in kind. If someone shakes your hand, return the shake. If someone initiates an exchange of kisses on the cheek, you can return it.

Time Different cultures have different understandings of time. In North American culture, time is considered a resource—time is money. North American businesspeople place great importance on punctuality and meeting deadlines.

In other cultures, the expected arrival time for a meeting is more flexible. It might be considered rude to show up twenty minutes late for a meeting in Toronto, but it would not be at all inappropriate in some countries in Latin America. In terms of deadlines, some cultures take for granted that we can't predict the future, and therefore deadlines are looser, more apt to change without notice. In North America, we expect that a deadline will be met or that we will receive notice in advance that the deadline must be changed.

For a Canadian travelling outside of Canada, it is a good idea to arrive on time for meetings. Even if members of a culture arrive late for meetings, they might consider it rude if a foreign businessperson arrived late. You will also want to find out what is considered culturally appropriate for social occasions—showing up either too early or too late can be considered impolite.

For people from cultures that have a more elastic view of time than North Americans do, the best practice is to show up on time when doing business in Canada and to communicate delays in advance if for any reason you cannot be on time for a meeting or will not be able to meet a deadline.

Chapter Summary

We started this chapter by looking at the importance of intercultural communication in today's world. We considered whether communication between men and women can be viewed as a form of intercultural communication.

We then looked at two cultural patterns: high context versus low context, and communitarianism versus individualism. We identified strategies to communicate successfully with people whose cultural pattern is different from our own, such as by identifying some things that people from low-context cultures should be aware of when communicating with people from high-context cultures.

Next, we looked at the importance of a culture's self narrative. A culture's history is not just in the past. It lives in the present as part of the way the culture understands itself. Specifically, we looked at elements of First Nations history and self narrative.

Finally, we discussed five non-verbal behaviours that differ among cultures: gestures, regulators, personal space, touch, and time. We provided strategies for approaching each of those differences.

Thinking and Writing Exercises

1. **High-Context and Low-Context Cultures**
   For each pair of countries below, identify which one has the more high-context culture and which the more low-context culture. Use any print or online resources you need.

   a. Denmark, Guatemala

   b. Singapore, Australia

   c. Canada, France

   d. Italy, England

   e. Canada, United States

   f. Germany, Japan

   g. Saudi Arabia, Netherlands

   h. Spain, China

   i. Israel, Sweden

   j. Czech Republic, Canada

2. **Communitarianism and Individualism**
   Use the same country pairs from the exercise above, and identify which of the countries in each pair values communitarianism more, and which one values individualism more.

   Did you find any correlation between where a country falls on the high-context/low-context continuum and where it falls on the communitarianism/individualism continuum?

3. **Exploring Canada's Self-Narrative**
   Answer the following questions based on your own experience of how Canadians talk about themselves.

   a. What do you think mainstream Canada's narrative is regarding Europeans settling here and founding Canada?

   b. What do you think mainstream Canadians think of themselves?

   c. What specific words resonate with meaning for Canadians?

   d. How do you think people from other cultures view Canadians?

   e. Is there anything you would like to see change in the way Canadians understand themselves?

4. **Making Small Talk**
   Those topics that are considered polite and those that are off limits can vary among regions and cultures. For example, New Yorkers will ask people they just met how much rent they are paying. In most places, however, asking someone a question about money would be considered rude.

   a. In Canada, what topics are often used when someone wants to make small talk?

   b. What topics are better avoided in Canada when making small talk?

   For questions (c) and (d), pick a culture other than your own. Use any print or online resources you need to answer the following questions:

   c. What topics are used for small talk in the culture you chose?

   d. What topics are considered off limits when making small talk in the culture you chose?

5. **Experiencing Cultural Differences**
   Answer the following questions based on your personal experiences. If you have not had a relevant personal experience, imagine how you would feel.

   a. North American society places a heavy emphasis on eliminating body odours. If you are a product of that North American culture, how do you feel about a culture where body odours are seen as natural, and no attempt is made to cover them? If you are from a society where body odours are considered more natural, how do you feel about mainstream North America's focus on covering body odours with scented soaps, deodorants, and perfumes?

   b. Have you ever travelled to a city, region, or country where you thought the people were rude? Can you objectively explain any differences you found there—that is, without making judgments (such as "the people are rude") about the region and its people but by describing specific actions (such as "no one stopped to say hi"). After completing this exercise, do you still feel the same way about the region?

c. Have you ever travelled to a place where people have a different conception of punctuality than you have? Did the people show up later than you for meetings, or did you feel as if you were regularly being judged as late? If you think of punctuality as a cultural expectation, what does that do to your perception of those experiences?

6. **Researching Cultural Differences**

Go to a library and identify six resources that would be helpful in researching cultural differences. Make sure that three of those resources are general—that is, they have information relevant to all cultures—and that the other three resources provide information on one or more cultures of particular interest to you.

Go online and identify six websites that would be helpful, again including three that are general and three that are related to specific cultures.

Class members may want to share and compile the lists to create a master list of useful resources for everyone.

Writing Skills Checkup: Capitalization

Rewrite the following sentences, capitalizing letters where necessary.

Example: the bookstore in madrid where I worked last summer was called librería manzanares.

Correction: The bookstore in Madrid where I worked last summer was called Librería Manzanares.

1. the african proverb "it takes a village to raise a child" expresses a communitarian value.
2. what sort of value does the proverb "the squeaky wheel gets the grease" express?
3. knowing that china is a more high-context culture than canada does not mean all chinese people in all situations will exhibit high-context communication patterns.

4. spanish is the common language throughout latin america, except in brazil, where they speak portuguese.
5. what effect do historical wars, like the war of 1812, world war I, and world war ii, have on the canadian self narrative?
6. the shuswap nation is located to the east of the fraser river.
7. emily howard stowe founded the canadian women's suffrage association (cwsa).
8. in south america, people from the united states are called *norte americanos,* or north americans.
9. people sometimes mistakenly think islamic countries are arabic countries—iran, for example, is islamic but not arabic.
10. "advance australia fair" is australia's national anthem.

Meetings

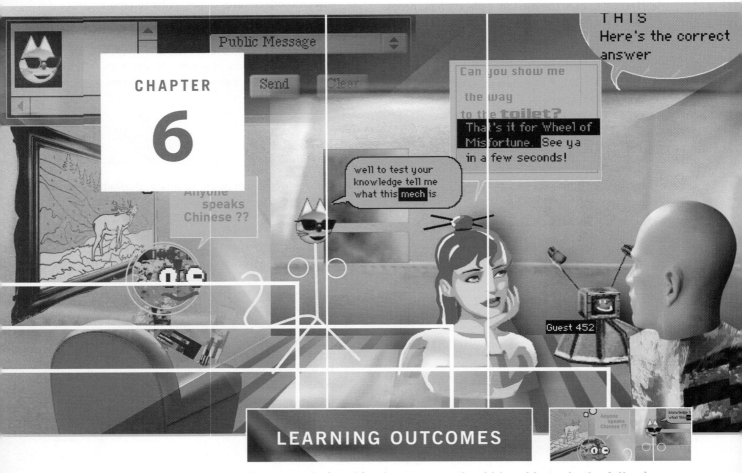

CHAPTER 6

SIMPLE MEETINGS CAN BE COMPLEX

A businessperson named Carol was in a restaurant, waiting for a very important client who was apparently running late. While in the lounge, she saw Donald Trump, famous businessperson and host of a popular reality show, sitting on the sofa enjoying a drink.

On a whim, Carol decided to introduce herself to him. Much to her surprise "the Donald" turned out to be very nice and not at all like his television persona where he inevitably says, "You're fired" to hapless business management contestants. She explained to Mr. Trump that she was about to close a very important business deal and that she would be very grateful if he could say a quick "Hello, Carol" to her when she was with her client. Mr. Trump agreed to do just that.

Later, while Carol was speaking with her client, she saw Donald Trump approach her table. Carol's client turned around and looked at him as he said, "Hi, Carol. What's going on?"

To which Carol smoothly replied, "Not now, Donald. Can't you see I'm in a meeting?"[1]

This story pokes fun at the famous billionaire businessperson and host of *The Apprentice*, but it also communicates two important points:

1. The reason that a businessperson receives an invitation to a meeting is not always obvious: There may be a private agenda.

2. Networking opportunities can arise in unexpected places. The way you make use of them is up to you.

In the story, Carol wants to impress her client. Donald Trump understands this and assumes that he can help her by pretending to know Carol. But Carol has other plans: She creates the illusion that she is ignoring the famous business tycoon to pay more attention to her client. Of course, this is a joke, and you get a laugh at Donald Trump's expense, but perhaps you also wondered whether the client is left thinking, "Is Carol important enough to ignore Donald Trump? Will she eventually ignore me too?"

Behind even a seemingly simple encounter between businesspeople, such as the one we just looked at, is the shared knowledge that meetings are indispensable in virtually every aspect of successful

Meetings are important to any successful business.

businesses. Meetings are organized for a variety of purposes, including planning, decision making, problem solving, communicating, and exchanging information. Planning effective meetings can be both challenging and highly rewarding.[2] Meetings are complex enough to deserve their own chapter in this book.

ISSUES
in Communication
The Obama Visit

Meetings can involve every level of management or staff. Whether the purpose is to share ideas, make decisions, build consensus, or introduce new people to the process, meetings matter.

After taking office as president of the United States, Barack Obama arrived for his first official visit to

The ultimate power meeting

Canada on February 19, 2009. Before aides from both countries met for a formal meeting, Prime Minister Harper and President Obama met privately for 33 minutes. They had been scheduled to meet for 10 minutes. The additional time was not enough to affect the schedule for the rest of the day, but it was enough to suggest that the national leaders had a productive first introduction. CBC News quoted a senior prime minister's office official as saying that the private meeting gave the leaders a chance to establish a "good rapport. This was a good start and bodes well for the rest of the day."[3]

Prime Minister Harper and President Obama outlined three main priorities for their countries' relationship:

1. working together to restore economic growth
2. creating a new initiative on environmental protection
3. making a commitment to stabilize the political situation in Afghanistan

Obama's visit prompted Harper to schedule a visit to the United States to continue the dialogue soon afterward.

Many Canadians were interested in Obama's visit, and thousands turned out to catch a glimpse of the popular new U.S. president. Before leaving to return to Washington, Obama was quoted as saying, "I love this country and I think we could not have a better friend and ally."

DISCUSSION

1. List three reasons that agendas are important in meetings. Then, still bearing agendas in mind, discuss why the first official meeting between Stephen Harper and Barack Obama went over the allotted time. Why might this be important to relations between Canada and the United States?

2. The prime minister and the president met for 33 minutes, but the meetings of their aides lasted hours. What do you think the aides talked about after the initial meeting between the leaders had ended?

3. After the leaders' meeting, they outlined three main priorities of the bilateral relationship. Discuss why each item is so important to Canada and the United States. Why is it important to recap the high points of a meeting immediately afterward?

4. What additional priority would you have included if you had been at the meeting? Why?

WORKING TOGETHER
TO MAKE MEETINGS SUCCEED

✓•—[Practise]

In today's increasingly complex business world, the ability to work with others is more important than ever. As authors Akehurst, Comeche, and Galindo put it: "In the current global corporate climate that surrounds us, firms would do well to encourage the talent and creativity of their employees to achieve success. This is achieved, not by giving priority to individual talent, but by optimizing the collective as a whole and with the firm's activities based on teamwork and joint effort."[4]

When it comes to meetings, unfortunately, many people do not understand the importance of working together to get the most done. Like all relationships, effective meetings take time and energy—and sometimes more than a little compromise.

In every meeting, different roles and responsibilities must be managed before the event can be called a success. At least five roles are involved:

1. organizer
2. chairperson
3. timekeeper
4. minute taker
5. attendees

In smaller organizations, or for meetings of relatively low importance, the organizer and chairperson may be the same person. The same is true of minute taker and timer.

In the next section, we will discuss how these roles come together and explore the duties of each in a well-run meeting. What is important here is to realize that successful meetings depend more on good planning, good execution, and good follow-up than on simple good luck.

1. The Organizer

Before any meeting is set up, there needs to be a clear purpose for getting people together. Author Bruce Lee identifies defining the purpose as the first step in successful meeting management.[5] You should not have a meeting for the sake of a meeting—that is a waste of valuable time. You must always have a purpose or a reason to get people together. "Knowing the destination" involves both the general purpose and the specific purpose, and—as the meeting facilitator—the organizer needs to know both. For example, sometimes the meeting's purpose is to bring people together to discuss issues or to generate new ideas through brainstorming. These are worthwhile purposes and getting consensus from the group can make future decision making easier.

The chairperson and attendees cannot have a successful meeting if they do not know what it is they are supposed to accomplish. It is important for all people involved with meetings to work well together, and good communication is a major part of that success. Who is asked to attend the meeting depends on many factors. The chairperson will often determine the list of

Consider the needs of all your attendees.

attendees for the meeting, but it is important for the organizer to know exactly who is attending.

Organizers find it helpful to set up a meeting planner (or schedule) to keep track of the many details required for successful meetings. The meeting planner should include the following:

- a list of attendees and their contact information
- the name, location, and description of the meeting place (for example, the description could include whether food or beverages are available on-site or whether the meeting room is accessible for people with disabilities)
- information on the status of reports, minutes from previous meetings, related information, and so on

2. The Chairperson

The decision of who needs to attend a meeting is important. If the meeting involves internal staff, then it is vital to involve the right departments based on the purpose. People will often be invited based on their position within the organization. For example, if you hold a meeting with your staff to discuss the planned changes to the health benefits package, you would likely include someone from human resources (HR) who is knowledgeable about the package. This would not likely be the head of HR, who may have arranged the deal, but it would likely be someone who is familiar with the details of the plan. The HR person must be knowledgeable because your staff will likely have specific questions.

Meetings of external partners, or those from outside your organization, are a little more complicated but follow the same logic.

If you are the chairperson, you need to include the agencies that have a direct effect on, or are directly affected by, the purpose of the meeting. The attendees will be the communication link between the organizations. If the meeting concerns the day-to-day issues of the organization, you likely would not include anyone in a senior management position. Conversely, if you need people to make decisions or commit resources at your meeting, you want the people with that authority to attend.

If possible, try to make sure that all attendees are at approximately the same level on the organizational charts of their organizations. For example, when you draft the membership of the meeting, ask yourself if all members are middle managers or supervisors or frontline workers. Having people from similar levels can often help improve communications among attendees, but it may not always be possible. The obvious exception is an informational meeting specifically designed to include an entire organization. For example, an annual general meeting can include people from all levels of an organization, because it can involve information that affects everyone.

Efficient meetings must be managed carefully to the best use of people's time. It is imperative to develop an agenda that allows your group to cover all the issues they need to discuss with sufficient time allocated to each item. It is important to have enough time so the items are discussed in full, but not so much that meeting time is wasted with conversations or awkward silence.

Remember that the meeting chairperson is not supposed to be the one talking all the time. You run the show, introduce the items, and manage the flow of the discussions. You must be tactful to make sure that everyone has a chance to speak and make sure that a few outspoken people do not dominate the conversation. If you believe that some group members are trying to take over the meeting, or be bullies with their opinions, respectfully acknowledge their contribution and then move to another in the group. This may be someone who is quieter but whom you know you can rely on to share his or her point of view. The perspectives of these quieter attendees are often very valuable, because these people may be more thoughtful in their response. A chairperson's tact and diplomacy are very important here, because no one should feel slighted but at the same time no one should feel obligated to talk. If you are the chairperson and you know that you have many quiet people attending the meeting, consider asking attendees to submit their thoughts in writing and in advance.

A last but very important point is whether or not to meet, which is usually up to the chairperson. If the meeting has no clear purpose, or if key invitees will be missing, then the meeting should likely be cancelled or postponed.

3. The Timekeeper

The timekeeper helps the chairperson to keep the agenda on schedule. If you are the timekeeper, you will be required to do the following:

- Make note of the exact time the meeting started and when each item was introduced.
- Check with the chairperson before the meeting to set the time for each item, if an item does not have one on the agenda.

TAKE IT FURTHER

Time Is Money

Many people complain about the time that they have to spend in meetings, and one company has done something about it. Meeting Miser is a web-based gadget that keeps a second-by-second estimate of the cost of a meeting based on the job titles and locations of the participants. That information can then be projected on a screen for all to see.[6]

Do you think such a tool as this can make meetings more efficient?

■ Warn the chairperson when the time allocated for a particular item is nearly complete. This will be a signal to the chairperson to conclude the topic and move to the next agenda item. The chairperson may choose to seek approval from the group to extend the time allocated to the discussion.

■ Take note of when the meeting is officially over.

■ Give all your notes on time to the minute taker for his or her use in summarizing the meeting.

Since the duties of the timekeeper are fairly simple, you might be an active member of the group and participate in the discussions.

4. The Minute Taker

The minute taker's role is very important. During the meeting, for example, the minute taker must keep track of three distinct sets of items:

1. the main points of the discussions
2. who contributed ideas
3. the final decisions

Most organizations do not use word-for-word, or verbatim, minutes anymore because this format is too long and cumbersome.[7] Unless the meeting is recorded with some mechanical device, mistakes or omissions are easy to make. If a recording device is used, be sure to let attendees know in advance. In some meetings, such as discussions about a complex legal situation or possibly a media interview, absolute accuracy of minutes is essential.

If you are the minute taker, finalize the minutes as soon as possible after the meeting to avoid two common problems: listening inefficiency and memory loss. Ralph Nichols showed that most people listen with only 25 percent efficiency. Put another way, people may miss or misunderstand 75 percent of what is said to them.[8]

The more time that passes between the meeting and the recording of minutes, the more likely the minute taker is to make mistakes. You should draft the minutes for the chairperson's review within 24 to 48 hours.

I'M AFRAID TURNOUT ISN'T AS HIGH AS WE'D HOPED. THREE OF THEM MISHEARD THE DATE, FIVE GOT THE TIME WRONG AND EVERYONE FROM SALES WENT TO A HOTEL IN SCARBOROUGH BY MISTAKE!

Active listening is not the same as simply hearing.

In preparing the minutes, you will use your notes taken during the meeting, and you may also have the notes of others, including the timekeeper and the chairperson. These notes are never truly complete and short-term memory can be used to fill in the blanks when the notes are not enough. Unfortunately, short-term memory cannot retain for long the details of who said what and when. The longer the minutes take to write, the more likely it is that problems will show up later.

5. The Attendees

If you are asked to attend a meeting, you have at least three responsibilities before you agree:

1. It is important to know the purpose of the meeting in advance because this will help you to decide whether you are the best person for the appointment. Maybe someone else in your organization is better suited to attend than you. If so, you should suggest the alternative to the chairperson.

2. You should know how long the meeting is likely to last so that you can be certain that you will be able to be present throughout.

3. You should know whether follow-up meetings are likely going to be required. If you cannot commit to attending all the meetings, let the chairperson know in advance so he or she can decide whether to include you as an invitee.

Once you have committed to attending the meeting, be sure to come prepared:

- Know what is expected of you (why you have been chosen to attend).
- Read all materials that are sent out to meeting members in advance.
- Most of all, be ready to participate in the discussions, deliberations, and decisions (if any).

Because you have been chosen to come to the meeting for a specific reason, you must do your part to make the meeting productive.

The role of meeting members includes more than just a commitment of time. It also involves active listening. This is much more than "hearing" because it involves paying close attention to the speaker, thinking about what is being said, and participating in discussions. Active listening is a difficult skill to learn but one that is critical to success in business.

Active Listening in Action   Many speakers talk far more slowly than they need to for the audience to absorb their words. The average formal presentation is about 120 words per minute, while most people can effectively listen up to 400 words per minute.[10] The key to active listening is to focus on the topic and actually think about what is being said.

As you listen to the speaker, try to think of examples within your experience that support the speaker's point of view. When appropriate, ask short and relevant questions to ensure that you have understood the main ideas. Some speakers prefer questions at the end of a presentation, and some prefer questions during the presentation. Be sure to find out the timing that your presenter prefers so as not to distract her or him from the presentation.

Take notes of the key points of the discussion, and once again think about connections with your own experiences. As you are listening, think about whether you agree or disagree, but be sure to keep an open mind. Do not prejudge a person or an idea before you have had a chance to think for yourself.

Another tip for good active listening is to engage your presenter with non-verbal signals to show that you understand what is being said:

- Keep eye contact.
- Nod when you agree.
- Lean toward the presenter to show interest.

Do not allow yourself to be distracted by the presenter's clothes, hairstyle, speech pattern, or other superficial characteristics. What is being said is more important than how it is said or even by whom.

Telltale signs of a distracted or disengaged attendee include the following:

- fidgeting
- doodling
- reading non-meeting related material
- daydreaming (or worse yet, sleeping)
- whispering side conversations with others in the meeting
- sighing, crossing arms, rolling eyes, leaning back (or away) from the speaker
- taking no notes (or excessive notes)
- using a cellphone or other electronic device
- being argumentative
- acting overly emotional

When you are listening to a presenter, you can process information faster than the presenter can speak. Use that extra brainpower to help yourself absorb the information more effectively. Try to relate the presenter's message to your business activities. Use the information to think of relevant questions for later discussions. Try not to let your mind wander to other (sometimes more interesting) ideas.

If you are the presenter, use this information to tell whether an audience is engaged with your presentation. The key is to look for trends: If one person is showing one or more of the signs above, take note but continue. If more people start to show signs, or the same person increases the level of disruptive activity, then you must decide whether to continue or stop and refocus the discussion. Stopping will naturally be disruptive to the flow of the presentation, but a disengaged audience is even more disruptive.

✳ Explore PREPARING TO HOLD A MEETING

Looking at what typically happens before, during, and after a meeting will help put into perspective the many tasks required to organize, implement, and follow up after a good meeting. It will also set the stage for a discussion of who should do what jobs.

Let us assume that you are the person who is organizing the meeting. Most of the time this means that you will also be the chairperson, but not always. For example, the chairperson role may be given to someone in your organization who is at a higher level or has more experience than you. These types of chairpeople do not organize the meeting or make it happen but they get to chair the meeting because of their position, power, expertise, or experience.

What Is the Purpose?

As mentioned earlier, it is essential to have a clear definition of the purpose of the meeting. If you, as the organizer, do not know what it is that you are supposed to accomplish, it will be very difficult to keep the group focused and on track. Attendees will not know why they are there or what needs to be done. Without clear instruction and direction, the meeting is likely to go off on some tangent that does not relate to the reason the meeting was set in the first place.

Remember that the time commitment required from attendees can be significant. The attendees must prepare for the meeting, clear schedules to attend, and, of course, actively participate in the discussions. There may even be follow-up work required of some members so, as the organizer, make sure you do everything possible to use their time wisely.

Who to Invite?

Once you have a clearly stated purpose, the next question you should ask is who needs to attend. The best meetings have memberships that are small enough so that everyone is engaged in the discussions but big enough to make sure that the proper resources are present to accomplish the purpose.

Too few people will result in little work being done because of a lack of resources, and too many people will result in little work being done as everyone competes for some of the discussion time, leaving little time for decision making or progress to fulfill the purpose. People are invited to a meeting because of their position, but most often they are invited because they have specific skills, knowledge, experience, or decision-making responsibility that is needed to fulfill the group's purpose.

What Is on the Agenda?

After carefully considering the purpose and the attendees, draft the meeting agenda. Make sure to allocate enough time to each item so that it can further the meeting's purpose. Estimate the time required for each item as closely as you can, because this will serve as a guide in the timing of the meeting itself. The chairperson, with the help of the timekeeper, must work diplomatically and tactfully guide the discussion to the desired decision or outcome. It is often a good idea to have various group members lead different parts of the agenda. This varies the presentation style and makes the meeting more interesting.

People are invited often because of their expertise, and so getting more people involved makes good sense. Just ensure that all participants know what items they are supposed to address and what exactly is expected for a presentation. As you draft the agenda, be sure to include the date, time, location, and other details for the meeting attendees. (See **Figure 6-1** for a sample agenda.)

When you are developing the agenda, keep in mind the dynamics of your group and the meeting's purpose. Consider these two different scenarios:

- If your meeting is with people from within your organization and the purpose is to communicate some basic information, you can do this in a direct way. The attendees may already know much about the issue, and so

FIGURE 6-1   **A Sample Agenda**

Rainbow Fashion Agency
Budget Meeting Agenda
Location: 123 Century Street, Room 311
Date: January 17, 2010
Time: 9:00–10:30 a.m.

1. Welcome and roundtable introductions (5 minutes)

2. Approve and adopt previous meeting minutes (5 minutes)

3. Announcements (5 minutes)

4. Discussion topics (60 minutes total)
   a. Review annual budgeting process
   b. Brainstorm new program delivery ideas
   c. Discuss new policies from finance committee

5. New business (10 minutes)

6. Choose time and set agenda for next meeting (5 minutes)

Close

less background information is required. If you do not expect any resistance, you will not likely need to soften the message for the audience. The process used here is similar to that used for writing good news or routine messages in Chapter 8. State the news up front and then the reasons why, and end on a positive note.

- If you are meeting with people outside your organization, then more background information may be required. You will need to introduce yourself and spend more time describing the purpose of the meeting, the important issues, and the problems being resolved during it. If you expect that the audience will be resistant to your purpose, you will need to provide more details about the problems or issues.

  For example, suppose that you are the manager of a neighbourhood library. Because of budget cuts, you must reduce library hours and close on Saturdays. You may want to soften the message by providing more of the reasoning for the closure at the beginning of the meeting. This is the same as the buffer used in writing letters relating negative news, discussed in Chapter 10.

  Another helpful tip on defusing negative reactions is to call key individuals in advance of the meeting. Let them know what is coming and try to get them to understand the reasoning behind the meeting. You may never get their full support, but by being diplomatic and cushioning the bad news with legitimate reasons, you can often defuse at least some of their resistance.

  Bear in mind four etiquette points before the meeting:

1. The agenda should always be delivered to attendees a few days in advance of the meeting. This allows them to look at the agenda items, think about the issues, and develop their own points of view.

2. If background material has to be reviewed before the meeting, it is a good idea to get it to your attendees well in advance. A week or two is usually enough time, unless the background reports are lengthy or complicated. If so, then give your group a little more time to prepare. The last thing you want to do is hand a package with the agenda, minutes from the previous meeting, and background reports to attendees as they enter the meeting room. This is highly disrespectful and will likely result in less than effective discussions. Some people may not even attend if they do not have the materials ahead of time.

3. Be sure to consider the needs of your meeting attendees as you arrange the final details of the meeting:

   - Have you arranged for parking?

   - If the meeting is long, or near a regularly scheduled mealtime, will you provide refreshments or food?

   - If you do supply food, do any of the attendees have allergies or other food considerations? These considerations may be cultural, religious, or personal, and your meeting attendees will appreciate your thinking of their unique needs.

4. Consider the meeting facility itself carefully. Ask yourself several questions:

- Is the location well known? If not, consider providing an easy-to-read map, highlighting important information like major street names, parking, bus routes, and so on.

- Is the meeting room big enough to seat everyone comfortably? Remember that a room that is too big can be as uncomfortable as one that is too small.

- Is there ample lighting, adequate temperature control, and easily accessible washroom facilities? If not, you may want to find a more suitable location.

- Finally, is the building and meeting room itself accessible for people with disabilities? This is most important if any attendees have a known disability.

All this information needs to be communicated to your meeting attendees in advance so they will not worry if they have unique needs.

THE ACTUAL MEETING

What follows is only one suggestion of how to manage a meeting. If you are not familiar with the technical process of managing meetings, there are many good resources to turn to, including *Robert's Rules of Order,* which was specifically developed to facilitate effective meetings.[11] This process is recognized around the world as the ultimate guide to managing professional meetings.

Using a step-by-step guide can bring more organization to your meeting, and although more formal, it can help focus the attendees on the task at hand.

Starting

If you are the chairperson, always be punctual and start the meeting on time. If the weather is unseasonably bad or some other unexpected problem delays attendees, it is acceptable to start a meeting a few minutes late. Do not make it a habit to start a meeting late, however. By waiting for late arrivals to start, or, worse yet, restarting the meeting after their arrival, you are rewarding negative behaviour. This is disrespectful to those who made sure to arrive on time, and it takes valuable time away from agenda items.

Once the appointed time arrives, start the meeting promptly by offering a few words of welcome and a brief description of the purpose of the meeting. You then have several choices:

- A great way to get started, especially for meetings with outside organizations, is to have attendees introduce themselves, tell what organizations they represent, and even what they hope to achieve in the meeting. This will help facilitate discussions later, as attendees have a better understanding of the perspectives around the meeting table.

- For simple meetings, involving staff from one department, the chairperson can usually start the meeting with a statement of purpose and then get right into the agenda items. Less time is needed with introductions and other formalities because everyone likely knows one another already.

The exception might be when new staff are attending a group meeting for the first time.

Once the introductions are finished and members have settled in, take the time to review the agenda, item by item. It is important to tell people what it is you hope to achieve with the meeting. Relate each agenda item to the purpose, so that members can see why each is important to the final goal. Ask the group if other issues need to be covered. Then you are ready to begin.

Follow the sequence and timing of items on the agenda as closely as you can. Often, people will be overly chatty in the beginning of a meeting when they are energetic. As meeting fatigue sets in, attendees can become quieter. This is not because the items late in the agenda are less important but because attendees are just more tired. If you are not careful, the group will spend too much time on the items that are early in the list and not enough time on items at the end of the agenda.

If the group is not ready to end a topic when you have reached the allotted time, ask for an extension. If approved, this will mean that another item, later in the agenda, gets shortened or moved to the next meeting. As much as you can, let your group be your guide regarding time, because they will not want to be rushed just to meet your assignments of time. Again, tact and diplomacy are important here, because the chairperson cannot lose control of the meeting.

Keeping Everyone Focused

As you are working through each item, be sure to keep the group focused on the issues that are the most important. It is easy, especially with groups

TAKE IT FURTHER

Robert's Rules of Order

For a quick online version of *Robert's Rules*, visit www.robertsrules.org.

In a small group, discuss the pros and cons of using *Robert's Rules of Order* in a typical business meeting. Be sure to discuss what types of business meetings could do without formal rules of order and what types absolutely require them.

Keep focused on the agenda to avoid getting sidetracked.

TAKE IT FURTHER

Dealing with Conflict

Leadership expert Todd Pittinsky had this to say about dealing with conflict: "CEOs must nudge their executives to rise above divisional turf battles. . . . Leaders can no longer just rally the troops. Instead they must employ more positive means to span boundaries, affirm identity, cultivate trust, and collaborate productively."[12]

Suppose that you are the chairperson of a meeting in which two members have an emotional disagreement over a key issue, without resolution. How would you handle the situation?

of outgoing and talkative people, for the discussion to become sidetracked. The side discussions may be interesting to some people, but they may not relate to the purpose of the meeting. However, if a side discussion is related to the purpose of the meeting, it is acceptable for the chairperson to intervene and ask the group to become involved. The side discussion could become an agenda item in the current meeting or part of a future meeting.

Remember that it is the role of the chairperson to keep the group on task, even if it means interrupting the discussion and refocusing attendees on the agenda. This should be done without insulting those involved in the discussion. For each agenda item, be sure to focus on the main point, even referring back to the purpose of the meeting.

For the sake of the record, clarify main points as they are discussed. Restate any conclusions or future work to be done, by whom, and by when. These details must be recorded by the minute taker, who, because of the more difficult duty of writing down the key points of the discussion, is usually not involved in the discussion itself.

As the meeting progresses, take note of who is doing most of the talking and who is not. As chairperson, it is usually in your best interest to draw out the ideas and opinions of all group members, not just the ones who talk first, longest, or loudest. Remember that the minutes will be reviewed as the record of what was discussed, and all opinions should be noted. Conflicts may arise because some people do not like to have their point of view challenged. Remember that confusion and chaos often come from a lack of understanding, so try to focus the discussion on the facts, rather than on opinions or emotions. If you find an issue that is dividing your meeting's membership, have each side clearly state and explain its perspective. You may not reach a resolution to the disagreement, but often it is enough to have all perspectives recorded in the minutes. Skills in conflict management and communications are very important to any chairperson, and many resources are available to help you better understand the many different personality types and how they can best work together.

As the agenda items are addressed, be sure to keep track of time left and time allocated to discussions. Although the timekeeper watches the clock and supports the chair, it is the chairperson who guides the discussion and decides when to move to the next agenda item. Make sure that the meeting ends on time, because meeting attendees may be heading to their next appointment. If your meeting goes overtime, they may be late to their next meeting. A good way to close discussion on the agenda topics is to allow for some time to discuss items that were not a part of the agenda. This allows attendees to bring forward anything that is important to the meeting.

Closing Actions

Before you close the meeting, consider making the following moves:

- Restate the purpose and quickly summarize the agenda items and outcomes. This is a great way to let people know what progress has been made.

- If people have been assigned or have volunteered for work, revisit these commitments now so that everyone is clear about who is doing what and by when. Identify someone as the lead on getting these materials collected and distributed to group members before the next meeting.

- If a follow-up meeting is required, it is often easier to set the time and date while all the attendees are still present. Often, people will have access to their meeting schedules and the meeting can be set up with far less frustration than trying to find an appropriate date and time via email.

AFTER THE MEETING

What happens after a meeting can be more important than what happens during the meeting. There are several obvious steps to take just in terms of getting the facts straight:

- As the meeting chairperson, give any notes you have jotted down to the minute taker.

- Make sure that the person drafting the minutes compares all notes against the agenda and against the notes she or he wrote during the meeting. (The goal of the minute taker is to summarize the key discussions and the final decisions only, not to have a word-for-word replay of the entire meeting.)

- Once you have the draft minutes, double-check to make sure that the summaries and tasks were properly recorded. Check names, grammar, and other technical information to make sure that what the minute taker recorded was what actually happened.

- Work closely with the minute taker to finalize the minutes within two days of the meeting.

- Send the minutes to all members within a week or two. If a follow-up meeting is required, these minutes will need to be reviewed and then accepted by the membership at the next meeting. The more accurate the minutes, the easier their approval becomes, and work can progress more quickly. Even if a follow-up meeting is not required, the minutes are often part of the permanent record of the organization, and they may be read in the future.

See **Figure 6-2** for a sample of good meeting minutes.

Quite often, many tasks will require follow-up before the next meeting. As the meeting chairperson, it is your responsibility to make sure that these tasks are done in a timely way.

Sometimes this means sending a separate reminder to someone who volunteered to complete a task. If a report is required, make sure that it is done well in advance of the next meeting. Chances are that it will need to be included in the next meeting notice, which goes to attendees anywhere from a few days to a few weeks before the next meeting date. Do not allow your members to bring these reports to the meeting without giving others

| FIGURE 6-2 | **Good Meeting Minutes** |

Rainbow Fashion Agency
Budget Meeting Agenda
Location: 123 Century Street, Room 311
Date: January 17, 2010
Time: 9:00 a.m.–11:00 a.m.

Committee chair: Charlie Hanover
Minute taker: Ken Diba
Present: Carol Dyer, Marco Smith, Wanda Neilson, Mina Patel
Absent: Jerry Downs

Topic	Presenter	Points of Discussion	Decision/Deliverable	Responsibility	Due Date
1. Welcome	Charlie	Introductions of new staff.	None	None	N/A
2. Review and approve previous minutes	Charlie	Reviewed: no omissions or errors.	Approved as written.	Ken	N/A
3. Announcements	Carol	a. Supervisors are asked to submit holiday plans for summer break by May 1. b. Office renovations may affect customer walk-ins during June.	a. Holidays allocated by seniority and position title. Report requested of implications to staff. b. Supervisors to submit workflow changes.	a. Marco and Wanda b. All supervisors	a. Feb 12 b. Feb 28
4. Discussion topics	Wanda				
a. Review annual budgeting process	Mina	Preliminary budget estimates will follow similar process as last year, except management must reduce discretionary costs by 10%.	The 10% reduction in department budgets can be achieved at the discretion of managers. Operations may be cut more than 10%, some less, so overall reduction is 10%.	Charlie	Feb 7
b. Brainstorm new program delivery ideas	Marco	Increased competition felt from large box stores. We need a new strategy for customer attraction and retention.	Loyalty program. Emphasize total quality concept in new ads. Hire local celebrity for endorsement.	Ken to set up working group to develop program and return to committee	Mar 15
c. Discuss new policies from finance committee	Wanda	Growth of international sales division has increased travel and related expenses.	Update needed to old travel expense forms.	Mina	Feb 28
5. New business	Charlie	Reduced fees for monthly parking.	Memo needed for affected staff.	Marco	Jan 31
6. Next meeting	Charlie	Today's minutes will be ready by Jan 19	Meeting date Jan 31, same location.	Charlie	Jan 31

Meeting minutes are the lasting record.

the benefit of being able to read them in advance. The follow-up meeting is not the time for attendees to read past meeting minutes or reports for the first time.

TIPS FOR SUCCESS

Productive meetings are clearly no accident. They require careful planning, assignment of roles and responsibilities, clear communication, and follow-through. Put another way, meetings most often fail because they lack a clear purpose, have the wrong person as chair, have the wrong people attending, or have logistical problems, like poor timing or location.

You can improve the chances of success by following these simple tips:

- Start and stop on time. This means arriving a little early and being prepared to participate right away.
- If you are not sure how to find a meeting's location, try to find it the day before the meeting. Be sure to locate local parking, bus stops, entry and exit points, and so on.
- Turn off all electronic devices before the chairperson starts the meeting. Cellphones, pagers, and other gadgets are often a nuisance in meetings. If it is an emergency or you need to take an important call, turn the phone to silent (or vibrate) mode and take the call after you have left the meeting room.
- If you know you must leave the meeting, make sure to let the chairperson know in advance. Sit as close to the door as possible so that you do not disturb the meeting when you leave.
- Come prepared by reading the minutes from the last meeting. If there are errors or omissions, the chairperson will often allow the minutes to be altered to reflect the changes, provided that other attendees agree with the changes.
- Study any background reports in advance. Take careful notes of your thoughts and be prepared to share these at the meeting.
- If you expect an emotional discussion on a difficult issue, jot down your thoughts in advance to remind you of the key points as the discussion progresses.
- Volunteer only for tasks that you are sure you can complete fully and on time.
- If you need to set up a short meeting on a simple topic with just a couple of people, try a *walking meeting* instead of using the usual meeting room. It is a great way to foster a discussion while getting some exercise—just be sure to write down the highlights of the discussion.

VIRTUAL MEETINGS

Developments in technology, such as teleconferencing and internet-based meetings, have changed the nature of the modern business meeting. Attendees no longer have to be in the same room, the same city, or even the

The virtual meeting

same time zone to have a productive meeting. Businesspeople from around the world organize, meet, and do work every day without ever meeting in person. This puts more responsibility on the organizer, the chairperson, and the minute taker.

In a meeting that uses telephone-based technology, it is sometimes difficult to know who is speaking, although some tips can help:

- Have speakers identify themselves before talking. This makes it easier for everyone, including the minute taker, to make note of who said what.
- Similarly, the chairperson can facilitate a more orderly discussion by calling on specific speakers in turn, rather than relying on the most outspoken attendee to take the floor and talk.

In internet-based meetings, attendees can type in comments or questions to the chairperson as the meeting progresses. This real-time interaction allows for a more dynamic discussion.

Chapter Summary

Productive business meetings require a defined purpose, clear assignment of roles and responsibilities, careful logistical planning, coordinated execution, and accurate and timely follow-up. The type of meeting will depend, in part, on what you hope to achieve, who will be participating, where the meeting will be held, and whether a follow-up meeting is required.

Remember that a good meeting uses the best of your communications skills. From planning to preparation, execution, and delivery, the meeting is really an exercise that uses all forms of communication: written, verbal, and non-verbal. Whether your part of the meeting is as organizer, chairperson, timekeeper, minute taker, or attendee, you have a definite role to play to make the meeting a productive success.

mycanadianbuscommlab Visit www.mycanadianbuscommlab.ca for everything you need to help you succeed in the job you've always wanted! Tools and resources include the following:

- Composing and The Writer's Toolkit
- Document Makeovers
- Video Case Studies
- Grammar exercises and much more!

Thinking and Writing Exercises

1. **The Need for a Purpose**
   Defining the purpose statement for a meeting is critically important to the success or failure of the meeting. Discuss the pros and cons of a clear statement and the likely outcome if a group does not know the purpose of the meeting.

2. **The People Factor**
   The membership of a meeting helps determine its success. Describe the types of people who should be invited to a meeting to develop a company policy on when people can and cannot take their vacations.

3. **The Role of Minute Taker**
   Some companies realize the importance of the role of minute taker and will provide extra training for people suited to the task. Use the internet to research, and then describe, in your own words, three important skills that minute takers should possess.

4. **Ways to Keep the Group Focused**
   The chairperson needs to be diplomatic when guiding a group discussion, especially when the focus wanders from the intended agenda item. Suppose the group is small. Discuss how you would try to return the focus to a key topic. Which would likely be the most effective step and why?

5. **The Process of Active Listening**
   As a group member, you must be an effective active listener. Describe the process and tips involved with being an active listener. Why is this skill important to a meeting?

6. **Making Meetings More Productive**
   It is easy to criticize a meeting as being useless or a particular presenter as being uninteresting. As a group member, describe what you can do to make the meeting more effective and productive.

7. **After the Meeting**
   Follow-up after a meeting is important to the overall success of the meeting. In a small group, discuss the merits of quick and accurate follow-up, and name three reasons that it is so important.

8. **Unproductive Meetings**
   Not all meetings end well. Discuss meetings that you have attended that were not a success. Identify the main reasons for the failure, linking them to what you have learned in this chapter. Describe what could have been done differently to make the meeting more successful.

Writing Skills Checkup: Writing Minutes

Suppose you are an assistant manager and the chairperson of a meeting. The set of draft minutes in **Figure 6-3** is given to you to review. Rewrite the minutes in a more appropriate format, including only the information necessary.

FIGURE 6-3   **Draft Minutes**

Rainbow Fashion Agency
Budget Meeting Agenda

- We met at the normal meeting place on the 17th at 9ish

- Everyone was there except some came in late.

1) Welcome–Charlie started the meeting late and told us about his weekend. He said the washer broke down on Friday and spilled water everywhere. He and his wife spent all of Saturday looking for another one. Ken asked what they bought and where. Charlie said they spent too much but it was a cool one. I didn't hear where exactly. The new people introduced themselves. Mina or Jenna just came over from head office. She didn't like the atmosphere there as much as here.

2) Previous minutes–Charlie handed out the minutes from the previous meeting and read them out loud. It was awhile ago so some people coupln't remember exactly what we said. Ken asked about point number 2. All voted to approve and move the agenda along.

3) Carol talked and talked about office stuff that is coming up. When are we taking holidays? Renovations again??? Charlie said they still haven't finished the baseboards in his office from the last renovations. Also what colour? Marco said that he hired some workers to redo his basement and it was very expensive. He wondered what the cost of the office renovations would be and did we really need to spend the money on paint and wallpaper when the sales team is crying for new promotional brochures. Carol said the renovations would be finished on time but we needed to submit work org/flow/charts by Tuesday. Marco asked Charlie if the water spill made any lasting damage and he knew some contractors that could fix it.

4) Discussion

a) Annual budgeting process is the same as always except everyone needs to cut 10%. Wanda asked if the 10% had to be in each line of business or just the department total for 10%. Mina said all lines but then she changed her mind. Charlie volunteered to take a first stab at getting the numbers down even if it didn't make sense to him. How can we do the job if we keep getting downsized? Strike that from the minutes. Charlie would be happy to do the first estimate and pass it around.

b) Brainstorm new program delivery ideas. Marco explained what brainstorming is and that no ideas are bad ones (duh?). He set up the easel and started taking notes. Everyone started talking at once . . . very confusing . . . Marco to come up with some sort of summary report. Time for a break says Charlie as he answers his cellphone. Be back as soon as you can.

5) New business–Meeting is way overtime so everyone wants to get done. This is cancelled.

6) Decide on time and agenda for next meeting. Charlie says let's set the next meeting over lunchtime so we can order sandwiches. He'll set it up and let everyone know the agenda.

These minutes are in need of a rewrite.

Oral Presentations:
The Counterintuitive Speaker

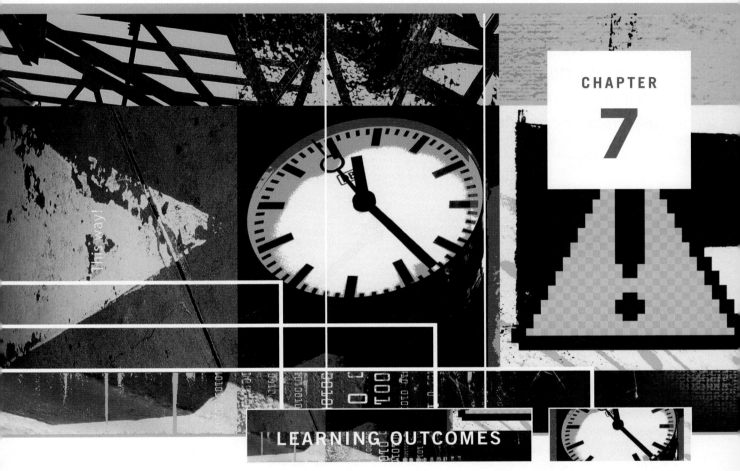

CHAPTER

7

LEARNING OUTCOMES

After completing this chapter, you should be able to do the following:

7.1 List the main ways in which a good speaker differs from a mediocre or poor speaker

7.2 Develop and deliver a focused

presentation that covers your key points while holding your audience's interest

7.3 Use visuals, including technology,

to improve your presentation

7.4 Look back and wonder what took you so long to enjoy speaking in public

THE FIRST THING YOU NEED TO KNOW

coun·ter·in·tu·i·tive [kòwntər in tχitiv]: contrary to expectations: not in accordance with what would naturally be assumed or expected[1]

One word contains the key. Memorize this word and use it whenever you need to speak before a group:

Counterintuitive

Here is what it means: Do the opposite of what convention tells you to do and what the audience expects you to do. When everyone else is marching in step clockwise, turn around and explore what lies off the beaten path.

Edward Tufte has become an international communications expert precisely, it can be argued, because he has gone his own way and explored the path less travelled. Part of his story follows below. Read it and consider whether the message resonates with you.

ISSUES
in Communication
"PowerPoint Is Evil"

In January 2003, the American Space Shuttle *Columbia* broke up as it was re-entering Earth's atmosphere after a two-week mission. All seven of its crewmembers died. Two months later, highly respected American academic Edward Tufte posted an analysis of the disaster on his website. His analysis, which would later gain notoriety as the misleading "PowerPoint Is Evil" thesis, laid part of the blame for those seven deaths on the way that PowerPoint was used.

Here is a quick look at what happened and why these events led to Tufte making a connection between the choice of popular Microsoft software and the deaths of seven astronauts:

- Eighty-two seconds after take-off, a piece of the shuttle's foam insulation broke off and hit the wing, causing a small hole. This damage would ultimately be the direct cause of the explosion.

- NASA (the U.S. National Aeronautics Space Administration) engineers on the ground were aware of the damage and its possible consequences for the shuttle's re-entry. They presented their findings to senior management via 28 PowerPoint slides. This presentation method wasn't unusual. In fact, it was expected; like many organizations, NASA often relied on briefings in the form of PowerPoint (PP) as opposed to more densely written reports. But, as Tufte points out, as the major information source, this form of presentation contained serious—in this case, fatal—flaws. (See **Figure 7-1**.) A mass of bulleted lists with six different levels of headings, crammed slides, and abbreviated notes hid some key facts. Based on these slides, however, the high-level NASA officials whose job it was to decide whether or not the shuttle was safe concluded that no further action was necessary.

Tufte insists that this disastrous outcome could have been avoided—and lives saved—if the findings had been presented in a conventional

FIGURE 7-1   Tufte's Critique of a NASA PowerPoint Slide about the *Columbia*'s Damaged Left Wing   ✓•—Practise

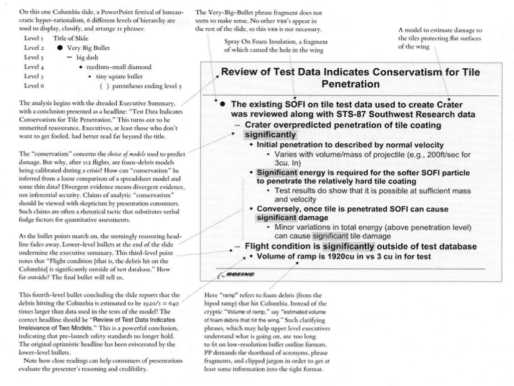

Source: From Tufte, Edward. "PowerPoint Does Rocket Science—and Better Techniques for Technical Reports." Ask E.T. 6 Sept. 2005. Web. 31 July 2009.

written report format. The standard PowerPoint presentation, with its characteristic bulleted lists and shortened forms, cannot convey complex information. (Imagine if we got rid of the text in this book and replaced it with page after page of bulleted lists.) Tufte has also argued that the standard PowerPoint presentation gives format more importance than content, showing "an attitude of commercialism that turns everything into a sales pitch."[2]

Five months after Tufte's website analysis, the Columbia Accident Investigation Board at NASA released its own report on why the space shuttle burned up on re-entry. It, too, identified NASA's dependence on PowerPoint as a contributing factor. In fact, the board members cited Tufte's analysis in their final report.

They were not the only ones who agreed with Tufte.

Tufte's comments on PowerPoint have caused a stir in boardrooms and classrooms around the world. A Google search of his name paired with "PowerPoint" yields 351 000 hits in less than one second—of course, not all of those articles support Tufte's view, but a good many do. And among those supporters are some who wield a fair bit of influence, such as Clive Thompson, writer for the *New York Times*, whose view is summed up in his article's title: "PowerPoint Makes You Dumb."[3]

It also makes you bored—and boring—say its critics. The person who coined the phrase "Death by PowerPoint"[4] was not making a tasteless reference to the Columbia space shuttle victims. In fact, she used the phrase two years before the shuttle disaster. The victims she is referring to are the audiences who have to endure speakers reading slide after slide of dense, bulleted entries that appear to bear little relationship to one another and indicate almost no sense of priority—despite their bolded fonts and

FIGURE 7-2 **Artwork from Alexei Kapterev's 2003 slideshow "Death by PowerPoint (and How to Fight It)"**

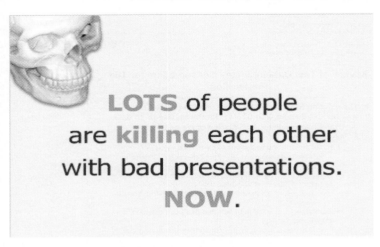

Source: From Kapterev, Alexei. "Death by PowerPoint (and How to Fight It)." The Content Wrangler. 26 Oct. 2007. Web. 31 July 2009.

animated features. And a lot of those speakers are out there: Microsoft estimates 450 million PowerPoint users in the world.[5] Quite a few of them are lethally boring.

Quite often, unfortunately, their audience is you (see **Figure 7-2**.)

THE COUNTERINTUITIVE APPROACH IN ACTION

Whether or not you agree with Tufte's views on PowerPoint, those views have earned him respect and positive attention from a widespread audience.

And what exactly did Tufte do to draw and keep this attention? He did the unexpected.

His analysis of the Columbia disaster referred to "velocity," "angle of incident," and "statistical significance"—all issues that we would expect to hear from someone who was investigating the impact of 750 grams of foam insulation hitting the wing of a space shuttle.

But then he turned a corner that most people would have ignored. He paired what appear to be two completely unrelated events: a space shuttle that burned up and a briefing made in PowerPoint. And he supported this connection with logic and detail, so that suddenly his readers were seriously considering a question that earlier would have seemed outlandish: Could a popular software program play a role in the deaths of seven astronauts?

Based on the evidence Tufte provides, the answer is "yes, apparently, it could."

One reason for Tufte's success as a communicator is that he surprised his audience with the unexpected connections he made. He chose to make his own path—but he also made sure it didn't lead him off a cliff. He didn't just present an unexpected point of view; he also supported it with logic and specific examples. In other words, he strengthened his creativity with a foundation that has been strong enough to withstand inspection by a great many people.

Tufte did a few more things along the way, which are discussed in the pages that follow. But the theme that unites many of them is the same. You know it. Remember it:

Counterintuitive

DISCUSSION

1. **Not everyone agrees with Tufte's view of PowerPoint's limitations. What arguments can you make against his opinion?**
2. **What exactly does Tufte mean when he says that PowerPoint has "an attitude of commercialism that turns everything into a sales pitch"? Do you agree or disagree? Why?**
3. **Why, in the face of all this criticism, do we continue to rely so much on PowerPoint?**
4. **Science, particularly quantum physics, contains some well-known counterintuitive thinkers, including Galileo, Newton, and Einstein. Who are some influential counterintuitive thinkers in other fields?**

HOW TO USE
THE COUNTERINTUITIVE APPROACH
✓•⎯Practise

Being a counterintuitive speaker requires action even before you face your audience. For most of the remainder of the chapter, we will go through the steps that you need to take to get through the four main stages of your speech:

1. preparation
2. the introduction
3. the body
4. the conclusion

We include a variety of exercises along the way. The steps for each stage are summarized in **Table 7-1**, later in the chapter.

1. PREPARATION

Let's see how many more preconceived ideas we can reconsider.

Approach in Your Own Presentations

Focus on Yourself   The best speakers do the following:

- They tailor their speeches to their audience.
- They address their audience's needs.
- They make their talks audience centred.

You have heard and read advice like that many times. It's become a cliché. That is why, just for the time being, we are asking you to reject it and embrace, instead, the opposite statement:

> **The best speakers attend to their own needs before they address their audience's concerns.**

It may be difficult to say openly that you are going to put your own needs before others'. After all, people feel a sense of nobility when stepping aside and ushering others ahead of them. One exception is, of course, flight attendants. Anyone who has travelled with a commercial airline has surely heard a flight attendant heartlessly announce: "In the event that it becomes necessary, put on your own oxygen mask first before you help anyone else."

Those flight attendants might be on to something.

They know that to help someone, you first have to be in good form. You have to possess a strong frame of mind to be able to breathe calmly and deeply in times of great stress.

The same principle applies to making a speech. So much of the effectiveness of a speech, and therefore the audience's enjoyment of it, depends on the speaker's frame of mind. The best speaker is able to take a deep breath right at the start and *genuinely know* that he or she is capable, in control, and focused on presenting something that is valuable. In contrast, if the speaker feels unsure, unworthy, or boring (and many speakers, despite their attempts to mask it, do feel this way about themselves), then the presentation will probably reflect those qualities. And the audience will suffer as a result.

Therefore, it makes good sense for a speaker to take the advice that runs counter to convention and expectations, and to say without apology, "First, I focus on my own needs."

And what are your own needs? That's easy: Your primary need is to feel good about yourself. Meeting this need, however, may require some disciplined—and counterintuitive—practice.

The next time you have to speak in front of others, whether it's a large group or a handful of people, resist the natural inclination to focus on how you feel right at that moment (because we suspect that many of you feel something between mild stress and total terror right before making a presentation). Focus, instead, on how you could feel at the end of your successful talk. Here is an exercise to help give you that practice.

Self-Focus in Action

Repeat the following statements to yourself as you prepare for your next presentation:

When I walk out the door after my presentation I want to be able to

- call the person whose opinion matters most to me and say, "I just gave an incredible talk!"
- smile at everyone I encounter
- truly look forward to the challenge of my next presentation

Continue the list with more statements that show how good you will feel about yourself after you give a successful presentation.

Continuing this list is important because it reinforces within your own mind, right from the start, that a successful presentation involves much more than simply standing up and speaking before a group. It also involves walking out the door afterward and feeling good about yourself because you did a difficult job well, and a room full of people witnessed your success. That experience is good for anyone who needs a boost to his or her self-esteem—which is probably most people. It's an experience that starts and ends with feeling good about yourself. Therefore, before you focus on anyone else, take time to focus on yourself and on how good you are going to feel at the end of this talk. It's a self-centred focus, true, but it's also one that will motivate and help you to develop and deliver an exceptional presentation.

Always Do What You Are Afraid to Do

If you found the above exercise difficult or if you dismissed it as nonsense or if you couldn't come up with any more entries to complete the list, one obstacle is probably in your way: lack of confidence. This is the number one barrier to giving good speeches. And the number one way it shows up is not through poor speeches but through no speeches at all. A person who lacks confidence will do whatever he or she can to avoid speaking in public. But avoiding opportunities to speak means avoiding opportunities to feel good about yourself.

Read the following passages and ask yourself if any of them apply to you:

a. I usually don't speak up in class or in meetings because most of the others know more than I do about the topic being discussed. They have more valuable things to say than I do and I don't want to waste their time.

b. When I am called on to speak up in a class or meeting I feel uncomfortable, as if everyone's looking at me and judging me. I just want to get it over with, and so I give the briefest possible answer.

c. Even though I'd like to speak up sometimes in a class or meeting, I have trouble quickly putting my thoughts together and finding the right words. I'm afraid of looking foolish and inarticulate in front of everyone else. They all speak so much better than I do.

d. I have completely different views from everyone else in the room, and if I speak up to let others know about these views, I'll end up being even more marginalized and isolated than I am already.

If you identified with any of the four passages, you could, no doubt, spend hours combing through your personal history trying to uncover childhood events or traumatizing relationships that prevent you, to this very day, from speaking up. And you would have the added bonus of being able to vent at all the injustices you have suffered over the years. This kind of self-analysis, the kind that involves poking at wounds to see why they stubbornly resist healing, is common. But a counterintuitive speaker doesn't take the common route. Instead, counterintuitive speakers who want to increase their confidence do something entirely unexpected: They search for a solution not within themselves and what they see as their own inadequacies but instead within their audience. Counterintuitive speakers know that the path to feeling good about themselves lies within feeling good about their audience.

This last statement makes sense because the persistent theme in passages (a) to (d) is not just lack of faith in your own speaking ability; it's also lack of faith in your audience—lack of faith in the audience members' capacity to empathize, to support, and to listen. This lack of faith can also involve fear of

TAKE IT FURTHER

Glossophobia

Glossophobia is the fear of public speaking. It's one of the most common phobias. In fact, many people claim they would rather die than give a speech.[6]

How did you feel when you did your first presentation in school? How did you get through it?

the audience. When speakers say that they fear being criticized, judged, or ignored, they are essentially saying that they are afraid of their audience. Fear is the reason that they avoid speaking.

But fear is *precisely* the reason they should speak up. American writer Ralph Waldo Emerson said it best more than a century and a half ago: "Always do what you are afraid to do." He was part of the original American "counterculture movement," and he would have agreed wholeheartedly with the idea that if you want to feel good about yourself, you need to face what frightens you.

You may be starting to feel that the counterintuitive theme is becoming tiresome, especially now that it involves facing something you genuinely fear. You would much rather do what most people do when faced with something scary: quietly avoid it (e.g., avoid enrolling in courses that require oral presentations or participation grades; avoid jobs that include public speaking) or run away from it (e.g., fake illness or plead to be excused for any number of imaginative reasons from any public speaking engagement for the rest of your life).

But your audience is not scary at all, not in most cases, anyway. In fact, in most cases you have ample reason to feel good about your audience.

Remember the Key Words: *Content* and *Connection*

Most audience members, whether in a classroom or in a boardroom, are supportive. They want you to do well. If you doubt that, just think about all the times you have listened to a reluctant and nervous speaker. Remember how you felt: uncomfortable and quietly hoping that he or she would pull things together and get through this speech. Your listeners want you to do well, if for no other than selfish reasons: It's uncomfortable for them if you flounder.

It's also a waste of their time if you don't do well. They want to get something valuable from you.

Now, here is what separates the exceptional speakers from all the rest: Exceptional speakers know exactly what that "something valuable" is and they deliver it. If you remember the following advice, you are well on your way to joining that group of exceptional speakers.

Your audience wants two things from you:

1. focused and clear content
2. a sense of connection

Most, if not all, speakers know about the first element. That is why so many of them spend 95 percent of their preparation time focused on the content—gathering it, memorizing it, transferring it onto handouts and PowerPoint slides, trying to cram it all into their allotted presentation time, and then apologizing for not being able to cover all of it.

That is also a major reason so many presentations fail to make any lasting positive impression on their audiences. The speaker, in his or her single-minded focus on content, fails to address the second element: connection. It's a strange oversight because the word *communication* means "common union," connecting with others. Any speaker who wants to communicate successfully with the audience needs to satisfy this second element.

What exactly does *connection* mean? At its most successful and profound, it means forging some sort of bond with your audience, where you all walk out the door afterward feeling somehow changed for the better because of this presentation. It's an elusive feeling to describe, dismissed by some as "touchy-feely," but this characterization is inaccurate because a connection doesn't necessarily involve some kind of emotional "feel good" response. Such a response is, of course, wonderful when it happens, but it happens rarely. (Speakers and audience members alike would be dooming themselves to failure if they expected this response every time they delivered or attended a presentation.) A connection can simply involve connecting your material to the audience's lives so that they see its relevance. They see that it really matters and that being present at your talk is the best possible use of their time right now. And when they walk away from your talk, they feel good about what just happened—not necessarily on some "touchy-feely" level, but on the level of knowing that someone understood what they needed and tried to serve those needs.

Nothing feels better for you, as a speaker, than knowing that you have helped foster this kind of connection.

Connecting with Your Audience: A 15-Minute Exercise

Think back to the teachers you have had. Who are the ones that made a significant positive impact on your life? (And *everyone*, even the most reluctant student, has had at least one teacher like that.) Write down all the qualities and characteristics that define those teachers.

Chances are what distinguished them for you in a really positive way was this simple fact: They connected with you, which is another way of saying they communicated well with you.

Now, try writing your own list. What are the qualities and characteristics you would like your audience members to see in you?

Review this list often and remember to consciously show these qualities and characteristics in giving your next presentation. That is one straightforward way to connect with your audience.

The following section discusses two more ways to connect with them.

"Don't Follow Leaders" Bob Dylan didn't just write those words; he also used them to build his career as one of the world's most influential singer/songwriters. And they're good words to follow when it comes to making counterintuitive speeches.[7]

Winston Churchill: "We shall fight on the beaches."

John F. Kennedy: "Ask not what your country can do for you—ask what you can do for your country."

Martin Luther King: "I have a dream."

There. They've been cited: three of the greatest public speakers of the last 100 years whose words have inspired and elevated millions and whose names are mentioned with awe in public speaking texts and instructors' comments everywhere.

Good.

Now you can move on.

And as a counterintuitive speaker, you know what direction you are *not* moving in: You are not going to follow, or even attempt to follow, in the footsteps of those great speakers cited above (or any others, for that matter). Other speakers, as wonderful as they may be, cannot clear the path for you. You have to figure it out for yourself, because the main quality of the exceptional speaker is uniqueness. An exceptional speaker is different, in a positive way, from all the other speakers. And this difference helps the exceptional speaker make a strong connection with the audience.

If you have trouble understanding or accepting this last statement, consider the following.

Most presentations fail to rise above the ordinary because the speaker fails to hold the audience's attention. That is not surprising in light of what the typical audience has already been exposed to: the entire world, really, via television, movies, and the internet. Little remains that this information-overloaded, attention-span-shortened audience has not watched, heard, or googled. There is little that audience members don't know about, at least on a superficial level, or think they don't know about.

Except for one thing: They don't know about you. They don't know your personality or your unique way of looking at things, of phrasing, of explaining. Therefore, if you want to keep your audience's attention, don't try to imitate other speakers you have heard about or listened to, because it's a safe bet that your audience has also heard about and listened to those same speakers and all the others who are imitating them. Your audience is likely bored by all this repetition and wants something new. You can present something new by being yourself. Because you will then be taking a path that is yours only and not anyone else's, it will offer a view that your audience has never seen before: a view based on new examples, new phrasing, a new way of looking at things. That is why the audience will be more likely to pay attention and to connect with what you are saying.

Connecting with Your Audience: A 30-Second Exercise

Take 30 seconds to summarize what you think are the most important ideas or points that you have learned so far from reading this chapter. You can write out your summary, say it aloud, or simply think it. Whatever method you choose, though, *make sure you use your own words.* Don't try to imitate the style of this chapter or this text; don't try to sound educated; and don't try to sound as though you are lecturing a class or running for public office. When you try to do those things, as so many speakers do, you are imitating someone else's idea of good speaking. *Just get comfortable with using your own well-chosen, precise, and appropriate words to express what you think is most important.*

Lose the Desire to Be Perfect   Perfection is so misunderstood. An average speaker would tell you that a perfect public speaker never stumbles, hesitates, or starts a sentence with "um." The average speaker would tell you that a perfect public speaker never loses his or her place and *always* knows what word comes next. The average person would also tell you that almost all speeches, perfect or not, are boring.

What the average speaker would not tell you, because he or she doesn't know it, is this: It's their so-called imperfections that often make speakers interesting and that help them forge a closer connection with their audience. Audiences do not really respond well to perfection as defined above, simply because it increases the gap between their imperfect selves and the presenter who never falters. Perfection is hard for the audience to relate to.

Perfection is also hard for the speaker to keep up with any degree of authenticity and comfort. Everyone, the best speakers included, will sometimes trip over the projector cord, momentarily forget an important name, and unknowingly make an inappropriate pun. It's simply part of being human. The best speakers, though, don't become stuck in embarrassment, an apology, or berating themselves. They accept their missteps with good grace, learning from them and moving on. That is one reason audiences consider them the best speakers.

Real Perfection   In the audience's eyes, real perfection comes when a speaker offers an authentic presentation, shortcomings and all. Counterintuitive speakers know this and therefore are not unduly preoccupied with projecting a perfect image. Instead, they focus on sincerely trying. They know that sincerity counts for quite a bit.

That's why the counterintuitive speaker can confidently make the following statements. Try repeating them yourself:

a. When I start to speak, I don't want to prove that I'm the smartest person in the room; the only thing I want to prove is that what I have to say is thoughtful and respectful.

b. People appreciate direct, simple language. I'm so much easier to understand when I use short sentences and plain English.

c. They're just views I am expressing. That's all. They don't define who I am or how I should be regarded. And even if they do, someone else's opinion of me, good or bad, really isn't any of my concern.

d. Most, if not all, of the people listening to me are kind and considerate.

e. Even though I find it difficult to speak up, if I take a risk and try, I'll feel more connected to all the other people here, I'll feel more included, and I'll feel so much better about myself and them when I walk out the door.

This is the foundation material. It's meant to guide and support your development as an exceptional speaker. Now we can turn to more concrete details on how to develop and deliver an exceptional presentation.

2. THE INTRODUCTION

Your audience is already bored with you.

You didn't expect that, did you? Not after the discussion about how audiences are generally kind, understanding people who want you to do well and who empathize with your so-called flaws as a presenter. Here are two lessons to consider from this:

1. It's possible, in fact it's likely, that the people in your audience (a) want to like your presentation but (b) are not prepared to *work* to like your presentation. In other words, they are probably nice people who just happen to get easily bored.

2. If you want to prevent the people in your audience from getting bored, give them something unexpected—and try starting with the title of your presentation. Edward Tufte demonstrated this principle with the title of his *Wired* article "PowerPoint Is Evil." Audiences don't expect this sort of provocative language, especially from an academic; as a result, when they hear it, they tend to pay attention.

Both lessons lead to the same conclusion: An exceptional speaker starts from the premise that the material is uninteresting. This statement may well run completely counter to all the advice you have been given by communications teachers and every communications textbook you have read. Perhaps all of them have encouraged you to choose topics that you are passionate about—as if passion were the starting point. For a lucky few, this may be the case, but for most people, plodding away day to day, the starting place is often to sift through all the information that confronts them, so that they can figure out what to do with it. It's an unromantic view, but it points the speaker toward success. Expecting first the speaker and then the audience to be passionate about, or at least seriously interested in, the topic right from the start is bound to lead to disappointment and frustration. It sets an extremely difficult goal.

Consider, instead, a strategy based on the opposite assumption: Passion is not the starting point. Do not assume that the people in your audience are going to be completely enraptured with your topic. Assume instead that they are going to be dismissive of it, bored with it, and skeptical about its importance. With this assumption in place (and with your confidence fully intact because you have already worked on it in the previous section of this chapter), you can see that your job is to create interest, enthusiasm, and maybe even passion.

We will now look at ways to do just that.

Startup in Action Try connecting your topic to something that the audience is already interested in and enthusiastic about: their own lives and their own well-being. Average speakers focus solely on the topic at hand. They don't move beyond the confines of its material: underlying causes of the mortgage crisis in the United States; marketing strategies for the Millennial Generation; effects of rising fuel prices on Canadian tourism. Exceptional speakers, conversely, take on the challenging—and time-consuming task—of pushing their topic beyond its own, predictable boundaries into the lives of the audience members. Now, everything is related, but everything is not clearly and obviously related.

The exceptional speakers are able to discover the subtle interrelationships and work out a way to shine a light on them. They figure out, for example, why the American subprime mortgage crisis is relevant to their twenty-year-old Canadian audience members who still live at home. This connection then becomes a central theme of their talk, introduced at the very start and referred to throughout.

You Need to Know

Exceptional speakers work harder on developing their presentations than all the other speakers do. They know that their presentation involves more than just the topic content of, say, mortgages or marketing or tourism trends. It also involves their audience members' lives. Almost anyone can give a speech that relates to just content. Only exceptional speakers can give a speech that relates to people's lives.

If you have trouble accepting what we have been saying, consider the case of a famously successful communicator: comedian Jerry Seinfeld. He created and co-wrote a show so successful that it continues to be part of popular culture years after its final episode aired in 1998. A good part of that success involved Seinfeld's ability to relate to his audience through using a counterintuitive strategy. He knew that a "show about nothing" (as *Seinfeld*

TAKE IT FURTHER

Toastmasters International

Toastmasters International is an educational, non-profit organization that is dedicated to helping its members improve their public speaking and leadership skills. It's a highly respected organization that has more than 226 000 members worldwide. Check out its website at www.toastmasters.org.

What does *toastmaster* mean?

Jerry Seinfeld, a counterintuitive communicator

was famously dubbed) was actually a show about everything. After all, it's the small details of everyday life—stopping at the bakery to buy a loaf of rye bread, waiting for a table at a popular Chinese restaurant, or standing in line for takeout soup—that the audience can relate to. It's those small, seemingly insignificant details that Seinfeld put in the spotlight. They formed the foundation of his work—and his success at connecting with his audience.

Getting the Audience's Attention: A 15-Minute Preparation Exercise

The First 5 Minutes

1. Think about a specific presentation that you will be giving. Keep in mind that "presentation" can refer to any number of situations, including a formal speech to your class, a work-related proposal to your boss, a short talk in front of a hiring committee, and even a detailed response to a question posed during a class or meeting.

2. Picture the audience members.

3. Write down everything you can think of about them—their backgrounds, ages, interests, and, *most important, their priorities.* Priorities will, of course, vary from audience to audience (and from audience member to audience member), but broad examples include career, education, environmental issues, ethics, family, friends, finances,

grades, personal growth, and so on. Your list, because it's based on a specific topic and specific audience, will be much more focused.

The Next 10 Minutes

4. Visualize yourself starting your presentation by announcing your topic and then posing the following question to your audience: "Why is this relevant to you?"

5. Now brainstorm all the possible answers to this question. Some of your answers may be related to your audience's backgrounds, ages, and interests, but all of them should be related to your audience's priorities. In other words, practise acknowledging right at the start that your audience is important by relating the topic to what matters most to them.

Connecting: Your Ego May Be Getting in the Way

Some speakers regard connecting with the audience as pandering to them and therefore dismiss this approach as belittling to the speech material. Certain types of academics, in particular, love to create the feeling that their sacred work exists on a higher plane, accessible only to the smartest audience members—and even then only if those members stand on their tiptoes and strain for a glimpse of the speaker's brilliance. You may have known a teacher or two like this. And you may even have aspired to be like that teacher, if for no other reason than for the sheer number of hours you have been exposed to this sort of presentation style. You may have come to believe that this is the proper way to present a speech.

Consider another way. Consider that speakers who place their material on a higher level than the audience's interests, who say "It's not my job to motivate my audience to listen; my material speaks for itself" may be misguided. They may be placing their own egos on a higher level than anything else, and so they may be doing their material an injustice. Information or ideas or data that are not effectively conveyed to the intended audience are wasted. Raising your audience's awareness or understanding through connecting the material to their lives is not pandering. It's honouring the importance of both the material and the audience.

Concrete Tips to Help You Get Started

Most people need to warm up to a topic. Here are some tips that will help you and your audience generate enthusiasm, and maybe even passion, for your topic.

Develop a Focused and Specific Topic   It's almost impossible to get too specific. This strategy may involve resisting your inclination to choose a *big* topic. Many speakers want to choose a big topic for the following two reasons, both of them negative:

1. *They are unable to work out the separate issues that emerge from the larger issue,* which might be the economic outlook for the next year or top marketing trends or implications of the environmental crisis or whatever the broad topic is.

   The problem, though, is that a big topic cannot be dealt with effectively in one speech: There is just too much to cover and too little time to cover it. The task of trying to do so becomes overwhelming. The following pre-presentation panic is typical of a speaker who chooses a big topic: "I don't know what to do. I've started a dozen times and I still don't have anything. I don't want to do this speech any more. How can I get out of it?" The following post-presentation lament is typical of a speaker who wasn't able to get out of it and went ahead with the big topic: "I could have done so much better if I had only had more time. I had no idea they were going to be serious about enforcing the time limit. It was hard getting through the last 15 slides in two minutes." If you've ever said or thought that, try narrowing down your topic next time. A specific topic is the most effective way of ensuring that your presentation material has a strong foundation.

2. *They are afraid of not having enough material to fill up the allotted presentation time.* If this concern troubles you, consider the following: No matter how witty, insightful, or engaging you are as a speaker, almost all audiences are happy when they hear the words "In conclusion" or "To sum things up." No one, in other words, is likely to get upset if you end a bit early. There is no need to be offended by that; it's just the nature of audiences.

Establishing a Strong Foundation for Your Talk: An Exercise

The left column in the table below lists some big topics. Practise revising these so that they are focused and specific. To get you started, two revisions are given, along with some notes.

Big Topic That Doesn't Work	*Focused and Specific Revised Topic That Does Work*
Immigration to Canada	Immigration's impact on Canada's hospitality workforce (Note: Sometimes you can focus a big topic simply by adding modifiers, as illustrated here.)
The airline industry after September 11, 2001	Economical and environmentally friendly alternatives to air travel (Note: Sometimes your revised topic bears no obvious resemblance to the original big topic. In this case, the revised topic represents one aspect only of the original multi-faceted big topic.)
The popularity of volunteer tourism	
The failing auto industry in North America	
Corporate social responsibility	
Finding a job	
Globalization and the environmental crisis	
North America's top employers	
Business ethics	
Trends in post-secondary education	
Social networking sites	
Gender differences	

If this exercise took longer than you thought it would, you are probably on the right track. If it made you feel uncharacteristically impatient and frustrated, you are probably on the right track. Sometimes a rocky start is a good sign, because it means that instead of relying on a generic template to guide you, you are relying on your own sense of analysis, insight, and creativity.

Craft a Title That Gets Your Audience's Attention—and Have Fun Doing It

Tufte isn't the only successful communicator who uses this strategy. Note some example headlines from the cover of *Maclean's* magazine:

- "Hasta La Vista, Baby"—about the ailing Fidel Castro's transfer of power to his brother and its implications for Cuba's future[8]

- "Crushing Poverty the Microsoft Way"—about Bill and Melinda Gates's philanthropic work and its implications for broader corporate social responsibility[9]
- "Flying Is Hell"—about the future of airline travel in light of increasing fuel costs and security concerns[10]

You can provide a serious study of an issue, keep your credibility, and still be creative with your title. Because the title is what the audience hears first, some unexpectedly creative phrasing will help get their interest and establish you as someone who is different from all the other speakers they have heard.

An Exercise to Get Both You and Your Audience Intrigued by Your Topic

Choose three of the specific topics you developed in the previous exercise and do the following for each:

1. Craft a creative title, one that generates the audience's interest in both the topic and the speaker.
2. Place a colon after your creative title.
3. Write a more businesslike and informative subtitle, one that guides the audience toward the focus of your talk and establishes that you have a serious, credible message to give.

Example:

"Air Travel Takes a Nosedive: Consumer Dissatisfaction with the Airline Industry and Its Implications"

Introduce Your Focused and Specific Topic Near the Start of Your Talk
Most audiences become immediately discouraged when they hear broad opening lines, such as "Throughout the history of the world," or "Since the beginning of humankind." It's boring.

Explain to the Audience Almost Immediately, Perhaps Even before You State the Topic Itself, How or Why They Will Benefit from Being Present at This Talk Of course, this strategy requires that you identify the audience benefits before the presentation, while you are still in the planning stages of developing your talk. (See the 15-minute preparation exercise to get the audience's attention on page 150.) It's a good strategy because it means that you will then refer to these benefits throughout the presentation.

Provide a Quick Overview of Your Presentation's Structure Right at the Start Audiences generally like a talk to have a logical, predictable structure. If they can clearly see the presentation's organization without any effort at all, they can then focus their attention and effort on the most important aspect of your presentation: what is actually being said. Two examples follow. The first is for a long presentation, and the second is for a shorter presentation.

Example 1:

"First, I'll briefly provide some background information about Dubai (its location, history, and population profile); next, we'll view a slide show of Dubai's recent hotel developments and tourist attractions; and then we'll spend the last half of the presentation discussing the major challenges that Dubai will face in the future. And if you have any questions or need anything clarified, please feel free to interrupt me at any time."

Example 2:

"I'm going to take the next five minutes to explain the three most important characteristics we should all look for in choosing a life partner. Afterward, you'll have time to pose questions and contribute your own views."

3. THE BODY

Here are some instructions that most speakers, probably including you, can easily list about developing the body of their presentation:

1. Restrict yourself to three to five main points.
2. Organize those points into a logical structure, such as problem-solution, cause and effect, comparison and contrast, chronological, or specific to general.
3. Develop each point through supporting detail and concrete examples.
4. Use transitions (e.g., "First . . . Second . . . Third . . .") to help the audience follow along and to strengthen the presentation's coherence.

Anyone reading this text probably has at least a decade's worth of classroom practice in applying these instructions to written assignments and oral presentations. That fact alone tells us these principles work. After all, they have stood the test of time. But that fact alone may also partly explain why so many presentations become robotic exercises, with the speaker dutifully trudging back and forth between principles (a) to (d) hell-bent on getting through his or her sheaf of notes or index cards or PowerPoint slides.

If that scenario sounds familiar, consider the following statement: Relying on time-tested principles is a good thing only if the speaker is aware that these principles are not a paint-by-numbers template that precludes any thinking or creativity. In other words, mindlessly following these principles isn't enough. If you want to be an exceptional speaker, embrace them, but move beyond them.

Here are some strategies to help you move beyond them as you develop your presentation.

Find Your Own Voice

Many speakers rely only on other people's opinions. They research their topic to find out what others have said about it and then they develop their presentation around those findings. These presenters don't venture off the path that has been travelled by others, so that they essentially become a mouthpiece for the views of others. As a result, their presentations are often quickly forgotten. They lack the spark of originality that's ignited by a speaker who has truly thought about the material and developed his or her own credible views on it—views that go beyond what was uncovered in the research.

If you would like your audience to truly think about your presentation material, to become engaged in what you are saying, then you need to demonstrate that you have thought deeply and independently about the material. Counterintuitive speakers know this. They do their research so that they are aware of what has been written and concluded about their topic. They then use this material to form a strong foundation for their presentation. But what they build on the foundation is their own original material. No one else's. That is also why counterintuitive speakers are often really passionate about their material—because, after all, it's *their* material. No one else's.

Finding Your Own Voice: A Four-Step Journalling Exercise

For this exercise, begin by writing down your topic. Make it as specific and focused as you can, but keep an open mind. As you progress through this exercise, you might decide to change your topic. In fact, changing your mind and revising your topic during these beginning stages are often very good signs that you are on the right track.

Now, begin your four-step journalling:

STEP 1: *What you already think or know about your topic.* Write down any opinions and factual knowledge you already have about the topic. You could draw on relevant personal experiences; conversations you have had; courses you have taken; websites, newspapers, and magazines that you have read—any exposure that you have already had to this particular topic.

STEP 2: *What your credible research sources think and know about this topic.* Write down notes from your research, taking care to include proper reference citations. Your research notes could include corresponding entries to what you wrote in step 1, but they will also include completely new information that you didn't touch on at all in step 1.

STEP 3: *What you now think about the material you have collected so far.* Your immediate objective here is to decide whether each entry should be used, abandoned, or modified. The more entries that fall into the "modified" category, the *stronger* your own voice will emerge.

STEP 4: *What conclusions you now draw about your topic.* Here's a tip: You'll know, without a doubt, that your own strong voice is emerging if you draw your conclusions from the entries that you have modified.

This process has no easy short cut, but counterintuitive speakers don't actually want one anyway. They like to forge their own trails.

Here's an abbreviated example (without the reference citations for step 2) of the four-step process:

Topic: The Impact of Immigration on Canada's Hospitality Industry

STEPS 1 AND 2: COLLECTING THE MATERIAL

what i think or know about the topic	what my research sources think or know about the topic
There's a danger of too many immigrants coming and taking jobs away from Canadians who have been here a long time.	Three categories of immigrants: family class (people who are closely related), independent immigrants (whose admission is based skill, wealth, and labour-market requirements), and refugees.
i couldn't get a co-op placement in a resort in Banff. Too many people are competing for the same jobs. we don't have enough jobs as it is for the people who are already here.	Canada plans to maintain its open immigration policy, even in light of the current economic recession. China, india, and the Philippines are among the top source countries for Canada's immigrants. Alberta has a severe shortage of lower-skilled hospitality workers. $26 636 is the median income of recent immigrants versus $57 656 for average Canadian-born person.

STEP 3: ASSESSING THE MATERIAL

what i think or know about the topic	what my research sources think or know about the topic
There's a danger of too many immigrants coming and taking jobs away from Canadians who have been here a long time. ⬆ Modify because the research says that this isn't happening; in fact, recent immigrants often have much lower-paying jobs. i couldn't get a co-op placement in a resort in Banff. Too many people are competing for the same jobs. we don't have enough jobs as it is for the people who are already here. ⬆ abandon because it's a generalization based on one personal example	Three categories of immigrants: family class (people who are closely related), independent immigrants (admitted on the basis of skill, wealth, and labour-market requirements), and refugees. ⬆ Abandon because it's not relevant to my topic. Canada plans to maintain its open immigration policy, even in light of the current economic recession. ⬆ Modify by pointing out that our open immigration policy needs to be changed to allow lower-skilled immigrants into the country. China, india, and the Philippines are among the top source countries for Canada's immigrants. ⬆ Modify by pointing out the significance of this entry: it illustrates the diverse cultural backgrounds of recent Canadians and therefore the need for employers who can manage this diverse workforce.

STEP 3: ASSESSING THE MATERIAL *(Continued)*

what i think or know about the topic	what my research sources think or know about the topic
	Alberta had a severe shortage of lower-skilled hospitality workers. ⬆ Use as one example. $26 636 is the median income of recent immigrants versus $57 656 for average Canadian-born person. ⬆ Use as supporting information.

STEP 4: DRAWING YOUR OWN CONCLUSIONS

My Conclusions

The hospitality industry needs recent immigrants to fill entry-level jobs.

Managers within the industry will increasingly need strong intercultural communication skills.

A poorly motivated and disengaged workforce is a real possibility if new immigrants are kept indefinitely within poorly paid, entry-level positions.

A plan is needed to attract immigrants with the required skills.

Hospitality professionals need to become more politically aware and active in order to shape immigration policies that affect their industry.

Think of It as a Conversation that Involves *You*, *We*, and *Us* If you think of yourself as engaging in a conversation with the audience (even if it is one in which you will do most of the talking), you will naturally start using pronouns. *You*, *we*, and *us* are the best ones to use: They carry an important psychological message.

For example, by directly addressing the audience as *you*, the speaker actively draws individual audience members into the presentation, affirming that this material is connected to each person's life. And by using the pronoun *we* (as opposed to *I*), the speaker closes the gap between himself or herself and the audience; it's not speaker versus audience as two separate entities— it's speaker and audience as one collective *we*.

This strategy won't work if the speaker views it only as a quick trick to get the audience on his or her side. It's more than that. It's a way of reminding you that one of your jobs as a presenter is to truly connect your material to the audience members' lives.

Seeing Is Believing: Using Visuals in Your Presentation   Most speakers have a limited view of what "a visual" is. For them, it's either overheads or PowerPoint and perhaps a handout. That's it. Audiences, however, are accustomed to the multimedia possibilities of the internet and movies—they dwell in a world of unlimited possibilities when it comes to presentation visuals. And although sitting through consistently boring presentations has trained your audience not to have high expectations, it has not curbed their desire to be proven wrong.

The counterintuitive speaker knows this. And therefore he or she rates the use of visuals to enlighten—and entertain—the audience as a high priority. See "The Little Extras" section later in this chapter for ideas.

Involve the Audience

Some speakers avoid getting the audience involved because they think the audience is too big, the time too limited, or the material too complex. But participation can work even under those circumstances. Possibilities include posing short-answer questions; asking for a show of hands; giving a simple task, such as writing down a quick answer or briefly consulting with a seatmate.

Other speakers avoid participation because it's too much of a risk. Allowing audience participation amounts to giving up control of the presentation and possibly exposing themselves to a situation they can't handle. It's too nerve-racking. Counterintuitive speakers take the opposite approach. They know that audience involvement is one way for a presenter to feel more relaxed and comfortable during a presentation. It's a boost to the speaker's

An Exercise in Constructive Pessimism and Audience Involvement

If you are reading this chapter, you probably have a presentation coming up. Base your answers to the following questions on that presentation.

1. Write down one question you can ask your audience that involves either a short answer or a show of hands.

2. Brainstorm all the responses to this question you hope you won't get. In other words, what are the most terrible, embarrassing, unexpected, and completely discourteous responses you could receive?

3. Now, in the unlikely event that those responses actually materialize, what will you do? How will you respond, for example, to the following?

   ■ an audience who stares blankly at you and doesn't appear to understand your question

   ■ an answer that is completely opposite to what you had expected

   ■ (Complete the list with the other items in your brainstorming list and your responses to those scenarios.)

confidence to see an engaged audience rather than an audience that's passively staring at the speaker.

The best speakers, true to their counterintuitive natures, ignore the common advice of "Be positive." They think of negative outcomes, and then they figure out how to avoid the negative situation completely or how to deal with it constructively. In other words, they are constructive pessimists who are not afraid to get the audience involved because they have figured out beforehand how to handle *any* situation.

Everyone Has a Perfect Personality

Everyone has a perfect personality, including you. That is why management expert and noted public speaker Tom Peters advises, "If you are a dour sourpuss, learn to give good dour sourpuss speeches. Don't try to be something you're not."[11] You don't need to try to change your personality to be more outgoing or funny or authoritative. That would ring false to the audience. You already have the personality that perfectly suits who you are and that distinguishes you from everyone else—and being different from everyone else, in a positive way, is exactly what you are aiming for in your speech.

So let your perfect personality shine throughout your presentation:

- *Cite brief examples from your own experiences to illustrate a point you want to make.* Be sure to keep them brief because these are meant to *support only*, not to serve as the main point. Then, ask the audience if they have encountered anything similar. This strategy will put a human face on the topic and help the audience connect to what is being said. Avoid generic examples—they are colourless, predictable, and, ultimately, forgettable. Draw on your own experiences or, better yet, experiences that the audience has shared.

- *When appropriate, use self-deprecating humour.* It can signal to the audience that you are far greater than your ego and that you are an approachable person. You don't take yourself too seriously; therefore, you have the time and energy to take your material—and the audience—seriously.

- *Use your own words.* Of course, you will use appropriate, professional language when speaking to your audience, but the words, expressions, and phrasing will be your own. They won't be taken word for word from a textbook or a journal or a website, because then you would be memorizing or reading someone else's words. Aside from the potential problem of plagiarism, this approach is boring for the audience and stressful for you.

Repetition Can Be Good

At some point, no matter how riveting the material and dynamic the presentation style, various audience members will start to daydream, drifting off into a chain of thoughts that have absolutely nothing to do with what you are saying. Accept it. Attention spans are short and the mind loves to wander. One way to deal with it is by using internal summaries: quick overviews of what you have just said, provided at appropriate intervals throughout the presentation. Your audience will appreciate the opportunity to catch up with the material they have just missed. And you will appreciate the opportunity to stay focused and organized by pausing to review the key points.

You can increase the effectiveness of these internal summaries by prefacing them with an enthusiastic "To recap," or "Here's what we've covered so far," or "The most important points to remember from all this are." These are good transitions that will help daydreaming audience members snap back to attention.

If the length and complexity of your presentation warrant it, try incorporating internal summaries into your talk. Everyone benefits from them.

Learn to Love the Audience from Hell (They're Not Leaving Anytime Soon)

Do you recognize any of the following statements?

- Studies show that people fear public speaking more than death or financial ruin. (A frequently referenced finding)
- "Most people at a funeral would rather be the one in the coffin than the one giving the eulogy." (A well-known joke from Jerry Seinfeld)
- Visualize the audience in their underwear. (Oft-repeated advice on overcoming public speaking anxiety)

The ongoing studies, jokes, and advice about public speaking anxiety didn't just appear out of thin air. Something must have prompted them, and every speaker knows what that is: the fear of encountering an audience that contains one or several of the following elements:

- non-stop whispered conversations
- audience members completely engrossed in their laptops or in sending text messages
- a self-proclaimed expert who regularly interrupts to challenge or correct you
- a ringing cellphone
- someone who answers a ringing cellphone

Welcome to your audience from hell.

If you are like most speakers, how you handle this audience is predictable. Depending on your personality and the specific context, you might do the following:

- Assume a good-natured attitude and soldier on through all the distractions and interruptions as if to say, "Yes, I understand. I am kind of boring and inadequate, but thank you for being here anyway."
- Forge ahead, determined to overpower all the annoying distractions by the volume of your voice and strength of your persistence.
- Cast irritated glances at the offenders as you continue.
- Stop when you finally can't take it any more and sternly rebuke the offending parties or, perhaps, everyone in the room, about the inappropriate use of cellphones, texting, laptops, and poor manners generally.

In other words, if you are like most speakers, you will get offended—and it will show.

But getting offended is not a satisfactory strategy in the long run. It may help you achieve the short-term goal of quieting down the audience and re-focusing their attention on your presentation, but it probably will not help you achieve your long-term goal: to feel really good about yourself when you walk out the door after your presentation. That is because getting offended simply reinforces your sense of discomfort and displeasure; and if you experience discomfort and displeasure enough times as a speaker, you will end up disliking audiences and looking for ways to avoid public speaking. Or if you can't avoid public speaking because of your program or your job, you will end up a victim of stress and burnout. Either way, you will not end up being a good speaker who can truly connect with the audience.

Now, many would argue that you have good reason to feel offended by audience members who ignore you and derail the presentation in some way. Such behaviour is disrespectful of audience members who do want to listen and it dishonours the speaker's efforts.

The Counterintuitive Speaker in Action   The counterintuitive speaker would not disagree with that last comment but would take another approach to solving the problem—one that's based on the motto "to serve and respect."

When your focus is directed outwardly toward serving the audience, rather than inwardly toward serving your ego, you will not view disruptive or discourteous behaviour as a personal affront. You will view it from a more detached perspective that's based not on your feelings but on this key value: respect for everyone, even the most difficult audience members, and respect for your function, which is to serve the needs of the group.

Shaping your approach with this value sends the following message to a disruptive audience: "I can do a better job for you if the laptops are closed, the texting postponed, and the chatter quieted." To an individual audience member who is monopolizing the discussion, this approach says, "Although I respect your views, we need to hear what others have to say," or "There's not enough time to do justice to everything that you're raising. We'll have to move on."

And if you truly mean what you are saying, your sincerity will be reflected in the tone and volume of your voice, your body language, your facial expression, and in your behaviour. All this should help you create a positive and strong connection with the audience.

And, by the way, serving the audience by dealing with everyone with respect—even the difficult ones—is easier on you, the speaker. It takes away a lot of stress when you can say to yourself (and truly mean it), "I don't take this personally; I'm not offended." When you foster this kind of attitude within yourself, you are also fostering something else: confidence that you can handle any difficult audience you might encounter. And that's one of the biggest reasons you will feel good about yourself when you walk out the door.

Some experienced speakers will dismiss all this as idealistic and naive. They will recount horror stories of belligerent, immature audiences, and they will suggest that only misguided candidates for the martyrdom would ever want to approach such an audience armed only with the wimpy mantra "to serve and respect."

They have a point. It *is* hard to stand in front of such an audience and not fall back into feeling offended and upset. The fact that it's a challenge, though, doesn't mean it's not worth the effort. Here is a suggestion that may help you:

Picture what your difficult audience members were like as children With some people, it's easier to do than with others, but with all people it's possible. If you try hard enough, you can see within that group of whispering conversationalists the chatterbox who sat beside you in Grade 3; the audience member with the persistent and often pointless interruptions becomes the precocious know-it-all from your adolescence; and the one in the back row with the MP3 player, studiously ignoring you, is the quiet one who never ventured far from the schoolyard's edge.

It's possible, when you engage in this exercise, to see your difficult audience members in a more vulnerable and less intimidating light. This light will allow you to more easily practise your mantra of "serve and respect."

4. THE CONCLUSION

Finally, we get to an easy part of the speech, the conclusion. Now you are in the home stretch (see **Table 7-1**) and the rules are simple:

1. *Signal to the audience that you are about to conclude.* The old standby transitions "In conclusion" or "To wrap things up" are fine. They alert the audience that the presentation is almost finished and that now is their last chance to hear your summary of main points.

TABLE 7-1	Overview of Your Presentation Structure

First impressions: A title that gets their attention

Presentation strategy: clear thinking made visible

The Introduction (not necessarily in this order)
— Explain your specific topic right away
— Focus on how or why the audience will benefit from this presentation
   (e.g., "Why is this relevant to you?")
— Provide an agenda, so that everyone knows what to expect

The Body
Develop your points by using
— a logical, clear structure (rather than a series of diverse points)
— audience participation
— supporting details that the audience can relate to
— conversational pronouns (*you, we,* and *us*)
— visuals (not necessarily overheads or PowerPoint; consider props also)
— reminders of how the audience benefits from this
— internal summaries, if needed

The Conclusion
— Signal the audience that your presentation is concluding
— Summarize the key points and their relevance
— Give the audience something to remember your key points
— End on time and leave feeling good

2. *Summarize the main points.* Everybody in the audience has been, at some point, daydreaming during your presentation. That means everybody has probably missed something important. Now is the time to remedy that by recapping the important points.

3. *Don't get derailed from your conclusion by introducing something new.* This will frustrate your audience. Even the best audiences attending the most riveting presentations are happy when the talk concludes. Don't push your luck by extending it beyond the agreed-on time; it's tedious for everyone.

The first three rules are the straightforward ones that everyone already knows. They are just meant as reminders. Now here are the rules that only the counterintuitive speakers know about:

4. *Acknowledge the restless audience that starts gathering books, putting on jackets, preparing to depart prematurely, before your presentation has finished.* Most speakers pretend not to be aware of this behaviour; they don't want to draw attention to the fact that some people seem anxious to make a quick exit from their presentation. But few things are more disheartening to a speaker than a view of the backs of people's heads as they rush to the exit door while he or she is still talking. A simple reassurance that you will finish on time is often all that is needed (e.g., "I'm aware of the time, and we'll be wrapping this up within the next 60 seconds"). The counterintuitive speaker has the ease and confidence to intervene directly like that.

5. *Memorize your concluding lines.* This is heresy! All the communication books say so. They say that, above all, you are not to memorize word for word your presentation. But this book is not like all the others, and neither are you. Go ahead and memorize word for word the final couple of lines. That way you will end the presentation on a polished note as opposed to "Well, I guess that's it" or "I'm done" or just standing there awkwardly until someone in the audience starts applauding simply to break the strained silence. Try to avoid that.

6. *Don't rush from your memorized, polished conclusion to the ungrammatical and usually futile "Is there any questions?"* First, the grammatical issue: the proper phrasing is "Are there any questions?" because your subject ("questions") is plural. Next, the futility issue: This question is almost always guaranteed to be met with a few moments of strained silence before someone starts applauding simply to break the strain (see the previous rule). The question also undermines your polished conclusion. Counterintuitive speakers who want questions from the audience don't rush to ask for them. They know that most audiences need a moment or two to digest all the information and that some see immediately raising their hand to make a comment or ask a question as unseemly haste to grab the spotlight. They want a moment or two. Give it to them by delaying the question until after the applause.

7. *Give them something nice to remember your talk by.* Counterintuitive speakers know that it's possible to be smart and considerate at the same time. That's why they will often bring a small gift for their audience—something

tangible, like a bookmark or chocolate, or something intangible, like a telling quotation or a parting suggestion. The gift is in some significant way related to a key theme of their talk.

THE LITTLE EXTRAS

Counterintuitive speakers are creative thinkers. Our list of little extras starts with two visual elements that offer great possibility and that every speaker has access to but few think of using.

Movement

Do something when you give a presentation beyond simply standing, feet riveted to the floor, directly behind the lectern. If you think once again of the meaning of *communication*, you will know what to do. It means "common union" or, in other words, making a connection. That lectern or that gaping space between you and the audience represents a barrier, not a connection. So remove it. If appropriate, move away from the lectern and closer to your audience. Aside from this symbolic value, movement can also lend a sense of energy and perhaps unpredictability to your presentation as the audience follows your movements and wonders what you will do next.

Props

You may be reluctant to move away from the safety of the lectern. You may actually want a barrier between you and the audience because you would feel too vulnerable and exposed standing closer to the audience without anything to hold on to.

Therefore, give yourself something to hold on to: a prop that physically illustrates a point you are making. Examples include the following:

- During a talk on time management, try holding up an oversized clock or appointment book.
- A talk on the plunging economy? Pull out your empty wallet.
- The effects of osteoporosis on bone density? Crush a hollowed egg in your fist.

Remember, the more senses you appeal to, the more successfully you will reinforce the points you want to make.

The possibilities for you to enlighten the audience while also entertaining them with your creativity are endless. Just make sure your visual is large enough that everyone in the audience can see it. As an added benefit, your prop can also steady your nerves. You don't have to feel that all eyes are trained on you; now they are all focused on what you are holding or pointing to.

These props don't need to cost a lot of money or involve a lot of effort. They just require your willingness to do something different and creative. Most speakers can't be bothered. The counterintuitive speaker, though, knows it's worth the effort.

PowerPoint that Respects the Audience

 Explore

Visuals do not work if they are used as a novelty only—a way of momentarily attracting the audience's attention for no reason that's related to the presentation material. And they fail totally if they are used as a crutch for the presenter, a way for him or her to avoid speaking directly and clearly to the audience. PowerPoint is often used in both ways, and as a result its use can often lead to audience boredom.

Edward Tufte wrote: "PowerPoint is a competent slide manager and projector. But rather than supplementing a presentation, it has become a substitute for it. Such misuse ignores the most important rule of speaking: Respect your audience."[12]

"Respect your audience" means don't waste their time by reading screen after screen of PowerPoint slides to them as if they were children.

"Respect your audience" means acknowledge that many of them would like to participate actively in your presentation rather than sit passively in a darkened room and stare at a list of bulleted points.

And, finally, "Respect your audience" means don't ask them to show up on time only to have to wait while you try to resolve technical problems with your PowerPoint slides—a process you are determined will take as long as necessary because you are completely dependent on PowerPoint. Without it, you have no presentation.

To be honest, if any of the above paragraphs resonate with you, you really don't have much of a presentation anyway, even with PowerPoint.

Some suggestions on creating a PowerPoint presentation that respects the audience appear in **Table 7-2.**

TAKE IT FURTHER

"The Magical Number Seven, Plus or Minus Two"

In a 1956 paper George Miller concluded that most people can remember only seven (plus or minus two) pieces of dull, unrelated data.[13] Based on this, someone devised the oft-repeated but misleading six-by-six rule for PP slides: Each slide should contain no more than six lines with each line no longer than six words. But, as Edward Tufte points out, Miller was referring to people's capacity to remember nonsense data, which does not, presumably, describe the content of your PP slides.

Why is readability important in PP? ■

This Exercise Could Take Some Time (but You Won't Mind)

Part One: Create a PowerPoint presentation to introduce yourself to your class. You might include details about your family background, academic interests, career aspirations, and extracurricular activities. The introduction should not last longer than two minutes.

Part Two: Create a second PowerPoint presentation to introduce yourself to your class by using the same material and time limit as above. This time, though, do not use any text. Use only pictures.

Part Three: Compare and evaluate the two presentations. What do you conclude about effective PowerPoint presentations?

Figuring Out What to Wear

Henry David Thoreau's advice to "beware of all enterprises that require new clothes" does not apply to public speaking. When people look around the room, they should know right away that you are the speaker, because you are dressed a little nicer than they are.[14] And they will be quietly flattered that you took the time to do this. Dressing up a little bit sends a message that you have prepared for this talk, you respect the audience, and you care what they think of you. By dressing up, you might also be sending a message to yourself. Many people feel more prepared and professional if they are well dressed.

TABLE 7-2	Guidelines for PowerPoint Presentations that Respect the Audience	
	Conventional Speakers	**Counterintuitive Speakers**
Audience Response		
Content	Bulleted lists of information. No clear indication of how the bulleted entries are related.	PP slides are organized so that they lead coherently and logically to a main conclusion.
Individual Slides	Crowded with detailed notes. Small font (less than 20 pt).	Key words and phrases only. Large font. Photos that illustrate key points.
Design Principle	"Bells and whistles." Many different colours, fonts, and slide transitions.	"Less is more." Consistent colours, font, and slide transition.
Room Lighting	As dark as possible.	As light as possible. Keep the audience awake and within view.
Technical Knowledge	Limited. No back-up plan.	Limited at first. Spend time learning the technology. Prepare coloured overhead transparencies of PP slides as a backup.
Preparation	Assume the presentation room is set up for PP; assume someone else will take care of the technical details in setting up.	*At least one day beforehand:* Rehearse in the presentation room to confirm how to set up and to ensure slideshow clearly projects onto the big screen. *On the presentation day:* Arrive early to set up. Any audience members who arrive early are greeted by the title slide already projected onto the big screen.
Delivery	Mostly reading from the screen.	Focus on the audience, not the screen.

Here is a quick guideline to help you figure out what to wear to your presentation:

- "Dressing up a bit" is not going to make or break your presentation, but it will send a positive message to your audience and it may help you focus more sharply on your topic.
- If you are the sort of casual person who isn't used to "dressing up a bit," try doing it in such a way that you still feel comfortable. Try combining casual with dressy—a suit jacket with jeans; wearing a collared shirt instead of a T-shirt, dress shoes instead of running shoes.
- If you are the sort of "extroverted dresser" who uses fashion to draw people's attention and make a statement, you might want to tone down your appearance for this particular speech. The focus should be on what you are saying, not on what you are wearing or how you look.

■ If you are the sort of person who thinks that "dressing up a bit" is a superficial strategy to get the audience's respect, you are probably right. But that doesn't mean it's not an effective strategy.

And no matter what sort of person you are, choose underwear that requires no adjusting at all during your presentation.

Three Final Tips on Your Delivery . . . and on Practising in front of Your Dog

The best way to introduce these final three tips into your presentation is by practising.

1. Consciously inject enthusiasm and expression into your voice. To your ears, you may sound exaggerated and over the top, but to your audience, you will sound passionate.
2. Keep sustained eye contact with your audience. This means that you need to know the material. You can't rely on reading your notes.
3. Use big gestures. Small, subdued gestures say you are timid and uncertain. Generous, open gestures show confidence and energy.

Practice doesn't mean sitting down and reading your notes. Practice means standing up and delivering the presentation just as if the audience were sitting before you. It doesn't matter if the audience in your practice session is your roommate, your dog, or the four walls of your bedroom. It just matters that you practise as if the audience were in front of you—and as if both you and they are enjoying every moment of your presentation.

Visualize your spellbound audience.

Chapter Summary

Counterintuitive speakers stand apart from many other speakers in two ways: (1) their material is based on both strong research and independent thinking; and (2) they see every presentation, even those involving difficult audiences, as an opportunity to create a connection based on serving and respecting their audience. Accomplishing these two goals means counterintuitive speakers put more effort into their presentations than most speakers. But they would say the extra effort is worth it because it brings them closer to achieving their ultimate goal: to be able to walk out the door, after the presentation, feeling good about themselves.

---

mycanadianbuscommlab Visit www.mycanadianbuscommlab.ca for everything you need to help you succeed in the job you've always wanted! Tools and resources include the following:

- Composing and The Writer's Toolkit
- Document Makeovers

- Video Case Studies
- Grammar exercises and much more!

Thinking and Speaking Exercises

1. Choose one topic from the list below. Consider the topic for one minute, and then deliver a two-minute presentation on it to the rest of the class, using techniques discussed in this chapter.

   a. Finish and explain the following sentence: "After I graduate, I am most interested in . . ."

   b. If your house were on fire, what is the one (only one) object you would grab as you escaped? Why?

   c. Identify one person, incident, or thing you encountered this week that you feel grateful for. Explain why.

   d. Finish and explain the following sentence, "One thing most people would be surprised to know about me is . . ."

   e. Explain what stresses you most about speaking in public. (Choose this topic only if you suffer, to some extent, from glossophobia.)

   f. Explain what you love the most about public speaking. (For those who don't have a problem with glossophobia.)

2. As you listen to each classmate deliver his or her presentation, make a list of all the techniques discussed in this chapter that you see in the presentation—or that you think would improve the presentation. The debriefing session that follows each semi-impromptu delivery will give you a chance to share what you noted about each speaker's presentation.

3. *Class exercise:* Based on the debriefing of each speaker's presentation, develop a grading rubric that can be used in two ways: (a) as a quick reminder of the key elements that make up a successful presentation, and (b) as an evaluation guideline.

4. Obtain a recent issue of *Maclean's* and note the cover headlines (the length, wording, and style). Now try creating a similar type of title for the impromptu presentation you gave in Exercise 1.[15]

5. Consider the debriefing you received on your impromptu presentation; revise the presentation, and deliver it once again as a seven-minute presentation. This time, along with the revised content, you will add PowerPoint to your presentation. Make sure that your PP slides reflect the "respect your audience" guidelines provided in the chapter. Make sure, too, that your presentation reflects the guidelines contained within the grading rubric that your class developed.

Writing Skills Checkup: Adjectives and Adverbs

An adjective is a word used to modify or describe a noun or pronoun. An adverb is a word used to modify or describe a verb, an adjective, or another adverb. Sometimes people have trouble figuring out whether they should use an adjective or an adverb.

> Example: I did (well, good) on my PowerPoint presentation.
>
> The correct answer here is the adverb "well" because it's being used to describe the verb "did."

For each sentence below choose the correct form of the word from the pair offered.

1. You, however, wouldn't be feeling so (bad, badly) _____ about your presentation, if you had followed my advice.
2. For example, use font colours that contrast (deep, deeply) _____ with the background.
3. This combination will work (good, well) _____ together.
4. You also spoke too (quick, quickly) _____.
5. Next time, don't show more than two slides per minute. That will encourage you to go (slow, slowly) _____.
6. At the start, the audience seemed (real, really) _____ subdued.
7. You, however, (sure, surely) _____ changed that by getting them involved.
8. Some of them looked (apprehensive, apprehensively) _____ about participating, but you made sure that no one was asked to do anything they found uncomfortable.
9. I liked, also, the way you used actual photographs in your PowerPoint presentation, rather than relying only on text. The website with the free pictures (**http://office.microsoft.com/en-us/clipart/default.aspx**) provided you with some great photos. Perhaps you didn't do so (bad, badly) _____ after all.
10. I'm sorry if my original assessment made you feel physically ill. I hope you're feeling (good, well) _____ now.

Writing Routine Letters, Memos, and Emails

CHAPTER

8

LEARNING OUTCOMES

After completing this chapter, you should be able to do the following:

8.1 Decide what information needs to be included in routine messages and what should be left out

8.2 Compose subject lines that provide an accurate description of the

contents of a message

8.3 Structure routine messages to begin with a key idea followed by necessary supporting details

8.4 Format email messages, letters, and memos to follow

standard business conventions

8.5 Write clear, courteous email messages that are sent only to the appropriate readers

THE COST OF COMMUNICATION

An article in the *Globe and Mail* estimated that if a $40 000-a-year employee spent two hours a day reading and writing email, the annual cost would be $9000. The writer noted that both the $40 000 salary and the two daily hours spent communicating were probably conservative examples.[1] Communication is expensive.

The cost of communication is undeniable, but it is an expense that most businesses consider worthwhile. What is more, good communication skills can provide a valuable boost to your career. An article in the journal *Supervision* described how one man's career progressed over five years from a low-level supervisory job in the computer department to a management position that paid three times his original salary. The author attributed this meteoric rise to the man's carefully prepared presentations, which improved his image as "a resident communicator" and earned him a reputation as the department problem solver.[2]

The era we live in is often called the Information Age, largely because the explosive growth in computers has made information a valuable product and communication a useful tool. The cost of communication comes both from the 25 percent of their day[3] that people devote to managing their written communications and from the supporting infrastructure: hardware, software, networks, printers, and paper.

Learning how to fine-tune routine communications—letters, memos, and emails—can be invaluable to your career.

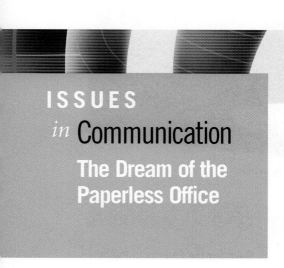

ISSUES
in Communication
The Dream of the Paperless Office

The dream of the paperless office was around long before the first computer was introduced. More than a century ago, inventor Thomas Edison predicted that his phonograph would allow office workers to record their words

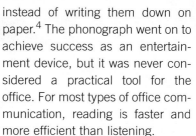

instead of writing them down on paper.[4] The phonograph went on to achieve success as an entertainment device, but it was never considered a practical tool for the office. For most types of office communication, reading is faster and more efficient than listening.

During the 1970s, the increased use of computer technology gave rise to numerous predictions about the declining role of paper in the modern office.[5] Such predictions have a logical basis. Paper is expensive to produce, bulky to store, and awkward to transport.

Nevertheless, such predictions have not become reality.

PROLIFERATION OF PRINTING

Paper is not disappearing. Walk into any office in the country and you will see numerous printers, photocopiers, filing cabinets, staplers, and all the other tools used to process paper. Our volume of paper use has not declined either. World office paper consumption almost doubled between 1980 and 1998.[6]

Paper remains a common sight in almost every office—in some more than others.

With computers, the internet, and email, people are now reading and writing more at work than ever before. A study conducted for Lexmark found that 40 percent of workers in small- to medium-sized businesses print correspondence that is received electronically. Two-thirds of all information created is printed at some point.[7]

People often prefer paper when composing, editing, and reviewing documents because it allows them to pencil in quick comments and annotations. People also often prefer to deliver paper copies of completed reports, partly because of the increased feelings of security that come with a tangible product, and partly so that they can answer

TAKE IT FURTHER

Covering the Country in Paper

In 2003, Canadians consumed 91.4 kilograms of paper per person. This is almost 20 000 pages for each person, enough to cover an Olympic swimming pool.[8]

Canada is one of the world's leading producers of paper, yet the paper industry is in trouble. Should people be increasing their use of paper products to support the industry?

questions and maintain a more personal relationship with their readers.[9]

The rising consumption of paper does not mean that people and organizations are rebelling against electronic information. Far from it. Businesses are bypassing paper for many routine transactions. More and more employers pay their employees through electronic direct deposits rather than the pay envelopes filled with cash that were used a generation ago or the paycheques used a decade ago.

TAKE IT FURTHER

The Paperless Office in Canada

The widespread increase of computers that began in the early 1980s sparked predictions of "the paperless office," in which all information would be transmitted electronically. Instead, Canada's consumption of printing and writing paper more than doubled between 1983 and 2003; Canada Post deliveries grew by 60 percent during the same period.[10]

Assuming that email and electronic bill payments have reduced Canada Post's volume, how do you account for the net increase?

INCREASING USE OF ELECTRONIC COMMUNICATION

Email is used heavily. One study says that the typical American spends about half an hour each workday processing email—about ten incoming and five outgoing messages. About 15 percent of workers process more than 50 emails a day, and 4 percent spend more than four hours a day doing email.[11] When email was new, and a novelty to many people, it was a routine for many people to print out all the messages that they received—perhaps one or two a week.

Paper will always have a use around the office.

TAKE IT FURTHER

Email: An Investment in Time

Another study estimated that, in 2006, people in business spent 26 percent of each workday reading and writing email.[12]

Do you think that email helps people use their time efficiently?

Many North Americans use scanning technology to process information that originated on paper. Documents can be digitized and stored electronically, usually as PDF (portable document format) files. An ever-increasing proportion of most college and university libraries consist of digitized journal articles stored in electronic databases. In offices, blueprints, reports, research articles, and other company records can all be stored this way, saving space and improving efficiency.

THE PERSISTENCE OF PAPER

Not all documents lend themselves to electronic transmission and storage, though. For now, contracts and documents requiring original signatures will continue to be printed. People resist having their personal notes saved for posterity, out of fear that their rough work will be misinterpreted or subpoenaed for court cases. The paperless office is unlikely to become a reality any time soon, but the way everyone uses paper will continue to evolve.

Individuals can make a big difference in the volume of paper being used by paying attention to their own printing habits. People are relying more on printers and less on photocopiers, which indicates that they are printing documents on an individual basis rather than making multiple copies for distribution. (Between 1988 and 1993, the number of photocopiers in use around the world rose by 5 percent, while the number of office printers jumped by 600 percent.[13])

If people can choose to print a document, in many cases they can also choose to view it electronically instead.

THE FUTURE OF THE PAPERLESS OFFICE

Undeniably, both computer use and paper consumption have been increasing. This has two implications for students:

1. Being able to write routine documents has increased in importance and will continue to do so.

2. People are growing increasingly alarmed at the costs associated with paper consumption.

Thomas Edison's vision of an office driven by recorded voice messages was never realized. However, the foremost technological innovator of our time, Bill Gates, has predicted an increase in the sophistication of speech recognition tools that allow people to dictate directly into their computers while the program converts their speech to text.[14] Widespread use of this technology will reduce keyboarding time but generally not affect the writing process. The skills required to organize and plan routine messages will likely change very little.

If speech recognition does make it easier to produce documents, it will likely bring about a further explosion in the amount of written material produced (with further implications for the amount of paper used).

Companies have introduced some measures to reduce paper use (such as by increasing the use of web-based documents), but individuals will find ways to reduce their own use of paper.

TIPS FOR REDUCING PAPER USE

The following ideas can help you make a difference:

- Learn to edit on-screen. Many word-processing programs come with tools to improve the writing process: outlining features that assist planning; spell and grammar checkers that help with proofreading; and reviewing tools that facilitate collaboration.

- Decide whether a printed version is necessary. Some media, such as visual presentations and documents containing hyperlinks, work better electronically.

- When printing is necessary, maximize the use of space. Reduce the size of margins and fonts. Print on both sides of a sheet and single space documents if possible. If you must print slides from a visual presentation, put six slides on a page.

- When printing revisions to a document, check to see which pages have changed, and print only those.

DISCUSSION

1. **Have you noticed paper being wasted at your educational institution? Who are the biggest culprits: students, instructors, or administrators? Give some examples. Consider how people at your college or university could be influenced to reduce paper usage.**

2. Why has the number of printers worldwide soared while photocopier installations have remained almost constant?
3. What advantages are there to reading from a computer screen over reading from paper? What are the advantages of reading from paper?
4. Voice recognition software allows a person to dictate into a microphone and have the computer convert it to text. What impact could widespread use of that technology have on people's writing?

THE PURPOSE OF ROUTINE MESSAGES

Routine messages keep business operations going. Most routine business messages fit into one of these three categories:

1. Providing information: "Our meeting will be postponed until after the contract is settled."
2. Asking for information: "Have you heard any more information about contract negotiations?"
3. Requesting action: "Please update the other group members on the status of the negotiations."

There is nothing sexy about any of these—no drama, no emotion, no empires won or lost. Routine messages are, by their very definition, routine (some would say boring). Anyone who has ever worked in an office can confirm this simply by reading emails or letters written a year or two ago. For example, an email advising employees that the cafeteria will be closed on May 10 may be important at the time, but after that date it no longer has any value. Once a routine message has been dealt with, it is usually deleted and has no further interest to the reader.

Routine messages may be boring to read and tedious to write, but that does not mean they are unimportant. If you are looking for strong emotion, you will find it instantly if you lose an email that told you the location of an important presentation. If you need drama, see what happens if you accidentally send a complaint about a dishonest customer back to that customer instead of to your supervisor.

Competent writing at work may not even be noticed; it is expected. The time anyone's writing skills are noticed is usually when problems occur. This also applies to associated skills, such as proofreading. A supervisor who sends a memo announcing changes that will affect people on the "late shaft" will be the target of rude jokes from the people receiving that message. A job applicant who writes about the "fast paste" environment of her last job will likely spend more time looking for work.

What would you do if you received an email that contained the following line: "I updated the Status report for the four discrepancies Lennie forward us via email (they in Barry file)."[15] If the writer was a co-worker, you might have to write or call to find out what the message meant. If the person wrote that way consistently and you were a supervisor, you might have to take stronger actions. Bad writing wastes time and costs money.

Even though routine office communications may not have the glamour of a celebrity news release or the complexity of a business plan, showing that you have developed these basic writing skills will improve your chances of obtaining a good job and future promotions.

Considering Message Outcomes

Each message you compose at work has two main outcomes:

1. It will communicate a set of ideas.
2. It will convey an image of you.

1. Communicating the Ideas You would not begin writing unless you had something to say. When you have something to communicate in routine letters, emails, and memos, remember that all good business writing shares these characteristics:

- *Good organization.* Competent writing starts with a main idea and then provides any necessary details. Understanding the audience will help you to decide which ideas are most important.
- *Audience awareness.* The information a co-worker requires may not be the same information that your supervisors need, so messages must always focus on the needs of a specific audience.
- *Clarity.* Competent writing is simple and clear. Big words do not impress people.
- *Conciseness.* Competent writing is as long as it has to be, but no longer than that. No one appreciates having to read any more than is necessary.
- *Courtesy.* It is sometimes necessary to be firm with people, but it is never acceptable to be insulting or abusive.
- *Correctness.* Providing inaccurate information or using bad grammar and spelling can damage your credibility.

It's easy to draw up such a list but not always easy to follow it. If it were easy, communication books, such as this one, would be unnecessary and people would not be drowning in a sea of poorly written and useless messages.

It is true that competent writing skills are a basic expectation in business and that poor writing ability will short-circuit a person's career, and it is also true that people who display superior writing skills are likely to make a favourable impression in any organization. When someone rises above mediocrity, those in authority take notice.

2. Creating Your Written Image The second outcome of business messages—image—is often overlooked. The initial impression someone has of you often comes from a written message that you have prepared. That impression affects the reader's image not only of you but also of the organization you work for. Just as polished shoes and a neatly tailored suit will create a far more favourable impression of you in a job interview than cut-off jeans and a T-shirt, careful attention to spelling and capitalization will help you to project an image of professionalism to your clients and to your employers.

Think of every letter, memo, report, or email message that you write as a sales letter. The product you are selling is your image and that of your employer. Attention to detail, good grammar, and a well-organized writing style will have as much impact on the image you project as a designer jacket and a $300 pair of shoes.

Beginning Employees An American survey of 120 corporations employing nearly 8 million people described workplace writing as a "threshold skill" for hiring and promotion among professional employees. The term "threshold skill" is perhaps best explained by the survey's no-holds-barred title: *Writing: A Ticket to Work . . . Or a Ticket Out.*

Many personnel officials said that they did not believe that salaried employees with poor writing skills would reach the point where they would ever be considered for promotion. Good writing skills were considered a basic expectation of all employees looking to advance. Poor writing skills were, however, an important factor in decisions to terminate employees.[16]

STRATEGIES FOR WRITING ROUTINE MESSAGES

Email, memos, and letters all have their place in routine business communication. Email has replaced many paper-based documents, but it is still worth knowing that memos, letters, and email can all be used well—and badly—for getting your point across.

Choosing Email and Memos

Email is the most common form of written communication used in offices today. It long ago overtook letters and memos as the primary means of communication for routine business messages. It is fast, cheap, and efficient. Email messages are used for both internal messages that stay within an organization and for external communication with people outside the organization.

At one time people would write a memorandum (usually shortened to memo) when they wanted to send an informal written document to co-workers, subordinates, or supervisors inside the organization. They would send letters to communicate with people outside their organization. Today, memos are used mainly in organizations in which some employees may not have easy access to computers. A memo announcing a change in work procedures could be posted on the wall of a break room, for example.

TAKE IT FURTHER

Phishing

The *Oxford English Dictionary* says that the term *phishing* was coined in 1996 and refers to internet fraud; specifically, "the impersonation of reputable companies in order to induce individuals to reveal personal information, such as passwords and credit card numbers, online."[17]

What is the best way to educate people about the danger of phishing? ▪

The format and writing style of memos and email messages is similar. The biggest difference between the two media is the audiences for each:

- Memos are used strictly for internal documents.
- Emails are used for both internal and external communication.

Both documents are relatively informal and are usually unsigned, meaning that they do not carry the same weight as more formal letters or contracts.

Although the absence of a signature makes emails informal documents, the tone and writing style of emails vary greatly with the audience. A quick note to a co-worker or a friend may contain misspellings or grammatical errors that the writer does not bother to correct—errors that are usually ignored as long as the message is understood.

Longer messages or those that are sent to people who are less well known to the writer require the same care and attention as any other written document and for the same reason: People are judged by the style of their writing.

An email containing technical errors could be dismissed as spam or "phishing" if it is sent to a stranger, even if the message is legitimate. Because many fraud artists disguise their messages as ones that come from legitimate organizations, the appearance of spelling and keying errors are seen as signs of a scam.

The importance of a good writing style increases in direct relation to the size of the audience and to your difference in familiarity with your reader(s). You may be able to get away with writing "C U l8r" in an email to a family member or a close business associate but not in one sent to a larger group or to your company president.

Bad Email   Look at **Figure 8-1** to see an example of a poorly written email message.

The message doesn't contain any spelling or grammatical errors, but it is poorly written for four reasons:

1. *Poor organization.* The most important information is buried in the middle of the document.
2. *Key information missing.* How will the new ID codes work with the new printer?
3. *Unnecessary details.* It is not necessary to provide detailed descriptions of the ways that people waste paper.
4. *Confrontational tone.* Several negative expressions, such as "heads will roll," needlessly antagonize readers.

Good Email in Action   Solving all the problems with the poorly written email in **Figure 8-1** requires two steps:

1. making a few minor changes to the content of the message
2. taking a more structured approach to the way it is organized

In **Figure 8-1**, the outcome was a vague threat of the consequences if printing was not reduced during the next three months. The revised version of the email message in **Figure 8-2** explains the introduction of the new

| FIGURE 8-1 | A Poorly Written Email Announcing a Change | ✱ Explore |

From:	Wai-Fong.Leung@internationalco.ca	Sent: Thu 8/27/2009 10:28 AM
To:	accountingstaff@internationalco.ca	
Cc:		
Subject:	Printing	

Printing costs are out of control.

I am not sure what everyone is printing or even who is doing all the unnecessary printing, but a look in the recycling bin showed a number of areas of waste:

– Printouts of email messages
– Unneeded copies of documents
– Draft copies of documents containing errors
– Blank (or almost blank) sheets containing only page numbers or empty spreadsheet cells

This wasteful practice has to stop. Therefore, I had no choice but to remove all printers and photocopiers from the office and replace them with a single printer/photocopier.

This, of course, means that printing will not be as fast or as convenient as it has been, but the old machines were noisy, inefficient, and a possible cause of indoor air pollution, so I know that everyone will welcome the change. I expect everyone to work toward reducing their thoughtless use of valuable resources by not printing out email messages, finding other ways to reduce paper waste, and sending large orders to Document Processing.

To ensure that this happens, the new printer/copier will require you to enter an individual ID code before printing so that print volumes can be recorded. No further action will be taken with this information right now, but if wasteful printing is not reduced during the next three months, heads will roll.

The subject line is vague.

The body of the message includes unnecessary information.

The main idea is buried in the middle of the document.

Important details are omitted.

The tone is too negative.

No signature or contact information is provided.

The email takes too long to get to the point and includes irrelevant chatter while omitting important information.

| FIGURE 8-2 | An Improved Email Message Announcing a Change | ✓ Practise |

From:	Wai-Fong.Leung@internationalco.ca	Sent: Thu 8/27/2009 10:28 AM
To:	accountingstaff@internationalco.ca	
Cc:		
Subject:	New Office Printer/Copier	

Good morning.
To help reduce printing costs, the photocopier and the four printers in the office will be replaced next week by a single networked printer/copier. The new machine will be quieter, more efficient, and faster than the old equipment. It will print on both sides of a page, which will help to lower paper consumption. Its eco-friendly design will reduce indoor air pollution.

Each person will be given a code so that printing volumes can be tracked. The codes will be distributed by email next week. When you print from your computer, start the printing process, and then enter the code when prompted. When using the photocopier, first press the ID button, and then enter your code.

Having only one printer will create some congestion if we print as much as we have in the past. We need to cooperate to reduce the amount of printing we do without reducing efficiency:

– Consider whether you really need a printout.
– Print only the number of copies that you need.
– Don't print emails, in most situations.
– Preview your documents before you print them to avoid printing blank pages.
– Send print jobs of more than 100 pages to Document Processing on the first floor.

Page limits are not being set, but that may change after three months if printing costs haven't decreased. Please share any suggestions you have for cutting printing costs further, and contact me if you have any problems with the new system.

Wai-Fong Leung, manager of accounting
416-555-1234

This email may contain confidential material. If you were not an intended recipient, please notify the sender and delete all copies. We may monitor email to and from our network.

The subject line is informative.

The message begins with the main idea, followed by the necessary supporting information.

The important details are included.

The tone is more positive and cooperation is stressed.

The signature block has additional contact information.

A confidentiality notice is included.

machines in more detail and presents the information in a less confrontational way that is less likely to anger the readers.

Luckily, similar messages have already been written. We will discuss those patterns next, and you can use them in your own writing.

"Begin at the beginning," the King said gravely, *"and go on till you come to the end: then stop."*

—*Lewis Carroll,* Alice's Adventures in Wonderland

Beginnings and Endings for All Messages

Some of the truest words about business writing appeared in Lewis Carroll's classic book *Alice's Adventures in Wonderland*: "Begin at the beginning," the King said gravely, "and go on till you come to the end: then stop."

Business messages have no set length. Many email messages are only a few words long. Some letters go on for two or three pages. Your job, when writing, is to focus on accomplishing a specific goal—for example, answering a question, making a sale, or organizing a meeting.

Often the hardest part of the job—especially if you have little experience writing at work—is to decide where to begin, where to end, and when to stop.

Some inexperienced writers start letters or email by introducing themselves. "My name is . . . and I am a. . . ." Such an approach may work in a few limited situations, such as a new sales representative introducing herself to clients in her area. In almost all other situations, though, it is unnecessary. Your name always appears in the signature block of letters and at the top of email messages. It does not need to be repeated in the opening sentence of a message. It is also not usually necessary to begin with polite chat about the weather or the state of anyone's health.

Psychologists say that the placement of information has an impact on how it will to be noticed and remembered. People have the best memory of the information they read first and the information they read last. Since people do not always read documents through to the end, the most important information should be placed at the beginning of most routine documents. If you are making a request or asking a complicated question, it may be necessary to explain yourself, but this information can follow the main idea.

Beginnings and Endings in Action   **Figure 8-3** and **Figure 8-4** are two versions of a letter to the local city council requesting information about the development of a meat-processing plant. Notice how long the first version (Figure 8-3) takes to get to the point.

Figure 8-4 contains the same message, but it has been restructured. It begins with the main idea and is more polite and easier to understand than the first version.

After reading the opening sentence in Figure 8-4, the reader would understand the key point of the request. The body of the letter explains the reasons for the request and presents further details about the exact requirements. The ending presents a specific date by which the information is needed, along with a reasonable justification.

Knowing When to Stop   The letter in Figure 8-4 was simple and polite. The writer's objective was to obtain information about a prospective city development. There was no political agenda and no attempt to convince the reader of anything.

The first letter (Figure 8-3) put the reader on the defensive by using intimidating language and threatening a lawsuit against someone whose only role is to distribute information. Strong language does have a time and a

✓•─Practise   FIGURE 8-3   **A Poor Request for Information**

Two Rivers Taxpayers' Federation
Box 1991A
Winnipeg, MB R2R 2G9
204-555-2345
www.TTTF.ca.

April 7, 2010

City Clerk's Department
Council Building, 510 Main Street
Winnipeg, MB R3B 1B9

To Whom It May Concern:

SUBJECT: Pork Processing Pollution

We, the members of the Two Rivers Taxpayers' Federation, strongly protest the move by Concarné Foods to begin construction of a hog slaughtering plant in the Two Rivers Industrial Park. An industry such as this will do irreparable damage to our businesses, to the neighbourhood surrounding the park, and to the city in general. We will be doing everything in our power to put a stop to this ill-advised proposal.

As such, we demand that you provide us with copies of the Clean Environment Commission's report, a poll that was commissioned on the Concarné hog plant, and information provided by Concarné on its efforts to control odours both at the Two Rivers plant and at its other operations.

We have a legal right to this information under the Access to Information Act, and we will be pursuing legal action if the documents are not forthcoming.

Sincerely,

Bob Knolten

> The tone is emotional and demanding.

> The request being made is unclear and the language is confrontational.

> The closing includes a threat.

The angry tone of this request would do little to ensure the cooperation of the employee being asked to provide the information.

place, but the writer has to choose the circumstances carefully to avoid alienating the reader.

An employer was once sued by a former employee whose job had been eliminated when a manager writing a letter about the need for more efficient production equipment explained his needs but then made the mistake of going on to write about "getting rid of deadwood" and "targeting those over 55 for early retirement."[18] If the writer had known when to stop writing, he would have saved his company an expensive lawsuit.

FIGURE 8-4   **An Improved Request for Information**   ✱⦁Explore

Two Rivers Taxpayers' Federation
Box 1991A
Winnipeg, MB R2R 2G9
204-555-2345
www.TTTF.ca

April 7, 2010

City Clerk's Department
Council Building, 510 Main Street
Winnipeg, MB R3B 1B9

SUBJECT: Information request: Concarné Foods' Proposal to build a pork
          processing plant

Please provide us with information regarding the proposal from Concarné Foods
to build a pork processing plant in the Two Rivers Industrial Park. The Two Rivers
Taxpayers' Federation is concerned that the plant may have a serious impact on
existing businesses.

Specifically, we are requesting the following documents:

• The Clean Environment Commission's environmental assessment of the plant's
  operations
• The results of a taxpayer-funded poll on the Concarné processing plant
• The report provided by Concarné Foods on the effect that its plants have had on
  other municipalities and the measures it uses to control odours

The TRTF will be meeting on June 1 to discuss its position on the Concarné
proposal. We would appreciate having the documents by May 15 so that we can
distribute copies to our members and give them time to study the information.

Sincerely,

Alice Strongpela
President, TRTF

> The subject line is specific.

> The request is clear and uses neutral language.

> The specific documents needed are listed.

> A reasonable date for delivery and an explanation are given.

> The writer's signature and title are included.

The formal request for information is assertive yet polite.

Applying a Pattern to Your Writing

Reading in the workplace is work. People have deadlines to meet and do not
enjoy wading through unnecessary details to get to important information.
They expect the messages they receive to be structured in a way that makes it
easy for them to extract the information they need. They may still get that
information if it is found at the end of a long, rambling document, but they
will be as annoyed at having to sort through the irrelevant information as
they would be at receiving their pay a week late.

There are several reasons why you should not let the idea of writing with a pattern intimidate you:

- It will not stifle your creativity.
- It will not make your writing tedious to read.
- Over the years, simple patterns for writing have evolved for many types of communication. The writers of murder mysteries, for example, use a structure where the crime is committed at the beginning of the book and solved at the end. People who watch slasher movies know the fate of the first person to explore the basement alone.

Simple structures impose order on the writing process, but they do not necessarily inhibit the writing—they can enhance it. They provide a framework for your creativity. If you begin a writing task knowing that you will begin with a key idea and then deal with a number of related issues, you will be able to concentrate on identifying those ideas rather than on trying to sort out other less important issues.

When you are writing at work, you want people to pay attention to the quality of your ideas. In almost all cases, that means beginning with the most important ideas and ending when you have provided all the necessary information. Providing unnecessary details can be almost as bad as leaving out important information.

Blaise Pascal, the French mathematician and philosopher once wrote, "I am sorry for the length of my letter, but I had no time to write a short one."[19] Pascal's point was that it takes time and effort to separate the key ideas from all the other useless information that surrounds them.

The Direct Pattern   Business writers apply different patterns to different types of documents. There are patterns for writing persuasive documents, for refusing requests, and for writing employment application letters.

Most routine workplace documents follow the fairly simple direct pattern shown in **Figure 8-5,** which can be applied to most common letters, emails, and memos.

Main Idea   The most important information should appear at the very beginning of the message—often in the first sentence. People will not always read the entire message, but they will usually read the first part. (Some email programs even encourage the practice by flashing the first few words of incoming messages in the corner of the recipient's computer screen.) The main idea should be thought of as the information that the reader needs most. Often it is a summary of the entire message.

In the example that appeared earlier, the writer began with a blunt statement that printing was out of control, followed by a list of complaints about wasted paper that would probably have most people's eyes rolling at the thought of a highly paid manager chasing after them for a few dollars' worth of excess printing. The most important information in this case is the fact that the printers and photocopiers are being replaced, a statement that does not appear until the middle of the message.

FIGURE 8-5 **The Direct Pattern for Writing Routine Messages**

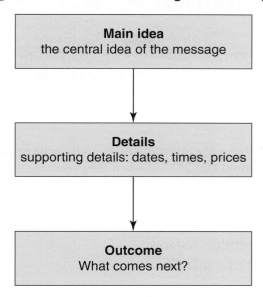

Details   All the information that supports the main idea should be placed in the middle of the document. In the case above, the details are the information relating to the installation of the new printer/copier. In other cases, the details might include background information on an issue, dates of an event, prices of equipment, or names of key personnel—anything that helps the reader to understand the main idea. Often the middle section is the longest part of the message.

Figure 8-5 implies that the entire message is made up of three paragraphs. It could be, but if the message is detailed, then the details section itself could be much longer.

The only details of the original message that need to be included from the example above are the reasons for replacing the old machines (cost, noise, indoor air pollution) and the fact that the new machine will require passwords.

Details that should have been included are the dates for the changeover, information on how passwords will be distributed, and explanations of how to use the new machine.

Outcome   The final section should tie everything together by explaining what happens next. It could be an explanation of what the writer intends to do next or a question or a request.

Lists in Documents

Letters, emails, and other business documents frequently contain lists of various types. Sometimes they are numbered; sometimes they are set off with bullets.

Lists help readers to find important information quickly. This improves reading efficiency and shortens documents. Lists can be made up of a group of items, steps in a procedure, or key points for discussion. Your lists will be more effective if you follow these four guidelines:

1. Keep lists brief—three to six items.
2. Keep items short—a few words or a sentence at most.
3. Use lists sparingly—no more than one list per page.
4. Introduce lists with a sentence that leads smoothly into the list—usually ending with a colon (i.e., :).

Bullets or Numbers?   Use numbered lists to indicate sequence or importance. Numbers should also be used when the preceding text emphasizes the number of items, as above, or when a later paragraph refers to a specific item.

For example, a memo to workers in a factory may list the company's priorities this way:

1. Eliminate all lost-time accidents!
2. Increase customer satisfaction.
3. Improve productivity.

This list indicates that safety is the company's top priority, with customer satisfaction and productivity coming next in importance.

Instructions for operating a fire extinguisher would also use a numbered list:

1. Remove the pin.
2. Direct the nozzle at the base of the flames.
3. Pull the trigger.
4. Spray the foam in a fanning motion.

The steps for these instructions (and most others) have to be followed in this precise order for the equipment to work properly.

However, when there is no intent to indicate chronology or importance, neutral bullet points should be used. For example, a meeting reminder might ask participants to come prepared with a number of items:

- year-end reviews
- monthly departmental reports
- proposals for next year's campaign

In this case, the sequence of the items is unimportant, so no numbers are needed.

Consistency of Lists   Items in a vertical list should follow a consistent style. Make each item in the list grammatically parallel with the others. These guidelines will help:

- Try to start each point with a key word, often a verb or a noun.
- Ensure that verbs are all in the same tense, usually either the present or the past tense.

- ▩ Capitalize the first word on each line.

- ▩ Use punctuation at the end of the line if the points are sentences; otherwise use no punctuation.

Remember that lists should be used sparingly. A document that has more bullets than narrative is usually thought of as an outline. Although outlines are a useful tool and you should definitely make use of them when planning documents, your readers will think your message is incomplete if you use too many lists.

Choosing between Letters and Email

Letters have not completely disappeared as a tool for conducting routine business, but their use is rapidly declining. Two main reasons for this are as follows:

1. *Speed.* Traditional letters are often called "snail mail" and with good reason. A local letter may take a few days to be delivered; an international letter could take several weeks. An email usually arrives in minutes, no matter where in the world it is being sent.

2. *Cost.* Email is usually cheaper than traditional mail. As long as both parties are connected to an email network, the only cost of the email message is the time it takes to write and to read the message. Traditional letters have the same costs in the time it takes to write them, along with the additional costs of printing the message and delivering it to the recipient. The additional delivery costs for a single message may amount to only a dollar or so, but with a mass mailing, which could involve a thousand letters or more, the costs will begin to add up fast.

Reasons in favour of choosing letters over email include the following:

- ▩ *Confidentiality.* Letters are a more secure form of communication than email and are useful when confidentiality is an issue. Although letters do not ensure complete confidentiality—they can always be photocopied or scanned and sent to unintended audiences—they are more secure than emails. Emails can be forwarded to unintended audiences with a click of a mouse, sometimes unintentionally, sometimes on purpose. Stories frequently appear in the news media about people who have been publicly embarrassed—or worse—when their email messages were read by unintended audiences.

- ▩ *Formality.* Letters also convey more formality than email messages. It is easy to include pictures and graphics in an email, or even animations and sound, but it is not possible to include embossed paper, genuine watermarks, or original signatures. Although the importance of paper-based letters as a tool for conducting routine business may be declining, letters will continue to be a common business tool for many years to come.

- ▩ *Signatures.* Letters carry signatures. In legal documents or in situations in which it is necessary to verify the identity of the sender, a letter (or other paper document) may be the only medium that the receiver will accept. In situations in which the information could be considered confidential, a signed letter may be required.

TAKE IT FURTHER

Document Security in an Earlier Time

Long before computers and document encryption, document security was protected with sealing wax. A blob of hot wax imprinted with the writer's seal was used to close a folded document. This acted both as a signature and as a means of preventing unauthorized people from reading or altering documents. Sealing wax is used today as a decoration, not as a security device.[20]

Many business emails come with a warning that readers should ignore and delete any messages they receive by mistake. Are these warnings useful? ▩

Wax seals were once used to guarantee documents' authenticity and to prevent them from being read by unauthorized readers.

In some special situations, writers may prefer to use letters for other reasons. Many direct marketing campaigns depend on the sales or fundraising letters that people find in their mailboxes every day. Job applicants are often encouraged to write a cover letter when submitting their resumés, and employers may write letters of reference to recommend job candidates. People may write letters when making complaints, or when responding to them. Letters can convey a more personal touch than email messages.

Goodwill Letters   In some situations, the formality that letters provide may be far more important than the speed email offers. Although a quick email message may be appropriate to thank a co-worker who has done a favour for you, a formal letter of thanks would be far more appropriate to acknowledge the services of a long-time business associate. See **Figure 8-6.**

Letters of Condolence   A letter or a card can be used to express emotion far more effectively than any electronic medium. If, for example, you need to express sadness for the loss of a business associate, it may be preferable to use a handwritten letter or card, rather than typing the message. Messages of

FIGURE 8-6   **An Appropriate Goodwill Message**

Blue Skies Development
2175 Avenue Road.
Regina, SK S3T 1S9
306-555-0987

February 10, 2010

Troy Eastwood
CEO, Prairie Interweb Design
41 Albert Street
Regina, SK S4R 2N3

Dear Mr. Eastwood:

Congratulations on winning the Most Innovative Website regional award from the Canadian Society of Graphic Designers. When I saw the announcement in last Tuesday's *Leader Post*, I immediately agreed with the judges' choice. Your design showing a banjo morphing into a football was brilliant. I'm sure that the recognition that accompanies the award will help create a bright future for your company.

Since our first meeting, I have continually been impressed by the professionalism and creativity of your web designers. Their ideas are always fresh, their attention to detail is exceptional, and our deadlines are always met. I am happy to have chosen your firm to design and maintain our website.

Again, let me offer my sincere congratulations. I am confident that the website will go on to win further awards when it is entered in the national competition next month. Good luck.

Sincerely,

Nickolas Scratch

Nickolas Scratch
Manager of media relations, Blue Skies Development

| FIGURE 8-7 | An Appropriate Letter of Condolence |

> Dear Alecia,
>
> I was deeply saddened to learn of your loss. Fred was one of the most cheerful people I have ever met. He never had an unkind word for anyone.
>
> If there is anything that I can do for you, please give me a call. You will always be a part of BRL Electronics.
>
> Jesse Armstrong

condolence are usually short. They express sympathy over the loss, share a personal memory of the person, and offer any assistance that you may be able to provide. See **Figure 8-7.**

Even though such messages are usually very short, tone is important. Do not try to minimize the person's pain with banal expressions, such as "Sally is now in a better place." Do not go to the opposite extreme either by focusing on the difficulties yet to come: "I know how hard it will be for you to continue without Bill." Instead, share a sincere message showing what the person meant to you: "Sheila was always the first person to offer her assistance whenever she saw someone needing help."

Layout of Letters Many computer programs contain templates for writing letters that help with some of the formatting. Four commonly used styles follow. The key differences relate to the placement of the inside address, date, and signature blocks:

1. The *full block* style (see **Figure 8-8**) is the easiest to remember; everything lines up with the left margin.

2. The *modified block* style is the same as full block but the date and signature block are centred.

3. The *semi-block style* is the same as modified block, but the first line of each paragraph is indented.

4. The *simplified* style is perhaps more logical that the other three. It omits the salutation entirely (Why do we refer to strangers as "Dear" anyway?) and replaces it with a subject line. This style leaves out a complimentary close for the same reason (Does "Sincerely" have any meaning at all in the closing of a letter?). When writing in the simplified style, some people insert the reader's name into the opening line to give the letter a more personal tone. "We have received your application, Ms. Jones, and will be reviewing it during the next week."

Although this style may be logical and more practical than other styles, it is considered less formal and may not be acceptable for more formal situations.

Punctuation Options in Letters Punctuation in the body of letters follows the standard rules of writing. However, addresses and salutations in letters

FIGURE 8-8   **Letter in Full Block Style with Mixed Punctuation**

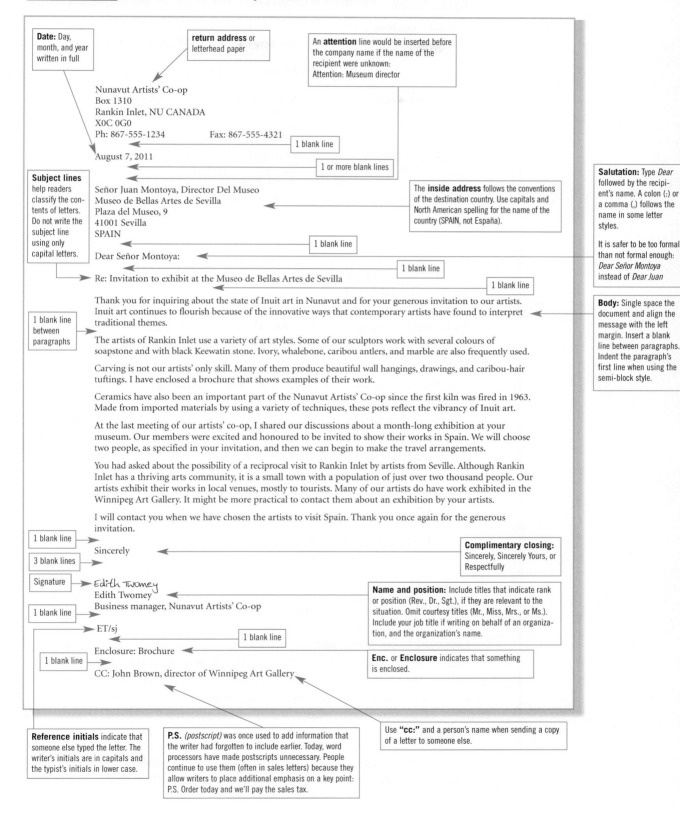

Date: Day, month, and year written in full

return address or letterhead paper

An **attention** line would be inserted before the company name if the name of the recipient were unknown: Attention: Museum director

Nunavut Artists' Co-op
Box 1310
Rankin Inlet, NU CANADA
X0C 0G0
Ph: 867-555-1234   Fax: 867-555-4321

1 blank line

August 7, 2011

1 or more blank lines

Subject lines help readers classify the contents of letters. Do not write the subject line using only capital letters.

Señor Juan Montoya, Director Del Museo
Museo de Bellas Artes de Sevilla
Plaza del Museo, 9
41001 Sevilla
SPAIN

The **inside address** follows the conventions of the destination country. Use capitals and North American spelling for the name of the country (SPAIN, not España).

1 blank line

Dear Señor Montoya:

1 blank line

Re: Invitation to exhibit at the Museo de Bellas Artes de Sevilla

1 blank line

Salutation: Type *Dear* followed by the recipient's name. A colon (:) or a comma (,) follows the name in some letter styles.

It is safer to be too formal than not formal enough: *Dear Señor Montoya* instead of *Dear Juan*

1 blank line between paragraphs

Thank you for inquiring about the state of Inuit art in Nunavut and for your generous invitation to our artists. Inuit art continues to flourish because of the innovative ways that contemporary artists have found to interpret traditional themes.

The artists of Rankin Inlet use a variety of art styles. Some of our sculptors work with several colours of soapstone and with black Keewatin stone. Ivory, whalebone, caribou antlers, and marble are also frequently used.

Carving is not our artists' only skill. Many of them produce beautiful wall hangings, drawings, and caribou-hair tuftings. I have enclosed a brochure that shows examples of their work.

Ceramics have also been an important part of the Nunavut Artists' Co-op since the first kiln was fired in 1963. Made from imported materials by using a variety of techniques, these pots reflect the vibrancy of Inuit art.

At the last meeting of our artists' co-op, I shared our discussions about a month-long exhibition at your museum. Our members were excited and honoured to be invited to show their works in Spain. We will choose two people, as specified in your invitation, and then we can begin to make the travel arrangements.

You had asked about the possibility of a reciprocal visit to Rankin Inlet by artists from Seville. Although Rankin Inlet has a thriving arts community, it is a small town with a population of just over two thousand people. Our artists exhibit their works in local venues, mostly to tourists. Many of our artists do have work exhibited in the Winnipeg Art Gallery. It might be more practical to contact them about an exhibition by your artists.

I will contact you when we have chosen the artists to visit Spain. Thank you once again for the generous invitation.

Body: Single space the document and align the message with the left margin. Insert a blank line between paragraphs. Indent the paragraph's first line when using the semi-block style.

1 blank line

Sincerely

3 blank lines

Complimentary closing: Sincerely, Sincerely Yours, or Respectfully

Signature

Edith Twomey
Edith Twomey
Business manager, Nunavut Artists' Co-op

Name and position: Include titles that indicate rank or position (Rev., Dr., Sgt.), if they are relevant to the situation. Omit courtesy titles (Mr., Miss, Mrs., or Ms.). Include your job title if writing on behalf of an organization, and the organization's name.

1 blank line

ET/sj

1 blank line

Enclosure: Brochure

Enc. or **Enclosure** indicates that something is enclosed.

1 blank line

CC: John Brown, director of Winnipeg Art Gallery

Reference initials indicate that someone else typed the letter. The writer's initials are in capitals and the typist's initials in lower case.

P.S. *(postscript)* was once used to add information that the writer had forgotten to include earlier. Today, word processors have made postscripts unnecessary. People continue to use them (often in sales letters) because they allow writers to place additional emphasis on a key point: P.S. Order today and we'll pay the sales tax.

Use **"cc:"** and a person's name when sending a copy of a letter to someone else.

TABLE 8-1	Punctuation Choices for Letter Addresses and Salutations
Mixed Punctuation (the most common approach)	– No punctuation at the end of lines in the inside address – A colon follows the salutation (after the name, not between the "Dear" and the name) – A comma follows the complimentary closing
Open Punctuation	– No punctuation at end of lines in the inside address – No punctuation following the salutation or the complimentary closing
Closed Punctuation	– A period follows the date and the last word of the inside address – A colon follows the salutation – A comma follows the complimentary closing

follow three different approaches: (1) open, (2) closed, and (3) mixed punctuation. See **Table 8-1.**

Addressing Envelopes   To improve the speed and accuracy by which addresses are scanned by computerized postal equipment, Canada Post provides these guidelines for addressing mail:

- Write addresses entirely in capital letters (although lower-case letters are acceptable).
- Place postal codes on the same line as the province or territory, written in two blocks of three characters with a single space between them (no hyphens). (See **Table 8-2** for provincial, territorial, and state abbreviations.)
- Do not use underlining, the # symbol, or any punctuation that is not part of a name.[21]

Following the Canada Post guidelines results in the following address style:

SUM SOO DIRECTOR OF MARKETING

ASIAN-CANADIAN IMPORTS

10-123 MAIN ST NW

PORT ALBERNI BC V9Y 2P6

Layout of Email Messages   Email toolbars vary depending on the program you are using. Typically they allow you to change the formatting of the message, or to insert pictures or attachments. Since email was designed with efficiency in mind, the date and footers found in most email messages are inserted automatically, and you can insert addresses with a few clicks of a mouse.

The Address Lines   *To* contains the email address of the main recipient(s). You can type in the address directly, but a single typing error will prevent the

| TABLE 8-2 | Canadian and U.S. Postal Abbreviations |

Canadian Postal Abbreviations

Alberta	AB	Nunavut	NU
British Columbia	BC	Ontario	ON
Manitoba	MB	Prince Edward Island	PE
New Brunswick	NB	Quebec	QC
Newfoundland and Labrador	NL	Saskatchewan	SK
Northwest Territories	NT	Yukon	YT
Nova Scotia	NS		

U.S. Postal Abbreviations

Alabama	AL	Montana	MT
Alaska	AK	Nebraska	NE
American Samoa	AS	Nevada	NV
Arizona	AZ	New Hampshire	NH
Arkansas	AR	New Jersey	NJ
California	CA	New Mexico	NM
Colorado	CO	New York	NY
Connecticut	CT	North Carolina	NC
Delaware	DE	North Dakota	ND
District of Columbia	DC	Northern Mariana Islands	MP
Federated States of Micronesia	FM	Ohio	OH
Florida	FL	Oklahoma	OK
Georgia	GA	Oregon	OR
Guam	GU	Palau	PW
Hawaii	HI	Pennsylvania	PA
Idaho	ID	Puerto Rico	PR
Illinois	IL	Rhode Island	RI
Indiana	IN	South Carolina	SC
Iowa	IA	South Dakota	SD
Kansas	KS	Tennessee	TN
Kentucky	KY	Texas	TX
Louisiana	LA	Utah	UT
Maine	ME	Vermont	VT
Marshall Islands	MH	Virgin Islands	VI
Maryland	MD	Virginia	VA
Massachusetts	MA	Washington	WA
Michigan	MI	West Virginia	WV
Minnesota	MN	Wisconsin	WI
Mississippi	MS	Wyoming	WY
Missouri	MO		

Source: "Addressing Guidelines." Canada Post. 22 June 2009. Web. 31 Aug. 2009.
"Official USPS Abbreviations." United States Postal Service. Web. 20 Oct. 2009.

message from reaching the desired recipient. Most people and organizations use contact lists or address books containing the addresses of people with whom they communicate. Many programs also allow people to set up group address lists so that by selecting a single entry, you can send the same message to all the people in your department, customer list, or workgroup.

Cc originally stood for "carbon copy" and now means either "courtesy copy" or "computer copy." The abbreviation itself is old-fashioned, but its use continues. The Cc line functions exactly the same as the To line, but it indicates to the reader that he or she is receiving a copy of the message that was sent to the main audience on the To line. Often this implies that the person receiving the Cc is being included in the information chain as a courtesy and is not expected to reply. Workers will often send a Cc to their supervisors to update them on the progress of their work.

A Cc may also be used strategically, almost like a 10-year-old saying "I'm telling Mom." If, for example, you have a disagreement with someone and attempts to resolve it have failed, it may be appropriate to send a copy to other people with authority to resolve the problem. Such people could be your Member of Parliament, the person's supervisor, or an official in a regulatory body. Keep in mind, however, that whenever you bring outsiders into a dispute, you are escalating the conflict.

Be careful, as well, about sending copies of routine correspondence to people who do not need the information. People find it annoying to receive needless copies of emails that do not concern them.

Bcc is a variation on Cc, but the B stands for "blind." The Bcc button has two uses: It is handy when a message is being sent to a very large group of people. Putting all the names on the Bcc line makes the email shorter when people do not have to scroll through a long list of names to reach the main message.

You can also use Bcc when you are sending a document to a list of people and you do not want each person to see the names of the others. People receiving a message from the Bcc function see only their own name and email address plus that of the sender. The identities of all other readers are concealed.

Be careful with this function. It is often useful for readers to know the names of others who have received the message.

Subject Lines Subject lines are a crucial part of most messages. Because people receive so many email messages—many of them junk—they frequently use the subject line to help them decide whether to read the rest of the message. A vague or missing subject line could cause the message to be deleted unread. Subject lines should contain the main idea of the message expressed in a few words. Since many people use spam filters that automatically filter out messages containing suspicious words, be careful about including such words as *free* or *urgent* in your subject line, since these are also common in many illegitimate messages.

Some guides recommend that you write the subject line using only capital letters (SUBJECT: SALES MEETING ON APRIL 1). This may not be a good idea, because spell checkers can be set to ignore words that are spelled in capitals so that they do not flag initialisms, such as HBC or RBC, as errors. If you depend on your spell checker and you write everything in caps, you may inadvertently introduce an error into your document. It is far safer to write the subject line by following the conventions you would use for any other title (Subject: Sales meeting on April 1).

Effective Subject Lines in Action   All email messages and memos begin with a subject line that usually summarizes the main idea. Many letters include one as well. The reason is the same. People are exposed to an enormous amount of information. To help manage this information, most people look at the name of the sender and the subject line before deciding when to read the messages (or to delete them). Subject lines are titles that help readers identify the contents of the message.

Subject lines speed the flow of information and improve people's efficiency by allowing email recipients to judge the level of urgency of messages. Although a message from your supervisor with the subject line "Meeting in 15 minutes" may require your immediate attention, you may not rush to read one from a co-worker labelled "Photocopier malfunction" (unless, of course, you need to copy something). You will probably delete, unread, an email message from a stranger that has the subject line "Discount inkjet cartridges by mail."

Subject lines should contain enough information for people to identify the contents of a message. Make the subject line is as specific as possible. See **Table 8-3.**

In some organizations, people transmit short messages by using only the subject line. If only a few words are needed to respond to another message, putting all the information in the subject line will save the other person the trouble of opening the message. Those who adopt this strategy often use a notation system to identify brief messages. Some people use an asterisk (*) or the letters "EOM" (end of message) to identify such messages. Thus, a response to an email asking when a meeting will be held may have this response: "Re: Time of sales meeting—3 p.m. Room 403 EOM."

Such strategies will save time only if everyone in the organization understands the abbreviations and agrees to use them. If you try implementing

TABLE 8-3	**Subject Line Examples**
Vague	**Specific**
Meeting	Safety committee meeting Friday @ 1 p.m.
New staff	Welcome Sally Smith to the marketing department
Proposal	Call for proposals—Canada Revenue Agency
Question	Location of your new branch office?
Health benefits	Health benefits will increase next year
Environmental options	New telecommuting positions becoming available

such a practice without consulting others, you will waste time answering inquiries about the meaning of EOM and explaining why the body of your message is blank.

Salutations   Salutations are becoming increasingly common in email messages. Since email tends to be less formal than many other forms of communication, one common approach is for people to begin with "Hi" followed by the recipient's first name. However, a more formal approach may be more appropriate when the writer and reader are unknown to each other or when there is a big difference in the people's levels of authority.

Footers   You can add these automatically to messages. Some people set the footer to include the writer's name, title, phone number, and mailing address. Others include a confidentiality warning telling people not to forward a message or to delete it if they have received it in error. Many workplaces have specific guidelines on the information that should be included in the footers.

Last Word on Memos

It is no coincidence that the format for memos is very much like that of email messages. Memos (or memoranda) were used in offices long before computers were invented. Memos were designed to transmit information efficiently and this format was imitated when electronic mail was invented.

Although email is used for both internal and external documents, memos are typically reserved for documents that stay within the organization. You may need to send a memo to people in your workplace who do not have access to email.

Memos in Action   See **Figure 8-9** for an example of a bad memo providing information to people in an office and **Figure 8-10** for an example of a good memo.

EMAIL ETIQUETTE

Email has become the main vehicle for much of the written communication in the workplace today, mostly because of its efficiency. However, this ease of use is also becoming one of its drawbacks. People are sending more and more emails because it is so easy to send them—and others are complaining about receiving too much email. Aside from the issue of junk mail or spam, which is a separate problem, people complain about being sent messages that they have no reason to receive.

A person in one department, for example, may send out a message to all staff within an organization that her office will be closed for an afternoon staff meeting "just in case" someone needs to contact them. Meanwhile countless people in the organization who have no need to contact anyone in the department will have to filter the message and delete it.

| FIGURE 8-9 | **A Poorly Written Memo** | |

Watrun Industries
670 King Street
Fredericton, E3B 1G1
506-555-2468
www.watrun.com

Date: April 4, 2010

To: All occupants of office 234

From: Darryl Harding DH.

Subject: Complaints

A few people have complained to me about the noise levels in the central office. I looked into it and asked around. Most people said that they were not bothered by the noise, but a few kept insisting that they are unable to concentrate. So for their sake, I looked into the matter further.

I found that a lot of people were engaging in personal discussions that should not be taking place in the workplace. You are not being paid to talk about the fight at last night's hockey game or to relay the intimate details of your domestic difficulties to other people. Even legitimate business meetings should not be taking place in an open office. This area is intended for quiet work only. PLEASE CONDUCT THESE DISCUSSIONS SOMEWHERE ELSE!

I also went a lot of trouble to measure the noise levels in the room and found that there is no cause for alarm. Everything is well within the limits that the CSA considers safe, so the complaints have little justification. The measurements show a level of 52–62 dBA, depending on where and when the measurements were taken. The CSA does recommend a design goal of 45–48 dBA for occupied "busy open offices," so technically, we are a bit on the high side, but once again, I must repeat, you are not in any danger.

Just to be on the safe side and to ensure that we finally get some quiet around here, I've arranged for the photocopier to be moved, and I've had the maintenance department replace a faulty compressor. I've also asked senior management to look into the installation of some other things that will control noise levels. White noise generators and sound-dampening materials are expensive though, so don't hold your breath waiting for these purchases to be approved.

I hope that settles things.

Marginal notes:
- The subject line is vague.
- The opening paragraph belittles the people who are complaining.
- Sarcasm does not contribute to the message.
- The request should come at the end of the memo, and more information is needed.
- Never use all-capital letters.
- The abbreviations CSA and dBA are never explained. The tone is disrespectful.
- More detail is needed about how this addresses the problem. The issue has not been resolved.

This poorly written memo has problems with both tone and organization.

Someone else will send a Cc to his supervisors or co-workers to keep them informed of work that he is doing even if these people have no real need for the information. The result is that many people are beginning to think of email as more of a time-wasting curse than a convenience.

Some organizations have even instituted email-free Fridays in which employees are required to phone people or walk over to talk rather than sending electronic messages.[23]

✳ Explore   **FIGURE 8-10**   **An Improved Memo**

Watrun Industries
670 King Street
Fredericton, E3B 1G1
506-555-2468
www.watrun.com

Date:	April 4, 2010
To:	All occupants of office 234
From:	Darryl Harding
Subject:	Noise-reduction changes to room 234

In response to complaints about noise in the central office, some changes have been made, and several larger changes have been recommended.

Office employees were consulted, and many expressed concern about their ability to concentrate because of the noise. Others said that they were not bothered by the noise.

The Canadian Standards Association (CSA) recommends occupied "busy open offices" have noise levels of no more than 45–48 decibels (dBA). We had noise-level measurements taken in our office, which ranged from 52 to 62 dBA, depending on the room activity and where in the office the measurement was taken.

These noise levels are well below what that the CSA considers hazardous to hearing; however, they are slightly above the recommended levels. Improvements will be made to reduce the noise levels:

- The photocopier has been moved to the outside wall beside the washroom and kitchen area. The interior walls should also help dampen the noise.

- Noises coming from the ventilation system have been corrected. A faulty compressor that was causing a rumbling noise throughout the office has been replaced.

- The installation of sound-dampening materials and a white noise generator have also been recommended. These modifications need senior management's approval.

These changes should help reduce the noise, but please remember that this is a large office and we all need to be considerate of our co-workers. Please conduct meetings in one of the meeting rooms rather than in the open office. Personal discussions should be held in the cafeteria or other common areas of the building.

I will keep you informed about any other changes that take place. If you have any further concerns, please call me at extension 3434 or drop by my office.

Side annotations:

- The subject line summarizes the content.
- Key information is given in the opening paragraph.
- Neutral, unemotional language is used.
- The terms *CSA* and *dBA* are explained.
- An explanation of the changes being made to address the problem is provided.
- The tone is respectful.
- The ending invites more discussion because the problem is not completely resolved.

This memo provides the readers with the necessary information in a diplomatic and well-organized manner.

Here are ten guidelines that may help prevent you from annoying people with your email messages:

1. *Do not ignore the basic rules of writing.* Email may be less formal than many other forms of communication, but you will be judged by the people who read your messages. If you are careless with your grammar and spelling, or you do not bother to put capital letters at the beginning of names or sentences, your lapses will reflect poorly on you.

2. *Avoid cuteness.* Emoticons, such as :) or :(, are commonly used by many people. Some programs will even convert them automatically to more recognizable icons: ☺ ☹. Emoticons have no place in business writing. Shorthand expressions, such as LOL (laughing out loud) and IMHO (in my humble opinion), are fine in chat rooms and personal communications but not in the office.

   A few shorthand expressions, such as FYI (for your information) and FAQ (frequently asked questions) have made their way into common usage in many offices. Your employer may also use other expressions that are specific to the organization, but the general rule to follow when deciding whether or not to abbreviate is "When in doubt, write it out."

3. *Do not contribute to information overload.* Many people complain about receiving too much email. Before using the Reply to All button, ask yourself whether everyone on the list needs to hear from you.

   - Sending people emails thanking them for sending you things is necessary only if the information was very important or if you know they had to work hard to give you the information.

   - Do not pass along chain letters, virus warnings, or other such messages that waste people's time and clog the system. Most of these warnings are hoaxes. Your employer's network administrator will inform you of the correct procedure to follow when you come across suspicious messages.

   - Do not reply to spam. It simply encourages people to keep sending it.

   - Do not click the "remove me" link in a spam message. This confirms that your address is active. Although your name might be removed from one delivery list, it will likely be added to several more. However, you should use the unsubscribe link to remove your address from any legitimate mailing list that you voluntarily subscribed to but no longer want to receive.

4. *Keep it brief.* Try to restrict your email messages to one screen or less so that people do not have to scroll through your message to read it all. If you have longer messages to deliver, consider sending them as attachments.

5. *Limit each message to one topic.* Email is cheap. If you have two or three messages to the same person or group, send them more than one email. That will help readers organize their information and reduce the chances of some of the information being missed or accidentally passed along to the wrong people.

6. *Find out your employer's policy for personal email use.* Some employers allow a reasonable amount of personal use of company email accounts; others forbid it entirely. Even if you are allowed to use your work account for personal reasons, be very careful about the information you send. Email is not private; do not send emails containing information that could embarrass you if read by the wrong person. Personal email accounts

are cheap and easy to set up. It is far safer to have one account for work and another account for your private life.

7. *Watch the tone of your messages.* The convenience and speed of email can be a drawback if you respond too quickly to messages that you find upsetting. It may be better to wait and calm down before replying to emails that bother you rather than dashing off a reply that you will later regret. WRITING EVERYTHING IN CAPITALS IS CONSIDERED SHOUTING.

8. *Remember that email is forever.* If you have information that is confidential or that could be used against you if read by the wrong person, consider sending it through a different channel. Even deleted messages can be recovered.

9. *Do not annoy people with technology.* Many programs contain features that allow people to attach an icon to a message indicating that it is urgent. Although the urgent indicator is a useful tool for messages that must be dealt with immediately, it loses its effectiveness and annoys readers when it is used with unimportant email. It conveys the message that the writer has no regard for the time of the reader or that the writer has an inflated sense of self-importance.

   Delivery receipts can be included with an email to send a message back to the sender that the email has been received. However, unless the email is very important or time sensitive, most people want to manage their email in private. When they see a pop-up box that says someone wants a return receipt for non-urgent email, they will get the feeling that they are not being trusted to manage their mail.

10. *Do not use email for sensitive matters.* If you need to make a serious complaint to a manager, discipline someone, or lay off staff members it is better to use a channel other than email. Face-to-face communication or a telephone call will allow two-way feedback as well as better expression of emotion, while a signed letter will provide more formality than an email message.

Chapter Summary

In today's business world, where computers sit on an overwhelming number of desks, email has become one of the primary communication tools in business. Writing is a basic skill in all areas of business, and writing skills have never been more important. Your writing style is an important factor in determining the impression that you make on other people.

Email is the most common channel for communicating routine information, but letters and memos are also used frequently. Whatever channel you use, messages should start with the main idea and then include any supporting ideas. Subject lines should be planned carefully because they will often determine whether the message is read or deleted. The final thought will point to the outcome. Messages do not have to be long—most people prefer brevity—but they must contain the necessary information written in a clear and well-organized manner.

Thinking and Writing Exercises

1. **Composing Subject Lines**
   Write a suitable subject line for each of the situations described below. For example:

   A request to a computer technician for instructions on how to defragment your computer's hard drive

   Defrag question

   a. an announcement that a payroll-deduction option is available for employees wanting to purchase Canada Savings Bonds

   b. a request for a co-worker who lives close to you to give you a ride to work tomorrow because your car will be in the repair shop

   c. a message to a regular customer announcing that the delivery date for his latest order of office supplies has been delayed a week to November 10

   d. a reprimand to an employee who has been coming in late and missing work without offering any excuses (This is a trick question.)

   e. a question to your supervisor about whether he wants you to include statistics about employee turnover in a report he has asked you to write about your company's hiring practices

2. **Organizing a Message about Reducing the Use of Paper**
   Assume that you work for the human resources department of a large bank that is attempting to reduce its paper consumption. Write a message to bank employees encouraging them to submit ideas for a new employee awareness program. Workers should be encouraged to submit ideas on ways to reduce paper waste in return for cash prizes. Answer the following questions to plan the message:

   a. Which two of these groups would be the audience for this document?

   b. Pick two channels that would be the most effective in delivering the message to your target audience.

   c. What would be a suitable subject line for the message?

   d. What main idea should be found in the opening line of the document? Identify one idea from the list below that would not likely be included anywhere in the document.

   - One litre of oil can contaminate 1 million litres of water. Dispose of hazardous materials properly!
   - Employees' suggestions on ways to reduce paper use could earn cash prizes while helping the bank protect the environment.
   - Last year your bank employed approximately 38 000 employees worldwide and had $11.3 billion in revenue.
   - The bank's paper purchases have decreased from 2100 tonnes in 2002 to 1650 tonnes in 2008, a reduction of 21%.
   - Canada signed the Kyoto Accord in 2002 but has never come close to meeting its energy-reduction commitments.
   - In 2001 Canada was producing almost 60 million documents a day—enough to form a pile 27 kilometres high.
   - Company vision statement: "Our vision is to be recognized as the leader in customer service. To get there, we have made commitments to deal with each of our stakeholders in a friendly, profitable, and environmentally responsible manner"
   - In some countries, almost 50 percent of paper is made from recycled fibres, wood chips, and by-products from forestry.

   e. Select two items from this list that would be contained in a section of the document explaining how to submit ideas. Pick one idea that would not likely be included in the final draft because it does not help to send the message on the need for employees to submit ideas. One of these ideas would likely be moved to another part of the document. Which idea is this and why?

- Ideas may be submitted online—a form is available on the company's website.
- Suggestion boxes and forms are found in all lunchrooms.
- Installation of double-side copying machines saved $50 000 in paper costs last year.
- Suggestions are to be restricted to ideas about paper use only.
- Forms that contain unprofessional comments will result in disciplinary action.
- Employees need to identify areas where paper is being wasted.

f. Select all the items that would be contained in a section of the document explaining how prizes will be awarded.

- Winning entries selected by a committee of labour and management representatives
- A yearly award of $500 for the idea that saves the most in printing costs
- Names of winners posted in the monthly newsletter, Banking News
- Descriptions of the winning ideas posted in the monthly newsletter
- Monthly prizes of $100 drawn from a list of all people whose ideas have been selected

g. What would be the most suitable way to close this message?

Using the ideas that you have selected, write the complete message about the paper-saving incentive program.

3. A Memo Encouraging College Students to Conserve Paper

Assume that you are the director of information technology in a small business college that has several computer labs that students use both to learn business applications and to complete their assignments. Each lab contains a networked printer that students can use for printouts. During the last several years, you have become concerned with the amount of wasted paper and unnecessary printing taking place in the labs. During random checks of the printouts left behind in recent months, you have observed multiple printouts of resumés containing the same error, PowerPoint presentations printed with one slide to a page, and spreadsheets containing only a single number.

Over the last year you have tried various approaches to reduce printing costs.

You have already tried restricting the amount of paper put into printers each day, posting signs by the printers encouraging conservation, and asking instructors to monitor students' printing habits more closely. None of these measures has caused a significant drop in the amount of paper being wasted.

Printing costs have reached an intolerable level—both in terms of the expenses associated with paper and printing supplies and in terms of the environmental damage caused by such waste.

Therefore, you have decided to implement a different solution. Beginning next term, all printing from labs will be charged to the students, just as it is now for photocopying. Here are the new procedures:

- Students will receive 50 pages of free printouts at the start of each term.
- When printing, students will have to enter their passwords and log on to their college accounts.
- Students' print balances will be recorded on their college accounts.
- Cost of additional printouts: $10 for 100 pages.
- Printouts can be purchased at the college bookstore and added to their accounts.
- Students who have used all their printing credits will not be able to print until they have purchased more credits.
- Bookstore hours: 9 a.m. to 5 p.m. every weekday.

An email has already been sent to all students in the college informing them of the new printing procedures. Many students do not use their college email accounts on a regular basis so you will also be posting the information in a memo on the bulletin board next to each printer. It is not necessary to use all the information above, but you will have to explain the new procedures carefully so that people do not lose the ability to print. You will need to win support for the new procedures (or at least minimize complaints) so your announcement should present the information in a positive way.

4. An Email Inquiring about Implementation of a Paperless Office

Assume that you are the vice-president in charge of customer relations in a company that installs specialized telecommunications equipment for large corporate clients. The company recently changed from a paper-based system to a computerized approach in an attempt to remain competitive in a changing marketplace.

The sales department was chosen to be the first to move toward digital information because it interacts with all other departments within the company as well as dealing extensively with clients—producing complex multi-page documents that contain details of new projects.

The move to a paperless approach within the sales department consisted of a two-part plan:

i. Improving the bidding process so that the various departments involved with preparing cost projections can store their estimates in a central database and update information rapidly when conditions change.

ii. Providing sales representatives with laptops and a database containing information on their customers' technical requirements that will allow the reps to share information with other people within the company about the customers' needs.

You are happy to see that the sales department has made a relatively smooth transition to the new system. The new graphical interface produced fewer technological problems than expected. Sales representatives working in the field and engineers and technologists working in the office were able to work out the details of the new bidding process so that it is workable by everyone concerned.

However, the transition from the older system of sales reps keeping their clients' records in personal notebooks to the new digital database has not gone as smoothly. Some of the sales representatives have entered some data into the customer database, indicating that there are probably no technical problems, but much of the information is too general to be very useful. Write an email to Justin Gavoya, manager for sales and client accounts, to find out the cause of the problem.

Select information from this list for your message. You do not need to use all the information.

- Details that would enable the company to gain a better understanding of its customers' requirements were often entered just before a contract was drawn up, too late to be useful.

- Sales representatives spend much of their time on the road, meeting with clients, and socializing with customers during luncheon meetings, hockey games, and other face-to-face contacts.

- Unlike the engineers and technical people who work at the main office, the sales reps spend only a day or two each week in the office.

- A shared database of customer information should facilitate contact among sales representatives and between the sales department and the main office.

Ask Gavoya to pass on your appreciation to the sales representatives for the smooth transition to the paperless bidding system. Ask him for an explanation for the vague information about clients that is being entered into the customer database. Find out if the problem is due to a technical glitch, a lack of time on the sales reps' part, or some other reason.[24]

5. Email about the Ownership of Sales Data

Assume that you are the manager for sales and client accounts for the telecommunications company described above. This morning you received an email inquiry from the vice-president in charge of customer relations. Sabrina Winzinowich congratulated you on your department's relatively smooth transition to the new system. However, Winzinowich expressed concern that the database of customer information contained far less data than expected, much of it vague. She has asked you to explain why your sales representatives have been reluctant to enter the data and instead have continued to store the information in paper notebooks.

After talking with your sales reps, you have assembled a list of their comments. Write a reply to Winzinowich's email by using some of the information below:

- Much of the work of sales representatives involves "relationship management" with key people within the customer organizations.

- Information on customers was acquired through lunch meetings, golf games, and other face-to-face contacts.

- Reps' notes often contained information on customers' leisure activities, family lives, and personal characteristics.

- The notes also included the names of people with whom they did not want to negotiate, as well as their reasons for wanting to avoid particular people.

- The sales representatives insisted that the information was subjective and useful only to the reps themselves.

- Some of the information could be considered libellous if released to the wrong people.

- Others felt that sharing the information with others in the company would make the sales representatives easier to replace, thus jeopardizing their long-term job prospects.

- Most sales reps insisted that they would continue to keep the information in their own notebooks, releasing only the most general information into the company database.

- They argued that as long as they did their jobs, the information that they kept on their clients was of no business to anyone else within the company.

- Several reps threatened to quit (and take their notebooks with them) if any further attempt was made by pushy members of upper management to coerce them into providing the company with personal data from their client lists.

Respond to Winzinowich's email, explaining that the sales representatives are willing to enter customers' technical requirements into the database but will continue to record personal information about the clients in their own notebooks.[25]

6. Letter Informing Bank Customers about Online Banking

Assume that you are part of the environmental working group at the Bank of Yellowknife. In 2004, the group was asked to create an environmental policy for paper use. The policy gives direction on paper conservation efforts and on improving the environmental qualities of the bank's paper choices, such as the use of recycled content and the introduction of measures to reduce paper use. The policy was reviewed by an external group of stakeholders and was launched in 2006.

Your task is to write a letter to account holders inviting them to convert their existing accounts to online accounts that use less paper.

Use some, but not all, of the information from the list below to explain the features of online banking:

- Electronic banking accounts are paper-free and eco-friendly.

- Online accounts do not require passbooks or mailed monthly statements.

- Accounts record 24 months of online transaction history.

- Online banking customers can receive and pay bills online, saving postage and transportation costs.

- Customers can find out more information and begin the process of converting their accounts by going to the bank's website: **www.bankofyellowknife.ca/online_accounts**

- The Bank of Yellowknife introduced paperless record keeping for all Canadian staff in 2005.

- The bank does not use email to warn customers of security risks. Any email messages claiming to be from the bank and asking for account information should be reported to the bank, but phishing attempts should never be answered.

- The use of passwords and 128-bit encryption makes online banking a safe alternative to traditional banking.

- During 2007, more than fifteen thousand employees switched to online banking.

- The bank now has more than fifty-one thousand paperless employee accounts.

- Internet banking requires a computer and an internet connection.

- The bank has already saved millions of printed pages as a result of the implementation of paperless staff accounts.

- At the head office in Yellowknife, more than 70 percent of waste has been diverted from landfill through recycling programs.

7. Email Informing Staff of a Conversion to a Paperless Office

Assume that you are the assistant to the manager of engineering at an engineering consulting firm. Yesterday, Steve Grey, the manager of engineering, informed you that he had finally received approval to convert the office to a new operating mode that relies more on electronic communication and less on paper. Grey has asked you to pass on the news to the other people in the office.

The conversion will require changes in three key areas:

i. a greater use of email for communication with clients and co-workers

ii. increased use of databases and electronic forms for customer orders and client records

iii. scanning of old paper-based files so that they can be stored electronically

The increasing dependence on email and electronic communication should produce few problems, but Grey expects that the scanning of the old files will be met with resistance.

He wants you to take steps to make the work go as quickly as possible.

"We do not expect the office staff to do the actual scanning, but we do want the technicians' work to go as smoothly as possible," says Grey. "I want you to write an email informing the engineering staff of the change. Some of those people have two or three filing cabinets filled with files they haven't looked at in years. They should welcome the opportunity to get rid of some of their junk. Unfortunately, some of them will be annoyed. You've got to convince them that a purge will be good for everyone."

He goes on to tell you the specific details of how the transition will work. The rough notes from your meeting with Grey appear below. It is not necessary to use all the information:

- Staff will now be allotted one drawer of a filing cabinet for paper files related to their current projects.

- All other information will be stored electronically.

- Place unneeded files in a disposal bin for shredding.

- Place archival information into the basket (provided) to be scanned.

- Archive signed contracts, records of meetings, correspondence, reports more than three years old.

- Filing cabinets will be collected in one month and replaced with new, smaller units.

Some people have a difficult time accepting the concept of the paperless office.

- More than 16 tonnes of paper is expected to be shredded from this office.
- Electronic files will be stored in a secure location and backed up every night.

8. Best Places to Work Contest: Letter Requesting Information

Assume that you are the manager of human resources for your employer. At a meeting of the company's managers, your company's CEO, Ali Stein, produced a copy of the article entitled "50 Best Employers in Canada" and said, "We should be on that list. Our company is making a profit, our employees are content, and our products are selling well. Please look into it and get back to me."

After reading the article and looking into the website that was set up to explain the contest, you reported the information found below to Stein. "All of this is good," he said, "but before I can commit to the project, we need more information. See if you can get a copy of each of the surveys. Also find out what it would cost to provide us with a detailed analysis of the results. And ask them for a more detailed description of the analysis.

"Also I need you to find out how many companies have entered the contest; it's not very flattering to be in the top 50 if only 55 companies entered. See if you can find out whether the losing companies' names are released as well. I'm not sure if we will want to be a part of this if they are.

"Some of this sounds too good to be true. I know the website says it's free and that they even pay the postage, but they have to get their money from somewhere. See if you can find out if there's a catch."

As your instructor directs, write either a letter or an email message to Hewitt Associates requesting further information. Here are the company addresses:

Hewitt Associates

1111 West Georgia Street

Suite 2010

Vancouver, British Columbia V6E 4M3

bestemployerscanada@hewitt.com

9. Best Places to Work Contest: Email Informing Employees

Assume that you work in the human resources department of a medium-sized business. Since the company began in 1995, it has gained a positive local reputation as a good place to work. Your company has grown from a small business employing 20 people to its present position of employing almost 800 full- and part-time employees, making it one of Canada's fastest-growing businesses.

Yesterday in a department meeting, the manager of human resources, Amelie Trebeck, announced that the company was planning to enter the *Globe and Mail Report on Business Magazine's* "50 Best Employers in Canada" contest. The annual contest surveys employees to identify the best places to work in Canada. According to Trebeck, the company's CEO, Ali Stein, is thinking of expanding the company's operations to other provinces, and he believes that the publicity of winning a place on the list should provide a boost to the company's reputation. "In addition," Trebeck pointed out, "winning such an award will enhance the department's reputation as well. And it won't hurt anyone in the department when it comes time for year-end bonuses to be awarded."

She goes on to explain that a company's standing is based on the results of several surveys that are to be completed by employees. Use any (but not all) of the information from the list below that will help you to prepare the email.

- All surveys are anonymous, so employee participation cannot be made mandatory.
- Entrants must have operated in Canada for at least three years and have 400 or more permanent employees.
- Participating organizations are required to administer all three of the following surveys in their organization:
  - i. Leadership Team Survey—completed by all members of senior management. The online survey takes 45 minutes to complete.
  - ii. Employee Opinion Survey—completed by 60% of your employees (480 people). The online or paper-based survey takes 35 minutes to complete.
  - iii. Human Resources Survey—completed by the head of HR. The online survey takes two hours to complete.
- The service is free to the company. Both online and paper-based surveys are provided free of charge. Postage is also paid by Hewitt Associates.
- Data is analyzed by Hewitt Associates, an international company that specializes in providing human resource services to companies around the world.
- Surveys must be submitted by June 30.
- Winners will be announced in the January issue of *Report on Business*.

- All companies participating will receive a standard report of the results. Further, more detailed analysis can be arranged at a cost.

- The survey measures three elements of employee engagement: whether workers speak positively about the organization to others, have a desire to remain a member of the organization, and are dedicated to helping the business succeed.[26]

Trebeck announces that you have been appointed to the position of survey coordinator. Your job, she says, is to encourage employees to participate in the surveys and to deal with the agency conducting the contest, Hewitt Associates. Your company will be included in this year's contest only if a sufficient number of employees complete the survey. Write an email to all employees in the company, explaining the contest and encouraging them to participate.

10. Letter Inquiring about a Rewards Program

Assume that you are employed by a locally owned credit union that provides financial services to the community in which you live. You have been looking for ways to improve employee morale. Employees are relatively content with their wages and benefits package, so you have decided to look into award vouchers that will allow your better workers to choose from a few luxury items for themselves rather than monetary awards, which would probably go toward paying bills. Rather than managing the program yourself, you have decided to contract the plan out to a business that specializes in such things, but you need to find out more information.

If all you wanted to do was present gift cards to employees, you could pick them up at any local mall but you want more than that. You need an organization that will allow managers to award a few points for coming in early and many points for winning a major contract. Employees would then redeem the points for various gifts.

Write a letter to a potential supplier asking about its rewards program. Your address is Precambrian Credit Union of Ontario, Box 1222, Sundridge, Ontario, P0A 1Z0. Before you agree to such a service, you require further information. Use some, but not all, of the ideas in the following list to help you put together your questions.

Background information:

- Precambrian Credit Union pays better wages than most other similar employers in the area.

- Sundridge is located between Toronto and North Bay.

- Last year out of a total staff of 20, you lost 3 employees and hired 4.

- Half of your employees are male; half are female.

- Employees already have a dental plan and government health insurance.

Information needed:

- procedure for employees to redeem points

- procedure for managers to award points

- evidence that reward programs improve employee performance

- catalogue of available prizes

- cost of the service

- Are rewards considered taxable income? If so, does the employee or the company pay?

11. Memo Soliciting Volunteers

Assume that you are the human resources director at Peak of the Market, a community-minded company that processes and sells fresh vegetables to markets across North America and Asia. Part of your company's mission is to serve the community. Last year the company donated more than 400 000 kilograms of fresh vegetables to various community-based foodbanks.[27]

As HR director you believe that employees want more from a job than just a paycheque at the end of the week. In addition to their regular paycheques and benefits, your employees receive other rewards from helping others that go far beyond money. Sometimes your company's community service activities give you the opportunity to reward workers in other ways. Assume that Peak of the Market has been asked to provide volunteers to collect food donations for a local food bank from people attending a local sporting event. You have been asked to recruit volunteers. Use some, but not all, of the information below in your memo or email to all employees:

- This is a playoff game. Tickets are hard to find.

- You have made a similar offer during other games this year. Support has been good but not great.

- So far this year volunteers have collected almost one tonne of canned and dried food.

- This is the first time in five years that the team has made the playoffs.

- The team missed the playoffs last year because of a coaching error in the final game of the regular season.

- All volunteers receive a ticket to the game plus a voucher for a burger and soft drink.

- Employees' spouses or children may also volunteer provided they are able to perform the required duties. (Children under 16 are ineligible.)
- People may sign up either by email or on one of the sign-up sheets posted in the break rooms.
- People should sign up only if they actually intend to volunteer. (You haven't had a problem with no-shows in the past, but you don't want to start now.)
- Volunteers need to indicate which position they are volunteering for and the ages of any children who will be assisting.
- The deadline for signing up is the first of next month.
- The game is on the tenth of next month. Game time is 2 p.m. Volunteers should be there by 1.
- Tickets and vouchers will be distributed by the supervisors a few days in advance of the game.

Duties of Game Day Volunteers:

- staff drop-off booths
- load donations onto trucks (some lifting required)
- arrive an hour before game time and to miss the first 30 minutes of the game

Duties of Pre-game Volunteers:

- organize volunteers into work teams and notify them of their drop-off stations
- notify media outlets of the food drive
- complete advance work a week before the game and an hour before the games
- involves no lifting
- expect to see most of the game

Duties of Post-game Volunteers

- return to the warehouse after the game and sort donations (estimated time about 90 minutes)
- do some lifting
- expect to see the entire game
- do not consume alcohol during the game to ensure safety

12. **Letter Inquiring about an Overseas Business Opportunity**

Assume that you work for the marketing department of Ten Thousand Villages, a business that specializes in fair trade marketing. Ten Thousand Villages helps artisans and food producers in developing countries market their products across North America so that they receive fair value for the work that they do.[28] In addition to operating retail stores in many cities, it also offers its products for sale over the internet at **www.tenthousandvillages.ca**.

Product offerings range from chocolate purchased from farmers' co-ops in Central and South America, drums and handicrafts from a non-profit marketing outlet in India, and hand-knotted oriental rugs from the Middle East to soapstone bookends from an artisan group in Kenya.

Ten Thousand Villages is always interested in expanding its product line as long as the profits go directly to the producers and are not absorbed by brokers or intermediaries. Recently a colleague returned from the South Pacific country of Papua New Guinea (PNG) with a number of fascinating artifacts that she suggested that you look into carrying. The crafts are indeed interesting, but before you can carry them, you have to ensure that you will be able to stay faithful to the principles of the store and ensure that the producers receive maximum benefits of their work. After doing some research on the country by using the internet, you have come up with a potential source of information about village cooperatives in PNG. Write a letter to the following address explaining the idea behind Ten Thousand Villages and asking whether they can put you in contact with artisans' cooperatives so that you can purchase locally produced crafts from PNG:

Village Development Trust

PO BOX 2397 Lae 411

Papua New Guinea

You will need to find out details of existing cooperatives that could supply your store and whether there are any government or environmental regulations on the types of purchases you make. Since shipping costs from the South Pacific could add up, you are especially interested in products that are easy to ship.

Some of the information in the following lists may be useful in your letter:

- Papua New Guinea has a population of about 5 million people and more than 700 native languages are spoken.
- PNG was a colony of Australia until 1975 and is now a member of the British Commonwealth, governed by a parliamentary democracy.
- PNG is home to 3000 different kinds of orchids and 30 species of the bird of paradise.

Your colleague has told you about these village-made crafts:

- net bags, or *bilums*, made by hand from natural fibres
- stone axes that were once used as tools and weapons but that are now purely ceremonial
- masks made of wood and clay and decorated with shells and pigs' teeth
- carved walking sticks, stools, and tables
- handheld Kundu drums shaped like an hourglass
- carved wooded storyboards that illustrate incidents of village life[29]

Here is further information about Ten Thousand Villages:

- You work with more than one hundred artisan groups in more than thirty countries in Africa, Asia, and Latin America.
- Your work is based on the principle that trade should have a conscience.
- You choose handicrafts that reflect rich cultural traditions, that are environmentally sensitive, and that appeal to North American consumers.
- Ten Thousand Villages was started in 1946 by Edna Ruth Byler, a Mennonite Central Committee worker.

Writing Skills Checkup: Using Numbers in Business Writing

(For more detailed guidelines on presenting numbers, see page 473.)

Numerals are used in the following situations:

- showing precision (a 2.1 percent increase)
- expressing large quantities (178 cars in the lot)
- stating money, serial numbers, phone numbers (416-555-6789)

Numbers are written as words in these situations:

- beginning a sentence (Twenty-one people signed the petition.)
- expressing numbers ten or less and common fractions (She ate half of the chocolates right away.)
- showing approximate amounts (Almost fifty people entered.)

Combinations of words and numerals are sometimes needed for clarity:

- showing very large numbers (Canada has a population of 33 million.)
- when two numbers appear together (I ordered 25 eighty-page booklets.)

Numbers with symbols are used in these cases:

- showing specific amounts of money (They received a $1.25 increase in hourly wages.). More general references use words (That is as phony as a three-dollar bill.)
- showing serial numbers (We requisitioned a new computer: #123abc456.)

- indicating percentages in tables or in scientific writing; business writing usually uses the word "percent" (Productivity increased by 13 percent.)

In statistical writing and other documents that make frequent use of numbers, numerals and symbols are often used instead of words.

Correct the use of numbers in these sentences. Some are correct. An example is shown:

Incorrect: Reformatting a property tax form to save paper saved one county twenty seven thousand dollars and twenty-five hundred kilograms of paper[30]

Correct: Reformatting a property tax form to save paper saved one country $27 000 and 2500 kilograms of paper.

1. It has been estimated that one market-size pulpwood tree makes about twelve thousand sheets of standard writing paper.
2. Some experts claim that electronic records will be readable for only a fraction of the two- to 300-year life expectancy of acid-free paper.
3. Worldwide in 1998 there were 218 000.000 printers, 22 000 000 multifunction machines (printer, scanner, and copier in 1), and 12 000 000 copiers.[31]
4. The average employee in a large company in Canada prints almost fifty pages a day, while the average employee based in a small-to-medium-sized environment (fewer than 500 employees) prints 35 pages a day.

5. Business documents represent 62 percent of pages being printed, while email and Internet printing represent averages of 16 and nine percent of total print volumes.[32]

6. In 2003, the TD bank evaluated all paper reports sent to retail branches and eliminated approximately twenty-five % of all existing reports or converted them to an online format, reducing the amount of stationery consumed each year by approximately forty-four and a half million sheets.[33]

7. Online banking offers the convenience of banking 24 hours a day, 7 days a week, and can save 100s of dollars each year in postage and travel expenses.

8. Currently, the average U.S. office worker is estimated to use a sheet of paper every 12 minutes—a ream per person every 2 1/2 working weeks—and to dispose of 50 to 90 kilograms of paper every year.

9. To store 2 000 000 paper documents, an organization can expect to spend between $40 000 and $60 000 on filing cabinets alone. Those same files could fit on fewer than ten CD-ROMs and require considerably less rented floor space.

Writing Persuasive Messages

LEARNING OUTCOMES

After completing this chapter, you should be able to do the following:

9.1 Create an audience-focused message

9.2 Use AIDA (attention, interest, desire, action) to structure persuasive messages

9.3 Choose the close that will move your audience to take action

9.4 Balance the logical and emotional appeal of your message

9.5 Identify the different types of persuasive messages

MAKE ANYONE DO ANYTHING

People like to get what they want, in the business world as much as in any other area of life. And you have likely seen websites, books, and ads for workshops and seminars that promise to give you the secret of getting others to do what you want. A Google search on "sales persuasion" brings up close to 2 million hits.[1]

But are people that easily persuaded? Are there reliable techniques for always getting others to buy your product, to give you a raise, to go out with you?

Think about times in your own life when someone was trying to sell you something. Chances are that you have bought something that you didn't want just because the salesperson had a persuasive approach. Being talked into buying something happens to almost everyone—most people have a treadmill or bread machine or snowboard gathering dust in their home. But how often are people talked into making a large purchase they didn't want? Consider whether you have said "no" to lots of salespeople.

Regardless of what some websites, books, and workshops claim, no foolproof techniques exist for persuading someone to do what you want. No magical phrases can close every deal. This chapter will not teach you to "make anyone do anything."

You can, however, make people more likely to listen to your request and to act on it. By making your case to people who are already receptive to what you have to offer, you can avoid wasting both your and your audience's time. By focusing on the needs and values of your audience, you can present your

"The salesman swore it would pay for itself within three months. I forgot to ask him what it did."

request in such a way that your audience is more likely to respond positively. By learning how to craft persuasive messages, you can become much more effective at presenting yourself and your ideas to others.

ISSUES
in Communication
The Nag Factor

The amount that companies in North America spend annually on marketing to children grew from US$100 million in 1983 to almost US$17 billion in 2007.[2] Since children seldom have the money to buy things themselves, many of the ads target what has been called the "nag factor" or "pester power." The goal of the ads is to get children to nag their parents for the advertised food or toy until the parents break down and buy it for them.

Marketers have split the type of nagging into two categories: (1) persistence nagging and (2) importance nagging.[3] Persistence nagging is what it sounds like—children keep nagging, repeating what it is they want, until their parents give up and buy it. "Please, can I have it? Please. Please. Please get it for me."

Importance nagging is based on the value of the item, often playing on parental concerns that their child fit in and that their child have high self-esteem. "I have to have a Spaceman Todd—all the kids have Spaceman Todd."

Marketers have divided the target of the nagging—parents—into four categories:[4]

- Kids' pals want to be their children's friends. They buy games and toys they can play with together.
- Indulgers give their children whatever they want—often in response to guilt over spending too much time at work.
- Conflicted parents try to balance a desire to get nice things for their children with a desire to resist giving their children every new thing that comes along.
- Bare necessities parents believe in getting their children only what they need. Because these parents are unsusceptible to whining, marketers target them with importance nagging.

Armed with that analysis, marketers are able to design ads to get children to nag in the most effective way given the various types of parents.

The problem is that these ads might not simply end up costing parents money—they might be harmful

"IS SUPERROBOTMAN SUPPOSED TO SOUND LIKE STEPHEN HAWKING?"

"The Omega 5000 was so last year, Mom."

for children. Research shows that preschool children do not distinguish between shows and commercials on TV.[5]

As Susan Linn points out in her book *Consuming Kids*, children as young as 1 year old pick up emotional cues from TV, and so "they are prime targets for manipulation, especially because they don't have the cognitive capacity to mediate their emotional responses."[6]

In addition, promoting unhealthy foods could damage children's health. The U.S. Center for Science in the Public Interest has found links between the advertising of junk food to children and growing rates of obesity.[7]

Is advertising aimed at children a problem? As a society, should we be doing something? As a businessperson, how would you handle marketing products for children?

DISCUSSION

1. How effective do you think advertising that tries to get children to nag their parents for something is at getting parents to buy?

2. Do you think television ads marketed to younger children should be banned? Why or why not? If you do think television ads aimed at children should be banned, up to what age?

3. If you were in charge of marketing for a toy company, where would you draw the line on what sorts of marketing strategies and ads were allowed?

4. Do think that advertising aimed at children is a problem? If so, who do you think should do something about it: society or businesspeople?

KNOW YOUR OBJECTIVE

What, Specifically, Do You Want to Happen?

Before you can persuade people to do something, you need to be clear about what you want them to do. The more concretely you can define your objective, the better the chance of crafting a message that will persuade your audience.

Suppose you believe your company would be more successful if everyone were better trained on your product line. You could send out a request to senior management suggesting they should hold more product training for staff. They might agree in principle and still not take any action because it's unclear what exactly "better trained" means and how best to achieve whatever it is. If you can make your objective more concrete—for example, "We should implement a one-week product training workshop for all new employees and annual three-day refresher workshops for all staff"—you provide your audience members with the specific step you would like to see them take. What is more, specific recommendations are more persuasive because they demonstrate that you have thought the problem through and realized the action that is needed to solve it.

You should limit yourself to one objective in a persuasive message, if possible. You want your audience to have a clear sense of what needs to be done. Trying to achieve multiple objectives at once increases the chance that your message will be unclear and that your audience members will not know exactly what you want them to do.

KNOW YOUR AUDIENCE

Who, Specifically, Are You Asking?

The key factor to creating persuasive messages is to know your audience. Whenever you ask people to do something for you, to buy something from you, or to donate money to your cause, at some level they ask themselves, "What's in it for me?"

In some cases, this is a very direct question. If you ask an investor to put $25 000 into your new business venture, she will want to know what she will get in return—such as the percentage of profit, ownership stake, or regular dividends. Imagine this is your message:

> Please invest $25 000 in my business. Otherwise I won't have enough money to pursue my dream of opening my own sandwich shop, and I will end up spending the next five years working behind the counter at fast-food restaurants.

Why would an investor, unless he or she also happens to be your parent, care whether you work in a fast-food restaurant? To appeal to investors, you need to have a business plan to show that you have thought through how your new business will make a profit, and you need to tell them how much return they can expect on their investment.

At other times, the "What's in it for me?" question might take a subtler form. If you ask someone to donate money for a new wing for the town library, he won't expect a direct payout for his donation. But he will weigh your request against other places he could put his money, using his personal values to judge where he would most like to spend it. Let's say you need to raise money to build a new computer centre for the local library and this is your message:

> The new library wing will hold internet-linked computers—to be donated by local companies. It will allow us to provide computer and internet access to all library patrons. In particular, after school the room will be set aside for student use. This will help our community provide students of all economic levels the opportunity to become proficient with new technologies and to access the wealth of knowledge available online.

Does that tell our audience what's in it for them? The fact is you cannot answer that question without knowing more about the audience. If you are addressing the parents of children in the local school system, then the message might be effective. If you are addressing someone who would like to see children, in general, reading more, a better message might be to focus specifically on the news, literary, and informational sources that a student can read online.

Whenever you need to create a persuasive message, remember to think about your audience on three levels:

1. Individual Ask yourself:

- Who is my audience?
- What's in it for these people?

Stakeholder

A stakeholder is any person or group who has an interest in an initiative, a decision, or a communication. For example, when someone puts up a new building, people who live nearby and care about the noise and air quality during construction are stakeholders—they care how the project is done. When a dam is built, environmentalists who want to protect the local ecosystem are stakeholders.

If your university or college decided to construct a Centre for the Study of Business Excellence, who would the stakeholders be?

■ What are the values they will hold when they consider my request?

2. Role Ask yourself:

■ What role is my audience in? Are the audience members my manager, my client, my peers?

Managers expect to be addressed differently than peers do. Investors you want funding from expect to be addressed differently than do relatives you are asking a favour from.

3. Cultural Ask yourself:

■ Does my audience have any cultural expectations?

Different cultures value different things, and in Chapter 5, we discussed the different meanings simple emblems or gestures can have in different cultures. In addition to your audience's individual reaction to your message, you also have to consider the cultural reaction of your audience members.

Understanding your audience members—who they are, what their role is, and whether they have any cultural expectations—enables you to create a message that tells them how your request fits their needs and values. This allows you to answer each audience member's question: What's in it for me

✱ Explore   AID FROM AIDA

One common approach to creating persuasive messages is to use AIDA—attention, interest, desire, action. If you structure your message to grab your audience members' attention, build their interest, create desire, and, finally, motivate action, you increase the chance that you will be able to persuade them to take the action you want them to.

Attention

Your opening has to grab your audience's attention. If you want people to keep reading, you have to engage them from the beginning. The best way to do this is by stating something that is true, direct, and important to your audience.

Everyone who has an email account receives spam that makes all kinds of claims while trying to sell products. Think about the amount of junk email you bother to read. Most people are sophisticated enough to recognize promises that are too good to be true. Although you might like to "make a million dollars a month watching TV at home," no one believes that is possible. Openings that do not ring true do not grab our attention.

Most people are also busy, and many things are competing for their attention. A request that is slow and indirect will lose the audience's attention before it gets a chance to make its point. Be direct—make sure your audience knows up front why they are reading your message.

Finally, as discussed in the section on knowing your audience, things that people care about grab their attention. Make sure you know what your audience wants and values, and make sure your opening lets people know why they will want to read the rest of your message.

"One of the most compelling graphic
presentations I'VE ever seen!"

"Before you start talking water purification systems, you have to get their attention."

Interest

Once you have your audience's attention, you need to build interest. Two key ways of doing that are by

1. expanding on the relevance of your message to the audience
2. demonstrating how you and your proposal or request can deliver what the audience wants

Expanding on the relevance of your message to your audience members can be done either directly or indirectly. When their wants are subtle—perhaps they are not even fully aware of what they value in the situation, for example—then you can build their interest by showing insight into what they want. If a young couple is looking to buy a house, perhaps expanding your message to include the high quality of the local school system will help build their interest by reminding them that they aren't just looking for a house but a home and a community in which to start a family. When the wants of your audience are obvious, often you don't need to state them directly. In a message to a potential investor, for example, you do not need to say, "You want to make money from this." You can proceed to tell her what sort of returns she can get from her investment.

Once your audience members know you understand what they value, they want to know that you can deliver.

The second way to build interest is by making it clear how you and your approach differ from others they might have seen. Consider exactly how you can give them what they want, exactly how their saying yes to your request fits their values, and exactly how your product or service delivers what they need.

Desire

Once you have your audience interested, you want to build their desire to adopt your proposal or to make the change you are requesting. You build desire by showing the benefits and by addressing any concerns.

The benefits of your proposal can be concrete (e.g., "Our money market fund offers a return of 5 percent"). Or they can be intangible and reflect your audience's bigger goals (e.g., "With our diversified investment portfolio you can achieve financial freedom"). Being specific about the benefits your audience can get from going along with your proposal or request moves audience members from interest into a desire to act.

One thing to be aware of, though, is that as someone reads your message, he will most likely come up with questions, or even objections, to what you are proposing. So the other side of creating desire is addressing the questions and objections that arise in your audience's minds. You probably regularly see stores offering sales that require no money down, which is a way of addressing the buyer's objection that she doesn't have the money for a big new TV right now. (It is, of course, another point whether it is in the buyer's best interest to get that TV if she does not have the money to buy it.) If you are selling a sophisticated software package, making sure prospective clients know it comes with a week of free onsite user training helps address any concern about whether their organization will be able to learn about and use the software effectively.

By providing your audience with benefits, and addressing concerns and objections that might arise, you move your audience from interest into a desire to act.

Action

You want to move your audience to action. The key here is to give audience members a specific action you want them to take and to provide a time frame for that action. As Brian Tracy says in the introduction to his book *The Art of Closing the Sale*, "I learned later that the words, 'Let me think it over' . . . are polite customer-speak for 'Good-bye forever; we'll never meet again.'"[8] The goal is to get your audience to do something. And the best way to do that is to provide a specific action and time frame. *The more specific, the better.* Rather than end your message with a vague request to "Give me a call soon to discuss," provide your audience with a very specific action that will move your proposal forward: "Call me tomorrow morning at 555-555-3658 and we can finalize details."

USE THE RIGHT CLOSE

Salespeople use a number of techniques to close—that is, to end their sales presentation in a way that leads their prospective clients to buy their product or service. Persuasive messages of all kinds can use those closes. Here are three strategies you can use to close a persuasive message.

1. Presumptive Close

The presumptive close presumes the person will do what you want. For example, "Please sign the attached contract. I will schedule a team to begin work first thing on Monday." The strength of the presumptive close is that it creates momentum, leading people forward into the action you want them to take. The danger is that if they are not ready to take action, the fact that you presumed they were ready could make them feel pushed, could make it seem as though you are doing a hard sell, and could therefore undermine the relationship of trust you have built—or would like to build.

2. Alternative Close

The alternative close is what it sounds like—it means giving your audience a limited number of alternatives to choose from. "If you are ready to get started, please fax me back a copy of the signed contract. I can have a team start work on Monday. If you have any questions, we can schedule a follow-up meeting to finalize any details tomorrow morning." This approach gives your customers the chance to choose the option that works for them while making sure that all the offered choices involve taking action to move things forward. The strength to this close is that it keeps things moving ahead while giving your customers the freedom to choose which specific action they want to take next.

3. Conditional Close

The conditional close can be effective if you have already been working with someone on the details, and only one or two outstanding issues remain. Consider this close: "I'll verify whether the software will run on workstations still using Windows 2000. If so, I can stop by tomorrow with the contract to sign, and we can start work on Monday." In this situation, one or two issues have not been resolved yet, and you make moving forward conditional on the resolution of those open issues.

Using the right close for the situation can help your audience bridge the gap between thinking about your proposal and taking action. The trick is to close in a way that makes it easy for people to follow through with the action you want them to take, without appearing to push them towards that action.

CRAFT A MESSAGE THAT APPEALS TO BOTH LOGIC AND EMOTION ✸ Explore

The best persuasive messages appeal to both emotion and logic. That is, they make a rational argument why the audience should follow the proposed course of action while also creating in people an emotional response that makes them want to take action. That said, although most persuasive messages appeal to both logic and emotion, what is effective, or even acceptable, varies in different situations. People do not like to be manipulated, so if your message is inappropriately emotional your audience will likely respond negatively.

If you have to miss a job interview and you want to reschedule, in your request to reschedule you will want to include a brief reason for why you have to miss the interview. However, if you include a long sob story about how tough your life is right now, with no money in the bank and your mother needing expensive medicine not covered by insurance, you are not doing yourself any favours. The interviewer will likely feel you are trying to manipulate her, thereby making it less likely she will grant your request to reschedule the interview. If you briefly say you are caring for an aging parent and must take him for a treatment on the morning of the interview, the message will make rational sense to the interviewer, and she will also likely identify with the emotional aspect of needing to care for a loved one. Given the reasonableness of both your situation and the emotional reaction it creates, if the interviewer has the flexibility to reschedule, she most likely will.

Logical Appeal

The logical appeal of your message comes from a clear presentation of the reasons for doing something. You should clearly state the benefits to the audience and demonstrate the way in which following your suggestion will achieve those benefits. You provide reasons that you (or your approach) are the best way to achieve those benefits. Each conclusion you draw should be based on the evidence you present. You should address any reasonable concern the audience may have about your proposal—perhaps explaining why that concern won't happen, why it won't be a problem if it does happen, or why the benefits outweigh it.

The style of the presentation should be clear. You can use visual presentations to make the meaning clearer and bullet points either to show the audience which steps to follow or to present a list of the benefits. See Chapter 7 for more information on using visuals effectively.

For centuries, no one tested Aristotle's explanations of how the world worked.

An appeal to logic depends on the strength of your evidence and the structure of your argument. Good evidence, presented so that each point you make leads logically to your next point, provides the audience with a rational reason for following your suggestion.

Emotional Appeal

People often make decisions based on reasons that are not purely rational. Although you always want to use care not to create overly emotional requests—so that you avoid seeming manipulative—consider the following ways of appealing to your audience's emotions:

a. Relationship Many companies give their salespeople expense accounts to take clients and potential clients out to lunch or golfing, or to pick up tickets to a concert or sporting event. The reason is that those companies realize that most customers would prefer to do business with people they know. In their private lives people certainly know that a friend is more likely to give them a ride to the airport than is someone they happen to sit next to at Tim Hortons.

One of the strongest emotional appeals to do something comes from having an existing relationship with someone. Even when you don't already know someone, calling or stopping by to introduce yourself adds a human element to your request. If someone will be evaluating proposals, a call to clarify requirements can help make your proposal stand out from the pile—as long as the call is quick and shows you have already read all available materials.

b. Authority Although "appeal to authority" is considered a logical fallacy (see **Take It Further**), the fact is that authority can persuade people. If you have authority in a given area, that makes your message more persuasive. Where appropriate, include information that increases your credibility, such as your professional qualifications.

If you do not have personal authority, using sources that carry authority lends credibility to your message. Carefully consider the sources you use. If you need to use population figures to make your case, you probably don't need to ask anyone if you would be better off getting them from Statistics Canada or Big Bo's Website of Trivia. Studies published in peer-reviewed journals carry authority because both the methodology and the results go through a careful vetting process. Articles published in the *Globe and Mail* carry an authority that blog entries do not.

c. Sympathy Readers who feel sympathy are motivated to take action to help. At times, this sympathy can be quite direct. Think of TV ads requesting donations to help children who lack food, medicine, shelter, and education—things people take for granted in Canada. Those ads explicitly try to get viewers' sympathy. One reason they can be so explicit is that the donations are meant for someone else's benefit.

When you are making a request for yourself, you have much less leeway to explicitly ask for sympathy. You can, however, include background information that will tend to make your reader sympathetic to your request. If you have to request that a business meeting be rescheduled at the last minute because you have to take your father to the emergency room, it is a good idea to include that reason in your message.

TYPES OF PERSUASIVE MESSAGES

Persuasive messages fall into several categories, depending on what you are trying to persuade your audience to do. We discuss five categories below, each with its own special considerations.

1. Simple Request

If your request is simple—for example, you need to ask someone to do something that is a standard part of her job—you do not need to make use of all

FIGURE 9-1 **A Simple Email Request (Sample)**

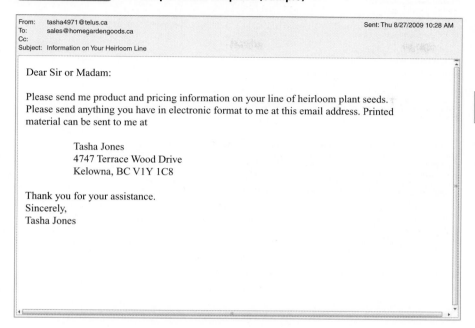

From: tasha4971@telus.ca
To: sales@homegardengoods.ca
Cc:
Subject: Information on Your Heirloom Line

Sent: Thu 8/27/2009 10:28 AM

Dear Sir or Madam:

Please send me product and pricing information on your line of heirloom plant seeds. Please send anything you have in electronic format to me at this email address. Printed material can be sent to me at

Tasha Jones
4747 Terrace Wood Drive
Kelowna, BC V1Y 1C8

Thank you for your assistance.
Sincerely,
Tasha Jones

> Email makes a direct statement of the simple request.

the persuasive techniques we have discussed. In these cases, a direct request is usually sufficient. If you want a company to send you information on its product line, simply ask for the material. The company wants you to know more about its product line and will be glad to send you the requested information. For example, the email to make the request could read as in **Figure 9-1.**

You can handle simple requests directly, with a polite request for the desired action.

2. Requests for Action

When you are asking someone to take an action, it's important to consider what objections or questions she will want you to address before she acts. As you are building interest and desire, demonstrate to your reader that you understand her concerns and that your proposal takes these into account. Think through the questions and concerns you would have if someone made the request of you, and address those questions and concerns in your message. At a minimum, your reader will want to know the following:

- What specifically are you asking him or her to do?
- What is the benefit for this person?
- Are there any risks or costs of taking this action?
- If so, how are those risks or costs going to be handled?

For example, imagine you are a project manager, and your team has just worked two consecutive weekends and a series of late nights to deliver the first phase of the project on time. Even though you still have an aggressive schedule to make the phase two deadline, you want your manager to approve a

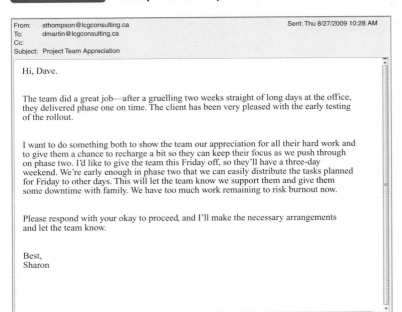

FIGURE 9-2   **Sample Email Request for Action**

ATTENTION: Grab attention by highlighting a company success.

INTEREST/DESIRE: Build interest and desire by highlighting the benefits of rewarding the team while addressing any concern that this will slow down phase two.

ACTION: Request a specific action that is easy to perform.

From: sthompson@lcgconsulting.ca   Sent: Thu 8/27/2009 10:28 AM
To: dmartin@lcgconsulting.ca
Cc:
Subject: Project Team Appreciation

Hi, Dave.

The team did a great job—after a gruelling two weeks straight of long days at the office, they delivered phase one on time. The client has been very pleased with the early testing of the rollout.

I want to do something both to show the team our appreciation for all their hard work and to give them a chance to recharge a bit so they can keep their focus as we push through on phase two. I'd like to give the team this Friday off, so they'll have a three-day weekend. We're early enough in phase two that we can easily distribute the tasks planned for Friday to other days. This will let the team know we support them and give them some downtime with family. We have too much work remaining to risk burnout now.

Please respond with your okay to proceed, and I'll make the necessary arrangements and let the team know.

Best,
Sharon

three-day weekend for the project team. Thinking through the situation from your manager's point of view, you identify that his main question is going to be whether giving the team this three-day weekend will put everyone behind schedule for phase two. While making sure to address your manager's concerns, you could structure your request as in **Figure 9-2.**

The email gives Dave the details of the benefits: Showing company appreciation for hard work will prevent employee burnout that could cause problems delivering phase two. It also addresses Dave's main concern: Since the project is at an early stage in phase two, it's possible to adjust the schedule to accommodate the day off. The email then requests a simple action: Please respond to this email with your okay.

3. Complaints

When a product or service does not work as it should, you can file a complaint or request a refund. When the request is simple and straightforward, you can use the direct approach shown above for simple requests. In some cases, you may want a company to do something beyond its normal policy, and you will need to make your complaint persuasive.

When making a complaint, it is important to state the facts in objective terms. If both you and the company can agree on the facts, you will have made a lot of progress toward a fair resolution. Taking a negative tone when stating the facts will tend to work against you, and it will make the person reading your message likely to disagree. If you say, "The cheap materials you use broke when I tried to put the desk together," you are putting the reader on the defensive. Keep your tone neutral (or even positive, if appropriate),

FIGURE 9-3   **Sample Complaint**

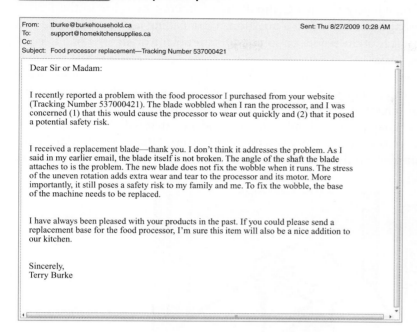

From: tburke@burkehousehold.ca   Sent: Thu 8/27/2009 10:28 AM
To: support@homekitchensupplies.ca
Cc:
Subject: Food processor replacement—Tracking Number 537000421

Dear Sir or Madam:

I recently reported a problem with the food processor I purchased from your website (Tracking Number 537000421). The blade wobbled when I ran the processor, and I was concerned (1) that this would cause the processor to wear out quickly and (2) that it posed a potential safety risk.

I received a replacement blade—thank you. I don't think it addresses the problem. As I said in my earlier email, the blade itself is not broken. The angle of the shaft the blade attaches to is the problem. The new blade does not fix the wobble when it runs. The stress of the uneven rotation adds extra wear and tear to the processor and its motor. More importantly, it still poses a safety risk to my family and me. To fix the wobble, the base of the machine needs to be replaced.

I have always been pleased with your products in the past. If you could please send a replacement base for the food processor, I'm sure this item will also be a nice addition to our kitchen.

Sincerely,
Terry Burke

> ATTENTION: Identify the problem and make sure the company has any information it needs to check previous correspondence.

> INTEREST/DESIRE: Thank the company for its initial response and explain why this response is not sufficient. Maintain a polite, matter-of-fact tone.

> ACTION: Request a specific action to resolve the issue.

and your words descriptive. For example, you might say, "When I followed the instructions to push brace C into slot D, the wood cracked."

Be specific about the problem you want resolved. Don't include a long list of complaints—include only things that are relevant to the action you want taken. If you are trying to get a replacement part for a piece that broke during assembly, the fact that customer service kept you on hold for 35 minutes is probably not relevant.

Many companies use account numbers for clients and assign tracking numbers to reported problems. Be sure to include—at the beginning of your message—any information the company needs to look up your file. See **Figure 9-3.**

Most companies value good customer experiences and the repeat business and positive word of mouth they generate. Companies want to deal with problems fairly. If you can explain the problem in clear, descriptive terms and suggest a resolution that is fair both to the company and to you, you can usually get companies to take care of problems that arise.

4. Sales Messages

The goal of a sales message is to persuade a potential customer to buy your product or service. This is one of the tougher forms of a persuasive message, because many people toss sales messages aside, or if they do read them, they read them critically. The people in your audience know you want them to spend their money, which means the message must give them a compelling reason to buy.

It is therefore important that sales messages grab the attention of the reader immediately by saying something of interest or value to the reader. Such messages can start with a question, a compelling fact (perhaps one that plays on a fear of the reader), a solution to a problem, or an offer of a free gift or product trial.

As soon as they have the reader's attention, sales messages should clearly describe the product or service being sold and provide the benefit to the reader of buying it. Each message should answer any questions or concerns the reader may have. It should provide evidence that will be meaningful to the reader. Concrete evidence will be more powerful than general statements. For example, "Studies show that using our ergonomic keyboard reduces

© Mike Baldwin / Cornered

"Your call is important to us.
Please stay on the line until your call
is no longer important to you."

For many businesses, customer service may be the only communication experience the majority of their customers have.

FIGURE 9-4   **Sample Sales Message**

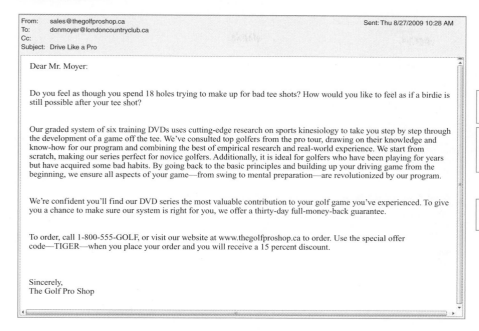

carpal tunnel syndrome by 73 percent over standard keyboards" is better than "Using our ergonomic keyboard reduces the likelihood of developing carpal tunnel syndrome." Evidence provided by independent evaluators carries more weight. For example, "*Keyboard and Mouse Magazine* named our ergonomic keyboard number one in computer-user comfort" is better than "Our keyboard creates a comfortable user experience."

Finally, sales messages should make it as easy as possible for the reader to buy. See **Figure 9-4**.

Readers often have their guard up when you are trying to get them to spend their money on your product or service. It is important that sales messages grab the readers' attention right away and not let up on generating interest and desire.

5. Fundraising Messages

Fundraising messages have similarities to sales messages—in both cases, you are asking people to spend their money. The difference is that where sales messages ask the reader to buy something that will directly benefit him or her, fundraising messages ask that the money be donated to a cause, to help others. Therefore, fundraising messages depend much more on appealing to the values of the reader. To get the reader to donate, you must convince him or her of the value of your cause or the need of those you want to help. See **Figure 9-5**.

The key to successful fundraising is to identify an audience that shares your mission's core values and show them how your organization furthers those values.

FIGURE 9-5   **Sample Fundraising Message**

ATTENTION: Start with an issue of concern.

INTEREST/DESIRE: Continue with benefits and raise the central issue—some students cannot afford the program.

ACTION: Provide an easy action to take.

From:	StephenDarrow@sciencecentre.ca	Sent: Thu 8/27/2009 10:28 AM
To:	kathy@kwilliams99.ca	
Cc:		
Subject:	Summer Science	

Dear Sir or Madam:

Canada will remain competitive only if it produces the expertise in science and technology that the modern global environment requires.

Students who attend the Science Centre's Summer Science program score at the top of their class in math and science, and many have gone on to attend the top universities in the world. Not everyone in our community, however, can afford to attend. The cost to Canada—both economically and ethically—of not supporting the full development of all its children, regardless of their family's income, is immeasurable. And so we are reaching out to all our members to help us make sure every student who wants to study can attend Summer Science at the Science Centre.

Please adopt a student today. Visit www.sciencecentresummerscience.ca and click "Yes, I want to adopt a student." Payment can be made by any major credit card, or you can arrange to be billed in easy monthly payments. Your contribution will ensure that every student who wants to work hard and learn will have the opportunity to succeed, for themselves, for our community, and for Canada.

Sincerely,
Stephen Darrow
Executive Director, Science Centre

CLICK, WHIRR

Many researchers have focused on the subject of influence and persuasion. Certain situations trigger automatic responses—what Robert Cialdini refers to as "*click, whirr*" responses—where we act without fully thinking through why we are acting, as if someone flicked a switch and turned on a machine. Two kinds of situations Cialdini looks at in his work on persuasion are reciprocity (or give and take) and consistency.[9]

a. Reciprocity

When someone does something for us, we tend to feel that we owe that person a favour in return. This is not a bad thing—it's good that we repay kindness with kindness. However, this trait can be used to influence your choices. For example, many makeup counters in department stores will have a salesperson do a woman's makeup for her. This is a good investment of time, because the woman then feels the urge to reciprocate, or give something back, which in this case means buying one or more of the products being sold.

Cialdini suggests that when dealing with salespeople or organizations that use this tendency to reciprocate to influence your actions, make sure to distinguish between real favours and sales techniques. In the case of a real favour, it's good to do something nice back. If it's just a sales technique, you do not need to feel any obligation—the company was never doing it as a favour in the first place.

b. Consistency

"What happens to a person's private opinion if he is forced to do or say something contrary to that opinion?"[10] This is the question that begins Leon Festinger's early paper on cognitive dissonance. This theory says that people like their ideas and behaviours to be consistent. When they are inconsistent, people experience mental discomfort (cognitive dissonance).

This desire for consistency gives rise to techniques that salespeople can use to trigger our *click, whirr* response. For instance, if a salesperson is hoping to get us to make a big commitment later, it is in his or her best interest to get us to make a small commitment up front. Many places that process phone orders will start by taking your personal information even if all you want them to do is answer a question. If you have already given them the information, it seems consistent for you to want to continue and make the purchase after they have answered your question. By taking the information before answering the question, they try to influence you to continue with an order.

In this case, being aware of our desire for consistency is a good defence. Just because a company makes us give information to get an answer to a question does not mean we called for any reason other than to get the information.

One reason to be aware of research on how people are influenced is to use those techniques to create persuasive messages. But another reason, just as important, is to protect yourself when others are trying to influence you to do something that perhaps is not in your best interest. Be aware of situations where you think someone might be trying to trigger your *click, whirr* response.

Chapter Summary

In many situations in business and life, you need to ask someone to do something for you. It is possible to make those requests more persuasive.

First, make sure you know your objective. What do you want to happen? If you want to craft an effective persuasive message, you have to know precisely what you are asking for. Then, make sure you know your audience. The way to persuade your audience members to take action is by showing that you understand their concerns and that what you are requesting benefits them.

Use AIDA (attention, interest, desire, action) to structure your persuasive message. Start out by grabbing your readers' attention. Then build interest and desire by showing them how your request will benefit them. Address any questions or concerns they may have. Finally, ask them to take a specific action, making it as easy as possible for them to act. You can use the presumptive close, the alternative close, or the conditional close to create a request for action your audience will go along with.

Understand what type of request you are making—simple request, request for action, complaint, sales, or fundraising—and create your message to meet the specific needs of that type of request.

Thinking and Writing Exercises

1. **Persuasive Techniques**

   a. What are some ways to grab your reader's attention at the beginning of a persuasive message?

   b. How can you build your reader's interest?

   c. How can you create desire in your reader?

   d. What makes a request for action effective?

   e. What are the three closes covered in this chapter? When might you use each? When would you not use each?

   f. How do make sure your persuasive message appeals to logic?

   g. How might you add emotional appeal to your message? Are there any risks in adding emotional appeal?

2. **Writing Persuasive Messages**

   Write a persuasive email appropriate for each of the following situations:

   a. You purchased a used laptop over eBay. The product works, but you are unhappy with it and would like to return it. Write the seller and ask to return the item.

   b. You hear about proposed legislation to provide zero-interest loans to students who maintain a B+ or better average. Write to your member of the legislative assembly and request he or she support the legislation.

   c. Your Student Business Association would like to establish a speaker series. Write a request to the dean of your business school for funding for the series.

3. **Know Your Audience**

   Visit a website that publishes RFPs (requests for proposal)—for example, www.bcbid.gov.bc.ca/open.dll/welcome. Pick an RFP of interest to you and come up with as complete a picture as possible of the audience who will be evaluating the proposal. In addition to the RFP itself, you may use the web to find out more background on the organization and people who put out the RFP.

4. **Effective and Ineffective Email**

   For the next week, monitor the email requests you receive. Find one example of an email sales or fundraising message that you think is effective. Find one example of an email sales or fundraising email that you think is poorly done. Print out both examples and be ready to discuss in class why they are effective or ineffective.

5. **Rewriting**

   Take the ineffective email message from exercise 4 and rewrite it so that it is effective. Use the AIDA structure, as well as any other techniques from the chapter that will make the message more persuasive.

6. **For Discussion: The Ethics of Persuasion**

   a. What is the difference between persuasion and manipulation? If you think they are the same thing, do you think manipulation is sometimes justified?

   b. Are there some persuasive techniques you find more ethically questionable than others? Which ones? Why do you find those techniques more problematic than others?

   c. What responsibility do companies and salespeople have to make sure that their customers understand what they are buying and have thought through their decision? Do they have any responsibility? Or should the saying "Let the buyer beware" govern the marketplace?

   d. Does your answer to question (c) change if you are selling to children?

Writing Skills Checkup: Pronoun Case

For each sentence below choose the correct pronoun from the pair offered. (Some sentences have more than one pair.)

Example: Susan and (I, me) like to go hiking.

In this sentence, the correct choice is I.

1. Joe and (I, me) _____ went to the sporting goods store.
2. Javid went to the store with Joe and (I, me) _____.
3. Jessica said that (she, her) would like to see for herself.
4. Between you and (I, me) _____, (I, me) _____ think the homework will be easy.
5. (We, us) _____ students want the student union to be open all night during the exam period.
6. (Who, whom) _____ are you talking to?
7. I gave the novels from class to (he, him) _____.
8. There are several things (we, us) _____ have to get done before (he, him) arrives.
9. I don't know where the two of (we, us) _____ went wrong.
10. If (she, her) _____ comes in before noon, I can make sure she/her gets an interview.

Dealing with Negative Information

LEARNING OUTCOMES

After completing this chapter, you should be able to do the following:

10.1 Discuss why businesses must deal with both positive and negative information

10.2 Write complaint letters that produce a positive outcome

10.3 Answer well-founded complaints from customers in a way that retains their goodwill

10.4 Deliver bad news in a sensitive manner by using the indirect writing formula

THE VALUE OF BAD NEWS

A common belief, which you can find in numerous self-help books, is that the Chinese characters for *crisis* consist of the symbols for *danger* and *opportunity*. This interpretation has been criticized as being an overly optimistic translation of the Chinese symbols meaning "danger" and "a time of incipient change," but the popular culture version has an element of usefulness. Looked at from the proper perspective, a complaint or any other negative information can produce a positive outcome. When things go wrong, whether it is because of tough economic times or because someone has made a mistake, people will make changes. Your task is to communicate negative information in such a way that the changes people make will produce the best results for both your organization and theirs.

The Chinese characters for crisis

In an ideal world, people would not make mistakes, and complaints would not be necessary. The business world is not ideal, though. Problems will occur and you will have to deal with them. Rather than dreading complaints, try following the strategy of one salesperson: Whether you are delivering bad news or responding to complaints, think of these as an invitation for more business. "It's like saying this is what you can do for me if you want to make me a happy customer. They're begging for you to make them happy and I'd like to do just that."[1]

This chapter is about bad news. It covers making complaints, dealing with legitimate complaints, and rejecting unfounded complaints. It provides plans that you can use to communicate bad news as humanely and tactfully as possible. The thought of dealing with bad news may seem unappealing, but those who deal with it well have opportunities to shine.

MAKING COMPLAINTS

When you receive poor service or experience some other form of mistake, your first step in dealing with the problem is to make a complaint. Preparing a complaint follows the same organizational process as other communication tasks. You need to choose the following:

- the appropriate medium and audience for the complaint
- the information to include when expressing your dissatisfaction
- the words to convey those ideas appropriately

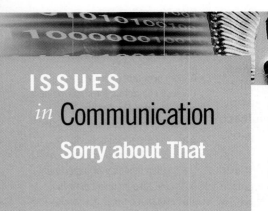

In the 1949 movie *She Wore a Yellow Ribbon,* John Wayne spoke this line: "Never apologize. It's a sign of weakness."[3]

Unfortunately, many businesses and organizations seem to have accepted this advice. In a 2003 study conducted by the Customer Care Alliance, almost 45 percent of American consumers indicated that they had experienced serious problems with a product or service in the past year. Of those people, 59 percent indicated that they would have liked to have received an apology for their troubles, but only 5 percent indicated that they had been offered one. Furthermore, 90 percent of the unsatisfied customers said that they had mentioned their displeasure to someone else.[4]

When people experience someone else's mistakes—and everyone makes mistakes—they expect an apology. When they do not receive one, they complain—often to many other people. When people have a legitimate claim for a legitimate problem, an apology will go a long way toward repairing an organization's image (especially when the organization intends to make some kind of restitution).

Sometimes people use apologetic language simply to explain their actions: "I'm sorry I'm late; I had trouble finding your office," for example. This approach may be acceptable for explaining away minor problems, such as arriving a few minutes late for a routine meeting. That is not a real apology though.

A genuine apology requires action, which becomes increasingly important as the severity of the damage increases. Getting lost, for example, might be an acceptable excuse for coming late to a meeting, but it would be inadequate as an apology for the late arrival of a fire truck. People would expect to know what the fire department was doing to prevent the problem from happening again, and what, if anything, the city was offering to the victims of the fire.

Here is a four-step plan for preparing an effective apology when someone has suffered a significant wrong:

1. Express sincere regret that the error occurred.

2. Explain how the mistake happened.

3. Describe the actions that have been taken to prevent a reoccurrence.

4. Offer to compensate for the damages.[5]

Once it has been determined that an organization is at fault, it should offer an apology as quickly as possible. Any apology should be sincere. A grudging apology or one that is forced out of someone does little to repair the damage.

When you are apologizing, be sure to look at the problem from the perspective of the person who was wronged. For example, if a software malfunction on your company's computer network caused the problem, your clients will be focusing only on the billing mix-up that caused them to be overcharged. You need to apologize for the billing error and not for the computer glitch.[6]

REASONS TO APOLOGIZE

Businesses make mistakes. When they do, a heartfelt apology coupled with an appropriate offer of compensation may help restore consumers' confidence. Businesses work hard to gain and keep the loyalty of their customers. They risk losing that goodwill if their clients feel that they have been treated poorly.

Several months after the launch of the iPhone, for example, Apple cut its price by $200 and angered many of the loyal customers who had been first to buy the new product. Apple's CEO Steve Jobs responded in less than a day, offering previous buyers a $100 coupon and an apology.[7]

When dealing with serious claims, some argue, an apology may defuse anger and cause people to reconsider launching a lawsuit. One American law professor said that apologies from doctors would have prevented 30 percent of medical malpractice suits.[8]

REASONS NOT TO APOLOGIZE

Concern about compensation is a major reason that organizations think carefully about making an apology. Many companies will gladly provide an apology and a replacement for small items, such as a box of stale chocolates. They may even offer something extra to make up for the inconvenience and to ensure the customer's continuing loyalty. Organizations face more of a dilemma when dealing with larger issues, such as medical errors or possible employee negligence. Compensation in such cases can amount to large sums of money and involve insurance companies and legal departments. Many corporate insurance policies expressly forbid their clients from apologizing for wrongdoing.[9]

One legal expert dismissed the idea of apologies in the legal system by bluntly stating, "The role of the tort system is compensation, not apology."[10]

APOLOGY LAWS

Several Canadian provinces and territories, and some American states, have enacted legislation that allows people to apologize without it being considered an admission of liability. Some of these jurisdictions allow people to provide an expression of sympathy or regret without admitting liability. Others state that damages may still be claimed if the person admits fault for the mistake.

A report by the British Columbia Ministry of the Attorney General states that "many disputes could be resolved earlier, more effectively and less expensively if apologies were promoted within our legal system."[11] By the end of 2009, British Columbia, Manitoba, Saskatchewan, Yukon, and Ontario had passed such laws. The report from British Columbia expressed concern about several aspects of these laws:

- Public confidence in the courts may be affected if a person admits fault and is then found not liable.

- Insincere and strategic apologies may occur.

- Apologies might cause some plaintiffs to accept settlements that are too low.

In the end, British Columbia decided that the benefits outweighed the drawbacks and that apology laws encouraged people to resolve disputes quickly, to communicate with each other after injuries, and to take responsibility for their actions after injuring someone.[12]

DISCUSSION

1. Why do many businesses not apologize after making mistakes that cause their customers inconvenience?
2. If you had bought one of the first Apple iPhones, would you have been satisfied with an apology and a $100 discount coupon after later purchasers benefited from a $200 price drop?
3. Do you agree with the conclusions of the report from British Columbia that says an apology law will "encourage people to engage in the moral and humane act of apologizing after they have injured another and to take responsibility for their actions"?[13]
4. Suppose that you are the victim of a serious error. What difference would it make to you to receive a letter expressing empathy for your pain or an apology from the person who made the mistake?

Choosing the Medium for the Message

Negative word-of-mouth publicity is harmful: Unsatisfied customers frequently take their business elsewhere, and their stories may make other people think twice before patronizing the offending business. One study indicates that the potential profits that are missed when a customer is lost are almost six times what it costs to satisfy an existing client.[14]

Most businesses and organizations know that unhappy people complain, often to many other people. Most organizations prefer that you take your complaints directly to them rather than sharing stories of your dissatisfaction with friends and colleagues. (Your friends and colleagues might appreciate it as well.) Complaints provide organizations with valuable feedback that allows them to improve their operations.

Most businesses realize the importance of having an effective way to handle complaints.

Where to go with a complaint depends on the degree of the problem.

Straightforward Complaints   These complaints can be handled quickly and efficiently either in person or over the phone. Some problems, such as merchandise that is clearly defective or orders that are missed because of simple clerical errors, can often be solved without the need for any written communication.

More Complicated Problems   These problems, such as billing errors or criticism about employee ineptitude, may require the organization to verify information and conduct an internal investigation before reaching a decision. In cases when it will not be possible for an organization to make an immediate adjustment, it may be better to put your complaint in writing. Nevertheless, it is still necessary to decide who should receive the complaint.

Most organizations have some sort of consumer affairs department dedicated to solving problems experienced by their clients. Companies usually make the contact information for such departments easy to find. They may provide toll-free numbers, email addresses, or mailing addresses to help with the process:

- A phone call is quick, cheap, and relatively easy, but it does not allow for the exchange of large amounts of information.
- Email or other electronic complaints allow more information to be exchanged, and the receiver can forward them easily, but they do not make it easy to attach other information, such as receipts.
- Letters require more time and effort, but they are necessary in some cases.

Further Problems   If the problem goes beyond a routine error, or if initial attempts to resolve it have not produced satisfaction, it may be a good idea to involve people outside the consumer affairs department. Writing to someone directly involved with the situation—a manager, supervisor, or department head—may produce results when using established channels has been ineffective. Whenever possible in such cases, address the person by name rather than "To Whom It May Concern." Finding such information may take more effort, but it is far harder for a person to ignore a complaint when it is addressed to him or her specifically.

Thinking Big

One further media decision you need to consider is whether to share the complaint with people outside the company. Some organizations can exert influence over decisions. Professional bodies that govern lawyers, engineers, or doctors have their own review boards. The Better Business Bureau mediates in complaints against its members. Governments often have an ombudsman. In many places rental disputes are handled by a government agency. Members of Parliament often intervene on behalf of their constituents.

Finally, do not ignore the power of publicity. The local television news may not consider it newsworthy to write a story about a minor consumer complaint, but it may be interested if the same problem has happened to many people, or if your problem is unusual or serious enough to capture their attention.

Getting satisfaction can take work, however, and the bigger the complaint, the more you will likely have to do to get it resolved. Persistence is key. Bigger complaints often require more than one letter or email to resolve. If you are convinced that you have been treated unjustly, and your initial attempts to resolve the situation have failed, try taking it to other people both inside and outside the organization. Be prepared to work to achieve satisfaction; settling claims can be difficult.

Tone

Tone is an important part of any complaint. Although you may be livid at the late delivery of the merchandise that you counted on to make your spring sale a success, it will not help your situation to take out your anger on the clerk at the other end of the line. Even though your claim may be directed toward a multi-million-dollar corporation, it is being handled by a live person who experiences emotions.

Whether you are talking on the telephone or writing a letter or an email, it is important to remember that the loser is usually the first person who gets angry.

The person dealing with the complaint is not likely the same person who caused the original error, but he or she might have the authority to fix the problem. You will find it far more productive if you are able to get the other person to work with you to solve a mutual problem than to leave the other person feeling defensive and wanting to get rid of you quickly to avoid facing any more insults or unfair accusations.

Remember the following:

- Use a non-accusing tone and perhaps a touch of humour.
- Try expressing disappointment in receiving less-than-adequate service from an organization that has always provided you with superior service in the past.
- Couple persistence, which has already been mentioned, with honesty.
- Take your complaint to more than one person or department if you must to get it resolved. Remember, though, that the people dealing with that complaint will talk with each other and verify the information relating to your claim. If you start exaggerating the information or conveniently "forgetting" to include facts that do not support your case, other people will provide the correct information, and your credibility will suffer. Tell your story honestly and completely to as many people as it takes to win your case.

Formula for Making Complaints

As with most business writing, complaints usually follow a formula, which is simply a variation of the direct pattern described in Chapter 8: (1) Begin with the main idea, then (2) include any relevant details, (3) and close by asking for a specific outcome.

1. Main Idea Your opening paragraph will, of course, state in general terms that you have a problem with a product or service, but it should also attempt to establish some sort of relationship with the reader. Start with a compliment about the company perhaps, or mention the long-term relationship you have had with the business. Then indicate surprise at the unexpected poor performance that you received.

2. Details of the Problem The body of the letter or email should include a detailed description of the problem. Describe the original transaction. Include dates, prices, and serial numbers. Explain why you are dissatisfied.

Remember that although most organizations are quite diligent in trying to correct problems for which they are clearly at fault, many situations have grey areas regarding the exact cause of the problem. Persistence is important in gaining satisfaction, but remember that one way to stall or deny a questionable claim is by writing back to insist on more complete information. Be prepared when you are explaining the details. Provide copies of receipts, warranty information, and any other information that may be required to settle your claim.

3. Outcome Once you have made the case that you deserve better treatment, you need to ask for a settlement. What will the organization have to do to regain your satisfaction? In some cases the desired resolution may be obvious. If you have been billed incorrectly, you may simply want the excess charges removed. In other cases, though, it may be necessary to explain whether you want a refund, a repair, a replacement, or something else. If the problem is more serious and damages have resulted from the mistake, then the settlement request is likely to be much more complicated.

Try to end on as positive a note as possible:

- You might mention your long history as a customer.
- You could describe how your organization has always been happy with the treatment it has received.
- You might state that all of your acquaintances have had good things to say about the organization.

Although these are all positive statements, they are also all veiled threats. Saying that your company has always appreciated the service it has received is also a subtle way of saying that that business will be withdrawn if you do not receive satisfaction. The same is true of such statements as "I am confident that we will continue to have a positive business relationship in the future."

Do not end your complaint with abusive threats or describe how you will ensure that the business does not survive if the company does not solve your problem. Even if you are completely correct in your complaint, your objective is to solve the problem, not to anger your reader. Remember, the first person who gets angry loses.

Excerpt from a Collection Letter from 1812

"Enclosed is your account, and I am sorry the statement of your mode of living, which has been reported to me, is such, that I must, in justice to myself, demand an immediate payment of the balance. It is not my disposition to act unkindly, or distress any man, but when I see people, with my property in their hands, squandering away their substance in wanton extravagance, it becomes necessary for me to see a little to my affairs."[18]

How much influence does a borrower's lifestyle have on a bank's willingness to lend today?

✳─[Explore

RECEIVING VALID COMPLAINTS

You will sometimes be on the receiving end of complaints, when you or someone else in your organization will be held responsible for an error that has occurred. When this happens, and happen it will, dealing with the initial anger and guilt will not be pleasant, but answering the complaint will require a straightforward response. You will have several objectives:

- Inform the reader immediately that you are willing to settle the problem.
- Apologize, if you have done something wrong.
- Regain the confidence of the client.

Follow these steps in the order in which they have been presented. Many people have heard so many empty apologies and have been handled by so many public relations representatives that they are distrustful of words. Offering them a concrete and fair settlement may be enough to lower their level of suspicion and have them listen to your apology and perhaps continue their patronage with your organization. Until the people have heard what you are doing to settle their complaint, they will be suspicious of anything else that you have to say.

You do need to regain the client's confidence, and your letter should not be defensive or attempt to explain why you are not to blame. Once the decision has been made to accept blame, you need to show what you are doing to prevent the same mistake from happening again.

For example, in 2008 meat products produced by Maple Leaf Foods caused an outbreak of food poisoning that killed 20 people and made thousands of others sick across Canada. The president of the company was praised for the way he dealt with the crisis. As soon as the full details of the problem emerged he went on air in a series of television commercials in which he accepted responsibility for the outbreak, apologized sincerely to his customers, and promised to set things right.[19]

Direct Formula for Resolving Complaints

The formula for resolving complaints is a variation of the standard three-step formula for direct messages (see **Figure 10-1**):

1. Begin with the main idea.
2. Follow it up with the relevant details.
3. Conclude by indicating what happens next.

GIVING BAD NEWS OR REJECTING REQUESTS

Anyone who has ever observed a customer making outrageous demands knows that the cliché "the customer is always right" is not true.

It is an unfortunate part of life that we sometimes need to turn down requests, to say no, or to give bad news. The best way to approach the rejection will depend on the way you think the person receiving the news will react.

FIGURE 10-1   **The Direct Formula in Action**   ✳ Explore

Norwegian Health Spa
2221 Victoria Avenue East
Regina SK S4N 6E4

June 11, 2010

Sophie Knutsen
1880 Saskatchewan Drive
Regina SK S4P 0A8

Dear Ms. Knutsen:

I have instructed the staff in the accounts receivable department to reverse the
$149 membership charges for May from your June 15 bill. After checking our records,
it was clear that you followed all procedures correctly and informed the gym staff
that you would not be renewing your introductory membership to the Norwegian
Health Spa.

> Good news is announced immediately.

Unfortunately, that information was not sent to our billing office in time for us to adjust
the billing information before your bill was created. That has now been corrected and your
membership has been cancelled, as you requested. I apologize for the inconvenience.

> An explanation is offered, along with an apology.

We will now be able to close your account. If, in the future, you decide to reactivate your
membership, please call me, and I will help you with the arrangements.

> The closing shows confidence in future business.

Sincerely,
Freda Anderson
Freda Anderson
Assistant Manager

> The writer's signature and title are included.

In some cases, when the rejection is not likely to cause any strong emotional reaction on the part of the person receiving the news, it is often better to give the bad news directly. Few people would be offended, for example, if they asked an acquaintance in the next cubicle to go for lunch and the person said, "I can't. I'm on my way to a meeting. Let's try again tomorrow." Such rejections are so routine that they usually receive little attention. That routine rejection fits neatly into the direct formula that is used for most writing (main idea, details, and outcome).

Not all negative information can be delivered this painlessly.

Presenting Bad News Directly

Strong emotions of any sort (anger, sadness, even joy) tend to affect people's ability to process information. Those who are disappointed or angry are not prepared to listen to explanations. When you are relaying bad news, you want your audience to understand the reasons behind your decision, but that may not happen if you present the main idea too quickly.

In **Figure 10-2** a company will not cancel a customer's contract.

This letter follows the direct formula. It is not bad, but its blunt tone is not likely to appease the customer or gain the company any repeat business.

FIGURE 10-2   **An Unsatisfactory Direct Letter**

> Norwegian Health Spa
> 2221 Victoria Avenue East
> Regina SK S4N 6E4
>
> June 11, 2010
>
> Sophie Knutsen
> 1880 Saskatchewan Drive
> Regina SK S4P 0A8
>
> Dear Ms. Knutsen:
>
> We cannot remove the $149 charge for your March membership from your credit card statement.
>
> Your introductory membership to the Norwegian Health Spa includes three months of unlimited use of our facilities. The contract that you signed *clearly* states that the first month is billed at an introductory rate of $49, but the fee reverts to the regular rate of $149 for each of the second and third months. Those charges remain in place even if you choose not to continue using our facilities. If you are moving to a different location, your membership will be honoured at any of our locations across Canada.
>
> Your membership will end on March 31, after which no further membership charges will be billed to your credit card statement. You will not be entitled to use the facilities after this month ends. If you change your mind, you may rejoin the Norwegian Health Spa at any time without penalty, but you will no longer be eligible for our special introductory rates.
>
> Sincerely,
> *Freda Anderson*
> Freda Anderson
> Assistant Manager

The blunt opening will likely anger the customer.

The explanation makes no attempt to build goodwill. The word clearly *places all blame with the customer.*

The writer's signature is not included.

With the rejection in the first line, the reader may not read the rest of the letter or may be so annoyed that he or she misses potentially useful information, such as the offer to transfer the membership to another branch.

Presenting Bad News Indirectly

Bad news that could upset the receiver may require an indirect approach. Essentially this means providing an explanation before the bad news. People will not likely be happy about receiving the news, but they will at least read the explanation if for no other reason than to reach the main idea. Consider **Figure 10-3.**

FIGURE 10-3   **A Good Indirect Letter**

Norwegian Health Spa
2221 Victoria Avenue East
Regina SK S4N 6E4

June 11, 2010

Sophie Knutsen
1880 Saskatchewan Drive
Regina SK S4P 0A8

Dear Ms. Knutsen:

Thank you for writing to us about your membership at the Norwegian Health Spa. The three-month trial period was chosen to allow sufficient time for clients to make regular exercise a part of their lifestyle. The special introductory rate includes a charge of just $49 for the first month and $149 for the next two months. We received your membership application on January 3 and have since received payments for the first two months of our agreement. One more month remains in your current contract. It is not possible to cancel our existing agreement, and I do hope that you will resume your pursuit of a healthy lifestyle.

The Norwegian Health Spa is open from 9 a.m. to 10 p.m., seven days a week. The staff at our facility will help you find exercise times that will suit your schedule. Memberships at the Norwegian Health Spa are valid at all 20 locations across the country, so even if you move, you are welcome to use any of our other locations. A directory of our facilities can be found at www.Norwegianhealthspa.ca. Thank you for being a customer of the Norwegian Health Spa.

Sincerely,
Freda Anderson
Freda Anderson
Assistant Manager

> The letter begins with a review of the charges and an explanation of the contract.

> The refusal is part of a longer sentence that is placed in the middle of the letter.

> An alternative solution is offered.

> The letter ends on a positive note.

> The writer's signature and title are included.

Notice that the explanation comes before the bad news, which is then softened somewhat by offering alternatives. The objectives when presenting bad news indirectly are to present the information clearly and to convince the reader to accept the bad news with as little animosity as possible toward the organization.

INDIRECT FORMULA FOR PRESENTING BAD NEWS

Using the four-part formula that appears in **Table 10-1** is one way of dealing with bad news. Depending on the circumstances, you may choose to leave out some of the steps or to modify the formula. The key principle is to present the explanation before the bad news when dealing with information that people may find disappointing.

Notice that the main idea (the bad news) is presented in the middle of the letter, a place where it will receive the least emphasis. The reason for placing it in the middle is not to hide the news but to control the timing. You want the reader to pay attention to the explanation, so it comes first. Presenting the alternative immediately after the bad news helps ease the unpleasantness.

Identifying the Positive Aspects of Negative Information

It is usually easier to present goods news than to present bad news. When messages contain a mixture of positive and negative information, the information can be structured in such a way that the good news softens the impact of the bad.

Some writers automatically try to insert positive information at the beginning and end of bad news letters, regardless of the main idea of the message. But consider the following:

- Bad news messages often begin with a buffer that identifies the general nature of the topic. If you use buffers, they should be short and neutral. Their purpose is to prepare the reader for the bad news that is to follow. A buffer that is too positive is cruel. It will raise the reader's hopes only to have the rest of the letter crush those expectations. (*I was delighted to receive your request.*)

- A buffer that is negative defeats the purpose of the indirect strategy. (*I will present the reasons for your dismissal.*)

TABLE 10-1	Bad News Letter Formula
1. **Explanation**	An unemotional account of the reasoning behind the bad news
2. **Bad news**	A clear statement of the bad news, presented as tactfully as possible
3. **An alternative**	Options that the reader can take to reduce the impact of the news
4. **Closing**	An ending that is as positive as it can be under the circumstances

TABLE 10-2 Writing a Buffer	
Express appreciation toward the reader.	Thank you for taking the time to write to us about your concerns.
Introduce the topic in general terms.	I have been asked to respond to your concerns about your December bill.
Find a point of common ground.	The recent downturn in the economy has been hard both for the company and for its employees.

- A buffer that is too long will simply annoy the reader. People often expect that the letters and emails that they read will open with the main idea. Although they will tolerate a certain amount of deviation from that pattern, they will quickly become annoyed at buffers that dwell too long on information that they find irrelevant.

See **Table 10-2** for a few possible approaches to writing a buffer.

It is often better to skip the buffer entirely and begin with your explanation. If you are writing a letter to people who have been interviewed for a position but are not being offered the job, a buffer will not help. People are almost always offered positions with a phone call, while rejections (when they are even sent) are delivered with a letter. Applicants who receive a letter from a prospective employer a few days after an interview will likely know what it says even before opening the envelope. A buffer in such circumstances is likely to annoy the readers with a needless delay, especially when they are already fairly certain that they have been rejected.

The same can be said of positive endings. People who are already disappointed at receiving bad news are not likely going to be made any less unhappy by the addition of news about future sales, new product offers, or statements indicating how much your organization values their input. People cannot be manipulated with a few positive words, and they are insulted when writers think that a few optimistic observations can make a difference.

In one study, a researcher presented the same message both directly and indirectly. The researcher found that "in negative letters, buffers do not matter, strong resale is counterproductive, and giving a brief reason before the refusal makes people more likely to say that the decision is fair but does not affect what their attitudes are toward the organization or what they would say about it to someone else."[20]

The same study criticized organizations that try to sell something to a consumer immediately after rejecting some other request. (Is it ethical, for instance, for a business to reject someone's request for a higher credit limit and then urge her or him to spend money at an upcoming sale?)

Putting the Indirect Formula into Practice

The main reason for presenting bad news with the indirect formula is that it allows you to present your explanation before you give the bad news. It should not be used to try to hide the bad news.

Communicating with angry people can be difficult.

Presenting Reasonable Explanations   Give explanations in a clear and logical manner. Ideally, you should begin by reviewing details that both sides agree on or by using information that cannot be refuted. After that, you can introduce details that may be contentious. At no time however, should you include weak or easily refuted explanations. Readers will try to refute your reasons, and if they find a flaw in even one of your arguments, they will expect you to give in. It is better to include no reasons at all than to give bad explanations for your decisions.

Make your explanations as meaningful as possible. Saying that "company policy prevents me from returning your deposit" is simply saying "because I said so" in a way that is only slightly less annoying than the original. However, telling the customer that "the deposit has already been spent on hall rentals and booking fees" may make the refusal seem more reasonable.

Giving Bad News Sensitively   The explanation should lead smoothly to the bad news. If you present your explanation logically, the bad news should not be a surprise to the reader. Ideally, the reader will see that your bad news is the only reasonable response to an unfortunate situation.

Even when readers do anticipate the bad news, it must be presented sensitively. Choose your words carefully to avoid the brusqueness that comes with such expressions as "your request is impossible," "I must reject your proposal," or "it is unreasonable to expect us to. . . ."

Do not apologize for presenting the bad news unless you have done something wrong. If your decision is reasonable and has been carefully considered, an apology will imply that you are uncertain about the decision and perhaps willing to change. You will not do anyone any favours by giving the reader false hope or prolonging an unpleasant process.

In such situations as layoffs, where you might genuinely regret having to deliver the bad news, it is certainly appropriate to show empathy with the readers' situation, or to express sadness at their circumstances, but it is still not necessary to apologize in such cases. Apologies should be reserved only for those times when you have done something wrong.

When delivering bad news, you need to convince the reader that the information, unpleasant as it may be, is fair and reasonable. **Table 10-3** shows a few strategies for presenting the bad news as sensitively as possible.

It may be necessary to present the bad news in a detailed sentence, but once that news is delivered, consider the following:

- It is not necessary to repeat the message or make further reference to the bad news.
- Do not offer additional detail as to why the reader is responsible for the problem.
- Do not explain what the reader could have done to avoid the difficulties.
- Do not say anything that will place further blame on the reader.

Your responsibility, once the news has been delivered, is to help the reader deal with the bad news.

TABLE 10-3	Ways to Present Bad News		Practise
How to Present the News	**Instead of This**	**Try This**	
Put the bad news in a long sentence.	I cannot offer you a job.	Although your credentials were impressive, several other applicants had even more experience than you do, and we chose a candidate who had an MBA and extensive experience in the field.	
State the news by using positive language.	You may not use your company email account for personal correspondence.	Company email accounts should be reserved for business purposes.	
Imply the bad news.	You cannot take all four weeks of your vacation during July.	It would not be fair to the other employees to make an exception to our practice that limits employees' vacations to two weeks during the summer months.	
Use the passive voice.	We will not be able to provide you with a free rental car while yours is being repaired.	Free rental cars are available only to those customers who purchased the premium insurance policy.	
Present the bad news in the same sentence as an alternative.	You are fully responsible for all repair costs.	Even though the repair costs cannot be covered under warranty, we can offer you a 25 percent discount on the purchase of a new stereo.	

Offering Alternatives People want to have control over their lives. It is sometimes necessary to disappoint them, but whenever possible you need to allow people to regain dignity by presenting them with options. Unfortunately, options are not always available.

One reason that tragic news is so sad is that the receiver has few alternatives. The police officers who inform family members of a fatal accident can offer them no choice but to deal with the bad news.

Business decisions, though, usually do allow a certain amount of latitude. Whenever possible, give readers a choice, or even the illusion of a choice over the news. You do not want to give the reader the impression that you are willing to change the decision; that will simply prolong the inevitable. Instead, you want to explain what the reader can do to cope with the bad news:

- When you deny someone credit, you can say that cash purchases are welcome.
- When you lay off employees, you can offer them employment counselling, severance packages, or assistance claiming employment insurance benefits.
- When you deny someone's request for an extended summer vacation, you can offer her the alternative of taking the time during the winter holiday season.
- If your business is out of stock on a hard-to-find product, customers will appreciate (and remember) your telling them where to find it.

Closing Closings in documents dealing with bad news are similar to those in routine messages. End by explaining what comes next:

- Some situations will require you to explain the various actions that the reader needs to take.
- In other cases, you may have to remind the reader what you will be doing and when.

TAKE IT FURTHER

Good News about Bad News

In a survey of 900 000 workers at 68 companies, 49 percent of the workers questioned between 1991 and 1995 said that they felt encouraged to report bad news to their managers. When asked the same question between 2001 and 2005, 65 percent of employees said they were encouraged to report negative information.[21]

Why do more than a third of businesses continue to discourage employees from reporting bad news?

TABLE 10-4 **Bad Endings**

Repeating the bad news	Once again let me remind you that we cannot . . .
Apologizing	I am deeply sorry that we could not . . .
Anticipating problems	If you are still not satisfied, you can . . .
Including insincere clichés	It's been a pleasure to . . .
Expressing doubt about the client's loyalty	I hope that this will not affect our future relations . . .

- At times, you may need to ask for additional communication with the reader, but do not end every bad news letter by inviting the reader to call.

- In many situations, one of your objectives in writing is to rid yourself of troublesome people. Inviting such people to call is counterproductive.

If the bad news is mild, and the reader is not likely to be upset, it may be appropriate to provide resale information about your company or its products. If, however, you have just refused to replace the motor on a customer's year-old sports car, it will be of little use to tell the reader about the many other fine products that your company has to offer.

All writing requires you to be sensitive to the feelings of the reader, and this is especially true when you are dealing with bad news. Try to end on as helpful a note as possible without being cheerful or overly pessimistic. **Table 10-4** suggests some wording you should avoid in endings.

Chapter Summary

Dealing with bad news can be difficult, but complaints and other negative information can provide useful feedback about a business's performance. Ignoring negative information not only will have an adverse affect on customer relations but will also take away opportunities to improve.

Complaints should follow the direct formula, beginning with a general statement expressing dissatisfaction, then listing the full details of the problem, and ending with a request for a solution.

Responses to valid complaints should also follow the direct formula, with an initial promise to resolve the problem, followed by details of how that will be accomplished.

You should take an indirect approach when rejecting complaints or giving other bad news that is likely to upset readers. Give carefully reasoned explanations, followed by a tactful statement of the bad news. Whenever possible, offer readers helpful alternatives. You should offer apologies only when you have done something wrong.

PEARSON
mycanadianbuscommlab Visit **www.mycanadianbuscommlab.ca** for everything you need to help you succeed in the job you've always wanted! Tools and resources include the following:

- Composing and The Writer's Toolkit
- Document Makeovers
- Video Case Studies
- Grammar exercises and much more!

Thinking and Writing Exercises

1. **Buffer or Not?**

   A buffer is a short but neutral statement that is some-times used to prepare the reader for the bad news that is coming. Discuss the need for buffers in the following situations:

   a. A client visited your office last month to inquire about a mortgage. At that time you told her that you were optimistic about being able to approve the paperwork once it was submitted. Since then market conditions have changed dramatically and your requirements have become much stricter. Do you use a buffer when informing her that you cannot approve her request?

   b. You need to send an email message to a customer telling him that the book he ordered is temporarily out of stock and delivery will be delayed for two weeks. Do you use a buffer?

   c. You need to send a customer a letter explaining why you are refusing to repair an electric razor that is still under warranty but had been plugged into a 240-volt outlet, which voided the warranty. Do you use a buffer?

   d. You need to send a rejection letter to three of the four candidates who made it through the second round of interviews for a new position in your business. Do you use a buffer?

2. **Closings for Messages**

   Write the closing line for each of the following messages.

   a. a letter refusing to replace a cellphone that was almost new but was dropped in a swimming pool, thus voiding the warranty

   b. a letter from an airline refusing a refund for a missed flight

   c. a letter to employees containing details of an unexpected layoff resulting from a weak economy

   d. a letter refusing to grant a line of credit to a customer whose business may be facing bankruptcy soon

   e. a letter rejecting a job applicant for a position as an administrative assistant; the applicant has several years of practical experience but no formal training for the position

   f. a letter refusing to grant a line of credit to a store owner in a company town in which the local sawmill will likely be closing in the next year

   g. a letter from an insurance company refusing to repair the damage that resulted from burst pipes that froze when a woman's furnace broke down while she was away on a two-week winter vacation

3. **The Bad News Boars**

   Wild boars were brought to Alberta in the 1990s to be farmed for meat and hunted for sport. Thousands of wild boars have since escaped and are running loose in Alberta. They are able to survive and reproduce in the Canadian climate.

   These non-native animals have destroyed crops and burrowed holes in the ground throughout southern Alberta. When cornered, they can be aggressive. Pork producers have expressed concerns that the wild boars could spread disease.

   In 2008, Alberta passed a law declaring wild boars that have escaped from game farms to be pests. Animals that stray from the property of their owners can be killed. No hunting licence is necessary, but the landowner's written permission is required. A $50 bounty has been offered for each feral pig that is killed. Landowners must now report and wipe out non-captive boars; otherwise provincial officials can kill the animals and send a bill to the landowner.[22]

   Not everyone welcomes such legislation. Informing other people presents numerous communication challenges. Answer the following questions based on Alberta's anti-boar law.

   a. Would it be more appropriate for the provincial government's announcement of the new legislation to follow a direct or indirect organizational strategy? Why?

   b. Assume that a boar rancher wants to decline a request from his neighbours to allow them on his land to hunt boars that have escaped from his pens. Should his response follow a direct or indirect organizational strategy? Why?

   c. Which of these opening lines would be most appropriate in a letter from the provincial government informing all farmers and large landowners of the new legislation?

   - Wild boars are aggressive, feral animals that were introduced to Alberta during the last decade.

   - The Government of Alberta has passed legislation requiring landowners to eradicate wild boars roaming loose on their property.

- Wild boars have the potential to spread disease to domestic pigs, posing the potential risk of a devastating livestock epidemic.

- Because of the irresponsible actions of a few game farmers, the Government of Alberta had no choice but to enact legislation requiring landowners to exterminate all feral wild boars.

d. Which of these would be the best opening line for a complaint from a landowner to a local wild boar rancher over damage caused by escaped animals?

- Your wild pigs are killing my horses.

- I had no problems with your game farm when it opened a few years ago, and since that time I have been pleased to see that it is becoming successful, but the boars that have escaped in the last few years have started to become a nuisance.

- I am sure that you are aware that the provincial government has ordered the destruction of all wild boars in the province.

- I am sorry to be the one to bring this to your attention, and I hope that I am not being too much of an inconvenience, but I think that I have seen a few of your escaped animals in my vegetable garden.

e. Which of the following lines would be an appropriate explanation and refusal for a game farm owner to use when replying to neighbours asking to come onto her land to shoot boars that have escaped from captivity?

- It is possible that some animals have escaped from my ranch and strayed onto your property after fences were cut by poachers. You have every right to exterminate those animals. I am concerned, though, for the safety of the clients who have booked the guest facilities of my ranch. Allowing unregulated hunting on my ranch would expose my guests to a significant degree of risk and so it is necessary to decline your offer.

- The provincial legislation does allow you to kill any boars that stray onto your property. There is, however, no legal obligation for me to allow hunters to trespass onto my ranch.

- Last month, my ranch played host to three different groups of guests who had come to hunt my boars. These clients bagged a total of nine

boars during their visits and brought close to $7000 to the local economy. It is unrealistic to expect my ranch to give up a lucrative source of income to provide complimentary game animals to local hunters.

- Wild boar has a sweet, nutty flavour that makes the meat much in demand by people who enjoy fine dining. It is no surprise to me that you would like to come onto my property to harvest this delicacy at no cost to you. Although I will gladly support local community functions with a donation of fresh meat, it will not be possible to open my land to unrestricted hunting.

f. Which of these would be appropriate alternatives that a game rancher could offer after refusing to allow unrestricted hunting on his land?

- We will continue diligently monitoring our fences and will now prosecute anyone found damaging our property.

- I will be happy to lend my assistance in helping exterminate any animals that have escaped from my property.

- If you want to hunt wild boar, you are welcome to register for one of our scheduled events. A price list is available on our website.

- Since the law has some obvious flaws, I will gladly offer my assistance in lobbying to have it changed.

4. **Sorry for My Pigs**

Assume that you are the owner of Wild Boar Game Ranch and Specialty Meats near Mayerthorpe, Alberta, a business that sells meat and offers hunters the opportunity to hunt boars that are released in a large, fenced-in area of dense bush. In recent years some boars have been released from your farm after fences were deliberately cut. You assume that this was done by people attempting to lure pigs from your compound so that they could hunt them without having to pay your outfitting fees.

Some of the escaped animals have caused significant damage to surrounding property. Write a letter to the owner of a neighbouring farm, apologizing for the damage caused by your escaped animals and offering to help prevent future occurrences. You may want to use information from question 3 and any of the relevant details found below:

- Your staff will join in any hunting parties to eradicate escaped animals living on neighbours' farms.

In 2008, Alberta declared wild boars to be a pest.

- The meat from such hunts will be dressed for free by Wild Boar Game Ranch and Specialty Meats.
- Fences will be inspected more often. Repairs to cut fences will be done as soon as they are discovered.
- Male wild boars can weigh up to 275 kilograms. They are aggressive and can be dangerous.
- Females can have yearly litters averaging nine piglets.
- They prefer to live in dense forest.
- You support the new law and believe that it will help eradicate feral pigs.

5. Refusing a Charity's Request

Assume that you are the manager of the Grand Dome Resort at Grand Beach Manitoba. Today you received a letter from Ivan Burlakow, director of the Manitoba Philanthropic Society, a prominent charity. He wants to use the resort as a site for his group's charity telethon. He sent the letter that appears on the following page.

You have a high regard for the Manitoba Philanthropic Society and for Mr. Burlakow. You cannot meet his request though. It is impractical for you to reopen your resort in the off-season simply to offer his group a giveaway, even if it is tax deductible. You are willing to give a reasonable donation or discount to a worthy cause, but Burlakow is asking for too much.

Write a tactful letter replying to him. You may use any of the information below to assist you, but you do not have to use all of it.

- The resort closes between September 31 and May 1 each year.
- Only a few maintenance workers remain during the winter.
- All seasonal kitchen and cleaning staff are laid off.
- It would cost too much to rehire workers for two or three days.
- Last year Burlakow was inducted into the Order of the Buffalo Hunt for his many years of charitable work, an award you felt he richly deserved.
- No food is left in the resort over the winter.
- Water in the resort is turned off in winter and access roads are not plowed.

The Manitoba Philanthropic Society
56433 Corydon Ave.
Winnipeg MB R3P 9S5

October 25, 2010

Sam Ateah, Manager
Grand Dome Resort
PO Box 23
Grand Beach MB R0E 0T0

Dear Mr. Ateah:

The Manitoba Philanthropic Society will be holding its annual charity telethon on February 15 next year. We would like to use the Grand Dome Resort for this two-day charity event. The telethon will be televised throughout Manitoba and will generate a great deal of publicity for your resort.

We selected your resort both because the scenic beauty of the dunes in the background will look good on television and because February is not likely a very busy time of year at Grand Beach. We are confident that you will be able to accommodate our group of about 50 staff and volunteers.

The Manitoba Philanthropic Society is run almost entirely by volunteers. Of every dollar donated, 95 goes directly toward assisting the victims of disaster and misfortune within the province. During the 1997 flood, we helped more than 100 families find much-needed accommodation. Now we are concentrating our efforts on improving the living conditions of inner-city residents of Winnipeg and Brandon. We expect that the annual telethon will help us meet our annual fundraising goal of $250 000.

We realize that it is too much to expect you to support the entire cost of running the telethon, but we hope that you will be able to provide us with accommodation and a hall in which to stage the show. The province-wide television exposure that we would generate in the two days would more than pay for the cost of the facilities we would use. In addition, we would purchase all our meals from your dining room. Since the resort is vacant at this time of year, our group should not be displacing other guests who might have wanted to book the resort.

I believe that this is a win-win situation for both the Manitoba Philanthropic Society and the Grand Dome Resort. You will obtain valuable publicity at no cost and a tax deduction for your expenses. We will have a place to operate our telethon. Please let me know by November 20 so that I can continue making arrangements.

Sincerely,
Ivan Burlakow
Ivan Burlakow
Director

- Some resorts do remain open all winter long to host conferences, retreats, and meetings. Moose Horn Resort in the Riding Mountains is one of them.
- You admire the work his organization has done. Your brother-in-law from Letellier received help during the flood of 1997.
- Grand Beach was once selected by *Playboy* magazine as one of the top ten beaches in the world.[23]
- You usually have your own vacation in February. This year you are planning a trip to Jamaica.
- Even if the resort were still open when they wanted to hold the telethon, you couldn't afford to give free accommodation to 50 people for a weekend.
- Free publicity for your resort in the middle of February is not likely to be that valuable to you. By the time summer begins, most people will have forgotten about it.
- This summer's cool and rainy weather was not good for beach resorts. You barely broke even and may be in financial difficulty if the weather is the same next year.
- You might be able to offer a reduced rate for future telethons if they are held during a quiet time of the year when the resort is just opening (early May).

- Grand Beach has three kilometres of white sand beaches and as many as 20 000 visitors during a warm summer day.

- You were able to assist other Manitoba charities last season. You hosted the events from the Pan-American Games and gave financial support to the United Way.

6. Modem Hijacking

Suppose that you live in a rural area in which the World Wide Web can be accessed only by using dial-up internet service. When your latest phone bill arrived, you noticed several long distance calls to a number that you could not identify and an extra charge of almost $100 on your bill. Further research indicated that the phone calls had been placed to Sao Tome, a tiny country off the west coast of Africa—one that you had never even heard of before this incident.

You emailed the customer service department of the Manitoba Phone Company (MPC). It offered the following advice: "The easiest way to prevent these types of calls is to make sure that when you are on a website, and it prompts you to accept or decline, accept only when you are 100 percent sure you will not be charged in any way." Attached to that reply was a copy of a dialogue box from a website labelled "Sexy Girls." That dialogue box carried a clearly worded warning that charges would be applied to the user's phone bill.

The response from MPC went on to say that your next month's bill would also contain a further $75 in charges from the same site that had not yet been recorded on this month's bill.

As you were reading this message, your telephone disconnected itself from the internet and began dialing the same number that had resulted in the earlier charges, all without any actions from you. To disconnect the modem from the computer, you had to shut down the computer. No dialogue boxes appeared at any time.

Write a letter to the customer service department of the Manitoba Phone Company, 56 Sparks Street, Winnipeg, MB, R3H 1J7. Ask that the excess charges be removed from your bill.

Your address is Box 1250, Pine Falls, MB, R0E 1M0.

Decide which of the following information should also be included in your letter. It is not necessary to use all the information:

- Express your concern about the customer service representative's assumption that you had been using your computer to view pornography.

- Your phone number is 204-555-2313. Your MPC account number is 45J345X.

- Insist that the customer service representative be disciplined for insensitivity.

- Ask that the access to the number in Sao Tome be blocked by MPC so that no more innocent customers receive the same fraudulent treatment.

- Request that other customers who had been similarly victimized also receive reimbursement.

- Suggest that a class action lawsuit from angry consumers could result in bad publicity and major losses to MPC.

7. Compensating a Customer's Hijacking Claim

As a customer service representative with the Manitoba Phone Company, you have been assigned to respond to the complaint described in question 6. You have been authorized to send a cheque for $175 to cover the charges incurred by the customer. Describe how the overbilling occurred and explain what the customer can do to prevent a reoccurrence.

Your address is Customer Service Department, the Manitoba Phone Company, 56 Sparks Street, Winnipeg, MB, R3H 1J7.

Here is the customer's information:

- The customer's address is Box 1250, Pine Falls, MB, R0E 1M0.

- The customer's phone number is 204-555-2313.

- The customer's MPC account number is 45J345X.

Decide which of the following information should also be included in your letter. It is not necessary to use all the information:

Facts about Dialer Programs

- Can cause the computer's modem to dial to internet service providers located overseas

- Can originate in such countries as Sao Tome, Nauru Republic, Madagascar, the Cook Islands, Tokelau, and New Zealand

- Are sometimes downloaded onto a user's computer through a program that changes a computer's settings

- Are sometimes installed without the users' knowledge or permission after users accept a service agreement for a different program

- Terms of agreement may not include any information about the secret dialer being installed

- Users are responsible for paying all long distance charges resulting from their computer activity, regardless of whether it was initiated from their direct actions

Preventative Measures

- Install anti-virus software and a firewall before accessing the internet.
- Consider the source and the potential risks before downloading and installing any software.
- Read all users' agreements and information on websites and pop-up boxes before clicking any Accept buttons.
- Protect yourself, since dishonest website operators shift locations and telephone numbers frequently.
- Monitor your modem while you are on the internet to ensure it does not disconnect and dial another number.
- Be aware that unscrupulous companies may not include any information about secret dialers being installed.
- Unplug your modem and restart your computer if you notice the modem trying to connect to an unfamiliar number.
- Consider connecting manually to the internet each time, instead of having the modem connect automatically.
- Remember that no anti-virus software or firewall is 100 percent effective.[24]

8. **Rejecting a Hijacking Claim**
   As a customer service representative with the Manitoba Phone Company, you have been assigned to respond to the customer's letter described in questions 6 and 7. MPC has decided that customers are responsible for all charges resulting from their computer activity. You have been told to explain how the modem began dialing a different number from what was originally entered and then to inform the customer about the steps that can be taken to prevent a reoccurrence. Express empathy for the customer's situation, but insist that the customer is responsible for all activity on his or her computer, including the $175 in calls made through the secret dialer.

9. **Writing a Real Complaint Letter**
   Write an actual letter of complaint to a hotel, a restaurant, a business, a government agency, or an educational institution. Explain why you are unsatisfied with the product or service that has been provided and ask for a fair resolution to the problem. Then send a copy to that organization.

   Wait one month, and then answer the following questions:

   a. What medium did you use to deliver your message: letter, email, website?
   b. Did you receive a response?
   c. If you received a response, did you receive an apology?
   d. If you received a response, did the organization offer a settlement or promise to resolve the problem?
   e. Are you satisfied with the response?
   f. Would you recommend the organization to other people?

   As a class, brainstorm any additional questions that you would like to know about the results of the letters. Then tabulate the results obtained by members of your class.

Writing Skills Checkup: Active and Passive Voices

PASSIVE VOICE

The passive voice emphasizes the action being performed rather than the person doing it. The passive voice has two main uses:

1. To present ideas objectively, showing that the results are more important than the person doing the work: "The surveys were tabulated."
2. To avoid using names or assigning blame: "An unfortunate error has occurred."

Construction of Passive Voice Sentences

a. Sentences in the passive voice begin with a thing rather than a person.
b. They use a two-word verb (*is* or *was* followed by a past-tense verb).
c. They sometimes end with a phrase starting with "by" that identifies the doer of the action.
d. "All decisions were approved by the manager."

ACTIVE VOICE

The active voice is preferred for most types of business writing because it is shorter, more personal, and more forceful.

   a. In active voice sentences, the subject of the verb performs the action.
   b. "I sold my mutual funds."
   c. "You made a mistake."

INSTRUCTIONS

Decide whether each of the following sentences uses the active or passive voice. Then decide whether you should change it from one to the other. Be prepared to justify your answer. When necessary, write down the revised version. An example is done for you:

> We cannot replace your cellphone under warranty because you left it in your car on a hot day and the temperature exceeded 50°C. (Active voice)

> Your cellphone cannot be replaced under warranty because it was left in a car on a hot day and the temperature exceeded 50°C. (Changed to passive voice to avoid placing blame)

1. I cannot approve your loan until you have provided us with collateral.
2. Someone left the window open last night and the cold killed all the plants.
3. We made a major error by spelling our client's name wrong in the contract.
4. The typing of the financial reports was done yesterday afternoon by the clerical staff.
5. You failed to submit the mortgage application before the first of the month.
6. We should not have gone to the expense of ordering laptop computers for the cleaning staff and cafeteria workers.
7. Even though hydroelectricity is generated from water, you should have known that using the hair dryer in the bathtub is dangerous.
8. We must delay filling your order because of problems with our supplier.
9. An additional payment of $45 is required before your order can be processed.
10. The graphics card was installed incorrectly on your computer.

Writing Instructions, Explanations, and Definitions

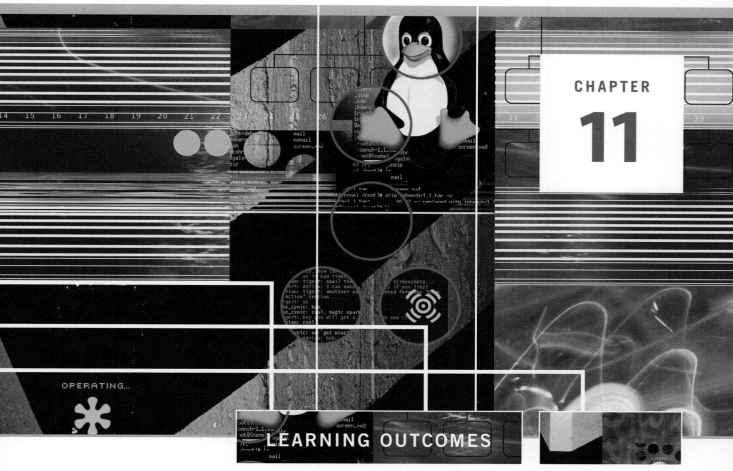

LEARNING OUTCOMES

After completing this chapter, you should be able to do the following:

11.1 Analyze the needs of audiences so that you can produce instructions that focus on users' needs rather than a product's features

11.2 Write simple instructions that are easy to follow

11.3 Identify and clarify the meaning of specialized terms or jargon

11.4 Submit instructions to members of a target audience for review before releasing them to all readers

✔•⎯[Practise] ## THE NEED FOR GOOD INSTRUCTIONS

Good instructions can save lives. Consider, for example, how clear instructions given over the phone by emergency personnel could help a parent save a child who has just swallowed poison and is waiting for an ambulance.

In everyday life, though, people do not always hold instructions in high regard. This is particularly obvious with instruction manuals, which people often do not bother to read at all—you can likely think of an example from your life. At times this happens for good reason. Many instructions are simply not needed and are included only to satisfy legal requirements or to protect against lawsuits. How many people, for example, read the instruction manual that comes with a toaster? If manufacturers left the instructions out, though, they could face legal challenges from every person who received a shock after using a fork to rescue a stuck piece of toast. Manufacturers, therefore, continue to include detailed instructions, written in several languages, explaining all the possible uses and abuses of their product.

Nevertheless, people need well-written explanations. Think of the number of times each day that you have to deal with instructions. From updating your computer's virus checker to clearing a paper jam on your photocopier, modern life often presents us with many different reasons to read instructions.

Instructions can be difficult to write. The fact that they are usually written for people who do not know how to do something means that writing a set of instructions requires even more planning than most documents. Think about the frustration you experienced the last time you read a set of instructions that contained errors, lacked vital information, was out of date, or was so badly translated that you could not understand what was required.

The purpose of this chapter is to help you write clear instructions that will provide people with the information that they need.

✱⎯[Explore] ## TYPES OF INSTRUCTIONS

The types of instructions you deal with every day vary greatly. This chapter does not detail all of them, but you should at least be familiar with some of the forms of instructions you will come across on a regular basis:

- Guidebooks contain suggestions for dealing with different situations.
- Operator manuals provide detailed instructions for operating equipment.
- Policy manuals list the rules that govern an organization.
- Reference manuals usually provide detailed information on hardware or software and are organized for quick reference.
- Service manuals are used by service technicians to fix problems.[1]
- Training manuals are designed to teach readers something new.
- User manuals contain instructions for specific procedures. They are organized in consecutive order, according to what the user can or must do.

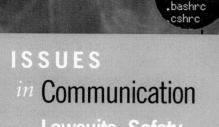

ISSUES
in Communication
Lawsuits, Safety Warnings, and Hazardous Coffee

In 1992 a woman in the United States sued McDonald's Restaurants after a cup of coffee that she was holding between her knees spilled on her lap while she was taking off the lid to add cream and sugar. After McDonald's refused to pay $20 000 for her hospital expenses, she sued and won an award of about $500 000. (The exact figure was never released.)

The case received a great deal of attention worldwide. Some people argued that she was holding the restaurant responsible for her carelessness. Others noted that McDonald's coffee at the time was served at a much hotter temperature than coffee sold by other restaurants or coffee made at home. Many other customers had experienced similar accidents.[2]

PRODUCT WARNINGS WITH QUESTIONABLE VALUE

After the accident and lawsuit, McDonald's and many other restaurants began serving their beverages at a less hazardous temperature and printing a notice on all cups: "Warning: Contents hot." Although the effect of reducing the temperature of the coffee is obvious, the benefits of the warning label may not be. Look at almost any product and you will see similar warnings pointing out what should be self-evident. We are warned not to use hair dryers in the shower, that beach toys are not life-saving devices, and that sleeping pills might affect our ability to drive. Numerous websites and contests have been created with the purpose of identifying the ever-more-foolish warnings that keep appearing as manufacturers go out of their way to protect themselves from lawsuits.

WARNINGS WITH POTENTIAL

Some warnings seem designed only to protect the manufacturers from frivolous lawsuits, but others have clearly proven their effectiveness. For example, the graphic pictures and warnings that are required on the front of all Canadian cigarette packages have had a positive impact. Smokers have said that the warning labels have prompted them to think about the consequences of their habit and to smoke less.[3] The success of such campaigns has caused some people to lobby for warning labels on liquor, wine, and beer about the dangers of drinking during pregnancy.

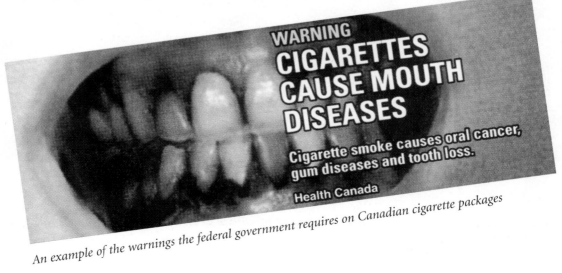

An example of the warnings the federal government requires on Canadian cigarette packages

MAKING WARNING LABELS EFFECTIVE

Labels that warn people about dangers can be useful, especially when the hazards may not be immediately obvious. If your company decides it needs a warning label and if you truly want it to be understood, consider these factors:

■ *Warnings must be easy to understand.* In this multicultural world, that might mean using pictures. Replace complicated terms (e.g., carcinogen) with simpler alternatives. Death may not be a pretty word, but it is easier to understand than "may produce adverse physical reaction."[4]

■ *Warnings must be practical.* They will be useless if it is impossible for people to carry out the actions that will ensure their safety. Consider, for example, that Canada has been criticized for selling asbestos to developing countries, at a time when the dangers associated with inhaling asbestos dust have led to a virtual halt in the use of asbestos within Canada. The government's defence that workers can avoid these dangers by wearing appropriate dust masks is impractical in countries where many industrial workers do not even wear shoes, let alone have access to dust masks.[5]

■ *Warnings must change people's behaviour.* They must be visible to users and last for the life of the product. They will not be useful if they are ignored. Placing a warning about the dangers of speeding on the speedometer of a high-powered sports motorcycle would not likely produce much of a change in a person's driving habits.

In the end people are usually held responsible for their own actions, but warnings that are well written and well placed can sometimes help protect people from their ignorance or carelessness.

These international symbols for safety equipment are intended to be understood easily by people who speak any language.

DISCUSSION

1. Was McDonald's justified in not offering to compensate the woman who spilled hot coffee on her lap? Are warnings placed on coffee cups an effective way to warn people about the danger of hot beverages?
2. Why do you think some car seat manufacturers came up with the idea of a sign that parents can hang in the car window to warn other drivers that babies are in the car? Do you think that such signs an effective safety measure?
3. Do you think that graphic warnings about the perils of a product, such as those found on cigarette packages, automatically reduce sales of the product?
4. Should beer, wine, and liquor containers carry warnings about the dangers of drinking during pregnancy?

TAKE IT FURTHER

You Put What? Where?!

These are actual warning labels people sent in to the Michigan Lawsuit Abuse Watch (M-LAW) Wacky Warning Label Contest:

- "Remove child before folding." (label on a baby stroller)
- "Harmful if swallowed." (brass fishing lure with a three-pronged hook on the end)
- "Do not use for personal hygiene." (flushable toilet brush)
- "Never force any body part into the backrest area while the rollers are moving." (a massage chair)[6]

Identify an example of a warning that you consider unnecessary. Explain why and see whether others in your class agree with you.

All these types of instructions serve different audiences and have different purposes, but they share certain characteristics: Good instructions concentrate on providing users with explanations of how they can accomplish certain tasks.

The key to planning any set of instructions is to identify the tasks that readers are likely to be doing and then to focus on meeting their needs. The two major areas of focus to choose from are (1) a product focus or (2) a user focus.

1. Product Focus

A product focus is seldom recommended. You may have encountered so-called *instructions* that simply describe a device without explaining its operation. A toaster may come with a sheet of paper that contains safety warnings, identifies the various buttons or controls, and shows the location of features that might be missed, such as crumb cleanout trays. This may be the only type of instructions the manufacturers provide. For a device as simple to operate as a toaster, a *product focus* approach may be sufficient. Most readers would find it unnecessary and possibly even insulting to read a guide telling them to place bread in the slot, set the doneness control, and press the toasting lever.

A product focus may be acceptable for explaining such straightforward devices as toasters, but the approach is not useful for explaining how to perform more detailed jobs. For example, you may have been frustrated at times by software that comes with instructions written with a product focus—a list describing the operation of each command or button but nothing that tells you how to do the task that you require.

Thank You for Explaining

The following quotations came from actual instruction manuals that users submitted to COREComm's Worst Technical Writing Contest:

- ■ "Type the field name Name in the Field Name field."
- ■ "To undo undo please do please do redo."
- ■ "Use non-gender-specific language. Keep in mind that a reader may be both male and female."

Find a confusing line from a set of instructions that you have read. How could it be made clearer? ■

2. User Focus

A user focus is usually recommended. Unless the operation you are writing about is self-evident (e.g., loading a toaster), every list of instructions that you write should have a *user focus*.

The instructions should (1) anticipate the various tasks that someone will need to perform and then (2) provide a sequential list of the operations needed to accomplish those goals.

As an example, consider how to write the instructions for a word-processing program: One section will describe how to start a new document, and the instructions will include such topics as saving the file in a particular format and selecting a template to apply. To perform any of the tasks that the program covers, readers need to choose commands from a variety of program menus—actions that you could not explain simply by listing the options that each menu item provides.

Instructions for completing an expense account will tell you what information needs to be included, how it needs to be submitted, and what specific documents need to accompany the paperwork.

WRITING INSTRUCTIONS

At some time you will need to explain to someone how to fill in an expense account or install some software. The instruction-writing process has several stages. The major ones are planning and structure.

Planning

The planning process for a list of instructions requires you to make decisions about (1) ideas, (2) words, and (3) media, just as you would for any other documents that you prepare. Note that you will not necessarily face these decisions in the sequence described below—the decisions you make in one area will often affect decisions in other areas.

1. What to Say (Ideas) When you are deciding what information to include in a set of instructions, you need the following:

- ■ a clear reason for your communication
- ■ a good idea of what the audience already knows about the subject, so that you are not providing them with unnecessary information or assuming they know things that have not been explained

Write down the purpose of your instructions and any preliminary requirements or materials needed. Then make a list of all the steps required to accomplish that purpose. If you are explaining a process, go through the required actions step by step. Take careful notes as you do so. As you are planning your instructions, ask yourself whether you are assuming that your audience knows any required information that has not been provided.

For example, a bank that is providing instructions on completing a loan application to corporate customers who are already familiar with the process might include such a line as this: "Send appropriate new account documentation to client file administration." However, instructions for small businesses or individual consumers would require a more detailed explanation of what is meant by "appropriate new account documentation."

2. How to Say It (Words) To make it as easy as possible for people to follow your instructions, remember the following:

- Keep your terms as uncomplicated as possible. Aim for specific wording— for example, do not say *several* when *four or five* is more accurate.

- Keep your terminology consistent. You may know that *computer screen*, *monitor image*, and *display* can refer to the same thing, but someone new to using computers might not realize that. Pick one term that explains your idea clearly and do not look for synonyms.

- Explain any terms that may be new or unclear to the audience. If your instructions are long, you may find it best to include a glossary.

How to Say It (Pictures) Because many people who should read the instructions do not do so until they are in trouble, one of your main tasks is to find a presentation style that makes the instructions easy to follow yet is brief.

Some assembly guides have managed to accomplish this task with pictures alone and no text. Although this is an admirable approach for writing a guide to assembling a bookcase, pictures alone may not be practical for explaining to employees how to prepare a month-end inventory report.

Pictures can be a helpful addition to many types of instructions, though. When they are included, pictures should be easy to view and up to date. Illustrations should include a caption and the relevant parts should be labelled. If the procedure that you are explaining relates to computer use, you can capture a screen shot with a few keyboard strokes or mouse clicks.

3. How to Send It (Media) Technology provides you with numerous ways to convey a set of instructions:

- written on paper
- delivered through different computer formats
- transmitted orally
- shown in videos

Each method has strengths and weaknesses, as **Table 11-1** demonstrates. Some media offer advantages that may not be immediately obvious. For example, walk through the aisles of a store that sells cookbooks and notice how many of these are spiral bound. Cooks find that form of binding useful because it allows a book to stay open when placed on a counter

---

TAKE IT FURTHER

Tying a Tie

A simple web search using the phrase "how to tie a tie" produces more than 100 000 hits, most of them containing either still pictures or video. It is possible to write instructions on tying a tie without using pictures, but visuals make the document easier to write and simpler to follow.

Without using visuals, try writing instructions on tying a tie (or a shoelace). Then test them on a classmate.

TABLE 11-1	Choosing How to Convey Instructions	
Option	**Strengths**	**Weaknesses**
On paper	The medium is familiar to most audiences; people can view the instructions without needing additional equipment.	Long paper-based instruction manuals can be expensive to duplicate, revise, and distribute.
On a website	Websites can offer extra features, such as hyperlinks and video, that can provide readers with supplementary information (and businesses with additional sales opportunities).	Readers need a computer and internet access.
Oral explanation	When working directly with someone, this can allow for a two-way exchange of information.	Two-way exchange is not always possible with large audiences, and presentations may change when repeated at different times.

and reduces the space taken up since the pages can be pulled behind the needed recipe.

Options in action   Often, you will need to tell people that they can choose the medium in which they receive their instructions.

Suppose, for example, that you are working for a health insurance provider and you need to explain to your clients how they can receive information about their personal accounts.

Your initial contact with new clients would most likely be in the form of a letter describing their options. These would probably include (1) calling a toll-free number, (2) receiving information by mail, or (3) logging on to a secure website.

Explaining the mail or telephone options would not likely require much more than giving the contact information and telling the audience to have their account numbers handy.

Explaining the process of setting up a confidential account could be more detailed, especially if the intended audience is unfamiliar with web-based tools. In addition to telling them the log-in address and reminding them to have their account numbers with them, it might be necessary to give them a systematic explanation of the steps required to set up an account. Showing pictures of the various screens could also be useful.

Structure

A helpful way to face the task of writing instructions is to consider that the basic form is often the same as for many other kinds of writing: (1) beginning, (2) middle, and (3) end.

1. Introductions   Many instructions follow a pattern that begins with an introduction containing general information about the operation: why it needs to be done, when, and by whom. Along with this information will be preparatory information, lists of required materials, and warnings and safety measures.

General information about the operation   People have very specific objectives for reading instructions—they generally do not read them out of interest or enjoyment. For this reason, you should begin by telling readers exactly what they can accomplish by completing the instructions.

A good example is the following statement, which appears in the Microsoft Word help guide, in a section entitled "Open a Word 2007 Document in an Earlier Version of Word":

> By using the Compatibility Pack for the 2007 Office system, you can open, edit some items, and save Office Word 2007 documents in previous versions of Word.[7]

After reading that introductory material, readers should have enough information to know if they are attempting the correct operation or whether they should look for information elsewhere.

Warnings   If the procedure involves any danger, whether to the reader or other people, or possible damage to equipment, you should give a clear warning at the beginning of the document. You should then repeat the information at the point where the cautionary note applies.

Three levels of warnings are commonly used. See **Table 11-2.**

2. Step-by-Step Instructions   Your instructions should follow a strict chronological order, organized into a list of numbered steps. Each step should contain enough information for the reader to be able to carry out the necessary action without referring to the instructions. But do not make steps so short that readers will need to read two or three actions for one step. The instructions in **Table 11-3** show a good and bad way of dealing with the same information.

TABLE 11-2   **Three Levels of Warning, from Most to Least Important**

Warning	Description	Example
1. Danger	Warns of hazards to people	Danger! Do not open this cover. This component contains an electrical charge that is dangerous even when the capacitor is disconnected from a power source.
2. Caution	Indicates the presence of potential threats that could damage equipment	Caution: Disabling the firewall will make the computer vulnerable to viruses.
3. Note	Reminds readers of information they might otherwise miss	Note: To qualify for preferred parking, carpools must be made up of three to six employees.

✔•─Practise

TABLE 11-3	Instructions for Locking a Door	

Bad (Too Many Steps)	Good (Sufficient Steps)
1. Insert the key in the lock.	1. Insert the key in the lock and turn it to the right until the cylinder clicks. Then, turn it back to the starting position and remove the key from the lock.
2. Turn the key to the right until the cylinder clicks.	
3. Turn the key back to the starting position.	
4. Remove the key from the lock.	
5. Check to see whether the lock is secure.	2. Always check that the lock is secure before moving to a different door.

It is usually best to avoid going to the opposite extreme and writing the instructions in the form of one long paragraph, as shown under the "Avoid" example in **Table 11-4.**

Be sure though that each step of the instructions contains an action that must be performed and not just a description of the result. With the "Good" example in **Table 11-4**, it would be an error to include this line as step 8: "The

Instructions should be short and numbered in correct order.

TABLE 11-4	Registration Information (Long and Short)
Avoid	**Use**
Online Registration Procedures	Online Registration for Courses at Regional Campuses
1. Go to the website of the campus that you want to attend. Our downtown campus specializes in business and computer-related courses, our suburban campuses teach trades and engineering programs, and our rural outlets offer a limited selection from several areas. From the list that is provided, select the program in which you are interested. To read a description of the course, click the button from the menu on the left side of the screen. Do not make any selections until you have ensured that a program of study is appropriate for you. Review the course's description and prerequisites. Applications will not be accepted for courses in which the prerequisites have not been met. Review the dates and times the course is offered by clicking "Availability by Term" from the menu on the left side of the screen.	To browse and then register online for a regional campus course, follow these steps: 1. Go to the regional campus website of your choice. 2. From the list of programs, select the program that interests you. 3. Click "Course Descriptions" from the menu on the left side of the screen. 4. Find the course you are interested in taking and review its description and prerequisites. Make sure that you have met all the requirements before selecting any courses. 5. Click "Availability by Term" from the menu on the left side of the screen to see the courses being offered by the regional campus. 6. Review the dates and times the course is offered.
2. Click "Register" for the class that you are interested in and follow the instructions on the new page.	7. Click "Register" for the class that you are interested in and follow the instructions on the new page.

registration page allows you to reserve a space in a course and explains your payment options."

Considering the details The more complicated the topic and the less sophisticated the audience, the more necessary a detailed list of instructions becomes. "Detail" in this case means including pictures, specific measurements, definitions of complicated terms, and anything that will reduce the amount of guesswork required by the reader.

As you go through the procedure, look for ways to divide the information into shorter sections. It is far less daunting for readers to deal with instructions that contain 4 sets of 5 steps than to have to deal with a single block of 20 steps. This method will allow readers to monitor their progress and to take breaks in between phases of the operation.

Surprises have no place in instructions. At every step of the procedure, readers should know exactly what to expect. If there is a possibility that the outcome of an action is unclear, be sure to explain it. For example, if you were explaining how to save a link to a webpage, you might tell readers to

1. Click *Favorites*.
2. Click *Add to Favorites*.
3. Click the button labelled *Add*.

TAKE IT FURTHER

Why Didn't You Say That the First Time?

Swedish researchers found that nurses performed a new administrative procedure faster and with fewer errors when their instruction manuals were rewritten to include shorter sentences written in the active voice and with less computer jargon and a more task-oriented approach.[8]

What else can writers do to improve user manuals and to ensure that people read them?

You would follow that with an explanation that a link to the site has been saved for future use.

Be sure to justify any actions that readers may be tempted to skip or whose purpose may be unclear. This is especially true if neglecting the instructions could result in danger to people or damage to equipment.

3. Conclusions   In the concluding section of your instructions—if you need one—provide readers with information about what comes next. If the operation is complete and if the results are self-evident, you may not need anything further. At other times you may need to describe the finished result and explain the readers' options. If the instructions are one phase of a larger set of instructions, you may need to summarize the results of one phase and show how it relates to the next. If the instructions are complicated and others have experienced problems in the past, you may need to include a troubleshooting section or answers to frequently asked questions.

Testing the Completed Instructions

People who write instructions usually (but not always) have a clear understanding of the operation being performed. At times you may be asked to write instructions for something that you do not know well, but even under those circumstances, by the time the instructions are completed, you will have repeated the operation so many times that you will be an expert on the procedure.

Having a high level of expertise can be a problem. Actions that may seem obvious to an expert may not be as straightforward to a beginner. That is why instructions cannot be considered truly complete until they have been tested by users. Ideally, the people selected to do the testing should be very much like the audience for the completed instructions. They should not be people who are already familiar with the product or procedure.

Testing in Action   Ask the test audience to follow the instructions and to note any parts where they found the instructions confusing or ambiguous or where they would have liked to see further information.

For example, if you have written instructions for performing a computer-based procedure, you may have abbreviated the words *yes* and *no* to "Y" and "N," only to find that some readers find the abbreviations unnecessary or confusing. Clarifying such potential problems is far easier during the revision stages than after the instructions have been circulated.

When you have revised your instructions based on the testers' criticism, try the instructions again with a different audience. It is far easier to correct problems for a limited audience than to have to deal with the confusion caused when poorly written information is distributed to a much larger audience.

Figure 11-1 shows instructions that you could present to a test audience.

| **FIGURE 11-1** | **A Guide to Conducting a Focus Group** |

A Guide to Conducting a Focus Group

Focus groups are a form of structured interview conducted with eight to ten participants. They can be an effective way to evaluate new ideas and are frequently used by marketers to assess the public's opinions of new products or advertising campaigns. Focus groups are also frequently used during election campaigns as a quick measure of candidates' effectiveness.

This guide explains how to conduct the three phases of a focus group: planning the session, facilitating the meeting, and analyzing the results.

> The introduction explains the purpose of the instructions, provides a brief definition, and gives an overview of the contents.

Planning the Session

1. Decide what information you require and identify the objective of the interviews.
2. Develop five or six open-ended questions that will assess the group's opinion on the issue. Be careful to use neutral wording.
3. Schedule the session at a time that is likely to be convenient for all participants. Sessions take between one and two hours.
4. Select group members who can give you the information you need. Members should have some common characteristics: such as familiarity with a product, interest in a political campaign, or membership in a specific organization. Try to select members who do not know one another.
5. Plan to hold the session in a convenient location for all group members, like a conference room. Send invitations to the members several days in advance, along with an explanation of your purpose and a brief agenda.
6. Prepare the conference room. Order refreshments for the participants, and arrange to have the session recorded.
7. Choose a facilitator who will keep the discussion focused on the questions and will not allow one person to dominate the discussion. The facilitator should not be a person who has authority over the participants.

> Each numbered point is an imperative sentence (it gives a command). Short related points are grouped together.

Facilitating the Meeting

1. Begin with an introduction that explains what a focus group is, the purpose of the meeting, and its length, and give brief introductions of all participants. Mention that the focus group will be taped to ensure that comments are recorded accurately.
2. Ask the first question. Make sure that each person is allowed a chance to speak. Use a round-table approach, with each person receiving a minute to discuss the question, before calling on the next person. Try to draw out the quieter members, and do not allow interruptions.
3. Follow this process with the other questions. Try to keep the discussion from wandering from the topic. If one or two people are dominating the discussion, ask one of the other members a direct question.
4. Stick to the time limits. At the end of the session thank the participants, and tell them how the information will be used. If you will be providing them with a copy of the completed report, tell them when it will be available.

> Headings are used to identify distinct phases of the instructions. Numbering begins at one after each heading.

Analyzing the Results

1. Immediately after the meeting, note any unusual events, such as equipment failures or unexpected behaviour from any of the participants.
2. Listen to the tape of the meeting and summarize the participants' answers.
3. Analyze the summaries by looking for trends in the participants' opinions. Note any unexpected comments.
4. Write the report. Explain the purpose of the focus group, include the questions and a summary of the responses, and write a conclusion that explains the significance of the information.

> Each step is explained in a complete sentence, with the function words left in place.

These sample instructions explain how to conduct focus groups, a procedure that is commonly used in business.

Sources: McNamara, Carter. "Basics of Conducting Focus Groups." Free Management Library. 1997. Web. 20 Aug. 2009; and "Conducting a Focus Group." Lehigh University. Web. 20 Aug. 2009.

The Principles of Writing Clear Instructions

The following principles will help you to present your instructions in a way that is likely to be understood.

- Maintain a strict chronological order for any instructions that you write. Always perform the actions yourself, and keep careful notes of the precise order of the operations.

▨ Write each step of your instructions by using commands.

Commands   Commands (also known as imperative sentences) have these advantages over other writings styles:

▨ Commands are an easy way to get your point across unambiguously. They are clear. They start with verbs. Sentences that begin with verbs are the most efficient way to tell people to do something. Consider the following sentence:

"The names and phone numbers of all temporary workers should be recorded in the folder near the telephone at the front desk. This will facilitate finding replacement workers when necessary."

▨ Is this telling the reader to write down the contact information for temporary workers so that others can use it? Or is it telling the reader that this is where the information can be located when he or she needs to call in a substitute? Or both? The instructions are ambiguous. Compare that version with the same idea expressed as a command.

"Record the names and phone numbers of all temporary workers in the folder located near the telephone at the front desk. Consult this list when calling in replacements for absent workers."

▨ Commands can be delivered quickly and efficiently. Compare these two sentences:

"It is important that employees make sure that this door gets locked at 10 p.m."

"Lock this door at 10 p.m."

The information is the same in both cases, but the second one is much clearer.

Tips   Bear in mind the following tips for commands:

1. *Do not omit function words (articles, conjunctions, and prepositions).* Although shorter is often better, brevity should not be achieved by sacrificing clarity. Function words, such as *and*, *the*, and *for*, indicate how one word relates to another, serving as the glue that holds sentences together. Compare these two sentences. The first one (labelled a.) has been written with few function words. Although it is shorter, it is also much harder to understand. (The function words have been underlined in both sentences.)

   a. To place long distance call, dial 9 for outside line. Dial 1 plus number. At tone, enter four-digit password.

   b. To place a long distance call, dial 9 to connect to an outside line. Then dial 1 plus the number. At the tone, enter your four-digit password.

2. *Tell readers what to expect.* Explaining the results of each action will justify any that may be unclear. For example, in a guide for calling in temporary workers, you may have to explain that three or four calls may be needed

to find one worker who is able to come in. Some workers may be available only for specific times. Union regulations may require that some workers be given precedence over others, so an explanation of how to determine which workers should be called first may be helpful.

3. *Organize your instructions into sections so that readers can chunk the information. Chunking* means grouping small bits of information into related sections to make it easier to understand. Telephone numbers facilitate chunking with a three-digit area code, a three-digit exchange prefix, and four additional digits, which is easier to remember than ten distinct digits. Books use chapters, headings, and paragraphs to accomplish the same purpose.

   You can also use bullets and numbers to chunk large blocks of material into shorter sections. (See Chapter 8.) When you are writing instructions, use numbers to indicate actions that must be followed in sequence; use bullets to indicate lists of items. If your instructions involve a long procedure, use section headings to identify each phase of the operation and restart the numbering at the beginning of each new section.

   Your instructions will be easier to understand if you group the information into logical phases, such as *preparation, assembly, operation,* and *maintenance.*

4. *Use parallel construction.* Your instructions will be easier to understand if they follow a consistent pattern. Usually, this means writing each step of the instructions as a command.

Table 11-5 contains two versions of instructions for multiplying two numbers by using a spreadsheet. Notice how much easier it is to understand the parallel version.

TABLE 11-5   **Parallel versus Non-parallel Instructions**

Not Parallel	Parallel
Please follow these instructions to multiply two numbers.	These instructions explain how to set up an equation that multiplies two numbers.
1. The first number should be entered in cell A1. Then the ENTER key should be pressed.	1. Click on cell A1, type the first number to be multiplied, and press ENTER.
2. After entering a second number in A2, you can move to cell A3 to create an equation that will multiply these two numbers.	2. Put the second number in cell A2, followed again by ENTER.
3. All equations start by clicking on =.	3. Click on A3, and press = to begin the equation.
4. Then click on cell A1.	4. Click on the number you entered in A1.
5. The multiplication sign is *.	5. Type * to enter the multiplication command.
6. Clicking on A2 again will put the second number into the equation.	6. Click again on A2 to enter the second number of the equation.
7. If you press ENTER again at this point the equation will be completed and the product of the two numbers will appear in A3.	7. Press ENTER to complete the equation. The product of the two numbers will be shown in A3.

The parallel version follows a consistent pattern in which each step of the instructions is written with a consistent pattern.

WRITING EXPLANATIONS

Sometimes you will need people to understand why or how something happens without presenting them with step-by-step instructions on how to deal with every aspect of the situation.

Guidebook

A guidebook contains explanations that may not always need to follow a sequential pattern. If, for example, you are writing a guide to accompany an emergency kit for people to carry in their trunks during extreme weather conditions, it would be far more important to make sure that all the necessary items were listed and to explain their purpose than to put the information in the guidebook into step-by-step instructions.

Instead, the guide would explain some of the general principles for dealing with various roadside emergencies: accidents, vehicle breakdowns, and cold weather emergencies. A section on being stuck in the winter might provide techniques for freeing a stuck vehicle, explain why people should stay with a stuck vehicle, and tell how candles could be used as an alternative to running the car to preserve heat.

Some parts of the guide would, of course, need to follow the same pattern as other types of instructions. Explaining how to use booster cables or emergency flairs, for example, would require readers to follow a specific set of operations.

Readers Select

Many other guides contain non-sequential aspects in which readers need to select only those sections that apply to their circumstances.

For example, guides for choosing a location for a retail outlet, orienting new employees to company procedures, or for reducing energy consumption around the office will contain a variety of techniques that will not apply to every situation. Readers must be familiar with the big picture and be prepared to select those parts of the guide that they can apply to their unique circumstances.

In these situations, you should begin with an introduction that explains the ultimate goal and presents any theory that may need to be explained first. The subsections that follow the introduction will explain the various approaches that readers need to consider when choosing the best way of reaching their goal.

WRITING DEFINITIONS

When people hear the word *definitions,* the first thing they think of is a dictionary. Certainly a dictionary is the obvious tool when it is necessary to find the meaning of an unfamiliar word. Writing definitions, though, is also necessary

The Benefits Agency is always willing to be flexible...but only under certain limited clearly defined circumstances

The way that terms are defined makes a big difference in how people interpret documents.

in business writing. Words frequently take on specialized meanings that go beyond those listed in many dictionaries.

In the world of computers, for example, such words as *menu* and *virus* have acquired meanings that are different from their everyday meanings.

Importance

Before any commercial transactions can take place, all people involved must agree on the terms of any deal. Business would stop if contracts and agreements did not include definitions, some of which can sometimes extend for pages.

Under some circumstances, even words that normally require no definition must be explained with great precision to avoid disagreements. In a rental agreement, for example, it is necessary to define *maintenance,* so that there is no confusion between the obligations of the tenant and the landlord. A clear definition allows all people involved to know who is responsible for cleaning specific areas; who must perform minor repairs, such as fixing leaking faucets; and who must do other work, such as painting or carpet cleaning. Without a precise definition of *maintenance*, both landlord and tenant would be able to argue that the work was the responsibility of the other side.

Other legal agreements require the same precision with language. A contract between workers and management must define *permanent employees* and *temporary workers*; a product warranty must define *defective*.

Special Needs for Business Definitions

When used in business writing, definitions are not simply used to clarify the terms of contract. Business, like any other field, has its own technical terms that need to be explained. Not all readers will readily know such terms as *holdback, tariffs,* and *perquisite*, so providing clear definitions is an important part of the writing process.

Definitions vary in complexity. See **Table 11-6.**

The decision of which type of definition to include (or even whether to include one) will depend on the purpose of the document and the needs of the audience who will be reading it. Definitions are used, of course, when it is necessary to explain unfamiliar terms to your audience, but they are also used when words are being used in a specialized manner.

TABLE 11-6 **Definition Choices**

Type of Definition	Explanation	Example
Parenthetic	Explains the meaning by using a word or short phrase set in parentheses	The records were audited (checked) every six months.
Formal	Sentence-length explanation similar to one in a dictionary	Capitalism is an economic system based on the private ownership of property and by competition in a free market.
Extended	Detailed explanation that may continue for several pages	Bankruptcy is a "legal procedure for liquidating a business (or property owned by an individual) which cannot fully pay its debts out of its current assets. Bankruptcy can be brought upon itself by an insolvent debtor (called 'voluntary bankruptcy') or it can be forced on court orders issued on creditors' petition (called 'involuntary bankruptcy'). Two major objectives of a bankruptcy are (1) fair settlement of the legal claims of the creditors through an equitable distribution of debtor's assets, and (2) to provide the debtor an opportunity for a fresh start. Bankruptcy amounts to a business-failure, but voluntary winding up does not."

Source for bankruptcy definition: BusinessDictionary.com. *WebFinance, Inc. n.d. Web. 14 Dec. 2008.*
"Entry for bankruptcy."

TABLE 11-7	Examples of Sentence Definitions	
Term	**Class**	**Differences**
A *perquisite*	is an employee benefit	given in addition to salaries and may include medical insurance, pension plans, company cars, and club memberships.
A *holdback*	is part of the payment to a contractor	that is retained by a customer until the job is finished to the customer's satisfaction.
An *annuity*	is a series of payments	made at specified intervals and guaranteed for a fixed number of years or the lifetime of the recipient.

The language used in the definition must be appropriate to the readers. If the audience needs a dictionary to understand the words used in the definition, the purpose of a definition is defeated.

Sentence definitions usually have three parts:

1. They begin with the term that is being defined.
2. That term is put into a class of related items.
3. An explanation is given of how the term is different from other items in the same class.

See **Table 11-7** for concrete examples of sentence definitions.

Tips for Writing Effective Definitions

1. Do not write circular definitions in which any form of the word being defined is part of the explanation.

   BAD: *Encryption* is the process of keeping information secret by encrypting data.

   BETTER: *Encryption* is the process of scrambling data so that it can be read only with the use of a key that decodes the information.

2. Do not use the introductory statement "is when" when defining a word.

   BAD: A *franchise* is when one company leases the rights to another's trademarks and operating processes.

   BETTER: A *franchise* is a leasing arrangement in which one company leases the rights to another's trademarks and operating processes.

3. Do not make your definition so narrow that it excludes information.

   BAD: *Government revenue* is money that the government receives from taxes. (This definition leaves out many sources of government income.)

   BETTER: *Government revenue* is money that the government receives from taxes, duties, fines, royalties, investment income, and other sources.

4. Do not make your definition so broad that it includes items that are not part of the class.

BAD: *Bandwidth* is a term used to describe the capacity of communications media. (This definition would also include communication media, such as notepads or film cameras, that do not measure capacity in bandwidth.)

BETTER: *Bandwidth* is a term used to describe the capacity of electronic communications media or computer networks.

5. Do not use language in your definition that readers would not understand.

BAD: *Telecommuting* is the substitution of telecommunications networks for transportation in a decentralized work arrangement.

BETTER: *Telecommuting* is the process of working at home, using a computer terminal and telephone linked to one's place of employment.

Chapter Summary

Providing people with clear instructions is a vital part of business. Good instructions focus on meeting the needs of the intended users. When planning instructions, writers have to make a careful analysis of the task involved and then divide the explanation into a sequence of short steps presented in a strict chronological order.

Language should be as simple as possible without being condescending. Instructions should be presented in the form of commands to make them short and easy to follow.

Explanations can be organized in a variety of ways, but the needs of the audience must always be considered when deciding what to explain and how much detail to include.

Definitions are used in business not only to explain things but also to clarify agreements. Definitions can range in length from a single word to several pages.

PEARSON mycanadianbuscommlab Visit www.mycanadianbuscommlab.ca for everything you need to help you succeed in the job you've always wanted! Tools and resources include the following:

- Composing and The Writer's Toolkit
- Document Makeovers
- Video Case Studies
- Grammar exercises and much more!

Thinking and Writing Exercises

1. **Collecting Examples of Poorly Written Instructions**
Obtain an example of instructions that you consider to be badly written. These instructions can be about anything at all: assembling toys, repairing a car, filling in a form, operating computer software, or installing some equipment. They may come from anywhere you choose: from the internet, accompanying a product or software, or purchased separately.

Identify the features that make the instructions bad. Then explain what needs to be done to improve them.

2. Revising a Policy on Using Cellphones While Driving
Rewrite this policy on using cellphones and two-way radios in company vehicles. The revised version should be shorter and clearer:

> Driving is currently the leading cause of fatalities in the Canadian oil and gas industry and we, the Senior Leadership Team in Canada, are committed to the safety of those that work for and with us. In Canada, we operate approximately 550 company vehicles on all types of roads and in all kinds of conditions so our risk exposure is high. One of the serious traffic safety problems in society is distractions while behind the wheel. In response, and to lead by example, the Senior Leadership Team has implemented important changes to our company-wide policy on the use of communication devices while driving. This policy is effective immediately.
>
> Policy: The use of any electronic communication device, including two-way radios, is prohibited while in urban areas or challenging driving environments. The use of properly installed hands-free devices and two-way radios is permitted for non-urban areas. In declared emergency situations an unaccompanied driver may use a cellphone/radio outside the restrictions of this policy.

3. Using Tax Software
Revise the following set of instructions for completing an income tax return by using tax preparation software:

> Install the software onto your computer and enter the code required to activate the program. The program will allow only a limited number of tax returns to be prepared. You must be connected to the internet in order for the software to be activated or the data to be sent to the Canada Revenue Agency. When your return is complete and you are filing it electronically by using NETFILE, you will need to enter the four-digit access code that is provided by the Canada Revenue Agency. Make sure that you have all your receipts available before you begin. Follow the on-screen instructions for entering personal and financial information into the program. You will be prompted to enter personal information—such as your name, address, and social insurance number—followed by information about your income taken from the receipts issued by your employer or financial institution. Also found on these information slips will be other financial information, such as union dues and Canada Pension Plan deductions. Information about your various deductions, tuition, health care expenses, and charitable donations will also be required. If you are filling in a return as part of a family, some of these may be transferred to a spouse or other family member. The program may offer suggestions to help you receive the optimum refund on your return. Depending on which province or territory you live in, there will be variations on the provincial or territorial taxes and tax deductions that apply to you. The program will lead you through the options.

4. Setting Your Email to Forward Automatically
Many colleges and universities assign an email account to students when they enrol. However, many students prefer to use their personal email accounts instead. If the institution sends emails only to the accounts that they have assigned, students who do not check their accounts may miss messages from the institution.

The solution for those who do not want to use their institutional account is to have messages forwarded to their personal accounts. Some people do not know how to do this, and so your job is to explain the procedure to them.

Check to see if your school account has the ability to forward email to other accounts. If so, first learn the process, and then write a set of instructions that explains to other students how they can set this up and avoid having to check both accounts.

5. Registering a Charity for Income Tax Purposes
Assume that you work for a community action group that helps other groups organize their charitable endeavours. Some of your clients have been involved in activities that may allow them to register as a charitable organization for income tax purposes. Many of these people are daunted by the procedures required to register their groups with the Canada Revenue Agency. (The application form is 12 pages long and the detailed instructions are 24 pages.)

Your task is to write a simplified version of these instructions that is about two pages long. All your clients have good hearts and a generous spirit, but many of them have limited education or a poor understanding of English, and so they are counting on you to explain the procedure in simple terms. Your finished product will not, of course, replace the longer version, but it should help your clients decide whether they should devote the time and expense needed to complete the application process.

a. Go to the Canada Revenue Agency's website (www.cra-arc.gc.ca) and download the application form "Application to Register a Charity under the Income Tax Act" and the document "Registering a Charity for Income Tax Purposes."

- After reading them, write short definitions of both registered charity and non-profit organization. Be sure to explain the differences between the two so that applicants can decide which category, if either, their group belongs to.

- Briefly explain the benefits that will come to their group from being accepted as either a non-profit organization or a registered charity.

b. Write a condensed version of the instructions provided by the Canada Revenue Agency, reducing them to a page or two.

6. **Explaining the Job Futures Website**
Write two sets of instructions for obtaining information from Service Canada's Job Futures website: www.jobfutures.ca/en/home.shtml.

a. The first instructions will be for people who are like you and have already chosen a career path similar to your own.

- Explain how to browse through an alphabetical list of job categories.

- Explain how to interpret the results in each of four categories: hourly earnings, work prospects, unemployment rate, and training required.

b. The other instructions are intended for people who have not yet chosen a career and are using the site to explore career possibilities.

- Explain how to choose a career path based on a person's education.

- Explain how to take a quiz to narrow career possibilities.

7. **Writing a Guide for Extending the Life of Laptop Batteries**
Assume that you work for an organization that issues many of its workers laptop computers. A common complaint that comes from those who are using laptops is that the batteries last only a year or so and then must be replaced—at a cost of about a hundred dollars each.

You know that they should last longer than that and that the company can save money by providing employees with tips on extending their computers' battery life.

Find several articles on how the lives of laptop batteries can be extended. Use this research to help you write a short guide for employees that explains what they need to do to make their computer battery last longer.

Writing Skills Checkup: Abbreviations, Acronyms, and Initialisms

Abbreviations are shortened forms of commonly used words (e.g., *St.* for *Street* and *Mr.* for *mister*). Acronyms are words that are formed by using the first letter of longer terms (*NAFTA*, for example, is an acronym of *North American Free Trade Agreement*). Initialisms are similar to acronyms but are not pronounced as words (*CGA* for *certified general accountant*).

The usage rules are too numerous to list here, but we have included some of the more common ones:

a. Abbreviations are less formal than the long form of terms. Terms for dates and measurement should be shortened only when space is an issue. For example,

use *February* or *metre* in the body of a letter or report rather than *Feb.* or *m.*

b. Abbreviate common courtesy titles when used together with a name (*Mr.* Aziz, *Ms.* Goldflamm).

c. Most acronyms and initialisms do not require periods (*RBC,* not *R.B.C.*). There are exceptions to this rule, such as *a.m.* and *p.m.*

d. Plurals of acronyms or initialisms are formed by adding a lower-case s (not *'s*): *several CDs.*

e. Acronyms and initialisms that may be unfamiliar to the audience should be written out the first time they appear: *Business Development Bank of Canada (BDC).*

f. In some cases, especially with technical terms, the initialism may be more familiar to the reader than the full version (*HIV* instead of *human immunodeficiency virus*). When using such terms, be careful not to use redundant terminology, such as *HIV virus*.

Correct the use of acronyms, abbreviations, and initialisms in the following sentences. An example is done for you:

Example: Unwrap your DVD's ASAP after purchasing them so that you can redeem any coupons before the end of Dec.

Correction: Unwrap your DVDs as soon as possible after purchasing them so that you can redeem any coupons before the end of December.

1. When connecting your PC to a LAN or WAN, it is especially important to use AV software to avoid viruses and worms.
2. All PFD's used in Canadian boats must be approved by DOTC, and they should only be used by people within their specified kg range.
3. Before purchasing a new prgrm for your pc, ensure that you are running the proper os and that you have enough RAM memory.
4. Keep your PIN number secure to avoid id theft. Do not release your S.I.N. number or PW over the internet.
5. The Canadian Centre for Occupational Health and Safety recommends that office workers take a 5–10 min. break for every hr. spent at the keyboard. The Canadian Centre for Occupational Health and Safety also warns that spending too long at a workstation can result in RSI's.[9]

Preparing to Write Proposals, Reports, and Electronic Presentations

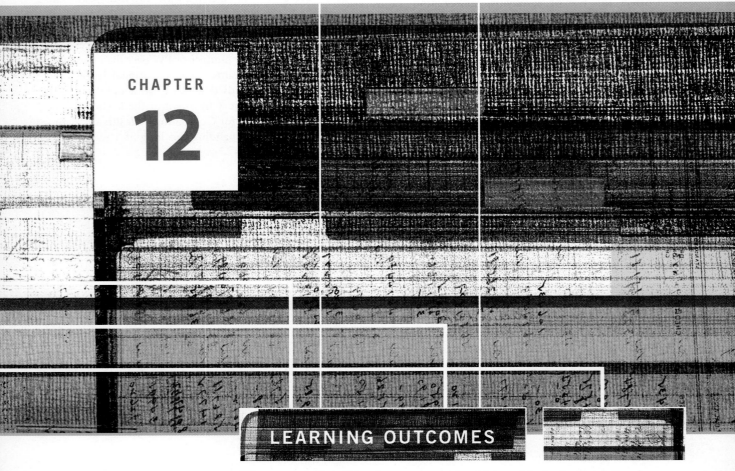

LEARNING OUTCOMES

After completing this chapter, you should be able to do the following:

12.1 Discuss different types of research and their advantages

12.2 Manage different information search techniques

12.3 Work out how best to visually present the results of your research

12.4 Make appropriate use of referencing and formatting

MANAGING INFORMATION

Businesses succeed—to some degree, at least—because they are able to meet customers' needs well while minimizing the cost to the company. Good decisions by management can be traced to good information management in the company, and the preferred method of managing information is the business report. In a world of fast-paced change, businesses must be able to change and adapt to new opportunities and challenges; a successful report or proposal often leads to such change within the company.

This chapter discusses the steps that you will need to complete successfully before you begin the process of actually writing proposals, reports, or electronic presentations. If you carry out the preparatory steps well, the writing stage itself becomes much easier. Research is an important part of preparation, and we discuss appropriate ways to prepare research for visual presentation, too, in tables, graphs, and PowerPoint presentations.

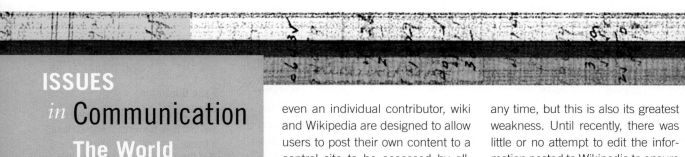

ISSUES
in Communication
The World according to Wiki and Wikipedia

Wiki, and in particular, Wikipedia, are websites with a difference. Rather than being hosted and created by a single organization, or even an individual contributor, wiki and Wikipedia are designed to allow users to post their own content to a central site to be accessed by all. Wikipedia attributes the origin of the name both to the Hawaiian word for "fast" and the acronym for "what I know is." The latter point demonstrates the sometimes uncertain information that wikis contain.

The strength of Wikipedia is that anyone can contribute anything at any time, but this is also its greatest weakness. Until recently, there was little or no attempt to edit the information posted to Wikipedia to ensure its accuracy. The result was a series of web postings that mimicked the children's game of broken telephone, where players sit in a circle and one person whispers a message to another, who passes it along quietly to another, until everyone has heard and retold the story. The last person says the message aloud. The

Is truth just a collective hunch?

final version rarely matches the original and the more convoluted the facts become, the funnier the outcome.

Much more serious is that a number of so-called editors are supplying information to Wikipedia that is known to be bogus. In one recent example, a student in Dublin, Ireland, purposely added a falsified quote to an entry on a recently deceased French composer. The student was interested in seeing how far and how fast the misinformation would spread. Wikipedia moderators eventually identified and removed the false information, but not before the fake quote was copied and pasted into many obituaries and related articles that ended up in such notable publications as the *Guardian*, the *Independent*, and *BBC Music Magazine*.[1]

In another example, a Wikipedia editor falsified his credentials to appear qualified to moderate online religious debates. The editor in question described himself as a professor of religion at a private university with experience teaching both undergraduate and graduate courses in theology. Known online as Essjay, he was in reality Ryan Jordan, a 24-year-old college student from Kentucky who used books, such as *Catholicism for Dummies,* to help answer more challenging questions. He has now retired from the site.[2]

Examples of purposeful misrepresentation abound, making Wikipedia an unpredictable source of information for any serious researcher.

Even with the editorial process that is now in place, significant lag time can occur between when bogus information is posted and when it is removed. This puts a pall on the site as a source of reference in any research project, because you cannot be certain that the information posted on the site is factual.

As a last example, consider the fake[3] town of Zhoda, Manitoba, where the local reeve race is determined by a wrestling match and the town's chief export is stray dogs. At the time of writing, the Zhoda page on Wikipedia had been online for over three years.

Always check with your instructors before using any wiki sites in a research project. Some may allow the reference but many will not, precisely because entries are not reviewed professionally or produced as part of a publication of merit.

DISCUSSION

1. How many people do you know who rely on Wikipedia for information? Do you think they know the site is not trustworthy?
2. If you were one of the reporters writing an article on the French composer, what type of sources would you have used?
3. How often do you rely on only the internet to supply you with information for your assignments?
4. What would make you rely on an internet site as a serious reference?

TAKE IT FURTHER

Fake Quotation

These words were posted on Wikipedia and said to be the words of Maurice Jarre, a famous composer who had recently died: "Music was my life, music brought me to life, and music is how I will be remembered long after I leave this life. When I die there will be a final waltz playing in my head that only I can hear."[4]

Why do you think experienced reporters were lured into believing this quotation was real?

TOO MUCH INFORMATION!

Managing information in an increasingly fast-paced business environment is becoming more of a challenge all the time. Because of new and refined access to information, a lack of information is rarely the problem. Rather, the new reality in the business world is how to handle too much information. Business proposals and reports, in all their varied forms to be discussed, are the key way business professionals make sense of the complicated data that help drive effective decision making. Let us begin by looking at the different types of research and their contribution to knowledge, the backbone of any business document.

PRIMARY VERSUS SECONDARY RESEARCH   ✱⌐Explore

When you write a business document, whether a report or proposal—or even a PowerPoint slide—you always need to look for information. Three factors are of note:

1. the accuracy of the information
2. the time required to collect it
3. the cost associated with its collection

Put another way, it is virtually impossible to have perfectly accurate information on a particular issue when you take little or no time to collect and analyze it and do so at little or no cost. Something has to give. Good researchers will mention any risks they have taken in their documents. For example, if speed is important and a deadline is looming, some loss of accuracy is often required if the research is to stay under a given budget. The question becomes how inaccurate can the data be and still be acceptable in terms of costs and timing?

The choice, then, is between primary and secondary research.

Primary Research

Primary research is information that a researcher collects to address a particular issue. It's called *primary* because, before the investigator created it, the research did not exist in that particular form. In terms of its accuracy, timeliness, and cost, primary research can be very accurate because the researcher can control the exact nature of the investigation. However, collecting data is time consuming and expensive. For example, if a manager is concerned about declining consumer confidence and its impact on sales, one possible solution is to create a survey and poll all customers as they leave the store. Assuming the proper polling techniques are used, this technique could give very accurate information, but it would take considerable time and cost quite a bit of money. Collecting the answers could be more expensive than the problem the information is being collected about. This leads to the need for a lower cost alternative, namely, secondary research.

Secondary Research

Secondary research is collected by someone else, somewhere else, and for something else. Secondary research may not be as specific as primary research, but the obvious advantages are the information already exists and the costs of its collection and analysis have been already borne by others. Secondary research is faster and cheaper than primary research, but it requires people to apply data from one set of circumstances to a different situation where it may not apply as accurately.

For our hypothetical manager, in the example under "Primary Research," who is looking for data on customers' degree of consumer confidence, one solution is to see whether these types of questions have recently been asked of other customers in other regions. The thorough researcher needs to ask

TAKE IT FURTHER

Meaty Research

In 2008, 22 people died in Canada after consuming meat products that were contaminated with bacteria known as *Listeria.* How to keep *Listeria* out of processed meat is the *primary research* question in a University of Guelph lab. One thing they're trying: adding viruses to the meat. Called bacteria phages, they infect only the dangerous bacteria and are harmless to people. The research is still in the early stages, but already Keith Warriner imagines some consumers might not like his idea.[5]

Why is it necessary to abandon secondary research to deal with *Listeria* bacteria outbreaks? ■

some obvious questions to help increase the usefulness of secondary research:

1. *How long ago was the data collected and have there been significant changes since the data was first collected?* These days, little remains constant and data may quickly go out of date as the observed behaviour changes.

2. *Was the target audience that was polled similar to the target audience under investigation now?* For example, consumers in Edmonton looking for winter clothing will have much more in common with consumers from Minot, North Dakota, than consumers from Victoria, even though Albertans and British Columbians are both Canadians.

3. *Is it clear that the original research was done to the highest possible standard?* This is really a question about the technical competency of the original researchers.

Although it is true that businesses would not usually spend a dollar to collect data to solve a problem that is worth a dime, it is equally true that good management decisions rarely come from bad information. Good research is often about balancing the need for accurate information with the real constraints of limited time and sometimes insufficient money or other resources. Compromise is often needed.

SOURCES OF INFORMATION

The Library

Unquestionably the most important source for information of all kinds is the library. It remains the leading storage place for facts, figures, data, and information.

This valuable source of secondary research can provide answers to most questions for most business situations most of the time. Chances are that data on the questions challenging the researcher have already been collected, analyzed, and recorded for use. The local library has a vast collection of business books, journals, periodicals, directories, government publications, almanacs, and newspapers. Apart from the wealth of information that is available at the researcher's fingertips, libraries are also home to librarians who are often professionally trained researchers and can help investigators to get the most out of the libraries' resources.

Today libraries usually have computers available for the public to use for web research. (See the next section.)

Online Research

Although libraries have historically been scholars' favourite research spots, the internet has grown in popularity because of its ease of use, its accessibility, and the range of available topics. Now, a lot of research can be done before stepping through the doors of a library.

TAKE IT FURTHER

Librarians

In a recent poll of non-librarians, author (and librarian) Catherine Jasper asked the question "What are three words or phrases that describe librarians (the actual people)?" More than half of respondents replied "smart/knowledgeable." In second place was "helpful," and in third place was "competent," though "nice" was close behind. Fewer than 10 percent of respondents described librarians with old stereotypes (glasses, sweaters, female, strict, old, and short). No one called librarians grumpy.[6]

In this age of increasing data digitization and the sheer volume of information available, what do you think it takes to be a good librarian?

Libraries are still the world's best information source.

Remember that not all information that is posted on the internet is valuable. In fact, much of what passes for content on the information highway is nothing but propaganda. Rather than aiming to increase human understanding, some websites use the internet to push a certain point of view.

Not all the information that is contained in the library is available online, so limiting research to only the web will leave out a lot of valuable information. We will now look at ways to judge what data are worthy of use by researchers and what are not.

The first distinction to be made is which internet we are talking about—more than one type of web is in existence. We will refer to the first as the *internet*, more because of the way the term is usually used than because it is strictly accurate.

The Internet (a.k.a. the World Wide Web)   The internet most people are familiar with is the one that we access through such common search sites as Yahoo.ca, Google.ca, and Bing.com. They all provide information through three key operations: *web crawling*, *results matching*, and *results ranking*. The details of how these operate are closely guarded corporate secrets, but in general the following definitions apply:[7]

- *Web crawling* uses programs called web bots that identify, download, and store potentially useful webpages.
- *Results matching* matches a user's search terms to the list of webpages while avoiding multiple links to the same site.
- *Results ranking* determines the order in which hits appear on a researcher's screen.

Each of these search engines uses slightly different techniques to provide results to searches of popular terms or phases called *key words*.

Yahoo! was launched in 1994; Google started up in 1998; and Microsoft entered Bing into the competition in 2009. Researchers, often referred to as surfers, type in a key word or phrase, the search engine combs through hundreds of thousands of possible websites, and it returns the ones most likely related to the search terms. Searches can produce thousands of hits, though, and many surfers look only at the first ten. For a fee, search sites will place a sponsored link at the top of a search list. Businesses sometimes hire *search engine optimizers,* who are consultants who help them manipulate their webpages so that their sites receive a higher ranking among the free links that search engines also provide.[8]

Unfortunately for the researcher, the organizations willing to pay the fee may not necessarily be the ones most sought after for information.

The real problem with all search engines of this type is the fact that they comb a largely unregulated and, as we've seen with Wikipedia, a sometimes unreliable data source. Anyone with access to the internet and a few dollars for development software can create a website to post information on any topic. A lot of garbage litters the so-called information highway.

Because the data that are posted on the internet are largely unsubstantiated and are not reviewed by knowledgeable experts before being posted, researchers seeking to quote leading references in a given field face problems. For this reason, more experienced researchers often avoid the internet if they are serious about looking for genuine information. These online investigators dive into the deep web.

The Deep Web   Increasingly used by serious researchers and scholars the world over, the deep web is a much more valuable source of information for academic and business writing, where accuracy is a priority. This is because the deep web contains information that typical internet search engines cannot access: university and college library databases, government databases, and other rich information sources that have a higher standard of informational content. Although many consider the amount of information that Google searches to be large, with its access to more than a trillion pages in its index,[9] the deep web is 500 times as large as Google![10]

By using any of the free deep web search engines—such as Completeplanet.com—a researcher will usually find legitimate information rather than popular trivia. The information accessible through the deep web has more likely been *peer reviewed* (examined by a panel of experts in the same field to verify for accuracy and technical competence) and even published, so the results of any inquiry are more likely to be true.

Even Google is getting into the deep web search action with its recent release of GoogleScholar.com, a beta version of a deep web engine. Each deep web search engine has its own specialties and if you are starting your researching, you should do some investigating and comparing before deciding which engine works best for a particular report in a specific area of research.

Assessing Web Sources   Following these simple rules to assessing online resources, adapted from the University of California, Berkeley, will help you avoid much of the trash and so help you to write a better report based on sound information:[11]

■ *Think about the source of the site.* If you are researching a particular industry, for example, and you reply on information from a company from within that industry, the information it presents may be biased. Remember that most commercial sites aim to convince the reader of their point of view, not to simply report the facts. A government website specializing in reporting business statistics will be a much more reliable source in this case than the data that are selectively reported on a particular business's site.

■ *Once you are satisfied that the site itself is sound, try to identify the author of the information presented and his or her credentials.* If no author is listed for the information or the analysis, an obvious question is "Why not?" What would the site hope to gain by hiding the author's credentials? If the author's name is listed, investigate further to see what makes this person worthy of your time. Remember, if you quote this reference, you are saying to the reader, "Trust this source and the point of view as true."

■ *Be careful about second-hand (or third-hand) information.* For example, if you find a website that reports the results of their secondary research, it is always a better idea to go to the original source. If you rely on getting the information from someone else, you also rely on the second author to accurately describe the original author's work. Errors in reporting are often made, especially if the author is trying to push a certain point of view.

■ *Ask yourself whether the site looks legitimate.* For example, a poorly designed website can mean a lack of resources to improve it. If the site has typing errors or other factual mistakes, you should assume that there are more mistakes that have not yet been discovered. If the website is old and not regularly updated or maintained, it may be obsolete and not used by its creator.

■ *Don't rely on a single source for information.* As a researcher, you are often describing the state of knowledge at a particular time. There should be many examples of similar perspectives for you to draw from. Of course, just because a mistake is repeated many times does not make it true (especially if these can all be traced to the same source).

Journal Databases

Journal databases are collections of abstracts, indexes, and articles from peer-reviewed and published journals. These databases are a tremendous resource for those who have access to them.

Most online journal databases operate on a user-pay-per-download basis or through some type of yearly subscription. Typically a student registered with a university or college is granted access to the library's site licence, which is paid for by student fees. The actual journal database will vary from school to school, but they are all based on similar technology. A journal database will often specialize in the types of information it holds. For example EBSCOhost is a journal database commonly used by academic researchers,[12] while MEDLINE is an online service of medical information dating back to 1948.[13]

How to Use Them   Journal databases will often be listed on the school library's website. This listing will be alphabetical, for those who know which database they want, and by subject area—which is especially helpful for researchers using the resource for the first time. Often, a single journal database contains dozens of smaller databases that are organized by specialty.

Thousands of entries are available for review and use. After accessing the larger database, you will be asked to choose which of the smaller databases to use. Of course, it is possible to "select all," but this choice unnecessarily slows down the entire process, because all entries must be searched and because some *hits* are certain to be of little or no use.

After you choose the database that is the most likely to have the information you need, a series of additional questions will help you further refine *the ask*. For example, you can often choose what types of information to query, including books, periodicals, reports, and newspapers. You can select from among many different types of entries, including full text, abstracts, bibliographies, speeches, and case studies. You can also focus your queries to certain periods, for example, anything produced within the last five years.

After you have completed the query refinement process, you enter a key word or phrase, similar to the process used in more traditional internet search engines like Yahoo and Google. If there are too many results on the key phase, you can be more exact by using quotation marks.

Effective research requires critical thinking at every stage, but the more you do it, the easier the process becomes.

Even the very best online journal database contains only a sampling of the information that is available from the actual bricks-and-mortar library. Researchers who do all their information searching online will see only a fraction of the total data, which will limit the researchers' results. For this reason alone, it is advisable to include the library in any information collection.

Database Example in Action   Let us look at a specific journal database search. Using a popular business-related journal database and typing in the words *business plan* yields 20 163 results. This is obviously far too many to follow up because it includes entries with the words *business plan*, *business*, or *plan* and various combinations and groupings of these key words, such as *businesses, planning,* and so on. You have some refining to do.

- To refine the search to only those publications that relate to a *business plan*, you can simply place the words in quotation marks. Using the phrase "business plan" (with the quotation marks) forces the search engine to look for this specific combination of words. The number of results drops from 20 163 to 2205.

- No one can consider 2000 entries and so further refinement is required. If your task is to develop a strategy to prepare a business plan, you could type in "preparing a business plan." The number of responses to this query drops to 12—a far more manageable number.

- The next step is to see if the actual hits returned are useful. If so, you can move on to the next steps of report writing. If not, you can change key words, change the previously selected subset of databases or perhaps even change the journal database itself.

PREPARING TO USE YOUR RESEARCH: THINK VISUALLY

The main function of any report is to transfer information from the writer to the reader. This is often done by using words, of course, but other media can carry the message. We pick up the writing side of the process in Chapter 13. First, we will consider the visuals.

Tables, Graphs, and Other Visuals in Reports

When you, as the writer, are thinking of ways to convey particularly complicated information, you may find it easier to use visuals rather than just words.

Take, for example, the task of communicating sales data over time. It is possible to write out the numbers as words over the period of interest. Much more effective, though, is creating a table of the actual numbers. Both methods are equally accurate in the information transmitted, but the table allows for this communication to occur much more quickly. Better yet, consider the use of a simple line graph that illustrates the numbers from the table. At a glance the reader can tell if the line is trending up or down and get some insight on whether sales are up or down.

These are very simple examples, but they illustrate that visual aids can sometimes carry a message more effectively than words can.

Tables   Tables are often used in report writing to summarize a large amount of related numerical data. Made up of a series of rows and columns, a table contains all the most valuable information that needs to be communicated, without all the supportive details that often need to surround the raw data in

"What's this, Dawkins—another of your 'visual metaphors'?"

A picture is worth a thousand words.

the written form. Because of the popularity of tables, most word-processing programs include simple table creation and insertion functions. A table is a useful way to communicate a significant amount of information in a highly organized and compact way. For example, a report on quarterly sales figures for a local gardening business could be listed in a sentence format:

> Northwest quarter-one sales were $12 000. Northwest quarter-two sales were $11 000. Northwest quarter-three sales were $12 000. Northwest quarter-four sales were $11 000. Northeast quarter-one sales were $8000. Northeast quarter-two sales were $7000. Northeast quarter-three sales were $6000. Northeast quarter-four sales were $5000. Southwest quarter-one sales were $2000. Southwest quarter-two sales were $4000. Southwest quarter-three sales were $8000. Southwest quarter-four sales were $12 000.

Reading this information is *boring* and even potentially confusing or misleading. For example, the fact that one section of the city has near constant sales while one section is declining slightly is not very obvious. If the reader gets bored and stops reading, the fact that sales in one section are exploding may be missed.

Consider the difference with the same information in a table format. See **Table 12-1.**

| TABLE 12-1 | **Making Data Interesting** | | | |

City Quarterly Sales Data for 2009				
	Quarter 1	Quarter 2	Quarter 3	Quarter 4
Northwest	$12 000	$11 000	$12 000	$11 000
Northeast	$ 8 000	$ 7 000	$ 6 000	$ 5 000
Southwest	$ 2 000	$ 4 000	$ 8 000	$12 000

Source: Corporate Sales Reports 2009, various quarters

The same data are being given but because they are better organized in the table, more information is being communicated. Trends over time and relative differences between city sections become obvious. This is enhanced further by slight additions to the table. (See **Table 12-2**.) Now you can start to answer the question "How is the company doing?"

Tips on creating tables   Keep the following points in mind when creating tables:

1. Create a rough draft first, to make sure the table is as easy to understand as possible. (Remember that readers tend to start at the top left side of a table, and then read to the right and down, ending in the bottom right corner.)

2. Use a clear table title to tell your reader what the table is about.

3. When an explanation accompanies the table, be sure it appears before the table. Otherwise, the reader is left wondering what to make of the table of numbers.

4. Use clear and explanatory column headings to keep the data organized.

5. The data contained within a table are often the result of other research, whether primary or secondary. Be sure to cite where your data came from, just as you would a quotation from a book or journal article. This source line comes after the table.

6. If you use more than one table in a report, be sure to number them sequentially and include descriptive titles for each.

7. Consider creating a summary of tables and other visual aids, their titles, and their page numbers at the beginning of the report, just after the table of contents.

| TABLE 12-2 | **Making Data Even More Interesting** | | | | |

City Quarterly Sales Data and Analysis for 2009					
	Quarter 1	Quarter 2	Quarter 3	Quarter 4	Change Q4 over Q1
Northwest	$12 000	$11 000	$12 000	$11 000	−8%
Northeast	$ 8 000	$ 7 000	$ 6 000	$ 5 000	−38%
Southwest	$ 2 000	$ 4 000	$ 8 000	$12 000	500%
Total	$22 000	$22 000	$26 000	$29 000	

Source: Corporate Sales Reports 2009, various quarters

Graphs   Graphs are visual representations of data from a table. There are many types of graphs, each with its own advantages and disadvantages. We will discuss a few common types.

Pie charts   A type of graph that is commonly used in business is the pie chart. It is used when describing the parts of a larger whole. The pie chart is helpful when comparing the size of one component against another. For example, the pie chart in **Figure 12-1** considers the quarterly sales for Product A.

    The reader can quickly see which quarter had the larger number of sales over the year, and which had the smallest. If you wanted to convey more information, say a comparison of quarterly sales by product type, then you would need another type of graph—the bar graph.

Bar graphs   Bar graphs are useful because you can illustrate more than one data stream at a time. (See **Figure 12-2**.) They allow you to communicate information, and perhaps relationships between the data, far more simply than with a table of figures.

Line graphs   The line graph allows for information to be linked over a series, such as time. Consider the data described in the bar graph in **Figure 12-2**. If your goal in writing a report is to show how the sales of each product are trending over time, a line graph may be a better choice. It uses the same data but presents them from a different point of view.

    In the example shown in **Figure 12-3**, the reader can clearly see the levels of sales in each quarter for each product, as was the case for the bar graph and the table. Notice, however, that the orientation of the trend line also conveys the information that sales in all product lines increased in the fourth quarter, suggesting that the company is doing better than in previous quarters. This is not as obvious in Figure 12.2. Remember, how you convey your message can be just as significant as what your message says.

FIGURE 12-1   **The Pie Chart**

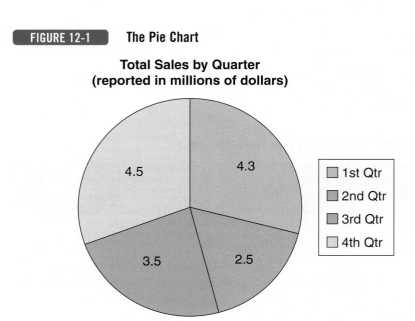

**Total Sales by Quarter
(reported in millions of dollars)**

 **The Bar Graph**

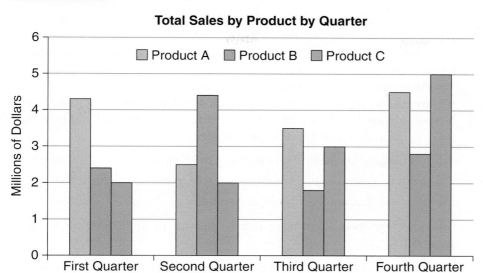

Source: Corporate Sales Reports 2009, various quarters

FIGURE 12-3 **The Line Graph**

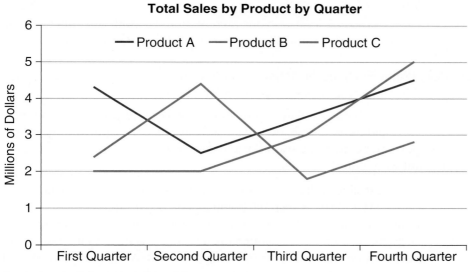

Source: Corporate Sales Reports 2009, various quarters

Visual Options With today's sophisticated word-processing programs and easy access to descriptive visuals on the internet, you have many possibilities for including visuals in a report: pictures, videos, clip art, predefined shapes, symbols, and anything else you can create.

It is important to remember, though, that just because new desktop publishing software makes it easy to insert all manner of visual aids, this does not mean that you should include them. The point of including the visual aid is to aid the reader in reaching a higher level of understanding. If you include unrelated imagery or misleading graphics, you may confuse the reader and lose any benefits of the visual aid.[14]

PowerPoint Slides

When you create a paper-based proposal or report, you will often need some type of associated presentation of the key points of the writing. As we noted in Chapter 7, PowerPoint is now used widely in workplaces as a computer-based presentation aid.

PowerPoint can help you to create a number of useful tools: on-screen presentations (or slide shows), audience handouts, speaker's notes, overheads, webpages, and 35 mm slides. If used well, PowerPoint can help liven up dry material. It also has other advantages:

- It is suitable for the different learning styles audience members may have.
- It can be posted online for those not able to attend the presentation.
- It is paperless and easy to reuse or modify.

However, PowerPoint may not be helpful in at least three kinds of situations:

1. If the presentation is made to a small group that is likely to be more participative or hands on, slide shows are a bit too formal.
2. If you are unsure about the technology available at the place where you are presenting, be sure you can complete your presentation without PowerPoint.
3. If there is a time limit on your presentation, be aware that once set, the course of the electronic presentation is harder to alter midstream.

✱ Explore **PowerPoint Planning in Action**   You have several issues to consider when preparing the actual slides for your presentation.

1. Design   Because the PowerPoint slide show is support for your presentation, it should never overshadow what you have to say. Keeping things simple is important, because you want the audience to focus on what you are saying and not what's on the screen.

- *Text.* Most slides will contain some text about your message. Use large and legible text and try to keep the bolding, italics, and underlining to a minimum, if you use them at all. Do not use full paragraphs or even full sentences for text—this is not your formal report. Use three to five bullets per slide, with no more than seven words per bullet. A bulleted point should nicely fit on one line of your slide to make it simple for the audience to read. Use an easy-to-read sans serif font, such as Helvetica, Arial, or Tacoma.
- *Colour.* Colour can add interest to your presentation, but use it wisely, and don't overdo it. Make sure that the colours you use for text and bullets go well together. Some colours clash and will be distracting for your audience. Some combinations are also hard to read. Avoid blue–black, brown–green, red–green, and blue–purple combinations.

2. Graphics and Animation   Images can help carry your message, but they can also be distracting if overused or improperly used. Any image that you include should be meaningful to your message. A picture may be worth a thousand words, but you should also use a few words to clarify the point of including the image.

Once you choose an image style, stick with it. For example, you can use photos for maximum impact or choose cartoons or other drawings, like clip art. Don't mix styles in a presentation.

Animation, with moving images on screen, is also a powerful tool to help with a presentation, but it is one that easily distracts the audience, so use it sparingly.

The use of images and animations has other considerations: (1) they significantly add to file size, which can make storage and transport more difficult, and (2) because additional computer processing is required to display these graphics, the computer you use for your presentation (especially if it is borrowed) may not be able to handle the larger file effectively.

If you do use photos in your presentation, you can reduce the file size by choosing a lower resolution. The problem then is that the picture becomes more pixelated and harder to see, especially if low resolution is accompanied by a large picture size. The file type can also make a difference. For example, JPEG compression loads more quickly and uses less space than other file types, such as bitmap or TIFF.

3. Templates   For ease in creating PowerPoint slides, the software includes many prepared slides or templates. These templates use different backgrounds, colours, and text options to help new or inexperienced users get started. Again, simplicity and clarity are important so be sure to choose a template that matches the message or theme of your presentation.

For example, if you are presenting profitability statements to a board of directors, do not choose a template with soft pastel colours or, worse yet, a party balloon motif. You can download many templates from the internet, and you can create your own template.

Whether you create a template or use one provided with the software, be sure to think about the presentation itself. In a darkened room, a dark background with lighter coloured text works well. If the room has any ambient or natural light, a template with a light-coloured background and dark text works better. If you are not sure, go with a light background.

4. Transitions and sound   As you make your presentation, transition becomes important. *Transition* is the process by which the program moves from one visual to the next. This might be from one slide to the next, one bullet to the next, one image to the next, or (in the extreme) one letter to the next.

The simplest option is to have the entire slide appear at once without any gradual transition. But you may not want to do this, especially for more complicated slides with a lot of content.

Another option is to have a bulleted point appear while the last one fades in colour as you are speaking. Timing can be automatic or determined by a mouse click by the presenter. Many options exist to transition from one slide to the next, including wipes, fades, page turns, and so on. Transitions can be very distracting so choose a simple option that works and use it throughout the presentation. If you change transitions from one slide to the next, your audience will spend more time trying to guess what the next transition will be than listening to you. Sound, such as clapping, barking dogs, glass smashing, or guns firing, can also be added to your presentation, but again, these can be more distracting than useful for making your point, so think carefully before using them.

Final Tips   If you are going to use PowerPoint, the key point to keep in mind is that if the slide show doesn't support what you have to say and bring your audience closer to understanding your message, then it pushes them further away from understanding. Simplicity, clarity, and thoughtful purpose should drive your PowerPoint decision making. Remember, just because PowerPoint can do something doesn't mean that you, as an effective PowerPoint designer, should use it.

Study **Figure 12-4**, an example of a good PowerPoint slide, and **Figure 12-5**, an example of a bad one. In your own slides avoid the following five major PowerPoint offences, as identified by Jamie McKenzie.[15]

1. having too many slides in quick succession
2. including too many slides for the presentation
3. reading from the slides
4. underutilizing PowerPoint's best assets, especially in graphics and animation
5. overusing PowerPoint assets, especially in special effects and readability

FIGURE 12-4   **A Good PowerPoint Slide**

The title is clear and explanatory.

Just a few fonts and colours are used. The fonts are easy to read.

The clip art is colourful and supports the text.

The items in the numbered list are short and clear.

The dark text on a light background is easy to read. Use a light background if you are unsure about the lighting in the room.

The template is visually pleasing.

| **FIGURE 12-5** | **A Bad PowerPoint Slide** |

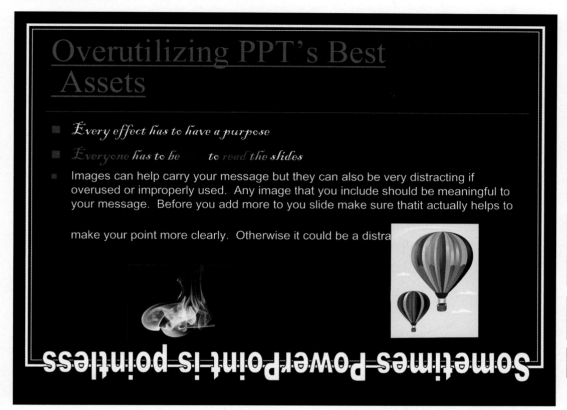

Try to get the title on one line.

Do not use more than three fonts or colours. Use fonts that are easy to read.

Keep bulleted points short. Wordy bullets are distracting.

Do not layer art and text.

Do not use dark text on a dark background—it is hard to read. A black background will not work in well-lit rooms.

Do not use both pictures and clip art. The art must relate to the message.

Do not use useless features.

REFERENCING

You need to give credit where credit is due—for the sake of fairness as well as to avoid charges of *plagiarism,* which means claiming someone else's work as your own.

Learning how to properly credit the work of other researchers can be confusing at first. Some students avoid giving proper credit because they are worried that the reference shows that they are taking the ideas of others. Nothing could be further from the truth. Knowledge is constantly changing, and you need to consider the works of past thinkers to better see where your understanding is now and where it might be headed. You will need to refer to older documents and other source material to explain how you formulated your ideas.

No leader in business, nor instructor in school, expects that you know everything about a problem you are investigating. Good research shows you the existing knowledge that will take you closer to a solution. Good referencing techniques tell the reader of your report that you did a good job of investigating what is already known before you added your contribution.

TAKE IT FURTHER

Who Said That?

In 2008 Prime Minister Stephen Harper and U.S. President Barack Obama were each caught reading speeches that were taken from the work of others. In the case of Obama, Senator Hillary Clinton pointed out that several of his speeches closely resembled those of Massachusetts Governor Deval Patrick. In fact, parts of the speeches were exactly the same, word for word. Harper was caught reading a speech that was a verbatim copy of a speech given earlier by then prime minister of Australia, John Howard, concerning the war in Iraq. It is unclear whether either Harper or Obama wrote the speeches he gave or whether they were penned by speech writers.[16]

Does it matter whether the North American political leaders wrote the speeches or not?

What (and What Not) to Reference

What exactly do you reference in a report? The answer to this question will be clearer when you understand how a typical report is put together.

An academic or business report of, say, 5000 words will cover about 10 to 15 typed pages and likely contain about 40 to 50 individual paragraphs. Each paragraph, if properly constructed, will have a single idea. These ideas, when strung together, should communicate your message (or thesis) to your reader. Many of these ideas will come from your secondary research on the work of others. You will have paragraphs of introduction, transition, and conclusion, if applicable, which likely won't have references. You will also write paragraphs of your own ideas that need no reference.

Each of the remaining paragraphs that discusses the ideas, words, and inventions of others should contain at least one reference to the originator of the information.

Don't Reference These   Here is a quick summary of what *not* to reference:

▪ Anything that comes from your own inspiration and is your own contribution does not need a reference.

"Intriguing proposal!
Give me some time to mull it over and co-opt it as my own."

Plagiarism is theft. It's that simple.

- Information that is common knowledge. For example, because the statement *the sun rises in the east* is common knowledge, it does not need to be referenced.

- Information that comes from an internal source of your business (say the accounting department) does not *necessarily* require formal referencing but, as we shall see, it is usually a good idea.

Do Reference These To avoid plagiarism, other information should be referenced, especially if there is doubt whether it is commonly known by the general public. If you are unsure, it is better to be cautious and include the reference. Several types of information should always be referenced:

- the precise words spoken by others

- other people's ideas, even if you have paraphrased these ideas

- other people's inventions, including charts, graphs, numbers, pictures, and so on

Types of References

Two basic types of references should be used in your report:

1. *Parenthetical in-text references.* To identify the source of the ideas, inventions, or words, insert the original author's last name, or the name of the source organization, in parentheses in your text. If the source is a published book, for example, include a page number to assist the reader to find the original information. The following is an example:

   The federal government has funded research concerning consumer protection and consumer transactions with online pharmacies (Food and Drug Administration 125).

   If the reader wants more information about the topic, he or she needs to look at the original source and find page 125.

2. *A reference or works cited list.* The reference list steers the reader to the source of the original work. It comes at the end of the chapters or sections instead of within the text itself. To help the reader find the original work, detailed information, such as the author's surname, given names (or initials), and bibliographical data, are part of the reference.

Reference Styles Standardized reference styles are available, which make it easy for the reader to explore the earlier works or to make judgments about the information being referenced. Most businesses and schools prefer one type over another. It is your responsibility to find out which style is preferred and to apply the rules of reference consistently. For readers, it is confusing to have references flip from one style to another or, worse yet, be a hybrid of the two. Two referencing styles are commonly used in business writing.

The *American Psychological Association (APA)* style of referencing uses the author-date method. Your citation of another person's work will include the original author's last name and the year of publication. Full bibliographical details are included at the end of the report in a list called References.

The newest APA guidelines specify the use of two spaces after punctuation marks at the end of a sentence, to improve the readability of draft manuscripts. Most other styles use only one space. For course assignments, use whichever style your instructor prefers.

- APA in-text citation of one author: (Jackson, 2010)
- APA in-text citation of two authors: (Applegate & Bombeck, 2010)
- APA in-text citation of one author with no date available: (Harper, n.d.)
- APA in-text direct quote from page 10: (Hamm, 2010, p. 10)
- APA in-text citation with no author but a title: ("Businesses Today," 2008)

The citation is usually inserted immediately after the mention of the document is made in your writing.

At the end of the report, all the APA references are listed alphabetically by author's last name. For example, a work by Anderson would be listed before another work by Zappa.

If the date of publication is known, put this in parentheses and place it immediately after the author initials. If two or more references by the same author are used, the older work is listed first:

Carr, D. (2008).

Carr, D. (2010).

If two publications are produced by the same author in the same year, then the years have letters to them (a, b, c). The letter given is determined by which publication is cited first in your work:

Bronwen, F. (2009a).

Bronwen, F. (2009b).

For the tiles of books, articles, brochures, webpages, and most other titles except those of journals, capitalize only the first letter of the title. The titles of books, magazines, journals, reports, and so on are italicized. The titles of articles are set in quotation marks.

When referencing periodicals, include the name of the journal, the volume number, the issue number (if the periodical is paginated by issue), and the page numbers. For example, if the volume number is 4, the issue number is 8, and the pages numbers for the specific article are 15 to 20, format is like this: *Journal Name, 4*(8): 15–20. Note that the name of the journal and the volume number are italicized.

If you are using an electronic reference, include the website address and the words "Retrieved from." No final punctuation mark is used at the end of the website address, and APA style does not include the date you visited the site: Retrieved from www.cbc.ca

You can find guides containing examples of APA referencing techniques and examples on the web, or you can purchase the APA's style guide. **Figure 12-6** shows part of a reference list completed in APA style.

The Start of a Reference List That Uses APA Style

References

Abramowitz, J. S. (2008). Obsessive-compulsive disorder. In W. E. Craighead, D. J. Miklowitz, & L. W. Craighead (Eds.), *Psychopathology: History, diagnosis, and empirical foundations* (pp. 159–197). Hoboken, NJ: Wiley.

Achenbach, T. M., & Edelbrock, C. (1983). *Manual for the child behavior checklist and revised child behavior profile.* Burlington, VT: University of Vermont.

Achenbach, T. M., & Rescorla, L. A. (2001). *Manual for ASEBA school-age forms & profiles.* Burlington, VT: University of Vermont, Research Center for Children, Youth, & Families.

Ackerknect, E. H. (1968). *Short history of psychiatry.* (S. Wolff, Trans.). New York: Hafner Publishing.

Ackerly, S. S., & Benton, A. L. (1948). Report of a case of bilateral frontal lobe defect. *Research and Publications of the Association for the Research of Nervous and Mental Disease, 27,* 479–504.

Adams, H. E., Lohr, B. A., & Wright, L. W. (1995, March). *Is homophobia associated with homosexual arousal?* Paper presented at the Southeastern Psychological Association Conference, Savannah, GA.

Adamson, S. J., & Sellman, J. D. (2001). Drinking goal selection and treatment outcome in out-patients with mild-moderate alcohol dependence. *Drug and Alcohol Review, 20,* 351–359.

Addiction Research Foundation. (1992). Abstinence and reduced drinking: Two approaches to alcohol treatment. *Best advice.* Toronto: Addiction Research Foundation.

Addiction Research Foundation. (1997). *Addiction Research Foundation Website.* Retrieved from http://www.arf.org. Now Centre for Addiction and Mental Health, http://www.camh.net

Ader, R., Felten, D. L., & Cohen, N. (Eds.). (2001). *Psychoneuroimmunology, Vols. 1 & 2* (3rd ed.). San Diego, CA: Academic.

Adlaf, E. M., Demers, A., & Gliksman, L. (Eds.). (2005). *Canadian campus survey 2004.* Toronto: Centre for Addiction and Mental Health.

Adlaf, E., Ivis, F. J., & Smart, R. (1994). *Alcohol and other drug use among Ontario adults in 1994 and changes since 1977.* Toronto: Addiction Research Foundation.

Adlaf, E. M., & Paglia-Boak, A. (2007) *Drug use among Ontario students: OSDUHS highlights 1977–2007.* Toronto: Centre for Addiction and Mental Health.

Albee, G. W. (1990). The futility of psychotherapy. *Journal of Mind and Behavior, 11,* 369–384.

Albee, G. W. (1991). No more rock-scrubbing, *The Scientist Practitioner, 1*(1).

Albee, G. W. (1996). Revolutions and counterrevolutions in prevention. *American Psychologist, 51,* 1130–1133.

Alberta Alcohol and Drug Abuse Commission (2004). *Tobacco basics handbook.* Edmonton: Alberta Alcohol and Drug Abuse Commission.

Alda, M. (1997). Bipolar disorder: From families to genes. *Canadian Journal of Psychiatry, 42,* 378–387.

Alden, L. (1989). Short-term structured treatment for avoidant personality disorder. *Journal of Consulting and Clinical Psychology, 57,* 756–764.

Alden, L. E., & Taylor, C. T. (2004). Interpersonal processes in social phobia. *Clinical Psychology Review, 24,* 857–882.

Alexander, F. (1950). *Psychosomatic medicine: Its principles and applications.* New York: Norton.

Alexander, F., & French, T. M. (1946). *Psychoanalytic therapy: Principles and application.* New York: Ronald Press.

Alexander-Passe, N. (2006). How dyslexic teenagers cope: An investigation of self-esteem, coping and depression. *Dyslexia, 12,* 256–275.

Alexopoulous, G. S., Katz, I. R., Reynolds, C. F., Carpenter, D., & Docherty, J. P. (2001). The Expert Consensus Guideline Series: Pharmacotherapy of depressive disorders in older patients. *Postgraduate Medicine, 110,* 1–86.

Alford, B. A., & Beck, A. T. (1997). *The integrative power of cognitive therapy.* New York: Guilford Press.

Allardyce, J., Gaebel, W., Zielasek, J., & Van Os, J. (2007). Deconstructing Psychosis Conference, February 2006: The validity of schizophrenia and alternative approaches to the classification of psychosis. *Schizophrenia Bulletin, 33,* 863–867.

Allebeck, P. (1989). Schizophrenia: A life-shortening disease. *Schizophrenia Bulletin, 15,* 81–90.

Allen, L. A., Woolfolk, R. L., Lehrer, P. M., Gara, M. A., & Escobar, J. I. (2001). Cognitive behaviour therapy for somatization disorder: A preliminary investigation. *Journal of Behaviour Therapy and Experimental Psychology, 32,* 53–62.

Source: From the References list of Wood, Samuel E., et al. World of Psychology, Sixth Canadian Edition, Pearson Canada Inc., 2011. Print.

As with APA style, in-text citations in the Modern Language Association (MLA) style include the original writer's last name, but this time a page number is used (if applicable). For example, an appropriate reference might be (Shakespeare, 221) indicating to the reader to look to the reference list, find the work cited from Shakespeare, and look at page 221 to find the passage of interest. If another quote from the same author follows closely after the first, you can provide only the new page number (222). The reader knows to look to the earlier author reference.

- MLA in-text citation of one author: (Stephenson 57)
- MLA in-text citation of two authors: (Wong and Sathi 109)
- MLA in-text citation with no author but a title: ("Business Reports" 28)

If more than one work from the same author is cited, include a short version of the title. For example, if Ansen Lee wrote an article entitled "Clear and

Present Writing" and a book called *Writing a Successful Business Plan*, your citations would look like this:

> Never underestimate the importance of clarity in communicating your ideas (Lee, "Clear" 47). And nowhere is clarity more important than in your business plan (Lee, *Writing* 109).

In MLA style a list called Works Cited includes all bibliographic information and comes at the end of the report. Entries are alphabetized by author's last name, or by the title if no author's name is included.

Capitalize the first letter of each main word in the titles of books, journals, articles, periodicals, and so on. The titles of books, magazines, journals, reports, and so on, are italicized. Titles of articles are set in quotation marks.

For journal articles, it is important to include the volume number, issue number, publication year, and page numbers. For example, if the volume number is 5, the issue number is 8, the year is 2010, and the pages numbers for the specific article are 500 to 510, format is as follows: *Journal Name* 5.8 (2010): 500–10. Note that the page span is contracted.

All MLA references should include the medium the source appeared in. Documents that are in print include the word "Print" at the end. If you are using an electronic reference, do not include the website address. Give the full bibliographic information, and include the word "Web" and the date you accessed the site: "Discussion Paper on Apology Legislation." *British Columbia Ministry of Attorney General.* 30 Jan. 2006. Web. 30 Mar. 2008.

Information and other examples of MLA formatting are also on the web. **Figure 12-7** shows part of a works cited list completed in MLA style.

FIGURE 12-7   **The Start of a Reference List That Uses MLA Style**

Works Cited

"About Zoocheck Canada." *Zoocheck Canada.* Zoocheck Canada, 2007. Web. 19 Apr. 2007.

Boehm, Ted. "A New Local Worry: Exotic Cats—Lion and Tiger Prices Fall, and Once Rare Pets Become a Costly Menace." *Wall Street Journal* 30 June 2000: B1. Print.

"Kenya." *Adoption Page.* Cat Tales Zoological Park, 1999. Web. 19 Apr. 2007.

Laidlaw, Rob. "Salmonella, Captivity-Related Stress and the Human Health Implications of Pet Reptiles." *WSPCA Canada.* World Society for the Protection of Animals, 2002. Web. 25 Apr. 2007.

Milloy, Ross E. "Banning Lions and Other Large Pets." *New York Times* 10 Dec. 2001: A19. Print.

Nikolovsky, Boris. "Critics Growl over Keeping of Exotic Pets: Zoo Animals Live in Basements and Backyards." *Toronto Star* 11 Aug. 1994: A18. Print.

"Stoli and Lil." *Adoption Page.* Cat Tales Zoological Park, 1999. Web. 19 Apr. 2007.

"Wild Animals Are Not Pets." Mission Statement. The Wild Animal Orphanage, 2001. Web. 19 Apr. 2007.

"Wild Animals Do Not Make Good Pets." *Animal Info.* Cat Tales Zoological Park, 1999. Web. 19 Apr. 2007.

Source: Adapted from Troyka, Lynn Quitman, and Douglas Hesse. Simon & Schuster Handbook for Writers. *Fifth Canadian Edition. Pearson Canada Inc., 2010. 130. Print.*

Chapter Summary

Careful preparation before writing proposals, reports, and electronic presentations is essential. Business owners, managers, supervisors, and staff make decisions every day and the best decisions are based on the best information.

That information can come from using secondary research that has already been collected and extrapolating to your own experience or from developing primary research to answer your unique questions. Information is available from many places, including your organization, various publications and trade journals, the internet, and, of course, the library.

Using visuals in a proposal, report, or electronic presentation can increase the interest and effectiveness of your work. Colours, fonts, tables, graphs, charts, and animation techniques are all options but should be used carefully to avoid distracting the audience from the main message of the project.

You will improve your business writing techniques by properly referencing the work of others when appropriate. Any time you use the ideas, words, or inventions of others, you should make a note of their contribution to your work. Proper referencing techniques help readers find additional information if they need more data and ensure that you avoid plagiarism. Often, a business or post-secondary institution will have a preference for using either APA or MLA style for citations and reference. You need to know which to use.

PEARSON
mycanadianbuscommlab   Visit **www.mycanadianbuscommlab.ca** for everything you need to help you succeed in the job you've always wanted! Tools and resources include the following:

- Composing and The Writer's Toolkit
- Document Makeovers
- Video Case Studies
- Grammar exercises and much more!

Thinking and Writing Exercises

1. **Finding Guides for Documenting Sources**
   Comprehensive guides for documenting sources are produced by both the Modern Language Association (MLA) and the American Psychological Association (APA). The websites of both organizations provide a limited amount of free information about how to document sources, but they understandably do not go into a great deal of detail. This textbook also provides some information but not enough to answer every question. Using any internet source that you choose, find links to at least five guides:

   - a simple version that provides rules and examples

   - a version that explains the rules by using PowerPoint (ppt)

   - a version that can be downloaded in portable document format (pdf) for easy printouts

   - an automatic version that allows researchers to enter the data while the website does the formatting

   - a commercial product that can be loaded in a word processor

   Save these links. They will be useful for papers that you will write in communication classes and in other courses.

2. **Using Wikipedia**
   Even if your instructor does not approve of Wikipedia as a source of information for a report, it can still be useful as a source for general information or for links to other sources.

   a. Use Wikipedia to look up information on one of the topics listed below. Then examine the sources cited in the entry (if any) and list those that you feel would be appropriate to include if you were writing a report on the impact that the issue has on Canada:

- public–private partnerships
- urban Aboriginal reserves
- diamond mining in the Northwest Territories
- fuel cell manufacturing
- the use of airships to carry cargo to the Canadian North

   b. Repeat your search by using one common search engine and another one that examines the deep web.

   c. List the number of potentially useful hits you received from each source.

3. **Benefits and Drawbacks of Research Types**
   Identify the major advantages and disadvantages of primary research and of secondary research. Which is better?

4. **Benefits and Drawbacks of Data Sources**
   Discuss the pros and cons of doing researching by using the library, the deep web, and the traditional internet. Which is better?

5. **Comparing Web Search Tools**
   Conduct a web search for information on a business-related topic by using at least two different web search engines and one that searches the deep web. (Your school library probably provides access to at least one of these.) A few suggested topics appear below. Your instructor may ask you to brainstorm additional topics:

- the North American Free Trade Agreement
- problems faced by Canada's forestry industries
- starting a small business
- the decline in the number of banks and credit unions in Canada's small towns and poorer inner city neighbourhoods

   a. Identify the key words that you used for each search.

   b. Identify the number of sponsored searches that you received from each search tool.

   c. Assume that you were writing a report dealing with the topic and needed to include five sources. Which search tool provided you with the most useful sources? List those sources by using standard MLA documentation style.

6. **The Benefits of Citations and References**
   Why is it important to use proper citation and referencing strategies? What are you telling your reader if you fail to acknowledge the words, ideas, or inventions of others? Why does this ruin your credibility?

7. **Tradeoffs among Report Accuracy, Timing, and Resources**
   Under what circumstances would you go to your supervisor or boss and ask for more resources to complete a formal report? Is it ever a good idea to sacrifice the accuracy of a report? Describe a situation in which you have made this difficult choice in either your work or school careers.

Writing Skills Checkup: Subject–Verb Agreement

Subjects and verbs are used to identify two essential parts of sentences. The subject of a sentence defines the focus and can be thought of as doing or being. When the subject is a noun, it is the person, place, or thing that is being or doing. For example, consider the following sentence:

The boss called a meeting of her staff.

The word *boss* is both a noun and the subject because it is doing the action of the sentence. Sometimes pronouns can act as the subject, and we could write "She called a meeting of her staff." The pronoun stands in for the noun to avoid repeating the noun again and again. A sentence's subject can be either singular or plural.

Verbs describe the action in the sentence or sometimes a state of being. In our earlier example, "She called a

meeting of her staff," the word *called* is the verb because it describes the action done by the subject. The verb can describe a state of being, as seen in the following: "The staff were happy the boss called the meeting." *Were* is the verb because it describes the state of the staff. Verbs can be present tense, past tense, or future tense. Verbs can also be singular or plural.

The following guidelines will help you decide whether you have subject–verb agreement in your writing.

1. Every verb must agree with its subject both in person (first, second, or third) and in number (singular or plural). If the subject is singular then the verb must also be singular.

   The employee is happy the boss called a meeting.

Because the subject (*employee*) is singular the verb (*is*) must also be singular.

2. If the subject is plural then the verb must also be plural.

The employees are happy the boss called a meeting.

Because *employees* is plural the verb (*are*) must also be plural.

The process of matching subject to verb is sometimes complicated when the subject itself is not obviously singular or plural. Sometimes a word like *staff* is used to mean one person and sometimes it refers to many people. This complicates the task of matching and the writer must look to other surrounding sentences to know if the subject is singular or plural. Alternatively, the sentence can be rewritten for added clarity.

Consider the following: "The staff (*was/were*) happy the boss called a meeting" is unclear because the subject itself is unclear. An alternative is to write "The staff member is happy the boss called a meeting" or "All the staff were happy that the boss called the meeting."

3. Business names can sometimes cause confusion because the name may suggest that the subject is plural when it is not.

Jeune Brothers is a famous store in Victoria.

The underlined subject suggests plurality, but there is only one store.

4. Quantities are sometimes singular and sometimes plural. If the quantity is the subject and it relates to a total amount, then the proper verb usage is singular.

Three weeks of vacation is a long break.

5. Alternatively, if the quantity relates to a countable unit then we apply a plural verb.

Ten dollars were left in the staff coffee fund to buy supplies.

Answer the following questions:

1. Choose the proper form of the subject to match the underlined verb.

   a. The (employee/employees) is leaving work on time _____.
   b. (She, her, they) called to say she's sick and won't come to work today _____.
   c. (Money, Monies) were left on the desk and handed in to Lost and Found _____.

2. Circle the proper form of the verb to match the underlined subject.

   a. The committee (is, are) meeting later today to decide about the project.
   b. Each board member (is, are) a volunteer from the business community.
   c. More than half of the desks (is, are) spoken for in the move.
   d. If I (was, were) the boss, I would be nice to staff.

3. Rewrite the sentences to make sure that the subject matches the verb.

   a. Data are useful in good decision making.
   b. The money in the budget are to be used to fund department priorities only.

Writing Proposals and Reports

CHAPTER

13

LEARNING OUTCOMES

After completing this chapter, you should be able to do the following:

13.1 Understand the various types of proposals and their uses in the workplace

13.2 Identify ways to use requests for proposals

13.3 Describe solicited proposals and unsolicited proposals

13.4 Understand the various types of reports and their uses in the workplace

READY, SET, . . .

Your organization is planning an event, and you are looking for sponsors and companies to donate prizes. Part of the process involves contacting corporations and foundations and asking them to participate. You will need to put the request in writing and submit it for review.

Writing a clear definition of the cause is critical to the success of any fundraising or sponsorship effort. You need to explain how the funds or goods will be used and what benefits the organization can expect from its investment. You also need to identify whether the cause fits with any mandate the individuals and organizations might have. To increase the chances of success, proposals made to foundations or businesses should explain how they will assist the funder in fulfilling the goals and objectives stated in the funder's mission statement.

Once you have secured the organization's support or interest, be sure to follow up with a formal letter of thanks. If you can, it is helpful to show that the event was a success and that the benefits you described in the proposal were achieved. Pictures of the funder's logo or signage, data on the number of exposures their message received, and information on total attendance at the event are all good measures of success and can provide positive closure to the event. They may even set you up for another successful partnership in the future.

PROPOSALS

A proposal is a suggestion, or offering, from one organization to another to do business or work together. The fundraising proposal just described is an example of a specialized proposal.

Proposals come in two types:

1. Internal: An offering from one unit within an organization to work with another unit within the same organization
2. External: An offering made to someone outside the organization

Writing Process for All Proposals

As for all communication tools, writing effective proposals follows a three-step process: (1) planning, (2) writing, and (3) editing. Before you begin writing the proposal, it is always helpful to define its purpose.

You need to create a clear statement of what you hope to achieve, in objective and measurable terms, from whom, and by when. This is called a purpose statement, and it usually begins with the word *To*. It then continues to say what is being proposed, for whom, by when, and why. For example, a proposal to expand the holdings in the school library could have a purpose statement like this:

> To increase the number of library books and journals by 5000 volumes in the next 12 months for use by students and faculty to increase access to knowledge and improve student outcomes

TAKE IT FURTHER

A Successful Proposal

In its initial proposal, Vancouver's Olympic Bid Committee promised to host, in 2010, the world's first environmentally sustainable Olympic Games. This promise fit Vancouver's and the International Olympic Committee's concern about the environment. But are the needs of hosting a mega-event compatible with the idea of sustainability? For example, protesters tried to stop road construction to protect the coastal rainforest habitat. Others pointed out possible disturbance of ancient native burial grounds.[1]

Are financial costs and economic benefits the only measures of support for a community event?

ISSUES
in Communication

The Art of Misgiving, Corporate Style

In many organizations, fundraising for charity work is an increasingly important aspect of business, for many reasons. Giving back to the community improves the organization's image in the minds of potential customers, which can also improve sales and profitability. However, corporations need to set specific guidelines for their sponsorships, which all applicants should follow. When either side misses a step, problems can result.

DOUBLE-DOUBLE, DAY OF TROUBLE

Tim Hortons learned the hard way in 2009 that corporate giving, when done incorrectly, can bring bad publicity.[2]

When the National Organization for Marriage approached a Tim Hortons executive for sponsorship,

"Excellent proposal. Let's take it upstairs and see if it flies."

Floating a new idea

the regional franchise owner agreed to donate coffee. Tim Hortons was promoted as a sponsor on flyers for "Rhode Island's First Annual Celebrate Marriage and Family Day!" However, the event was for heterosexual couples only.

Canada legalized gay marriage in 2005, and Tim Hortons quickly came under criticism in this country for supporting the anti-gay organization. Protests on Facebook and Twitter, and petitions on blogs, forced the chain to withdraw its sponsorship. In an attempt to recover from the bad publicity, the Canadian head office released a statement: "It has come to our attention that the Rhode Island event organizer and purpose of the event fall outside of our sponsorship guidelines." They added that their corporate guidelines specifically

state they will not sponsor religious groups, political affiliates, or lobby groups. However, the National Organization for Marriage's website clearly states its position on gay rights.

Neither party followed the correct process for sponsorship in this situation, and neither party received the outcome it had anticipated.

DISCUSSION

1. **Create some guidelines to help corporate sponsors make effective sponsorship decisions. What should corporate sponsors avoid?**
2. **Given the risk of negative publicity, why should any business offer sponsorships?**
3. **Should businesses support the same causes year after year? Why or why not?**
4. **As a business owner, you want to support a particular cause, but it is late in the fiscal year, and your sponsorship budget is depleted. How can you help?**

In that purpose statement, the reader knows exactly what is being proposed, who will benefit, and how success can be measured.

Once your purpose is clear, the process continues much as it does with other forms of writing. Proposals typically have three main sections:

1. the introduction, which often includes the background of the problem that needs to be solved
2. the body of the proposal, in which the details are described
3. the summary or conclusion, which brings the reader back to your proposed resolution and the reason that the proposal is the best course of action

How you prepare each section will vary according to the type of proposal.

Considering the Audience   Different audiences require different types of information and perhaps even different writing styles:

- *A proposal for upper management:* You may need to be very brief; this proposal is usually to get an agreement in principle for some kind of change. You can work out the details later, once the initial direction of change has been determined.

Proposals bring new ideas to life.

- *A proposal to middle or frontline management:* This type should contain more details of how the proposal will affect people and the jobs they do.
- *A proposal for staff:* This type needs even more detail and should describe exactly what the changes mean to people's day-to-day activities. At this level, there is no room for debate about whether the proposal is sound. The focus instead is on how best to bring about the change efficiently.

The degree of formality of the writing will also likely decrease from upper to middle management. You would usually use the most informal writing styles for staff.

As the author of the proposal, you want to do more than just present the idea—you want to get it approved. Understanding the needs of your audience is crucial. Ask yourself the simple questions: "What does the audience know now about this proposal and the issues it addresses?" and "What do they need to know to approve your proposal?" The answers will guide and focus your development of relevant arguments and help you write a more persuasive proposal.

Solicited and Unsolicited Proposals

A solicited proposal is one requested by your supervisor or boss. Your supervisor may be aware of a problem and ask you to prepare a proposal for its solution. Because the supervisor is already aware of the problem, you do not have to waste time and energy detailing the background.

Everyone is entitled to my opinion.

An unsolicited proposal is one you initiate to solve a problem. In this type of proposal, you may have to describe the background and the problem, especially if the audience is not aware of the issues that your proposal is intended to correct.

Almost all proposals involve change, which can be expensive and disruptive to staff, management, and even customers. The benefits of the proposal must outweigh the costs of doing nothing. If the supervisor does not agree that there is a problem, then little can be gained through change, and your proposal is more likely to be rejected.

To write your proposal, brainstorm ideas and relevant key issues, and then group them appropriately for an organized draft list. This can be in order of importance, by the sequence of time, by geographic region, by business unit, and so on. List ideas in the way that will make the most sense to the audience. Once the sequencing is complete, you are ready to begin the actual proposal writing. Proposals, like formal reports, can vary in length from a couple of pages to dozens, if not hundreds, of pages. The size of the proposal will depend, in part, on how big the problem is you need to address and the complexity of the proposed solution.

1. The Request for Proposal (RFP)

A request for proposal (RFP) is a unique type of formal solicited proposal that is often used in business. As the name implies, the RFP is a formal request made by one organization to another for proposed solutions to a defined problem.

In many cases, the RFP is the first step in getting an outside agency to complete a project or set amount of work. For example, suppose you are the manager of a small company. As a part of your organization's growth strategy, a new marketing campaign will be initiated to increase customer awareness, product acceptance, and sales. Because the company is small, you do not have a dedicated marketing department. One option is to send out an RFP to marketing and advertising specialists to give you ideas on what they could do for your campaign and how much it will cost. By using an RFP, you can meet the objective of launching a new marketing campaign without the expense of starting a new department.

Because the RFP is so common in today's business world, most organizations have already established a company process to either (1) initiate an RFP or (2) respond to an RFP. It is important to check with your organization about the approved process before beginning work.

Writing an RFP   Writing an effective RFP can be quite complicated, because it must be complete in all its details and highly accurate. Remember that the RFP is a guide for firms to set up their proposals. If you make mistakes or leave out important details, the proposals that come in will be flawed as well. If you want quality proposals, then you must supply a quality RFP.

The RFP not only describes the project and its parameters but also gives information on how companies should respond, how the proposals will be reviewed, and how to contact your company. These guidelines help contractors

"POLITICS-FREE CONTRACT THAT WAS ONLY A DREAM"

If you feather your nest with contractor kickbacks, prepare to eat some crow.

to include the right kinds of information in the right order, and they also help the company compare the responses.

Table 13-1 lists the sections that make up an RFP.

Each section will be discussed as we explore the process of responding to an RFP.

TABLE 13-1	A Typical Request for Proposal (RFP)
Section	**Description**
executive summary	summary of the entire proposal
statement of need	why the project is necessary
project description	what the final project will include and how RFPs will be evaluated
organization information	who the work is being prepared for
project schedule	when the project steps will be completed
budget	financial estimates of major tasks of the RFP and the total
conclusion	a summary of the proposal

TAKE IT FURTHER

Sweetheart Deals

After a public outcry over single-source contracts (single-source contracts are given to a single company with little or no competition process) for large companies working in the war efforts in Afghanistan and Iraq and the cleanup following Hurricane Katrina, the U.S. government changed its RFP policy. The concerns emerged after multi-million-dollar sweetheart deals were awarded to private sector contractors, some of whom had reported political connections. The share of work awarded by using full and open competition (open only to large firms) dropped from 65 percent to 55 percent, while the number of small-business contracts increased.[6]

How does the traditional RFP process help ensure fairness and efficiency in awarding contracts?

2. Proposal Responding to an RFP

The response to an RFP is also a solicited proposal. Because there are no absolute rules in writing an RFP, there are no absolute rules or guidelines for writing a proposal that responds to an RFP. An exception might be government agencies, which typically provide strict instructions to follow when completing the RFP. Contractors who do not complete each of the government RFP requirements risk having their proposal denied for non-compliance. Contractors must carefully study the RFP and write a proposal explaining how they can effectively meet the established needs.

The RFP is very detailed in describing the work required because the company that initiated the RFP has to be confident that the selected contractor can complete the work on time and on budget. For example, an RFP would never say its purpose is to improve sales by 10 percent in a given time. This is far too open to speculation of how to achieve the goal. An RFP may have that as the ultimate goal, but it will spell out how it is to be reached, for example, through a television-based advertising strategy running for three months, a public relations event, and a post-campaign evaluation of customer response. Details matter in an RFP, and it must state what is required of the contractor.

The components of a reply to an RFP will vary, but most will contain the sections shown in **Table 13-2**.

TABLE 13-2   **A Typical Proposal Responding to an RFP**

Section	Description
Copy of the original RFP	The copy is helpful because it lays out the parameters of what is required, for what budget, and by when.
Executive summary	Written from the responding company's perspective, this is a brief one- to two-page overview of how the responding company will provide the required work.
Body of proposal	The body includes the standard introduction section, details, and closing statements.
Title page	Often optional, the title page provides the RFP title, author name, organization, date, and other information pertinent to the reviewer.
Letter of authorization	This is the covering letter for the proposal from the responding organization to the company contact that issued the RFP.
List of illustrations and tables	The list summarizes the table names and page numbers.
Budget	Detailed costing information for each subtask is included, as well as the total budget. It may include additional information on timing, percent hold-back, and other related information.
Qualifications	This section details the background and experience of the major contributors to the tasks outlined in the RFP. For our previous example, if the RFP is to develop a television-based advertising campaign, then information on the previous experience developing television advertising campaigns will be important for the RFP reviewers.

The real key to writing a successful RFP response is to follow the RFP guidelines very carefully to make sure that your company complies with all RFP requirements of the issuing organization. This is especially true of government-issued RFPs, which are often subject to public criticism and calls for greater accountability and transparency in the process. Failure to completely and accurately comply with all the stated RFP requirements can result in automatic dismissal of the proposal, even if it is otherwise the best of all the submissions.

3. Unsolicited Proposals

Explore

Unsolicited proposals usually take more time and attention to write than solicited proposals, because the audience may not be aware of the problem the proposal is intended to solve. Even if they are aware of the issue, they are not likely aware that a proposal is being presented. Additional attention is needed in the introduction section to make sure that everyone understands the main issues.

Step 1: Planning A clear statement of purpose will help writers stay focused on what is important to the success of a proposal. For the example above, the purpose statement "to raise $5000 in the next three months to build an on-site playground for children in the company daycare" is much more convincing than say, "to improve staff morale."

Once the purpose is developed, a helpful exercise is to brainstorm the issues that relate to the purpose. For example, a sampling of issues could include the following:

- inadequacy of current playroom
- budget constraints
- installation logistics
- upkeep and repair costs
- use of licensed contractors
- age-specific playground activities
- building permits
- access routes
- perimeter fencing
- lighting
- liability issues
- accessibility for children with disabilities
- child safety and first aid

Once you have identified the main ideas, you need to sort the issues to give structure to the proposal. Issues can be sorted in many ways based on importance, chronology, cost, timing, or critical path to completion. As the writer, you should always think about how readers prefer to receive their information. This tactic increases readers' comprehension and perhaps even influences their opinions to be more favourable. Good planning and preparation should account for about 25 percent of the work required to write a good proposal.

Step 2: Writing a Draft With good planning and preparation of the key issues, the writing itself becomes little more than connecting the bits of relevant information, much like connecting the numbered dots of a dot-to-dot puzzle provides a complete image at the end.

Remember that the structure of business writing is somewhat different from other types of writing that you may have learned in the past. In creative writing, the writer drops hints throughout the story to build to a climax near the end. In business writing, the opposite happens.

Remember that you are providing information the audience needs to support your idea. Beginning with the strongest arguments for your idea increases the likelihood that your audience will read and understand these arguments. Often the most valuable asset a senior manager or business owner has is time, and to save time (and money) some decision makers will skip reading the ends of reports.

The same can also be said for constructing effective paragraphs. A common speed-reading technique is to read the first line in every paragraph to get the gist of the story. Knowing this, you can place the thesis statement (the meat of the paragraph) as the first sentence. The remaining sentences of the paragraph then become support for your paragraph's thesis.

Once you have drafted the body of the proposal, it is usually a good time to go back and write the introduction and the conclusion. Writers will often write the introduction after the body of the proposal, because it's not always possible to know all the details of the body before you actually write it. By writing the introduction afterward, you can include all the most relevant bits of information and improve the flow of information to the reader.

Writing the conclusion after the introduction allows you to revisit all the major issues presented in the introduction and remind the reader of these key points.

Step 2—or getting from the outline to the finished first draft—usually makes up about 50 percent of the work required to write an effective proposal.

Step 3: Refining and Polishing   Every proposal requires the audience to believe in your idea and so to believe in you. A proposal that has spelling errors, punctuation problems, sentence structure issues, or other formatting errors makes you seem less competent. A decent idea can become worthless if not properly presented with accuracy.

It is common for proposal writers to edit a report three or four times or more before submitting it. Do not use the spell checker and grammar checker of your word processor as a crutch. Many common errors are missed by these applications.

Consider editing the final proposal in stages.

First edit   Try reading the report aloud, following along with a pencil as you read. Errors become more apparent during this process. There are two reasons for reading aloud:

1. When you read the work silently, your brain automatically substitutes what you wrote with what you expect it to say.

2. When you read your work aloud, you are more likely to notice any mistakes you made in word choice, punctuation, and sentence structure.

Second edit   Next, go back and correct spelling errors. At the same time, identify any words that you have used that may not be clear or familiar to your audience. Have you relied on jargon, for example, that is known only to your own organization? How about acronyms? Will everyone who reads your proposal know what you mean? A common error is substituting a complicated word taken from a thesaurus for a simple word. Many writers think that big words make them appear smarter or make the proposal sound more sophisticated. Neither is true, and effective business writing puts clarity first. The simple choice is often the best choice.

Third edit   You can use this edit to manage sentence structure. Each paragraph should include mixtures of short and medium-length sentences—nothing overly complicated that requires a doctorate in punctuation to decipher. Variable sentence length makes the reading more interesting. Too many short sentences make for a choppier read, which can be frustrating to readers. Too many long sentences can be confusing.

Another set of eyes   As a last edit, it is helpful to get someone who is unfamiliar with the proposal to read it. If that person can understand it, the chances are good that it will be understandable to your audience, who, presumably, know more about the issue. Friends and family can be helpful here.

Timing Note   Try to break up the edits, with at least a few hours in between or, better yet, overnight. Looking at a piece of written work with a fresh perspective can often lead to more clarity in thinking and improved editing style. Of course, you may not always have the luxury of time, but with unsolicited proposals, the timing of the presentation is likely up to you as the initiator of the idea. The editing process can take as much as 25 percent of the total time needed for the proposal. Unfortunately, writers often overlook it by assuming that their first draft is adequate or that rushing to meet an artificial deadline is more important than producing a finely tuned and professional looking proposal.

Figure 13-1 is an example adapted from a student project proposing a new community youth drop-in centre. It contains many of the points described above and will give you an idea of what is involved in preparing an effective unsolicited proposal.

REPORTS: FORMAL AND INFORMAL

Reports, like all types of communications, play a role in business. They can be either formal or informal.

The formal report is the most technically demanding of all business reports, and, depending on the complexity of the problem and needs of the audience, can take weeks or months to prepare. It is not unusual for a very detailed formal report to be 50 to 100 pages or more, but most business reports are between 5 and 25 pages.

Informal reports tend to be significantly shorter, usually between two and ten pages. Easily the most common of all business reports, the informal

TAKE IT FURTHER

Holy head in the sand, Batman!

Baby boomers (born between about 1945 and 1962) aren't as healthy as they think, the Heart and Stroke Foundation said in a recent annual report. More than half of baby boomers were inactive, while obesity rates had climbed by nearly 60 percent in ten years for that age group. Although 58 percent of boomers think their weight has little or no effect on their heart health, the Heart and Stroke Foundation said 1.3 million Canadian baby boomers have already been diagnosed with heart disease, stroke, or high blood pressure.[7]

Despite this unsolicited report, obesity and inactivity in all age groups have increased. If you were the author of the report, what could you do to try to bring about real change?

FIGURE 13-1   **An Unsolicited Proposal Written by Students**

Mallory Rance
Trishia Siemens
(204) 555-2810

January 23, 2008

Ernest Bauer, Chief Administrative Officer
Box 152
Rosebloom, Manitoba
R0G 1W0

The formatting is correct throughout.

Dear Ernest Bauer:

SUBJECT: A PROPOSAL TO OPEN A YOUTH DROP-IN CENTRE

The purpose statement is clear.

As our society has changed over the past few years, more and more teens have turned to smoking, drugs, sex, and violence as sources of entertainment and fun. Starting a youth drop-in centre in Rosebloom will not only help stop these destructive behaviours but also prevent them from happening in the future.

Problem

In Rosebloom, a growing number of teens have turned to negative lifestyles as a form of entertainment. This is due to the fact that Rosebloom has nothing available for evening entertainment past 8:00 p.m. Underage teens have recently resorted to vandalism, drinking and driving, and other reckless behaviours.

Information is supported by research.

One of the many examples of these behaviours happened in the summer of 2005. Many teens looking for something to keep occupied resorted to jumping off the local bridge into the river below. This new activity started out as a simple concern to parents but seemed harmless to most. It ended up leading to a tragic accident on the bridge caused by the many distractions to drivers. An elderly woman died when she rear-ended another vehicle that was slowing down to watch the teens jump.

In efforts to decrease these reckless behaviours, we want to create a place where teens can go in the evenings to have fun and don't have to face the pressures of society, and starting a drop-in centre in Rosebloom will do just that.

FIGURE 13-1 (*continued*)

2

Proposal

When looking for a proper location for the Rosebloom Drop-In Centre, we decided it was best to rent an existing building. Currently, the back banquet room in the C.K. Café is not in use, and it would be the perfect size to accommodate all of our plans. This space is not in excellent shape and therefore needs to be completely renovated before opening the drop-in centre to the public.

Our renovation plan is 8 weeks long and consists of many factors:
- ripping out the existing carpet and installing new laminate flooring
- painting all walls and ceiling
- purchasing 7 tables and 28 chairs
- purchasing 4 sofas and 2 love seats
- installing one 50-inch flat-screen television
- installing a sound system
- purchasing 1 pool table
- constructing a juice bar
- purchasing 1 refrigerator to store drinks

Once our renovations are complete, we plan to operate from 7 p.m. to 12 a.m. on Monday to Thursday, and 7 p.m. to 2 a.m. on Friday and Saturday, and will be closed on Sunday.

Benefits

We believe this project will benefit Rosebloom in three main areas. It will first and foremost give teenagers a place to socialize in a safe environment. It will also give the parents of the teenagers peace of mind, knowing that their kids are safe in a controlled environment. The drop-in centre will also benefit the community by preparing the youth for the workforce by creating work positions at the centre.

> The solution is practical and creative.

> Bullets are used effectively.

> The benefits are clearly explained.

FIGURE 13-1   (*continued*)

3

Staffing/Qualifications

To effectively run the Rosebloom Youth Drop-In Centre, our staff for each shift will need to include two adults with one year prior experience in childcare, who possess general management skills, as well as two teens to run the juice bar and clean up at the end of their shift.

By allowing our team to operate this business, you can be assured that you will have a safer and more controlled community. It will also attract families to Rosebloom from surrounding communities and therefore generate more revenue for other local businesses. By investing in this project, you will give Rosebloom the chance to expand in different ways.

Schedule

The time of year when teens are the most anxious to find entertainment is in the summer. Therefore, we are aiming to have the drop-in completed and ready for business by June 1, 2008. Listed below are dates included in our time plan:

- March 1 – Sign contract with C.K. Café for renting the space starting April 1, 2008.
- March 1–15 – Purchase all materials needed for flooring, juice bar, and painting.
- March 16–31 – Make sure all volunteer helpers are contacted for work starting on April 1.
- April 7 – Have the existing floor ripped out as well as all preparation for the walls to be painted, such as taping and sanding.
- April 8–20 – Install all flooring as well as construct juice bar.
- April 21–30 – Prime and paint all walls and ceiling.
- April 21–30 – Purchase all accessories for the space, such as couches, pool table, television, sound system, refrigerator, and tables and chairs.
- May 1–15 – Install all electronics, arrange furniture, and finish any set-up needed before opening date.
- May 16–31 – Purchase and set up chips and drinks to be sold at the snack bar.
- May 16–31 – Tie up any loose ends.
- June 1 – Opening date.

The timeline is realistic and detailed.

FIGURE 13-1 *(continued)*

4

Cost

Most of our costs will be start-up costs. The only costs that will be carried on throughout the year will be the rental of the space (including the use of utilities), minimum wage salaries for the kids working the juice bar, and supplies for the juice bar. Please see our detailed list attached for all our expected expenses.

Our operating expenses for the year to follow will include:

Salaries Expense	$13 000
Operating Expense	9 600
Total Operating Expenses Per Year	$22 600

Evaluation

The success of this project cannot be well measured in profit, and so we plan to rely on surveys that will be distributed through the town of Rosebloom. A detailed, one-page survey will be given to any visitors of the drop-in during the week of September 1, three months after our opening date. We are also planning to distribute these surveys throughout the town by putting one survey in every mailbox in Rosebloom. This way we can be sure to get feedback from the teens, as well as their parents and local businesses.

To measure our success, the feedback will be graded by percentage. All questions on the survey will be answered on a scale of 1 to 10. These numbers will indicate a percent. For example, if one question is graded as a 2 out of 10, its outcome is 20%. We will take the average percentage of feedback on each question as well as the average final percentage of the whole survey. Looking at the average of each question will help us to know where we need to improve and where we are doing very well. Taking the average final percentage will help us know whether or not we have been successful. If our score is between 60% and 69%, we will continue with the drop-in and try to accommodate any changes that are needed to improve. If we score a final of 70% or higher, we will consider the drop-in a success.

We plan to take these surveys every three months for the first year, and afterwards, every six months. We want to keep track of our success rates to make sure everyone is continually happy about the drop-in centre's contribution to the town of Rosebloom.

Careful attention has been paid to spelling, grammar, and punctuation.

FIGURE 13-1 *(continued)*

5

Authorization

We would love for the R.M. of Morris to consider funding our project in hopes of improving our community. We want to create a safer place for teenagers where we can help kids socialize and feel connected to the community. We are requesting a final decision by February 15, 2008. If you decide that this is a positive movement for our town, we need all funds advanced to us via cheque by March 1, 2008, as well as an attached copy of this proposal signed by you, Ernest Bauer, the Chief Administrative Officer of the R.M. of Morris. We hope that you have found this proposal to be a start of a project that is well worth the time, effort, and finances it will take to start the operation by June 1. Please feel free to contact Mallory Rance regarding any concerns or information. We want to start the Rosebloom Drop-In Centre with the R.M. of Morris behind us.

Sincerely,

Mallory Rance

Trishia Siemens

Mallory Rance
Trishia Siemens
(204) 555-2810

FIGURE 13-1 (*continued*)

6

Detailed Schedule of Expenses and Purchases

Operating Expenses
Total: $22 600

Salaries
$13 000/year
This includes paying two teenagers per shift at minimum wage. These shifts are roughly 5 hours long with some additional clean-up. This total is estimated because of some unknown exact hours.

Rent Expense (Utilities Included)
$6600/year, $550/month
This includes utilities that the C.K. Café will be paying.

Food and Drinks Expense
$3000/year, $250/month
This includes all chips and drinks sold. This total is estimated because of some unknown variables, such as what the demand will end up being exactly.

Maintenance Purchases
Total: $1347.85

- Sico Paint – Primer, 5 gallons – $164.95, 32.99/gallon from Rona
- ceiling paint, 4 gallons – $147.96, $36.99/gallon from Rona
- wall paint, 6 gallons – $209.94, $34.99/gallon from Rona
- Rustin Elegance Vermont Maple Laminate Flooring – $825, $2.50/square foot from laminateflooring.org

Capital Purchases
Total: $17 183.97

- four Tylosand 4-seater sofa – $5996.00 from Ikea at $1499.00/piece.
- two EKTORP love seats – $1198 from Ikea at $599.00/piece.
- seven sets of Jans large table and 4 chairs – $1036.00 from Jysk at $148.00/set
- Bose Lyfestyle 28 Series sound system – $2999.99 from Future Shop
- Panasonic 50-inch flat-panel television – $2699.99 from Future Shop
- Samsung 18.8 cu. ft. refrigerator – $1249.99 from Future Shop
- "The Monaco" 7-foot pool table – $1145.00 from PoolTablesDirect.ca (reg. $3604.99)
- building supplies for juice bar – $859.00 as quoted by Rona Rosebloom

Total expenses for our starting year:
        $41 131.82

Source: Rance, Mallory, and Trishia Siemens. A Proposal to Open a Youth Drop-In Centre. *Unpublished assignment for Les Hanson, Instructor, Red River College. 23 Jan. 2008. Print.*

report can take the form of a letter, memo, or more stylized report with organizational headers and sections.

Using the proven three-step process of planning, analyzing, and writing can simplify the challenge of producing a report.

✓●─[Practise] # 1. Informational Report and Memo Format

Easily the most common type of report in business is the informational report that is presented in a memo format. The steps taken in this project are similar to those of other types of communication: planning, researching, and writing.

It is helpful to begin the process by answering some basic questions:

- What is the purpose of the report?
- What will the report be about?
- Who is the report for?
- What are the constraints, such as time to complete, length, and people involved?
- What should the final product look like?

The answers to these preliminary questions will help you narrow the investigation and analysis to only that information that will further the purpose. Taking the time to draft a plan with the answers to these questions can save a lot of time later, especially if the instructions you received in the request for the report are unclear. Consider getting approval of an overview document that details these answers to these questions before beginning the actual work.

The purpose of this informational report is to provide information to the reader in the form of a written document. This does not include either an analysis of the information or a recommendation for further action. The report will be about a particular set of data of interest, such as branch sales figures by quarter for the previous fiscal year. Informational reports are often intended for internal use within an organization and so will be sent to a supervisor, boss, or colleague.

Most informal reports in memo format will be short, a few pages at most. The major sections include (1) an opening summary, (2) a background, (3) current status, (4) future considerations, and (5) a summary and conclusions. Businesses will typically have an approved format and the sections may vary somewhat from the above list. You should investigate and follow any established ways of writing reports in your business environment.

As with all memos, the opening section includes necessary information:

Organization Name:

Date:

To:

From:

Subject:

The various parts of the informational report are as follows:

1. *Opening summary*: Describes the purpose for the report. We will continue to use our earlier example, and so the purpose is to report on quarterly sales figures by branch.

2. *Background*: Provides the reader with recent history about the purpose and puts the information in context to improve the understandability of the report. In our example of quarterly sales, a possible background statement might be "Further to the need to develop ongoing strategies to increase future sales, the following quarterly sales will be presented."

3. *Current status*: Describes the work done to date. These data are time sensitive and therefore subject to change as time passes and additional work is completed. Continuing our example, "The most up-to-date data available include January–March 2010."

4. *Future consideration*: If included, this section allows you to inform the reader of possible changes in the future. Continuing our example, "Sales in all quarters may improve when the overall economy improves."

5. *Summary and conclusions*: If included, this section provides a highlight of the major messages contained within the report: "The quarterly reports of sales show stable sales in most markets, with the exception of Midtown, which is decreasing."

See **Figure 13-2** for a sample of a report written as a memo.

Depending on the audience and the restriction on time or length, you may be able to cover the details of the report very briefly in a sentence or two. In very short reports of a page or two there is little value in having more formalized sections complete with headings. The information on background is still important and included as a part of the overall message. It just doesn't have a section of its own separated by a header.

2. Analytical Report in Letter Format

An analytical report in letter format is similar to the informational report, with one significant exception: The informational report conveys to the reader the data or information, often in its rawest form. The analytical report takes it further by adding the author's analysis of the information.

For example, the quarterly sales data by region is simply a list of numbers. The analytical report in letter format takes the process a step further and relies on the skill and expertise of the researcher to study the raw data and interpret what it most likely means. Rather than just giving information, you are now asked to provide insight on what might be influencing the information as presented. This *value added* component helps senior managers, owners, and decision makers to improve their understanding of what is happening and so improve their responses to changing business conditions.

A report like this needs additional space to present all the necessary details *and* the analysis. Again, if there are limits on length, for example, you need to explore all possible ways to present the information in the manner that will be most valuable, from the reader's point of view. **Figure 13-3** uses the same basic process as Figure 13-2 and expands it into an analytical report in letter format.

It is possible, of course, to provide more definitive explanations than in the informal analytical report, but this requires more time, expertise, and resources to complete. A report of this type is a formal report, to which we will now turn our attention.

FIGURE 13-2 — **An Information Report in Memo Format**

ACME Sportswear Company
Interoffice Memo

Date: January 15, 2010
To: Jane Gooding, Regional Vice-President
From: Tom Sleuth, Assistant Sales Manager
Subject: Quarterly sales figures, by region, for fiscal year 2009–2010

The purpose of this memo is to provide information on the total sales figures (in dollars) by region for the most recent fiscal year: 2009–2010. These data are provided in response to your request of January 2, 2010.

Reported sales by region were highest in Midtown, peaking in Quarter 1 at $3.8 million. From this high, sales dropped in Midtown for each successive quarter to a low of $2.8 million. Sales in Northtown were the next highest, reaching $2.6 million in Quarter 3. Sales in Southtown were the lowest of the three, ranging from a high of $1.9 million in Quarter 3 to a low of $1.3 million in Quarter 2. The details are shown in the following table.

Quarterly Sales by Region (in millions of dollars)

	Midtown	Northtown	Southtown
Quarter 1	$3.8	$2.5	$1.5
Quarter 2	$3.3	$2.4	$1.3
Quarter 3	$3.0	$2.6	$1.9
Quarter 4	$2.8	$2.5	$1.4

Source: Accounting Department, *Quarterly Sales Report*, Dave Stern

The store expansions in Northtown are now complete. Planned expansions to stores in Southtown are expected to begin in May 2010 and are scheduled for completion in October 2010. If the experience of the Northtown store expansions are any indication of what to expect in the Southtown expansions, we can expect delays of one to two months. To better plan for possible delays, I will prepare an interim report on sales and construction status by the end of Quarter 2.

The interim report on sales and construction will be completed by July 15 for your review.

FIGURE 13-3   **An Analytical Report in Letter Format**

ACME Sportswear Company
123 Dufferin Street
Anytown, MB R3Y 1G8
204-555-1234
www.acmesportwear.ca

January 15, 2010

Ms. Anita Wong, Board Chairperson
Integrated Sports Investment International
Suite 10001, Skyview Terrace
Toronto ON M4K 3Z4

Dear Ms. Wong:

The purpose of this letter is to provide information on the total sales figures (in dollars) by region for the most recent fiscal year: 2009–2010. These data are provided in response to your request of January 2, 2010. Sales for all regions totalled $29 million for the fiscal year, with a growing percentage of total sales coming from Northtown and Southtown. Reasons for these changes are related to worsening economic conditions in Midtown. Sales in Northtown improved after the renovations were completed, and it is expected that a similar rise in sales in Southtown will occur once the renovations there are complete.

> The purpose statement is clear.

Reported sales by region were highest in Midtown, peaking in Quarter 1 at $3.8 million. From this high, sales dropped in Midtown for each successive quarter to a low of $2.8 million. Sales in Northtown were the next highest, reaching $2.6 million in Quarter 3. Sales in Southtown were the lowest of the three, ranging from a high of $1.9 million in Quarter 3 to a low of $1.3 million in Quarter 2. The details are shown in the following table.

> The information is relevant.

Quarterly Sales by Region (in millions of dollars)

	Midtown	Northtown	Southtown	Total
Quarter 1	$3.8	$2.5	$1.5	$ 7.8
Quarter 2	$3.3	$2.4	$1.3	$ 7.0
Quarter 3	$3.0	$2.6	$1.9	$ 7.5
Quarter 4	$2.8	$2.5	$1.4	$ 6.7
Total	$12.9	$10.0	$6.1	$29.0

> Sources are cited.

Source: Accounting Department, *Quarterly Sales Report*, Dave Stern

FIGURE 13-3 (*continued*)

2

The cumulative impact on quarterly sales over the fiscal year can be seen more clearly in the following graph. The sales for Midtown were initially high after the renovations were completed in the last quarter of the previous fiscal year. Since then, quarterly sales have dropped, perhaps because of worsening economic conditions, which have also curtailed higher forecasted sales in Northtown expected after renovations. Southtown's sales have been fairly consistent over time, with the exception of the third quarter. A new residential development opened in Southtown during this period, which could help explain the increase in sales in that region.

> Good use is made of a visual to support the argument.

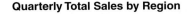
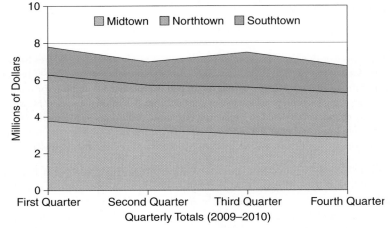

Quarterly Total Sales by Region

In summary, the store expansions to Midtown and Northtown are now complete. Planned expansions to stores in Southtown are expected to begin in May 2010 and are scheduled for completion in October 2010. If the experience of the Northtown store expansions are any indication of what to expect in the Southtown expansions, we can expect delays of one to two months. To better plan for possible delays, I will prepare an interim report on sales and construction status by the end of the second quarter. The interim report on sales and construction will be completed by July 15 for your review.

> The follow-up steps are listed.

If you or the board members have any questions, please do not hesitate to contact me at your convenience. My direct number is 204-555-1235.

> Contact information is provided.

Sincerely,

Jane Gooding

Jane Gooding
Regional Vice-President

> The writer's signature and title are included.

3. Formal Reports

Because they are intended to deal with more complex issues, formal reports require considerably more work in planning, research, writing, and editing than shorter informal reports. There are other differences, too:

- The style of the writing is different, with more formal use of language and grammar. For example, contractions, such as *couldn't*, are written in full as *could not*, and personal pronouns, such as *I, me, we,* and *us,* are not typically used.

- Word choice may be an issue in more formal reports, but remember that as the writer it is your responsibility to ensure that your point is being made clearly, accurately, and articulately. The formality of the report does not give you licence to grab the nearest thesaurus and replace simple words with longer, little used, and often misunderstood ones. *Clarity* should always be preferred over *perspicuity*. The italicized words are synonyms, but the first word is far more widely understood.

For especially long and complicated reports, it is usually advisable to have two versions:

1. one highly detailed and suitable for middle management, who require in-depth analysis
2. a second summarized version that is more suitable for upper management, who do not have the time to read a long, technical paper

The formal report writing process is similar to all other communications vehicles we have discussed. Although new and inexperienced writers are often overwhelmed with the idea of writing their first formal business report, using the three-step process can help overcome that anxiety by answering the first question: "Where do I begin?"

First Steps   Once again, the process begins with a statement of purpose. What is the intention of the report or, put another way, what does the writer hope to accomplish in writing the report?

If you need to satisfy a demand for information and analysis of the data, then an analytical report is likely the best option. If you need to communicate highly complex information, include analysis, and perhaps provide recommendations for future action, then a formal report is best.

As discussed earlier, a purpose statement is most effective when it begins with the word *To* and continues with an action verb. For example, the purpose of a formal report might read "To inform the board of directors of regional quarterly sales and reasons for change in fiscal 2009–2010, and to recommend possible actions to improve sales by 10 percent for the next fiscal year." This example is very detailed and this can help to focus the writer (and thereby the reader) to a particular outcome. In this example, the writer will show the readers how to improve regional (where) sales (what) by 10 percent (how much) within the next fiscal year (when).

The only question left unaddressed is how, and it is assumed from the purpose that the report itself will be the answer to this last question.

Detailed purpose statements also provide useful milestones for measuring success. For example, what if sales increased by only 8 percent? Are the report and its outcomes a failure? What if the increased sales of 10 percent do occur but this is done in 18 months (or 6)? Does this mean the report is a failure?

Consider What to Cover   Once the purpose of the report is set, it is often helpful to define the scope of investigation and analysis that goes into the report. Given enough time and unlimited resources, you could develop a very complex report. The question is whether such a report meets the needs and expectations of the readers. Too often report writers lose sight of the readers' needs and end up with a mountain of paper that is never read.

One way to limit the size of the report is to limit the kinds of questions it addresses and the types of research that you will do to answer them. Primary research can be more accurate than secondary research (both are discussed in Chapter 12), but it is much more expensive to collect, requires considerably more time to collect, and needs much more sophisticated analysis to make sense of the results. If time and resources are limited, secondary research may be preferable, because much of the work has already been done. It is a matter of whether the results of this earlier analysis are useful and applicable to your report's purpose.

When deciding where to do the research, start by considering internal versus external data. Internal data can come from any department within the organization, including accounting, marketing, sales, production, research and development, customer service, or finance. Internal data are often of high quality and usually easy to access. The quarterly regional sales data that we talked about earlier are an example of internal data. Internal data may not be useful for understanding what is happening outside the organization. The example in Figure 13-3 of the informal analytical report suggests that residential growth could have caused the rise in third-quarter sales in Southtown. Actual data of the number of additional residences could be more convincing and is an example of external data.

Once the purpose is complete, the writer has a sense of the direction that the report will take, as some measure for determining the success for the report.

How Much to Write   An element that should be addressed at this point in the process is the scope of the writing. What questions will be answered? What ones will be recognized as needing an answer in the future? What questions will be set aside completely? The solutions to these questions will require a careful analysis of the resources that are available to you to do the necessary background research, draft writing, and final editing of the report.

In the end, the solutions also depend heavily on how much time is available to you (or your writing team). Every report is a compromise among accuracy, time, and available personnel resources. If the complicated formal report requires 100 percent accuracy and must be done in a short time, then more resources will be required, adding an additional challenge of organizing everyone's efforts.

Formal reports usually deal with complex problems, analyses, and reviews of solutions. Formal reports are often read by readers outside the organization, who may not be familiar with the company's business.

The Audience   Whether audience members are inside or outside your business, they may not be receptive to your recommendations. You will need to address all likely complications before beginning the project, because each condition that the final report must meet (an unreceptive audience, for example) demands a slightly different style of writing to help you make your point.

- *For internal audiences,* or those from within your organization, a direct approach is often preferred because it gets more directly to the point and does not take the reader through unnecessary background information.

- *For an external audience* or an audience that may not agree with your summary and recommendations, an indirect approach is usually more successful because the buffer in the indirect approach helps to explain the need for the decision and the rationale for the ultimate direction of and recommendations in the report.

Two questions are useful to ask at this point:

1. "What does my audience know now about the issue?" This question sets up the information foundation that you need to establish in the background and discussion sections of the report.

2. "What does my audience need to know to make the decision that they make?" This question defines the information and analysis requirements that will help lead the audience to agree with the conclusions and recommendations in the report.

The final elements to consider are the report itself and how it will look. How long should the report be? Longer reports allow you more space to make a valid case for the issue, but longer reports are less likely to be read by people making the final decisions.

Editing Visuals   You need to reconsider how visuals will be included in the report.

In Chapter 12, we discussed different ways of presenting the results of your research visually when you are in the planning stage. Now that you have figures represented visually, you need to edit them, too. For example, consider the use of the pie charts in **Figures 13-4A** and **13-4B**. Which makes the point more clearly?

Does Figure 13-4A or Figure 13-4B represent more in total sales over the three-year period? Because of the size of the pie chart itself, the total sales for **Figure 13-4B** seems higher. In **Figure 13-4B**, which of the three years has the highest total sales? It probably seems as if 2010 does, because of the stretching that occurs in the three-dimensional option. The orientation of the 2010 piece makes it seem closer and larger, from the reader's perspective. The data used to create the two pie charts are exactly the same, and each year's results

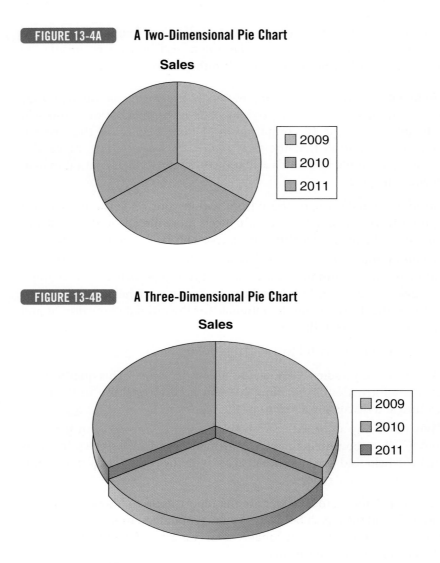

FIGURE 13-4A   A Two-Dimensional Pie Chart

Sales

FIGURE 13-4B   A Three-Dimensional Pie Chart

Sales

are exactly the same. Optical illusions are created by the choice of data representation. The two pie charts were created by using the default settings in a common word processor. The settings were not changed to make the final chart misleading. You have to be cautious in selecting and refining the options for your presentation.

For another example, consider the line graphs in **Figures 13-5A** and **13-5B**. Which shows a stronger growth in sales?

When your eyes see a steep upward-sloping line on a graph, as in Figure 13-5B, your brain automatically concludes "growth in sales is good." The truth is that the data tables used to create the two line graphs are identical. By altering the y-axis and starting at a number that is closer to the start of the data series, rather than at 0, as in Figure 13-5A, the slope of the data can be emphasized, even overemphasized. Total sales have increased by less than 1 percent over the ten-year period but the mind reads the graphs differently.

Make sure, during this editing stage, that your visuals are making the point you want them to—nothing more, nothing less.

FIGURE 13-5A   **A Line Graph Showing Little Line Slope**

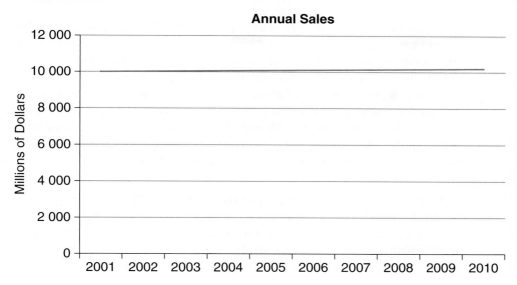

Annual Sales

FIGURE13-5B   **A Line Graph That Emphasizes Line Slope**

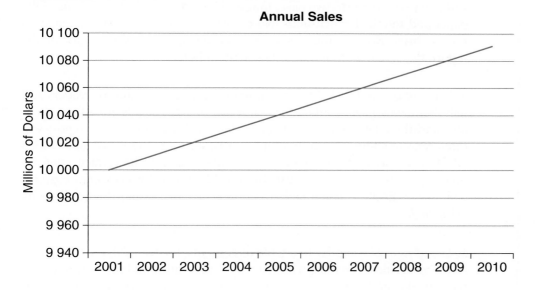

Annual Sales

Sections in a Formal Report   Most organizations will have an established format for the sections to be included in a formal report. This is because the organization wants to project a positive image, and a consistent format suggests that thought has been put into a communications strategy. A consistent format also improves the reader's ability to find the needed information because the report will have the same basic organizational structure regardless of who writes the paper. Formal reports, because of their size and complexity, are often broken into smaller and more manageable sections.

The following order of main sections is fairly common.

1. Letter of transmittal   The letter of transmittal is a letter or memo that introduces the report to the intended audience. It tells the audience who you are, where you work, and what the report is for, and it introduces the opportunity for future discussions about the report's findings. A letter of transmittal is especially important when a formal report is sent to an external audience or any audience that is not necessarily expecting to receive the report or remember why they are receiving it. Although the letter of transmittal accompanies a report in the same envelope, it is not always permanently affixed to the report itself and may not become part of the formal written record or file.

2. Title page   Truly the beginning of the report itself, the title page gives the reader a synopsis of key information, including the name of the report, who it was prepared for, who wrote it, and when it was finalized. The title page is traditionally unnumbered but considered as page i.

3. Executive summary   The executive summary is a summary of the report's key findings and recommendations, intended especially for senior management, who may not have time to read the entire report. A typical executive summary will be one to two pages long and include only the high points of the paper and the final conclusions. No discussion or examples are included, to keep it brief. Because the executive summary synthesizes the work of the report, the executive summary is best written last.

4. Table of contents   A table of contents is a fast access aid for readers and tells them what pages contain the major sections. No details other than headings and the related page numbers are included. Because a final report will often require adding, or subtracting, words, sections, and visual aids (which affects page orientation), the table of contents should be created after the final report is approved for distribution. Many word-processing programs will automatically create a table of contents if you format the headings by using *Styles*.

5. List of figures   Similar to a table of contents, the list of figures is a list of all the visual aids contained within a report, their titles, and the page numbers they appear on. For the sake of clarity, use the word *Figure* to describe a figure, *Table* to describe a table, and so on. Be sure to number each figure and table, starting at 1.

6. Report body   The body is the real substance of the report. In the body, you try to lead the reader through the maze of issues affecting the report's purpose and highlight the logic that supports the final conclusions and recommendations, when applicable. Because the report often goes beyond simply providing information, you need to try to anticipate as many questions and barriers to reader comprehension as possible and provide reasonable solutions.

The body is traditionally broken into subsections, again for the convenience of the reader and to help in comprehension:

- *Introduction:* This provides the reader with an understanding of the foundation on which the report is built. For example, the statement of purpose for the report is included in the introduction, although this will almost always be worded slightly differently than the working purpose statement developed earlier in the writing process. The purpose can include the details of the objectives we discussed earlier, but if these are included, they will naturally be used by the reader to gauge success or failure of the report. Sometimes it is advisable to withhold some of the details of the purpose from the final report to make the report less controversial. Information on the scope of the report and whether primary or secondary research was used are also contained in the introduction.

- *Background:* This is the section in which you provide the reader with the necessary history to better understand the issues. The background for an internal audience that is receptive to the report's findings can be fairly short because almost everyone agrees with the description of the issues and the most likely outcomes. A report for an external audience, or an audience that is not receptive to the outcomes of the report, may require more information on the historical background to better understand why the report's outcomes make the most sense.

- *Discussion section:* This part of the report body is the section in which you present the major issues and key arguments to the reader. Most problems or issues that require a detailed formal report have a series of key components that a reader needs to understand to come to the same conclusion as the writer did. A good writer will lead the reader through a series of small steps based on agreeable assumptions and logical arguments to arrive at the same conclusion. The major questions and their answers, as well as typical barriers to understanding, are all contained within the discussion section. By addressing the major concerns of the audience in a logical and sequential way, you can gradually eliminate most arguments against your final conclusions and recommendations. You take readers from where they stand in their understanding, feeling, and beliefs about an issue and lead them to where you need them to be at the end.

- *Summary and conclusions:* Sometimes the final section within the body (when no recommendations are made), this section is a restatement of the important points made within the body of the report and reminds the reader of what the obvious or logical conclusions are. This helps the reader to come away from reading the report with the same understanding of the problems as the writer has. It is important to remember that no new information can be introduced in the summary and conclusions section. It is simply a reminder of what has come before so that the reader is ready to move to the next step of the reading process.

- *Recommendations section:* This is sometimes required as the final section of the body. Rather than simply presenting the audience with a detailed description of a particular issue or problem and then leaving them on their own, the writer includes the recommendations section to go further and suggest the best course of action for decision makers. Recommendations should fall logically from the case made within the report itself. Not all of the audience will necessarily agree with the final recommendations, but if they agree with the initial background, the assumptions and methodology of the analysis, the description of the main points, and the measures of success, going against the recommendations becomes more difficult.

7. Appendix   You should always write a report from the audience's point of view. Everything that you do as a writer should try to assist the reader to take in the information as quickly and accurately as possible. Some information is not easily understood by readers. For example, a data table of detailed sales information by region, by month, and by store could be included within the discussion section of the report, but this level of detail is often well beyond what most readers need to know. The reader is relying on the writer to take the complicated data, analyze it, interpret the information, and present it in a more reader-friendly form. Rather than a listing of hundreds of data points, the reader needs to know what areas are succeeding, what areas are experiencing problems meeting their goals, and why. The details of the measurement of these outcomes are best moved to the appendix, where readers who are keen to see the details for themselves can do so. The trends or main messages within the data are presented in written form in a few sentences, and the stacks of numbers that accurately describe the trends are separated.

8. References or works cited   Whenever the words, ideas, or inventions of another person are used, it is proper to cite references in recognition of the work. To omit this recognition is to say "These are my words, ideas, or inventions," which is not true. It is plagiarism and equivalent to intellectual property theft. Most formal reports for internal audiences will rely heavily on data that was collected from within the organization, but the same rule applies: Give credit where credit is due. From the readers' perspective there is a more important reason to include references and works cited information: The references provide readers with a trail that they can follow if they want to investigate more deeply on their own. The readers of a report may include people some time in the future. Suppose, for example, that a boss comes across a report that was very helpful when it was created years earlier. The boss may ask to have the report updated but if the first writer did not provide references for where the information (words, ideas, or inventions) came from originally, it will be much more difficult for the second writer to replicate the report with updated data. This is especially true if the original writer is no longer working on the file or, worse yet, no longer working at the organization.

9. Glossary of Key Terms Particularly useful for external audiences, a glossary of key terms is your attempt to recognize that not all readers necessarily start with an equal understanding of the words used within the organization to describe its activities, challenges, and environments. Rather than write the report to the lowest level of knowledge on key terms (and so make the report overly detailed and cumbersome to those who know the terms), you should recognize where misunderstandings may occur and provide simple definitions to the key words or acronyms your organization uses.

See **Figure 13-6** for a good example of a formal report written by a student.

When real data can't be found . . . you may have to improvise.

Information Reports

You have already encountered a form of information report in the section on memo formats. Now we are looking at the formal information report.

The information that these reports contain can take many forms, such as numbers, dates, and facts, and these types of reports are often used by managers in the day-to-day operations of an organization. Information reports present data about a particular problem or issue, but they do not provide an analysis of the data or offer opinions or recommendations. There are many uses for information reports in business today, covering all aspects of the business.

Information reports include sales reports, annual reports, status reports, and progress reports, which we will look at individually.

These types of reports can be thought of as snapshots or pictures of a moment in time for an organization. Of course, anyone who has held a job at any level in an organization knows that it is in a constant state of change. It is not necessary or even desirable, to have a moment-by-moment update of sales for example. The costs of producing and maintaining such a system would be too expensive compared to the value of the added accuracy of the numbers.

1. Sales Report   Sales reports are interesting to readers because they give information about some of the many measures of output from a business. The number of sales last month is important by itself, but it becomes even more important when compared with the previous month's sales or the sales from the same month last year. The series of snapshots, when merged, give a more complete picture of trends over time.

2. Annual Reports   Annual reports are produced once each year and are required by law for some types of organizations, such as publicly traded companies and charities. Other organizations produce annual reports as a part of their commitment to sharing information with key interest groups and others. The purpose of an annual report is to give interested readers a perspective on the organization, where it is at the time of writing, and where the managers intend to take it in the coming months. Typical sections of an annual report include the following:

- a letter from the chair or chief executive officer to the shareholders
- financial highlights
- balance sheets
- profit-and-loss statements
- new business
- the year in review
- projections
- outstanding shares of stock and
- a complete list of board members

FIGURE 13-6   **A Formal Report Written by a Student**

Informational Report Assignment (CA/P Int.)

Date:	November 9, 2007
To:	Business Communication I Students
CC:	Les Hanson, Business Communications Instructor
From:	Shane Witwicki
Subject:	University of Calgary Teaching Malicious Coding to Students

Introduction

In 2005, the University of Calgary created waves in the computer industry by offering students a new course called *Spam and Spyware*. The course was created because the professor realized that there was a lot of information that needed to be covered that would not all fit into the controversial *Viruses and Malware* course that began two years prior to the start of *Spam and Spyware*.

The following report covers an overview of the *Spam and Spyware* course. Information presented here covers the criticism the course received, what was said in the course's defence, and how the university is taking precautions to ease the public's concerns on security in the classroom.

Research was gathered from various sources, including a report done by John Aycock, who was a professor in the Department of Computer Science at the UofC. Further information came from magazine articles, such as *PC Magazine*, the University of Calgary website, and even one of the UofC's newsweekly articles has been consulted.

Course Overview

Spam and Spyware is a course that the University of Calgary has been offering since the fall semester of 2005. The theory behind the course is that in order to teach a student how to become an effective security software developer, the student should know how malicious software works. In the classroom, students learn how to create types of spyware and spam, and then learn how to prevent those files from harming their computers.

Students taking the course learn more then just the coding behind the malicious and defensive software. The topic of fraud is touched upon, allowing the students to become aware of the types of scams that exist and have worked on people in the past. This is so the students can identify scams and have a general idea what schemes they should be wary of. Ethics were taught to the students, along with Canadian, United States, and Australian laws regarding spam and spyware. A lawyer is brought in at the beginning of the course as a guest speaker to provide additional information. (Aycock, p. 5)

Email is also covered in the course: how email works, from mail system architecture to mail headers. Since the course does involve spam and anti-spam techniques, detailed knowledge on how email works is a necessary prerequisite.

Phishing, a scam in which personal information is acquired by masquerading as a trustworthy entity in an electronic communication (Wikipedia), is also covered in the class. Like the topics on spyware and spam, anti-phishing techniques were also covered.

Assignments in spyware begin with the students writing offensive software. The software is aimed at capturing the user name and password of a user doing online banking. The bank was just a fake website set up on the classroom's network. Now that the student knew how spyware would capture a person's user name and password, the student exchanged the malicious program with another student, and developed software that detected and removed the spyware sample for the second assignment.

The formatting remains consistent.

The main ideas are easy to identify.

The background information is useful to the audience.

FIGURE 13-6 (*continued*)

2

Spam was handled the same way as spyware. The student sent multiple messages to one recipient in the class. The fourth assignment consisted of the student developing a spam filter. (Aycock, p. 4)

Criticism toward the Spam and Spyware Course

The research is thorough.

In 2003, when the *Viruses and Malware* class came into play, some of the public expressed concern over classroom security and anger over students being taught how to code viruses. There were even some anti-virus companies who refused to hire graduates who took the course, as they did not want to have the reputation of hiring virus coders. (CBC News)

Public reaction to *Spam and Spyware* was similar to that of *Viruses and Malware*, though not as strongly opposed as the course on viruses was opposed.

Sources are cited.

Clearswift's Threatlab manager, Pete Simpson, was reported as saying that the university's reason for teaching virus coding to students was a "dubious defence" and that using the same reason for the *Spam and Spyware* course was a weak argument. He also thought that spam tools could be a temptation, as the programs could be used as a source of income for a student since most students are usually in need of money. (Sturgeon)

Pete Lindstrom, research director of Spire Security, goes so far as to criticize not just the course but John Aycock and the UofC as well. Lindstrom's view is that the UofC is just seeking attention and doing nothing but causing damage. He even goes into saying that the security community should hold the university liable when the first student gets caught doing something illegal with the knowledge the student is taught, implying that at least one student will be irresponsible with the knowledge they have gained. (Lindstrom)

Some anti-virus companies have sworn to never hire students from the UofC if they have taken this course. These companies include top ranking anti-virus businesses such as McAfee and Sophos. They believe that students do not need to learn how to write malicious code in order to understand how it works. (Gaudiano)

Public Statements Supporting *Spam and Spyware*

Information is supported by research.

Ken Barker, head of the computer science department at the UofC, believes that in order to undo the harm any malicious software causes, a person has to know how to do it first. Meanwhile, John Aycock has done research with one of his students that proves that a new type of spam can be created that would likely bypass the best spam filters. These findings were presented at the annual conference of the European Institute for Computer Anti-Virus Research on April 15, 2006. Aycock has stated that he thinks the industry should be proactive towards trying to protect against malicious software and not reactive to malicious software. (Mikkelsen)

Members of the UofC are not the only people to speak out in defence of the course. In 2006, Christopher Allisson, a manager at Lavasoft Security Center, stated that a person who knew the inner workings of spam and spyware would be invaluable to the Lavasoft team. He also believes that a hands on approach is the only way to teach in being proactive against these kinds of malicious software. (Lavasoft)

Class Admittance

Headings and subject lines are thoughtful and effective.

With the amount of harmful software the class was handling, it is no surprise that the University of Calgary implemented an array of security measures to ensure the odds of anything malicious leaving the classroom was minimal.

FIGURE 13-6   (*continued*)

3

Getting into the course was not as easy as just submitting an application. The student needs a Grade Point Average of 3.0 or higher to even be considered. The student has to be at least in his/her fourth year of Computer Science, and needs to submit a one-page essay on why the student wants to take the class. The essays are evaluated by a committee. Graduate students need not write an essay, but a personal interview was held instead.

The identities of students attending the lectures were verified by the instructor. No one is allowed to "sit in" on the course. (Aycock, p. 1)

Laboratory protocol is important. Any student failing to abide by the protocol is immediately given a failing grade. The protocol is not only abided by the students but by the instructor and technical staff as well.

Students have to sign a legal agreement in order to take the course, which they can review with their own legal counsel if they wish. The legal agreement reinforced the rules set down for lab usage, specified liability, and listed penalties (both academic and legal) for violating the agreement. (Aycock, p. 2)

Classroom Security

Having already developed a secure classroom for their *Viruses and Malware* course, the University of Calgary followed basically the same steps in providing a safe lab for *Spam and Spyware*. The *Spam and Spyware* lab's security was designed to a bit of a lesser degree, as spam is not as dangerous as a computer virus can be.

At the beginning of the course, all students were issued a key to the lab. The only other people to hold a key were faculty members who dealt directly with the course. The lab had only eight computers, two students per computer, with padlocked cases, and unnecessary Input/Output devices disabled (such as USB ports or CD-ROMs). A locked cabinet contained the lab's server and backup information. The network was isolated to only the computers in the classroom, making it so only students could send spyware or spam to each other.

At the end of the course, all computers have their hard drives reformatted, and all backup tapes are erased. (Aycock, p. 4)

> Careful attention has been paid to mechanics, such as spelling and grammar.

Summary

Although the University of Calgary has raised some controversy with the *Spam and Spyware* course, the university has taken many steps to provide a secure classroom to conduct the teaching of the class. Additionally, the university has made many public statements justifying the reason why the course should be available to students.

Some anti-virus companies will still not be convinced, and will continue to believe that having employees who know how to write spyware and spam to be nothing but a tarnish to their image. There are many companies who are of the opposite viewpoint to these companies, believing that hands on teaching of how malicious software works is a great asset in being proactive in preventing these harmful programs from infecting computers.

> The report ends with a good, brief summary.

FIGURE 13-6 (*continued*)

4

Works Cited

"Phishing." *Wikipedia.* Wikimedia Foundation, 2006. Web. Oct. 17, 2007.

"Spyware School at Canadian University." *Lavasoft News.* Lavasoft, Nov. 2006. Web. 19 Oct. 2007.

"University to Offer E-Mail Spam Course." *CBC News.* Canadian Broadcasting Corporation, 5 Feb. 2005. Web. 5 Oct. 2007.

Aycock, John. "Teaching Spam and Spyware at the University of C@1g4ry." *Proceedings of the Third Conference on Email and Anti-Spam. 27*-28 July 2006. Mountain View: CEAS. 137-141. Web. 26 Oct. 2007.

Gaudiano, Nicole. "Controversial Course Teaches Spyware Writing." *InfoSec News.* InfoSec News, 1 Nov. 2006. Web. 2 Nov. 2007.

Lindstrom, Pete. "Learn to Write Spam, Spyware." *Spire Security Viewpoint.* Spire Security, 9 Feb. 2005. Web. 29 Oct. 2007.

Mikkelsen, Alana. "The Virus Guy." *University of Calgary OnCampus Weekly.* 28 Apr. 2006. Web. 19 Oct. 2007.

Sturgeon, Will. "University Offers Spam and Spyware Writing Course." *Silicon.com.* CBS Interactive, 8 Feb. 2005. Web. 18 Oct. 2007.

All works cited in the paper are documented.

Source: Witwicki, Shane. University of Calgary Teaching Malicious Coding to Students. *Unpublished assignment for Les Hanson, Instructor, Red River College. 9 Nov. 2007. Print.*

A company that collects money by selling shares often uses the information contained in the annual report to convince prospective shareholders that the company is a good investment.

3. Status Reports Status reports give information about the important measures of interest to the reader regarding a particular project, program, or issue. Unlike a sales report that focuses exclusively on product or service sales, the status report can be more inclusive of other types of information. For example, if the reader is interested in the human resource management aspect of a project, you can include information about the number of staff involved or the number of overtime hours dedicated to the project. A status can also include information about all aspects of an organization, from research and development to production, marketing, accounting, sales, and logistics.

4. Progress Reports Progress reports are often short updates to let supervisors and managers know about the progress of a project or task. These types of reports help to ensure that more complex projects are completed on schedule.

Analytical Reports

We first encountered a type of analytical report in the section on letter formats for reports. Now we are looking at the formal version.

This is similar to an information report, with the addition of the writer's analysis of the information. Often, analytical reports will include a summary and recommendations section to help decision makers to make more informed decisions. Better analytical reports will present the data of both sides of a particular issue and lead the reader through a series of logical conclusions to arrive at the preferred set of recommended actions or outcomes. (Note that proposals can be seen as examples of analytical reports because they address a particular problem and make a definite recommendation for a particular outcome.)

1. Feasibility Studies Feasibility studies investigate all aspects of a particular problem to see if it is technically possible for a proposed solution to solve the problem and at what cost. You can include estimates of profitability because the underlying objective of many business decisions is to increase profitability.

2. Evaluation Reports Evaluation reports take a slightly different perspective and do not address the question of "Is this possible?" so much as the one of "If we take this action, what are the likely implications to our business?" Businesses are not islands isolated in the middle of the ocean untouched by others but more like a thread in a large tapestry that is the economy or society, a tapestry in which each thread affects and is affected by all others. An evaluation report tries to predict all the possible and likely outcomes to a business as it makes smaller, and seemingly unrelated, changes to its operations.

3. Justification Reports   Justification reports look at information from an entirely different point of view. While feasibility studies and evaluation reports are prospective, looking into the future before a project starts, the justification report looks to the past and studies decisions that have already been made. The purpose of a justification report is to highlight the pieces of information that contributed to a past management decision. For example, a newly appointed human resources vice-president may ask a subordinate for a justification report on a past decision made by the former vice-president to curtail staff holidays during the summer. Rather than looking forward to explore the potential for change or the implication of change, the justification report tries to explain the rationale for decisions made in the past.

4. Problem-Solving Reports   Problem-solving reports are a common type of analytical report, especially for presentation to middle and upper management. Not surprisingly, problem-solving reports start with the description of a particular problem facing the business. This may require you to include some background information for the readers about how the problem arose in the first place. You then investigate the problem by using a combination of secondary and primary data.

Once the problem is fully identified, you turn to describing possible solutions, including the pros and cons of all reasonable alternatives. The problem-solving report typically ends with a recommendation to senior management on a particular course of action to solve the problem efficiently.

It is important to note that problem-solving reports are mainly used by middle and upper management because they rely on lower-level staff to develop solutions to many problems. Upper management especially may have become distanced from the day-to-day challenges of the business where so-called frontline staff and supervisors see the problems and possible solutions first hand.

Background Reports

Although much of the day-to-day management of business is forward looking, planning for the next month, next quarter, or next year, these types of decisions often require a good understanding of the status quo, answering the questions "Where are we now?" and "How did we get here?" A background report tries to answer the second question and can be an excellent source of information for new employees, managers, or committee members to get a better understanding of what has been accomplished so far on the issue.

Operating Documents: Policies and Procedures

Most businesses develop a series of rules that help to increase business efficiency, cost effectiveness, and employee and management decision making. These rules, if found to be particularly useful over time, may become policies and procedures that help guide others facing similar decisions. These decision rules can usually be found in a policies and procedures report.

An example of a business policy is the process required to deal with customer complaints and concerns. Obviously, this can be a difficult issue, because dealing with unhappy customers can be frustrating, but it is in the business's best interest to document the results of complaints so that they can fix the problem and avoid future complaints. Having a standardized policy of what to do in the case of a complaint allows for the right types of questions to be asked and the right types of procedures to be put into practice.

Chapter Summary

Reports and proposals are very common types of business communications. Good business decisions rely on good information, which is contained in the many types of reports and proposals. Some of these reports and proposals are intended for use within an organization (internal reports), while others (external reports) are intended for audiences outside the organization.

Requests for proposals (RFPs) are used by businesses when contracting tasks to outside agencies or businesses. To be effective, RFPs must be carefully crafted to make sure that the details of the task are clear to bidders. Those supplying a response to a proposal must also ensure that their proposal clearly meets or exceeds the expectations and specifications of the organization issuing the RFP.

There are many uses for both reports and proposals, and you should carefully plan and execute the writing to make the biggest possible impact with your audience. Using visual aids effectively can improve any report or proposal, but some caution is needed to make sure that the visuals support the message and don't overpower it.

Just as there are many uses for reports, there are also many different types of reports: information, justification, feasibility, evaluation, problem solving, background, and policies and procedures. Exactly which type of report you write will depend on the audience and what they need.

PEARSON
mycanadianbuscommlab Visit **www.mycanadianbuscommlab.ca** for everything you need to help you succeed in the job you've always wanted! Tools and resources include the following:

- Composing and The Writer's Toolkit
- Document Makeovers

- Video Case Studies
- Grammar exercises and much more!

Thinking and Writing Exercises

1. **Motivating Staff**
   Suppose you are in charge of organizing a fundraiser for co-workers at your job. The boss has asked that you write a one-page proposal to send to all staff via email. What do you think will be good motivators to get staff to donate money? What are some barriers that might hold them back?

2. **Proposing a Blood Donation Clinic**
   Suppose that you have been asked by the president of your student council to write an unsolicited proposal to the dean of student life. The goal is to host a blood donor clinic at your school. What do you think the benefits and costs might be from the students' perspective? How about from the perspective of administration?

3. **Considering Your Options**

   When writing a proposal, why should you always think about all the options (which sometimes include doing nothing)?

4. **Background Information**

   With unsolicited proposals, why is it important to spend time developing the background? After all, isn't every good idea obvious to all?

5. **Brainstorming Ideas to Improve Student Services**

   In a group, brainstorm about what facilities you have available at your school and those that are missing. Suppose that you have been asked for a proposal to improve services to students. Write the results of the brainstorming session as a report on the different facilities at your university or college.

6. **Evaluation Report on Increasing the Minimum Wage**

   Assume that you work for the economic development branch of your provincial or territorial government. The government is considering plans to increase the minimum wage by a dollar an hour in the upcoming year, a move that could have a major effect on fast-food restaurants, convenience stores, and other businesses that pay minimum wage. Write an evaluation report that considers the impact such a move will have on these businesses and on other organizations that might also be affected: food banks, charities, social services, high schools and post-secondary schools (dropout rates). You will not have access to primary information, but you can use secondary sources of information to see how other places have been affected by sudden increases in the minimum wage.

7. **An Internal Proposal to Improve Your Workplace**

   Choose a business or organization where you have worked recently, and write a proposal on one way to improve its operation. You could suggest ways that it could cut energy costs or reduce its waste of materials. Another approach might be to look at ways to increase the efficiency of the business or the scheduling of employees. Alternatively, you could suggest ways for the organization to expand its operations by moving into new areas or adding to its line of products or services.

8. **A Problem-Solving Report on Computer Abuse**

   Assume that you work for a medium-sized business that uses computers in its day-to-day operations. The network does have virus protection and firewalls to protect it from intruders, but the owner is concerned with employees who misuse the computers. Some spend too much time playing games, surfing the net, or sending personal emails. The owner wants to cut the worst abuses of the system. The business has no computer-use policy. You are assigned to find an inexpensive solution to this problem that still allows a reasonable amount of personal computer use.

9. **A Background Report on Music Piracy**

   Assume that you work for a business that sells music online. One of the problems that your industry faces is competition from people who distribute pirated music illegally. The industry has tried different ways to solve the problem, including technological innovations, creative marketing, and vigorous prosecution. Write a background report describing the different techniques that have been attempted worldwide.

10. **Feasibility Report for a Payday Loan Company**

    Assume that you work for a payday loan company in a province or territory that has enacted legislation regulating the interest rates and fees that your business can charge.[9] (If there is no such legislation where you live, use the regulations from a neighbouring province as a model.) Write a feasibility report analyzing whether it will still be possible for your business to remain profitable under these regulations.

    You will not be able to obtain primary information from a payday loan company, so you will have to rely on secondary information for your report.

Writing Skills Checkup: Colons and Semicolons

Semicolons are sometimes used instead of commas and conjunctions to join closely related clauses in a sentence.

Incorrect: Greg is an excellent artist, his paintings look like photographs.

Correct: Greg is an excellent artist; his paintings look like photographs.

They are also used in lists that already contain commas.

Incorrect: I sent copies of the report to Helen Pollard, president, Joanne Vermette, vice-president, and Ahmed Hafezi, chief financial officer.

Correct: I sent copies of the report to Helen Pollard, president; Joanne Vermette, vice-president; and Ahmed Hafezi, chief financial officer.

Colons are used to announce lists and quotations after a complete sentence. Colons are often used after the salutation in formal letters and emails.

Incorrect: All committee members attending the meeting should bring: progress reports, plans for the next quarter, and copies of the year-end review.

Correct: All committee members should bring these documents with them to the meeting: progress reports, plans for the next quarter, and copies of the year-end review.

Correct the following:

1. Hi, Dragan;
   I am reviewing your expense account and I need you to send me: hotel receipts, mileage figures, and itemized entertainment requests.

2. Charitable donations are tax deductable, entertainment expenses are not.

3. If you are looking for unusual statues you can find notable examples of them in many small towns across Canada; Wawa, Ontario, Vulcan Alberta, Flin Flon, Manitoba, and Duncan, British Columbia.

4. Consider the words of Mark Twain. "Some people get an education without going to college: the rest get it after they get out."

5. There are three kinds of lies; lies; damned lies; and statistics.

6. Mohandas Gandhi once had this to say about the free market system "Capital as such is not evil, it is its wrong use that is evil.

Writing Business Plans

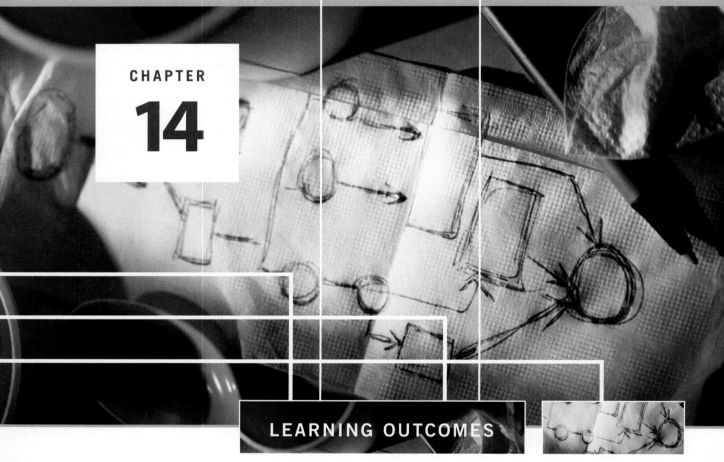

LEARNING OUTCOMES

After completing this chapter, you should be able to do the following:

14.1 Explain the purpose of a business plan

14.2 Write concise mission statements that define a business's reason for existing

14.3 Identify the central components of all business plans

14.4 Select the key information that needs to be placed in a business plan

14.5 Write sections of a business plan that present the required information in a persuasive way

THE IMPORTANCE OF PLANNING

About a thousand people across Canada and the United States were unsure, as this book went to press, whether they would ever get any money back after investing in a business in which they were supposed to raise pigeons that would be sold as meat. While squab is eaten in many places and the investors did receive the breeding birds that they had purchased, investors say the pigeon-slaughter facility they were promised was never built, and breeders were left with birds that they were unable to sell. After paying himself a salary totalling $1.2 million, the owner of the pigeon-breeding business declared bankruptcy, leaving behind assets of $46 000 and debts of more than $20 million.[1,2]

Several lawsuits were pending in late 2009, with the courts yet to determine whether the breeders were the victims of fraud.

This case is a good reminder that business plans are the way we ensure sufficient planning is put into a business. If you ever need to apply to a financial institution for funding to build a business, the first thing you will be asked to provide is a business plan. Such a plan is not written simply to satisfy a lender's needs. A high percentage of businesses fail during their first few years of operation, and having a good business plan could prevent your business from ending up as a financial casualty.

It's a good idea to write a business plan even when you are not looking for investors. It requires you to take a step back from your day-to-day business and examine your operations with a critical eye. The long-range planning required in preparing a business plan may help even established businesses improve their operations or branch out into other avenues while providing a benchmark to compare with future developments.

The story behind a famous business plan appears in the Issues in Communication box.

WHY WRITE A BUSINESS PLAN?

 Explore

A business plan is a document that shows the objectives of a particular business, along with detailed plans and budgets for achieving these objectives.

ISSUES
in Communication

Tiny Loans Become a Huge Success

An economics professor lent $27 of his own money to 42 stool makers when he visited rural Bangladesh, and he went on to receive a Nobel Peace Prize in 2006 for following through on the idea behind his gesture.

The economics professor is Muhammad Yunus, who founded the Grameen Bank, an organization based on the belief that the ability to control capital gives people the power to rise out of poverty. Not content simply to study the poverty in his country, he founded a bank that offered loans to poor people without requiring collateral.

The inspiration for the bank came during his 1976 visit to rural Bangladesh. The artisans he lent money to made bamboo stools and had been caught in a system of bonded labour that required them to borrow from money lenders to buy the raw materials to make their stools, and then to sell their finished product back to the money lenders for a few cents more than the cost of the materials.

Yunus's initial microloan allowed these women to break the cycle of poverty so that they could sell their stools at a higher price to other buyers. That allowed them to earn enough to repay the loans, buy more bamboo, and improve their standard of living.

More significantly, this small loan formed the humble beginnings of the Grameen Bank, which, since 1983 has lent more than US$8 billion to the people of Bangladesh, with a repayment rate of 97 percent.[3]

CREDIT AS A RIGHT

The small investment with the stool makers provided Yunus with the main premise of the Grameen Bank: Credit is a human right.

Yunus considered the initial loan an emotional act that by itself would do little to alleviate the country's widespread poverty. In order to convince banks to support such a program, he needed to overcome the banks' concern about whether people with no collateral would repay their loans. The banks were not convinced by his argument that the peasants' poverty was their collateral: Defaulting on one loan would mean an end to all further credit.

Yunus refined his business plan. He grouped the women (97 percent of the borrowers are

female) into groups of five. Two people in each group received an initial loan, followed by two others in the group a few months later, followed by the group leader. The members gave one another advice and moral support but were not jointly responsible for one another's loans. Group members received no further loans, however, when one member was in default.

The loans themselves are structured simply over one year, with small weekly payments. No legal papers are signed; no legal action is taken against defaulters. Interest rates are low. In late 2009 they ranged from 0 percent for loans made to beggars to about 19 percent for loans that generated income. Simple interest is calculated on loans, based on the remaining balance, which amounts to about 10 percent annually.[4]

Yunus was initially required to act as a guarantor before the banks would approve any loans, but he was concerned that requiring a wealthy person to act as a co-signer had the potential to turn that person into a tyrant. Still, the banks he was working with at the time insisted. More changes to the idea were required, which led to the establishment of the first independent Grameen Bank in 1983.

DEALING WITH CRITICS

The bank had to deal with its critics, who claimed that the application forms would cost more than the returns from the small loans and that illiterate applicants would not be able to complete them anyway. Therefore, loans were kept simple; paperwork was reduced to a minimum; and frontline bank workers were hired to circulate through the villages and collect the weekly payments.[5]

Religious conservatives argued that lending money to women violated the practice of *purdah,* which required women to stay in their homes unless accompanied by a male relative. The conservatives also said that the bank violated Islamic *Shariah* laws by charging interest on loans. Yunus countered that since

Muhammad Yunus and the Grameen Bank were awarded the Nobel Peace Prize in 2006.

the bank was set up as a cooperative, the borrowers were lending to themselves—an acceptable practice.[6] He argued that lending money to women allowed them to start home-based businesses so that they could stay at home and work, rather than being forced out on the streets to beg, thus making it easier for the women to honour the practice of *purdah*.[7]

Yunus started off small, with a basic idea for a new business concept. He gathered information and used it to refine that idea, listened to criticism, and refined the idea further. He kept building on the strengths of that original idea until the Grameen Bank reached its current form. A bank that began as one professor's economic experiment has now grown into the Grameen Group, a collection of businesses involved in enterprises as diverse as yogourt production, telecommunications, and renewable energy.[8]

The Grameen Bank now lends hundreds of millions of dollars to poor people every year, and the concept of microcredit has spread to dozens of countries.

DISCUSSION

1. The practice of offering microcredit loans to poor people has spread from Bangladesh to many other developing countries, but it has been slow to catch on in North America. Why?
2. What would need to change for microcredit to become more common in Canada?
3. Microcredit caught on first in rural communities in Bangladesh before making inroads into urban centres. If an attempt were made to introduce the practice in Canada, would it be better to start in the cities, rural areas, farming centres, or Aboriginal communities? Why?
4. Most of the borrowers (and shareholders) of the Grameen bank are women. If a similar approach were tried in Canada, would it be a good idea to focus on borrowers of only one sex?

TAKE IT FURTHER

The Meaning of *Grameen*

In Bengali, *Grameen* means "rural" or "of the village."[9]

Do you think this kind of bank could succeed in the big cities of the world?

This woman is both a client and a shareholder in the Grameen Bank.

All business plans have this purpose and many other features in common, but a business plan is not a one-size-fits-all document that can be adapted to suit any business. The differences depend on the nature of the business and whether the plan is being written for an existing business or a startup.

Templates for business plans are available on the internet, from reference books, and from vendors of every variety. These can be a useful starting point, and they will give you ideas on ways to organize your own business plan, but, again, every business is different. The information needed by investors for the expansion of a flower shop may be quite different from the information they need for a small manufacturing company startup.

When you are writing your own business plan, you may want to examine plans written by others or to examine some of the templates that are available, but you should do your own writing independently. The key reason that almost any potential investor requires a business plan is to ensure that you have planned every aspect of your business and are prepared for whatever is to come. Dropping your information into someone else's plan is not likely to result in your having a thorough understanding of all the problems and opportunities that your business is likely to face during the next few years.

STRUCTURE OF A BUSINESS PLAN

At minimum, all business plans should do the following:

- present a detailed description of the business
- explain how the product or service will be marketed
- give a detailed account of how the finances of the business will be structured

A good business plan includes not only those essential elements but several others too, which can be organized in a variety of ways, such as the following: (1) executive summary, (2) overview of the business, (3) description of the products and services, (4) overview of the industry in which the business will compete, (5) marketing strategy, (6) description of the management and staff, (7) implementation plan, and (8) financial plan.[10]

We will look at these elements in that order, but remember that the order should depend on what works best for a particular business plan. Nevertheless, unless your plan is very short, it will begin with an executive summary.

1. Executive Summary

No matter how much effort you put into writing a business plan, your intended audience may not read the entire document carefully. They will, however, read the executive summary, which should be only a page or two long. This will be the first section presented in the business plan, even though it will probably be the final section that you write.

© Mike Baldwin / Cornered

LOANS

Apparently, wild hopes and dreams, re-enacted by Barbie and Ken, are no substitute for a solid business plan.

Writing a business plan requires extensive research and planning.

Your executive summary should highlight the business's important features and describe the opportunities it presents. See **Figure 14-1** for an example of an executive summary.

2. Overview of the Business

Early in your business plan, you need to provide a brief description of your proposed business. Explain what you have done so far and what you hope to accomplish. The overview may include the following elements.

Background   If you are writing about an established business, provide a history of the business: when it was established and how it has changed since that time. Describe the location of the business and provide descriptions of any buildings or equipment you have.

✓•—Practise ▐ FIGURE 14-1 ▐ **Fitness Fifty-Five Executive Summary**

provides a brief overview of the business

describes the target market, business location, and competitor

describes its marketing strategy

lists the business's features and a competitive advantage

describes staff

summarizes financial information

closes with an optimistic prediction

Fitness Fifty-Five Executive Summary

Fitness Fifty-Five will be a fitness facility located in Victoria, British Columbia, that will cater to the specific health requirements of people over the age of 55. People's fitness needs change as they get older, and so the facility offers a medical-based fitness program that allows people to exercise safely, without damaging joints or aggravating existing medical conditions.

The 325-square-metre facility will be located on Douglas Street in James Bay, one of the oldest residential areas in Victoria. A large percentage of the people who call Victoria home are seniors. The potential client base is approximately fifteen thousand people between the ages of 55 and 80 who live within a 20-minute drive of the facility. One other fitness facility that caters to seniors already exists in the Greater Victoria area, but it is operating at capacity, leaving room for at least one more such business. Membership fees will be comparable, but rather than offering only yearly memberships, Fitness Fifty-Five will give clients additional choices of regular memberships, renewable every three months, and personal training memberships, which include one personal training session per month. Fitness Fifty-Five will be promoted with a series of advertisements and discount coupons appearing in local publications in the months leading up the business's grand opening.

Fitness Fifty-Five will offer a wide variety of exercise machines specifically designed to meet the needs of its members and organized classes, such as yoga, Tai Chi, Pilates, and other classes that focus on endurance, flexibility, strength, and balance training. It will also offer specialized exercise classes to members with heart disease, arthritis, or osteoporosis. It will be the only fitness facility in Victoria with a driving simulator, which members can use to keep their motor skills sharp.

The facility will be headed by medical exercise program director Fatima Michel, who is also a registered kinesiologist. She will ensure that all clients receive exercise programs in a safe and supportive environment. Ms. Michel will be assisted by four personal trainers and by administrative and maintenance staff. A dietician and physiotherapist will also be available to Fitness Fifty-Five members.

Fitness Fifty-Five will be privately incorporated. A total of $300 000 in start-up capital is available, financed by $15 000 investments made by each of the 20 shareholders, one of whom is the facility's program director. Start-up costs come to a total of $291 000. A return on investment of 3% is expected by its fourth year of operation, with steady increases in subsequent years.

Victoria has a rapidly aging population that is becoming increasingly concerned with maintaining wellness. Fitness Fifty-Five presents investors with an opportunity to capitalize on these factors while promoting a healthy lifestyle.

This executive summary presents an overview of a longer business plan.

Objectives   List your objectives for the next year or two. Are you trying to establish yourself in the market? If so, state what percentage of the market you hope to win. Are you trying to increase your market share or profitability? Whatever your objective, you must provide readers with realistic numbers so that they can assess whether your objectives are reasonable.

Legal Structure   You need to explain the legal structure of the business. Will it be a sole proprietorship? A partnership? Will it be incorporated? Answers to

TABLE 14-1	**Real Mission Statements**
WestJet	"To enrich the lives of everyone in WestJet's world by providing safe, friendly and affordable air travel"
Junior Achievement of Canada	"To inspire and prepare young people to succeed in a global economy"
Indigo Books	"To provide booklovers and those they care about with the most inspiring retail and online environments in the world for books and life-enriching products and services"
Loblaw Companies Ltd.	"To be Canada's best food, health and home retailer by exceeding customer expectations through innovative products at great prices"
Right to Play	"To improve the lives of children in the most disadvantaged areas of the world by using the power of sport and play for development, health and peace"

Source: "WestJet Culture." WestJet. 2009. Web. 20 Oct. 2009; "About JA." Junior Achievement of Canada. 2009. Web. 20 Oct. 2009; "Our Company." Chapters Indigo. 2009. Web. 20 Oct. 2009; "2008 Annual Report." Loblaw Companies. 2009. Web. 20 Oct. 2009; and "Mission, Vision and Values." Right to Play. 2009. Web. 20 Oct. 2009.

these questions will affect the decision-making structure of the business, the ways in which the owners are paid, and what will happen should it be necessary to dissolve the business in the future.

Mission Statement   A mission statement should be motivational both to clients and to employees, and easy to understand yet broad enough to encompass all aspects of the business.

A good mission statement gives readers an instant picture of the key principles of the business in a sentence or two. A mission statement can be used as a yardstick to see whether the business is remaining faithful to its central purpose. Mission statements may change periodically as the business evolves, but they should always be simply expressed and short enough so that workers, customers, and shareholders can get a picture of the business at a glance. Do not make the mission statement so general that it could apply to any enterprise, nor so specific that it will need to be rewritten frequently. See **Table 14-1** for examples of mission statements from Canadian companies.

3. Description of the Products and Services

Once you have provided the general structure of the business itself, you need to provide more detail about the product or service. Explain what the company does and how it will meet a need in the marketplace. List the specific advantages that you will be able to offer, such as

- a strategic location
- a unique product
- improved customer service
- more affordable prices

Your Competitive Edge   You need to describe your business model in such a way that the audience can see the feature that makes your business more attractive than the competition. Describing a video rental outlet as a store that "rents DVDs and video games" puts it in a class with every other video rental outlet and will not likely convince anyone of its value.

A more persuasive business model might show how the store is able to offer the following:

- better rates or selection
- a superior way of delivering the product to customers
- a bonus plan that encourages frequent rentals

The business description may elaborate on the initial idea that led to the creation of the business plan. This part, perhaps more than any other, will allow you to display your creativity. Be sure to write it in a persuasive way. Unsupported claims, however, will not help you. It is essential that you provide evidence to back up any claims that you make about the superiority of your product or service.

Your creative challenge has two goals:

1. to find a better way of doing business than the competition does
2. to convince investors that your new way will be profitable

Convincing Your Audience   As with any other document, consider the audience when choosing what information to present and how to present it. Identify the readers' needs and biases when describing the business. During the early stages of the Grameen Bank, when it still depended on other banks for funding, Muhammad Yunus needed to alter the terms of a business plan several times so that it would be acceptable.

Other banks rejected Yunus's early request for funding to provide Grameen's clients with small "home improvement loans" for sheet metal roofing because the $125 requested was considered too small to make significant improvements. The terms were revised to "shelter loans" but were rejected again because the loans brought in no return on investment, unlike earlier small loans that brought in income to repay the loans.

Undaunted, Yunus tried a third time, this time renaming the requests "factory loans" and presenting the argument that proper roofs over people's heads would improve the productivity of home-based businesses, thus producing income that could help with the repayments.[12]

The approach succeeded once the lenders saw that they could preserve the security of their investments while still realizing a profit.

Once you have written a description of the business, the remainder of the business plan will demonstrate that the business can succeed. You will show how you plan to market the idea and organize the overall business and, specifically, the financial aspects of the venture.

4. Overview of the Industry

Provide an analysis of your company's strengths that will help you succeed in the face of competition. To do this, of course, you will have to research the

TABLE 14-2	Direct and Indirect Competitors
Type of Competitor	Characteristic
Direct	Offers the same product to the same market
Indirect	Focuses on a similar product or market

competition. Identify all the businesses in your market area that offer similar services. Be sure to include both direct and indirect competitors. See **Table 14-2** for a description of each type of competitor.

Market Research   Your analysis will require extensive research on your part. Obviously you will have an advantage if you have existing first-hand knowledge of the business you are entering, but that by itself is not enough. Go to the library. Find as much publicly available information as you can about the industry you are entering. Explain how your business will fit into the industry. Ask yourself such questions as these:

- Is this a new industry with opportunities for innovative ideas?
- Is it a growth industry in which a unique approach might provide an advantage?
- Is the field changing?
- Is the field underserviced by existing competitors?

You may have a fabulous business idea, but if numerous others have flooded the market already with similar products or services, your chances of success will be slim.

Try to determine the areas in which your competitors are strong, as well as any weaknesses they may have. Your objective is to find a niche where your business can fit into the market.

Provide your audience with a forecast on the direction you expect the market to take in the next few years. Opening a business that sells luxury clothing may be difficult during a recession, for example, whereas one that offers an inexpensive selection may have a greater chance of success.

Sources of Information   Businesses carefully guard some information about their operations to avoid giving rivals a competitive advantage, but enough information will be available from newspapers, annual reports, and business directories to enable you to provide some background on the industry you are entering.

5. Marketing Strategy

 Explore

Closely tied to your analysis of your competition is knowing who your customers are. To develop a marketing strategy, you first need to identify your customers and any relevant characteristics that may help you determine the best way to sell to them. Then you can plan your strategy.

Conducting Research You can consider many questions at this point, such as the following:

- Who are your customers?
- How many customers can you expect?
- How much money can you expect them to spend?
- Are they willing to pay a premium price for high quality?
- Do they require a convenient location?
- Do warranties and good service plans play a big factor in their decisions?

Before you can market your product or service, you need to find out what would make your customers want to buy it. The more you know about your market, the better you will be able to tailor your marketing strategy to your potential customers.

The kind of business you have in mind will have a major impact on the amount and type of research that you conduct. For example, a store offering specialty products to a local retail market will require a different approach from a business offering its services to larger businesses in the area.

Demographics For some businesses it will be necessary to put together information about the *demographics* of your target market. *Demographics* are the characteristics of typical members of your target market, such as age, gender, and cultural background.

For some types of businesses, especially those offering retail services, you may have an idea of the demographics of your customers before you even do any serious research. You can further refine this rough picture with research from secondary sources. See **Table 14-3** for a list of some of the resources that you can use to refine the picture of your target market.

TABLE 14-3 **Resources to Help You Refine Your Target Market**

Source	What It Offers
Statistics Canada	sells demographic data that it collects from censuses, taxation records, surveys, and other government sources
E-Stat (more limited version of Statistics Canada)	provides information to students and educational institutions
Industry Canada	provides an online tool that allows potential entrepreneurs to compare financial data from their businesses to data from tax records of business in more than 600 business sectors across the country, to help small businesses predict how they will measure up against their competition
Surveys	allow you to ask specific questions to a wide variety of people; while online tools are available that will allow you to administer surveys to selected participants, a truly objective survey requires the assistance of an independent research company
Focus groups	consist of a group of eight or ten people who are specifically chosen to represent the demographics of your target market

Sources: For Statistics Canada: "Welcome to Statistics Canada." Statistics Canada. Government of Canada. 2009. Web. 8 Apr. 2009; for E-Stat: "Welcome to E-Stat." Statistics Canada. Government of Canada. 2009. Web. 8 Apr. 2009; for Industry Canada: "Performance Plus." Industry Canada. Government of Canada. 9 Feb. 2009. Web. 13 Apr. 2009.

Some types of data can be acquired only through more specialized research. In those cases, you may be able to use surveys or focus groups.

How a focus group works   A focus group typically has eight to ten people. A moderator leads them through a round-table discussion on a specific topic. The discussion is recorded and used to estimate the opinions of a larger population.

Although conducting a focus group can be both faster and cheaper than hiring someone to administer a survey, conducting primary research by using either of these methods can be expensive and will be available only to larger projects that have enough funding to use these tools.

Market share   Once you have determined the demographics of your customers, you will then have to determine what your share of the market will be. Estimating market share requires you to calculate the percentage of the total market for your product or service that you can expect to win from your competitors. This figure will be a part of your financial projections, so it is important that you come to a reasonable estimate and that you explain to your audience how you reached that figure.

Planning Strategy   Along with identifying the customers and the competition comes planning the marketing strategy, known as the four P's: (1) product, (2) price, (3) promotion, and (4) place. See **Table 14-4** for an explanation of each element. The combination of these factors is unique to every business.

Marketing decisions in action: restaurants   The restaurant section of your local phone book provides evidence of some restaurateurs' decisions relating

TABLE 14-4	Four P Planning	
The Four P's	**Explanation**
1. Product	What makes your product or service better than your competitors'? List its features, and then describe how these will benefit the customers. If one key characteristic stands out, draw the investors' attention to it.
2. Price	Explain how you have determined the price. Obviously, a cheaper product will be more attractive to your customers, but setting the price too low will not earn the business enough money to stay viable. You have to arrive at a figure that will please both the customers and the financiers. This will come after calculating your costs and predicting how much customers will be willing to pay for comparable services.
3. Promotion	How will customers learn about your business? You will need to determine whether to advertise and, if so, where and how. Media that may work for one type of business may be ineffective or too expensive for another type of business. Promotion will also include anything else that draws your customers' attention to the business: websites, signage, brochures, or a listing in the phone book.
4. Place	Although *place* is easy to remember as part of the four P's, it refers to far more than physical location. Place relates to all the distribution channels involved in getting the product to customers. How will you deliver your product to your customers? What shipping costs are involved? Where will your supplies originate, and how will they be warehoused? How large a territory will your business serve?

to one small aspect of the marketing process. The managers must decide how much money to invest in *Yellow Pages* ads. The nature of their product and their distribution network will determine how much money they spend.

Since the telephone is the key to the takeout business, any restaurants that depend on deliveries will likely invest heavily in large advertisements that include menus and price lists. Restaurants that take reservations will also try to attract patrons through the *Yellow Pages,* though they may decide not to advertise their prices. Other restaurants that do not depend on the telephone as part of their distribution network may still place ads, but they will likely be small and include only the business's name, address, and phone number. Restaurants that offer only dine-in or drive-through service usually choose other ways to promote their businesses.

Although *Yellow Pages* advertising is only one very small part of the marketing process, this example should illustrate that marketing decisions that work for one type of business may be unsuitable for another.

6. Description of Management and Staff

People are the key to any business. You must demonstrate that the people in your business have the drive and ability to make it a success. You need to describe the duties of each person and explain the following:

- how many staff will be present at any time
- what they will do
- how much they will be paid
- when they will work

You may include the resumés of key staff members in an appendix.

If you are operating a single-person business, the management and organization of the business will be easy to describe. As a business grows, its structure becomes increasingly complex and requires more intricate planning. You must show that you have allocated sufficient resources to allow the business to run efficiently yet not so much as to be wasteful.

Will any labour market issues affect your business in either a positive or a negative way? Starting a business in a booming economy may make it difficult to acquire and retain staff. Operating in a depressed economy may mean access to a plentiful labour force or government hiring incentives.

7. Implementation Plan

The implementation plan should describe how your business will function on an ongoing basis. You have several aspects to consider when you draw up your implementation plan.

Administration Administration of businesses varies greatly depending on the businesses' purposes, but you will need to demonstrate the complete chain of events, from where your supplies will come from and how your product will be produced to how you will meet the needs of your customers and what after-sales service you will provide.

Businesses range in size and complexity from the small hobby business operating in a garage to multinationals employing thousands of people. Regardless of the size of the business, the business plan should describe the equipment and facilities that will be used, the operating procedures followed, the responsibilities of everyone involved in the business, and any improvements required to the physical facilities.

If your business needs a computer network or extensive customer records, explain how data will be kept secure from theft, viruses, and accidents.

Legal Issues   Demonstrate that you have dealt with all the legal issues surrounding the business: licences, insurance, zoning requirements, contracts with suppliers and subcontractors, and trademark issues.

Risks   Any business entails a certain amount of risk. Depending on the business, such factors as bad weather, a declining economy, or theft, could destroy a business. It will never be possible to anticipate all the possible threats, but many can be identified. List as many significant risks as you can, the steps that have been taken to avoid them, and any plans that you have made to deal with them should they occur:

- In a partnership, what will a partner do if the other partner dies or decides to leave the business?
- In a family-owned business, what will happen in the event of divorce?

As unpleasant as it may be to speculate on such events, they must be considered. Explain any legal agreements that have been drawn up among the principals of the business and any insurance policies that have been taken out to guard against unforeseen events.

8. Financial Plan

The financial plan for your business will show potential investors the amount of external funding that the business will require. It will also demonstrate that the business will be financially viable. If the business plan is used to obtain external funding, the financial plan should begin by stating how much is needed and how it will be used, as well as the amount of your own money you are investing. Potential investors will be wary of any business plan in which they are being asked to assume all the risk.

If the business plan is for an established operation that is looking for external funding, it should include a summary of the company's financial operations for the last few years.

The plan will also need to include projections that (1) explain where the money will be used and (2) demonstrate how much return on investment the business is expected to produce.

Pro Forma **Financial Statements**   The financial section of plans for startup businesses will include three *pro forma* (projected) statements: (1) a cash flow statement, (2) an income statement, and (3) a balance sheet. See **Table 14-5** for an explanation of each statement.

Young Entrepreneurship Awards

What do these have in common: a business that creates wine cellars, an IT consulting firm, a dance academy, and a video surveillance business that uses cameras controlled over the internet?[14] They all won Young Entrepreneur Awards in 2008 from the Business Development Bank of Canada (BDC). The annual awards showcase the work of Canadian entrepreneurs aged 19 to 35. They are based on originality of business concept, company success and growth potential, and the team's community involvement.

What motivates organizations such as BDC to sponsor contests?

TABLE 14-5 *Pro Forma* **Statements**

Type	What It Does	Notes
cash flow statement	shows all the cash projected to come into the business and all the expenses that will need to be paid	serves as a budget and will need to be prepared on a monthly basis for the most volatile first year and less frequently for subsequent years
income statement	shows the profits and losses incurred by the business over a given time (usually the tax year)	should be prepared monthly during the startup period so that you can modify the timing of any actions, such as advertising or seasonal promotions, that do not necessarily have to occur at a given time
balance sheets	prepared annually and show a summary of the business's assets, liabilities, and equity	*equity* is the difference between the business's assets and liabilities; the owner's equity will have a major influence on the amount of capital that investors feel that they can contribute safely

Source: Balance sheet notes adapted from "Elements of a Business Plan." Entrepreneur Network. Entrepreneur Media, 2009. Web. 23 Apr. 2009.

Break-Even Analysis   Few businesses make money during their startup period. Adding inventory, buying equipment, and paying for other initial expenses means it will take a few years before most businesses can expect to turn a profit. The break-even analysis uses data from the *pro forma* statements to predict when that point will be.

It might be tempting to present a very optimistic picture of your business's financials, but one of your primary purposes is to establish credibility. If your predictions are not believable, or if you have omitted information that does not support your plan, your audience will have little faith in your idea.

Chapter Summary

A business plan is a document that presents a detailed description of a business, showing its objectives and detailed plans and budget.

It explains what the business does and how it will meet a need in the marketplace, emphasizing any specific advantages over the competition. It describes the way the business will be organized and provides information about its management structure.

A business plan provides information about similar companies operating in the same area. It identifies your customers and any relevant characteristics that determine the marketing strategy you have chosen. This includes information about the product itself, its pricing strategy, how it will be promoted to customers, and the distribution channels that will be used.

A business plan gives detailed statements showing how the finances of the prospective business will be structured: a cash flow statement, an income statement, and a balance sheet.

A business plan will assist you in planning a business, as well as in providing you with credibility among prospective investors.

Thinking and Writing Exercises

1. **Mission Statements for Kiva Borrowers**

   The Grameen Bank demonstrated that loan amounts do not necessarily have to be large. Business plans do not necessarily have to be long and detailed either. Kiva is a microfinance organization that matches lenders from affluent places with borrowers from developing countries.

   Go to the website at www.kiva.org. Read the profiles of several loan applicants. Then write mission statements for three prospective borrowers.

2. **Executive Summary of a Business Plan for a Financial Service**

   Across Canada, banks have been vacating many rural and lower-income neighbourhoods while consolidating their services in larger locations in malls and other high-traffic locations. People who do not have easy access to transportation are forced to use fringe financial services, such as generic banking machines, payday loan companies, and pawn brokers, for their routine financial transactions—services that are often far more expensive than those offered by banks or credit unions.[15]

   Assume that you have written a business plan for a financial service that is to be offered in a rural or an inner city area that has been abandoned by the mainstream banks and credit unions. Write the executive summary of the plan, emphasizing the business's more important features and describing the opportunities it presents.

3. **Description of the Ideal Video Rental Business**

   In about 300 words write the description of the products and services section of a business plan for a video rental business. Find a way to improve on the operations of existing video stores that you know about. Remember that your purpose is to convince an investor that your way of operating the business would be profitable. You need to balance the obvious attraction of low rental fees and wide selection with the need to generate income.

   Deal with some of the following topics:

   - rental periods and late fees
   - security and loss prevention
   - product availability and selling of old stock
   - membership fees and purchasing incentives (if any)
   - distributing the product to customers
   - extras that might attract customers to the store

4. **A Short Business Plan for a Small Startup Loan**

   Write a business plan in about 300 words.

   a. Ask for a startup loan of $20 to begin a real business that requires little startup capital: cleaning car windshields, raking leaves, shovelling snow, operating a lemonade stand, cleaning apartments, walking dogs, washing cars, or babysitting.

   b. Assume that you had begun the $20 business described above by using your own savings. Now, after it has been operating successfully for a week, you require $50 to expand. Write the business plan. Demonstrate how you could ensure that the investor's $50 would be returned. Once again, keep it to 300 words. Include the following sections:

   - company description: product or service, number of employees
   - marketing plan: four P's (product, promotion, price, place), competitors
   - financial plan: expenses, revenue forecast

5. **Business Plan for a Global Charitable Organization**

   After eBay had made him a wealthy man, its creator, Pierre Omidyar, became a philanthropist. Rather than simply giving his money to worthy charities, he applied the democratic concept of eBay to the world of philanthropy. The Omidyar Network joined forces with organizations, such as GlobalGiving, an organization that allows donors to connect directly with community-based projects around the world.[16]

Charitable groups submit proposals for projects that need support. Donors give money to projects that they consider worthy. The internet functions as an intermediary between donors and recipients, providing donors with feedback on how the money was spent and allowing them to see the tangible impact that their gifts have on the lives of the recipients.[17]

Go to the websites of the Omidyar Network (www.omidyar.com) or of one of the charities with which it is affiliated: www.donorchoose.org and www.globalgiving.com. Based on information found on their websites, construct a business plan written as if you were starting one of these organizations.

6. **A Preliminary Business Plan for a Microloan**
Write an outline for a business plan funded by a microloan. Start by identifying a person (possibly you) who could benefit from a microloan. Be as specific as possible. If you don't know such an individual, look through a newspaper or watch a news program and try to find someone who may have an idea in need of capital funding. Then, with a fictional loan of around $1000, make a list of the key features of the business. Use these headings to begin the planning process:

- Overview of the Business
- Products and Services
- Industry Analysis
- Marketing Strategy
- Management and Staff
- Implementation Plan
- Financial Plan

Writing Skills Checkup: Commas

Commas are used to group ideas or to indicate short pauses. The following guidelines and examples will help you to decide when to use commas in your writing.

a. Use commas after an introductory phrase.

Established in Bangladesh, the Grameen bank has spread to other countries.

b. Use commas to separate three or more elements in a series.

Microcredit operations have been established in Bolivia, Chile, India, and Vietnam.

c. Use commas to restate names or titles or to interject comments.

Muhammad Yunus, founder of the Grameen Bank, was originally a professor of economics. The bank uses borrowers' poverty, not their possessions, as collateral.

d. Use commas to join a dependent clause to the beginning of a sentence.

Because microloans are so small, traditional banks are often reluctant to deal with poor people.

e. Use commas to join independent clauses with coordinating conjunctions: *and, or, but, nor, so, for, yet.*

Groups of lenders are not responsible for each other's loans, but group members receive no further credit when one member is in default.

f. Do not use commas to separate a subject from a verb.

Microcredit financing institutions/ have not been widely established in Canada.

Insert commas where needed into these sentences. Remove any unnecessary commas.

1. By providing small loans to poor people, the Grameen Bank offers recipients, the chance to become entrepreneurs.
2. Microcredit gives borrowers the opportunity, to break themselves free from the cycle of poverty.
3. As microfinance institutions continue to grow financial institutions have begun to take notice.
4. In its broadest sense, microcredit includes the act of lending small amounts, often $100 or less, to borrowers who have been ignored by commercial banks.

5. Microfinance institutions have begun to offer other financial services such as, savings accounts flexible loan repayments pension plans and insurance policies.

6. Because many microfinance institutions have established positive returns microfinance is being seen by many professional investors as a profitable investment opportunity.[18]

7. Pure Grameen-style group lending schemes have not produced substantial results in the United States, but that is not to say that microcredit is not available to the poor.

8. Instead microfinance operations in the United States sometimes offer individual lending operations that require borrowers to attend small business training programs or offer loans to attend specialized schooling for particular professions.

9. The additional training substantially raises costs to the point where, instead of being self-sustaining, many U.S. microfinance institutions rely on grants and subsidies.

10. Committed practitioners a wealth of theoretical work and a surging demand for investment, have proven microfinance to be an effective and adaptable tool for improving the lives of poor people.

Writing Resumés

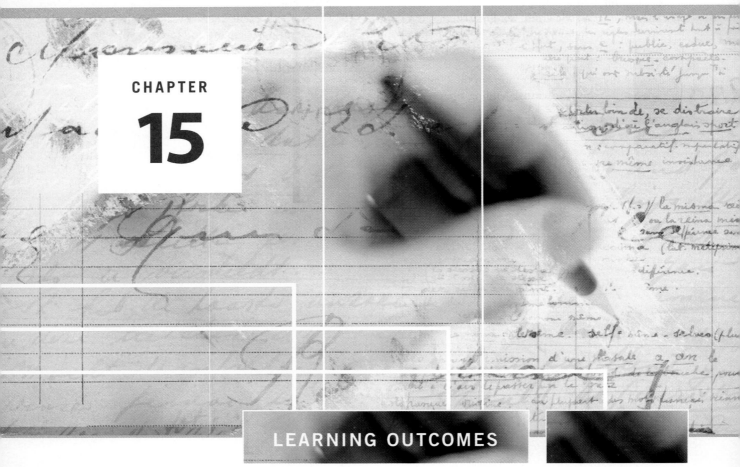

CHAPTER 15

LEARNING OUTCOMES

After completing this chapter, you should be able to do the following:

15.1 Find out what employers want most from their new hires

15.2 Develop a resumé to market your skills and abilities

15.3 Create an employment portfolio

15.4 Write persuasive application letters

FINDING YOUR CAREER

Students, like you, who are completing this course as part of their formal education will soon be entering a new phase of their working life: starting a career. Even though many students work in the summers and part time while in school, the change from casual or part-time work to full-time career-track employment can be intimidating. You need a clear vision of what you want to be doing while at work and where you want to be employed. This chapter, along with Chapter 16, addresses many of these concerns and can help you move into a rewarding career.

Many companies realize that with increasing competition, and the growing emphasis on providing excellent customer service, hiring the right person for the right job is more important than ever. In this chapter, we will discuss the process of the job search from both the applicant's and the employer's point of view. Understanding the process that employers go through will help you refine how you present your resumé, your application letter, and—quite possibly— yourself in the interview to follow. Although understanding the process cannot guarantee you the job you want, it can help you avoid common pitfalls that could result in your application being dropped from further consideration.

Where do you want to begin your career?

WHAT EMPLOYERS WANT

To be successful, job seekers need to consider what employers want in their new hires. The Conference Board of Canada has conducted research into this area, and the results of the "Employability Skills 2000+" are an excellent resource.[1] Look back to Chapter 1 (Table 1-2) to review the list. According to the Conference Board, employers' needs fall into three areas:

1. fundamental skills, including communications skills
2. personal management skills
3. teamwork skills

Of course, the specific skills and experiences that any particular company requires will be defined in the job posting. However, it is worthwhile to keep the general needs of the marketplace in mind as you prepare for a wider job search.

ISSUES
in Communication
Surfing for a Job

Like so many other tasks, searching for work is no longer the tedious process it once was. Thanks to new technology and information sharing across borders, time zones, and even cultures, such companies as Monster.com and others have recorded significant growth in operations and a tripling of profit rates.[2]

From their home, school, or office, job seekers can find, research, and compare job opportunities from a number of prospective employers without ever making a telephone call or setting up a meeting.

The internet has transformed the job-search process. Online employment sites have become increasingly popular, and they offer job seekers a wider market, instant accessibility to opportunities, and convenience. Thanks to a growing number of businesses and employment agencies that have gone online to advertise their need for new talent, job seekers can search for, analyze, and apply to a wide variety of job opportunities from their computer. But this way of job searching comes with an unfortunate cost: phishing.[3] *Phishing* is a form of online scam in which a legitimate-looking website or email is used to collect personal information to illegally acquire a credit card, gain access to a bank account, or engage in other fraudulent activity.

If you are using websites to look for jobs, you need to be aware of the many threats online. These threats come from individuals and organizations that try to steal personal information, social insurance numbers, bank account numbers, and other valuable data. According to a recent brochure from the US government, this information allows thieves to take out loans, get credit cards, and ruin a person's financial record.[4]

Job seekers can be tricked into thinking they are applying for jobs and are being asked to complete application forms. However, these forms have inappropriate questions,

TAKE IT FURTHER

The Best Job in the World

In 2009, tourism officials from Queensland, Australia, received 30 000 applications for a six-month position as caretaker of a tropical resort that required the winner to keep a blog about the island paradise. The campaign also resulted in millions of dollars of free publicity and increased bookings to the island.[5]

How could less glamorous businesses use this technique to generate publicity or job applications?

such as a request for a social insurance number.

Another common way that job seekers who use the internet are victimized is through fraudulent job offers. People who have posted their resumés publicly may receive unsolicited offers of work-at-home positions, job-placement assistance, or business opportunities that often turn out to be multi-level marketing programs (pyramid schemes). All these scams require the job seekers to make large up-front "investments" for which they receive little or nothing in return.[6]

Even the industry leader, Google, is not exempt and was the target of an elaborate phishing scam to try to steal clients' credit card numbers.[7] It was again attacked in 2009 by hackers trying to steal clients' personal passwords.[8]

If you are applying online, do not provide any information that could be used to steal your identify. Never consent to an online background check. Never pay a fee for a job placement or a work-at-home business. Remember, if it sounds too good to be true, it probably is.

SEARCH TIPS

The following tips can improve your online job search.

1. *Look at specialized sites:* Monster and Workopolis advertise heavily and do have many job openings, but they also attract many applicants. Do not ignore sites run by specific professional associations and those that focus on specific industries or geographic areas.

2. *Look at older listings:* People tend to focus on the newer listings, so if you apply to ones that have been there longer, you may receive greater attention from the prospective employer.

3. *Create an email address for job searches:* You will be able to focus your efforts more efficiently (and receive less spam) if you obtain an email address that you use solely for job searches. Ideally, it's better to have your name in the address than to have an alias or anything that conveys an unprofessional image.

4. *Manage your online image:* Many people post pictures or personal details about their lives on social networking sites. Many employers search for such information when screening applicants. Before beginning your job search, remove any information that might be considered unprofessional or controversial.

5. *Protect your identity:* Take advantage of online employment sites' offers to let you post resumés anonymously. Never include personal information such as birth date, social insurance number, home address, or anything else that an imposter could use to steal your identify.

6. *Focus your efforts:* Whether you are applying online or using a paper-based approach, a customized search will be more effective than flooding the market with as many applications as possible. Identify what the prospective employers are looking for, and then try to demonstrate that you can meet their needs.

7. *Do not restrict your search to the internet:* Online job search tools can be valuable, but they should not be your only tool. Continue to talk with friends, business contacts, and relatives about possible openings. Traditional approaches to job searching are still very effective.[9]

DISCUSSION

1. What do you think is the greatest benefit of using the internet to search for a new job?

2. What is a pyramid scheme? How do fraud artists target people who have applied for online jobs?

3. During your own online job searches, has anyone ever approached you and offered a product or service that you considered fraudulent?

4. During your own job searches, what have you found to be the most productive for job leads: the internet, friends, newspaper ads, referrals from other people?

TAKE IT FURTHER

Anatomy of a Fraud

One person who was hired as an online sales representative for a fraudulent company was instructed to open a bank account and to supply the company with the account numbers. The company deposited money into the account from so-called orders and instructed the victim to keep a small commission and send most of it to an offshore account. The money had actually been obtained from the accounts of other sales reps, and the victim was forced into bankruptcy.[10]

Should victims of fraud be held financially responsible for such crimes?

TAKE IT FURTHER

Top Five Skills

Business recruiters have identified these as the top five skills they look for in job applications: communication (oral and written), computer literacy, interpersonal/social, critical thinking, and leadership/teamwork.[11]

How can you prove on a resumé that you are skilled in these areas? ■

The work of the Conference Board shows that fundamental skills are the baseline on which future success in the workplace is built. Your skills in communications are the first and the most important:

- communicating through reading, understanding, listening, and speaking
- managing information by gathering, organizing, analyzing, and applying knowledge from a variety of sources
- using numbers for observing, measuring, calculating, recording, and estimating results
- thinking and solving problems by assessing the situation, seeking different points of view, recognizing the dimensions of the problem, identifying the root cause, exploring possible solutions, using science and technology, making decisions, and evaluating results

The Employability Skills 2000+ continues with an analysis of the personal management skills most sought by employers:

- demonstrating positive attitudes and behaviours
- being responsible, setting goals, and being accountable
- being adaptable to change
- learning continually to develop and grow your strengths

Finally, the survey highlights teamwork skills:

- working with others as a contributor or leader, as needed
- participating in projects and tasks from start to finish

BUILDING AN EFFECTIVE RESUMÉ

The resumé is a one- to two-page summary of your strengths that highlights the skills and experiences that are most desirable to potential employers. Like your experience, it is work in progress and should be updated every six months or so. The resumé is a written piece of communication, and just like the other types of communication you learned about in previous chapters, it requires the three-step process of planning, writing, and editing.

The purpose of the resumé is to get you an interview. You need to understand your audience so that you can answer some questions: "What makes you special?" "Why should I hire you?" Employers may have to read a hundred resumés or more from people who have similar educational backgrounds and even similar types of introductory-level work experiences. You need to supply them with information that will make you stand out.

Those who are granted interviews will likely have proven that they have positive experience in whatever skills the prospective employer values most.

The first step in creating an effective resumé is to examine the descriptions of the positions you are interested in applying for. The key requirements are often listed in the job posting (see Figure 15-1). By reviewing the posting and highlighting the important requirements, you will be able to address the employer's needs. Often, you will need to show how your skills match the requirements and answer some of the main questions the employer has in mind:

- Does the applicant value results? Does he or she have a proven ability to handle increasing levels of responsibility?
- Does the applicant have a strong work ethic and a drive to succeed?
- Can the applicant work well with others while focusing on doing a job well?

"Hey, I saw you on the cover of Assembly Line Illustrated!"

To get ahead, you need more than the basic skills.

Be prepared not only to list your skills but, as we mentioned above, to prove them. This means briefly showing how you used these skills in the workplace or your outside activities to achieve measurable results.

One Size Does Not Fit All

You don't need to create a unique resumé for every job that you apply for, but consider creating a unique resumé for each *type* of job that you apply for. For example, suppose that you have experience as a part-time cashier in retail sales and you are just completing academic training for accounting. The resumé that you use for sales-related jobs will be quite different from the resumé that you use for an accounting position. The first should focus on customer service and related people skills, while the second should emphasize such skills as accuracy, facility with numbers, and an ability to work independently. Of course, all the information you supply will be true, so many of the facts about you will be the same on both resumés. The difference comes in the placement of the skills and careful attention to the things that employers value in the candidates they interview and hire.

The resumé is a potential employer's first good look at your background. Because an employer is deciding whether you deserve an interview, it is critically important that your resumé have a consistent layout, good sentence structure, proper punctuation, concise bulleted lists, and parallel structure. (For more information on parallel structure, see the Thinking and Writing Exercises at the end of the chapter.)

First Things First It is important to keep in mind that any call for applications for a job opportunity can result in hundreds of responses. The resumé is initially used by employers to screen applicants *out*. Because it is not possible, or desirable, to interview every single applicant, some process of choosing only the most promising is needed. People will not necessarily read the entire document so making a good first impression is critical.

Spelling mistakes or grammatical errors often cause a resumé to be thrown out.[12] Even if there are no technical errors, your resumé will not always be read in its entirety, because resumés are often quite similar. Make sure that the most important information appears near the top of your resumé and that it is free from technical errors.

So how can you increase the odds that the employer will include your resumé for a second look? A good way to start is to deconstruct the potential employer's job posting itself to see what the employer is looking for in an ideal candidate. Once you know that, you can present your strengths more effectively. See **Figure 15-1** for an example of a deconstructed job posting.

Most job postings are constructed by using a similar format, although the specifics may vary. The key sections include the following:

- company background
- duties and responsibilities
- qualifications

We will discuss these in turn, but first, it will be useful to describe the role of action verbs in resumés, job postings, and applications letters.

FIGURE 15-1 A Deconstructed Job Posting

When deconstructing a job ad, start by identifying the tasks that you must be able to do to be hired. In this ad from a college in Manitoba, the duties that must be performed are underlined. Usually, the most important are listed first, so if you don't have experience in all areas (or room to list them all) choose the most important ones from the top of the list.

Next, highlight the action verbs, and try to use these when describing your experience. Doing so will help the application reviewer to clearly see your qualifications. These verbs are highlighted in yellow.

Then, closely study the qualifications required (bolded). Often, the human resource department will have a checklist to track whether an applicant has or doesn't have these requirements. Too many "Doesn't haves" and your application won't be considered. Make it clear to the reader exactly how you meet the minimum qualifications. Be explicit and don't rely on him or her to make the connections. Take the first line as an example. You could say, "Gained more than three years of administrative experience as the office manager of Local Co., where I was promoted twice and given a higher level of responsibility." Be specific on as many of these qualifications as possible. Remember, this is your chance to make a good first impression. Be sure to point out your successes with real and measurable results.

Finally, scan the ad for any other important information (in italics). In this ad, the college states its commitment to diversity. If you are a member of any of the subgroups mentioned (Aboriginal persons, women, visible minorities, and individuals with disabilities), you would be wise to mention it, perhaps in the closing lines of your covering letter.

Apply early and be sure to follow up by email before the closing date to ensure they received your application package.

RED RIVER COLLEGE
OF APPLIED ARTS, SCIENCE AND TECHNOLOGY

Administrative Assistant — Teacher Education

Red River College requires an administrative assistant to provide reception and administrative support duties to the Teacher Education department. Reporting to the Chair of Teacher Education, the administrative secretary provides support to the Chair and Instructional Staff.

Duties: Providing program information; ordering, purchasing and managing of materials for the department; assisting with organizing and promoting of department events; organizing meetings of the Department Advisory Committee; recording and distributing minutes of meetings; maintaining staff and student records; scheduling appointments; updating timetables and booklists; maintaining payroll timesheets and updating Program Handbooks, brochures and other materials required by the department; organizing and maintaining records and files in electronic and hard copy format; compiling reports; distributing mail and other duties as assigned.

Qualification Requirements
- Minimum three years of administrative experience;
- **Extensive knowledge and experience with Microsoft Office suite;**
- **Motivation, organization, flexibility, ability to work with accuracy and attention to detail;**
- **Ability to identify the presenting needs of students and refer to appropriate services;**
- **Superior interpersonal and communication skills;**
- **Ability to interpret situations and respond appropriately;**
- **Ability to work independently and within a team setting;**
- **Ability to work effectively with college faculty, support staff and the public;**
- Knowledge in Adobe Writer and Colleague would be an asset;
- Post-secondary education or business education training would be an asset.

We seek diversity in our workplace. Aboriginal persons, women, visible minorities, and individuals with disabilities are encouraged to apply.

Competition No.: *009-100A*
Closing Date: *October 2, 2009*
Salary: Commensurate with experience

Apply in writing to
Red River College
15 Notre Dame Avenue
Winnipeg, MB R3H 0J9
Fax: 204-555-1212
e-mail: *personnelresources@rrc.mb*

To view this and other employment opportunities online, visit us at www.rrc.mb.ca and select "Employment Opportunities" from the list of quick links on the right. We thank all applicants for their interest, but only those selected for an interview will be contacted.

Source: Job posting from Red River College. Used by permission.

TABLE 15-1	Action Verbs Relating to Communication Skills				
addressed	convinced	expressed	listened	promoted	solicited
analyzed	corresponded	formulated	marketed	proposed	specified
authored	defined	gathered	mediated	publicized	spoke
clarified	developed	incorporated	moderated	reconciled	suggested
collaborated	directed	influenced	negotiated	recruited	synthesized
communicated	discussed	interacted	observed	referred	transcribed
composed	drafted	interpreted	outlined	reinforced	translated
consulted	edited	interviewed	participated	reported	validated
contacted	enlisted	involved	persuaded	resolved	verified
conveyed	explained	joined	presented	responded	wrote

Action Verbs Action verbs are a specific set of words to describe your skills and experiences. They are used in your resumé, cover letter, and even during your interview to describe your successes in acquiring skills. Action verbs increase the strength of your message and make employers want to know more about you. Many action words relate to common job requirements. Some of these that relate to communication skills are listed in **Table 15-1**.

Many other action verbs relate to other types of job skills and experiences. An online source, such as QuintCareers.com, is an excellent resource for additional ideas.

Use an action verb to start your description of each skill or accomplishment that you describe in your resumé. This places emphasis on your activities and allows you to leave out such words as *I* and *was*.

Weak verb: I was responsible for the recruitment of 30 new clients in six months.

Action verb: Recruited 30 new clients in six months.

What to Watch For

Deconstructing a job ad is a little like building a jigsaw puzzle. The company gives you most of the pieces (what is important to the employer) and it is up to you to put it together, fill in any blanks, and show why you are the best person for the job. Remember that you are in a job competition, and you want to win. Read and reread the posting carefully. Examine the following sections of an ad closely and match the requirements to your skills when writing your resumé.

Company Background Usually, a brief description of the company and its areas of specialty is given. Pay particular attention to the action verbs they've used to describe their business. If you can, try to incorporate these same verbs into your covering letter or resumé.

Duties and Responsibilities In this section, a company describes the main responsibilities that it will require from any successful candidate. Usually, these are listed with the most important duty first and then in descending order. Use the same ordering for describing your skills and responsibilities in the covering letter. If your resumé has a Skills and Experiences section, you can address the company's main needs there, too. Try not to leave anything to chance—for example, list the employer's highest need as your top skill. Never falsify your application just to get the interview, but if it is just a matter of ordering or choosing the action verbs used to describe your skills, why not use the company's list of priorities? The company has already told you what it values most, so tell the company what it wants to hear. If you leave your strengths to the end of your resumé, like you might when writing the climax to a short story, then your best skills may never be read.

Qualifications This last section describes the types of education or additional training and experience that are needed. Often, these are considered as minimum qualifications, but occasionally a company may consider hiring a less-qualified candidate to a more junior-level position. If you do not have all the necessary qualifications, be sure to express an interest in pursuing the missing qualifications if you are hired. As you write, pretend that you are competing against a virtual ideal candidate. A hard-working team player with a positive attitude who is willing to learn is often a great candidate for any job.

Don't Forget As you create your resumé, think about what employers want and focus on how successful you have been in gaining that experience. That experience is best gained while on the job, but it can also come from school projects or even volunteer work in the community. Remember that your resumé is a marketing tool that you use to sell yourself to a potential employer. You must always tell the truth, but exactly how you portray your skills and experience is critical to your success. You can use organization and planning to emphasize what matters most to your future employer.

Before we turn to a discussion of resumé styles, one source of confusion is the inclusion of references in a resumé. Unless specifically asked, it is not a good idea to include references as a part of your resumé. If you are successful and get an interview, you will be asked to provide a reference list. Developing positive references and effective networks is addressed in Chapter 16.

RESUMÉ STYLES

You can choose from several styles of resumés. Here are the top three:

1. *Chronological:* Emphasizes work experience and is the most popular, and most traditional, style
2. *Functional:* Focuses on skills and capabilities
3. *Hybrid:* Combines the best features of the other two

We will be examining each of these—and some less common forms—later in this section.

After you have decided which style of resumé will portray your talents most effectively, you still have many choices to make. You will need to decide which components to include, the sequence in which to present them, and whether to include a number of optional features (to be discussed).

Objective Statement An objective statement (see the start of **Figures 15-3, 15-4,** and **15-5** later in this section) can help to focus your resumé, especially if you are prospecting for a job—that is, submitting an application without knowing whether the company has an opening.

Some feel that an objective is useful because it helps screeners identify the position for which you are applying and allows you to provide a marketing statement that describes how you meet their needs—for example, "To contribute my leadership skills to a growing company that needs an out-of-the-box thinker to improve delivery methods for their technical and marketing communication strategies."[13]

Others advise you to move your objective to the application letter or eliminate it entirely, calling it fluff that prevents you from delivering your key message in the first ten seconds the screener spends reading your resumé. Your true objective is, after all, to obtain the job that you are applying for.[14] These people suggest that you consider including a summary of qualifications.

Remember, as with all business writing, if information does not take you closer to achieving your goal—in this case, getting an interview—then it pushes you farther away. A vague or misguided objective statement could hurt your resumé, so it is better left out. If you are unsure whether you need an objective statement, your best option is to go for brevity and leave such a statement out.

Summary of Qualifications Instead of an objective, many people include a profile that summarizes their key qualifications (see **Figure 15-2**). A summary at the beginning of a resumé does the same thing as a summary at the beginning of a report: It presents the key information for those who do not

FIGURE 15-2   **A Summary of Qualifications**

A business administration specialist with three years' experience organizing day-to-day operations for a company with $25 million in annual sales and 20 full-time employees. First staff member to win the Outstanding Achiever Award for Customer Service in three consecutive fiscal quarters. Highly organized and competent in managing multiple priorities with excellent results. Outstanding computer skills, including a typing speed of 95 words per minute, specializing in Microsoft Office Suite, Adobe Writer, and other leading office management programs. An independent and creative problem solver who is innovative and enthusiastic, with proven abilities in interpersonal communication, team building, diplomacy, and exceeding clients' expectations.

have time to read the entire document. Thus, it is especially useful if your resumé is long.

Summaries should not simply restate details found later in your resumé; people will get bored, or even annoyed, at being asked to read the same information twice. Instead, the summary should include half a dozen key points that condense details of your education and transferable career skills. Transferable skills are skills you learned doing one task for one type of company that can be equally and successfully applied to another task with another company. For example, "providing outstanding customer service" is a skill that is transferable from one job to another.

Condensing similar experience is important. For example, a person who is applying for a marketing position could combine two sales jobs with two different employers as "five years of retail sales in home electronics."

Tips   Here are a few guidelines for writing a summary of qualifications:

- Keep your points brief—details that support each statement will appear later in the resumé.
- Consider the employer's needs when deciding which information to highlight at the top of your list.
- Focus on measurable achievements: such adjectives as *hardworking, dependable,* and *detail oriented* are useless unless accompanied by specific evidence.

Interests and Outside Activities   Generally speaking, it is best to restrict your resumé to your professional qualifications. Mention your interests and hobbies only if they have a potential use to the employer. The exception is volunteer work, which always looks good on a resumé.

Putting It All Together   Now that we have deconstructed the job posting, looked at important action verbs, and examined elements that make effective resumés, it is time to bring all the pieces together and decide which type of resumé works best for your experience.

1. Chronological Resumés

Chronological resumés, as we mentioned, are the most common type (see the example in **Figure 15-3**). They all contain two key sections:

1. One describes your work experience.
2. The other lists your education.

The order of these two sections will depend on your background. If you are a recent graduate or do not have strong work experience, describe your education first, because it is likely to be your strongest selling point. A few years after you have graduated and gained some relevant work experience, you should emphasize your employment history by placing it first.

Employment History   Work history begins with the most recent work first and lists positions chronologically backward in time. The longest entries

FIGURE 15-3 **A Chronological Resumé**

Relevant contact information is clearly placed and centred.

Objective is brief and clearly stated.

Experience is listed concisely with dates and achievements.

Action verbs show accomplishments.

excellent use of bullets and headings

Good spacing allows for easy reading.

Special skills are listed and easy to find.

Mackenzie Washington
122 Cloverplace Crescent
Anytown, MB R9A 1K5
204-555-1212
mwashington@shaw.ca

OBJECTIVE
To contribute to the success of a retail department through increased sales and improved customer satisfaction in an entry-level supervisor or management position

EXPERIENCE
Supervisor (part time), Hometown Hardware, Winnipeg, Manitoba
October 2007 to present
- Assisted with training, motivating, and supervising checkout clerks, and won Provincial Award for Employee Excellence two years in a row
- Improved customer satisfaction with detailed staff training on frequently asked questions, which increased customer retention by 10 percent

Concession clerk (summer term, full time), Everynight Movie Theatre, The Pas, Manitoba
May 2007 to September 2007
- Initiated a sales contest to increase multiple purchases, resulting in a 15 percent increase in theatre concession profit
- Created a staff checklist to organize and standardize counter cleanup for shift changeover

EDUCATION
University of Manitoba, Winnipeg, Manitoba
Completing a Bachelor in Business Administration
Graduating in May 2012
    Major Courses: Marketing and Sales
                                      Retail Merchandising
                                        Accounting

Red River College, Winnipeg, Manitoba
Diploma in Applied Commerce and Management
Graduated with honours in 2008
    Major Courses: E-Commerce
                                      Organizational Behaviour
                                      Human Resource Management

SKILLS
- Excellent communication skills gained by use of office computers and related software
- Effective management skills developed by initiating and leading many work improvement programs
- Teamwork skills built through leading staff discussions and employee improvement initiatives
- Proficiency with Windows, Excel, and PowerPoint

References available on request

should be for the most recent positions and those that are closely related to the job you are seeking. If you have a substantial number of entries in this category, you may want to omit some of your earlier low-level positions.

If, however, you are young and do not have a great deal of work experience to offer, do not downplay the significance of these low-level jobs. Do not make the mistake of leaving menial positions off your resumé simply because they do not relate to the position for which you are applying. All jobs require people to behave responsibly, to cooperate, and to do good work. Even unskilled positions will allow you to demonstrate these qualities.

When you are describing your jobs, focus on describing your accomplishments rather than your duties. Your goal is to demonstrate that you are a better prospect for the position than your competitors are. If you can prove that you have increased sales, improved productivity, or created something new, then you will be showing how you are a better fit for the position.

Entries do not need to be complete sentences—in fact, it is better to avoid sentences. Since the resumé is about you, and since you are trying to showcase your best points, each sentence would almost certainly start with the word *I* and reading about your activities would be very tedious. Instead write short phrases starting with *action verbs,* which we discussed earlier, that draw the readers' attention to your accomplishments.

Chronological resumés can be very persuasive for those with a long and strong work history, especially when the position you are seeking falls in line with your existing career goals and past job experience.

2. Functional Resumés

This format—sometimes referred to as a skills-based or accomplishment-based resumé—places greater emphasis on the transferable skills that you have learned while working rather than where you worked. (See **Figure 15-4** for a sample of this kind of resumé.) These resumés describe your accomplishments and try to match them with the needs of the employer. Functional resumés allow you to give equal emphasis to experience gained from volunteer work, paid employment, and education.

To write a functional resumé, you pool all your qualifications and then organize the information into categories. The categories you choose will depend on your background and should match the employer's needs.

As with a chronological resumé, the functional resumé will often have an objective statement or a summary of qualifications at the top. The functional resumé will then have three to five sections that highlight your skills as they relate to the position you want. The categories of skills that are important to the employer can usually be teased out of their advertisement in the list of duties and responsibilities. Because the list is driven by employer expectations, it is impossible to include here all possible categories to consider for your functional resumé. That said, based on the sample advertisement in Figure 15-1, possible categories could include Office Operational Management, Report Writing and Desktop Publishing, and Teambuilding. If you are unsure of what categories to include, it is helpful to look through the list of skills that are most sought after by potential employers, shown in **Table 15-2**.

FIGURE 15-4 **A Functional Resumé**

Relevant contact information is clearly placed and centred.

Objective is brief and clearly stated.

excellent use of bullets, headings, and spacing

Skills are organized by type and listed first.

Action verbs show accomplishments.

Experience is listed at end with employment dates.

Mackenzie Washington
122 Cloverplace Crescent
Anytown, MB R9A 1K5
204-555-1212
mwashington@shaw.ca

OBJECTIVE
To contribute to the success of a retail department through increased sales and improved customer satisfaction in an entry-level supervisor or management position

SKILLS

Communication Skills
- Excellent communication skills gained by use of office technology
- Proficiency with Windows, Excel, and PowerPoint

Management Skills
- Managed and created staff schedules for improved workflow and better efficiency
- Assisted with training, motivating, and supervising checkout clerks, and won Provincial Award for Employee Excellence two years in a row

Organizational and Problem-Solving Skills
- Improved customer satisfaction with detailed staff training on frequently asked questions, which increased customer retention by 10 percent
- Created a staff checklist to organize and standardize counter cleanup for shift changeover

Team Building Skills
- Initiated a sales contest to increase multiple purchases, resulting in a 15 percent increase in theatre concession profit
- Motivated new staff to improve product knowledge and customer service

EDUCATION
University of Manitoba, Winnipeg, Manitoba
Completing a Bachelor in Business Administration, graduating in May 2012
Red River College, Winnipeg, Manitoba
Diploma in Applied Commerce and Management, graduated with honours in 2008

EXPERIENCE
Supervisor (part time), Hometown Hardware, Winnipeg, Manitoba
October 2007 to present
Concession clerk (summer term, full time), Everynight Movie Theatre, The Pas, Manitoba
May 2007 to September 2007

References available on request

TABLE 15-2 Categories for a Functional Resumé and Their Descriptions

Interpersonal Communication	Personal Management Skills	Teamwork Skills
Communicate Effectively	**Demonstrate Positive Attitudes and Behaviours**	**Work Well with Others**
– Addressed the need for effective communications by regularly presenting complicated information in an under-standable manner (e.g., using audience-appropriate words, graphs, charts, diagrams) in staff meetings, resulting in positive audience evaluations	– Spoke with confidence . . .	– Understood and worked within the dynamics of a group . . .
– Developed excellent listening skills to appreciate the points of view of others to increase understanding with clients and co-workers	– Addressed people, problems, and situations with honesty, integrity, and personal ethics . . .	– Ensured that a team's purpose and objectives were clear . . .
– Enlisted appropriate information-sharing technologies, such as voicemail, email, fax, and computers . . . (you finish the points by filling in the [what you did] and [what was the outcome])	– Promoted other people's good efforts . . .	– Showed flexibility, respect, openness, and support for the thoughts, opinions and contributions of others in a group . . .
– Clarified ideas by using relevant scientific, technological, and mathematical knowledge and explanatory skills . . .	– Conveyed interest, initiative, and effort . . .	– Identified and respected people's diversity, individual differences, and perspectives . . .
Manage Information	**Be Responsible**	– Accepted and provided feedback in a constructive and considerate manner . . .
– Located, gathered, and organized information by using appropriate technology and information systems . . .	– Integrated goals and priorities, balancing work and personal life . . .	– Contributed to a team by sharing information and expertise . . .
– Incorporated knowledge and skills from various disciplines (e.g., the arts, languages, science, technology, mathematics, social sciences, and the humanities) . . .	– Reconciled the challenges of managing time, money, and other resources to achieve goals . . .	– Led or supported, when appropriate, a group for high performance . . .
Use and Understand Numbers	– Assessed, weighed, and managed risk . . .	– Understood the role of conflict in a group to reach solutions . . .
– Defined what data needs to be measured or calculated . . .	– Promoted accountability for personal actions and the actions of the group . . .	– Managed and resolved conflict when appropriate . . .
– Observed and recorded data by using appropriate methods, tools, and technology . . .	– Contributed to my community in a socially responsible manner . . .	**Participate Effectively in Projects and Tasks**
– Reported estimates and verified calculations . . .	**Be Adaptable**	– Planned, designed, and carried out a project or task from start to finish, with well-defined objectives and outcomes . . .
Think Independently and Solve Problems	– Conveyed an open and constructive response to change . . .	– Directed multiple tasks and projects . . .
– Assessed situations and identified problems . . .	**Learn Continually**	– Proposed innovative and resourceful ways to achieve goals and get the job done . . .
– Investigated different points of view and evaluated them based on facts . . .	– Embraced continuous learning and growing . . .	– Worked independently and as a part of a team . . .

TABLE 15-2   *(Continued)*

Interpersonal Communication	Personal Management Skills	Teamwork Skills
– Recognized the human, interpersonal, technical, scientific, and mathematical dimensions of a problem . . .	– Assessed personal strengths and identified areas for development . . .	– Learned from past mistakes and accepted feedback . . .
– Determined the cause of a problem . . .	– Initiated my own learning goals . . .	– Managed uncertainty in the team by . . .
– Proposed creative and innovative solutions to problems . . .	– Identified and accessed learning sources and opportunities . . .	– Ensured full participation of team members by . . .
– Integrated science, technology, and mathematics as ways to think, gain, and share knowledge, solve problems, and make decisions . . .	– Planned for and achieved learning goals . . .	– Promoted respect and professionalism by . . .
– Validated solutions to make recommendations or decisions . . .	**Work Safely**	– Guided group discussions to productive outcomes by . . .
– Verified that a solution works, and acted on opportunities for improvement . . .	– Verified personal and group health and safety practices and procedures, and acted in accordance . . .	– Followed up after team meetings with group support by . . .

Source: Adapted from "Employability Skills 2000+." Conference Board of Canada. *May 2000. Web. 29 Oct. 2007.*

When writing the bullets to support each of these categories, remember that you need to prove that you have related experience. You need to show the specific skills you have, what you did to develop the skills, and what the outcome was. Your opinion, plus measurable proof, is more convincing.

This kind of resumé can be useful for those with a limited work history or for people making a major career change, but it is often hard for employers to follow. The skills listed are no longer associated directly with work history and are therefore more difficult to check or even understand.

3. Hybrid Resumés

Both chronological and functional resumés have good parts, and so many people choose to combine them and use the best of both. The hybrid resumé is particularly useful to employers because it highlights the transferable skills that will be of use if the person is hired and details the development of the applicant over time. See **Figure 15-5** for a sample hybrid resumé.

4. Web-Based Resumés

The increasing use of the internet as a job-search tool has created the need for new resumé formats. For example, you may need to create a plain text (or ASCII) file that is easily scanned by computer. So-called scannable resumés allow potential employers to use their computers to quickly and easily scan

FIGURE 15-5   **A Hybrid Resumé**

Mackenzie Washington
122 Cloverplace Crescent
Anytown, MB R9A 1K5
204-555-1212
mwashington@shaw.ca

OBJECTIVE

To contribute to the success of a retail department through increased sales and improved customer satisfaction in an entry-level supervisor or management position

SKILLS

- Excellent communication skills gained by use of office technology
- Effective management skills developed by initiating and leading many work improvement programs, including schedules, checklists, and competitions
- Teamwork skills built through leading staff discussions and employee improvement initiatives
- Office operation skills increased with proficient use of Windows, Excel, and PowerPoint

EDUCATION

University of Manitoba, Winnipeg, Manitoba
Completing a Bachelor in Business Administration
Graduating in May 2012

Major Courses:	Marketing and Sales
	Retail Merchandising
	Accounting

Red River College, Winnipeg, Manitoba
Diploma in Applied Commerce and Management
Graduated with honours in 2008

Major Courses:	E-Commerce
	Organizational Behaviour
	Human Resource Management

EXPERIENCE

Supervisor (part time), Hometown Hardware, Winnipeg, Manitoba
October 2007 to present

- Assisted with training, motivating, and supervising checkout clerks, and won Provincial Award for Employee Excellence two years in a row
- Improved customer satisfaction with detailed staff training on frequently asked questions, which increased customer retention by 10 percent

Concession clerk (summer term, full time), Everynight Movie Theatre,
The Pas, Manitoba
May 2007 to September 2007

- Initiated a sales contest to increase multiple purchases, resulting in a 15 percent increase in theatre concession profit
- Created a staff checklist to organize and standardize counter cleanup for shift changeover

References available on request

Sidebar notes:
- Relevant contact information is clearly placed and centred.
- Objective is brief and clearly stated.
- Transferable skills are highlighted.
- excellent use of bullets, headings, and spacing
- Action verbs show accomplishments and are listed under work experience.

thousands of resumés and choose a small sample based on their own selection criteria. Here are some pointers for creating a scannable resumé from your existing resumé.

1. Begin by removing all text formatting, including bolding, underlining, and italics.

2. Next, remove any other page formatting options you may have used, such as reverse text or graphics.

3. Choose an easily scannable typeface, such as Times New Roman, Courier, Futura, Univers, or Helvetica.

4. Select a slightly large font size (up to 14 points).

5. Include a new section in the beginning that contains twenty to thirty common keywords that relate to your skills and experience. Be sure to use keywords from the job description, as well as those from similar positions elsewhere. See **Table 15-3** for examples.

6. Save the file under a new name and choose "Text only with line breaks" as the format.

TABLE 15-3	**Examples of Keywords**		
accountable	customer service	hard worker	problem solve
analytical	detail oriented	initiative	team player
communication skills	ethical	multi-tasking	think outside the box
creative	good listener	open-minded	willing to travel

5. Employment Portfolios and Eportfolios

Going beyond the traditional resumé, many people develop an employment portfolio—a collection of past successes, accomplishments, accolades, and activities that make them unique and more valuable as a potential employee.

An eportfolio is the electronic extension of this concept and includes a multimedia presentation of the experiences and skills that you have already developed and can transfer to your new job.[15]

Examples of work to include in your portfolio (electronic or otherwise) could be any of the following:

- school papers
- work projects
- solutions to difficult problems you have faced in the workplace or elsewhere

Remember, just like with a traditional resumé, if you want the portfolio to be useful in getting you the job you seek, it should address the main skills that are sought by most employers. As detailed in **Table 1-2**, Conference Board of Canada research shows that these skills include the following:

- fundamental skills, such as communicating, managing information, and problem solving

Start your list with the transferable skills that the employer wants most.

- personal management skills, such as adapting to change, portraying a positive attitude, and learning continually
- teamwork skills, such as working well with others, participating in projects from start to finish, and managing conflict effectively

If you choose to develop an eportfolio, you can distribute it in many ways. You can create a compact disk version and send it along with your resumé in the application process. You can also post the eportfolio to a dedicated website or a networking website. If you do post this information to the internet, be sure it does not include any personal information that could be used in online scams. Also, make sure that if you use examples of past work projects that this information is not sensitive or confidential.

LETTERS THAT CAN GET YOU WORK

Many job seekers wait until they see a job opening online or in the newspaper before they contact a company. The trouble with that strategy is that their application may be lost in the hundreds of other applications for the same job. Instead, try using a prospecting letter to get noticed.

TAKE IT FURTHER

The Cost of Mistakes

A survey of 150 senior staffing specialists from different companies asked how many typos in a resumé it took before an applicant would not be considered for a position with their company:[16]

- one typo: 47%
- two typos: 37%
- three or more typos: 13%

Three percent didn't know or didn't answer.

Why do recruiters place so much importance on an applicant supplying a well-prepared resumé?

The Prospecting Letter

A prospecting letter is an unsolicited letter that you write to a potential employer that you would like to work for. The purpose of the letter is to introduce yourself and your skills and abilities, and generate enough interest to be asked in for an interview. See **Figure 15-6** for an example.

Because the letter is unsolicited, meaning not asked for, you will need to spend some time establishing why you are writing to the company. It is important to remember that not all companies have job openings that relate to your experience, so the prospecting letter is more about generating interest that may someday land you a job.

As you would with any other correspondence, it is important to adopt the three-step process already described in this text (planning, writing, and editing). You must know your purpose and have a clear understanding of what you hope to accomplish. It is good to know who you are writing to, and this information can come from an internet search or a telephone call to the company to ask for the name of the person in charge of hiring employees.

Consider what the company needs to know for you to get what you want: an interview. Once you have your planning and brainstorming completed, write the letter, making sure to include the following points:

- Clearly state your interest in working for the company.
- Explain where you learned about the company.
- Sell yourself and your strongest skills and abilities, keeping in mind what you now know are the skills that employers seek.
- Follow with a specific action plan and a description of what you want to accomplish.
- Finally, close with a sincere expression of thanks for the person's time.

Letters about Advertised Positions

A letter that is written in response to an advertised job opening is called a solicited application letter. Although the letter is similar to the prospecting letter described above, it has some notable differences.

The main difference is that now you are writing to request and interview for a specific job, which makes your purpose clearer. See **Figure 15-7** for a sample solicited application letter.

Unfortunately, many people will likely be writing to the same company for the same job. Because of the sheer volume of applications that must be processed in a limited time, there is a greater chance that some of the details of your solicited application letter may be overlooked. This puts extra pressure on you to make sure that the letter is an effective sales pitch of you and your abilities. Of course, using the three-step writing process is the best way to start. The following tips can also help:

1. *Be specific:* The most important suggestion is to make sure that your application letter is specific to the job opening. Be sure to include the job title and unique job reference number, if one appears on the job posting. This will help ensure that your application is included in the right competition.

FIGURE 15-6   **A Prospecting Letter**

Mackenzie Washington
122 Cloverplace Crescent
Anytown, MB R9A 1K5

February 3, 2012

Mr. John Appletree
Sunrise Marketing
23 Riverside Drive
Anytown, MB R9A 1T9

Dear Mr. Appletree:

Your recent ad in *Canadian Business Weekly* for the Sugarfree Bagel Company featuring the dancing doughnuts was so creative and unique that I knew immediately that Sunrise Marketing is the company where I want to put my marketing research skills to work. I have extensive experience in the marketing industry, and I am eager to contribute to your company's bottom line. When a position as a market researcher becomes available, please consider me.

I am currently a student at the University of Manitoba, and I will graduate with a degree in Business Administration in April 2012. Through hard work and dedication, I have achieved a high grade point average and gained valuable experience by studying sales and marketing, business management, business accounting, and organizational development. I have led and participated in many research projects and business proposals whose goal was to solve difficult problems efficiently and cost effectively.

In addition to my studies, I have valuable work-related experience that is described in the attached resumé. As you will see, I have developed many professional and personal skills that are transferable to your company. These include effective communications skills, time management, multi-tasking, customer relations, team building, and adaptability. I would like to bring these skills to Sunrise Marketing and continue my lifelong learning.

I realize that you will you be very busy in March when the new ad campaigns launch. Perhaps you will require an experienced researcher before that time. Could we discuss my qualifications and the possibility of an opening? I will telephone your office on Tuesday, February 11th, to set a date and time that is convenient for you. If you have any questions before that time, please call me at 1-204-555-1212.

Sincerely,
Mackenzie Washington
Mackenzie Washington
ENCLOSURE

---

expresses knowledge of the company and grabs attention in the first paragraph

provides personal details not in resumé

displays industry knowledge and acknowledges the reader

FIGURE 15-7   **A Solicited Application Letter**

Mackenzie Washington
122 Cloverplace Crescent
Anytown, MB R9A 1K5

February 3, 2012

Mr. Jeffrey Baird
Silverton Inc.
350 Yonge St. N.
Anytown, MB R9A 1T9

Dear Mr. Baird:

provides reader with purpose of letter and introduces applicant's skills

I am writing to apply for the opportunity of assistant sales manager for the Midcity region (Posting # 13512) as described in the *Winnipeg Free Press* newspaper, February 2, 2012. I believe that my sales and management experience match the qualifications that you are looking for in this position.

matches skills and achievements with those listed in the ad

Your job posting noted that you are looking for a self-starter. In my current position, I identified a problem with the process of handling customer complaints. I studied the problem and developed a solution, with my supervisor's approval. Hometown started a pilot using the new complaint-resolution process I had created. The number of satisfied customers has increased by 25 percent, and repeat sales continue to increase. Your ad also says that being an effective team builder is important. I have led or participated in many team projects. For example, I implemented a process in which issues are anonymously brought forward in our regular office planning sessions. Proactively dealing with staff concerns before they became bigger problems improved the staff morale, and turnover and absenteeism were reduced. I have included my resumé, which describes my other professional and personal skills that are transferable to your company.

I am currently a student at the University of Manitoba, and I will graduate with a degree in Business Administration in April 2012. Through hard work and dedication, I have achieved a high grade point average and gained valuable experience by studying sales and marketing, business management, business accounting, and organizational development. I have led and participated in many research projects and business proposals whose goal was to solve difficult problems efficiently and cost effectively.

mentions enclosed resumé

requests a meeting

I hope to meet in person to discuss this opportunity further. If you have any questions or would like to arrange a time that is convenient, please call me at 1-204-555-1212.

Sincerely,
Mackenzie Washington
Mackenzie Washington
ENCLOSURE

This is especially helpful when applying to larger companies that may have many job competitions happening at once.

2. *Open well:* As before, the first paragraph is very important because it must tell the reader why you are writing and also stir some interest to get this person to keep reading. Chances are that a professional in the human resources department will review the letter, so it will be something this person *has* to do. So why not make your application letter more interesting than most so the HR person *wants* to read it and perhaps puts your application at the top of the pile for his or her supervisor to read? Remember:

   ▪ As we discussed earlier in the chapter, use the information provided by the company in its call for applications, or job posting, to customize your letter to its needs.

   ▪ Start with the duties that are most important to the company, and then clearly show how your skills and experience match them.

   ▪ Consider doing this for the top two or three most important qualifications and be sure to include similar words and phrasing as the company has. Of course this will not guarantee you an interview, but it will decrease the likelihood that your application is overlooked.

3. *Avoid being dropped:* The company you will be applying to will likely receive tens, if not hundreds, of applications from people with similar backgrounds to yours. Of course, they did not all go to the same schools or work at the same part-time and summer jobs as you, but the background of these other applicants is very similar to yours. Human resources people usually do the first read of applications to try to eliminate applications. At this point they want to eliminate the weakest applications: those that do not clearly have the required qualifications or those that did not bother to check spelling, punctuation, and grammar. It is not possible, nor desirable, to interview everyone that applies for a job to find the very best. A stack of, say, one hundred applications is cut to twenty-five, then down to ten, and then to three to five candidates who get a call for an interview.

   These first reviews aren't done to see who should be included but rather to see who should definitely be excluded from further consideration. To write an effective cover letter, don't give them any reason to drop your application from further consideration.

4. *Be purposeful:* After drafting the first paragraph that lists your interest in a particular job and where you learned of the opportunity, it's time for the harder part of the letter: the body. Rather than just talk about some generic skills that you hope they are looking for, be purposeful in your writing. Remember that they are working from a checklist of what they want, and if you don't show that your background measures up, then you will not be selected for an interview.

Read the job description carefully and identify the top two or three skills it says are needed. Sometimes the company will list them directly and sometimes these show up as "key responsibilities." In your letter's body, use the company terminology and then show how your experience matches. Don't rely on the person sitting in an office somewhere to connect the dots to see the bigger picture. Effectively say, "This is what I know you need; this is what I did to get the skills you need; and this was the outcome."

Solicited Application Letter in Action Suppose the job posting indicated "retail cash skills" as a required asset. Never use a line like "Handled cash" in your application letter (or resumé, for that matter). Everyone can say that they "handle cash," even a bank robber. You have to word your experience in a way that sizzles.

Consider saying something like "Took great care in following established cash-handling procedures and initiated a new checklist to improve cash balances to 100 percent accuracy." Never tell a lie in the application process, because your honesty is your greatest asset. How you describe what you did can be as important as what you actually did. Repeat this process for each of the main skills that the company says it needs. Finally, refer the reader to your attached resumé for additional details, and the body section is complete.

As before, close with a statement that you will be in contact about possibly arranging an interview, and thank them for their attention.

Chapter Summary

The process of finding and securing the ideal job is difficult. One way you can be prepared is by updating your resumé every six months or so. Use a chronological or functional resumé or a hybrid of the two, and make sure that your information is fresh and up to date. Including new responsibilities, skills acquired, and other related information every six months or so will ensure that your resumé never gets too far out of date. Taking it further by developing a web-based resumé or employment portfolio that can also be posted online uses technology to showcase your greatest asset: you.

Writing prospecting letters to companies that are not currently advertising job opportunities is a great way to learn more about companies that you are particularly interested in working for. Writing letters in response to advertised positions allows you to use details found in the job description to make your writing more specific and more successful. Clearly drawing the connection between the skills that the employer needs and the transferable skills that you already possess is the key to getting the interview. After that, getting the job takes additional skills that you can develop when you study Chapter 16.

PEARSON
mycanadianbuscommlab Visit **www.mycanadianbuscommlab.ca** for everything you need to help you succeed in the job you've always wanted! Tools and resources include the following:

- Composing and The Writer's Toolkit
- Document Makeovers
- Video Case Studies
- Grammar exercises and much more!

Thinking and Writing Exercises

1. **Identifying Accomplishments**

   Identify a job that you would like to have once you graduate. With that position in mind, answer the following questions:

   a. List five words that describe you positively.

   b. List three personal activities that other people have praised.

   c. List three academic strengths.

   d. List three things that you did well at your last (or current) job.

   Use this information to write three achievement statements that could be included on a resumé or application letter. Your achievement statements must describe a strength and provide evidence to support it.[17]

2. **Transferable Skills and How to Get Them**

   a. What are transferable skills and how do you get them?

   b. List your top three professional skills. How did you develop them?

   c. List the top four transferable skills most sought by employers. How do these compare with your strongest skills?

   d. If your strengths do not exactly match the skills sought by employers, name some of the ways that you can build the needed skills before you look for your next job.

   e. Why is it a good idea to build your transferable skills while you are currently working?

3. **General Resumé Questions**

   a. What is a resumé? What is its main purpose?

   b. What are the main parts of a resumé?

   c. What types of information should you never include in your resumé?

   d. Why should you never lie in your resumé? After all, isn't the point to get the job any way possible?

4. **Different Styles of Resumés**

   a. What is a chronological resumé? What are its main parts? List the emphasis of this type of resumé and its strengths and weaknesses.

   b. What is a functional resumé? What are its main parts? List the emphasis of this type of resumé and its strengths and weaknesses.

   c. What is a hybrid resumé? What are its main parts? List the emphasis of this type of resumé and its strengths and weaknesses.

   d. What is a web-based resumé? What are its main parts? List the emphasis of this type of resumé and its strengths and weaknesses.

   e. What is an employment portfolio? What are its main parts? List the emphasis of this type of presentation and its strengths and weaknesses.

5. **Letters about Jobs**

   a. What is a prospecting letter? What is its purpose?

   b. What are the key points to include in a prospecting letter?

   c. What is a solicited application letter?

   d. What are the key points to include in this type of letter?

   e. What is the most important detail to include in this type of letter?

   f. What are solicited application letters used for, especially in the early stages of a candidate review process?

   g. How can you better your chances of not being excluded from a competition even before the interview process?

Writing Skills Checkup: Parallel Structure

In parallel structure, one pattern of words shows that two or more ideas have the same degree of importance. The usual way to join parallel structures is by using coordinating conjunctions, such as *and* or *or*. Parallel structure can happen at the word, phrase, or clause level. The following guidelines will help you to decide when to use parallel structure in your writing.

PARALLEL STRUCTURE WITH WORDS

a. Not parallel

   My top three work-related skills are communicating, team building, and office management.

b. Parallel

My top three work-related skills are communicating, team building, and managing the office.

PARALLEL STRUCTURE WITH A PHRASE

a. Not parallel

The supervisor said that he was a poor worker because he waited until the last minute to start his shift, completed his duties in a careless manner, and his motivation was low.

b. Parallel

The supervisor said that he was a poor worker because he waited until the last minute to start his shift, completed his duties in a careless manner, and lacked motivation.

PARALLEL STRUCTURE WITH A CLAUSE

a. Not parallel

As team leader, I told my colleagues that they should set clear goals, that they should monitor their progress, and document the project's outcomes.

b. Parallel

As team leader, I told my colleagues that they should set clear goals, that they should monitor their progress, and that they should document the project's outcomes.

Correct the parallel structure, when needed, in these sentences.

1. I have managed an office and supervise workers.
2. In my current position I am responsible for balancing petty cash and audits.
3. I enjoy working with the public and answered many complaints.
4. In my previous job I opened the store, handled cash, and cleaned the storerooms.
5. I enjoyed working at my last job because my manager gave me more responsibilities, trained me to help with handling customer complaints, and better hours.
6. I decided to leave my last job because I wasn't getting enough hours, wasn't fully trained to handle the finances, and there were no holidays in summer.
7. I have completed a college certificate, completed professional training in customer service, and am learning accounting software.
8. After I finished school I travelled to Europe, volunteered with my community youth program, and play in a band.
9. Created an automated computer program to track inventory, created a word-processing program to send flyers to customers, and started a customer comment process.
10. Prepared reconciliation reports, balancing end of month sales reports, and prepared annual reports.

Networking, Developing Effective References, and Succeeding in Employment Interviews

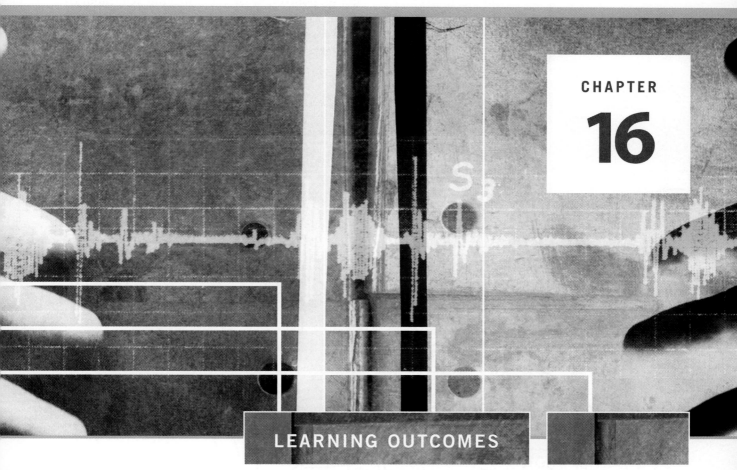

LEARNING OUTCOMES

After completing this chapter, you should be able to do the following:

16.1 Develop a career network to help you with a successful job search

16.2 Establish effective references

16.3 Identify and prepare for common interview questions

16.4 Understand the various types of interviews and how to prepare for them

16.5 Properly follow up after an interview

FINDING THE BEST OF THE BUNCH

Developing good references and finding jobs through networking can be challenging, but for most people, the most intimidating (and sometimes exhilarating) part of the job search process is the interview. Along with providing details on networking and creating references, this chapter discusses the types of interviews employers have devised to try to find the best people with the highest chances of future success in their companies. The reason is simple: If an employer chooses poorly and selects an incompetent candidate, the future costs to the company can be tens of thousands of dollars or more. These costs can come in the form of problematic behaviour (see the Issues in Communication box), unexpected training costs, poor job performance, and severance.

"Very impressive educational background...now let's discuss WHO you know."

Whom you know can help you make the best of what you know.

To help reduce the anxiety that often comes before the interview, we suggest you view the process as useful to everyone involved. True, the interviewer is appraising your skills and qualifications, but you also have an excellent opportunity to explore whether this is really the employer you want to work for. Understanding the lessons of this chapter will help you to get the job that best suits you.

NETWORKING AND THE HIDDEN JOB MARKET

Too many would-be job seekers forget about their most valuable asset as they are searching for a job: the people who know them. The world is filled with highly educated and well-qualified people, but not all these people will succeed in every type of work environment. *Networking* is the process of using your social and informal relationships to better your chances of landing a great job.

For many people, the network of family, friends, and acquaintances can make the difference in landing the perfect job. Many people do not realize that some jobs never make it to the formal competition process. Job seekers who rely only on public postings of job openings never even know of the jobs that got away.

The size of the so-called hidden job market is significant, and it exists in parallel with the one that most job seekers know about. Many jobs are filled without ever being posted in newspapers, on internet sites, or on company websites.

ISSUES

in Communication
Drugs and the Workplace

The idea of random drug testing in the workplace is controversial. Some critics see this method of identifying potentially problematic behaviour as an invasion of privacy and believe it should not be allowed under any circumstance. Furthermore, they

note, little evidence suggests that workplace drug tests are an effective way to deter "counterproductive behaviours on the job."[1]

Another claim is that the mere presence of an illegal or controlled substance on a test does not necessarily mean the person took the drug willingly (think second-hand smoke) or for its intoxicating properties (some over-the-counter cough medicines contain narcotics). Others claim that testing only verifies the existence of a particular substance and not the person's level of intoxication.

Supporters of the idea of workplace drug testing claim that public safety is more important than personal freedom and that drug testing is essential to make sure that the workplace is safe. They say that some jobs—on a police force, for example—require an even higher standard.

Advocates of random testing point to the New York Police Department, which has a random testing program for all officers, coupled with a zero tolerance policy. Any officer who tests positive for any

Olympic champion swimmer Michael Phelps has learned "A good reputation takes a lifetime to build, and a few minutes to lose."

type of banned substance is fired automatically.

Police departments in Canada have resisted following the example of New York, with the head of the Toronto Police Department's union describing mandatory drug testing as a "non-starter."[2]

In spite of mixed public reaction, recent court appeals in the United States have supported employers who want to drug test employees who have safety-related jobs. Four in ten American employers use regular drug testing, the highest rate of any country.[3] Data collected in the United States during random workplace drug testing shows fewer positive results in today's workers (where positive means there is evidence of drugs): The rate of drug detection in workplace samples has dropped by 66 percent since 1988.[4]

The decline in positive drug-related results is occurring in spite of more employers using drug testing in the workplace and even in pre-employment interviews. Statistics vary widely between the United States and Canada, with approximately 80 percent of U.S. employers testing job applicants and current employees, compared with 15 percent of Canadian companies.[5]

DISCUSSION

1. Do you agree with mandatory drug testing for all potential new hires as part of a screening process? Do you think that permanent employees should also be required to submit to periodic random tests? Why or why not?

2. How do you explain the falling number of positive workplace drug-test results if there is still a need for the current war on drugs?

3. Consider the two examples of police department attitudes toward drug testing. List three arguments for mandatory testing of police officers. List some arguments against mandatory testing. Assuming that mandatory testing of police is acceptable, what other types of jobs should have mandatory drug testing?

4. Suppose that you were asked to provide saliva, hair, or urine samples as a part of a selection interview process. What would you do? If the results came back positive and you believed it was because you were standing near some drug smokers at a local nightclub, how would you react?

Taking Action

The dedicated job hunter will use every avenue to achieve success. The following steps (which we will return to soon) can be particularly helpful:

- *Think about everyone you know:* That may be hundreds of names.
- *Build an online network:* You can tap into an online network of people with similar business interests so that you can help one another.

Good networks take time and attention to create, but the rewards can be life changing or, at the very least, career changing. Consider that once a job opening goes public via the internet, a newspaper, or another medium, the number of applicants for the position will increase drastically. This translates to more people chasing fewer jobs, equalling stiffer competition.

Building a Career Network

The first step in building a career network is to list all the people who could help you get your next job. This is like brainstorming, and so it is better to include too many names than to mistakenly eliminate someone too early in the process. Remember, none of these people may be your future boss, but one may hear of an opening that you are qualified for and recommend you.

Think in terms of circles of acquaintances. For example, do you have any family friends who might have contacts in the field or industry in which you want to work? If you do, then write their names down.

Once you have the list of family friends finished, continue the process with ever-larger circles of acquaintances:

- What teachers or school administrators have you met who likely have contacts in the areas in which you want to work? Jot their names down.
- What community contacts do you have? Do you volunteer, play sports, or go to church, shrine, synagogue, or mosque? Write down people's names.
- Do your friends have family members who could help? Jot them all down.

Your list likely now includes hundreds of names. Because this is a brainstorming exercise, it is more important to be thorough than to be accurate. You can reduce the list later as you refine your network. See **Figure 16-1** for ideas about who to include in your network list.

Your Field   It is always a good idea to include people who work in, or know about, the field that you want to work in:

- Start with a former instructor. If you wanted to be an accountant but did not know any accountants personally, you might contact your accounting instructor and ask for names of industry people to contact.
- Next, use your research techniques to explore companies in your industry of interest. Start with the ones that have the most to offer you: Do you want to travel or pursue advancements and promotions? If so, medium to larger companies that have offices in many regions may be of interest to you. It is easier to transfer within an organization and see different parts of the country or take advantage of openings than it is to quit your job and start again with a new company in a new region. Typically, rewards, such as pay raises and holiday allotments, increase as you gain experience with a particular company. If you quit to start with a new one, you may lose some or all of these rewards. Conversely, if you would like to stay where you are, geographically speaking, and get involved with a more diversified array of responsibilities, a smaller local company may be the route for you.
- Check out related professional sites on the internet. Also look at the websites of professional associations and Chambers of Commerce. Each of these is a direct link to people who are already working in your area of interest and may be of help in the future.

Start Expanding   The list of network contacts you have now is not the list you have forever. Even if you are still months or a year or more away from starting your career, start to expand and enrich your networks now.

FIGURE 16–1   **How to Build a Personal Contacts List**

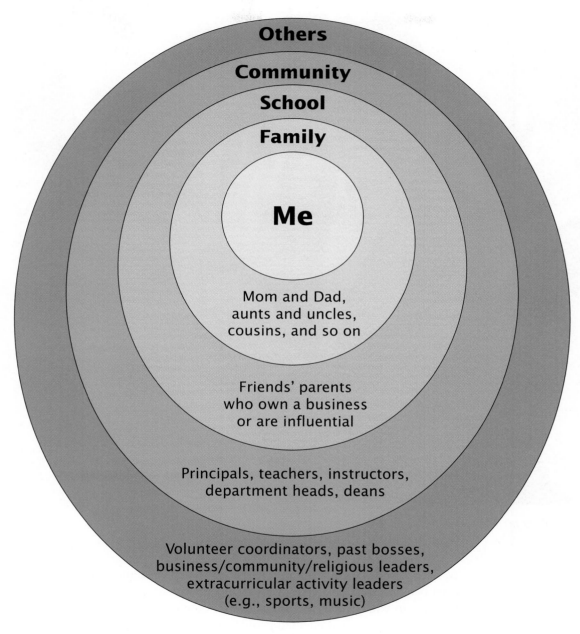

It can take many months, even years, to build a strong career network. In fact, it is never truly done because you will constantly be dropping people as they retire and adding new people you meet. Once you have your network complete, the work of contacting them for help finding a job begins.

It Works Both Ways   Having a network is not about taking advantage of someone to further your own career. In fact, it is just the opposite. Quite often you will be of some use to your contacts as well. Your career network

Always be on the lookout for network contacts.

contacts could even develop into personal friends or mentors, and one might even become your boss. The relationship should always be win-win. As you advance in your career and begin to hire employees yourself, you will find yourself taking note of talented people you want to join your team. Networks work for everyone.

Developing and maintaining a good network is perhaps the most important task that you can do to ensure a long-term, successful career. Although the old saying "It's not what you know; it's who you know" is not entirely true, it does have a logical base. Your network can open the door for you, but it is up to you to do a great job and make the most of the opportunities you have. A more appropriate saying in today's work world might be "Who you know can help you make the most of what you know."

Always leave a job on the best possible terms.

Timing The best time to look for a better job through your network is when you are already working. The fact is that most people will change jobs, even entire careers, many times within their working life. It is not because workers today are not dedicated to their jobs or their employers but because the nature of the workplace itself is changing rapidly. By focusing on your career path, you gain the advantage of time. This time can help you to find the great jobs that otherwise go by if you are not paying attention.

Planning Ahead If you find a great employer that you'd like to work for, consider calling the human resources department and setting up a meeting to get more information about the company and possible openings.

Great business contacts are everywhere, if you only look for them. Keep in mind that you should choose your next job—it should not choose you. If you don't plan ahead and establish your network, you may have to take the first job that comes along if the situation suddenly goes wrong. Perhaps the most devastating news you can get as an employee is that your company is closing and your job is finished. You could be the best employee at the organization, but if the company goes bankrupt or is taken over by another company your pink slip is the same colour as everyone else's. As they say: Take the time to dig your well before you are thirsty.

INTERVIEWS: WHAT TO PREPARE FOR

After your network list helps you find a job opening, you will need to focus on doing well at the interview. Before we can discuss how to prepare for an interview, it will be helpful for you to understand what you are preparing for. Interviews take many different forms, and each strives to fulfill a specific purpose for the potential employer. After discussing formal and informal interviews and interviews at the preliminary, final, and follow-up stages, we look at these specialized interviews: (1) stress, (2) behavioural, (3) group, and (4) new wave.

First, though, we start with a look at the general processes involved and the role you are expected to play as an interviewee.

Understanding the Process

When preparing for an interview, it is worthwhile to consider its purpose from the employer's point of view. You want the job and that is why you applied for it in the first place—that point instructs much of what you do, how you prepare, how you conduct yourself in the interview itself, and what you do afterward. Unfortunately, the employer's motive is not always as straightforward. Consider, for a moment, what the interview means for the employer.

The interview is an opportunity for employers to meet many candidates to see if any are qualified for the posted position. It is a competition, although it is quite possible that no one will win—the employer may not find anyone suitable among the available candidates. This brings up an important point: Candidates for a vacancy are not competing against each other as much as they are competing against an imaginary ideal candidate who has all the qualities and experience as defined by the employer. If you competed only against other candidates, someone would always be best and there would always be a winner. In reality, a number of competitions end without any job offers because the employer did not find the right person with the right combination of skills, experiences, and attributes. That search continues at a later date, perhaps with different search criteria.

If the position has an incumbent, that is, someone who already holds the job, it is difficult to know whether the competition is real. Perhaps the employer is perfectly happy with the performance of the person who has the job now and the competition is being held for some other reason, such as to fulfill a requirement of the collective agreement if the workplace is unionized. Alternatively, perhaps a former employee left suddenly and the current employee is an internal candidate who was asked to fill in temporarily until the competition could be organized. In this case, the incumbent may not be the preferred candidate and the competition is real.

The point to keep in mind is that the employers will be looking at several well-qualified candidates, any of whom could likely do the job. Just because you were invited to an interview does not mean the job is yours. Rather, with an interview pool of five or six other candidates, the job could be yours to lose. The pre-screening eliminated the most unlikely of candidates, and the people left are the best of the bunch. All candidates will likely have the minimum set of skills, experiences, and academic training as specified in the job posting. The difference between a successful candidate and the first runner-up can come down to the answer to a single question or, worse yet, something as seemingly trivial as showing up late, being flustered, or being dressed inappropriately. At this point in the process, everything matters.

Types of Interviews   The interview itself will often be as unique as the organization that is doing the interviewing. It could be done by someone acting alone: the boss, the supervisor, or someone from the human resources department. It could also be a panel of two, three, or even more people.

Formal interviews   Typically, formal interviews have a structure and a more rigid process. A list of questions is usually prepared in advance. The same questions are asked by the same people in the same order for all candidates. Usually, in panel settings, the person asking the questions engages the interviewee while the others write down the important points of the answer provided by the candidate. These notes are then used after the interview to grade the candidate against the ideal answer.

Here's a helpful tip for formal interviews: If you are talking and no one is writing down the information, chances are you are off track. Take a moment, ask clarifying questions to make sure you understand what they want, and restart your answer. It's better to lose a little time to get back on track than to miss an entire question.

Less formal interviews   Typically, less formal interviews are for less-senior-level positions and can be done by a single person without the benefit of a predetermined set of questions or much in the way of structure. These types of interviews can often appear disorganized and be unsettling for candidates. After all, you have likely spent hours, if not days, preparing and the interview can be over in minutes. It is up to the candidate to adjust and appear confident and calm in any type of setting.

We will now look at specific stages at which interviews are held.

Preliminary Stage   Some organizations use these types of interviews when they have an unusually large number of well-qualified candidates or when someone high up in the organizational hierarchy conducts the final interviews.

The interviews are preliminary in the sense that no one will be offered a job right away. Rather, it is a time for a sneak peek at many candidates so that—to borrow a phrase from a popular television program—they can "vote some people off the island" and reduce the workload of the more detailed interviews to follow.

For example, suppose that 300 people applied for an assistant manager position at a local office of a national finance company. No employer can interview all 300 applicants because the costs would easily exceed the benefits of closely looking at every possible candidate. The pre-screening of work experience, academic background, and transferable skills will substantially

"ANY OTHER REFERENCES BESIDES ME?"

Don't be voted off the interview island.

reduce the number of qualified candidates, say, to 50. This is still far too many to interview, and so the human resources department may hold a preliminary interview.

Typically, this involves bringing groups of people into the office for the following:

- a short presentation about the company
- a discussion of the process

■ perhaps a skills test, such as a timed writing assignment, a problem-solving exercise, or a technical test to make sure you have the needed skills for the position

The preliminary interview could also be a more typical format, with the candidates being asked a set of predefined questions. The preliminary review panel would then decide who goes on and who is dropped from the process.

The results of the preliminary interview will be graded and the top candidates invited to the next level of the competition. From the 50 candidates in our example, the company may choose 5, 8, 10, or perhaps more. The final number of interviewees is dependent on the time and availability of the interviewers, as well as the need for an immediate replacement.

Final Stage   The top candidates from the preliminary interview are then selected for the final interview, which could be in one of two main formats:

1. If the preliminary interview was skills based, meaning some type of assignment was completed, then the final interview will not likely include the same type of requirement. Instead, a panel with structured questions can be expected. The results of the preliminary interview may be considered but, chances are, the final candidates will be equal in skills.

2. If the preliminary interview was itself made up of questions and answers, the very same questions may be used in the final interview. This can be confusing to some candidates who are expecting something different. It is important in these circumstances to answer as completely as possible. Do not assume that your answers from the preliminary interview are used to judge the final interview. It is likely that the panel has different members, and the new members, maybe your prospective boss, were not there for the preliminary interview. Never assume that people know, or will remember, your strengths.

Follow-Up Stage   On rare occasions, such as when the top two candidates are extremely close in skills, experiences, and qualifications, a follow-up interview may be required. At this point, the interviewers can further explore certain areas of your background or experience or perhaps explore aspects of your personality to see if you will fit in with the existing team. In today's workplace, with its increased emphasis on teamwork and collective workloads, interpersonal skills and communication skills are highly desired. No employee works in a vacuum, and so it is important for supervisors, managers, and business owners to make sure that the new person will not disrupt the established work environment.

Tip   Remember that as a candidate for a position, it is your right to ask about the various stages of the interviewing process and what you can expect. This will help you to prepare yourself for the challenges ahead and give you the best chance to succeed. As we have said, it is not just about beating the other candidates—it is about beating the ideal candidate who exists in the minds of the interviewers.

Interview Formats

The interview technique an organization chooses can vary as much as the organization itself. Do not hesitate to ask for details about what type of interview technique will be used. The following are specialized interview formats.

1. Stress Interviews   Not as frequently used as they once were, these interviews were specifically designed to try to unsettle the candidates. The theory is that by subjecting a candidate to stress during the interview, the employer will gain insight into how that person might react under stress within the workplace. Examples of stress interviews include, but are not limited to

- asking probing questions
- subjecting candidates to criticism or even hostility
- using rapid-fire questioning
- interrupting answers midsentence with another question
- exposing candidates to prolonged periods of silence

The purpose of these types of interviews is to try to unnerve you, and so the longer you can keep your cool, the better your chances of success are.

2. Behavioural Interviews   Most employers have had the experience of hiring someone who answered questions well during the interview only to find out a few months later that the person was not well suited for the position. Interviews are, of course, an imperfect process—no one will ever be able to determine with total accuracy whether a candidate is right for the job based simply on a resumé, a reference check, and an hour-long interview. Hiring people is an expensive process, and so employers are always looking for ways to make the process work better.

One technique that is being used by more and more employers is asking people to describe their past actions rather than to answer hypothetical questions. The problem with hypothetical questions is that applicants may know what they are supposed to say, but they may not act that way once they are on the job.

Consider, for example, an employer with a retail business who wants to be sure that the people she hires will remain polite even when dealing with overbearing customers. A hypothetical question for such a situation might be "What would you do if a customer is rude with you when you make a mistake?" The problem with such a question is that even the most quick-tempered person would probably know enough not to admit it and to instead provide a more suitable answer.

A behavioural question, however, would call for the applicant to describe a real-life incident: "Tell me about the last time that you had to deal with a rude person. What made the person angry and how did you deal with the situation?" Although it is possible for someone to make up a totally fictitious answer to such a question, most people are not very good at lying, and the employer would probably quickly notice their attempts at deception.

Some applicants will at first try to answer behavioural questions with a hypothetical answer: "If a customer was rude to me, I would never...." At that point, a skilled interviewer will politely interrupt and ask for a specific example of an actual experience.

Answering behaviour-based questions   Behavioural questions require you to tell stories about yourself that illustrate your strengths. As with most stories they require a beginning, a middle, and an end. The formula in **Table 16-1** may help you organize your ideas.

It will not always be possible for you to instantly come up with stories to illustrate your talents. A good behavioural interviewer will realize this and encourage you to take your time coming up with an example.[9]

You can, however, prepare a collection of stories in advance to illustrate your best characteristics. Doing so will require you to think about your positive characteristics in advance. Such preparation will be useful to you whether or not you are asked behavioural questions.

Even if you are not asked these types of questions during an interview, these stories can be useful. Giving a detailed personal response to an interviewer's

TABLE 16-1   **A Formula for Answering Behaviour-Based Questions**

Stage of Your Answer	What to Say	Example
1. Start = Background	Begin by describing the circumstances surrounding the situation that you are trying to relate.	"A customer once got mad at me when I told her that the two-for-one special she wanted was available only on Mondays. I explained the situation to her, showed her where it said that on the coupon, and told her that she would have to pay full price. The customer yelled at me, called me stupid, and demanded to see my manager."
2. Middle = Action	The middle of your story should describe how you dealt with the problem.	"I did as the customer demanded. I called my manager over, explained the situation, and let her deal with the customer. Even though I was annoyed, I kept my temper and didn't let the customer see that I was angry."
3. End = Result	End your story by letting the interviewer know the outcome of the situation.	"Later, after the customer had left, my manager told me that I had done everything correctly. She said the same customer had caused trouble before and other people who had dealt with her had not always handled things as well."

Sincere impressions are lasting impressions.

hypothetical question can be an impressive tactic. Suppose, for example, that the interviewer asks applicants what they will do to ensure that they meet deadlines. One applicant might give a response saying that he has no trouble meeting deadlines and that he will work hard and stay organized. If you are able to respond to that question with an example that describes a situation in which you were able to cope with a tight deadline, most employers will be more impressed by your concrete example than by the general statement.

TAKE IT FURTHER

Number One Interview Question

One of the more common questions that interviewers ask is "What is your greatest achievement to date, and why?"[10]

Do you think interviewers are more interested in personal or professional accomplishments?

3. Group Interviews   Interviewers sometimes use group interviews to observe candidates within group settings, to see how they act and react in larger numbers. This can be helpful in organizations that want staff to work together as a supportive team. Candidates may be graded on how outgoing they are or how withdrawn. They may be judged on how open or welcoming they are to other candidates or how secretive or conspiratorial. How often does a candidate smile or take an interest in what another is saying? How often does a candidate truly listen to others? Does a candidate try to best another's experience with a story of his or her own?

4. New Wave Interviews   With the arrival of technology, such as the telephone, videoconferencing, and the internet, the old limitations of the interview

The virtual interview is everywhere at once.

process have changed. In the past, employers were often limited to interviewing candidates in the local region of the job opportunity. Promising candidates could be brought in to the final stages of the interview process but only at significant cost.

In today's work world, where technology is forever pushing the boundaries of the possible, virtual interviews are much more commonplace. Candidates from around the world may participate in preliminary interviews by submitting their answers by email or by completing a timed quiz online. From different time zones, countries, continents, or cultures, the reach of the interview process is limited only by the will of those organizing the process.

Successful candidates from these virtual interview processes typically are asked to visit in person for a final meeting before an offer is made.

Preparing for an Interview

Now that you know the kinds of interviews you might face, you are in a better position to start getting ready for the real thing.

Understanding What Employers Want   Before an interview, it is a good idea to review the results of the Conference Board of Canada survey on the major skills that employers look for in new applicants. (See Chapters 1 and 15.) The review will help you think about how to describe your skills and experience in the best way. You may think you know yourself well, but have you tried to describe yourself to a stranger in 30 seconds? What makes you special enough for the employer to forget the other applicants and hire you?

Think about the following:

- It is never enough to rely on the facts in your resumé. You should come to the interview prepared to prove how you developed the skills that you claim to have.
- Practical examples of past work are an excellent source of information.
- If you do not have specific experience from the work world, draw on experiences that you gained in school, as a part of your volunteer background, or from other projects that you have done.
- Once you have prepared the answers to the common interview questions, try practising these answers in front of a mirror or, better yet, in front of a friend or family member. Be sure to make good eye contact and don't stumble through your answer saying *umm* and *like.*

Research the Company, the Position, and the Industry Today's applicants have a wealth of information available through the internet. Most employers have some type of website that provides background information, company history, leading strengths, and sometimes even financial data. Taken together, these data provide applicants with valuable information on the company and department. Pretend you are a reporter doing a story on the organization and answer the basic questions:

Who?	Where?	Why?
What?	When?	How?

You should be able to describe the employer and the department in detail. Exploring outside the company is also a good idea. For example, you could find out the following:

- Who are the employer's major competitors and what is the employer's competitive advantage?
- How can the employer survive in an increasingly competitive world?
- What are the major challenges facing similar organizations?

Once again, think about how the organization you want to join is positioned to change with changing market conditions.

Looking Good

It takes just a second to form a positive first impression and forever to recover from a bad one. What you decide to wear to an interview can work for or against you. Decide what the typical work wear is in an office and then bump it up one notch for your interview. For example, if business casual is the dress code in the company, then consider wearing a business suit. If jeans and a

T-shirt are typical, then consider pressed pants and a well-ironed shirt or blouse.

Wear minimal jewellery, makeup, and scents. Style your hair in a professional, appropriate, and slightly conservative way. This is not the time to scream your individuality with piercings, tattoos, and unnatural hair colours. Remember, you are asking to join an established team, and it is up to you to show that you can fit in with the existing network.

Get the Paperwork in Order   It is always a good idea to bring a copy of your references along to the interview. Many employers use references to investigate the details of what you have told them in the interview, your resumé, and your covering letter. They also use references to ask additional questions about your skills in certain areas—teamwork, for example. We'll discuss references in the next section.

It is also a good idea to bring a few copies of your resumé and some blank paper or a notebook. The resumés can be distributed if, for example, this is a panel interview and the panel did not bring enough copies. Use the blank paper to write down the main points of the questions so that you can give more complete answers. In a highly competitive contest, the decision of whom to hire can sometimes be made based on the answer to a single question. Taking notes, asking the interviewer to repeat especially complicated questions, and jotting down key aspects of your answer before you begin your response can make all the difference. It also shows that you are organized, well prepared, and thorough.

REFERENCES

Before making a job offer, many companies will want to talk to your references: people who can speak about your past. They will check basic facts of employment, such as start and stop dates, job titles, and, perhaps, related duties. The purpose of the reference check is to get objective and impartial information about your skills and abilities and added insight into how you might succeed in the position if they hire you.[12]

Because potential employers are looking for objective assessments of your skills and abilities, friends and family do not make good references. A better solution is to include as references people who have different perspectives. For example, you would not want to include three school instructors as references, because chances are that they will all say similar things about you.

Choosing Good References

The most sought-after reference will be your current (or past) supervisor. Before you use a person's name as a reference, you should ask for his or her permission. If you do not want your current boss to know you are looking for a new job, then potential employers will understand if you choose a previous boss as a reference instead. At the interview, if they ask about references, be sure to let them know why you are not using your current boss. What if your

TAKE IT FURTHER

References Checks

According to the Society for Human Resource Management, nine out of ten employers check references.[13]

What can applicants do to ensure that the people that they use for references supply positive information about them to employers?

Know what your references are likely to say.

current boss doesn't like the work you do? You can use this same tactic and supply a reference from earlier in your career.

Other good references are people who work with you at the same level and have some experience seeing you in action. If your old position included supervisory responsibilities, you could include someone who worked for you.

Finally, a well-respected member of your community can be a great source of unbiased information. You may have met this person through volunteering or other related community work.

Be careful about whom you choose for your references. A negative, or even neutral, report from a reference could cost you the job. If you are not sure that a person will be positive, do not include him or her.

Tips   Do *not* include references directly in your resumé or initial application package unless asked. The reasoning is simple: Most employers check references but only for the candidates who succeeded in the formal interview process. It is a final check on your background, before a job is offered, just to make sure that the facts that you supplied are accurate.

If you are interviewed and asked for references, this means that you are in the running for the final offer. It is always a good idea to contact your references before the potential employer calls them. Consider sending them a copy of your current resumé so that they can see what you have been doing and maybe learn even more about your skills and strengths. By contacting your references directly, you can remind them that they may be called and provide additional information, like the job description, so they know what attributes to speak about on your behalf. If you supply your references in your resumé, the potential employer can call without your knowing it and possibly catch your reference unprepared. If the reference doesn't respond favourably, this could hurt your job search.

Concerns   The usefulness of reference checks can be reasonably questioned. Because of fears of possible financial liability, many companies have strict reference check rules that limit what their employees can say about past employees. For example, supervisors and managers can confirm that a person was an employee and the dates of employment, but that is all. These details provide little value added to interviewers' existing knowledge.

A more fundamental flaw warrants discussion. A bad reference can tarnish the applicant in the eyes of the interviewer, even eliminating the applicant from the competition. Because of this, applicants are more likely to include references who will speak highly of them than someone who is indifferent or, worse, negative. References almost always speak highly of those that they have agreed to speak for. In spite of these drawbacks, reference checks remain a part of the candidate search process.

THE DAY OF THE INTERVIEW

On the day of the interview, the best way to stay focused is to follow your usual routine. In addition, some practical recommendations can help:

- The day before the interview, travel to the location of the interview, if you can. Learn the route and find parking or the nearest bus routes.
- Make sure you are well prepared. This will help lessen the tensions and anxiety of the interview day.
- The night before, lay out the clothes that you plan to wear. Trying to find the perfect pair of pants or ironing your shirt the morning of the interview adds needless stress.
- The night before, try to relax before going to bed. Go to bed at your usual time.
- Get a good night's sleep. Do not stay up late cramming for your interview. It doesn't work well for school, and it won't work for an interview either.
- Get up a little earlier than usual the day of your interview. Think about setting a backup alarm in case there is a problem with the first.
- Have your usual breakfast, and take a piece of fruit or some juice to have just before the interview. Don't arrive over-caffeinated and jittery. The fruit has a natural sugar, which can give you an energy bump for the interview.

- Do as many of your normal tasks in your day as possible. People are creatures of habit so don't add to the tension by introducing new elements to your day.

Arriving for the Interview

Plan to arrive 15 to 20 minutes before you are scheduled to be interviewed. Not having to worry about being on time will help you to relax. Sometimes buses are late, or traffic is heavier than expected—the extra time ensures that you arrive on schedule and focused.

Most companies will have a waiting area for you to use. You may even see the candidate who was interviewed just before you. Don't let that psych you out. At this point in the process, everyone has an equal chance at success, and all you can do is your very best. The interview may start on time, but the process often falls behind schedule. Again, do not panic if no one is there to usher you in to the interview at exactly the right time. Use the time to relax.

Performing Well in the Interview

If you are invited for an interview, you likely have at least the minimum levels of skills and experience. The interview is your chance to enrich the details provided in your resumé and application letter. A successful interview can lead to a job offer, perhaps more than at any other stage in the search process.

Give enough information in the interview to show that you are the best candidate but no information that can be used against you in the evaluation process. For example, "Why are you leaving your current job?" is a typical interview question. The applicant who replies with an answer like "I am looking to further develop my skills and take my career to the next level" and ends the answer there will likely be more successful than the candidate who says this and continues by telling all the things that are wrong with his or her current boss. The added detail can reveal an overly critical person who cannot be relied on for loyalty or holding confidences.

Starting the Interview

Quite often, the interview will begin with introductions of the people on the panel and their respective roles. Be sure to write down the names of the interviewers and note who is sitting where. Later, you will want to address each by name. Your research should already have told you the name of the direct supervisor of the position you are applying for. Although it would be rude to direct all your answers to this person, it is still a good idea to pay attention to his or her body language and gauge your answers accordingly. Additionally, ask yourself such questions as these:

- Are the panel members listening intently?
- Are they writing down your answers as you speak?
- Do they seem distracted, preoccupied, or confused?
- Are they fidgeting?
- Do they seem bored?

Watch for all the verbal and non-verbal signs that you have learned as an effective communicator. This applies to all panel members but especially to those whose opinions likely matter most: your future boss and the person representing the human resources department.

The first question is often referred to as an "icebreaker" and it gives you the chance to settle in and get comfortable with the process. Be sure to answer succinctly and not to overdo it. You will be asked many questions that will allow you to clearly explain why you are the best candidate for the job.

Keep track of the questions and your answers. Most interviewers will allow you to return to a previous question if you want to add or even change your answer. The blank paper or notebook we mentioned earlier is useful here to help keep you organized. This is especially true for complicated and multi-part questions. Clarity, consistency, and comprehensiveness will make a positive difference in your answers.

Answering Common Interview Questions

It is surprising how small the total pool of interview questions is. Of course, every interview will be unique, and the questions asked should relate to the specific job being filled, but you can prepare in advance for many general questions.

The job description is the best source for figuring out what will be asked in the interview. In addition, look over **Table 16-2**, which shows 25 common job interview questions:

You can never be sure exactly what will be asked, but it is helpful to have prepared answers for as many questions as possible going into the interview. Very often, you will be asked to describe how your past experience relates to skills that the company is looking for. You can do this effectively by relaying a real experience and how you reacted.

Trying to think of related anecdotes from your past work can be tricky, especially in a stressful interview situation with a panel of strangers staring at you. The simple solution is to be prepared.

You can prepare answers to common questions well in advance of the interview. Take the time to practise your responses. A well-polished answer in the interview will give the impression that you are a quick thinker and well spoken. No one needs to know that you practised in front of the mirror for hours.

Staying on Track

Nervousness can ruin an otherwise positive interview. One natural reaction to being nervous is to rush ahead to answer the question as quickly as possible. The interview panel has probably been through this process many times, and they have allocated sufficient time for you to answer.

Rushing ahead to answer what you perceive to be the question may take you further from success, especially if you do not clearly understand what is being asked. Remember, if the panel isn't writing down your answers, or they look confused or are in obvious disagreement, you may be on the wrong track with your answer.

TABLE 16-2	Common Interview Questions

1a. Tell us a little about you.

1b. What did you do to prepare for this interview?

These are common icebreakers. The intention here isn't to collect information as much as to get you comfortable talking about yourself. Be sure to hit the high points only as there will be plenty of specific questions to come.

2a. What two or three words would your current boss use to describe you?

2b. How would your friends describe you as a person?

3. What is your definition of success?

4. Where do you see yourself five years from now?

5. Tell about a time when you suggested a change in your workplace. What was the outcome?

6. What do you like (or dislike) most about your current job?

7. Describe an ethical dilemma you faced at work. What did you do and what was the outcome?

8. Tell us about when you had a serious problem with your supervisor and what you did.

9. How do you feel about professional development, and what do you expect from us?

10. Why are you the best person for this position?

11. Do you work better alone or as part of a larger team?

12. Did you participate in any volunteer activities over the past year? What did you learn from this experience?

13. How do you manage your time at work?

14. What are your main strengths? What are your major weaknesses?

15. Think of the last time you had many tasks to do and not enough time to complete them all. How did you manage to cope with the situation?

16. What kind of client irritates you the most? What kind of colleagues bother you?

17. Tell us about your greatest success (or failure). What did you learn from the experience?

18. What do you know about this position and our company?

19. Why did you leave your last job?

20. How do you balance your work and family commitments?

21. What do you see as the greatest challenge of this position, and what would you do about it?

22. Apart from your experience, tell me why I should hire you for this position.

23. What are your starting salary expectations? When can you start?

24. What kind of a manager (supervisor, salesperson, . . .) are you?

25. Are there any questions you would like to ask us?

Source: Adapted from "Do You Know How to Respond to These Common Interview Questions?" Interview-Tips-and-Tricks.com. 2009. Web. 23 Oct. 2009.

Many questions are obvious and need little or no clarification, but if a question is unclear, stop and ask for an explanation. Try repeating the question or rephrasing it to make it clearer to you. Once you and the interviewer agree on what is being asked, write it down, jot down your answer, and respond. You won't be able to do this with every question, as the process takes too long, and asking for clarification every time would soon become tiresome to the interviewers.

Remember that multi-part questions require multi-part answers. Although it might be clearer to separate these complicated questions into separate queries, each with a single focus, the point may be to add additional stress and see how you do in organizing more complicated thought processes.

Be sure you answer only the question that was asked. Once again, nervousness, or even overconfidence, can be an interviewee's downfall. Because silence is awkward, people tend to want to fill the void. If you feel you have answered the question, stop and wait. Don't blather on just to hear someone talk. Sometimes, it is in these unrehearsed parts of the answer that something potentially damaging to your interview can leak out by accident. An example might be mentioning in passing that you are a perfectionist. Some people may think this is a positive trait but it can also be very stressful and difficult for co-workers, who may be made to feel inadequate.

Asking Questions during the Interview

Most interviewers will leave some time at the end of the interview for you to ask questions. Be sure to take advantage of this opportunity. Try to ask relevant questions:

- When does the panel hope to fill the position?
- Does the person in the position act independently or as a part of a team?

If you have a particular skill that did not come up in the interview, ask a related question and then provide the panel with the added detail.

Asking about the company, the department, or even the industry itself is a great way to show that you have spent time researching the job. Interviewers will not likely want to get into a discussion about the trials of the industry or the competition that is squeezing out the last of the company's profit, but they may want to know that you are aware of the challenges facing all businesses. Again, this is especially true if you can relate your past experiences in successfully dealing with similar circumstances.

Discussing Paycheques

Inevitably in your career, you will be asked how much money you are worth, and you will need to provide a reasonable answer. No company can afford to pay a person more than the value that he or she brings to the company. For some positions this value is easier to measure than for others. A salesperson can be judged by the number or profitability of sales made. Better salespeople can expect to make more money than less productive colleagues. But what about a clerical position, a supervisor, or a manager? How do you measure the output of management? Once again, your pre-interview research can help.

Many companies will post the range of salaries that apply to a particular job at the time of posting. This helps separate applicants who might apply, be chosen, and then refuse the offer because of insufficient pay. When no details are provided, information about pay scales of similar positions with other employers can be helpful.

Even with positions for which the pay scale is made public, where exactly you end up is often a matter of negotiation.

- Some employers start all new hires at the bottom of the pay scale that is associated with the job being filled.
- Employers may give credit for experience in a similar job with another company and start the new hire at a level that is more commensurate with experience.
- Other employers give credit for additional academic achievements beyond the minimum necessary for the position.
- Employers often use the tiers within a pay scale as a means of attracting good candidates.

The way pay is determined is impossible to know in advance, and so you need to be flexible.

The question of what you are worth is perhaps better put as what are you willing to accept to go to work for the company.

Closing Strongly

By the time the interview ends, you should have fulfilled your purpose of showing why you are the most qualified candidate and would be a positive addition to the team. Your answers should have provided all the necessary support to your resumé and covering letter. You can take the time for a short recap of why you are interested in the position, how it fits into your longer-term career goals, and what positive energy you could bring to the workplace. Don't repeat the details—just hit the high points.

You have now made the best impression possible. All that is left is to thank the interviewers for their time and consideration. Good eye contact, a firm handshake, and a warm smile are all positive ways to end the interview.

Following Up

The interview is over, and it went as well as you had expected. But you are not quite finished making a good impression.

Thank-You Letter   Immediately after the interview, prepare a formal thank-you letter for the interview panel. The purpose is to show your gratitude and highlight one last way that you are the best choice among the candidates. Be sure the wording is sincere and the names are all spelled correctly. If you are unsure of the spelling, call the public information line or the human resources department and ask for help.

Letter of Inquiry   If you have not heard the outcomes of the interview within two or three weeks, it is appropriate to write a letter of inquiry. The purpose of this letter is to investigate where the process is and when a decision will be made. Often, the reason for the delay is legitimate. At other times, because of budget cuts, for example, competitions are cancelled at the last minute, before any job offer is made. This is helpful information to know since it

---

TAKE IT FURTHER

Non-traditional Interview Questions

Microsoft has been credited with pioneering the use of brainteasers during interviews to test applicants' creativity and ability to think on their feet. Applicants have been asked to estimate how many golf balls could fit inside a school bus or to explain why manhole covers are round. Google sought out applicants by placing math problems on a billboard, with the correct answer leading to a website where they could submit resumés.[14]

How can applicants prepare for such questions?

means your job search must continue. An email can replace the formal letter of inquiry and may even speed the response.

Letter of Acceptance Probably the easiest letter you will ever have to write is the letter to accept a job. Often, you will simply be restating the important points and making a statement of your feelings about starting with the company. You will formally accept the terms and conditions of the job offer, including a specific start date, the location of work, the salary and position title, and any other details that are related in their offer of employment.

Letter of Refusal The second easiest letter to write is the letter of refusal. The purpose of this letter is again to thank the interviewers for their consideration and to formally refuse their offer of employment. You should not go into detail about why the offer is unacceptable, nor should you be anything other than grateful for the experience. You may find yourself in an interview for a different position before the same panel of the same employer in the future, and you don't want to ruin any opportunities.

Letter of Resignation Letters of resignation can be difficult to write, as are most bad news letters. The methods described in this text can help.

A good thank-you letter can keep future opportunities open.

As with letters of refusal, letters of resignation need to be done with tact and diplomacy. This is no time to tell your boss what you really think or criticize the company that has provided you with a paycheque. You never know what the future will hold, and you may be back working for the same company or even the same boss later. If you think the news will be taken badly, it is often best to use an indirect method of resignation. If the news is less of a surprise or will not be entirely unexpected, the direct method of writing is likely preferable.

Regardless of the approach, end on a positive note and thank the addressee for the experience. Remember, you learn life lessons from bad experiences as well as good. Dealing with adversity in the workplace is a necessary skill that you can benefit from.

Chapter Summary

Students who are about to graduate from university or college are often met with an entirely new challenge: getting started in their career of choice. While many have already gained valuable experience working part time or volunteering in the community, the types of positions that they will now be applying for are markedly different.

As you finish your formal academic training, a helpful first step is to develop a career network to help you with a successful job search. Your network of possible influencers is a constantly evolving list of people. Using your established list of personal and professional contacts will increase your chances of discovering that perfect job opportunity, maybe even one that is not public knowledge.

Once you have made the shortlist and been asked to come in for an interview, you can prepare to give the best possible impression by researching the job, the organization, and the industry. It is also possible to identify and prepare for common interview questions. Practising you answers ahead of time will make you appear more confident in the interview, which is often very important.

Many types of interviews are used in employee recruitment. It is helpful to understand the various types of interviews and how to prepare for them so that you can focus on getting the job. The last thing you want is to be flustered by the unexpected. Consider asking what type of interview will be used when you are called for the appointment.

Most businesses will check your references before offering you a job. Establish a list of effective references whom you can count on to speak positively about your qualities.

Successfully getting through the interview is not the end of your opportunity to make an impression. Properly follow up after an interview with a thank-you letter to the head of the interview panel or representative from the human resources department. After a few weeks, if you have not heard about the outcome, write a letter or an email requesting an update on the status of the competition. Although some businesses may be ready to hire a candidate on the spot, others may take weeks or even months to decide.

PEARSON
mycanadianbuscommlab™   Visit **www.mycanadianbuscommlab.ca** for everything you need to help you succeed in the job you've always wanted! Tools and resources include the following:

- Composing and The Writer's Toolkit
- Document Makeovers
- Video Case Studies
- Grammar exercises and much more!

Thinking and Writing Exercises

1. **Dealing with Interviews**

   a. An "elevator speech" is a 20- to 30-second speech that you use to introduce yourself at a business function. Write your elevator speech and practise it aloud. Be sure to include all the high points about what makes you someone to remember.

   b. It is important to engage the panel members of an interview. What tips could you use to show them that you are interested in what they have to say?

   c. It is important to know your competitive advantage, that special something that makes you different from other applicants. Knowing what specific skills in your background are of particular interest to interviewers can help you make a better impression. Name three sources of information that could help you decide what the interviewer really wants in a new employee.

   d. In the early stages of the application process, interviewers are trying to find ways to eliminate applicants. Why is this helpful when applying for a position?

   e. During the interview, an applicant will be asked many questions. Should the interviewee focus on one or two good work-related stories and keep coming back to these, or would it be better to think of a separate example for each major skill, such as team work, problem solving, communication, customer service, and so on. Why or why not?

   f. Suppose you are trying to change jobs because your current boss does not like you or the work you do. How would you explain this to a potential employer? How can you avoid using your current boss as a reference?

   g. Why do you suppose it is important to tell the truth in an interview? After all, isn't good marketing all about embellishing the truth?

   h. When a potential employer asks what your salary expectations are, what will you say? On what will you base your answer?

   i. Suppose that the interview process is running late, and, at the last minute, the panel rushes you into the interview room and tells you that your time has been cut in half. How should you respond?

   j. Suppose you are in an interview with two or more interviewees and you get the distinct impression that one of the members is hostile toward you. How will you respond?

2. **Behavioural Interview Questions**

   Prepare answers to the following questions with information from your personal experience.

   a. Describe a time when you had to convince someone to do something.

   b. Describe a time when you had to explain a difficult concept to someone who couldn't understand it.

   c. Tell me about a time when you had to deal with someone who didn't like you.

   d. Describe the most significant problem you faced in your last job or at school and explain how you solved it.

   e. Describe a dispute you had with a co-worker. What led up to it and how was it settled?

   f. Describe the last time you were asked to do more than your share of a task. What caused the situation and how did you deal with it?

   g. Describe a time when you had too many things to do within a limited time. How did you deal with the situation?

Writing Skills Checkup: Pronoun References

Pronouns are words that are used to replace a noun. They help you avoid repeating the same noun again and again. When the word that the pronoun replaces is plural, the pronoun also has to be plural. The following guidelines will help you to decide when to use pronouns in your writing.

a. A pronoun sometimes has multiple antecedents.

My previous bosses, Mike Chow and Nancy Andrews, went beyond *their* normal duties and wrote letters of commendation for me.

b. Unclear antecedents are a problem when choosing a pronoun. The best solution is to rewrite the sentence and repeat the nouns as necessary to improve clarity.

Mike Chow sent Brian Chalmers *his* thoughts on my work.

c. Gender-neutral pronouns are sometimes hard to use, but the pronouns *he* and *his* relate only to males and *she* and *her* relate only to females. Using the phrase *his or her* can be awkward, especially if it is repeated more than once in a document.

Each staff member had to make up *his* (not all are male) mind.

Each staff member had to make up *her* (not all are female) mind.

Each staff member had to make up *his or her* mind on what to include in *his or her* report that was due in *his or her* section of the final document. (awkward)

One solution is to rewrite the sentence to make the antecedents plural. For example:

All staff had to make up *their* minds on what to include in *their* reports that were due in *their* sections of the final report.

d. The case of a pronoun tells whether a pronoun is acted on or is acting. Consider the following example:

I sold more product than any other person at the store, and *I* got a promotion.

In this example, *I* did the selling (acting). Consider the change when the pronoun is acted on.

After *I* sold more product than any other person at the store, my boss gave *me* a promotion.

The appropriate pronoun becomes *me* rather than *I*.

e. Possessive pronouns show ownership or automatic association:

Her desk

His report

Their work

Its attributes (Note that the possessive form of *its* has no apostrophe.)

Choose the proper pronoun for the following sentences.

1. When I finished the petty cash audit I gave the results to (him, he). _____
2. When dealing with an angry customer, I try to calm (him, him or her, them) down first. _____
3. Our main competitor decided to change (their, its) strategy. _____
4. I advised my boss it was time to update (our, their) webpage. _____
5. To (whom, who) shall I address my thank-you letter? _____
6. As the party committee, Bruce and (I, me) are in charge of the staff luncheon. _____
7. The team members prepared guidelines for (its, their) clients. _____
8. Komar and Eileen have instructed (her, their) staff on the changes to the holiday schedule. _____
9. Few of the salespeople hand in (its, their) daily sales sheets on time. _____
10. It was either Sandra or Sharmila that left (her, their) goodbye note on my door. _____

Interpersonal Communication: Surviving Life on the Cube Farm

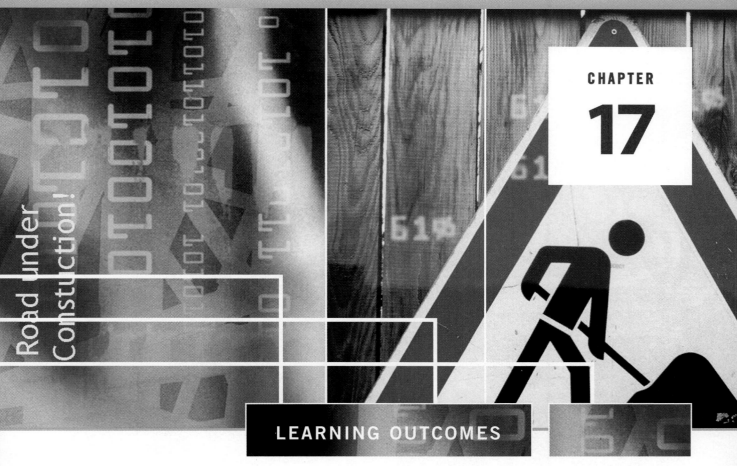

Road under Constuction!

LEARNING OUTCOMES

After completing this chapter, you should be able to do the following:

17.1 Choose from passive, aggressive, passive-aggressive, and assertive modes of communication when dealing with colleagues, clients, and supervisors

17.2 Identify the key qualities of emotional intelligence

17.3 Use appropriate interpersonal behaviour to promote a co-operative work environment

17.4 Make good career decisions when you move to a new office environment

THE OFFICE ENVIRONMENT

The term *cube farm* is said to have first appeared in print in 1997 as a slang term for office cubicles.[1] Other terms that are even less flattering have also been used to describe these fixtures of the modern office environment. Douglas Coupland, the Vancouver author who also popularized the term *Generation X*, referred to cubicles as *veal fattening pens* after the "pre-slaughter cubicles used by the cattle industry" and defined them as "small, cramped office workstations built of fabric-covered disassemblable wall partitions and inhabited by junior staff members."[2]

Office cubicles were introduced in 1968 as an improvement over the office environment that they replaced—open area offices with rows of desks that allowed even less privacy than the cubicles of today.[3] Although many Canadians may dream of occupying a private corner office on the penthouse floor, the reality for a large number will be to work out of a cubicle, the same type of environment as 70 percent of American office workers have.[4]

Working out of a cubicle measuring two by three metres does not have to be a dreaded fate. This chapter presents communication strategies for working effectively with others in this kind of environment. Topics include

Cubicles are now a common fixture in the office environment.

communicating assertively, using emotional intelligence, communicating effectively with your supervisor, communicating by telephone, and observing cubicle etiquette.

COMMUNICATING ASSERTIVELY

Conflict and competition are part of life. In business, as in all other fields, people have differences of opinions, and usually only one person comes out on top. The process of dealing with this conflict is important. Approaching it from the wrong perspective can lead to anger, resentment, hurt feelings—even sabotage.

Television stereotypes sometimes portray successful managers as despots who demean their employees with a constant barrage of swear words or keep them on their toes by shouting "You're fired!" when someone's performance is less than perfect. Such TV caricatures have no more connection to real life than talking tugboats or purple dinosaurs. Although some managers (and others) believe that shouting and screaming are the only ways to get people to pay attention, the vast majority of successful people have found that an assertive approach is far more effective.

ISSUES
in Communication
Workplace Bullying

In 2007, two Nova Scotia students distributed 50 pink shirts throughout their local high school to show support for a younger student who had been bullied for wearing a pink shirt to school. This began a "Sea of Pink Campaign" that spread across North America.[5] In Nova Scotia, the provincial government proclaimed the second Thursday in September to be "Stand Up against Bullying Day."[6] The movement grew the next year when provincial members of

the legislative assembly and union members in British Columbia joined, also wearing pink shirts to work to show their support.[7]

At one time people often dismissed bullying as something that occurred only on school grounds—something that people grew out of when they reached adulthood. Sadly, though, we now know that workplace bullying is more prevalent and more devastating to some than sexual harassment.[8]

Workplace bullying has been defined as any behaviour that intimidates, humiliates, or demeans a person. Such actions include physically aggressive behaviour, verbal abuse, persistent nitpicking, mali-

cious rumours, the undermining of or the taking of credit for the target's work, or unfair workloads.[9] Women make up 80 percent of the people who are bullied at work and 58 percent of the bullies. About 60 percent of the time, men bully men and women bully women.[10]

DEALING WITH WORKPLACE BULLIES

Workplace bullying can be stopped, but it requires effort and cooperation. Ignoring the problem simply allows it to continue. The obligation to prevent bullying also lies with employers. In 2006, a British Columbia police officer won a settlement of close to $1 million from the RCMP, after senior officers ignored her complaints about being harassed by her supervisor and other officers.[11]

Such legal actions are usually a last resort. You can try the following five communication strategies if you believe that you are the target of bullies.

1. *Document the abuse:* Keep a written record of bullying incidents. Record the date, time, and circumstances of the bullying behaviour, as well as the exact wording of any derogatory comments. If there are other witnesses, record their names as well. Bullies will find it harder to deny the abuse when presented with a detailed record. Documentation is even more effective when given to upper management along with published research that indicates the damage workplace bullying causes.[12]

2. *Approach the bully:* Raised in a locker-room atmosphere where shouting and swearing are the norm, some bullies may not even realize that they are doing anything wrong. Other bullies are cowards who will back down when confronted.

   Approach bullies in a non-confrontational way. Do not try to humiliate the abuser since most workplace bullies are managers who have the power to retaliate when they feel threatened. Do not seek revenge by adopting the same tactics as the bully or by reducing your level of output. The bully can end up using such actions against you.[13]

   Instead, describe the problem in an unemotional way and tell the bully what you would like changed. Be careful though. One expert cautions that in situations where organizations have left bullying unchecked, approaching the bully on an individual basis can make the situation worse.[14]

3. *Report the behaviour to people in authority:* Sometimes it is necessary to involve others in the dispute. The offender's supervisor can be made to intervene, and unions and employee support groups often provide representation. Use caution before reporting trivial problems to people in authority, however. A survey of nearly eight thousand American workers reported that in 62 percent of the cases where employers were made aware of bullying, they either did nothing or worsened the problem.[15]

4. *Band together:* One person can sometimes terrorize whole groups of people. A group of nurses in New Brunswick dealt with an abusive doctor by ensuring that he was never alone with either patients or nurses. When he did become abusive, thinking that he was unnoticed, they were able to document his behaviour and have him disciplined.[16]

5. *Move along:* Finally, sometimes it is best simply to leave, whether by arranging a transfer to a different department or by leaving the organization entirely. It may not be worth your health and happiness to stay in a position that causes you chronic pain. In a survey of people who had been bullied at work, the Canada Safety Council found that 70 percent either quit or were fired, and 17 percent were transferred to other positions. Thirteen percent of the bullies were punished for their actions.[17]

DON'T BECOME A BULLY

Some people honestly believe that a leader needs to intimidate people to gain respect. Fear may produce short-term results, but in the long run, people who are driven by fear will not do any more work than is necessary to avoid punishment.

Office bullies can be classified into four categories:

1. Screamers, who believe that raising their voices is the only way to get people's attention.
2. Gatekeepers, who control people's access to resources, usually in an uneven manner.
3. Nitpickers, who focus on tiny details rather than looking at issues from a broader perspective.
4. Snakes, who are openly pleasant but later bite people in the back.

It is more effective to ask for people's ideas than to scream at them, to help employees gain access to resources rather than try to find ways to restrict them, to assist people as they develop their ideas rather than find flaws with details, and to nurture co-workers rather than stab them in the back.[18]

It is also important to ensure that your workplace has a written policy on workplace bullying, that employees know about it, and that complaints are acted on. Let your staff know that bullying will not be tolerated. If you come across bullying, take immediate action. A well-run organization has no room for bullies.

Bullies hurt the productivity of organizations and reduce morale, but effective communication strategies can prevent them from causing further damage.

DISCUSSION

1. Under what circumstances, if any, is bullying justified in the workplace?
2. Why is it that 70 percent of people who are bullied end up either quitting or being fired, while only 13 percent of bullies are ever disciplined? How can those statistics be changed?
3. You or someone you know has likely been bullied at work. Ask someone who has been the target of bullies why people bully others in the workplace.
4. People who have been attacked by bullies are now referred to as *targets* rather than as *victims.* Why do you think that is? What is the difference in meaning between these two words?

TAKE IT FURTHER

The Targets of Bullies

The Canada Safety Council says that even though bullied people are commonly stereotyped as being weak, oddballs, or loners, the targets that adult bullies choose are often capable, dedicated staff members who are well liked by co-workers. Bullies are most likely to pick on people with an easygoing interpersonal style and an ability to cooperate.[19]

What characteristics do you think are shared by most office bullies?

Developing your skills at assertive communication is the key to avoiding both shouting matches and being taken advantage of by others. Assertion and

Such bosses as those portrayed in comic books or television shows may exist in the real world, but they seldom achieve the same levels of success as people who look after their co-workers' needs.

aggression are not the same, although they share some characteristics. Both involve standing up for your rights, but aggressive communication involves winning at all costs, while assertive communication considers the rights of all people involved.

Other styles of communication behaviour in difficult situations include the following:

- passive communication, which involves sacrificing your rights to avoid conflict
- passive-aggressive communication, which involves a combination of aggressiveness and passivity—it usually involves taking an outwardly passive approach while finding ways to subtly punish the opposition

Assertive behaviour is usually the best approach for both business and personal lives, but all modes of behaviour have their place.[20] **Table 17-1** provides examples of both appropriate and inappropriate use of these types of behaviour in a workplace environment.

Assertive communication is not always easy. At one time or another everyone has had to deal with someone who has behaved irresponsibly or made an unreasonable demand. Even if the first impulse is to either crush the person or ignore the problem, neither approach is likely to provide a long-term solution. An assertive approach aims to solve the problem in such a way that it does not happen again.

Assertiveness Rights and Responsibilities

Assertiveness involves claiming your rights, but it also means finding ways to avoid violating the rights of others. Assertiveness thus carries with it certain responsibilities, as listed in **Table 17-2** (on page 430).

Another way of looking at rights and responsibilities is to consider that while it is important to be able to assert your rights, assertiveness also requires you to recognize that other people have the same rights. It will sometimes be necessary for you to refuse to do a favour or to tell someone that you are angry, but you must assert your rights in a way that does not demean others or take away their rights.

Remember that you also have the right to not act assertively. An assertive solution may not be the best answer to all areas of disagreement. If an assertive solution causes more friction, makes extra work, or makes life more difficult, in some situations it may be better simply to accept a different alternative. In the words of two respected business writers, "People are entitled to establish their own priorities, to make mistakes, to suffer the consequences, and to be the ultimate judges of their own actions."[21]

Strategies for Disagreeing Assertively

You can use assertive communication to reduce negative feelings when dealing with differences of opinion. When doing so, you may need to take some of these actions:

- Describe the event to which you are reacting and the effect that it has had on you.

- Indicate that you understand the other person's position and the ways in which you empathize with it.
- List the changes that need to take place or offer to negotiate a reasonable solution.
- Give a non-threatening indication of the consequences that will follow if changes are not made.[22]

TABLE 17-1	Appropriate and Inappropriate Communication Behaviour in Difficult Situations	
Mode of Communication Behaviour	**Appropriate Behaviour**	**Inappropriate Behaviour**
Aggressiveness Claiming your rights without considering the needs of other people	Ordering two junior associates to immediately stop a practice that is both dangerous and illegal, even though the two employees want to wait until Monday so that they can see if the department head orders the change; they claim that your demands will make more work for them and they aren't yet convinced that their approach is wrong	Berating a new employee for half an hour after he makes an honest mistake
Passivity Sacrificing your own rights to avoid rejection or other problems	Complying with a border guard who insists on inspecting your passport for a third time	Agreeing once again to cover a co-worker's duties so that she can leave early for a social event, even though the co-worker has always found excuses not to return the favour
Passive-Aggressiveness Avoiding the appearance of confrontation, but later getting payback through other means	Missing a deadline after a domineering supervisor decided on a whim to increase everyone else's workload and then leaves for an unscheduled long weekend vacation during your busy season	Congratulating a rival for winning the promotion that you had both applied for and then making sure that your joint project goes over budget
Assertiveness Standing up for your own rights without trampling on the rights of others	Informing a supplier that any further cost overruns will put your company's further business relations at risk	Trying to be fair to everyone by insisting that a retiring employee maintain the same hours as everyone else during her final week on the job, even though all of her clients and duties have been handed over to other workers in the office

TAKE IT FURTHER

Your Mother Doesn't Work Here

In the workplace (or any other shared space) people sometimes get frustrated at the behaviour of others. One website posts notes, such as this one, that people have left anonymously: "Attention. Your mother doesn't work here. Please clean up your own mess!"[23]

What is an appropriate way to deal with workplace behaviour that annoys you?

TABLE 17-2   **Assertiveness Rights and Responsibilities**

Assertivenes Rights	Assertiveness Responsibilities
To refuse requests	To honour commitments
To act independently	To respect differences of opinion
To be treated as a capable adult	To treat others with respect
To get what you paid for	To provide fair value to others
To feel and express anger	To express anger in socially acceptable ways
To be competitive	To compete fairly
To make mistakes	To take responsibility for your mistakes
To have your opinion respected	To treat other opinions with respect
To choose not to act assertively	To make choices that benefit yourself and others

Source: Adapted from Loftus, A. Paul P. "Training." Industrial & Commercial Training 24.2 (1992): 4. Print.

It may not be necessary to use all of these strategies in all situations. When dealing with supervisors or people whom you depend on, it may be more effective to empathize with their position and to offer to negotiate a solution rather than taking the more drastic steps of listing the changes you need or indicating what will happen if these actions are not taken.

With co-workers it may be better to simply describe what it is that is causing difficulty and specify what you need the other person to do.

With strangers, it may be necessary to present more detail, describing the problem and its effects on you, and then listing what you expect to change and the consequences for non-compliance.[24]

Techniques for Being Assertive

As with many other aspects of communication, assertive communication has as much to do with the way that you communicate as it does with the information that you communicate. You can learn to follow these basic steps:

- Prepare your arguments in advance so that you know what you are going to say and you have the evidence to back up your points.
- Pay attention to your voice and body language. For example, (1) stand up straight, (2) maintain eye contact, and (3) speak in a clear, confident tone of voice.
- If you are interrupted or attacked unfairly, deal with the matter immediately by saying something like, "Please allow me to finish what I was saying."
- Do not apologize for your ideas or discount your own expertise.
- Express your ideas with confidence so that others focus on what you are saying rather than looking for ways to undermine your statements.

Descriptions of four different types of assertion follow.[25]

1. Empathic Assertion   It is often possible to express empathy for the other person's point of view, while maintaining your original position:

> "I realize that you've been waiting for 30 minutes, but the bad weather has caused delays. We should be able to assist you within the next half hour."

I *language assertion*   A variation on empathic assertion is to describe the effect that the other person's actions have on you:

> "When you raise your voice like that, I have difficulty understanding what you need. Please lower your voice and explain what you want."

2. Confrontive Assertion   Sometimes it is necessary to confront someone by comparing the present situation with a standard that had been established earlier.

> "You agreed to install the equipment on January 5. When I called on January 10 you told me that you had had to reschedule the work to February 1. Now it is February 10 and the equipment still has not been installed."

3. Broken Record   Calmly repeat your message, regardless of the other person's response.

> "You agreed to have your part of the project finished by today."

> "I need the work by today."

> "The work needs to be completed today."

4. Escalating Assertion   When these techniques are ineffective, it may be necessary to gradually increase the assertion without becoming aggressive:

> "I know you have your own ideas. You'll have a chance to present them when I have finished talking." (empathic assertion)

> "We agreed that we would each have five minutes to present our positions. I still have two minutes left." (confrontive assertion)

> "Neither I nor anyone else can hear when you keep interrupting me. Please let me finish." (*I* language assertion)

Although assertiveness is often needed in confrontational situations, it can also be valuable in more positive situations. Acknowledging the importance of a co-worker's hard work or providing an unsolicited recommendation of one client to another can also be considered forms of assertiveness.

Remember, though, assertiveness is not always the best strategy. It may not be the most appropriate mode of behaviour in situations where you are dealing with violent or unbalanced people, when nothing is to be gained by acting assertively, or when being assertive will cause you to lose more than you gain.[26]

EMOTIONAL INTELLIGENCE

Most people are familiar with traditional definitions of intelligence, which is usually tested by using a combination of verbal and mathematical questions that produce a numerical result known as an *intelligence quotient* or *IQ*. Intelligence is a quality that is highly valued in most workplaces.

Emotional Intelligence is less well known, but it may be even more important to your success in the business world than your technical skills or your IQ.[27] The people who succeed most often in business are not necessarily those with the highest marks in school but those who have the drive to succeed, the ability to read their emotions and those of others, and the judgment to act accordingly. Successful businesspeople need to motivate groups of people, to negotiate deals, and to solicit advice from others—all qualities that benefit from a high emotional quotient (EQ).

Emotional Intelligence Defined   *Emotional intelligence* has been defined as "a form of social intelligence that involves the ability to monitor one's own and others' feelings and emotions, to discriminate among them, and to use this information to guide one's thinking and action."[28]

Daniel Goleman, the psychologist responsible for spreading the word about emotional intelligence, identified five main characteristics:

1. *Self-awareness:* the ability to understand your own emotions and their effects on others
2. *Self-regulation:* the ability to control yourself, to suspend judgment, and to think before acting
3. *Motivation:* persistence, energy, and the capacity to work for reasons other than money
4. *Empathy:* the ability to interpret the emotions of others and to deal with people accordingly
5. *Social skill:* the ability to build teams, manage relationships, and negotiate with others.[29]

Increasing Your EQ

Emotional intelligence tends to increase as people age (*maturity* and *wisdom* are frequently used as synonyms). Goleman also said that reading about it or listening to lectures on it does not increase a person's emotional intelligence. Most EQ training involves a series of self-assessment tests, along with commentary from others in the workplace, to determine people's areas of strengths and weaknesses. This is followed by individual coaching and mentoring to help people find ways to overcome their deficiencies. Such techniques were found to be more effective at raising EQ than traditional classroom instruction.[30]

These techniques are expensive, and it is likely that only upper-level management would use them. You can do other things. Diann Daniel consulted with experts in the field and listed four other ways to improve EQ:

1. Learn to take responsibility rather than micromanaging or looking to blame people.

2. Practise public speaking to improve your persuasiveness and your abilities to read people.

3. Use yoga and meditation to improve both your focus and your ability to relax.

4. Take an improvisation course to improve your listening skills and your ability to build on the ideas of others.[31]

Maclean's magazine notes that many successful businesspeople, including Angus Reid, CEO of a large market research company, and Fred Jaekel, founder of a billion-dollar auto parts manufacturing business, had trouble in school but have high levels of emotional intelligence.[32]

Developing your emotional intelligence may not be easy, but doing so may help your career as much as earning high grades in school will.

COMMUNICATION SKILLS TO EARN THE COOPERATION OF OTHER PEOPLE IN THE OFFICE

You are likely to spend about 40 hours a week or more at work from the day you begin your next job until the time you retire. It would be unrealistic to suggest that you will become friends with everyone you meet or that every moment will be a rewarding experience, but a few common-sense strategies can make the work go more smoothly for you and for the people you encounter.

Decisions about your career—including promotions, layoffs, and transfers—are based partly on the economic climate, seniority lists, and your ability. Part of those decisions will also be based on factors that are hard to measure.

Communicating with Your Boss

Management genius Peter F. Drucker wrote that he could identify people in an organization who were destined for promotion and those who were not by watching the way that they dealt with their bosses. People who simply complained about their supervisors were not likely to go anywhere; those who were able to manage their bosses were likely to be promoted.

Drucker emphasized that "managing the boss" does not mean subjecting your supervisor to empty flattery. Instead, he provided four common-sense principles:

1. Recognize that every boss is a human being with a unique set of characteristics. Some bosses may respond well to flattery; others hate it. Some

prefer to receive written communication; others want to hear you explaining your ideas. Find out your boss's preferences.

2. Realize that the boss cannot read minds. Keep your boss informed about any projects that you are working on, and let him know about any decisions that you have made and any difficulties you are facing. Do not try to hide problems or withhold negative information; doing so is unfair to both of you.

3. Understand that the bosses does not give you or anyone else as much of their time as you really need, and so you need to manage what little of their time that you do have. Prepare for meetings so that the time gets used productively. Provide them with follow-up information so that any decisions made can be acted on easily.

4. Remember that underrating your bosses is far more dangerous than overrating them. People who hold their bosses in contempt will not last long. Drucker said that overestimating the boss's abilities is a less dangerous mistake but cautioned that when faced with an incompetent or corrupt boss, it is better to leave the position than be dragged down into failure.[33]

Fitting into Your Boss's Plans

Despite the best intentions of everyone involved, new employees sometimes do not work out, and so employers reserve the right to replace these people when necessary. Your first six months or so on the job will probably be a probationary period, a time when your employer can dismiss you without giving any cause. The following five guidelines can help you succeed in a new work environment:

1. Manage Your Career   If you intend to thrive in a new job, you will first need to survive the probationary period. That means getting along with your boss and co-workers while demonstrating that you can be a productive member of the team. Remember that your boss is responsible for a number of people, often with a diverse set of skills. You will find on occasion that you know far more about an issue than either your boss or your co-workers. That is normal. You will be expected to demonstrate expertise in your specific area of responsibility. Your manager is responsible for the success of the entire department and will be looking at the big picture when making decisions. He or she will have to consider such factors as budgetary restrictions and the broad strategic objectives of the organization. Sometimes this will mean making decisions that may be unpopular or that do not fit well with your plans.

2. Send Out Good Signals   Productivity and technical ability are both important, but other factors affecting your image are also important. Punctuality will be noticed, for example. Try to arrive for meetings a few minutes early. Be careful with your choice in clothing, jewellery, and hairstyle. (See "Cubicle Etiquette" later in this chapter.)

You will make mistakes, especially when you are beginning a new job. Errors are expected, but be sure that you take responsibility for your mistakes, and then work toward correcting them. When you are in doubt, ask questions. Your more-experienced co-workers know that it is far easier to avoid problems than it is to correct them once the damage has been done, and so in most cases they will be more than eager to give you advice.[34]

3. Be a Team Player To be considered part of the workplace team and to win the loyalty of your colleagues, you will have to demonstrate that you can fit into the working environment. This does not mean that you have to be friends with everyone you work with, but it does mean that you will be expected to be able to cooperate with everyone, even those you might not socialize with.

Show that you can work well with your co-workers. Volunteer for extra assignments on occasion, and do your work cheerfully. No one likes to work alongside someone who constantly complains. Show that you have a positive attitude.

4. Demonstrate Productivity Find out your manager's objectives and the strategies for achieving these goals and then look for ways that you can contribute to the overall plan.

Demonstrate that you can get the job done. One way to inspire your superior's confidence is to meet all deadlines that are given to you. Reliability is a valuable quality.

Most bosses will want to listen to your ideas and will even appreciate suggestions that will improve their ideas, but be constructive. Offer alternatives when you do find flaws in their plans, and avoid criticizing supervisors in front of other people, especially clients or upper management. If you have to raise serious objections, do so in private.

Consider talking with your manager about your career ambitions. He or she may be able to offer advice or give you assignments that will allow you to achieve your goals.[35]

5. Communicate Fairly Contribute your own ideas, even if they run against established thinking, but do so in a way that does not create enemies. Do not demean other people, even if you disagree with their approach. Do not criticize an idea without offering an alternative solution to a problem.

Do not expect all of your ideas to be accepted—other people will be looking at the issue from different viewpoints. The answer that is eventually chosen may be better at meeting the needs of those people, even if it does not work as well for you.

6. Acquire the Necessary Skills In one study, representatives from the Fortune 500 companies in the United States were asked to rate the importance of skills that entry-level accounting graduates possess.

Although accounting knowledge topped the list, and computer skills were listed as number five, the other key items in the top five were soft skills:

- communication
- problem solving
- group work/interpersonal skills

The people who were surveyed also felt that graduates' accounting knowledge was decreasing in importance, while communication skills, interpersonal skills, computer use, and problem-solving ability were becoming more important.[36]

Another U.S. survey of employers asked about the skills that beginning administrators need. It produced similar findings and also emphasized the importance of honesty, integrity, and a strong work ethic.

The employers who responded also commented that they were having a difficult time finding new graduates who were good at reading and writing, who could display maturity and business etiquette, and who had realistic expectations of professional life.[37]

Many managers consult with other people before making any personnel decisions, so getting along with co-workers and clients is important for your career well-being. If you are willing and able to work hard, demonstrate integrity, cooperate with others, and think on your feet, you should be able to expect a favourable review from your supervisor at the end of your probationary period.

Communicating with Frontline Workers

In almost every job that you will ever do, much of your interpersonal communication will be with frontline workers. The frontline workers are those who have the initial contact with clients, the general public, and their counterparts in other departments and who form the frontline of every business and government agency. Such people include the clerks, receptionists, administrative assistants, customer service workers, security personnel, and parking lot attendants. You may have already done such jobs. You may also find that you will be hired for such a position immediately on graduation before moving on to other jobs that pay more and carry more responsibility.

Many people do these jobs for their entire lives. In some ways these workers can be considered the lifeblood of any organization, but too often, frontline workers are ignored or looked down on. That is a serious mistake.

Whether you are a frontline worker yourself, and have to deal with others doing similar jobs, or you have to deal with people on the frontline in your own or other organizations, follow one rule above all others:

> Treat frontline workers with the courtesy and respect that they deserve.

Follow this rule and you will find that these people have ways to make your work go faster and more smoothly. Yell at them, make sarcastic comments, or do anything else that makes their job more difficult than it already is, and they will punish you with a dozen different passive-aggressive strategies—all the while smiling politely at you and wishing you a very nice day.

The people on the frontline usually do their best to help others. Sometimes, though, they have to refuse. They may be unable to comply with your requests for reasons that are beyond their control or because they are following instructions from their supervisors. Frontline workers do not usually have the authority to change policies, and so it is a mistake to blame them for decisions that they did not make.

People on the frontline do have a great deal of power, but for you to make that work to your advantage, it is important that you recognize the limitations of frontline staff so that you can avoid frustrating yourself and them by asking for the impossible.

What They Cannot Do   Frontline workers cannot change policies or overturn their supervisors' decisions. They have been given instructions to follow, and they risk being reprimanded if they do not follow them. They may not even agree with the rules they have been told to enforce, but they know that they must do so. When you come across situations in which an exception must be made to the rules or policies need to be changed, your only option is to deal with someone who has the authority to change the rules, rather than making life difficult for those who are only following instructions.

Remember, though, that people who work on the frontline communicate with one another and with their supervisors. If you push people to do something beyond their authority, or if you try to bully people or deceive them, they may not confront you directly, but they will share that information with others. If you are rude or dishonest with one person, you can expect that others in the organization will unite against you. You will find yourself spending extra time in waiting rooms and then being greeted coldly by the people you need to see.

What They Can Do   Many frontline staff are gatekeepers, with the job of assisting their supervisors by keeping them organized, supplying them with information, and filtering out unwanted visitors. This role gives them the power to influence many decisions:

- They can control the timing of the information that reaches their bosses.
- They can bring important information to the attention of their supervisors.
- They can summarize visitors' stories and advise their supervisors of any inconsistencies that they notice.

Provide them with the information that they need to do their jobs, but do not expect them to be able to make a major decision on your situation.

Treat the frontline workers with respect, and you will gain valuable workplace allies.

Some of the tasks that frontline staff perform are ones that you may not even notice. The people who deliver the mail, clean the office, and answer the telephones often have opportunities to perform tasks that are not listed on their job descriptions. Whether they do these extras for you or not will depend largely on the way you treat these staff members.

Of course, frontline workers are not the only ones who deal with the outside world by telephone. Almost everyone at work gets to do that at some point, which leads us to the following section.

COMMUNICATING BY PHONE AT WORK

The telephone is one of the key tools used in the office today. When you are speaking on your office phone, you are representing not only yourself but everyone else who works in the organization. It is important that you use your phone effectively.

Pay attention to your vocal qualities. Some people stand while they talk on the phone; others smile. Although neither practice will be noticed by the person on the other end, if it leads you to have a more expressive telephone voice, it will be well worth the effort.

Tips for Using Office Telephones

Remember that when you are using the phone at work, you are representing your employer. These tips will help you present a better image:

- Use a standard greeting when answering your office phone. This will usually mean giving your name and the name of your department or employer. Keep all greetings brief.
- Even if your telephone is equipped with caller ID, you should not answer your phone by addressing the caller by name. Someone else could be using the caller's phone.
- Give your full attention to the caller. Do not eat or chew gum while on the phone.
- Do not try to operate your computer or perform other tasks while talking on the phone.
- If you must put a person on hold or if you need to redirect the call to someone else, ask for permission first and politely explain to the caller what you are doing.
- When taking a caller off hold, always thank the person for holding.
- When placing a call, begin by stating your name and your employer's name. Then ask for the person that you are trying to reach. Do not begin calls by saying, "Who have I got?" even if you are calling a familiar number.
- Before you hang up, be sure that you have answered all the caller's questions. Let the caller hang up first.
- Look over **Table 17-3** for phrases to avoid.

TABLE 17-3   **Phrases to Avoid**

Try to be as positive as possible, even when giving bad news or dealing with difficult customers.

Avoid Saying This	Try This Instead
"I don't know."	"I'll try to find that information for you."
"It's not possible to do that."	"Here's what we can do."
"Just a second."	Give a realistic answer about how long it will take you to do whatever you are doing.

Phone Messages When taking phone messages, be sure to include the following information:

- the caller's name and company name if applicable
- the time and date of call
- a brief message
- the caller's phone number if a return call is required

When leaving voicemail messages, state your name and phone number clearly, and keep messages short.

Cellphone Etiquette

The following guidelines apply to all handheld devices:

- Turn off your cellphone before going into meetings, restaurants, or enclosed public spaces. Never have emotional conversations in any public place.
- If you must use your cellphone in a public place, keep your voice down, and stand at least three metres away from other people. Excuse yourself and leave any public gathering while taking a call.
- Avoid using loud or annoying ring tones.
- Do not multi-task by making calls while waiting in line or taking care of personal business.
- Tell callers that you are talking on your cellphone in case you have to deal with a distraction or the call becomes disconnected.
- Keep calls brief.
- Do not answer your phone or place a call while you are driving. Even hands-free cellphones pose a dangerous distraction. Texting while driving is as dangerous (and as socially unacceptable) as driving while drunk.

CUBICLE ETIQUETTE

Cubicles are a major feature of most modern offices. They may reduce building expenses and promote informality, but they also pose a number of challenges relating to noise and privacy. With no doors to hide you from the eyes of your neighbours, working in a cubicle can be somewhat like living in a fishbowl.

Inappropriate cubicle behaviour may not receive public comment from anyone. (Who can blame a supervisor for not wanting to ask someone to leave his shoes on and to stop putting his smelly feet on his desk?) Such behaviour does affect a person's reputation, though, and it can lead to long-term consequences.

Common-Sense Guidelines

Following these common-sense guidelines can make cubicle life smoother for you and everyone else in your office.

TAKE IT FURTHER

Flying with Cellphones

Airlines have the technical capability to offer cellphone service during flights, but they are struggling with the question of whether to do so. Although the service would allow people to use their time on an airplane more productively, it has the potential of annoying people who would be forced to listen to calls in cramped airplane cabins. Some airlines are restricting phone usage to text and data.[39]

Should people be allowed to use their telephones while flying?

1. Cut Out Strong Odours Many people do eat lunch or snacks at their desks, but food choices can present problems. Avoid foods that have a strong odour. Smells carry throughout an office, and your neighbour may not appreciate the aroma of your sardine and onion sandwich. The odour of some cooked foods, such as microwave popcorn, tends to permeate an entire workspace, especially if it is burnt.

Other foods pose a danger to those with allergies. Check with co-workers before bringing in common allergens, such as peanuts or shrimp.

When eating at your desk, try to select foods that can be eaten relatively discreetly. Most sandwiches can be eaten quietly and create little mess. Many people do eat potato chips, even though they are noisy and lead to greasy fingers. Such foods must be considered marginal. People who chronically snap their gum, crunch their ice cubes, or eat foods that bother others will prove to be an annoyance to their neighbours. It is best to avoid any foods that could be troublesome until you have seen what others in the office find acceptable.

Other odours Be cautious with anything else that may carry a strong odour. At one time or another you have likely walked past someone in a hallway who seems to buy cologne in litre-sized bottles. Imagine how stressful it would be to work in a cubicle beside someone who uses that much scent. Unfortunately, those who do apply excess quantities of cologne or aftershave may have overloaded their own senses to the point where they are not even aware of the strength of their scent.

The sense of smell is strongly linked to the emotional centre of the brain. An overpowering scent can produce a strong negative reaction in people without their realizing the basis for their distaste. A person could end up being punished for overusing perfume with neither the punisher nor the victim noticing the real source of the problem.

Even a small amount of perfume sometimes poses problems for people who have extreme sensitivities, so it is best to be very conservative with any scents until you know how other people are likely to react. Some workplaces even have no-scent policies in effect.

2. Respect the Common Areas Many offices contain a kitchen area with small appliances, such as a refrigerator, microwave, and coffee maker. Make sure that you do your part to contribute to the overall cleanliness of the area. Do not leave dirty dishes in the sink. Do not allow your food to turn into science projects in the fridge. If you make a mess, clean it up. No one wants to be your cleaner.

If you are heating food in the microwave or boiling water in the kettle, watch them so that you can turn them off when they are done. Your co-workers will not appreciate standing beside a steaming kettle or having to wait for you to remove your food so that they can prepare their lunches.

Find out the rules about communal appliances, such as coffee makers. In some workplaces, the employers bear the cost of coffee, sugar, and milk. In other offices people are expected to contribute to a fund that pays for such items. In some places people pay for each cup on an honour system. Be sure to follow the rules of the workplace. If you do not drink coffee, for example,

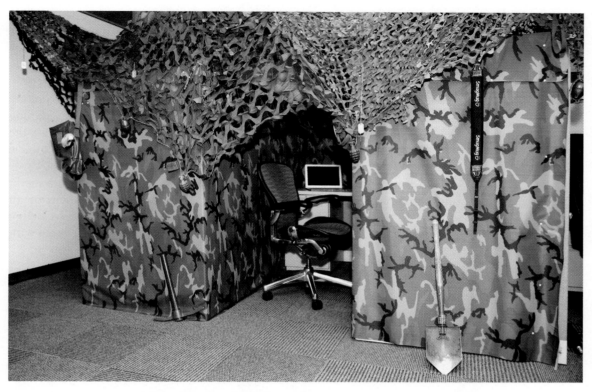

Some people may go to extremes when decorating their cubicles.

you should not feel obligated to contribute, but if you do—even occasionally—you should be prepared to contribute your share. That also means sharing in the upkeep. Do not leave a dribble of coffee in the bottom of a coffee maker and expect someone else to make the next pot. Either make a fresh pot for the next person or rinse it out and turn the machine off if the day is almost finished.

3. Watch Your Decor
Most employers allow staff to bring in personal items to decorate their workspaces. This improves morale and allows people to demonstrate their individuality. Remember, though, that the workplace is a shared environment. Keep your decorating modest. It is a workplace first and a personal space second.

Avoid risqué pictures or screensavers, and as a general rule do not post anything that carries a religious or political message.

Plants can be a welcome addition to any office, but remember to position them so that they do not cause damage if they leak water or tip over.

4. Don't Spread Germs
If you have an infectious illness, stay home. While you may feel that it is your duty to the employer to work even when you are coughing and sneezing, you will earn no praise from co-workers or clients if you infect them.

Action Offices

When office cubicles were introduced in 1968, their designer called them "action offices." Cubicles were an improvement over the office environment that they replaced—open area offices with rows of desks that allowed even less privacy than the cubicles of today.[40]

How can cubicles be improved without increasing their cost?

5. Interrupt Tactfully   It will at times be necessary to interrupt someone who is working in a cubicle. This can be problematic, especially if the person's back faces the cubicle entrance. To avoid startling a person who cannot see you coming, it is best to announce your presence by knocking on a solid surface or saying something like "excuse me" or "knock knock" before entering.

Prairie dogging is office slang that describes the practice of people poking their heads up over their cubicle walls either when they hear something unusual or when they want to initiate a casual conversation. Except for the briefest of exchanges, it is better to walk over to the other person's cubicle than to pop your head up or yell over the wall.

At times you will overhear people talking about a work-related issue in an adjoining cubicle. If you have useful information to offer them or an answer to their question, you may want to quietly interrupt them by saying something like, "I couldn't help overhearing . . ." and then provide them with

"Something has spooked the prairie dogs."

Prairie dogging is common in business cubicles.

the information they need. This, however, should not be taken as an open invitation to join in on every conversation that you overhear. The key factor that you should consider before intruding on someone else's conversation is whether your comments will be perceived as being helpful or not.

6. Consider Noise   One of the bigger challenges that comes with working in a cubicle is dealing with noise, both yours and others'. Sound carries very well in a cubicle environment. You need to find ways to keep from annoying others with your noise while blocking out the sounds that are made by other people.

Many workplaces do allow people to use their office phones for a reasonable amount of personal communication, but it is important to remember that everyone in your immediate area will be able to hear every word that you say. Do you really want your co-workers to know that you and your spouse are fighting, that your children are having trouble in school, or that you have an oozing sore on a private part of your anatomy? It is usually better to deal with private matters on a line where you will not be overheard by others. While your co-workers will make every effort to appear as though they are not eavesdropping on such conversations, they will hear every word, and they generally will not appreciate the interruption. For the same reason, do not take calls or replay voice messages on speakerphones.

The same principle applies to face-to-face exchanges. Short, quiet conversations are fine in a cubicle, but when you need to conduct a meeting with several people or exchange detailed information, it is best to move the meeting to a more suitable environment. It is especially rude to stand outside someone else's cubicle and carry on a conversation with a different person about the latest celebrity scandal or some other topic that is not related to work. Move your personal conversations to the cafeteria or lunchroom.

Blocking out noise   When you need to block out the noise that other people are making, do not just turn on a radio to drown out them out. That simply adds more noise pollution to the mix. Use earphones when you are listening to a radio or music player. But even then, a certain amount of care is necessary. Do not turn the volume up so loud that you cannot hear other office sounds. A person may need to speak with you in person and will want to get your attention without having to tap you on the shoulder.

If you are the type who sings along with your music, whether consciously or not, you should listen to talk radio or restrict your musical selections to instrumentals. Your co-workers do not want to be serenaded with your humming or foot tapping.

One rule of thumb that may prove useful is to avoid doing anything that you would find objectionable if done by someone else. Setting a good example for others is the first step in dealing with insensitive office behaviour. Of course, it is always possible that people could be unaware that one of their habits is objectionable to you or someone else. When that happens, let them know in a pleasant and non-threatening manner what it is that you would like changed.

"Haven't they ever heard of walls around here?"

Cubicles do not offer the same degree of privacy as walled offices.

7. Be Aware of Cubicle Fashions   Whether you like it or not, the clothes that you wear communicate a great deal about you. Choose clothing, jewellery, and a hairstyle that fits in with the workplace environment. Even in places that do not have dress codes or that observe casual Fridays, you should not dress the same way for work that you would for the beach or a night out. It is always better to be too conservative than too flamboyant. Clothes that are sloppy, unclean, or too revealing will attract negative attention, as will large tattoos, excessive makeup, or numerous piercings. The workplace is not the best place to make a fashion statement.

Chapter Summary

Effective interpersonal communication is an important quality in the environment of the modern office.

Assertiveness is a style of communication that involves a calm insistence on fairness to everyone. It is different from aggressiveness, where winning is the only thing that matters. Passive communicators allow other people to dominate them, while passive-aggressive communicators appear to give in, and then find subtle ways to get their revenge. Note that emotional intelligence, the ability to monitor the effects of the emotions of yourself and others, has been linked to the success of many people whose performance in traditional academic pursuits has been only average.

Office telephones and cellphones are important business tools, but you need to follow telephone etiquette so that you avoid annoying other people with your calls.

To thrive in the business world, it is necessary to cooperate with others, to fit in with the office culture, and to demonstrate initiative. Effective interpersonal communication requires you to deal with people at your own level, as well as with supervisors and frontline workers. Treat all these people with courtesy and respect, and you will discover numerous ways that they can contribute toward the success of your career.

Cubicles require people to deal with the noise and interruptions that are the inevitable result of working closely together. The importance of these skills is crucial to successful business relationships.

PEARSON
mycanadianbuscommlab Visit **www.mycanadianbuscommlab.ca** for everything you need to help you succeed in the job you've always wanted! Tools and resources include the following:

- Composing and The Writer's Toolkit
- Document Makeovers
- Video Case Studies
- Grammar exercises and much more!

Thinking and Writing Exercises

1. **Workplace Bullying**

   Without naming the names of the people involved, describe an incident in which a person was bullied in the workplace. Answer the following questions:

   a. Was the target male or female? What was the gender of the perpetrator(s)?

   b. Describe the professional relationship between the bully and the target. Was the problem between co-workers at the same level, between a client and a worker, or between co-workers at different levels?

   c. Describe how the situation was resolved. Was management involved in resolving the problem? Was the resolution successful?

2. **Communicating Assertively**

   Describe an assertive approach for dealing with each of the following scenarios.

   a. A co-worker says that she doesn't have time to attend all of your workgroup's regular weekly meetings but says that she will agree to whatever everyone else decides. She later meets privately with the manager to complain that the work is not being done properly.

   b. You're sitting in your cubicle trying to prepare for an important meeting that begins in an hour, but people in the next cubicle have been talking about last night's hockey game for the last half hour.

c. You think that you have found a solution to a problem that is costing your department a lot of money. You are reluctant to mention it at your staff meeting, though, because your approach is unusual and most of your co-workers have very conservative ideas. The last time you described one of your ideas, the other people thought it was silly and laughed at you.

3. **Passive, Aggressive, Passive-Aggressive, and Assertive Communication**

Each of the following situations contains four possible responses to a situation. First, classify the four responses as aggressive (AG), passive (P), passive-aggressive (PA), or assertive (AS), and then decide what you would do.

a. A person with whom you carpool is often late. The last two times when you arrived to pick him up at 7:30, he was not ready and caused you to arrive late for work. He calls today and asks if you can pick him up 15 minutes earlier than usual tomorrow, because he has an early meeting. What do you do?

- Say, "Sure, no problem," and hope that this time he is ready.

- Refuse. Remind him how rude and inconsiderate he has been by making you wait.

- Tell him that you will be at his house at 7:15 and if he is ready, he can ride with you. Otherwise, you will go on without him.

- Tell him that you will be at his house at 7:15, and then arrive at 7:40 so that you teach him a lesson.

b. You are the group leader on a project that has been very frustrating for everyone. When the project is close to completion, your people finally start doing everything according to your expectations. What do you do?

- Say nothing at all. They should have been doing this sort of work from the beginning of the project.

- Send the group members an email telling them that this is the sort of work they should have been doing all along. Remind that that if they fall behind schedule again, some people's jobs might be in jeopardy.

- At the next group meeting, congratulate them on doing a good job. Tell them that you are confident that this trend will continue.

- Send the group members an email congratulating them on finally getting things right. Then remind them that the group is still the least productive of the four groups in your division.

c. A person in the cubicle next to you spends an average of half an hour every day making romantic phone calls to her boyfriend in another province. You find that the calls interfere with your concentration. What do you do?

- Do nothing at all. Long distance romances rarely last very long.

- Say nothing to your colleague but send an anonymous message to your supervisor mentioning that your colleague's long distance calls are not being used for company business.

- Let your colleague know that her calls are interfering with your work, and ask her to call her boyfriend during her lunch hour or after work.

- The next time she takes a personal call, storm into her cubicle, tell her to keep the noise down, and hang up her phone.

d. A major client calls for the third time and insists that you adjust your delivery schedule so that he receives his shipments at the same time each week. This time he is angry and swears at you. Your company is able to guarantee a four-hour "window" for deliveries, but it is not possible to give a more precise delivery time. What do you do?

- Allow him to vent his anger, and then tell him that you realize how frustrating it is to be kept waiting. Tell him that you will pass his concerns along to the delivery supervisor, but inform the client that such adjustments may not happen overnight.

- Reply to the client by using language that is even more offensive than the words he directed at you. Insist that the next time he calls, he will begin by apologizing. Then hang up.

- Apologize for the problem with the delivery times and promise to do a better job next time.

- Apologize for the inconsistent delivery times. Then after hanging up, change the client's next morning delivery request to the afternoon.

4. **Dealing with Difficult Workplace Situations**

Form a group of three or four people and try to find a consensus on the best way to handle each of the following situations. Give a brief description of exactly how you would handle each situation, and then label the approach aggressive (AG), passive (P), passive-aggressive (AS), or assertive (AS).

a. You are being kept on the phone at work by your regular sales representative, who is trying to sell you something you don't want.

b. Your boss has just won an award from the local Chamber of Commerce for being entrepreneur of the year.

c. You are the fire marshal on the floor of your building. Someone smells smoke and pulls the alarm, but the people in the next office refuse to leave because it is "probably another false alarm."

d. Your doctor keeps you waiting more than 20 minutes even though when you made the appointment you informed the receptionist that your time was tight.

e. You receive a bill that seems unusually high for the service you received.

f. You see someone smoking beside a "No Smoking" sign at the entrance to the building where you work.

g. The person in the cubicle next to you asks you to show him how to do something on the computer just before you were about to leave on your break.

h. You are making an important presentation to a group of clients, and one of their cellphones rings.

i. During a meeting, a member of the committee interrupts your presentation by muttering jokes about the sound of your voice.

j. You receive an unfair comment from your supervisor during your annual performance review.

5. **Testing Your Emotional Intelligence**
Take a test of your emotional intelligence at one of the sites listed below. Read the analysis provided:

www.queendom.com/tests/index.htm

www.psychtests.com/tests/index.html

6. **Understanding Emotional Intelligence**
Your emotions have an effect on the people with whom you associate.[41] Understanding your own emotions and the impact they can have on others will help you to communicate better at work. Answer the following questions.

a. Think about a time when you did poorly on a school assignment or had problems with your work. Did other people realize that you had difficulties? What signals did you send that allowed them to gauge your mood?

b. Think about the last time that you had too many things to do and not enough time to do them. How did this affect other people with whom you work, live, or go to school?

c. Describe a time when one of the people that you live, work, or go to school with did something that you admired. How did you indicate your admiration? How did the other(s) react?

d. Think about a time when you received some bad news. Did others know that you had received bad news? What signs did you send? How did others respond to you?

e. Describe a time when other people did not perform according to your expectations. Did they know that you were disappointed in them? How?

f. Describe a time when one of the people that you live, work, or go to school with showed signs that they were experiencing difficulties with their work. What signals did they send? Describe your response.

g. Think about a time when you were angry with someone in your class. How were the others in your class affected by your mood?

7. **Dealing with Frontline Staff**

a. Describe the worst store clerk, bank teller, receptionist, or other frontline worker that you remember seeing in the past month. Explain what that person did (or did not do) that made that person's performance bad. What factors do you think contributed to his or her actions?

b. Describe the worst customer, client, or patron that you have seen dealing with a frontline worker in the past month. Explain what that person did (or did not do) that made that person's performance bad. What factors do you think contributed to his or her actions?

c. What can clients and frontline workers do to make each other's lives easier?

Writing Skills Checkup: Dangling and Misplaced Modifiers

Modifiers are words or phrases that add information to another part of a sentence. A misplaced modifier is placed incorrectly so that it modifies the wrong part of the sentence.

> Misplaced: Amina *nearly* edited the whole report.

> Correct: Amina edited *nearly* the whole report.

A dangling modifier is not properly attached to the rest of the sentence so that it modifies words not found in the sentence.

> Dangling: While reading my email, the telephone rang.

> Correct: While *I was* reading my email, the telephone rang.

Fix the modifiers in the following sentences:

1. Everyone nearly notices when people behave badly at work, but a few people only complain when people act that way.
2. A common part of workplace introductions, many people judge others by their handshake.
3. A handshake sends a message of a domineering or weak nature if done wrong.
4. When leaving the table during a meal, your napkin should be placed on your chair seat.
5. Establishing business relationships and conducting negotiations, business luncheons can be an important part of a business career.
6. Difficult to consume gracefully, people should avoid ordering such foods as spaghetti or whole lobster during business lunches.
7. When meeting with someone, your cellphone should be turned off and your voicemail should take incoming calls.
8. If taking messages for someone, the caller's name, time, and a brief message should be written in a brief note.
9. Instead of a desk or a public place, a washroom should be used to perform personal grooming.
10. When demonstrating good manners in the workplace, the office is a more pleasant place to work.

Grammar, Punctuation, and Plain English

Most college and university communication courses include little time to teach basic English, but you need to know how to use it properly. Your instructor's job is to ensure that you can write sentences that convey relevant meaning appropriate in a business context. This appendix can help you write what you mean by using clear, well-constructed sentences.

Sound funny your sentence does, mmm?

The appendix is *not* a buffet of appetizing apostrophes, crunchy conjunctive adverbs, scrumptious subordinate noun clauses, or tasty tenses. Instead, it is intended to be a *quick* reference for you, focusing on how to fix the common grammatical problems that cause many students to lose marks. (Telling you what a subordinating conjunction is does not tell you how to use it properly.) This appendix emphasizes how to correct common errors, not how to label parts of speech. If, for example, your instructor takes off marks because you have run-on sentences in your assignment, check out that section so that you will not lose marks to run-on sentence errors on new assignments. The sections that follow are simple and concise. Where appropriate, information has been condensed into tables, bad examples, good examples, and practice questions with answers. The appendix is divided into three main sections—(1) grammar, (2) punctuation, and (3) plain English—and includes numbers, abbreviations, and non-sexist writing.

FOUR PIECES OF ADVICE

Let's start with a little advice:

1. Never ever trust your word processor's grammar checker. Check the checker! Check every

indication of a grammar or spelling error, but even if the grammar or spell checker shows no sign of an error, assume your assignment is still a flawed masterpiece that requires further work.

2. Never submit a first draft. Proofreading while the pages are still warm from the printer prevents you from finding your mistakes, because your brain reads what it *thinks* you wrote. Always finish the first draft of your writing a few days before your deadline. Letting your writing "cool" for a few days improves your chances of finding errors. Reread your assignment and the related handouts several times, asking yourself whether you have done what you were asked to do. Proofread your assignment several times, looking for errors and wasted words.

3. If you do not understand something in this appendix, ask your instructor. Sometimes instructors have specific requirements. Be sure to find out what those requirements are.

4. Once you feel comfortable with the topics in this appendix, you may want to wander into a bookstore to buy a usable (by *your* standards!) grammar book. Some day you will report to a supervisor instead of an instructor, and your job of producing excellent written communication will continue. The need to write well never ends.

1. GRAMMAR

The grammar issues in this section are sorted alphabetically.

1.1 Adjectives and Adverbs

Most of us know the difference between adjectives and adverbs, but let us recap:[1]

- Adjectives describe nouns and pronouns.
- Adverbs describe verbs, adjectives, and other adverbs. Adverbs frequently, but not always, end in -*ly*.

Use an Adjective When You Want to Describe	Use an Adverb When You Want to Describe
Which one (*this, that*)	Where
What kind (*red*)	When
How many (*few*)	How How much/often/long
With linking (non-action) verbs (e.g., forms of *to be* [such as *was, is, are*] and *seems, appears, feels*)	With action verbs

Adjective (Describing Noun)	Adverb (Describing Where, When, How)	Adverb (-*ly* extension) (Describing Where, When, How)
She practised a *hard* piano piece.	He pounded the drums *hard*.	Billy *hardly* hit Justin.
He attends *high* school.	The bird flew *high* in the sky.	I *highly* recommend it.
We are *close* friends.	Sit *close* to me.	The girls are *closely* related.
Charlie is doing a *fine* job.	You are walking *fine* since the accident.	We need some *finely* chopped celery.
The magician put her in a *deep* trance.	She dived *deep* into the pool.	He felt *deeply* happy as he dug.
He is a *fair* player.	He's not cheating—he's playing *fair*.	He's playing *fairly* well.
He was in a *tight* situation.	Hold *tight*.	These ropes are *tightly* twisted.
You make a *right* turn at the next stop sign.	The teacher said I spelled it *right*.	She praised me *rightly*.
I took a *wrong* turn at the light.	The teacher said I spelled it *wrong*.	She accused me *wrongly*.
The *late* show starts at midnight.	I was *late* to class this morning.	I haven't been sleeping well *lately*.

Most of the time you can figure out which you need, but sometimes you may confuse adjectives and adverbs. Sometimes you may confuse just adverbs because sometimes they are the same word but used differently. To baffle you further, adverbs that have an -ly extension are used differently from the same word without an -ly and may have a very different meaning from that shorter word.

What is the difference between the following sentences?

I feel bad. This sentence means you are not feeling well. You may be feeling sick, guilty, nervous, or any other number of ailments. The sentence is describing the subject *I.*

I feel badly. This sentence means your fingers are not working very well.

Such words as *bad/badly, easy/easily, good/well, real/really,* and *sure/surely* are frequently misused. One common error occurs when adverbs (especially *only*) are misplaced.

Only *Tom found the third report.* This sentence means that Tom is the only person who found the third report.

Tom **only** *found the third report.* This sentence means that Tom only found the third report; he has not edited it or done anything else with it.

Tom found **only** *the third report.* Hmmm . . . where are the other reports?

1.2 Capitalization

The following list shows what to capitalize:

- names of people
- days, months, holidays (not seasons)
- title and position if used before a person's name
- geographic names, including specific regions
- historical periods
- names of the deity and sacred books
- religions, races, languages, countries, nationalities (Note: Hockey and other sports may be a religion to some of us, but sports are generally not capitalized unless the word begins a sentence, as in this example.)
- names of specific courses but not general courses
- specific facilities, organizations, and teams
- planets' names
- brand names
- stand-alone letters that begin a word (*X-ray*)
- names of movies, books, chapters, and articles (print and online)
- (optional) a statement after a colon, if the statement that follows the colon is a complete sentence

Having said all that, do not over-capitalize.

YOUR TURN!

Circle the correct word for the blank in the following sentences:

1. After cheating on the exam, Barnum felt (bad, badly) _____.

2. The Edsel was following too (close, closely) _____ behind us.

3. They knew not to bury the time capsule too (deep, deeply) _____ under the school's home plate.

4. The other company won the bid (fair, fairly) _____.

5. (Late, Lately), _____ students haven't been able to finish their assignments on time.

YOUR TURN!

Circle any of the following words that were not capitalized appropriately:

The department of Extended Family Services has a fund for Children's services. This Fund includes money for Projects involving Expectant Mothers, for Projects involving the protection of Newborns and Young Children from early childhood Diseases, and for Projects involving the detection of Learning Disabilities in Preschool Children.

1.3 Commonly Confused Words

Word	Meaning
a	an article that comes before a "hard" sound
an	an article that comes before a "soft" sound (*an MP*)
a lot	many
alot	**do not use**
accent	speech coloration
ascent	a rise upward
assent	agreement
accept	to receive, take
except	most commonly means "but"
adapt	to change
adept	proficient
adopt	to take on
advice	an opinion
advise	to give an opinion (Note: *-ice* is usually the noun; *-ise* is usually the verb)
affect	verb: to change, alter
effect	noun: a result; verb: to bring about
allude	to make indirect reference to
elude	to avoid
assure	to confidently tell someone
ensure	to make sure
insure	to protect by buying a policy
all ready	everyone or everything is ready (Note: you can usually delete *all*)
already	by now, done before
all right	all correct (Note: you can usually delete *all*)
alright	**do not use**
all together	everything or everyone
altogether	completely
altar	a place to worship
alter	to change
among	with three or more
between	with two
anyway	anyhow
anyways	**do not use**
as	preposition (links, compares)
because	shows cause and effect; *because* can be used at the start of a sentence
due to	means "caused by"; do *not* start a sentence with *Due to . . .*

Word	Meaning
	due to describes a noun and usually follows a form of the verb *to be*: The cancellation of the fair was due to rain. *because of* describes a verb and answers *why* (cause and effect): The fair was cancelled because of rain.
beside	located next to
besides	in addition to
borrow	to receive something temporarily Please, never say, "Please borrow me your communications book."
loan	to give something temporarily; lend
bring	assumes an item will be coming
take	assumes an item will be going
can	ability
may	permission
might	probability
canvas	a fabric
canvass	to take a poll
capital	main, most important; seat of government
capitol	a legislative building
cite	to quote or recognize
site	a location
complement	complete
compliment	praise
continual	in succession
continuous	without stop
council	a committee or group
counsel	to give advice; an attorney
device	a thing
devise	to make, develop
disinterested	impartial, fair, without prejudice
uninterested	not interested
emigrant	(Hint: *e* = exit) a person who leaves a home country
immigrant	(Hint: *i* = in) a person who comes (in) to a new country
eminent	noteworthy, distinguished
imminent	likely to happen soon
e.g.	give or list specific examples (for example)
i.e.	that is (in other words)
farther	reference to measurable distance
further	in addition to; verb: to promote

(Continued)

(Continued)

Word	Meaning
imply	to suggest
infer	to reach a conclusion with or without evidence
it's	it is
its	possessive pronoun
later	after
latter	the last of two or more things
lay, laid, laid	to place (takes an object and answers the question *what*)
lie, lay, lain	to recline (takes no object and answers the question *where*)
lead	a metallic element
lead	a position at the front
lead	to direct on a course
led	past tense of *lead* (to direct on a course)
me	See section 1.7: Pronoun Case
myself	
I	
precede	to come before
proceed	to move forward
persecute	to torment
prosecute	to bring to a trial
personal	private, related to one person
personnel	a group of employees
principal	adjective: most important, high ranking, main; noun: head of a school, a sum of money
principle	truth or idea, belief
prophecy	noun: a prediction
prophesy	to predict
regardless	despite
irregardless	**do not use**
respectful	with respect
respective	in regard to
stationary	not moving
stationery	writing supplies (hint *e* = envelope)
than	a comparative
then	a time reference
that	introduces an essential clause; do not put a comma before it
which	introduces a non-essential clause; usually surrounded by commas
who	introduces a question/clause about a person or animal (do not use *that* or *which* to refer to people)

Word	Meaning
whom	objective form of *who* (see section 1.7: Pronoun Case)
their	belonging to; showing possession
there	a location
they're	contraction of *they are*
to	preposition: shows action/condition (*to write*)
too	also, excess
two	number (2)
weather	climatic condition
whether	which one of two choices
we're	contraction for *we are*
were	past tense of *are*
where	location
who's	contraction of *who is*
whose	ownership

YOUR TURN!

Circle the correct word for the blank in the following sentences:

1. (its/it's): _____ a new policy of the company to call a meeting and explain to the staff _____ policies.

2. (principal/principle): The _____ reason to study business communication is to improve how we work with others.

3. (assure/ensure/insure): Let me _____ you that the best way to _____ you are compensated for your Porsche's value if it is stolen, is to _____ the vehicle through Acme Financial Services.

4. (to/too/two): We had _____ go pick up spaghetti from the grocery store for our _____ school projects. You needed spaghetti _____, didn't you? The bridge projects were _____ funny!

5. (can/may/might): After practising for months, I _____ complete the statistical analysis. If we get our homework done, we _____ be allowed to play football for a couple of hours. Depending on Anwar's schedule, he _____ come and help us with accounting.

6. (as/because): There was still time to submit the bid _____ the deadline was a week away. _____ the snow was falling heavily, no one wanted to stay late.

7. (affect/effect): He was not aware that missing Monday morning classes could _____ his mark so much. By not attending classes Monday morning, he would _____ a grade of D in communication.

1.4 Modifiers (Dangling and Misplaced)

See the table on the next page for an explanation and for good and bad examples:

Modifier Type	Ooo, Bad! ☹	Yeah, Baby! ☺
Dangling modifiers It is not clear what the modifier is describing. Note: Each of these examples begins with a phrase. The phrase should describe the subject that follows right after it.	By selecting this option, the software will freeze.	If you select this option, the software will freeze.
	If properly installed, you shouldn't be able to open the CD writer without first pressing the safety button.	If the CD writer is properly installed, you shouldn't be able to open it without first pressing the safety button.
	While turning the corner, the 27-storey office tower can be seen.	While you're turning the corner, the 27-storey office tower can be seen.
Misplaced modifiers The modifier is placed so that it is very likely describing the wrong noun.	The new executive was eating his hot dog in a blue suit.	The new executive wore a blue suit while eating his hot dog.
	The accounting department was reviewing the budget, which worked through the evening.	The accounting department staff, who worked through the evening, were reviewing the budget.

YOUR TURN!

Rewrite the following sentences so they are clear:

1. The supervisor was evaluating the newest hire with a checklist.
2. While bathing, my boss called with news of my promotion.
3. Nibbling on kibble, the staff liked to watch the deer feed.
4. The fax machine was spewing out paper with the red panel.
5. After installation, I knew the software wasn't working right.

1.5 Parallelism

Parallelism problems can be tricky, and they generally occur in the following three areas:

- lists (especially on resumés!)
- verb forms
- sentence voice (passive, active)

The best way to explain parallelism is to show you good and bad examples of each. See the accompanying table.

Case	Ooo, Bad! ☹	Yeah, Baby! ☺
Lists One of the easiest ways to explain parallelism in a list is "one of these does not look like the others."	There are several ways to make your sentences clear: – Use the same form of the verb. – Spelling out acronyms when they are first used. – Paragraphs should contain only one thought.	There are several ways to make your sentences clear: – Use the same form of the verb. – Spell out acronyms when they are first used. – Limit paragraphs to only one thought.
Verb forms In the bad example, the verbs are not of the same form: one is the infinitive [to + verb] *to determine* and the other is a gerund [ends in *ing*] for *measuring*.	Students were tested to determine their basic grammar skills and for measuring their improvement.	Students were tested to determine their basic grammar skills and to measure their improvement.
Sentence order In the bad example, the first part of the sentence is active, while the second part of the sentence is passive.	The students used [*active*] lighter wheels to increase the distance the car travelled, but the tendency for the car to veer from a straight path was made [*passive*] worse.	The students used lighter wheels to increase the distance the car travelled, but the car tended to veer more from a straight path.

YOUR TURN!

Rewrite the following sentences so they are parallel:

1. While at Acme, I performed the following tasks:
   - project reports
   - productivity reports
   - reporting on building comfort issues

2. He put supplies in new locations and having all folders in numerical order to make them easier to find.

3. I gained a great deal of knowledge on the software by doing all inventory, documented parts lists, and cataloguing of parts.

4. Last summer, I filled new cabinets, organized and labelled office supply locations, as well as lots of painting and service part organization.

5. I helped produce the operator's guides and was also involved with its distribution.

1.6 Pronoun–Antecedent Agreement

A pronoun can replace a noun. The following table summarizes English pronouns, specifically their person (first, second, or third) and number (singular or plural). It also shows possessive and reflexive pronouns.

Person	Number Singular			
	Subject	**Object**	**Possessive**	**Reflexive**
First	I	me	my/mine	myself
Second	you	you	your/yours	yourself
Third	he/she	him/her	his/her his/hers	himself/ herself
	Plural			
	Subject	**Object**	**Possessive**	**Reflexive**
First	we	us	our/ours	ourselves
Second	you	you	your/yours	yourselves
Third	they	them	their/theirs	themselves

Four rules govern which pronoun to pick:

1. The pronoun must agree in sex (*male or female*).

   The man studied hard for her exam.

   (This sentence is grammatically incorrect!)

   The correct sentence would be *The man studied hard for his exam.* Easy, right?

2. The pronoun must agree in person (*first/second/third*).

   If he had not prepared for the exam, your mark would not be very good. One minute you are in the third person, *he*, then you are in the second, *your*. (Did *he* write your exam?)

   The correct sentence would be *If he had not prepared for the exam, his mark would not be very good.* Easy, right?

3. The pronoun must agree in number (*singular/plural*).

   Each man studied hard for their test.

   The sentence starts out singular, *each man*, but at the end of the sentence there are several, *their*. The

correct sentence would be *Each man studied hard for his test.* This example shows a common error.

But what if the people are not all *he*?

Be careful with words like *everyone, anyone, anybody, each, neither, nobody, someone.* They may look plural, but they are singular:

> Incorrect: *Anyone* [singular subject] who *is* [singular verb] interested in buying the old photocopier can submit *their* [plural pronoun] bids by email.

The intention of this sentence is plural, so a better sentence would be: *All staff members* [plural] *who are* [plural] interested in buying the old photocopier can submit *their* [plural pronoun] bids by email.

4. The pronoun must refer clearly to a specific noun. Generally, a pronoun refers back to the closest noun. Sometimes that may confuse your reader as shown in the following:

Ooo, Bad! ☹	Yeah, Baby! ☺
Although the coffee mug fell on the proposal, it was not damaged. (*Is it the mug or the proposal?*)	Although the coffee mug fell on the proposal, the document was not damaged.
They are always having safety meetings here. (*Who are "they"?*)	Safety meetings happen frequently here.
Our salary increases are coming soon, which is great. (*What is great: the increase or when it takes place?*)	It is great that our salary will increase at the end of the quarter.
George worked in a marketing and advertising firm for the last three years. This may be what he'll be doing here. (*Be careful of words like* this, those, these, *and* that. *You know what you mean, but your reader may not.*)	George worked in a marketing and advertising firm for the last three years. Marketing may be what he'll be doing here.
Three cars stopped to help us, and they lifted the car off Terry's arm. (*How, exactly, did the other cars help lift the car off Terry's arm?*)	Three cars stopped and their passengers came to help us lift the car off Terry's arm.

See also "Modifiers (Dangling and Misplaced)." Pronouns must clearly replace nouns. Pronouns must also be balanced in sex, number, and person.

1.7 Pronoun Case

This section focuses on whether to use *he* or *him*, *she* or *her*, *I* or *me*, and so on. Grammatically speaking, you are concerned with using the correct subjective, objective, and possessive pronoun cases. Most grammar books will leave your head spinning with words like *subjective*, *objective*, *indirect object*, *object of the preposition*, and so on. Never fear—you can use some tricks:

Confusing Example	Remove-Word Trick	Add-Word Trick
	When you see the word *and*, remove the "easy" pronoun along with *and*.	Remember parallelism? Add words that emphasize parallelism.
Samson typed out the minutes for you and *I/me*.	Samson typed out the minutes for ~~you and~~ *I/me*. Ans: Samson typed out the minutes for you and *me*.	Samson typed out the minutes *for you* and *for I/me*. Ans: Samson typed out the minutes *for you and me*.
He/Him and I went to the satellite office.	*He/Him* ~~and I~~ went to the satellite office. Ans: *He* and I went to the satellite office.	*He/Him* went to the satellite office and I went to the satellite office. Ans: *He* and I went to the satellite office.
Dan got the promotion because he had more education than *me/I*.	In a comparison, try flipping the essential part of the sentence around: *I/me* had less education than Dan. Ans: Dan got the promotion because he had more education than *I*.	Dan got the promotion because he had more education than *me/I* did. Ans: Dan got the promotion because he had more education than *I* did.

(Continued)

(Continued)

Confusing Example	Remove-Word Trick	Add-Word Trick
Having smaller classes lets *we/us* students feel that our instructors are here to help.	**When removing the word(s) works** In *we/us students*, the word *students* describes *we* or *us*. Try taking out the descriptor to see what you have: Having smaller classes lets *we/us* feel that our instructors are here to help. Ans: Having smaller classes lets *us* students feel that our instructors are here to help. Better ans: Having smaller classes lets students feel that instructors are here to help.	

NOTE: In the preceding examples, it is considered polite to put ourselves (*I, me, we, us*) second to the other pronouns.

The following examples are both right, but they mean different things. Adding words allows us to see the different meanings.

Example	Explanation
The supervisor, Federico, paid me better than her.	The word *her* is an object. Objects receive action and usually come after a subject. To keep *her* as an object, you could add the subject in after the comparison words: *The supervisor, Federico, paid me better than he paid her.*
The supervisor, Federico, paid me better than she.	In this case, the word *she* is a subject. Subjects give action and usually come before an object. To keep *she* as a subject, you could add the object after the comparison words: *The supervisor, Federico, paid me better than she paid me.*

In the previous two examples, it is important to know what you want to say and not to leave the reader confused. You may leave the extra words in, so your reader can understand. Now that you've tackled *he/him*, *she/her*, *I/me*, *we/us*, you can relax knowing that the dreaded *who/whom* is tackled the same way: *Who* is the subjective case, and *whom* is the objective case. *Hint: Whom* should follow a preposition (*with whom, for whom, to whom*).

Reflexive Pronoun Misuse (The Hideous, Evil Misuse of *Myself*)

Do not substitute *myself* for the word *me* or *I*. This is a common mistake and the following Ooo, Bad! examples abound in every workplace:

Ooo, Bad! ☹	Yeah, Baby ☺
Send your suggestions to *myself*.	Send your suggestions to *me*.
Louisa works with Raymon and *myself*.	Louisa works with Raymon and *me*.
Myself and Ruth wrote the instructions.	Ruth and *I* wrote the instructions.
The boss and his apprentice told Fred and *myself* to take a hike.	The boss and his apprentice told Fred and *me* to take a hike.
Fred and *myself* took a hike.	Fred and *I* took a hike.

The word *myself* is reflexive. It needs to reflect back to its singular first-person subject, *I*.

So, when should you use the word *myself*? Use *myself* only if the word *I* comes before it in the same sentence.

See how the reflexive pronoun calls attention to the subject of the sentence:

> I completed the project.

> I completed the project myself. (No one else helped me.)

Use the other reflexive pronouns (*yourself, himself, herself, ourselves, yourselves,* and *themselves*) in the same way. Each reflexive pronoun must reflect back to a noun of the same gender and number.

YOUR TURN!

Circle the correct word for the blank in the following sentences:

1. Samson made _____ (him, himself) eat the tasteless rice cakes.

2. The company told _____ (myself, me, I) last Friday to take a hike.

3. When it comes to procrastination, I know _____ (myself, me, I) better than anyone else.

4. When you have finished your proposal, bring it to _____ (myself, me, I) for editing.

5. _____ (Who, Whom) shall I tell him is calling?

6. Look after _____ (you, yourself).

7. Sandu and Renata had not heard from Mortimer, _____ [who, whom] was on stress leave.

1.8 Run-On Sentences

Every sentence must have one subject (what the sentence is about) and one predicate (what the subject is doing, i.e., the verb). See **Figure A-1**.

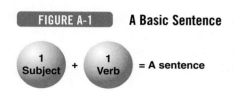

FIGURE A-1 **A Basic Sentence**

One perfectly fine sentence, for example, is *Rufus howled*. One subject and one predicate is all you need—no more! But what if you want to write more? How about *Rufus howled, Stuffy hissed*? The problem with this sentence is that you have exceeded the limit of one subject and one verb. This is called a run-on sentence. In fact, you have two sentences illegally joined.

To legally have more than one subject and one predicate, you have several tools you can use. See **Figure A-2** for ways to fix the sentence *Rufus howled, Stuffy hissed*.

Note that each fix may change the meaning of the sentence. The best way to fix a run-on sentence depends on what you are trying to say.

YOUR TURN!

Choose several ways to fix the following run-on sentences:

1. A run-on sentence is one thing a sentence fragment is something else.

2. There was a dangerous virus in the operating system unfortunately I didn't find it before it found me.

3. I have always wanted to drive a Bugatti I like fast cars.

4. The MAP sensor functions as two different sensors the MAP's primary function is to tell the ECM how much load is being placed on the engine.

HUMDINGER WARNING!

5. Be careful when writing emails and text messages:

   didn't you want to know how things went last week just to let you know also that im going to be taking that week before school starts off and really think im going to be done with the program cause i think i can't anyways cause i was on probation and because stan was being an ass i might not even have a gpa of 1 just to vent i guess lol i might come in sometime then when you going to be in

| FIGURE A-2 | Tools You Can Use to Fix Run-On Sentences |

Case	Pretty Graphic	Example
Period	SV1. SV2	*Rufus howled. Stuffy hissed.* **Note:** a comma is **not** enough to fix a run-on sentence!
Conjunction	SV1 **and** SV2	*Rufus howled **and** Stuffy hissed.*
Subordinate clauses	SV2 / SV1	Make the second part depend on the first part. *Rufus howled **while** Stuffy hissed.*
Subordinate clauses	SV1 / SV2	Make the first part depend on the second part **While** *Rufus howled, Stuffy hissed.*
Semicolon	SV1; SV2	(**Note:** the two sentences must be very closely related.) *Rufus howled; Stuffy hissed.*
Semicolon with a conjunctive adjective or transitional phrase (whoa!)	SV1; **however,** SV2 / SV1; **all the while,** SV2	**Conjunctive adjective** *Rufus howled; **however,** Stuffy hissed.* **Transitional phrase** *Rufus howled; **all the while,** Stuffy hissed.*

Case	Example	Correction
The sentence has no subject. Ask *who* or *what* the sentence is about.	I learned to use new software. Using Microsoft Project and Excel to do Gantt charts, progress reports, and project completion reports. *Note: This error is common. The first sentence is fine. The second sentence has no subject. Because of the first sentence, the reader is left to assume you are still talking about I.*	I learned to use new software. I used Microsoft Project and Excel to do Gantt charts, progress reports, and project completion reports.
The sentence has no main verb in it.	My apologies for not calling you last week. *Note: Action words inside phrases and clauses (e.g., calling) are not the main verbs in the sentence.*	I apologize for not calling you last week.
The sentence starts with a subordinating word (e.g., *because, although, that, which*) and the sentence has no logical completion.	Because the blizzard had turned the road from the chalet into ice. *Note: You can start a sentence with* because, *but be sure to finish the sentence!*	Because the blizzard had turned the road from the chalet into ice, the sales staff could not return from their meeting on Friday.

In some grammatical errors, the reader can guess what you meant. With sentence fragments, you cannot assume your reader knows what you meant. Essential information is missing, and you are the only one who knows what it is!

YOUR TURN!

Edit the following sentences to eliminate sentence fragments:

1. As I sat reading my clumsy instructions. I recalled my instructor in continuing education. Telling me how to write for the reader. And remembered what she taught me: all writing should be clear, concise, and correct.

1.9 Sentence Fragments

In a sentence fragment, a subject or predicate (action word) is missing. Use the following to test whether the sentence is a fragment:

2. It has been said that there are only three good operating systems. Linux, Windows XP, and Windows 2000.

3. We need to stop believing two myths about document design. That two spaces are required after a period and that you underline information to emphasize it.

4. When we downloaded the file. We saw the virus warning. A message inside a typical pop-up window.

5. I would like to learn more about manufacturing and enterprise resource planning to save time with filing and planning. Some of which were encountered this summer.

1.10 Subject–Verb Agreement

You would think that nothing could be simpler than ensuring your subjects and verbs agree. You would not say *The office manager are revising the accounting software*. Well, many disguises can hide your real subject. You need to do three things to keep your assignment marks high, in spite of this grammatical issue:

1. Find the subject.
2. Determine whether the subject is singular or plural.
3. Match the verb to the subject's number (singular or plural).

To help you with this supposedly simple task, let us examine three subject disguises.

Phrase Disguises

The photocopiers were recalled. No problem. *Photocopiers* is plural and so is *were*. All is well.

The number of the recalled photocopiers was/were small. What is the subject here? If you think it's *photocopiers . . .* sorry. The subject is *number*. The term *of the recalled photocopiers* is called a phrase and describes the noun number. *The number of recalled photocopiers was small* is correct. *The number of* is like *the group of*. The emphasis is on the size of the number, which is a single entity.

A number of the photocopiers was/were recalled. Even though this sentence seems similar to the previous, it uses *a* instead of *the*. *A number of* is very similar to the word *some* or *several*, both of which are plural nouns. *A number of [Some] of the photocopiers* were recalled.

How about this?

The office manager, along with her staff, is/are recommending the new project management software. Surely this is a plural subject. No. The words *along with her staff* form a phrase that could be removed from the sentence without changing the sentence's structure. You could use a compound subject and treat it as a plural entity instead. Use *and*: *The office manager and her staff are recommending the new project management software.*

Order Disguises

The greatest difficulty is/are the problems associated with discrimination. In this sentence the subject is at the beginning of the sentence. *The greatest difficulty* is singular, so use *is* regardless of the plural descriptor on the other side of the verb.

The staff members is/are Acme's greatest asset. In this sentence *The staff members* is plural, so use *are* regardless of the singular descriptor on the other side of the verb. All is well.

How about the following?

Accounting and engineering is/are moving to the other location. This should be easy. Use *are* because you have a compound subject.

Where is/are accounting and engineering moving to? Even though the sentence order is reversed because it is a question, the subject is still *accounting and engineering*. Use *are*.

There is/are many proposals still open. Frequently, the word *there* is a wasted word (i.e., *Many proposals are still open*). What is the real subject, and is it plural or singular? The real subject is *many proposals*, so use *are*.

Here comes an exception: The word *it* is similar to the word *there* in that they are both called expletives. They are placeholders and mean little. But *it* is singular, no matter what: *It is/are a shame that she didn't get a promotion.* No-brainer again: use *is*.

It is/are a shame and an insult that she didn't get a promotion. Even though a compound construction is on the other side of the verb, the sentence's verb is still driven by the word *it*, so use *is*. *It are a shame . . .?* That doesn't work!

It is/are many things to many people. Even though the plural construction on the other side of the verb is obvious, the sentence's verb is still driven by the word *it*, so use *is*.

Singular/Plural Disguises

Case	Words	Examples
Some nouns that look plural can have singular or plural meanings.	scissors, pants, pliers, tongs, odds, tactics, ethics	My scissors are lost. *In this case, it is not obvious how many pairs of scissors are lost. The usage is plural, but there may be only one pair.* The odds are against it.
Some nouns can be considered both singular and plural (*-ics* words).	politics, statistics fish	Politics is a fascinating subject. The new mayor's politics are frightening.
Some nouns look plural but take a singular noun.	news, Hearts (card game), mathematics, chicken pox	The news was sweeping through the office.
Collective nouns can be used as either	staff, family	The staff was queried by the RCMP. *This means the staff as a group was questioned.* The staff were queried by the RCMP. *This means each staff member was questioned individually.*
A compound entity, which is really one thing, is singular.	macaroni and cheese	My macaroni and cheese is fattening but delicious. The hammer and sickle is still a striking emblem.
Words adopted from Latin and Greek are not made plural by adding *-s*.	stimulus/stimuli, criterion/criteria, medium/media, phenomenon/phenomena, data (*dictionaries show* data *as either singular or plural*)	Office media include email, phones, and SharePoint. Weather phenomena are exciting to watch.
Nouns of amount can be singular or plural.	money, weight, time, and so on	Five times four is twenty. (Five times four *is a single concept.*) Five days is a long time to finish this assignment. Five hours were needed to finish this assignment. Thirty-five dollars is needed to pay the speeding ticket. Thirty-five loonies (Canadian, eh!) were found in the coffee cupboard.
Indefinite pronouns are misleading. Many people think *everyone* and *everybody* are plural, but they are not. Other examples are provided.	**Singular** everyone, everybody, everything, anyone, anybody, anything, no one, nobody, nothing, someone, somebody, something, each, another, either, neither, little, much	Much is covered in English grammar books. Sometimes too much is covered!
	Plural Both, several, few, many	Several employees were hanging around the water cooler.
	Depends Any, more, some, enough, all, most, who, half, none	None of the proposal is ready for editing. (Proposal *is a singular noun, so use a singular verb.*) None of the employees are ready for the presentation. (Employees *is a plural noun, so use a plural verb.*)

(Continued)

Case	Words	Examples
	either/or and neither/nor *Hint:* Look at the word that is closest to the verb to determine whether the expression is singular or plural. *Hint:* If you have plural and singular nouns in *either/or* or *neither/nor* expressions, the order doesn't matter. It may be better to put the plural noun at the end and use the plural verb.	Either Bill or Shareen is available to play baseball this year. Neither the employees nor the manager is taking a vacation this year. Neither the manager nor the employees are taking a vacation this year.

Whether a noun or pronoun is singular or plural may depend on how it is being used. Consider *bacon and eggs*, which has a plural focus, or *snakes and ladders*, which has a singular focus (i.e., *the game of*). Ensure you are using the subject correctly as a singular or plural entity.

YOUR TURN!

Correct the following sentences to ensure subject–verb agreement:

1. One of our friends are winning the city's Entrepreneur of the Year award.
2. Sixty dollars are the entrance fee.
3. We build trucks like a rock!
4. Everyone at Acme is required to have their work assessed on an annual basis.
5. The only benefit of switching our health plan for our staff members are the many ways of accessing the refunds.
6. Sally or the twins is usually late for the golf tournament.

2. PUNCTUATION

2.1 Apostrophes and Possessives

Use apostrophes in the following applications:

- possessives (*The manager's toy is a Jeep.*)
- contractions (*I can't see why she wanted a Jeep.*)
- replacement for missing letters and numbers (*Back in '08, all reports had to be done by 10 o'clock.*)
- uncommon plurals (*I got three A's on my transcript.*)

This section describes when not to use apostrophes, when to be extra careful, and where the apostrophe goes to show possession.

When Not to Use an Apostrophe

1. Do not use apostrophes with possessive pronouns (*its, his, hers, ours, yours, whose, theirs*). They already show possession.
2. Do not use apostrophes just because you have a noun ending in *-s*: *CFL players take a lot of abuse during a football game.* Plural nouns followed by a verb cannot be possessive. You can't own a verb.

When to Be Extra Careful

Many people mix up words like *there's/theirs, you're/your, who's/whose*, and, of course, *its/it's*. See section 1.3: Commonly Confused Words, and consider all the words in that table as red flags. When you need to use a red flag word, double check to ensure that you have used the right one.

Location, Location, Location

Where, oh where, does that little ' go when you need to show possession? This hint is going to make your life so much easier: Simply rewrite the expression backward and use the words *of (the)*. See the following example:

FERNANDOS SISTER

1. Flip it around to become *sister of Fernando*. (If you cannot flip it around, the sentence may not show possession.)
2. Draw a line where the expression ends (after *Fernando*).

   sister of Fernando/.

3. The line goes after the *o* and so this is where you put the apostrophe (Fernando's sister). Wherever you put the line at the end of the *of* phrase is where you put the apostrophe. Too easy!

Let us try more . . .

Example	Converting to *of the*	Putting the ' Where the Line Was
the Rough Riders win	the win of the Rough Riders/	the Rough Riders' win
the mens hats	the hats of the men/	the men's hats
the tables legs	the legs of the table/ (1 table) or the legs of the tables/ (more than 1 table) (*How many tables do you have? As the writer, you will know this.*)	the table's legs or the tables' legs
James math book	the math book of James/	James' math book or (*both are correct!*) James's math book Note: if *-s's* is awkward to pronounce, the last *-s* may be dropped (*Descartes'* ideas).
The locker shared by Liz and Lacey	the locker of Liz and Lacey/	Liz and Lacey's locker
What if Liz and Lacey each have their own lockers?	the locker of Liz/ and the locker of Lacey/	Liz's locker and Lacey's locker or Liz's and Lacey's lockers
my mother-in-laws locker	the locker of my mother-in-law/	my mother-in-law's locker
What if you have two mothers-in-law and they both have lockers? (*Just kidding! How could you have two mothers-in-law?*)	the lockers of my friends/ mothers-in-law/	my friends' mothers-in-law's lockers (scary but correct)

Last, but not least, how do you remember *its* and *it's*? The hint is easy: If you can separate *its* into *it is* or *it has,* then the contraction needs an apostrophe.

Examples:

1. *Give the dog its bone.* Can you say *Give the dog it is bone*? No, and so there is no apostrophe.

2. *I like going to class when its not snowing.* Can you say *I like going to class when it is not snowing*? Yes. You can separate it, and so you need an apostrophe: *I like going to class when it's not* snowing.

Another way to remember *its* versus *it's* is that none of the possessive pronouns (*his, hers, ours, yours, theirs*) has an apostrophe, so *its,* as a possessive pronoun, does not get one either.

YOUR TURN!

Add or delete apostrophes as required in the following sentences:
1. The dog ate its biscuit greedily.
2. Mens and womens washrooms are located in the stores basement.
3. In the 80s, the Blue Bombers talent was as good as anyones.
4. Kids clothes are on the second floor.
5. Keeping up with the Joneses is difficult since the Jones house is such an expensive one.
6. The house was hers, the car was his, and the children we're theirs'.
7. Its a mystery why Lois measles don't clear up.
8. We bought more than fifty dollars worth of meat.
9. All of the secretarys desks were moved to clean the office.
10. Last weeks work remained unfinished because many employee's were off sick.

2.2 Brackets

See section 2.7: Parentheses and Brackets.

2.3 Colons and Semicolons

Colons	Semicolons
Use a colon after an independent clause to introduce a list, an appositive, or a quotation: **A list** (*following*, or *as follows* **is commonly included**) Writers should be experts in the following areas: grammar, punctuation, and plain English. **An appositive** My program is guilty of two problems: crashing and freezing. **A quotation** Consider the words of Steve DeMarco: "You cannot control what you cannot measure."	*Use a semicolon between closely related independent clauses not joined by a coordinating conjunction (e.g., and).* A run-on sentence is one thing; a sentence fragment is something else.
Use a colon between independent clauses if the second summarizes or explains the first. Minds are like parachutes: they function only when open.	*Use a semicolon between independent clauses linked by a transitional expression (conjunctive adverb or transitional phrase).* A run-on sentence is one thing; however, a sentence fragment is something else. A run-on sentence is one thing; on the other hand, a sentence fragment is something else.
Other uses Salutation (Dear Madam:) (using a colon at the end of a salutation is considered very formal) Time (5:30 p.m.) Ratios (2:1) Title and subtitles (*Xena: Warrior Princess*) Bibliography (London: Associated Press) Biblical reference (John 3:16)	*Use a semicolon between items in a series that contains internal punctuation* Several characters appear in both *Hercules* and *Xena*: Hercules, with his sidekick, Iolaus; Atolicus, by himself; Aries, with his sidekick, Discord; Joxter, with his stupid hat; and, of course, Xena and Gabrielle, with their assortment of well-used weapons.
Colon misuses *Between a verb and its object or complement* (do **not** place a colon here) Good courses for technical writers to take are ⊗ planning, manuals, plain English, and document design. *Between a preposition and its object* Their manuals consisted of ⊗ a cover, a title page, a table of contents, an introduction, and a conclusion. *After the words such as, including* They took some of their favourite courses, such as ⊗ math, English, and physics.	

YOUR TURN!

Edit the following sentences. You may have to add or delete colons and semicolons, or change them to more appropriate punctuation.

1. The business world really needs workers who see the bigger picture work with others well and put the company's goals first.
2. Please follow these three simple steps when completing the form print your last name first, your first name, and then your middle initial.
3. Kim achieved her goals in life she became an accountant and a mystery writer.
4. The new computer store is open instead of selling new PCs, it sells only used ones.
5. I really like Accounting Wizard for this application you should try it.
6. I find Acme's products easy to use however I also find they crash easily.
7. We recommended several changes at work, such as: taking regular breaks working with subject matter experts and peer editing each other's work.
8. Bill's office party list included: beer, wine, and coolers.

2.4 Commas

Ho hum . . . yawn! Why would you need a lesson on commas? As it turns out, the kamikaze comma is

Case	Ooo, Bad! ☹	Yeah, Baby! ☺
Use a comma before a coordinating conjunction (*and, but, for, or, so, yet*) that introduces an independent clause (a clause that can stand on its own as a sentence).	The office party got totally out of hand, I got sick. (*See also run-on sentences.*)	The office party got totally out of hand, and I got sick. *Note: If both independent clauses are short, you may omit the comma.*
Use a comma after a coordinating adverb (*finally, furthermore, however, indeed, meanwhile, nonetheless, otherwise, therefore, unfortunately*).	Everyone at the office party had a great time, however I got sick. (*See also run-on sentences.*)	Everyone at the office party had a great time; however, I got sick.
Use a comma after an introductory phrase or clause (subordinate).	Because everyone at the office party had a great time I was reluctant to tell anyone I was sick. *Note: The guideline states that if the introductory statement is short you may omit the comma, but check out the following:* While I was eating my supervisor called with news of my termination. *Note: Eating your supervisor pretty much guarantees your termination!*	Because everyone at the office party had a great time, I was reluctant to tell anyone I was sick. While I was eating, my supervisor called with news of my termination. (*See also modifiers.*)
Use commas to emphasize adverbs.	Jon prepared quickly the budget for the meeting.	Jon prepared, quickly, the budget for the meeting.
Use commas around a word or group of words that come after but describe a noun. This is called an *appositive*. Note that the subject and verb are too far apart without the commas.	The new supervisor all tanned and fresh from her vacation locked herself in her office to start next year's budget.	The new supervisor, all tanned and fresh from her vacation, locked herself in her office to start next year's budget.
Use a comma when emphasizing an aside.	The office party crazy as it was was a good chance for staff to lighten up.	The office party, crazy as it was, was a good chance for staff to lighten up.
Use commas in lists. Most people know to use commas in a list, but two problems remain: 1. How to use a comma with semicolons (described in section 2.3: Colons and Semicolons). 2. When do you use a comma before the last item? In the previous example, either sentence is fine because the list items are simple. If the list items are complex or contain *and*, use a comma to avoid confusion.	This sales office supports Manitoba Saskatchewan Alberta and British Columbia. When the boss is on holiday the staff enjoy setting up mini-golf in the cafeteria, playing charades and playing board games and cards during lunch.	This sales office supports Manitoba, Saskatchewan, Alberta and British Columbia. This sales office supports Manitoba, Saskatchewan, Alberta, and British Columbia. When the boss is on holiday, the staff enjoy setting up mini-golf in the cafeteria, playing charades, and playing board games and cards during lunch.
Use a comma between consecutive adjectives as appropriate. This one is a bit tougher but there a couple of tricks you can use. – If the word *and* would fit between the adjectives and the sentence still makes sense, use a comma. – If you could switch the order of the adjectives, use a comma. Do not put a comma before the noun being described.	The photocopier was dark, beige, small, and fast. *Note: You cannot switch* dark *and* beige. *Putting* and *between* dark and beige *doesn't work either. Dark describes the shade of beige, so no comma goes between these words.*	The photocopier was dark beige, small, and fast.
Use a comma after open and closing salutations in a closed punctuated letter. (Open punctuation letters do not have punctuation after the salutations.)		Dear Sir, Dear Ms. Jones,
Use a comma to directly address someone.	I've told you Cindy to stop lurking at the water cooler.	I've told you, Cindy, to stop lurking at the water cooler.
Use a comma in addresses and dates.	The incident occurred in Thunder Bay Ontario on August 17 2008.	The incident occurred in Thunder Bay, Ontario, on August 17, 2008.

Avoid the "comma-kazi" comma.

the most common and most misused punctuation mark. The problems with commas are that sometimes they must be used, sometimes they cannot be used, and sometimes they are optional. If you insert commas when you are writing, you may end up inserting them every time your brain goes off to think deep thoughts. If you insert commas when you are proofreading, you may insert them where you pause naturally. Neither of these methods ensures you are following the rules. To avoid the "comma-kazi" comma, see the guidelines on the previous page.

YOUR TURN!

Edit the following sentences. You may have to add commas, delete commas, or change a comma to more appropriate punctuation.

1. When the secretary went to the conference the staff were exhausted trying to answer the phones pacify angry customers and get all their own work done.
2. Because, no one had time to complete the media brief I was upset when the job became my responsibility.
3. The golf game went really well, I won.
4. The presentations all completed in the latest software refused to load on the comptroller's laptop. We searched with great haste for another laptop.
5. As I explained to you Mr. Black the company should have changed suppliers.
6. While I was washing my brother called with news of a possible job.

2.5 Dashes (Em and En!)

Em Dashes

An em dash is a lively way to emphasize an expression. Do not use two hyphens. If your word processor

does not automatically convert two hyphens (- -) to —, then type [Alt+0151] on your keypad, or insert the em dash as a special character. You don't need to include spaces before and after the em dash (although some style guides include them as a style choice).

Use	Example
To link to related parts of a sentence	Always buckle your seat belt—it's the law.
To emphasize a parenthetical expression	Business communication—the language of the workplace—must be concise.
To separate a long appositive (words that describe the subject) or an appositive with lots of commas	Our office requires that writers use plain English—a way of writing that ensures everyone who reads your information will understand it the first time.
To sum up a list or expand a concept	Organization, formatting, and plain English—these are the writer's tools.

En Dashes

An en dash usually replaces the word *to* and is generally used with numbers. In MS Word, you can insert one by typing [Alt+0150] by using keypad, or you can insert the en dash as a special character. Note that there is no space before or after the en dash.

Use	Example
Distance range	4–6 km
Time span	2008–10; 6–8 seconds
Page numbers	Information on that subject is found on pages 234–237.

2.6 Hyphens

Hyphens create a single unit from two or more words that may mean something different from the individual parts. See the examples that follow:

Use	Example
Two or more words functioning as a single unit (see also "Compound adjectives and adverbs," below)	state-of-the-art
Compound adjectives and adverbs	**Compound adjectives** The *heavy-duty* photocopier took on a devilish green glow. His *full-time* job was at night. His job was *full time* and it was at night. (*Notice that when the adjective comes after the noun it describes, it does not need to be hyphenated.*) *Here's another example:* I gave him a *short-term* loan. The loan I gave him was *short term.* **Compound adverbs** The *hard-hitting* batter had four home runs last game. The group congratulated Stefan on his *well-written* report. *Note: In general, do not hyphenate adverbs ending in -ly or adverbs that follow whatever they are modifying:* The team felt they had written a *poorly* conceived document. The document was *poorly* conceived. *Dictionaries can also help you if you need to argue your point with your instructor!*
Two-word numbers when they are written out	thirty-six
Words combined with certain prefixes (*ex-*, *quasi-*, *semi-*, and *self-* use hyphens when used as prefixes and placed in front of other words)	ex-husband quasi-scientific semi-retired self-guided
Prefixes when the first letter of the next word begins with a capital letter	When the national anthem began, all the pro-Canadian fans rose to their feet.
A way to eliminate confusion	recover (*to find, or to get better*) re-cover (*to put a new cover on*)
Words that are suspended in a sentence	The lease can be offered with either a three- to four-year buyout option. *Note: If dangling hyphens make you uncomfortable, try rewriting your sentences to avoid them:* The lease can be bought out after three or four years.
Phone numbers	604-555-1212
Numerical unit adjectives	Most instructors find a ten-point font too small to read comfortably.

How are you going to remember which words are hyphenated and which are not? Don't trust your memory or your spell checker. Use a good dictionary and be consistent.

Some basic rules follow for where you put the hyphen at a line break:

- Do not hyphenate short words. It is better to extend slightly into the margin or manually place the word on the next line. To do this in some word processors, put your cursor before the word you don't want hyphenated and press shift+enter.

- Use a dictionary to show you where to hyphenate, especially those words with double consonants.

- Do not hyphenate if you will leave only one or two letters alone on a line.

- Do not use a hyphen to begin list items. Use en dashes or bullets instead.

YOUR TURN!

Edit the following for en-dash, em-dash, and hyphen misuses.

1. A meaningful job, a loving spouse, and a car that won't break down, these are the things new graduates want.

2. Jun. 2009 – Sept. 2011

   My work included

   - filing clients' invoices
   - calling clients to set up scheduled maintenance visits
   - logging maintenance visits into service schedules

3. You should write thirty three as 33.

4. After he had recovered from the flu, he had to recover his grandmother's sofa.

5. I request, no, I demand, that you stay late to finish the presentation.

2.7 Parentheses and Brackets

Parentheses ( ) are used in pairs (open and closed) around extra information in a sentence, similar to dashes. Parentheses are used when you want to whisper the extra information; dashes are used when you want to shout the extra information. Do not overuse parentheses. Parentheses are used as follows:

Case	Example
To add supplemental information	The third proposal (due March 30) was never submitted.
To add numbers, such as in lists run into the text or set as a displayed list	To run the new copier, (1) press the ON button, (2) clear all previous jobs, (3) insert your original, and (4) pray. or 1) Press the ON button. 2) Clear all previous jobs. 3) Insert your original. 4) Pray.

Brackets [ ] are used in pairs (open and closed) for writing your personal or "editorial" comments to your reader, as shown in the following typical uses:

Case	Example
To add extra information to a direct quotation	The RRR Agency reported, "New generations [e.g., Gen Y and Gen X] are having a profound impact on the busyness [*sic*] environment."
To show that the original quote contained an error [*sic*]	

Always consult your American Psychological Association (APA), Modern Language Association (MLA), or other required style guide when quoting sources.

2.8 Quotation Marks

Use quotation marks[2] (" and ") in the following cases:

- direct verbal quotations (exactly what someone said)

  Note: Unspoken thoughts do not need quotation marks.

- direct written quotations (exactly what someone wrote)

  Note: If you are required to comply with a specific format specified by a style guide, such as the *Publication Manual of the APA*, the *MLA Style Manual*, or the *Chicago Manual of Style*, refer to the specific style guide. Be especially vigilant when referencing citations.

- doubts or sarcasm (*You want me to use this "computer"? My gerbil runs faster.*)

- definitions (*The project management institute defines project management as "the application of knowledge, skills, tools, and techniques to project activities to meet project requirements."*)

- sayings (*The new employee was "as dumb as dirt."*)

- labels (*The front panel said, "Disconnect power before opening."*)

- silly use of a word or slang (*The new cafeteria serves "double-doubles."*)

The table shows on the next page how quotation marks work with other punctuation.

Other Punctuation	Rule	Example
, or .	Always go inside the quotation marks	Marty said, "Hello." "Hello," Marty said.
; and :	Always go outside the quotation marks	Anwar said, "I'll make sure the proposal goes out on time"; I'll believe that when I see it. Anwar meant one thing when he said, "Get the proposal out on time": my job was on the line.
' and '	Quotation inside a quotation	Morticia said, "Herman had replied, 'Over my dead body,' to my sheer delight."
!	Placement depends on whether the sentence or the quotation requires the exclamation	*The sentence is an exclamation* I will scream if he says, "You have homework tonight"! *The quotation is an exclamation* "Be careful!" the instructor yelled. *Both the sentence and the quotation are exclamations* I will scream if he exclaims, "You have a lot of homework tonight!"

2.9 Semicolons

See 2.3 Colons and Semicolons.

3. PLAIN ENGLISH

Just because something has been written in a grammatically correct way does not mean it has been written in plain English. The mechanics of plain English entail writing in a way that your reader can understand your words the first time they are read. Plain English is clear and concise, and embraces the keep-it-simple (KIS) concept. In this fast-paced technological age, it is sometimes difficult—but it is essential—to use plain English.

Several concepts are associated with plain English: active and passive voice, wasted words, nominalization, and lists. Three other concepts covered in this section are numbers, abbreviations, and non-sexist writing.

3.1 Active and Passive Voices

The active voice (doer → action → receiver) is usually shorter and much more straightforward. It is more direct and active! Take a look at the following two sentences:

Active: The office manager rejected the new lease agreement. *Notice how the order here is doer → action word → receiver.*

Passive: The new lease agreement was rejected by the office manager. *The passive voice follows the order of receiver → action → doer.*

But how do you know if the voice is passive or active? How do you know which is the doer and which is the receiver of the action?

> Note: Passive voice is not the same as past tense.

You can tell in three ways whether a sentence uses active voice:

- If the order of the sentence is receiver → action → doer, the sentence is passive.
- If you see *by* followed by a doer, the sentence is passive.
- If you see a form of the verb *to be* (e.g., *are, is, was, were*), the sentence is likely passive.
- If you cannot find a doer, the sentence must also be passive (e.g., *The new lease agreement was rejected*).

Note that the doer does not have to be a person (e.g., *The printing was done by our in-house photocopier* [passive] versus *Our in-house photocopier did our printing* [active]).

How do you convert a passive sentence to active? Let's try another example:

The reports were completed by the new staff.

Step	Action	Result
1	Find the verb.	*completed*
2	Find who or what is doing the work of the verb.	Who is completing something? Right! *The new staff*
3	If the doer of the verb does not come before the verb, move it so it does. Delete excess words, such as *by* and *were*.	*The new staff completed*
4	Put the receiver of the action after the verb.	*The new staff completed* the reports.

Is this fun or what?

Note that the passive voice (receiver → action → doer) is not incorrect, but you should try to use the active voice, except for the following three cases:

- You don't know who the doer is (e.g., *The office downtown was set on fire*).
- You don't want to blame the doer (e.g., *The customer's equipment was poorly maintained*).
- You don't care who the doer is (e.g., *My Bugatti Veyron was delivered this morning*). This final case occurs frequently in business and technical writing because what happened is more important than who did it.

YOUR TURN!

Convert the following sentences to active voice:[3]

1. April's project meeting minutes were approved by the district manager, Anil Khalek.
2. We shipped the new software by noon, but the customer still hasn't received it.
3. The corporate bully was fired last Monday for harassment.
4. The marketing department's computers at Acme will be networked by a central file server that was designed by the Atlantis IT department.
5. It was recommended by the project manager that the proposal should be proofread again by the team.

HUMDINGER WARNING!

6. Verification of the agreement was indicated by the signing of the contract by members of Acme's union.

3.2 Wasted Words

Wasted words are words that either don't need to be in the sentence or can be simplified to make the sentence's meaning clear. Wasted words may be

- low information content (LIC)[4] words
- repetitions
- clichés
- idioms
- jargon

Some LIC expressions appear in the accompanying table.

LIC	Replacement	LIC	Replacement
a majority of	most	in order to	to
a number of	many, several	in our opinion	we believe
as a means of	for, to	in reference to	(delete)
as a result	so	in such a manner as to	to
at the rate of	at	in terms of	in, for
at the same time as	while	in the course of	during
at this point in time	now (or delete)	in the direction of	toward
by means of	by	in the event that	if
by use of	by	in the form of	as
due to the fact that	because	in the matter of	(delete)
during the time that	while	in the vicinity of	about, near
for a period of	for	for a purpose of	for, to
if and when	(delete)	involves the use of	employs, uses
in an area where	where	it can be seen that	so, therefore
in an effort to	to	it will be necessary to	we, you, they must
in close proximity to	close to, near	please feel free to	please
in connection with	about	with reference to	(delete)
in fact	(delete)	13 cubic metres in volume	13 cubic metres

Before: In a majority of cases, the template can be used.

After: In most cases, the template can be used.

Clichés

Avoid using the following clichés.[5] They are overused and have little meaning.

as a matter of fact	enclosed herewith
at this point in time	in the matter of
in reference to	it has come to our attention that
please feel free to	attached hereto
you are hereby advised	in our opinion
as per	last but not least

Idioms

Although every language has idioms, they are not professional, they do not make sense in our culturally diverse workplaces, and they do not translate into other languages. Do not use them.

as clear as day	dead as a doornail
busy as a bee	keep your eye on it
starting out at the bottom of the ladder	playing with fire
like water off a duck's back	blind as a bat
reinvent the wheel	raining cats and dogs
dog tired	stubborn as a mule

Before: We should keep an eye on the compressor failure rates.

After: We should monitor/track/record failure rates.

Jargon

Many people say you should not use jargon, but in many cases you must. If you are using jargon, always use the jargon your audience expects and understands.

You can dazzle your friends by generating incomprehensible sentences. Simply combine statements from each of columns A, B, C, and D in the table on the following page.

Not convinced that jargon is a problem? Let us see if you understand what the following two sentences mean:

1. When a dependent clause starting with a subordinating conjunction comes before an independent clause, a comma usually separates the clauses.[6]

2. Did you know that if you put a slot in the top of your principal, you'll make it sound horny?[7]

Chances are good that if grammar is not your strong suit, the first sentence won't help you much. If you don't understand the second sentence, you don't play the organ, and you're likely thinking it means something totally different! If you are writing to grammarians, organists, and others, use the jargon they understand.

Useless Repetition

Such expressions as the following are wordy:

alternative choices, basic fundamentals, final conclusion, end results, past experience, advance warning

Choices are alternatives, fundamentals are basic, and experience did occur in the past. The adjectives are redundant and not required. Rather than state *The course covered the basic fundamentals of the new office software,* try *The course covered the basics of the new office software.*

Vague Words

There were many fatalities in the past few years.

For this sentence to have some value, *many* and *few* should be more precise.

Column A	Column B	Column C	Column D
1. In particular,	1. a large portion of the interface coordination communication	1. must utilize and be functionally interwoven with	1. the sophisticated hardware.
2. On the other hand,	2. a constant flow of effective information	2. maximizes the probability of project success and minimizes the cost and time required for	2. the anticipated fourth generation equipment.
3. However,	3. the characterization of specific criteria	3. adds explicit performance limits to	3. the subsystem compatibility testing.
4. Similarly,	4. initiation of critical subsystem development	4. necessitates that urgent consideration be applied to	4. the structural design, based on system engineering concepts.
5. As a resultant implication,	5. the fully integrated test program	5. requires considerable systems analysis and trade-off studies to arrive at	5. the preliminary qualification limit.
6. In this regard,	6. the product configuration baseline	6. is further compounded, when taking into account	6. the evolution of specifications over a given time period.
7. Based on integral subsystem considerations,	7. any associated supporting element	7. presents extremely interesting challenges to	7. the philosophy of commonality and standardization.
8. For example,	8. the incorporation of additional mission constraints	8. recognizes the importance of other systems and the necessity for	8. the greater fight-worthiness concept.
9. Thus,	9. the independent functional principle	9. effects a significant implementation of	9. any discrete configuration mode.
10. In respect to specific goals,	10. a primary interrelationship between system and/or subsystem technologies	10. adds overriding performance constraints to	10. the total system rationale.

Source: Honeywell's Buzzphrase, Buzzword Generator. *copywriting-on-demand. Web. 31 July 2009.*

YOUR TURN!

Fix the following sentences.

Hint: First identify the wasted word problem (low information content, repetitions, clichés, idiom, jargon).

1. The new software was implemented for the purposes of increasing managers' efficiency.

2. Although we had other alternative choices, the final end result was equally as effective as what our past experiences had predicted.

3. In the legal statements below, you will be asked to make these long, complicated sentences into something that is readable and a little clearer.

4. It has come to our attention that in the matter of the graffiti on our building's west wall, you are hereby advised that a professional will remove it on Wednesday.

5. It was just a shot in the dark, but I thought the office manager was wrapped around the axle about something.

6. It will be necessary to involve the use of staff evaluation forms to effect an improvement in customer service.

7. The HP5P is accessed from my CPU by using an IEEE-488 bus. [Eh?]

8. I'll send it to you next week.

3.3 Nouns to Verbs

For most daily writing tasks, write to inform rather than to impress. One way writers try to impress readers is by using longer, more formal sounding words. One way they do that is to turn clear, simple verbs into longer nouns. This is called nominalization. Nouns that end in *-ment, -tion, -sion, -ity,* and so on frequently have vibrant, active verbs struggling to get out! Here are several examples: decision (decide), reimbursement (reimburse), examination (examine), inspection (inspect), and payment (pay).

Release your active verbs.

Before: The group arrived at the decision to cancel the trip.

After: The group decided to cancel the trip.

YOUR TURN!

Convert the following sentences to plain English by "freeing" the verbs:

1. Acme's director has come to the decision that the most efficient way to make improvements with the problem of employee absenteeism is to implement a strategy of termination for staff who are away without authorized absenteeism.
2. The completion of this report will bring to a conclusion the project for the Acme Corporation.[8]
3. While doing an analysis of the managerial style of the manager, her supervisor determined that acceptance of difficult assignments appeared to be a problem for her.
4. The prospectus showed that computation of the annual revenues had been calculated properly.
5. If Acme arrives at the conclusion it would be necessary to make obsolete its preprinted letterhead service, it will make an announcement indicating the reasons for its decision.

HUMDINGER WARNING!

6. The implementation of the rule by the Director necessitated a reassessment of the policy by the management.[9]

3.4 Listing Important or Detailed Information

Making a list of major or complex information lets the reader see the details more quickly and easily. Consider the side-by-side examples below:

Canadian Public Health Association Seminar: Managing Stress		
All staff members are requested to return the enclosed reply cards by the due date, stating their interest in attending a seminar on managing stress, sponsored by CPHA, on May 5 from 9:30 a.m. to 4:00 p.m. The seminar will be held in the CPHA boardroom and should be of benefit to all who attend. CPHA will provide a light lunch. Seminar materials cost $12.00. Please register by April 15. If you need more information, call Fred at 555-999-1234.	**Date** **Time** **Place** **Price** **Lunch** **Sign up by** **More info**	May 5 9:30 a.m.– 4:00 p.m. CPHA boardroom 329 Richmond St. 3rd Floor $12.00 for seminar materials Provided by CPHA April 15 Fred at 555-999-1234

YOUR TURN!

In the following sentence, the information should be broken out into a list because it is very detailed. Listing it will help the reader understand it better the first time. Careful! We've added a trick or two to this one.

Because a significant portion of Acme's business involves the design, programming, and maintenance of document management software, and the design is selected from a set of Acme proprietary options that are used in many other firms, and Acme has committed to long-term support of the software as a part of their offer, Acme is a good candidate for winning this proposal.

3.5 Numbers

Use the following general guidelines for numbers:[10]

- Use the most readable format.
- Use the simplest format.
- Be consistent with the rest of the report or with corporate guidelines.

Use Figures for Numerical Data When	Spell Out the Number When
Writing numbers higher than ten (see exceptions below in "Special number formats")	The number is ten or less (and doesn't conflict with when you should use figures)
Writing about specific technical information test results: – dimensions, tolerances, statistics, data (tables)	The number is an approximation or estimate: *There are about fifty people waiting outside the bookstore.*
Writing numbers before a symbol or a unit of measure: – 7 kg, 5 psi, 14 A, 32°, 65%, 65¢	The number is a common fraction: *The midterm will compose half of your final mark.*
Writing several numbers in one sentence when some numbers are less than ten and some are higher than ten: *On January 5, we shipped 6 boxes of resistors, 18 relays, and 10 consoles.*	The number begins a sentence. If the number is awkward to write out, try to rewrite the sentence. *3456 books of the library's holdings were destroyed by fire.* *Of the library's holdings, 3456 books were destroyed by fire.*
Writing placards on equipment Numbering sections of a manual: – volumes, chapters, parts, pages, figures, tables	
Writing fractions, percentages, and decimals: – decimals are easier to write than fractions	
Writing years, dates, times, addresses	
Writing sums of money	
Writing people's ages	

Special Number Formats

Several special number formats follow:

- Spell out one of the numbers if you have two numbers written consecutively (pick the simplest expression):

  36 fifty-watt amplifiers

  or

  thirty-six 50-watt amplifiers

- Put a 0 before a decimal: 0.187 rather than .187.

- Be careful about different formats for numbers. Either state which system you are using or use the same system that your reader does. If you can, use the style your customers are used to:

  2 078 000 means the same as 2,078,000

  2,367.48 francs means the same as 2 367,48 francs.

3.6 Abbreviations

Abbreviation is a general word that describes the various ways you can shorten terms. The following table defines, shows examples, and provides guidance on how to use the forms of abbreviations. Remembering what type of abbreviations you are using is not as important as the guidelines for using them. Be careful when using any type of abbreviation. Use the guidelines on the following page to ensure consistency and to ensure your reader understands your writing.

3.7 Non-sexist Writing

Sexist writing uses words such as either *his* or *her* when both sexes should be included. The sentence *Everyone in the organization is required to have his work assessed annually* assumes that the organization employs only males. In today's modern business environment the words *he* and *his* are no longer acceptable when discussing males and females. The reverse is also true: saying *she* or *her* when referring to both sexes is equally wrong but far less prevalent. Many corporate style guides (e.g., the Department of National Defence) specify that documents must not contain sexist language. Sometimes you may not even be aware that you are using sexist language. An example of such stereotyping follows:

A good accountant never leaves his spreadsheets lying around.

A good accountant never leaves his or her spreadsheets lying around is awkward, but you can, fortunately, use several ways to improve this sentence and

Type	Example	Guidelines
Initialisms Each letter is spoken.	RCMP, NRC, SOP, LAN	Many people refer to initialisms as acronyms. Follow these guidelines when using them: Do not put periods between the letters. Define them when they are first used: "We used the Standard Operating Procedure (SOP) to extract the chemical from the solution." After defining the initialism, you can just use just the letters. In a longer document, if you have not used the initialism for several chapters, you may spell it out again. Use initialisms consistently. If you have used *PC* for *programmable controller,* the first time you used it, you cannot use it to mean *personal computer* later. If you have a lot of initialisms, refer readers to an alphanumerically sorted table. Use initialisms that are common to your workplace or industry.
Acronyms The letters form a word.	RAM, laser, scuba	Many of these words are defined in dictionaries and have become part of our language. You do not need to spell out what each letter means.
Portmanteaux	modem, Wikipedia	These are words that have been created by combining two other words. Words like these have become common within certain industries.
Short forms	tech	*Tech* most likely means *technician*, but there is room for error when using short forms. Notice there is no period after the short form, unless the short form looks like a real word, such as *in.* for *inches* and *in* as a preposition, or *no.* for *number* versus *no* as a denial. If you need a period at the end of the short form for clarity and the short form ends the sentence, do not use two periods.
Technical units (*Metric units are considered symbols, not abbreviations.*)	dB, ft, nmi	Write in roman (not italic) type. Write in lower case (unless the abbreviation was named after someone).

eliminate *she/he, her/him,* and *his* or *her* by using the non-sexist writing techniques listed.

Action	Result
Eliminate the pronoun, if possible.	A good accountant never leaves spreadsheets lying around.
Use *you* or *your.*	Don't leave your spreadsheets lying around. (*Command form of the verb.*)
Use the plurals *they* or *their.*	Good accountants never leave their spreadsheets lying around.

Other methods of avoiding sexist language include

- replacing masculine or feminine pronouns with the person's position (abbreviate, if necessary)
- using tables or lists
- replacing sex-specific titles, such as the following, with neutral terms:

Sex-Specific Terms	Neutral Terms
husband/wife	spouse
chairman	chair, chairperson
salesmen	sales representative, salesperson
mailman	letter carrier, mail carrier
mankind	people
spokesman	spokesperson
boy(s)/girl(s)	child/children

YOUR TURN!

Improve the following sentences using non-sexist writing techniques, and try to do so in more ways than one.

1. The employee logs on using his or her password.
2. If a student has questions about grammar, he should consult a grammar text.
3. We were away when the repairman came to fix the microwave so he wasn't able to complete his repairs.
4. Everyone at Acme is required to have their performance assessed annually.
5. man-machine interface

Answers to Your Turns

1.1 Adjectives and Adverbs
1. bad
2. close
3. deep
4. fairly
5. lately

1.2 Capitalization

The Department of Extended Family Services has a fund for children's services. This fund includes money for projects involving expectant mothers, for projects involving the protection of newborns and young children from early childhood diseases, and for projects involving the detection of learning disabilities in preschool children.

1.3 Commonly Confused Words
1. It's/its
2. principal
3. assure/ensure/insure
4. to/two/too/too
5. can/may/might
6. because/Because
7. affect/effect

1.4 Modifiers (Dangling and Misplaced)
1. The supervisor was using a checklist to evaluate the newest hire.
2. While I was bathing, my boss called with news of my promotion. (Don't forget the comma!)
3. The staff liked to watch the deer nibble on kibble.
4. The fax machine with the red panel was spewing out paper.
5. After I installed the software, I knew it wasn't working right.

1.5 Parallelism
1. While at Acme, I performed the following tasks:
   - writing project reports
   - completing productivity reports
   - reporting on building comfort issues
2. He put supplies in new locations, and he put all folders in numerical order to make them easier to find.
3. I gained a great deal of knowledge on the software by doing all inventory, documenting parts lists, and cataloguing parts.
4. Last summer, I filled new cabinets, organized and labelled office supply locations, painted, and organized service parts.
5. I helped produce and distribute the operator's guides.

1.6 Pronoun–Antecedent Agreement

Questions for Pronoun–Antecedent are covered elsewhere, in section 1.4: Modifiers (Dangling and Misplaced); 3.7: Non-sexist Writing; and 1.7: Pronoun Case.

1.7 Pronoun Case
1. Samson made himself eat the tasteless rice cakes.
2. The company told me last Friday to take a hike.
3. When it comes to procrastination, I know myself better than anyone else.
4. When you have finished your proposal, bring it to me for editing.
5. Who shall I tell him is calling?
6. Look after yourself. (Note: The "you" is implied.)
7. Sandu and Renata had not heard from Mortimer, who was on stress leave.

1.8 Run-On Sentences

Several answers are possible for fixing run-ons. One solution has been provided for questions 1 to 4.
1. A run-on sentence is one thing; a sentence fragment is something else.
2. There was a dangerous virus in the operating system. Unfortunately, I didn't find it before it found me.
3. I have always wanted to drive a Bugatti. I like fast cars.
4. The MAP sensor functions as two different sensors; the MAP's primary function is to tell the ECM how much load is being placed on the engine.
5. There is no answer here, but the point is be careful when emailing and text messaging. Think about to whom you're writing.

1.9 Sentence Fragments
1. As I sat reading my clumsy instructions, I recalled my instructor in continuing education telling me how to write for the reader. And I remembered what she taught me: All writing should be clear, concise, and correct.
2. It has been said that there are only three good operating systems: Linux, Windows XP, and Windows 2000.
3. We need to stop believing two myths about document design: that two spaces are required after a period and that you underline information to emphasize it.
4. When we downloaded the file we saw the virus warning: a message inside a typical pop-up window.
5. I would like to learn more about manufacturing and enterprise resource planning to save time with filing and planning. We encountered some of these tasks this summer.

1.10 Subject–Verb Agreement
1. One of our friends is winning the city's Entrepreneur of the Year award.
2. Sixty dollars is the entrance fee.
3. We build a truck like a rock! or We build trucks like rocks!
4. All staff at Acme are required to have their work assessed on an annual basis. (Although *everyone* is singular, the plural form *their* is preferred over *his or her*.)
5. The only benefit of switching our health plan for our staff members is the many ways of accessing the refunds.
6. Either Sally or the twins are usually late for the golf tournament.

2.1 Apostrophes and Possessives
1. The dog ate its biscuit greedily.
2. Men's and women's washrooms are located in the store's basement.
3. In the '80s, the Blue Bombers' talent was as good as anyone's.
4. Kids' clothes are on the second floor.
5. Keeping up with the Joneses is difficult since the Jones's house is such an expensive one.
6. The house was hers, the car was his, and the children were theirs.
7. It's a mystery why Lois's measles don't clear up.
8. We bought more than fifty dollars' worth of meat.
9. All the secretary's desks were moved to clean the office. Note: If you were describing more than one secretary, the answer would be *All of the secretaries' desks were moved to clean the office.*
10. Last week's work remained unfinished because many employees were off sick.

2.2 Brackets
See Parentheses.

2.3 Colons and Semicolons
1. The business world really needs workers who see the bigger picture , work with others well , and put the company's goals first. (No : or ; required.)
2. Please follow these three simple steps when completing the form : print your last name first, your first name, and then your middle initial.
3. Kim achieved her goals in life : she became an accountant and a mystery writer.
4. The new computer store is open ; instead of selling new PCs, it sells only used ones.
5. I really like Accounting Wizard for this application ; you should try it.
6. I find Acme's products easy to use ; however , I also find they crash easily.
7. We recommended several changes at work, such as taking regular breaks , working with subject matter experts , and peer editing each other's work.
8. Bill's office party list included beer , wine , and coolers. (No : required.)

2.4 Commas
1. When the secretary went to the conference, the staff were exhausted trying to answer the phones, pacify angry customers, and get all their own work done.
2. Because no one had time to complete the media brief, I was upset when the job became my responsibility.
3. The golf game went really well. I won.
4. The presentations, all completed in the latest software, refused to load on the comptroller's laptop. We searched, with great haste, for another laptop.
5. As I explained to you, Mr. Black, the company should have changed suppliers.
6. While I was washing, my brother called with news of a possible job.

2.5 Dashes (En and Em!)
See Hyphens.

2.6 Hyphens
1. A meaningful job, a loving spouse, and a car that won't break down—these are the things new graduates want.
2. Jun. 2009–Sept. 2011
My work included
   - filing clients' invoices
   - calling clients to set up scheduled maintenance visits
   - logging maintenance visits into service schedules
3. You should write thirty-three as 33.
4. After he had recovered from the flu, he had to re-cover his grandmother's sofa.
5. I request—no, I demand—that you stay late to finish the presentation.

2.7 Parentheses and Brackets
No exercises.

2.8 Quotation Marks
No exercises.

2.9 Semicolons
See Colons and Semicolons.

3.1 Active and Passive Voices
1. Anil Khalek, the district manager, approved April's project meeting minutes.
2. We shipped the new software by noon, but the customer still hasn't received it. (Both parts of the sentence are already active.)
3. The corporate bully was fired last Monday for harassment. (Passive, doer unknown. You cannot change this one because you do not know who fired the corporate bully.)
4. The Atlantis IT department designed a central file server to network the marketing department's computers at Acme.
5. The project manager recommended that the team proofread the proposal again.
6. When the members of Acme's union signed the contract, they verified the agreement.

3.2 Wasted Words
1. The new software was implemented to increase managers' efficiency.
2. Although we had choices, the result was as effective as what our experiences had predicted.
3. Make the following legal statements readable.
4. A professional will remove the graffiti on our building's west wall on Wednesday.
5. It was just a guess, but I thought the office manager was upset about something.
6. We need to use staff evaluation forms to improve customer service. (Note: This example also requires noun-to-verb practice; see next section.)
7. The printer is accessed from my computer's central processing unit (CPU) by using an IEEE-488 bus (parallel cable). (Note: Be careful. This kind of information is suitable only for specifice audiences.)
8. I'll send it to you next week. (Vague information: What will you send me? How will you send it? What day will you send it?)

3.3 Nouns to Verbs

1. Acme's director has decided that the best way to improve the problem of absent employees is to terminate (fire) staff who are away without authorized absenteeism (or without authorization).
2. When this report is done, the project for the Acme Corporation will be complete.
3. While analyzing the manager's style, her supervisor determined that she had a problem accepting difficult assignments.
4. The prospectus showed that the annual revenues had been calculated properly.
5. If Acme decides to discontinue its preprinted letterhead service, Acme will let us know why.
6. When the Director implemented the rule, management had to reassess the policy.[1] (What is going on with this sentence? Hint: There are two plain English problems with this sentence. One problem is passive voice, the other is the verb-to-noun problem.)

3.4 Listing important or detailed information

1. Acme is a good candidate for winning this proposal because
   - a significant portion of Acme's business involves designing, programming, and maintaining document management software
   - the design is selected from a set of Acme proprietary options used in many other firms
   - the offer includes long-term support of the software
   Note: Unless each list item is a full sentence, and the introductory statement is complete, capitalizing the first word or adding end-of-line punctuation is not necessary.
   Note: Keep it parallel!

3.5 Numbers

No exercises.

3.6 Abbreviations

No exercises.

3.7 Non-sexist Writing

1. Employees log on using their passwords. Log on using your password. The employee logs on using a password.
2. If students have questions about grammar, they should consult a grammar text.
3. We were away when the technician came to fix the microwave so the repairs weren't completed. (Note the acceptable use of passive voice.)
4. All employees at Acme are required to have their performance assessed annually.
5. user interface

Endnotes

CHAPTER 1

1. "Timeline of Cell Phones and Wireless Communications." *Cell-Phone-Accessories.com*. Web. 7 Aug. 2008.
2. King, Rachael. "Companies Shed Initial Resistance to iPhone." *Business Week Online* (5 May 2009): 1-1. Web. 4 July 2009.
3. "A BlackBerry in Every Pocket." *Communications News* 44.11 (Nov. 2007): 8. Print.
4. Tugend, Alina. "BlackBerry Jam." *Government Executive* 36.19 (1 Nov. 2004): 40–46. Print.
5. "Think You Might Be Addicted to Email? You're Not Alone." *AOL*. Web. 26 July 2007.
6. O'Reilly, Sally. "System Overload." *Personnel Today* (28 Nov. 2006): 35–35. Print.
7. Tugend, Alina. "BlackBerry Jam." *Government Executive* 36.19 (1 Nov. 2004): 40–46. Print.
8. "Obama's BlackBerry Victory Raises Security Questions." *CBC News*. Canadian Broadcasting Corporation, 23 Jan. 2009. Web. 24 Jan. 2009.
9. Messmer, Max. "Soft Skills Are Key to Advancing Your Career." *Business Credit* 109.4 (Apr. 2007): 34–35. Print.
10. "Employability Skills 2000+." *Conference Board of Canada*. May 2000. Web. 29 Oct. 2007.
11. Associated Press. "RadioShack Layoff Notices Are Sent by E-Mail." *New York Times* 31 Aug. 2006. Print.
12. McLuhan, Marshall. *Understanding Media: The Extensions of Man*. New York: McGraw-Hill, 1964. Print.
13. Saroyan, William. *The Human Comedy*. Don Mills: Longmans Canada, 1964. Print.
14. The Playboy Interview: Marshall McLuhan, *Playboy Magazine* March 1969. Print.
15. Leacy, F. H., ed. "Historical Statistics of Canada." *Statistics Canada*. 1983. Web. 26 Aug. 2009.
16. Bell Canada. 2009. Web. 26 Aug. 2009.
17. *OED Online*. Oxford University Press. Entry for "spam." June 2001. Web. 10 Oct. 2007.
18. "E-mail-Free Friday to Encourage Verbal Communication." *Global: Ideas: Bank*. Nicholas Albery Foundation. Web. 15 Feb. 2008.
19. Carnevale, Dan. "E-Mail Is for Old People." *The Chronicle of Higher Education* 6 Oct. 2006. Print.
20. Agar, Jon. *Constant Touch: A Global History of the Mobile Phone*. Cambridge: Icon, 2003. 176. Print.
21. Ibid., p. 177.
22. Norrie, Justin. "In Japan, Cellular Storytelling Is All the Rage." *Sydney Morning Herald* 3 Dec. 2007. Print.
23. Tiltman, David. "New Gadgets, Same Teenage Kicks." *Marketing* 25 July 2007: 28–29. Print.
24. *OED Online*. Oxford University Press. Entry for "multi-tasking." March 2003. Web. 10 Oct. 2007.
25. Lohr, Steve. "Slow Down, Brave Multitasker, and Don't Read This in Traffic." *New York Times* 25 Mar. 2007. Print.
26. Harbluk, Joanne L., and Y. Ian Noy. "The Impact of Cognitive Distraction on Driver Visual Behaviour and Vehicle Control." *Road Safety Directorate and Motor Vehicle Regulation Directorate*. Transport Canada. Feb. 2002. Web. 15 Oct. 2008.
27. Lohr, Steve. "Slow Down, Brave Multitasker, and Don't Read This in Traffic." *New York Times* 25 Mar. 2007. Print.
28. Nugent, Helen. "Texting While Driving Is More Dangerous Than Drink-Driving." *Times Online*. Times Newspapers, 18 Sept. 2008. Web. 17 Aug. 2009.
29. Leo, Peter. "Tag You're Fired: Big Businesses Behaving Badly." *Pittsburgh Post-Gazette* 8 Sept. 2006. Print.

CHAPTER 2

1. Chhatwal, Kyl. "Still a Divided People; Mirabel Airport Fiasco Stands as a Glaring Example of the French-English Divide." *Waterloo Region Record* 28 Mar. 2008: A11. Print.
2. Lahey, Jen. "Mirabel Finally Grounded in Reality." *Capital News Online*. Carleton University, 22 Oct. 2004. Web. 9 July 2009.
3. Canadian Press. "Mirabel Airport to Be Turned into Amusement Park." *CTV News*. CTVglobemedia. 21 Feb. 2006. Web. 17 Aug. 2009.
4. Spivey, Angela. "Plastic Bags—Prolific Problem." *Environmental Health Perspectives* 111.4 (2003): A208. Print.
5. "China Bans Use of Disposable Plastic Bags." *BioCycle* 49.6 (2008): 12-12. Print.
6. "Partnerships Promote Wise Use and Recycling of Plastic Bags." *Alberta Plastics Recycling Association News*. Alberta Plastics Recycling Association, Spring 2008. Web. 8 Mar. 2009.
7. "Plastic Shopping Bags . . . Use Them Wisely, for Everything They're Worth." *Canadian Plastics Industry Association*. Web. 8 Mar. 2009.
8. Carlson, Deborah, and Paul Lingl. *Doing Business in a New Climate: A Guide to Measuring, Reducing and Offsetting Greenhouse Gas Emissions*. David Suzuki Foundation, 2008. Web. 17 Aug. 2009.
9. "Loblaw Kicks Off the New Year by Launching Its Plastic Bag Reduction Program in the City of Toronto Stores and Announcing Partnership with WWF-Canada." *George Weston Limited*. 11 Jan. 2009. Web. 17 Aug. 2009.
10. "The Way We Do Business: Loblaw Companies Limited 2008 Corporate Social Responsibility Report." *Loblaw Companies Limited*. April 2009. Web. 13 Apr. 2009.
11. Pearce, F. "The Consumers Are Not So Green. *New Scientist* 13 (June): 14. Print.
12. "Loblaws Pay-Per-Bag Fee Starts Monday." *CTV Toronto*. CTVglobemedia. 11 Jan. 2009. Web. 7 Mar. 2009.
13. "Sobeys Shopping Bag for Life." *Greenthinkers blog*. N.p. 5 June 2007. Web. 7 Mar. 2009.
14. "Markets for Recycled Film." *Canadian Plastics Industry Association*. 2009. Web. 8 Mar. 2009.

15. Overcash, Craig. "But TIGER's the real $$$ deal." *Fort Worth Business Press* 16.20 (2003): 34. Print.

16. Maddox, Kate. "Marketing Messages Missing Mark." *B to B* 88.1 (2003): 3. Print.

17. *The Columbia World of Quotations.* Columbia University Press, 1996. Web. 14 Aug. 2008.

18. Osborn, Alex. *Applied Imagination: Principles and Procedures of Creative Problem Solving.* New York: Scribner's, 1963. Print.

19. Hempel, Jessi. "Big Blue Brainstorm." *Business Week* 7 Aug. 2006: 70. Print.

20. *QuotesDaddy.com.* Eds. Eyal Yaakov and Maya Elhalal. Quotes Daddy, 2008. Web. 9 July 2009.

21. "Young Entrepreneur Awards 2008." *Business Development Bank of Canada.* 2008. Web. 17 Aug. 2009.

22. Service Corps of Retired Executives. "Business Plan for Startup Business." *Microsoft.* 31 May 2008. Web. 17 Aug. 2009.

CHAPTER 3

1. Pinker, Steven. *The Stuff of Thought: Language as a Window into Human Nature.* New York: Viking, 2007. Print.

2. "OED Online." *Oxford University Press.* June 2001. Web. 17 June 2008. Entry for "skyscraper."

3. Abley, Mark. *The Prodigal Tongue: Dispatches from the Future of English.* Toronto: Random House Canada, 2008. Print.

4. "AskOxford: The Americas." *Oxford University Press.* Web. 14 Aug. 2008.

5. "OED Online." Oxford University Press. 1989. Web. 17 June 2008. Entry for "tuque."

6. Murphy, David. "26 Jargon Words to Avoid (Like the Plague)." *The Tendo View.* Tendo Communications, 12 May 2009. Web. 15 Aug. 2008.

7. Nunberg, Geoffrey. "Usage in the *American Heritage Dictionary.*" *The American Heritage Dictionary of the English Language.* 4th ed. Houghton Mifflin, 2000. Web. 19 Aug. 2008.

8. Roberts, Tim. "Cold Pasteurization of Food by Irradiation." *Virginia Cooperative Extension.* Virginia Tech. Publication Number 458-300. Aug. 1998. Web. 18 Aug. 2008.

9. "OED Online." *Oxford University Press.* June 2001. Web. 17 June 2008. Entry for "weblog."

10. Lutz, William. *Doublespeak: From "Revenue Enhancement" to "Terminal Living," How Government, Business, Advertisers, and Others Use Language to Deceive You.* New York: Harper & Row, 1989. Print.

11. Ibid.

12. "Canadians Want Action, Vision, Leadership on Climate Change." *Vancouver Sun.* Canwest Publishing, 27 Oct. 2007. Web. 14 July 2009.

13. Bogomolny, Laura. "The Name Game." *Canadian Business* 12 Sept. 2005: 134–35. Print.

14. Zhang, Shi, and Bernd Schmitt. "Creating Local Brands in Multilingual International Markets." *Journal of Marketing Research* 38 (2001): 313–25. Print.

15. "OED Online." *Oxford University Press.* June 2008. Web. 17 June 2008. Entry for "Ms."

16. Communications Branch, Indian and Northern Affairs Canada. *Words First: An Evolving Terminology Relating to Aboriginal Peoples in Canada.* Indian and Northern Affairs Canada, Oct. 2002. Web. 13 July 2009.

17. Shewchuk, Blair. "Men, Women, and Fishers." *CBC News.* Canadian Broadcasting Corporation, 24 Aug. 2000. Web. 13 July 2009.

18. "Manual or Automatic?" *Toronto Star* 25 Oct. 2003. Print.

19. *The American Heritage Dictionary of the English Language.* 4th ed. Houghton Mifflin Company, 2004. Web. 11 Aug. 2008. Entry for "standard English."

20. "OED Online." *Oxford University Press.* June 2008. Web. 17 June 2008. Entry for "gay."

21. "OED Online." *Oxford University Press.* 1989. Web. 17 June 2008. Entry for "ridiculous."

22. *The American Heritage Dictionary of the English Language.* 4th ed. Houghton Mifflin Company, 2004. Web. 11 Aug. 2008. Entry for "anxious."

23. *Webster's Revised Unabridged Dictionary.* MICRA, Inc. Web. 19 June 2008. Entry for "anxious."

24. "Big Stuff, Little Stuff: A Decennial Measurement of Executives' and Academics' Reactions to Questionable Usage Elements." *Journal of Business Communication* 38.4 (2001): 439. Print.

25. "Clarifying the Bureaucratese." *Toronto Star.* thestar.com, 25 Oct. 2004. Web. 11 Aug. 2008.

26. Kimball, Roger. "Political Correctness or, the Perils of Benevolence." *National Interest* (Winter 2003). Web. 11 Aug. 2008.

27. Whorf, Benjamin Lee. *Language, Thought and Reality: Selected Writings of Benjamin Lee Whorf.* Ed. John B. Carroll. Cambridge: MIT, 1956. 207–19. Print.

28. *Canadian Oxford Dictionary.* Toronto: Oxford University Press, 1998. Entry for "rule of thumb." Print.

29. "OED Online." *Oxford University Press.* 1989. Web. 3 Mar. 2009. Entry for "rule."

30. Communications Branch, Indian and Northern Affairs Canada. *Words First: An Evolving Terminology Relating to Aboriginal Peoples in Canada.* Indian and Northern Affairs Canada, Oct. 2002. Web. 13 July 2009.

31. American Psychological Association. *Publication Manual of the American Psychological Association.* 6th ed. Washington, DC: American Psychological Association, 2010. 75. Print.

32. Woodlee, Yolanda. "D.C. Mayor Acted 'Hastily,' Will Rehire Aide." *Washington Post.* Washington Post Company. 4 Feb. 1999. Web. 10 Aug. 2008.

33. *Dictionary of Canadian Quotations.* Ed. Winnie Caw. Folk Corporation, 2004. Web. 12 July 2008.

CHAPTER 4

1. Based on Hale, W. G., Venetia A. Saunders, and J. Philip Margham. *Collins Dictionary of Biology.* 3rd ed. Glasgow: Harper Collins Publishers, 2003. 495. Print.

2. Griffith, John, dir. *Bride Has Massive Hair Wig Out (ORIGINAL).* Video. YouTube.com. Burnout Productions, 2007. Web. 6 June 2009.

3. "YouTube Seed Blossoms into Bloomin' Bridezilla." *Toronto Star.* thestar.com, 6 Feb. 2007. Web. 8 June 2009.

4. Wells, Jennifer. "Invasion of the Stunt Marketers." *Globe and Mail.* CTVglobemedia, 31 Mar. 2009. Web. 8 June 2009.

5. "Two Held after Ad Campaign Triggers Boston Bomb Scare." *CNN.com.* Turner Broadcasting System, 1 Feb. 2007. Web. 6 June 2009.

6. Eichenwald, Kurt, and Jack Lynch. "Arthur Andersen Charged with Obstruction of Justice." *New York Times.* New York Times Company, 14 Mar. 2002. Web. 18 Aug. 2008.

7. Cialdini, Robert. *The Psychology of Influence.* rev. ed. New York: William Morrow. 1993. 171–72. Print.

8. "Student Recruits Unfit for Service, Say Former Border Guards." *CBC News.* Canadian Broadcasting Corporation, 1 Oct. 2007. Web. 7 Jun. 2009.

9. Ibid.

CHAPTER 5

1. Imen, Wallace. "Tougher for Women to Work for Women: Study Finds More Mental, Physical Problems Than If They Work for a Man. *Globe and Mail.* CTVglobemedia, 10 Sept. 2008. Web. 18 Feb. 2009.
2. Ibid.
3. Tannen, Deborah. *You Just Don't Understand.* New York: William and Morrow, 1990. 18. Print.
4. Ibid., p. 24.
5. Ibid., p. 25.
6. Ibid., p. 77.
7. Ibid.
8. *Canadian Dictionary of the English Language: An Encyclopedic Reference.* Scarborough: ITP Nelson, 1997. Entry for "intercultural." Print.
9. Ibid., entry for "cross-cultural."
10. "Africa & Middle East: United Arab Emirates, Country Profile." *Berlitz Career Services.* Berlitz International Inc. Web. 23 Aug. 2008.
11. Hall, Edward T. *Beyond Culture.* New York: Anchor Books, 1989. Print. The section on high-context and low-context cultures is based on the work of Edward T. Hall. See also Lustig, Myron, and Jolene Koester. *Intercultural Communication: Interpersonal Communication across Cultures.* 5th ed. Boston: Pearson Education, 2006. Print.
12. Brown, Nina. "Edward T. Hall: Proxemic Theory, 1966." *CSISS Classics.* Center for Spatially Integrated Social Science. Regents of University of California, Santa Barbara. Web. 1 June 2009.
13. Onishi, Norimitsu. "For Japanese Hostages, Release Only Adds to Stress." *New York Times.* New York Times Company, 22 Apr. 2004. Web. 23 Aug. 2008.
14. Ibid.
15. Ibid.
16. Ibid.
17. Ibid.
18. Hofstede, Geert. *Culture's Consequences: Comparing Values, Behaviors, Institutions and Organizations across Nations.* 2nd ed. Thousand Oaks: Sage Publications, 2001. Print. The section on communitarianism and individualism is based on the work of Geert Hofstede. See also Lustig, Myron, and Jolene Koester. *Intercultural Communication: Interpersonal Communication across Cultures.* 5th ed. Boston: Pearson Education, 2006. Print; and Hofstede, Geert. *Cultures and Organizations: Software of the Mind.* London: McGraw-Hill, 1991. Print.
19. Baird, Chief Kim. "Making History: Tsawwassen First Nation First Urban Treaty in Modern-Day British Columbia." *Chief Kim Baird's Historic Speech to the BC Legislature.* Tsawwassen First Nation. 15 Oct. 2007. Web. 31 Oct. 2007.
20. Ibid.

CHAPTER 6

1. Adapted from "The Business Meeting." *Only Funny Stories.* Ed. Marc Dussault. 2009. Web. 14 Sept. 2009.
2. Henkel, Shri. *Successful Meetings: How to Plan, Prepare and Execute Top Notch Business Meetings.* Ocala: Atlanta Publishing Group, 2007. Print.
3. "PM, Obama Talk Trade, Afghanistan, Pledge 'Clean Energy Dialogue.'" *CBC News.* Canadian Broadcasting Corporation, 19 Feb. 2009. Web. 14 Sept. 2009.

4. Akehurst, Gary, José Manuel Comeche, and Miguel-Angel Galindo. "Job Satisfaction and Commitment in the Entrepreneurial SME." *Small Business Economics* 32.3 (2009): 277–89. Print.
5. Lee, Bruce. "Management: Meetings That Count." *Canadian Consulting Engineer* 43.6 (2002): 73.
6. "PayScale Meeting Miser." *PayScale.* 2009. Web. 16 Sept. 2009.
7. Beavers, John P., and Kevin M. Kinross. "Corporate Minutes: When Less Is More." *Corporate Board* Mar./Apr. (2008). Print. See also Hayman, Russell, Mark Milhanovic, and Michael Peregrine. "Corporate Minute Taking: A General Counsel's Guide." *Venulex Legal Summaries* 4 (2005): 1–6. Print.
8. Nichols, Ralph G. "Listening Is a 10-Part Skill." *Nation's Business* 75.9 (1987): 54–60. Print.
9. Leverentz, Frances, and Garman, Dorothy. What was that you said? *Instructor* 96.8 (1987): 66–68. Print.
10. Jensen, J. Vernon. *Perspectives on Oral Communication.* Boston: Holbrook Press, 1970. Print. For more recent findings, see also Colbert, Kent. "A Quantitative Analysis of CEDA Speaking Rates." *National Forensic Journal* VI (1988): 113–20. Print.
11. *RobertsRules.org.* Ed. Beverly Kennedy. Robert's Rules of Order, 1997. Web. 17 Sept. 2009.
12. Pittinsky, Todd, ed. *Crossing the Divide: Intergroup Leadership in a World of Difference.* Boston: Harvard Business Press, 2009. 1. Print.

CHAPTER 7

1. *MSN Encarta: Online Dictionary.* Microsoft Corporation. Entry for "counterintuitive." Web. 31 July 2009.
2. Tufte, Edward. "*Columbia* Evidence—Analysis of Key Slide." *Ask E.T.* 18 Mar. 2003. Web. 31 July 2009. Tufte, Edward. "PowerPoint Is Evil." *Wired* 11.09 (2003): n.p. Web. 31 July 2009.
3. Thompson, Clive. "PowerPoint Makes You Dumb." *New York Times.* New York Times Company, 14 Dec. 2003. Web. 31 July 2009.
4. Garber, Angela. "Death by PowerPoint." *SmallBusinessComputing.com.* WebMediaBrands, 1 Apr. 2001. Web. 21 July 2009.
5. "Killer Presentations—Wake Up Your Audience!" *Microsoft at Work.* Microsoft Corporation. 20 Sept. 2006. Web. 21 July 2009.
6. *Do You Suffer from Glossophobia?* Glossophobia.com. Web. 9 Aug. 2008.
7. Line from Dylan, Bob. "Don't Follow Leaders." *Subterranean Homesick Blues.* Sony BMG Music Entertainment, 2008. CD.
8. "Hasta La Vista, Baby." *Maclean's* 3 March 2008: Cover. Print.
9. "Crushing Poverty the Microsoft Way." *Maclean's* 21 July 2008: Cover. Print.
10. "Flying Is Hell." *Maclean's* 28 July 2008. Cover. Print.
11. Peters, Tom. *10 Vital Rules for Giving Incredible Speeches . . . And Why They're Irrelevant.* Lakewood: Richardson Company Training Media, 1990. Print.
12. Tufte, Edward. "PowerPoint Is Evil." *Wired* 11.09 (2003): n.p. Web. 31 July 2009.
13. Miller, George A. "The Magical Number Seven, Plus or Minus Two: Some Limits on Our Capacity for Processing Information." *Psychological Review* 63 (1956): 81–97. Print.
14. Toff, Ron. *I Can See You Naked.* Kansas City: Andrews & McMeel, 1992. Print.

15. The idea for this exercise came from Bergells, Laura. "Cosmopolitan PowerPoint." *Maniactive*. N.p. 28 Feb. 2005. Web. 3 Aug. 2009.

CHAPTER 8

1. Wilkie, Helen. "Communicate Well and Prosper: Poor Interaction Costs Companies More Than They Realize—Or Can Afford." *Globe and Mail*. 27 Feb. 2004. Print.
2. Dreyfack, Raymond. "The Write Way to Jump-Start your Career." *Supervision* 65.4 (2004): 13–15. Print.
3. Wilkie, Helen. "Communicate Well and Prosper: Poor Interaction Costs Companies More Than They Realize—Or Can Afford." *Globe and Mail* 27 Feb. 2004. Print.
4. Sellen, Abigail J., and Richard H. R. Harper. *The Myth of the Paperless Office*. Cambridge: MIT Press, 2002. Print.
5. "The Office of the Future" *Business Week* 30 June 1975: 48–70. Print.
6. Sellen, Abigail J., and Richard H. R. Harper. *The Myth of the Paperless Office*. Cambridge: MIT Press, 2002. Print.
7. "Study Says Paperless Office a Myth." *Computer Dealer News* 18 Apr. 2003: 19. Print.
8. Sciadas, G. *Our Lives in Digital Times*. Connectedness Series. Cat. no. 56F0004MIE, no. 14. Ottawa: Ministry of Industry, 2006. *Statistics Canada*. Web. 21 May 2008.
9. Sellen, Abigail J., and Richard H. R. Harper. *The Myth of the Paperless Office*. Cambridge: MIT Press, 2002. Print.
10. Sciadas, G. *Our Lives in Digital Times*. Connectedness Series. Cat. no. 56F0004MIE, no. 14. Ottawa: Ministry of Industry, 2006. *Statistics Canada*. Web. 21 May 2008.
11. Fallows, Deborah. "E-mail at Work: Few Feel Overwhelmed and Most Are Pleased with the Way E-mail Helps Them Do Their Jobs." *Pew Internet and American Life Project*. 2002. Web. 28 Apr. 2008.
12. *Addressing Information Overload in Corporate Email: The Economics of User Attention*. Radicati Group. Apr. 2007. Web. 10 Mar. 2008.
13. Sellen, Abigail J., and Richard H. R. Harper. *The Myth of the Paperless Office*. Cambridge: MIT Press, 2002. Print.
14. Fried, Ina. "Gates Still Finding his Voice." *CNETNews.com*. CBS Interactive, 19 Oct. 2007. Web. 24 Apr. 2008.
15. Dillon, Sam. "What Corporate America Can't Build: A Sentence." *New York Times* 7 Dec. 2004. Print.
16. National Commission on Writing for America's Families, Schools, and Colleges. *Writing: A Ticket to Work . . . Or a Ticket Out: A Survey of Business Leaders*. College Board, 2004. Web. 4 July 2008.
17. "OED Online." *Oxford University Press*. 21 Mar. 2008. Web. 25 Apr. 2008. Entry for "phishing."
18. Shea, Gordon F. "A Case for Clear Writing." *Training & Development* 46.1 (1992): 63. Print.
19. Pascal, Blaise. *Lettres Provinciales*, letter 16. 1657. Print.
20. "The History of Sealing Wax." *Nostalgic Impressions: The Timeless Art of Writing*. n.d. Web. 6 Aug. 2009.
21. "Addressing Guidelines." *Canada Post*. 22 June 2009. Web. 1 Sept. 2009.
22. Duchemin, Claude, and Brian J. Mallet. *Structural and Regulatory Changes and Globalization in Postal and Telecommunications Services: The Human Resources Dimension*. International Labour Office, 1998. Web. 1 Mar. 2008.
23. Kessler, Michelle. "Fridays Go from Casual to E-mail-free." *USA Today* 5 Oct. 2007. Print.
24. Based on a case described in Sellen, Abigail J., and Richard H. R. Harper. *The Myth of the Paperless Office*. Cambridge: MIT Press, 2002. 40–49. Print.
25. Ibid.
26. "50 Best Employers in Canada." *Hewitt Associates*. 2008. Web. 15 Jan. 2008.
27. "Mission and Values." *Peak of the Market*. Web. 2 Jan. 2008.
28. "About Us." *Ten Thousand Villages*. 2008. Web. 5 Jan. 2008.
29. *Papua New Guinea Tourism and Business Directory*. n.d. Web. 5 Jan. 2008.
30. Sarantis, Heather. *Business Guide to Paper Reduction: A Step-by-Step Plan to Save Money by Saving Paper*. ForestEthics, 2002. Web. 5 Jan. 2008.
31. "The Elusive Paperless Office." *Awake!* 8 June 1999. Print.
32. "Study Says Paperless Office a Myth." *Computer Dealer News* 18 Apr. 2003: 19. Print.
33. *The Future Matters to Our Environment: Corporate Responsibility Report 2003*. TD Bank Financial Group, 2003. Web. 1 Mar. 2008.

CHAPTER 9

1. Search completed on Google.ca. Web. 18 Mar. 2009.
2. "Resources: Marketing to Kids." *CBS News*. CBS Interactive, 17 May 2007. Web. 19 Mar. 2009.
3. Bakan, Joel. *The Corporation*. Toronto: Viking Canada. 2004. 120. Print.
4. Ibid., p. 120.
5. Linn, Susan. *Consuming Kids: The Hostile Takeover of Childhood*. New York: The New Press, 2004. 2. Print.
6. Ibid., p. 51.
7. Center for Science in the Public Interest. *Pestering Parents: How Food Companies Market Obesity to Children*. Washington, D.C.: CSPINET, 2003. Web. 18 Mar. 2009.
8. Tracy, Brian. *The Art of Closing the Sale*. Nashville: Thomas Nelson, 2007. v. Print.
9. Cialdini, Robert. *Influence: The Psychology of Persuasion*. rev. ed. New York: William Morrow, 1993. Print. The sections entitled "Reciprocity" and "Consistency" are based on Cialdini's book.
10. Festinger, Leon, and James Carlsmith. "Cognitive Consequences of Forced Compliance." *Journal of Abnormal and Social Psychology* 58 (1959): 203–10. Print. Rpt. in Green, Christopher. *Classics in the History of Psychology: An Electronic Resource*. 3 Oct. 2004. Web. 7 Mar. 2009.

CHAPTER 10

1. Michelson Jr., Michael W. "Turning Complaints into Cash." *American Salesman* 48.12 (2003): 22–25. Print.
2. Mair, Victor H., Denis Mair, and Zhang Liqing. "'Crisis' Does NOT Equal 'Danger' plus 'Opportunity': How a Misunderstanding about Chinese Characters Has Led Many Astray." *Pinyin.info: A Guide to the Writing of Mandarin Chinese in Romanization*. 2004. Web. 10 Oct. 2008.
3. *She Wore a Yellow Ribbon*. Screenplay by Frank S. Nugent. Dir. John Ford. Prod. Merian C. Cooper, Lowell J. Farrell, and John Ford. Perf. John Wayne and Joanne Dru. 1949. RKO Radio Pictures. *IMDB: Internet Movie Data Base*. Web. 11 Aug. 2009.
4. "Did You Know? Most Customers Want an Apology When a Mistake Is Made." *Floral Management* July (2004): 12. Print.

5. Kiger, Patrick J. "The Art of the Apology." *Workforce Management* 83.10 (2004): 57–62. Print.
6. "Artful Apologies." *Wearables Business* 11.9 (2007): 26. Print.
7. Arellano, Jonah. "Say You're Sorry." *Rural Telecommunications* 27.2 (2008): 9. Print.
8. Dresser, Rebecca. "The Limits of Apology Laws." *Hastings Center Report* May–June (2006): 6–7. Print.
9. Quinley, Kevin. "Risk Management." *Claims Magazine* May (2008): 14–16. Print.
10. Keeva, Steven. "Does Law Mean Never Having to Say You're Sorry?" *ABA Journal* Dec. (1999): 64–48, 95. Print.
11. "Discussion Paper on Apology Legislation." *British Columbia Ministry of Attorney General.* 30 Jan. 2006. Web. 30 Mar. 2008.
12. Ibid.
13. Ibid.
14. Clark, Gary L., Kaminski, Peter F., and David R. Rink. "Consumer Complaints: Advice on How Companies Should Respond Based on an Empirical Study." *Journal of Consumer Marketing* 9.3 (1992): 5. Print.
15. Grainer, Marc. Customer Care: The Multibillion Dollar Sinkhole: A Case of Customer Rage Unassuaged. *Customer Care Measurement & Consulting* Oct. (2003). Web. 25 Nov. 2008.
16. Lutz, William D. "Corporate Doublespeak: Making Bad News Look Good." *Business and Society Review* Winter (1983): 19–22. Print.
17. Gaunt, Jeremy. "Corporations Are Becoming Expert at Doublespeak to Mask Bad News." *Los Angeles Times.* Tribune Interactive, 2 Dec. 1990. Web. 31 July 2009.
18. *The Modem Letter-Writer, or Whole Art of Polite Correspondence.* Gainesborough: Henry Mozley, 1812. 66–67. Cited in Locker, Kitty O. "'Sir, This Will Never Do': Model Dunning Letters, 1592–1873." *Journal of Business Communication* 22.2 (1985): 39–45. Print.
19. Greenberg, Josh, and Charlene Elliott. "A Cold Cut Crisis: Listeriosis, Maple Leaf Foods, and the Politics of Apology." *Canadian Journal of Communication* 34.2 (2009): 189–204. Print.
20. Locker, Kitty O. "Factors in Reader Responses to Negative Letters: Experimental Evidence for Changing What We Teach." *Journal of Business and Technical Communication* 13.1 (1999): 5. Print.
21. "Bad News Gets Easier." *T+D: Training and Development* 59.11 (2005): 16–17. Print.
22. Cotter, John. "Alberta Orders Landowners to Help Eradicate Wild Boars" *Canadian Press.* Canadian Press, 8 July 2008. Web. 8 Nov. 2008.
23. "Grand Beach and the East Beaches Area Visitors Guide." *Grand Beach Tourism.* n.d. Web. 25 Nov. 2008.
24. "Phone & Internet Security." *SaskTel News* 36 (2006). Web. 20 Nov. 2008.

CHAPTER 11

1. Kent, Duncan. *Writing Revisable Manuals: A Guidebook for Business and Government.* Duncan Kent & Associates, 2006. Web. 19 Nov. 2008.
2. "Stella Liebeck & McDonald's Coffee: Classic Example of Public Misconceptions Embraced by Tort Reformers." *Coalition against No-Fault in BC.* n.d. Web. 20 Nov. 2008.
3. Hammond, David, Geoffrey T. Fong, Paul W. McDonald, K. Stephen Brown, and Roy Cameron. "Graphic Canadian Cigarette Warning Labels and Adverse Outcomes: Evidence from Canadian Smokers." *American Journal of Public Health* 94.8 (2004): 1442–44. Print.
4. Davis, Phillip M. "Nine Paths to Effective Warnings." *Design News* 45.21 (1989): 218. Print.
5. "Our Asbestos Gambit." Editorial. *Toronto Star* 3 Nov. 2008: AA06. Print.
6. "M-Law's Wacky Warning Labels." Michigan Lawsuit Abuse Watch. 2008. Web. 20 Nov. 2008.
7. *Microsoft Office Word 2007.* Redmond: Microsoft, 2007. CD-ROM.
8. Allwood, Carl Martin, and Tomas Kalen. "Evaluating and Improving the Usability of a User Manual." *Behaviour & Information Technology* 16.1 (1997): 43–57. Print.
9. "Office Ergonomics." *CCOHS Canadian Centre for Occupational Health and Safety.* 2009. Web. 1 Mar. 2009.

CHAPTER 12

1. "Late Great Prank." *Sunday Times* [London] 10 May 2009: 10-11. *EBSCOhost.* Web. 27 May 2009.
2. "Fake Professor in Wikipedia Storm." BBC News. BBC MMIX, 6 Mar. 2007. Web. 2 Oct. 2009.
3. http://en.wikipedia.org/wiki/Zhoda,_Manitoba.
4. Butterworth, Siobhain. "Open Door." *Guardian.* Guardian News and Media Limited, 4 May 2009. Web. 1 Oct. 2009.
5. *National.* CBC News. CBC, Winnipeg, 28 Aug. 2008. Television.
6. Kneale, Ruth. "Librarians and Pop Culture: What's the Skinny, Anyway?" *Oregon Library Association Quarterly* 14.1 (2009): 21, 28. Web. 2 Oct. 2009.
7. Thelwall, Mike. "Quantitative Comparisons of Search Engine Results." *Journal of the American Society for Information Science & Technology* 59.11 (2008): 1702–10. Print.
8. Stone, Brad. "Hotwiring Your Search Engine." *Newsweek* 146.25 (2005): 52–54.
9. Wright, Alex. "Searching the Deep Web." *Communications of the ACM* 51.10 (2008): 14–15. Web. 2 Oct. 2009.
10. Boswell, Wendy. "The Invisible Web: How to Find and Search the Invisible Web." *About.com.* New York Times Company, 2009. Web. 2 Oct. 2009.
11. "Evaluating Web Pages: Techniques to Apply and Questions to Ask." *University of California Berkeley Library.* Regents of the University of California, 2009. Web. 2 Oct. 2009.
12. "About EBSCOhost." *Ebsco.com.* Ebsco Publishing, 2009. Web. 2 Oct. 2009.
13. "Welcome to PubMed." *PubMed.gov.* U.S. National Library of Medicine and the National Institutes of Health, 2009. Web. 2 Oct. 2009.
14. Campanazi, Jane. *Effective Writing for the Quality Professional: Creating Useful Letters, Reports, and Procedures.* Milwaukee: Quality Press, 2005. Print.
15. McKenzie, Jamie. "Scoring PowerPoints." *From Now On: Educational Technology Journal* 10.1 (2000). Web. 2 Oct. 2009.
16. Reid, Tim. "Hillary Clinton Hits Barack Obama with Plagiarism Allegation." *Times.* Times Newspapers, 19 Feb. 2008. Web. 23 Oct. 2009; and *National.* CBC News. CBC, Winnipeg, 30 Sept. 2008. Television.

CHAPTER 13

1. Levitz, Stephanie. "Anti-Olympic Protesters Want World Media to Know They Oppose 2010 Games." *Prince George Citizen.* Prince George Citizen, 11 Nov. 2008. Web. 17 Oct. 2009.

2. Powell, Kimahli. "Double-Double Day of Trouble." *Torontoist* 11 (2009). Web. 15 Oct. 2009.

3. Hennig, Scott. "Globalfest in Calgary Gets Federal Funds." *Canadian Taxpayers Federation.* 9 Sept. 2009. Web. 15 Oct. 2009.

4. "Big Red Ball of Government Spending." *Small Business Grants, Loans and Other Goodies.* Small Business Finance Centre, 16 July 2009. Web. 15 Oct. 2009.

5. "Adscam's Tab Keeps on Rising." *Record* (Kitchener). Metroland Media Group, 15 Mar. 2006. Web. 17 Oct. 2009.

6. "Major Shift Seen as over Half of Key Federal Contracts Now Set Aside for Small Businesses after Flaps over Iraq, Afghanistan and Katrina Sole-Source Contracting." *Business Credit* 109.6 (2007): 69.

7. "Is 60 the New 70?" *Report Cards on Health, 2006.* Heart and Stroke Foundation, 2007. Web. 21 Oct. 2009.

8. Bray, Chad. "Madoff Begins First Day of 150 Years." *Wall Street Journal* (Eastern Edition). Dow Jones & Company, 15 July 2009. Web. 21 Oct. 2009.

9. "Poverty Activists Cheer Payday Loan Legislation." *Ottawa Citizen.* Canwest Publishing, 2 Apr. 2008. Web. 17 Oct. 2009.

CHAPTER 14

1. Howitt, Chuck. "Pigeon King Creditors Pursue Galbraith's Personal Assets." *Record* [Waterloo]. Metroland Media Group, 14 Nov. 2008. Web. 11 May 2009.

2. Krugel, Lauren. "Feather Flap." *Winnipeg Free Press.* Winnipeg Free Press, 19 July 2008. Web. 13 Apr. 2009.

3. "Statement No: 1, Issue Number 338." *Grameen Bank.* Grameen Communications, 11 Mar. 2008. Web. 13 Apr. 2009.

4. "Grameen Bank: Banking for the Poor." *Grameen Bank.* Grameen Communications, July 2009. Web. 20 Sept. 2009.

5. Yunus, Muhammad. *Banker to the Poor: Micro-Lending and the Battle against World Poverty.* New York: Public Affairs, 2003. 70. Print.

6. Ibid., 110.

7. Ibid., 107.

8. "Grameen Family." *Grameen Bank.* Grameen Communications, 19 Apr. 2009. Web. 23 Apr. 2009.

9. Yunus, Muhammad. *Banker to the Poor: Micro-Lending and the Battle against World Poverty.* New York: Public Affairs, 2003. 93. Print.

10. "Interactive Business Planner." *Canada Business: Services for Entrepreneurs.* Government of Canada, 21 Sept. 2007. Web. 29 Apr. 2009.

11. Roehl, Richard, and Hal R. Varian. "Circulating Libraries and Video Rental Stores." *First Monday* 6.5 (2001). Web. 12 Oct. 2009.

12. Yunus, Muhammad. *Banker to the Poor: Micro-Lending and the Battle against World Poverty.* New York: Public Affairs, 2003. 128–130. Print.

13. "Frederick W. Smith." *Academy of Achievement.* 9 Jan. 2008. Web. 8 Apr. 2009.

14. "Young Entrepreneur Awards." *Business Development Bank of Canada.* Government of Canada, 2008. Web. 13 May 2009.

15. Buckland, Jerry, and Thibault Martin. *Fringe Banking in Winnipeg's North End.* Winnipeg: Winnipeg Inner-city Research Alliance, 2005. Web. 18 May 2009.

16. Conlin, Michelle, and Rob Hof. "The eBay Way." *Business Week* 29 Nov. 2004: 96-98. Print.

17. Home Page. *GlobalGiving.com.* n.d. Web. 21 May 2008.

18. Questions 6 to 10 are based on Sengupta, Rajdeep, and Craig P. Aubuchon. "The Microfinance Revolution: An Overview."

Federal Reserve Bank of St. Louis Review Jan./Feb. 2008: 9–30. Web. 13 Jan. 2009.

CHAPTER 15

1. "Employability Skills 2000+." *Conference Board of Canada.* May 2000. Web. 16 Mar. 2009.

2. Monster Worldwide. "SWOT Analysis: Key Facts." *Company Report 2008.* 2009. Web. 15 June 2009.

3. Stark, Betsy. "Stealing You." *World News Tonight.* ABC, Burbank, 8 Feb. 2006. Television.

4. Board of Governors of the Federal Reserve System et al. *You have the power to stop identity theft.* Washington: Federal Reserve, 2009. Print.

5. Montagne, Renee. "Search Over: Best Job in the World Filled." *Morning Edition National Public Radio.* 8 May 2009. Transcript.

6. "Steer Clear of Online Job Scams." *Consumer Reports* July 2003: 53. Print.

7. Charny, Ben. "Fake Google Toolbars Go Phishing." *PC Magazine* 6 Dec. 2005: 33. Print.

8. "The Good, the Bad, and the Ugly." *Network World* 26.9 (2009): 5. Print.

9. Willmer, Dave. "Eight Tips for a Better Online Job Search." *Office Pro* 68.7 (2008): 6. Print.

10. "Beware the Hidden Monsters on Job Search Websites." *Hamilton Spectator.* Metroland Media Group, 14 Sept. 2007. Web. 2 Nov. 2009.

11. Moody, Janette, Brent Stewart, and Cynthia Bolt-Lee. "Showcasing the Skilled Business Graduate: Expanding the Tool Kit." *Business Communication Quarterly* 65.1 (2002): 21–36. Print.

12. "Don't Forget the Spell-Check." *OfficeTeam Specialized Administrative Staffing.* OfficeTeam Press Releases. 6 Sept. 2006. Web. 10 June 2009.

13. Bailie, Rahel Anne. "Using a Résumé to Showcase Your Talents." *Intercom* 50.8 (2003): 15. Web. 2 Nov. 2009.

14. Lankford, Kimberly, and Jessica Anderson. "A New Resumé for a New Year." *Kiplinger's Personal Finance* 59.1 (2005): 87–88. Web. 2 Nov. 2009.

15. Rowh, Mark. "Building an E-Portfolio." *Career World* Nov./Dec. 2008: 26–28. Print.

16. "Don't Forget the Spell-Check." *OfficeTeam Specialized Administrative Staffing.* OfficeTeam Press Releases. 6 Sept. 2006. Web. 10 June 2009.

17. Smart, Karl. "Articulating Skills in the Job Search." *Business Communication Quarterly* 67.2 (2004): 198–205. Print.

CHAPTER 16

1. Powell, Betsy. "Random Drug Testing Is Routine for NYPD." *Toronto Star.* thestar.com, 28 Feb. 2004. Web. 18 Apr. 2009.

2. Ibid.

3. Armour, Stephanie, and Del Jones. "Workers' Positive Drug Tests Decrease." *USA Today.* 20 June 2006. Web. 23 Oct. 2009.

4. Seijts, Gerard H., Daniel P. Skarlicki, and Stephen W. Gilliand. "Canadian and American Reactions to *Drug* and Alcohol Testing Programs in the Workplace." *Employee Responsibilities & Rights Journal* 15.4 (2003): 191–208. Print. Refers to earlier work of American Management Association. *Workplace Drug Testing and Drug Abuse Policies.* New York: American Management Association, 1996. Print.

5. Brown, Peter. "Drug-Testing at Work." *Times* (UK).Times Newspapers, 1 July 2004. Web. 4 Oct. 2009.

6. "Canadian Snowboarder Retains Olympic Gold Medal after Testing Positive for Marijuana; Canadian Debate on Marijuana Decriminalization Prompted." *Newsbriefs*. National Drug Strategy Network. Feb. 1998. Web. 23 Oct. 2009.

7. "Plus: Olympics; Marijuana Becomes Banned Substance." *New York Times*. New York Times Company, 28 Apr. 1998. Web. 23 Oct. 2009.

8. Associated Press. "Phelps: Photo with Marijuana Pipe Real." *ESPN.com*. ESPN Internet Ventures, 2 Feb. 2009. Web. 4 Oct. 2009.

9. Spak, Jan. "Talking Shop." *Winnipeg Free Press* 14 Feb. 1998: 1–2. Print.

10. Foord Kirk, Janis. "Make Most of No. 1 Job Interview Question." *Toronto Star*. thestar.com, 1 Dec. 2001. Web. 23 Oct. 2009.

11. "Blue Hair, Body Piercings—Do Employers Care?" *Occupational Outlook Quarterly* 50.3 (2006): 24. Print.

12. Fernández-Aráoz, Claudio. "The Definitive Guide to Recruiting in Good Times and Bad." *Harvard Business Review* 87.5 (2009): 74–84. Print.

13. Burke, Mary Elizabeth. *2004 Reference and Background Checking Survey Report*. Alexandria: Society for Human Resource Management, 2005. 1. Web. 22 Oct. 2009.

14. Kaplan, Michael. "Job Interview Brainteasers." *Business 2.0* 8.8 (2007): 35–37. Print.

CHAPTER 17

1. *OED Online*. Draft Entry. Oxford University Press. Entry for "cube." Sept. 2006. Web. 17 Aug. 2008.

2. Douglas Coupland. *Generation X: Tales for an Accelerated Culture*. New York: St. Martin's Press, 1991. Print.

3. Cullen, Lisa Takeuchi. "Redrawing the Cube." *Time* 17 July 2006: 42–44. Print.

4. Ibid.

5. "Bullied Student Tickled Pink by Schoolmates' T-Shirt Campaign." *CBC News*. Canadian Broadcasting Corporation, 19 Sept. 2007. Web. 14 Oct. 2009.

6. "Stand Up against Bullying Day Proclaimed." *Nova Scotia Department of Education*. 25 Sept. 2007. Web. 14 Oct. 2009.

7. "CUPE Members Part of Pink Wave against Bullying." *CUPE.Ca*. 28 Feb. 2008. Web. 14 Oct. 2009.

8. Kim, Jane N. "The Cubicle Bully." *Scientific American Mind* (June 2008): 13. Print.

9. Bernardi, Lauren. "Bullies at Work: A Legal Perspective." Annual Meeting and Professional Development Institute. Blue Mountains. 12 June 2006. Lecture.

10. Namie, Gary. "Workplace Bullying: Escalated Incivility." *Ivey Business Journal* Nov./Dec. (2003): 1–6. Print.

11. Scott, Sarah. "You *#%&!." *Maclean's* 3 Sept. 2007: 40–43. Print.

12. Lutgen-Sandvik, Pamela. "Take This Job and. . . : Quitting and Other Forms of Resistance to Workplace Bullying." *Communication Monographs* 73.4 (2006): 406–33. Print.

13. "Bullying in the Workplace." *Canadian Centre for Occupational Health and Safety*. 8 Mar. 2005. Web. 14 Aug. 2008.

14. Lutgen-Sandvik, Pamela. "Take This Job and . . : Quitting and Other Forms of Resistance to Workplace Bullying." *Communication Monographs* 73.4 (2006): 406–33. Print.

15. Namie, Gary. "U.S. Workplace Bullying Survey." *Workplace Bullying Institute and Zogby International*. Sept. 2007. Web. 10 Oct. 2009.

16. Cornwall, Claudia. "Working with Difficult People." *Reader's Digest Canada* Feb. 2005: 59–63. Print.

17. "Targeting Workplace Bullies." *Canada Safety Council*. 2005. Web. 27 July 2008.

18. Locander, William B., and David L. Luechauer. "Don't Be a Bully." *Marketing Management* 14.4 (July 2005): 48–50. Print.

19. "Targeting Workplace Bullies." *Canada Safety Council*. 2005. Web. 27 July 2008.

20. Eastmond, Steven. *Passive, Aggressive, and Assertive Communication: Understanding Communication Styles*. n.d. Web. 14 Aug. 2008.

21. Hulbert, Jack E., and Hulbert, Doris. "The Value of Assertiveness in Interpersonal Communication." *Management Review* (Aug. 1982): 23–26. Print.

22. Waters, James A. "Managerial Assertiveness." *Business Horizons* Sept./Oct. 1982: 24–29. Print.

23. *PassiveAggressiveNotes.com*. Ed. Kerry Miller. Passive Aggressive Notes. n.d. Web. 14 Oct. 2009.

24. Ibid.

25. Osborne, Becky. "Assertiveness Workshop." Danville Area Community College. 2002. Web. 21 Aug. 2008.

26. Loftus, A. Paul P. "Training." *Industrial & Commercial Training* 24.2 (1992): 4. Print.

27. Sardo, Serge. "Learning to Display Emotional Intelligence." *Business Strategy Review* 15.1 (2004): 14–17. Print.

28. Salovey, Peter, and John D. Mayer. "Emotional Intelligence." *Imagination, Cognition, and Personality* 9.3 (1989–1990): 185–211. Print.

29. Goleman, Daniel. "What Makes a Leader?" *Harvard Business Review* Nov. 1998: 93–102. Print.

30. Ibid.

31. Daniel, Diann. "4 Ways to Boost your Emotional Intelligence." *CIO* 20.21 (2007): 13–16. Print.

32. Scott, Sarah. "Do Grades Really Matter?" *Maclean's* 10 Sept. 2007: 70–74. Print.

33. Drucker, Peter F. "How to Manage your Boss." *Management Review* 66.5 (1977): 8. Print.

34. Bartlett, Dede. "The Next (Real) World: Part Two: How to Help Students Survive Their First Job." *University Business*. Aug. 2006. Web. 28 Aug. 2008.

35. "How to Boss your Boss." *FinancialManagement* Nov. 2000: 57. Print.

36. Lee, Dong-Woo, and Carol Blaszczynski. "Perspectives of 'Fortune 500' Executives on the Competency Requirements for Accounting." *Journal of Education for Business* 75.2 (1999): 104. Print.

37. U.S. Department of Labor, Bureau of Labor Statistics. *Occupational Outlook Handbook, 2002–03 edition. Job Outlook 2003*. Washington: 2003. Print. Cited in Hartman, Diane B., Jan Bentley, Kathleen Richards, and Cynthia Krebs. "Administrative Tasks and Skills Needed for Today's Office: The Employees' Perspective." *Journal of Education for Business* 80.6 (2005): 347–357. Print.

38. "Drunks, Thieves and Potty Mouths Need Not Apply." *CBC News*. Canadian Broadcasting Corporation, 29 Nov. 2007. Web. 14 Oct. 2009.

39. "Getting the Message, at Last." *Economist* 15 Dec. 2007: 18. Print.

40. Cullen, Lisa Takeuchi. "Redrawing the Cube." *Time* 17 July 2006: 42–44. Print.

41. This section is based on an idea from Lynn, Adele B. *The Emotional Intelligence Activity Book*. New York: Amacom. 2002. Print.

APPENDIX

1. Adapted from Elliott, Rebecca. *Painless Grammar.* New York: Barron's, 2006. Print. Rebecca Elliott's work was invaluable as a reference in the writing of the appendix.
2. Ibid.
3. Some of the sentences in this "Your Turn" are adapted from Blicq, Ron S., and Lisa Moretto. *Technically-Write!* 5th ed. Toronto: Pearson Prentice Hall, 1998. Print.
4. Ibid.
5. This section and the next ("Idioms") are adapted from Blicq, Ron S., and Lisa Moretto. *Technically-Write!* 5th ed. Toronto: Pearson Prentice Hall, 1998. Print.
6. Troyka, Lynn Quitman. *Concise Handbook.* rev. ed. New Jersey: Simon & Schuster, 1992. Print.
7. Norman, Herbert J. *The Organ Today.* London: Barrie & Rockcliff, 1966. 119. Print.
8. Adapted from Blicq, Ron S., and Lisa Moretto. *Technically-Write!* 5th ed. Toronto: Pearson Prentice Hall, 1998. Print.
9. Human Resources Development Canada. *Plain Language: Clear and Simple.* Ottawa: Canada Communication Group—Publishing, 1996. Print.
10. This "Numbers" section is summarized from Blicq, Ron S., and Lisa Moretto. *Technically-Write!* 5th ed. Toronto: Pearson Prentice Hall, 1998. Print.

Answers to "Your Turn!" Questions

1. Human Resources Development Canada. *Plain Language: Clear and Simple.* Ottawa: Canada Communication Group—Publishing, 1996. Print.

Credits

Chapter 7

Page 137: Alamy Images; *p. 139:* Mike Margol/PhotoEdit; *p. 140:* Alexei Kapterev, kapterev.com; *p. 149:* Kevin Mazur/WireImage/ Getty Images; *p. 166:* Table 7-2, (a) Big Cheese Photo LLC/Alamy; (b) PhotoAlto/Alamy; *p. 167:* Courtesy of Joan Flaherty.

Chapter 8

Page 170: Alamy Images; *p. 172:* SuperStock/MaXx Images; *p. 173:* Mike Flanagan/Cartoonstock.com; *p. 180:* Mary Evans Picture Library; *p. 188:* gladcov/Shutterstock; *p. 205:* Fran/Cartoonstock.com.

Chapter 9

Page 211: PhotoDisc Images; *p. 212:* Fran/Cartoonstock.com; *p. 213:* Dan Rosandich/Cartoonstock.com; *p. 217:* Chris Wildt/ Cartoonstock.com; *p. 221:* The London Art Archive/Alamy; *p. 226:* Mike Baldwin/Cartoonstock.com.

Chapter 10

Page 232: Alamy Images; *p. 236:* Mike Baldwin/Cartoonstock.com; *p. 246:* Brand X Pictures Image/JupiterImages Unlimited; *p. 252:* Zoran Mijatov/Shutterstock.

Chapter 11

Page 257: Alamy Images; *p. 259:* BC Intellectual Property and Pierre Roussel/Getty Images; *p. 260:* designalldone/Shutterstock; *p. 266:* Larry/Cartoonstock.com; *p. 273:* Fran/Cartoonstock.com.

Chapter 12

Page 280: Eyewire Images; *p. 281:* DILBERT: © Scott Adams/Dist. by United Feature Syndicate, Inc.; *p. 285:* Shalom Ormsby/MaXx Images; *p. 290:* Jim Sizemore/Cartoonstock.com; *p. 296:* Figure 12-4, kabliczech/Shutterstock; *p. 297:* Figure 12-5, (a) williammpark/ Shutterstock; (b) Luhanor/Shutterstock; *p. 298:* Shannon Burns/ Cartoonstock.com.

Chapter 13

Page 306: Alamy Images; *p. 308:* Mike Baldwin/Cartoonstock.com; *p. 310:* Dean Mitchell/Shutterstock; *p. 311:* Dave Carpenter/ Cartoonstock.com; *p. 313:* Fran/Cartoonstock.com; *p. 337:* Patrick Hardin/Cartoonstock.com.

Chapter 14

Page 348: PhotoDisc Images; *p. 350:* Kalyan Chakravorty/The India Today Group/Getty Images; *p. 351:* RAFIQUR RAHMAN/Reuters/ Landov; *p. 353:* Mike Baldwin/Cartoonstock.com.

Chapter 15

Page 366: Digital Vision Images; *p. 367:* Creatas Images/JupiterImages Unlimited; *p. 371:* Andrew Toos/Cartoonstock.com; *p. 385:* Monkey Business Images/Shutterstock.

Chapter 16

Page 393: Digital Vision Images; *p. 394:* Dan Rosandich/Cartoonstock. com; *p. 396:* ZENG YI/Xinhua/Landov; *p. 400:* AVAVA/Shutterstock; *p. 401:* Dmitriy Shironosov/Shutterstock; *p. 404:* Dave Carpenter/ Cartoonstock.com; *p. 408:* Adam Gregor/Shutterstock; *p. 409:* Thinkstock Images/JupiterImages Unlimited; *p. 412:* PhotoAlto/ Alamy; *p. 419:* Zsolt Nyulaszi/Shutterstock.

Chapter 17

Page 423: Alamy Images; *p. 424:* Chad McDermott/Shutterstock; *p. 427:* Images.com/Corbis; *p. 441:* Photo courtesy of Chris MacAskill, SmugMug, www.smugmug.com; *p. 442:* Jim Sizemore/Cartoonstock. com; *p. 444:* Thomas Bros./Cartoonstock.com.

Appendix

p. 449: Alamy Images; Cartoon Network.

Index